Realm of the Saint

Realm of the Saint

POWER AND AUTHORITY IN MOROCCAN SUFISM

BY VINCENT J. CORNELL

UNIVERSITY OF TEXAS PRESS
Austin

The publication of this book was assisted by a grant from the Andrew W. Mellon Foundation.

Printed in the United States of America
First edition, 1998

♾ The paper used in this publication meets the minimum requirements of American National Standard for Information Sciences—Permanence of Paper for Printed Library Materials, ANSI Z39.48-1984.

LIBRARY OF CONGRESS CATALOGING-IN-PUBLICATION DATA

Cornell, Vincent J.
Realm of the saint : power and authority in Moroccan Sufism / by Vincent J. Cornell. — 1st ed.
p. cm.
Includes bibliographical references (p.) and index.
ISBN 0-292-71209-X (alk. paper). — ISBN 0-292-71210-3 (pbk. : alk. paper)
1. Sufism—Morocco. 2. Morocco—Religious life and customs.
I. Title.
BP188.8.M6C67 1998
297.4'0964—dc21 97-32878

To Muḥammad ibn Sulaymān al-Jazūlī and the Moroccan ṣāliḥīn:
May this work be a worthy legacy.

To the people of Morocco:
May this work help you rediscover your heritage.

Contents

List of Maps and Figures

MAPS

FIGURES

Preface and Acknowledgments

North African historians often complain that the study of their region gets little respect on the other side of the Atlantic Ocean. Whether or not these concerns are justified, American scholars have indeed deferred to European academics for much of their information on premodern Morocco, Algeria, and Tunisia. Although this stance is logical, given the long history of French and Spanish involvement in the Maghrib, it has led to two unfortunate consequences. First, the continued reliance on colonial-era studies has allowed certain outmoded paradigms to outlive their usefulness, thus distorting the image of North African Islam among European and North American scholars. These paradigms will receive critical attention in the chapters that follow. Second, the disengagement of American scholarship from the premodern Maghrib has created a level of indifference that is an anomaly in the field of Islamic Studies. This indifference is doubly problematical. In the first place, it prevents American researchers from drawing their own, independent conclusions about the history of a major part of the Muslim world. In addition, it precludes them from becoming acquainted with modern scholarship on the Maghrib in Arabic, which is at least as significant as that written in European languages.

This book was written to rectify this situation and to restore a sense of geographical balance to the study of Islamic mysticism. As such, it is primarily directed at three audiences. One audience consists of students of Islamic Studies, who have not yet been exposed to the wide range of mystical traditions to be found in the Muslim West. Without an understanding of the history of Sufism in this region, the importance of the Maghrib to the development of Islamic thought remains unappreciated. A second audience is made up of those who are interested in saints and sainthood in the major world religions. For such scholars, a focus on the Mediterranean basin in medieval and early modern times requires attention to holiness as a social phenomenon expressed similarly on both sides of the Muslim–Christian divide.

The third audience consists of those who specialize in Maghrib Studies. In this field, intellectual history has not been subjected to the same rigorous analysis that it has enjoyed in the study of other regions of the Muslim world. By relating formal and practical conceptions of Moroccan sainthood to the development of social and political institutions, this book posits a direct relationship between the religious teachings of Islam and regional models of authority. Such an approach makes it easier to understand popular religious movements without resorting to reductionist paradigms. Insofar as it brings the social and intellectual history of Moroccan Islam into the wider orbit of Islamic theology and mysticism, it also demonstrates that the North African "periphery" of Islamdom has never been an intellectual backwater. Finally, in opening up the historiographical discourse of Maghrib Studies to more "subaltern" voices, it pays particular attention to the writings of contemporary North African scholars. In this regard, the footnotes and bibliography may be a useful guide to indigenous research.

Several Moroccan historians have assisted me personally in the twelve years that I have spent on this work. I am particularly indebted to the late Muḥammad Ibrāhīm al-Kattānī, director of the manuscripts section (*qism al-wathāʾiq*) of the Bibliothèque Générale et Archives, Rabat, for his patient friendship and advice. I am also grateful to Muḥammad al-Manūnī, ʿAbd al-Karīm Krīm, Ahmed Toufiq, Halima Ferhat, and Zakia Zouanate for their kind help and advice. Others whom I have not met in person but whose ideas have influenced my own include Ahmed Boucharb, Muḥammad Ḥajjī, Mohamed Kably, and Abdellah Laroui.

I should also acknowledge the non-academic persons who have assisted me in Morocco. The first is Mūlāy Muḥammad at-Tilmudī, administrator of the shrine and mosque of Muḥammad ibn Sulaymān al-Jazūlī in Marrakesh. This descendent of Imām al-Jazūlī, whose family has maintained the saint's spiritual legacy for four centuries, has helped me to appreciate the importance of the Muḥammadan paradigm in Sufi doctrine and practice. He and the members of his house will always have a place in my heart. Equal in importance is Mūlāy ʿUmar ar-Rīsh of Rabat, who has nurtured me with his wisdom and friendship for more than sixteen years. In knowing this Idrisid sharif, *ṣāliḥ,* and *ʿārif bi'llāh,* I have drunk from a spring of traditional knowledge that is all too rare in the modern world.

Other resource persons in Morocco include Muṣṭafā an-Nājī, who, before opening the bookstore he now co-owns in Rabat, was the best locator of academic texts and Islamic manuscripts in the country. This work would not have been possible without his involvement. Muṣṭafā's current business partner, Mohammed el-Alami el-Ouali should also be mentioned as one of Morocco's important resources. The clothing and tailor shop owned by this idiosyncratic intellectual is a primary site for academic discourse in Rabat, where on almost any occasion the visitor can find historians, sociologists, economists, Sufis, and even Islamists carrying on discussions over mint tea or Coca-Cola, which el-Alami calls "Islamic whiskey."

Despite my interest in promoting Moroccan scholars, I must not neglect those in America who have helped bring this work to fruition. First, I must thank my academic *shaykh at-tarbiyya,* Michael Morony of the University of California at Los Angeles, and my academic *shaykh at-tarqiyya,* Bruce Lawrence of Duke University, for their friendship and guidance. I doubt that more incisive critics could ever be found. Thanks also go to those at UCLA who helped me through the initial stages of this study. These include Ismail Poonawala, Jacques Maquet, Amin Banani, Afaf Marsot, Thomas Penchoen, and Georges Sabagh. At Northwestern University advice was provided by John Hunwick, Carl Petry, and Richard Kieckhefer. At Duke University thanks must go to Mel Peters, Kalman Bland, and Stanley Hauerwas for giving me invaluable advice on how to make my arguments more clearly understood. Also helpful were Dale Eickelman of Dartmouth College, Miriam Cooke of Duke University, Carl Ernst of the University of North Carolina at Chapel Hill, Alan Godlas of the University of Georgia, and Arthur F. Buehler of Colgate University. All of these colleagues provided important advice on how to clarify a work of great scope and complexity. Finally, I must thank my students Eric Boyd, Frederick S. Colby, Richard Lamar Collier, Scott Kugle, and Behdad Shahsavari, who either helped me prepare the manuscript for publication or provided feedback in my attempt to trace the Moroccan saint's "road map to God."

Financial support for this work was provided by the Social Science Research Council, the U.S. Department of Education through the Fulbright–Hayes program, the Del Amo Foundation of California, the American Institute of Maghrib Studies, and the Academic Research Council of Duke University. Institutional support was provided in Rabat by the Bibliothèque

Hassania and its director, Muḥammad al-ʿArabī al-Khaṭṭābī and the Bibliothèque Générale et Archives and its director, ʿAbd ar-Raḥmān al-Fāsī. Support was also provided by the Bibliothèque Ben Youssef of Marrakesh and its director, Mūlāy Ḥasan aṣ-Ṣabāḥ, and the Bibliothèque al-Qarawiyyīn, Fez, to which access was arranged by the Moroccan Ministry of Culture. In Europe, thanks should go to the staffs of the British Library in London, the Bibliothèque Nationale in Paris, and the Biblioteca Nacional in Madrid.

Above everyone else, I owe a debt of gratitude to my wife, Rkia Elaroui Cornell. Maintaining her faith in this project through good times and bad, she remains my best friend and inspiration, serving as critic, interlocutor, and resource in the Arabic and Berber languages. Along with our daughter, Sakina, she has also been a fellow traveler on this path, exploring with me the religious heritage of the country that has become ours together. I hope that this book reflects our appreciation for both Morocco and Islam while remaining true to the ideals of Euro-American intellectual engagement.

List of Abbreviations

AM	*Archives Marocaines* (Paris, 1927)
Ar.	Arabic
Ber.	Berber
BG	Bibliothèque Générale (*al-Khizāna al-ʿĀmma*), Rabat
BH	Bibliothèque Hassania (*al-Khizāna al-Ḥasaniyya*), Rabat
BL	British Library, London
BNM	Biblioteca Nacional, Madrid
BNP	Bibliothèque Nationale, Paris
BQ	Bibliothèque al-Qarawiyyīn (*Khizānat al-Qarawiyyīn*), Fez
BSOAS	*Bulletin of the School of Oriental and African Studies*
BY	Bibliothèque Ben Youssef (*Khizānat Ibn Yūsuf*), Marrakesh
Dial. Ar.	Dialectical Arabic
diss.	dissertation
DKM	Dār al-Kutub al-Miṣriyya, Cairo
EI	*Encyclopaedia of Islam* (EI[1] first edition, EI[2] second edition)
GC	Garrett Collection, Princeton University Library
IJMES	*International Journal of Middle East Studies*
JAAR	*Journal of the American Academy of Religion*
lith.	lithograph
ms.	manuscript
ROMM	*Revue de l'Occident Musulman et de la Méditerranée*

Transliteration of Foreign Terms

Arabic and Berber names and terms in this book will be transliterated according to the usage of *The International Journal of Middle East Studies.* Certain commonly used Islamic terms, which have been incorporated by the field of Middle East Studies into standard English, will not be transliterated. These include "Qur'an" instead of *Qur'ān,* "hadith" for *ḥadīth,* "ulama" for *ʿulamāʾ,* and "caliph" for *khalīfa.* In addition, well-known names of cities and geographical locations will not be transliterated but will appear in their common English spelling (e.g., "Marrakesh" for *Marrākush,* "Tangier" for *Ṭanja,* "Tetuan" for *Ṭitwān* or *Tīṭāwīn,* and "Rif" for *ar-Rīf*). Certain place-names, however, whose Latinized spelling has distorted the Arabic or Berber original, will be transliterated in their original form (e.g., "Shafshāwan" instead of "Chaouen" and "Sabta" instead of "Ceuta"). Frequently used Arabic terms, such as *ṣāliḥ* and *uṣūlī,* will fall out of italics after being mentioned several times in the text.

Dates include both common era (C.E.) and Islamic (*anno Hegirae* or A.H.) forms. When the two appear together, the Islamic year precedes that of the common era. For example, the year in which Baghdad fell to the Mongols is written as 656/1258. This corresponds to A.H. 656 and 1258 C.E. The common era dating is used instead of the A.D. (*anno Domini*) form in order to maintain a religiously neutral stance.

MAHJOUBI AHERDAN, *Aguns' n Tillas* (HEART OF DARKNESS, RABAT, 1985).

Que dire
de ceux que l'on vénère?
Que dire
des hommes-dieux
des saints
des sages
que l'on prend pour exemple
et pour guides?
Que dire de ceux
qui sèment aux vents
paraboles et versets?

[What should be said of those whom we venerate? What should be said of the holy men, the saints, the sages whom we take as examples and guides? What should be said of those who scatter parables and verses on the winds?]

INTRODUCTION

Morocco and the Problem of Sainthood in Islamic Studies

Naming Muslim Sainthood: Walāya *or* Wilāya?

The problematic of Muslim sainthood begins with its very name. When one translates (literally, "carries over") a word from a foreign language into one's own tongue, the classic translator's dilemma arises: a good translation must be both faithful to the meaning of the foreign term and also fully expressive of its own language. In effect, a double translation must be created.[1] Since this is impossible in an absolute sense, every translation is inadequate. This limitation is all the more present with regard to religious concepts, where even a small difference in meaning can lead to serious misunderstandings. Such is the case, for example, when one uses the English word "sainthood"—a concept associated with Christianity—for the Islamic terms *walāya* or *wilāya.* Once taken out of its original context, each term runs the risk of being rendered contextless, and as such would not be recognized by the audience to whom it was first addressed.[2]

But the Islamic case presents its own paradox: although *walāya* and *wilāya* are related in meaning, they are nonetheless different. The real issue is therefore one of "double subjectivity" rather than of true objectivity.[3] A problematic exists on both sides of the equation. Should not one be equally as attentive to Muslim interpretations of *walāya* and *wilāya* as to their English translation?

This problem is seldom recognized in the field of Islamic Studies. *Walāya* and *wilāya* are used interchangeably by most Western scholars of Islam, just as they are in informal Arabic. Recently, however, a debate over these terms has arisen among specialists in Sufism in Europe and America.[4] Some scholars maintain that what we in the West think of as sainthood is most accurately conveyed in Islam by the term *walāya.* This conclusion comes from a strict etymological analysis of the Arabic root *waliya,* which means "to be near or close." Thus, *walī Allāh,* the compound word most often translated as "saint" in English, means an "intimate" or a "friend" of God.[5]

But the actual use of an expression does not always correspond to etymological ideals. When the word *walī* is used in the Qur'an, it does not necessarily mean "friend." More often, it carries the power-laden connotations of "manager," "guardian," "protector," or "intercessor"—concepts that are more in the semantic domain of *wilāya* than *walāya.*[6] Even *walāya* itself, which is used twice in the Holy Book, does not always connote friendship.[7] Only when *walī Allāh* is used in the plural, as in the verse: "Verily for the *awliyāʾ Allāh* there is no fear, nor shall they grieve" (X [*Yūnus*], 62), is the idea of closeness to God foregrounded. Thus, according to Qur'anic usage, the term *walī Allāh* has a social as well as a metaphysical signification: the Muslim saint protects or intercedes for others as Allah's deputy or vicegerent.[8]

In the Islamic Middle Period, the question of whether *walāya* or *wilāya* was the "correct" verbal noun of *walī* was widely discussed by grammarians.[9] Ibn Kathīr, for example, came down on the side of *wilāya,* which he defined as authority, power, or the ability to act. To Ibn Sīdah, *wilāya* and *walāya* were more or less identical. For Ibn as-Sikkīt, *wilāya* meant governmental authority (*sulṭān*), while both *wilāya* and *walāya* denoted assistance or support (*nuṣra*). According to the strictly formalistic Sībawayh, *walāya* was a verbal noun whereas *wilāya* was an abstract noun. Yet both meant essentially the same thing: either command (*imāra*) or delegated authority (*niqāba*).[10]

Despite their best efforts, neither alternative, *walāya* nor *wilāya,* could be put forward by medieval grammarians as the "correct" verbal noun of *walī.*[11] Given this fact, it should come as no surprise to find that the meaning of these terms was also debated by Sufis. In the early fourteenth century, the Indian master Niẓām ad-Dīn Awliyāʾ (d. 725/1325) discussed the difference between *walāya* and *wilāya* in a lecture that found its way into the pages of Amīr Ḥasan Sijzī's *Fawāʾid al-Fuʾād* (Morals for the heart):

> The saint possesses both *walayat* and *wilayat* at the same time. *Walayat* is that which masters impart to disciples about God, just as they teach them about the etiquette of the Way. Everything such as this which takes place between the Shaykh and other people is called *walayat*. But that which takes place between the Shaykh and God is called *wilayat*. That is a special kind of love, and when the Shaykh leaves the world, he takes his *wilayat* with him. His *walayat*, on the other hand, he can confer on someone else, whomever he wishes, and if he does not confer it, then it is suitable for God Almighty to confer that *walayat* on someone. But the *wilayat* is the Shaykh's constant companion; he bears it with him (wherever he goes).[12]

For Niẓām ad-Dīn, it is *wilāya* that connotes closeness or love, whereas *walāya* connotes authority. This is not the case, however, for Aḥmad ibn Ibrāhīm al-Māgirī (fl. 696/1297), an Egyptian contemporary of Niẓām ad-Dīn and great-grandson of the Moroccan shaykh Abū Muḥammad Ṣāliḥ (d. 631/1234). For this writer, the semantic ambiguity of *walāya* and *wilāya* is resolved in favor of authority:

> We say (and with God is the approval): *Walāya* is a verbal noun and *wilāya* is a gerund [*ism maṣdar*]. The meaning of both is "assistance or support" [*nuṣra*], according to Sībawayh. Al-Azharī, however, says that *walāya* means "most clearly related" [*aẓhar fi'n-nasab*], while the idea of assistance or support comes from the saying, "a patron by virtue of authority" [*walī bayna wilāya*]. *Wilāya*, therefore, is like a command [*imāra*], as in the saying, "governing by virtue of [delegated] authority" [*wālin bayna wilāya*].[13]

When all is said and done, *walāya* and *wilāya* are best seen as semantic fraternal twins that coexist symbiotically, like yin and yang. Each relies on the other for its meaning. This interpretation is confirmed by etymology and Qur'anic usage alike. It also corresponds to actual experience. A person can only exercise delegated authority over another by being close to the one who bestows authority in the first place. This closeness can be expressed literally, in terms of physical proximity, or metaphorically, in terms of status. When this logic is applied to the Muslim saint, the following argument pertains: Allah is the source of all power and authority. Since the *walī Allāh* is Allah's "friend," he must be close to Allah. Therefore, he is seen by others as Allah's protégé, just as the friend of a king is seen as a protégé of that king. Protégés of the powerful benefit from their links to their patrons by acting as intermediaries for those who are below them. As an intermediary, the protégé is also a patron, for others rely on him to intercede for them before the ultimate source of authority. Thus, the *walī Allāh* is both an intermediary and a patron for his clients.

How does this relate to the semantic problem discussed above? If translation means that fidelity to the original can only be found in exact replication, then distortion and infidelity are the lot of every translation. Does this prove the old adage *Traduttore traditore* ("The translator is a traitor")?[14] Not necessarily. George Steiner has noted that the academic debate about translation is based on two mutually exclusive premises. The "universalist" premise argues that all human languages share a common structure. If this were the case, then it would be possible for the researcher to delve beneath surface differences to find common similarities. The "relativist" or "monadist" premise, on the other hand, views languages as so different from each other that comparison cannot comprehend them. If this were true, then the interpretation of *walāya* and *wilāya* as "Muslim sainthood" would be so inaccurate as to be meaningless.[15]

But the mere fact of difference does not mean that one cannot translate. Such a conclusion would be absurd, since human beings translate all the time. Every good translator is aware that since translation involves interpretation, no translation can be exact. From this perspective, translation is subsumed under the wider category of representation, analogy, and metaphor—what Wittgenstein called "family resemblances."[16] If all translation is mimetic, then any carefully conceived analogue in any language can serve the task of translation equally well. Whether we use sainthood, *sainteté, hagaia, santidad,* or any other comparable term for *walāya* and *wilāya* is unimportant, so long as we do not claim that it conveys the full meaning of the Arabic concepts.

This point has also been made by Jacques Derrida. For him, "Une 'bonne' traduction doit toujours abuser."[17] Derrida is saying more in this statement than that "a good translation must always abuse." Rather, he reminds us that in every act of translation, the interpretive process distorts the original in new and sometimes imaginative ways. According to Derrida's specialized lexicon of deconstruction, translated concepts are said to be "*ab*-used." It is often forgotten that the Arabic terms *walāya* and *wilāya* are themselves interpretations, since together they represent a concept whose full meaning goes beyond the semantic range of either word when taken by itself. Put another way, they too are "*ab*-usive" of a greater reality. Thus, the English term "sainthood" need not be any more abusive of the larger reality than the Arabic words it replaces. When we translate *walāya* and *wilāya* as "Muslim sainthood," we are simply trying to "understand other cultures as far as possible in their own terms but in our language."[18] Such is the nature of all comparative analysis, whether linguistic or otherwise. Although we should not trivialize foreign concepts by disregarding their historical, cultural, and lexicographical contexts, we may unpack or deconstruct them on different levels.

Why Study Morocco?

The aim of this book is to examine the relationship between sainthood and authority in Morocco, the Far Maghrib (Ar. *al-Maghrib al-Aqṣāʾ*) of the premodern Islamic world. Although this region was not a "nation" in the modern sense, its spatial and cultural contours were more clearly defined than in other areas of Islamdom.[19] To the north, it was bounded by the Mediterranean, which formed both a natural border and a means of access to Muslim Spain. To the west was the Atlantic Ocean, an expanse which Moroccans never crossed. To the south was the Sahara desert, a "sea" unto itself, which also acted as a border. The only undefined border was to the east, where the Taza gap opens onto the city of Tlemcen and the Algerian Ouarsenis. Here, cultural and political barriers made up for the absence of geographical limits. After the thirteenth century, it became increasingly difficult to conceive of Tlemcen—a city so near yet so far away from Morocco proper—as part of the Far Maghrib. After the Ottoman occupation of western Algeria in the sixteenth century, the separate identity of this city and its region became an accepted fact.

Premodern Morocco is important to the study of sainthood for several reasons. First, this part of the world has been studied extensively by Western social scientists. However, since anthropological and sociological studies of religion are concerned primarily with behavioral and social-structural issues, social-scientific investigations of Moroccan sainthood have focused on the social aspect of this phenomenon instead of its doctrinal or metaphysical aspect. Although such research is useful, it tells only part of the story. If the doctrinal aspect of Muslim sainthood is not explored, the important relationship between Sufism and the Moroccan cult of saints is liable to be ignored or misunderstood.[20]

Second, although Morocco has received plenty of attention from social

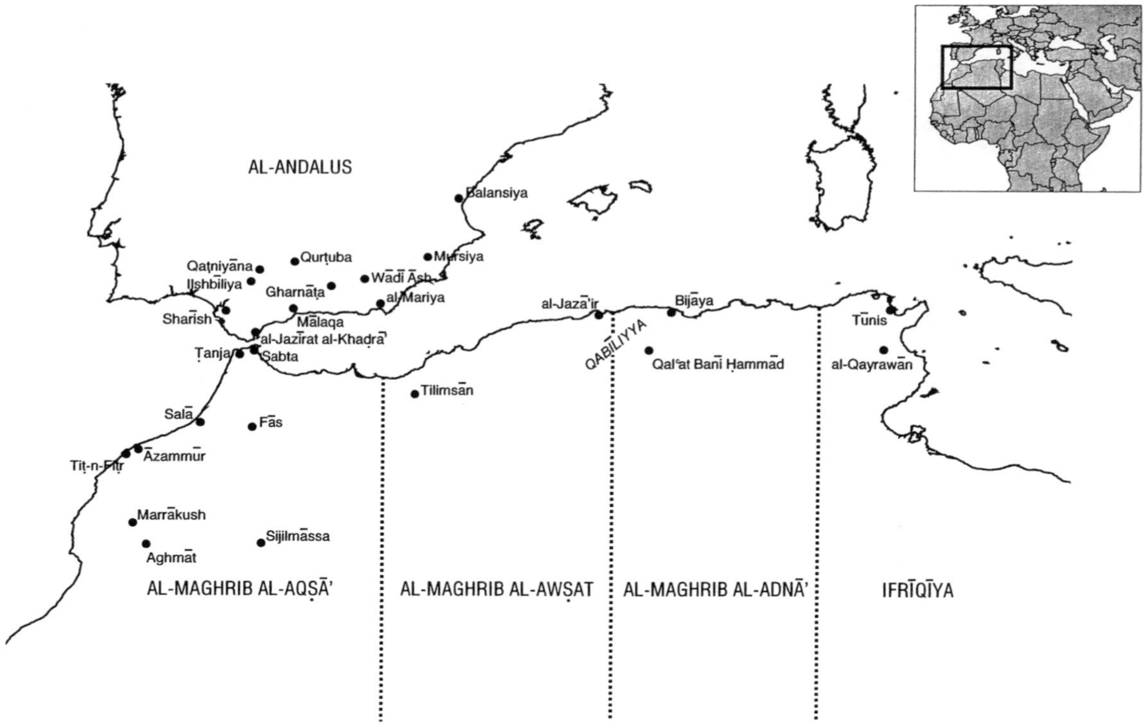

MAP ONE
The Premodern Maghrib

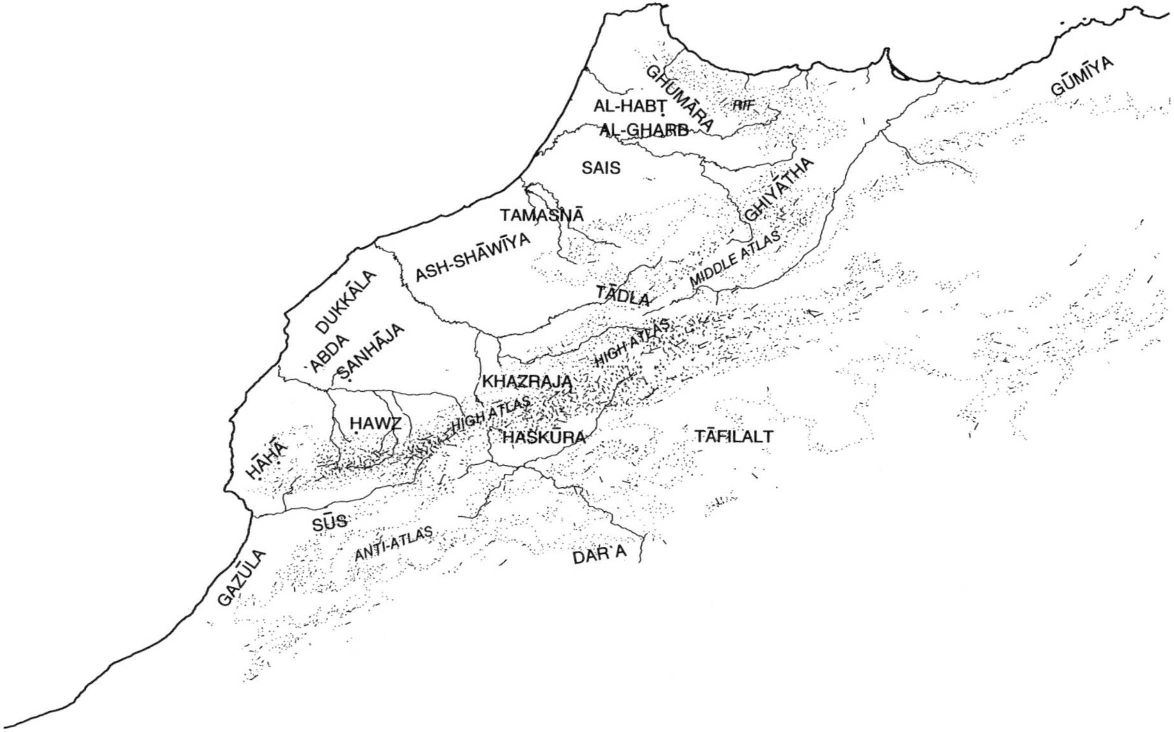

MAP TWO

Regions of Premodern Morocco

scientists, it has been overlooked in the field of Islamic Studies. This is particularly true of Moroccan Sufism.[21] While a number of Moroccan Sufi texts have been edited in Arabic and one or two have appeared in French, no detailed study of Moroccan Sufism has yet been written in any language. This problem is all the more acute because the Far Maghrib has long been one of the most important crucibles of Islamic mysticism. The wide geographical extent of the Shādhiliyya and Tijāniyya Sufi orders underscores the importance of this lacuna. In addition, recent studies of so-called neo-Sufism have shown that the transregional character of this concept extends to, and must include, Moroccan Sufism.[22]

North Africa was never the backwater that many orientalists and social scientists have assumed. While Muslim Spain (Ar. *al-Andalus*), with its sophisticated intellectual life and "civilized" ways, is often highlighted in surveys of Islamic civilization, the premodern Maghrib is still dismissed as either an appendix of Islamic Iberia or a mere subregion of a peripheral and marginalized Islamic Africa. But the historian who looks at North African primary sources without prejudice finds that such an extreme center–periphery approach distorts reality. Rather than making a peripheralized North Africa dependent on Muslim Spain, it is better to view the entire Islamic West—al-Andalus, the Maghrib, Muslim Sicily, and parts of West Africa—as a single, relatively unified cultural entity. In this wider region, ideas were freely exchanged and innovations were adopted as readily as anywhere in the Muslim world. Most importantly, religious and intellectual movements from Morocco and other parts of the Maghrib often created ebb tides of intellectual and cultural influence that flowed toward the East. Instead of being merely imitative, many of the doctrines and institutions that were created in western "subcenters" such as Fez or Marrakesh had profound effects on the rest of the Islamic world.

Only by embracing a more open-minded approach to the premodern Maghrib can we fully understand the relationship between Islam, authority, and mysticism in Morocco. Why, for example, is Muslim sainthood referred to as *walāya* in Sufi texts but as *wilāya* in Moroccan Arabic? Can this difference be dismissed as the result of dialectical euphony or were there different modalities of sainthood in premodern North Africa?[23] Can one bridge the gap between Sufism and popular religion without having to rely on etymological explanations? How much have North African Sufis assimilated the concept of *wilāya* into their own understanding of sainthood? Was there, in fact, a Sufi order that stressed *wilāya* as part of its doctrines?

If so, how was the interrelationship between *wilāya* and *walāya* articulated in theory and practice? All of these issues, and more, will be addressed in the following chapters.

Sainthood and Social Science in Morocco

When social scientists discuss sainthood in Morocco, they seldom use either *walāya* or *wilāya.*[24] Instead, they talk about charisma, which they equate with the Arabic term *baraka*—a concept whose definition has run the gamut from "blessed virtue" and "spiritual potency" to "power" and even "luck."[25] Since European saints are said to be charismatic figures, charisma is also assumed to be central to the Moroccan conception of religious authority. For this reason, the Moroccan saint is most often defined as a *baraka*-laden individual.[26]

But how is the holy person characterized in Morocco itself? In actual practice, what is doctrinally known as a *walī Allāh* can be designated by any one of several terms, either masculine or feminine: *ṣāliḥ/ṣāliḥa* (Ar.), *shaykh* (Ar.), *murābiṭ* (Ar.), *siyyid/siyyida* (Dial. Ar.), *agurram/tagurramt* (Ber.), and *amghār* (Ber.).[27] Yet despite this range of alternatives, social scientists most often refer to the Moroccan saint as a marabout, a Francophone corruption of the Arabic term *murābiṭ* that was used in Algeria to designate rural holy men.[28] This "abuse" of an indigenous concept has become so prevalent that today even North Africans often use *marabout* in place of *walī Allāh.*[29]

In examining the role of the saint in Moroccan society, social scientists often base their discussions on *La Religion musulmane en Berbérie* (1938) by the French historian Alfred Bel. According to Bel, North African Islam was heavily influenced by pre-Islamic Berber religiosity. This he defines as a predilection for sacrifice, a belief in the dualistic opposition of good versus evil, and faith in the power of charms and amulets. These pre-Islamic beliefs, which were driven underground after the Arab conquest, supposedly reemerged from the soil of the Maghrib after the introduction of Sufi mysticism in the eleventh and twelfth centuries.[30] Into what Bel saw as the "Arab" ethos of Islam—dominated by a remote and "terrible God" (*dieu terrible*) who permits no communion, no intermediary, and no contact between Himself and His creatures—Sufism introduced the concepts of mysticism, divine love, and belief in a beneficent deity who bestows *baraka* upon favored protégés.[31] Over time, a syncretistic form of religiosity, neither specifically Berber nor properly Muslim, metamorphosed out of this admixture of Berber spiritualism, Arab Islam, and Sufism. After gaining the approval of a sufficient percentage of the scholarly elite, this new syncretism supposedly evolved into an intolerant form of popular Sufism and a self-satisfied fatalism that contributed to the overall decline of Islamic civilization.[32]

According to Bel, the key figure in the development of popular Islam in North Africa was the marabout. Originally a point man in the Islamization of the rural Maghrib, he was seen by the masses as a theophany or "human fetish" (*homme fétiche*).[33] Based in a rural hermitage located far from the influence of cities or governments, the marabout performed important social functions, such as teaching Islam and mediating disputes. By thus making himself indispensable, he could compete with urban scholars in influencing the beliefs and practices of his followers. The marabout dominated Moroccan Islam from the beginning of the sixteenth century, when a so-called "epidemic of sharifism" was started by the followers of the Sufi shaykh Muḥammad ibn Sulaymān al-Jazūlī (d. 869/1465). In the early modern period, marabouts began to ascribe false prophetic lineages to themselves, replacing a paradigm of holiness based on asceticism and heroic virtue with one that was based on genealogy alone.[34]

Although Bel does make some valid historical points, his paradigm of "maraboutism" was heavily influenced by his political agenda. The overall purpose of his book was to explicate North African Islam for colonial officials who had little sympathy for the religion of their native subjects. These officials were most concerned with countering the influence of Islamic reformists in Algeria, who had begun to add their voices to the call for independence.[35] The concept of maraboutism was well-suited for creating an artificial dichotomy between the supposedly "natural" religious syncretism of the Berbers and an "Arab" Islamic orthodoxy. Until the end of the colonial period, the official French policy toward religion in the Maghrib was to distinguish the supposedly sober, authoritarian, and culturally alien ethos of classical Islam from the affective, syncretistic, and Mediterranean ethos of the Berber "state of nature."[36]

Despite its lack of objectivity, some of the most prominent anthropologists, social historians, and political scientists working in Morocco still regard Bel's model of North African Islam as definitive.[37] Others have tried to improve upon it by examining his paradigm of maraboutism through the lens of social anthropology, basing their findings on structural–functional studies of holy families and tomb complexes.

Ernest Gellner exemplifies this approach. Gellner sees maraboutism as one side of a dichotomy between urban and rural types of religious expression. In *Saints of the Atlas* (1969), he postulates an egalitarian, scripturally oriented, and urban Islamic orthodoxy, opposing it to a hierarchical, ritually indulgent, and rural heterodoxy.[38] Grafting Max Weber's ideal-type model of Protestant and Catholic religious culture onto an alien context, he epitomizes the conflict between these contrasting interpretations of Islam by drawing on an oppositional pair from medieval Europe: the "doctor" (an urban legist) versus the "saint" (a rural marabout).[39] Although Gellner tries to indigenize his model by identifying the ascribed and acquired traits that Moroccans associate with sainthood, these after-the-fact explanations do not extricate him from the mire of reductionistic and tautological definitions. Why is a Moroccan marabout or *agurram* a saint? "A person is a [saint] by virtue of being held to be one."[40]

Although Gellner's analysis of Moroccan sainthood provides certain insights into the nature of holy-family politics, it does not solve the problem of maraboutism. Claiming that a person is a saint because others treat him as such may help one understand why the descendants of a saint are considered holy, but it tells us little about the original, living saint himself. Also, one must ask: how can typologies drawn from localized case studies, such as Gellner's Aḥansal marabouts of the Atlas mountains, represent Muslim (or even Moroccan) sainthood in every respect? Finally, Gellner seems to contradict himself. Despite his stated aversion to the reification of tradition, he affirms the immutability of social structure by applying analytical tools developed for the study of small-scale societies to the complex and often literate world of Islamic Morocco.[41] Part of his problem lies in the anthropological disposition to favor the present over the past. If the present is not systematically compared with the past, it is easy to imagine that premodern institutions do not change. But traditions are ideational complexes, and ideas change all the time. It is not, therefore, more logical to assume that Moroccan ideas about holiness have changed as well? And may not local conceptions of sainthood reflect more than just local paradigms?

Other anthropologists and social historians have tried to overcome such difficulties by interpreting Moroccan sainthood in terms that are more universally Islamic. Émile Dermenghem (1954), for example, draws a distinction between "hereditary sanctity" and "initiatic sanctity" and focuses on three Islamic ideal types: the *walī* (the one who is close to God), the *ṣāliḥ* (the pure), and the *ṣiddīq* (the just).[42] Dale Eickelman (1976), on the other hand, concentrates on the idea of closeness (*qarāba*), which is both a doctrinal and a cultural metaphor.[43] These approaches indeed point academic inquiry toward categories that are used throughout the Muslim world. But before they can be worked into a general theory of sainthood, the extent of their applicability must first be established by comparative research.

The most fundamental problem with the neo-Weberian approach to Muslim sainthood, however, lies in Weber's paradigms themselves. This is particularly true of his model of charismatic authority. In Moroccan Studies, this concept is commonly used to explain the phenomenon of hereditary sainthood. In place of the prophet, Weber's ideal-type charismatic leader, neo-Weberians substitute the marabout; for charisma, they substitute *baraka*. As for the *ribāṭ* (the marabout's home base), its institutional development is assumed to follow the pattern of Weber's charismatic state.[44]

According to Weber's theory of the transformation of charisma, the charismatic authority of a religious leader changes after his death into a hereditary charisma that is retained by his descendants. To preserve their position in a competitive world, these second- and third-generation charismatic leaders rely on the artificial proof of miracle working and magic to attract a clientele. Since pure charisma can no longer be maintained, hereditary authority instead becomes dependent on social-structural and economic criteria. This "routinization of charisma" dulls the creative aspects of charismatic authority after only a few generations. Now stagnant, religiously legitimated leadership comes to rely on traditional forms of authority that have little of the original, creative character of charisma itself.[45]

At first glance, this approach seems ideally suited to the study of institutionalized sainthood. Recent historical and anthropological studies have indeed demonstrated that a number of North African marabouts presided over micropolities or "charismatic states."[46] What remains at issue, however, is Weber's inability to clarify the premises on which the phenomenon of charismatic domination is based. Among recent anthropologists, only Michael Gilsenan (1982) has attempted to identify the epistemological foundations of a Muslim holy man's charisma. To do so, however, he is forced to go outside the boundaries of classical Weberian sociology.[47]

Bryan Turner (1978) has attempted to modify the neo-Weberian discourse in Muslim sainthood by rejecting the terms "saint" for *walī* and "charisma" for *baraka*. Taking the monadist position on translation, he asserts that the Christian term "sainthood" is of little use in an Islamic context. Using the Roman Catholic process of canonization as his basis of comparison, he points out that this formal and highly bureaucratic procedure for recognizing posthumously the holiness of theologians and clerics has little to do with the informal and often ad hoc sanctification of living persons in the Islamic world. For Turner, since these Arabic concepts have little or nothing in common with Christianity, it is best to leave them untranslated.[48]

Yet the point made earlier about translation is equally valid for sociology. Differences in expression do not necessarily imply differences in the phenomena that words describe. While it is correct to say that a European "saint" and a Moroccan *walī Allāh* are not exactly the same, cultural relativism can be taken too far.[49] Turner's cultural purism is based on the premise that difference is fundamental whereas similarity is not. But if this were true, how could cross-cultural comparison be at all possible? To put it another way: If a *walī Allāh* looks like a saint, acts like a saint, and speaks like a saint, why not call him a saint?

Turner's relativistic argument is further weakened by misconceptions about the nature of sainthood in Islam and Christianity alike. First of all, the term "saint" is not inherently Christian. Like the term "religion," it has a polytheistic origin that is significantly different from its monotheistic present character.[50] Second, premodern Muslim sainthood (which Turner calls "Islamic maraboutism") can in no way be considered "formally and practically heretical."[51] Chapters One and Three of this book will show that jurists and similar "clerical" types were just as important to the hagiographical tradition of Morocco as they were to that of Europe. Furthermore, studies of sainthood in medieval Europe have demonstrated that whatever the official Church position on sainthood might have been, the vox populi was just as clearly heard in Latin Christendom as it was in Moroccan Islam.[52] Finally, Turner takes no account of the fact that even a Roman Catholic saint has to be recognized as holy in life before being canonized after death. This means that any serious investigation of sainthood—whether in premodern Europe, North Africa, or anywhere else in the Christian or Muslim worlds—must be conducted among the living as much as among the deceased.[53]

The Sociology of Sainthood

Unfortunately, the problematic of sainthood has not been resolved for any case under scholarly examination. If the relationship between holiness and authority in medieval Europe is imperfectly understood, how can one compare Islamic and Christian ideal types—even superficially? Must the student of Muslim sainthood forever rely on simplistic models? Can we do no better than Dermenghem's facile distinction between "popular saints" and "serious saints"?[54] Are we left with Clifford Geertz's (1968) cynical vision of marabouts as "vivid" manipulators of the masses who gain power by "contriving" to make things happen?[55] Although Geertz has provided a novel twist to the analysis of maraboutism, is charisma-as-showmanship the definitive explanation of this phenomenon?

One certainly hopes not. Sainthood as a characteristic of living men and women deserves more than to be dismissed with offhand or reductive explanations. If modern scholarship is to understand what it means to be a Muslim saint in both doctrinal and social terms, we cannot assume, as Geertz does, that the concept of holiness is ineffable. Lacking sufficient analytical tools in one discipline, we must turn to others until we find the right one. In other words, we need a multidisciplinary approach that is also cross-credal and transregional.

The most significant advances in the study of sainthood have come not from the field of Islamic Studies, but from historians and sociologists working within the Christian tradition. This research is indebted methodologically to the Bollandist cleric Hippolyte Delehaye, who sought to rationalize the study of sainthood in the Catholic Church by subjecting the *vitae* of saints to critical historical analysis. In his influential work *Sanctus* (1927), Delehaye attempted to come up with a normative paradigm for the Christian saint by analyzing early Church doctrines and the veneration of holy persons in late antiquity. He was most concerned with drawing a distinction between saints per se, who appear in the hagiographical record as martyrs and confessors, and the public cult of saints, which he traced to pagan antecedents.[56] Only in the last section of his work does he discuss the concept of sainthood (*sainteté*) itself.

For this Catholic priest, *sainteté* is an act of divine grace that manifests itself in several dimensions at once. In the most general sense, the saint is a friend of God whose virtue makes him the object of divine consideration. More narrowly conceived, he is also a member of a spiritual elite whose heroic acts elevate him above other human beings. Finally, as an individual exemplar, he is something different for different people at different times: in late antiquity he was a martyr or an ascetic; in medieval times he was a mystic or a miracle worker; in modern times he is a practitioner of charity. In the end, however, Delehaye's definition of sainthood remains suspended between Church doctrine on the one hand and the elusiveness of charisma on the other: sainthood is a quality of the individual soul whose effects can be seen by men but whose reality is known only to God.[57]

Although Delehaye's overt Catholicism limited the usefulness of his conclusions for secular historians, his attempt to create a sociohistorical model of sainthood aroused the interest of a fellow Belgian, the sociologist Pierre Delooz. Combining Delehaye's purely historical approach with the *Annaliste* concern for the study of mentalities, Delooz produced *Sociologie et canonisations* (1969), a historical-sociological study that gave birth to a new discipline known as the "sociology of sainthood."[58]

Going beyond Pitrim Sorokin's (1950) naive vision of sainthood as a form of idealized altruism,[59] Delooz examines holiness as part of a wider issue: the sixties-era interest in a sociology of knowledge. In his view, the cult of saints, as expressed in "sacred biography" or hagiographical literature, is uniquely able to satisfy the requirements of such a discipline.[60] First, it provides a precise type of social perception that can be assessed quantitatively. Second, because the production of hagiographies has persisted over so many centuries, the researcher can observe variations in the perception of sainthood over extended periods of time.

Delooz's starting point is the premise that a saint's reputation for holiness is socially generated: "to be a saint is to be a saint for others."[61] Although this statement appears on the surface to agree with Gellner's tautological definition of sainthood, in reality it says more. Like Delehaye but unlike Gellner, Delooz draws a fundamental distinction between the perception of living saints and the reputation that is ascribed to saints after death. Most saints, he claims, are "real" individuals who reside in the social imaginary. The raw data of this collective memory consist of accounts about the conduct of a holy person that are recorded during the saint's lifetime. Witnesses to the holy person's behavior "selectively perceive" the saint's actions according to their shared experiences, faith, and religious doctrines. After the holy person dies, these understandings help to redefine and transform the recollection of the saint within his or her community, so that only certain traits are reinforced and retained, while others are blurred and forgotten with the passage of time. In this way, the image of the saint is continually being remodelled according to the expectations of the saint's audience. In time, the saint who is the focus of cultic practices becomes what Delooz calls a "constructed saint"—one for whom the collective recollection is defined on the basis of universal paradigms. In the most extreme cases, the totalizing character of these paradigms might even lead to the fictional construction of a saint's reputation. This victory of the imaginary over the real is illustrated in Delooz's book by the Italian "Saint Priscilla of the Via Salaria," a woman whose only objective existence consisted of an empty Roman tomb discovered in 1802.[62]

Because of Delooz's affinity with the *Annales* school of social history, he is particularly sensitive to the issue of class. Although the canonization process in Roman Catholicism is notorious for its politics and bureaucratic legalisms, he found that the initiative in proposing an individual for sainthood usually came from the lower classes; it was they who aroused the interest of the Church hierarchy in the first place. Seldom did such initiatives come from either the nobility or the upper levels of the clergy.[63] Even in modern times, the Church has remained aware of the fact that although individual saints may have been princes, bishops, kings, or popes, the saint cult as an institution is maintained by the common people who visit saints' shrines. Significantly, Delooz's investigations could uncover no instance in which the canonization of a saint was the result of a purely political or top-down imposition of a holy reputation.[64]

Delooz's hypothesis of the "construction" of saints significantly advances our understanding of the relationship between living sainthood and tomb cults. Rather than assuming that the occupant of a tomb is venerated simply because others treat him as a saint, Delooz reminds us that the cult of a holy person is closely linked to the memory of who (or what) the saint was during his or her life. Whether this recollection is true or not is of little importance. What is significant is the fact that the collective memory of a saint's past attributes is based on a living model.

The American historians Donald Weinstein and Rudolph Bell have brought this paradigm into clearer focus by subjecting the *vitae* of European saints to a statistical analysis of traits and behaviors. The key to their monograph *Saints and Society* (1982) is the often-neglected concept of piety. For these scholars, who take a Durkheimian rather than a Weberian approach to the study of religion, piety is a speculum that the researcher can use to investigate social norms: "We study saints in order to understand piety; we study piety in order to understand society, for it is one of our basic premises that the pursuit as well as the perception of holiness [mirrors] social values and concerns."[65]

To Weinstein and Bell, sainthood is more than a mere tableau of individual and collective perceptions. Rather, it is a dynamic concept, both conditioned by and acting upon the society of which it is a part. In contrast to the dominant social-scientific tradition, which dismisses heroic piety as a passive–aggressive rejection of the material world,[66] they conceive of the saint's approach to God as "active, world-denying, God-seeking. Ordinary piety was more likely to be passive and favor-seeking, the majority of the faithful blurring the goals of purification and reverence with those of petition and covenant."[67] The dialectic engendered between ordinary and extraordinary forms of piety produces in turn the "paradox of the two spheres of sanctity" that is the leitmotif of their book.[68]

The centerpiece of *Saints and Society* is a computer-based, multivariate analysis of the *vitae* of 864 European saints who lived between the years 1000 and 1700 C.E. The authors' purpose in subjecting sacred biography to quantification is to study modal differences in sainthood for each region of Europe. As a result of their efforts, they identified variations specific not only to individual regions but to different time periods as well. For example, the majority of eleventh-century saints were noble wielders of power, twelfth-century saints were monastic reformers, and thirteenth-century saints were déclassé individuals who practiced humility as members of mendicant orders.

Weinstein and Bell also subjected their data to collective analyses in order to discover patterns not anticipated at the start of their research. By comparing data on the childhoods of saints, they were able to establish that the concept of the affective family was known in medieval society. Also significant was their discovery that differences in social demography were reflected in the meanings that people gave to the central paradigms of sainthood—a controversial point that attempts to resuscitate Delooz's earlier link between the study of sainthood and the sociology of knowledge.[69] Although Weinstein and Bell rely too heavily on official hagiographical lists as sources of data,[70] their research further highlights the relationship between a saint's posthumous cult and his or her prior life—a connection that was more logical to the medieval mind than to our own.

What This Book Will Demonstrate

The investigations of European sainthood begun by Delehaye and continued by Delooz, Weinstein and Bell, and others[71] suggest useful directions for the study of sainthood in Morocco and elsewhere in the Muslim world. In particular, these attempts to understand the medieval concept of holiness on its own terms rather than on the basis of theoretical hindsight alone open up the possibility of making systematic comparisons for the first time.

In both Islamdom and Christendom, a major problem for both religious authorities and modern researchers has been what to make of the two worlds of sainthood that existed in premodern society: the way of piety and mysticism as expressed in doctrinal writings and the way of power and miracle as expressed in the cult of saints. In Islam and Christianity as well, it was so-called popular religiosity that gave rise to the saint cult. Similarly, the proofs of sainthood often consisted in both cases of exceptional and miraculous occurrences. The collective appreciation of holiness was also expressed in terms of vaguely defined properties such as charisma (Christian) or *baraka* (Muslim). In both Christendom and Islamdom, the recollections of a saint's contemporaries were codified in literary form—through biographies (both collective and individual), memoirs, and accounts of memorable acts. In both doctrinal environments, such works helped to secure the acceptance of saint cults by religious officials, who consecrated and legitimized traditions that were instituted from below.

Such correspondences are sufficient to demonstrate that approaches used for the study of Christian sainthood can also be relevant to the study of *walāya* and *wilāya* in Islam. The present research builds upon such foundations by applying sociological and sociohistorical research methods to the study of sainthood and authority in premodern Morocco. Unlike previous works on Moroccan sainthood, however, its scope is not limited to the social-scientific alone. Instead, it is both revisionist and multidisciplinary. It is revisionist in that it approaches Islamic history from the methodological edge—by tracing the development of Moroccan Sufism and Moroccan sainthood without focusing on states or dynasties.[72] Its main characters are scholars and mystics, not sultans and viziers. Although these developments are periodized according to well-known eras and regimes, the latter are important only insofar as the politics of the times impinge on specific doctrines or modes of thought. In general, dynastic histories tell us little about what went on in premodern Muslim societies beyond the palace walls.[73] Those who wish to know more about the political history of the Maghrib should consult standard historical surveys of this region, such as Abdallah Laroui's *The History of the Maghrib, An Interpretive Essay* (1977) or Jamil M. Abun-Nasr's *A History of the Maghrib in the Islamic Period* (1987).

This research is multidisciplinary in that it employs the methodologies of narrative history, social history, rhetorical studies, and historical anthropology in a single work. A chronological approach is necessary because the history of Moroccan Sufism, the intellectual tradition in which Moroccan sainthood was embedded, has yet to be written. It makes little sense to draw conclusions about the nature of sainthood and authority in Muslim Morocco without first detailing the evolution of these concepts.

The historical narrative of this book will trace the development of Moroccan Sufism as an institution and Moroccan sainthood as a concept from the introduction of Islam through the end of the sixteenth century. As social history, it is concerned with how the perception of sainthood affects social action—what historians of the *Annales* school call the "history of public opinion."[74] As a study of the social uses of rhetoric, it also examines the role of hagiography in the development of the Moroccan paradigm of sainthood. Finally, as historical anthropology, it investigates the "logic of culture" in rural and urban society and across ethnic and regional boundaries.

The conceptual thread that ties the chapters of this book together are the themes of sainthood as a metaphysical "closeness" to God (*walāya*) and sainthood as the exercise of power and authority on earth (*wilāya*). In Morocco, as elsewhere in Islam, both aspects of sainthood are thought to be personified by Sufi teachers or spiritual masters (Ar. *ustādh, shaykh, murshid*). Consequently, it is impossible to disassociate the study of Moroccan sainthood from that of Sufism. Certainly, not all Muslim saints are Sufis. Martyrs, Companions of the Prophet, Shiʿite imams, and Kharijite ascetics might also be called *awliyāʾ Allāh.* But the existence of a few exceptions does not alter the general rule. Sufism and sainthood must be studied together because the Moroccan hagiographical tradition conceives of them as related. Whether or not a saint actually followed Sufi teachings or belonged to a Sufi order matters less than the fact that he (and occasionally she) is assumed to have done so.

The symbiotic relationship between Muslim sainthood and Sufism also underscores the limits to the sociological investigation of sanctity. Even if one accepts the premise that sainthood is a matter of social perception, the mystical-philosophical discussions of the subject found in Sufi treatises indicate that this perception operates on more than one level at the same time. This observation tells us that another version of Weinstein and Bell's "two spheres of sainthood" existed in premodern Morocco: the *walī Allāh* as seen by the Muslim masses versus the *walī Allāh* as seen by an inner circle of mystics and intellectuals.

Although different, these two modes of perception are not completely separate. Rather, they influence each other reciprocally: the "popular" image of the *walī Allāh* may also be shared by Sufi specialists, who reinterpret it according to their own doctrines. This "eternal point" of conjuncture, as one sixteenth-century Moroccan Sufi called it—the bridge between mystical doctrine and sainthood as experienced by the majority of Muslims—is most clearly visible in the saint who is the greatest of his time: the so-called Axis of the Age (*quṭb az-zamān*). The most important axial saint in early-modern Morocco was Muḥammad ibn Sulaymān al-Jazūlī, the very person blamed by Alfred Bel for causing the decline of Moroccan Islam. Far from introducing an unorthodox model of Islamic leadership as Bel surmised, the image of al-Jazūlī as a *walī Allāh* was modeled on the paradigm of the Prophet Muḥammad. Thus, the collective recollection of his sainthood reflected not just local norms but a more universal "tropics of prophethood" that pertained to Islam as a whole.[75]

Al-Jazūlī's appearance, however, culminates a process that requires detailed investigation. Therefore, this study of Moroccan sainthood must begin in the institution's formative period—the eleventh and twelfth centuries C.E. This era roughly matches, but is not identical to, the temporal extent of the Almoravid and Almohad empires.

Chapter One introduces the reader to the concept of the *ṣāliḥ,* a term which epitomizes Moroccan sainthood in early hagiographical texts. In the cities, the *ṣāliḥ* was often revered as an "anchor of the earth" (*watad al-arḍ*). In this role, he was a religious leader (*imām*) whose knowledge of Islamic law and moral uprightness kept the social fabric intact. As an "anchor" of his society, he was first and foremost a juridical scholar (*faqīh*): one who exercised interpretive authority over the *Sharīʿa,* the divine law. When the paradigm of the *ṣāliḥ* was incorporated into Sufism, it came to symbolize the perspectives of "Sunni internationalism" and *uṣūl ad-dīn,* a hermeneutical method that based normative Islamic practice on the Qur'an and the traditions of the Prophet Muḥammad. As both Sufi and *uṣūlī,* the *ṣāliḥ* advocated a consensus-based interpretation of Sunni Islam against regional forms of sectarianism.

Chapter Two examines rural sainthood in Morocco from the standpoint of historical anthropology, focusing on the rural saint's dependence on urban intellectual traditions. As Alfred Bel surmised, the rural saint was a spokesperson for normative Islam and played a vital role in the Islamization of the countryside. But the rural saint was more than just a marabout. Although Bel popularized this particular persona of the rural saint, he ignored two others of equal importance: the rural legist and the rural Sufi shaykh.

Often, a marabout might double as both legist and shaykh. Yet even when these roles were embodied in different persons, each drew on similar epistemologies and played similar social roles. In addition, all three figures saw themselves as legitimate bearers of religious authority and members of the ulama, the scholarly class.

The relationship between rural sainthood and authority was most clearly visible in the context of the *ribāṭ,* the institutional center of rural Sufism. From this site the rural saint taught Islamic dogma and dispensed justice to tribal clients. Since the *ribāṭ* also served as a teaching center for normative Islam, it complemented rather than opposed urban Islamic institutions. In addition, its position astride multiple social and intellectual networks allowed it to play an important role in the development of institutionalized Sufism. In Morocco, the earliest Sufi confraternities were *ribāṭ*-based. These brotherhoods fostered the normative homogeneity of Sunni Islam by combining mystical doctrines that originated in lands far removed from Morocco, such as Egypt and eastern Iran, with criteria of membership that were based on ethnic or tribal ties.[76]

Chapter Three examines Moroccan sainthood as visualized in the hagiographical monograph made up of "exploit narratives" (Ar. *manqaba,* pl. *manāqib*), focusing in particular on the role of the urban jurist in establishing the limits of saintly authority. By examining a work on the rural holy man Abū Yiʿzzā (d. 572/1177), it explores how an urban legist and arbiter of tradition can reconceptualize the "meaning" of a rural charismatic. In the case of Abū Yiʿzzā, this process of redefinition involved turning the saint's reputation for miracle working into an argument for divinely guided leadership. The second half of the chapter examines how the saint himself might participate in the interpretation of sainthood. The subject of this section is Abū'l-ʿAbbās as-Sabtī (d. 601/1204), the patron saint of Marrakesh. In contrast to the power-wielding Abū Yiʿzzā, as-Sabtī is concerned to portray himself as an ethical exemplar and defender of the poor, whose miracles are designed to raise the social consciousness of his audience.

Chapter Four concludes the first part of this book by examining the genre of the hagiographical anthology, the *rijāl* literature. After addressing the interpretive nature of this tradition, 316 saints who flourished in the Almoravid and Almohad periods are analyzed sociologically, based on the methods introduced by Delooz and Weinstein and Bell. The information in these notices is examined according to multiple criteria, including ethnicity, urban origins, education, and social status. Other criteria, such as spiritual practices, significant signs of holiness, and types of miracles are also examined to arrive at a typicality profile of the Moroccan *walī Allāh.* A major goal of this chapter is to demonstrate that although Delehaye may have been right when he asserted that the full reality of the saint is known only to God, sainthood as a concept is by no means ineffable, and can be traced by sociological investigation.

The second part of this book details the institutionalization of the Moroccan paradigm of sainthood in a specific corporate body: the Sufi order (*ṭāʾifa*) founded by the axial saint (*quṭb*) al-Jazūlī. Chapter Five sets the stage for this discussion by providing an overview of Moroccan institutional Sufism in the two centuries before al-Jazūlī. Here Sufism is examined in the context of Marinid-era intellectual life, which was characterized by the attempt to institutionalize and standardize most branches of Islamic thought. This process of institutionalization affected Moroccan Sufism as well and resulted in the creation of the corporately organized Sufi confraternity. Two groups of regional confraternities are discussed in this chapter: those stemming from the way of Abū Madyan (d. 594/1198), which drew from both Andalusian and Moroccan antecedents and was influential as far away as Egypt, and those tracing their roots to Abū'l-Ḥasan ash-Shādhilī (d. 656/1258), which helped introduce the sharifian model of authority into Moroccan Sufism.

The crux of this book lies in the final three chapters, where the interrelationship between *walāya* and *wilāya* in Moroccan Sufism is examined through a study of the doctrines and activities of the Jazūliyya Sufi order. These chapters constitute the first in-depth study of this important confraternity in any language. The writings of al-Jazūlī and his successors demonstrate that these mystical leaders conceived of their order as a vehicle for new and revolutionary ideologies. Through the concepts of the "sovereignty of saintly authority" (*siyādat al-imāma*) and the "Muḥammadan Way" (*aṭ-ṭarīqa al-Muḥammadiyya*), the Jazūliyya *ṭāʾifa* was more than just a vehicle for religious reform. It also promoted the political ideology of sharifism and helped to define Morocco as a country with a unique Islamic identity.

Chapter Six is a literary-biographical study of the founder of the Jazūliyya Sufi order in light of the political, social, and intellectual life of fifteenth-century Morocco. The impact of al-Jazūlī's doctrine, which combined Shādhilī, Qādirī, and even Persian perspectives, was so great that it dominated Moroccan Sufism for two hundred years. In fact, it was practically impossible for one to be a Sufi in sixteenth-century Morocco without calling oneself a Jazūlite. Al-Jazūlī's personification of power and authority was no less important than his doctrine. More than just a spiritual master and doctrinal innovator, he was also regarded as the long-awaited "just Imam"—a divinely guided leader whose persona reflected the paradigms of both Sufism and sharifism. Although he was a sincere Sunni Muslim and disapproved of Shiʿite comparisons, his concept of authority was at least partly dependent on ʿAlid paradigms.

Chapter Seven is a study of the main pillar of Jazūlite ideology, the doctrine of the Muḥammadan Way. The roots of this model of authority are traced to the "imitatio Muhammadi" paradigm of Islamic pietism and Idrisid sharifism, which conceived of the Muḥammadan paradigm in genealogical terms. The Jazūlite concept of Muḥammadan sainthood is next traced doctrinally from al-Ḥakīm at-Tirmidhī (d. 298/910) to Ibn al-ʿArabī (d. 638/1240) and ʿAbd al-Karīm al-Jīlī (d. 805/1402–3), and ending with the Jazūlite shaykhs ʿAlī Ṣāliḥ al-Andalusī (d. before 914/1508–9) and ʿAbdallāh al-Ghazwānī (d. 935/1528–9). The writings of these last two figures reveal that in Morocco at least, the Muḥammadan Way constituted a model of authority in which sainthood and religious leadership were predicated on the assimilation of the Prophetic archetype. This merging of Prophet and saint was most clearly expressed in al-Ghazwānī's doctrine of the "sovereignty of saintly authority" (*siyādat al-imāma*), in which the paradigmatic Sufi saint takes on many of the characteristics of the ʿAlid Imam.

Chapter Eight concludes the narrative sequence of this book by taking al-Ghazwānī's concept of the "sovereignty of saintly authority" into the material world and detailing how the shaykhs of the Jazūliyya aided in the creation of sharifian Morocco. This involvement in political activism was different from the so-called Maraboutic Crisis described by colonial-era scholars. Rather than reflecting the fissiparous tendencies of traditional Moroccan society, the doctrines and actions of Jazūlite shaykhs helped to unite Morocco against its Portuguese invaders and gave a new sense of legitimacy to the state and its institutions. Contrary to the assumptions of Alfred Bel and his followers, the leaders of the Jazūliyya did not see themselves as rivals for the throne but as religious guides and moral guardians, and they tended to support any claimant for power who agreed with their agenda. When al-Ghazwānī and his followers finally cast their lot with the Saʿdian sharifs of southern Morocco, they attained their immediate objectives but created the conditions for their eventual undoing. In the end, the sharifs prevailed over the shaykhs of the Jazūliyya as divinely sanctioned imams because their ascribed *wilāya,* based as it was on genealogical closeness to the Prophet, was more easily reckoned than the acquired *wilāya* of their Sufi mentors, which was based on the elusive criterion of closeness to God.

Texts and Sources

This study relies extensively on primary sources of information: the treatises, aphorisms, and sayings of Moroccan saints themselves, notices and memoirs composed by their followers, and hagiographical materials from later generations. In the field of Islamic Studies, the use of biographies as sources for social history is a relatively new, but by no means unheard-of approach. Richard Bulliet's *The Patricians of Nishapur* (1972) and L. Carl Brown's *The Tunisia of Ahmad Bey* (1974) were ground-breaking attempts in the use of such materials.[77] Carl F. Petry's (1981) use of biographical dictionaries to study the ulama of fifteenth-century Cairo provided a wealth of information on late Mamluk society.[78] Similar work has yet to be done, however, with hagiographies.[79] To a large extent, this is due to the fact that the canons of Western rationalism have led contemporary Islamicists and social scientists to doubt whether the saints described in sacred biography are actual historical personages. This is also a reason why anthropologists, assuming that the "real" individual at the heart of a saint cult lies beyond objective verification, tend to avoid the doctrinal aspects of Muslim sainthood, preferring instead to concentrate on more "objectively" visible concepts such as *baraka* and the routinization of charisma.

The ineffability of religious experience is a central premise of Durkheimian sociology, which views religion as a closed cultural system that reflects the ethos of the host society. This perspective is evident in Clifford Geertz's famous definition of religion as a cultural system: religion is "a system of symbols which acts to establish powerful, pervasive, and long-lasting *moods* and motivations in men by formulating conceptions of a general order of existence and *clothing* these conceptions with such an *aura of factuality* that the moods and motivations *seem* uniquely realistic" (italics added).[80]

Geertz's definition can be challenged in at least three ways. First, if religions could not transcend cultural boundaries, then conversion would require a process of re-enculturation whereby the convert would exchange not only his or her religious identity but also the entire cultural matrix in which his or her identity has been formed.[81] If this were the case, the practical barriers to conversion would be nearly insurmountable, and conversion from one religion to another would not be as easy or as rapid as it clearly has been. Second, the vocabulary used by Geertz in his definition "poisons the well" against spiritual realities and strips religion of its claim to truth: *moods* are changeable emotional states; *clothing* implies a sense of fashion or even dissimulation; *aura of factuality* refers to something that is not really there, a false consciousness or a psychic delusion; and *seem* connotes appearance rather than reality, a distortion of the facts, and reality seen "through a glass darkly." Finally, Geertz's premise of ineffability renders the academic study of sainthood all but impossible. While it is true that the boundaries between the sacred and the profane have become more permeable in the social-scientific study of religion, the modernist bias of "perspectivist" models such as is displayed here still precludes any dialectic between the sacred and concrete, lived experiences. Without such a dialectic, there can be no place for either saints or miracles.[82]

Postmodern literary criticism and historiography have demonstrated that the politics of data selection can provide an image of former events that reflects the consciousness of the present as much or more than that of the past. Hayden White and others have additionally pointed out that the process of hermeneutics can alter the "facts" that are retained by later generations.[83] It is often forgotten, however, that such caveats are equally applicable to a Western historian's own reconstruction of non-Western "facts." To use but one example, many have assumed, on the basis of present custom, that descent from the Prophet Muḥammad is a near-universal prerequisite for Moroccan sainthood. An examination of premodern Moroccan hagiographies, however, reveals that prior to the sixteenth century the possession of a Prophetic lineage, although highly valued as a marker of social status, was largely irrelevant to the attribution of sainthood.[84]

There are a number of ways to look at the texts that provide information about a Muslim saint. One approach is to view all accounts—first-hand, second-hand, premodern, or contemporary—as literature. Those who adhere to this perspective tend to view both history and biography as rhetorical exercises that say as much about their writers as they do about their subjects. On the radical side are post-Nietzschean deconstructivists, whose "metaphysics of the nihil" cause them to regard all historical writing as fiction.[85] A more fruitful approach is that of Hans-Georg Gadamer or Alasdair MacIntyre, who see the history of ideas as the product of ever-changing contexts and epistemologies that leave tradition dynamically suspended between the present and the past.[86] Similarly, Hayden White contends that the "fictions of factual representation" are relative rather than absolute, and Paul Ricoeur argues that a time-based "narrative understanding" lies at the heart of all historical writing.[87]

Although the rhetorical approach to history is both beneficial and thought-provoking, having too much faith in the concept of tropes can lead to two major pitfalls. One is the idea that premodern peoples could not or would not distinguish between fact and fantasy.[88] If this were the case, then why did medieval hagiographers in both the Christian and the Islamic worlds make such an effort to prove the validity of their claims? In answering this question, the tropological extremist can only fall back on the fallacy of the unverifiable assumption and assume that these authors' concern for the truth was no more than a mystification created by the rhetoric of *instructio.*

Another, more subtle error is to assert that the study of premodern religiosity should be concerned with perceptions rather than facts. This premise, which is a corollary of Durkheimian sociology, assumes, without adequate corroboration, that the notices contained in hagiographical literature are latter-day expressions of ideal sainthood, not representations of real people.[89] This perspective also begs the question of verifiability by implying that divine revelations, extraordinary virtues, or paranormal phenomena do not exist.[90] Although the epistemological problem of differentiating fact from fantasy is undeniably difficult, it is simply not true that all sacred biography represents only *topoi* and not real human beings. The Moroccan hagiographies discussed in this book contain too much quotidian information to dismiss their subjects as mere tropological ideals.

A different approach to hagiography can be found in the so-called traditionalist perspective, which views the contents of sacred biography as expressing a "human margin" that obscures an underlying spiritual reality.[91] Frithjof Schuon, the most notable proponent of this approach, would agree with rhetoricians and tropologists that the "exaggerations and platitudes" of hagiographies render them "practically unreadable for anyone who is looking for a concrete and lifelike picture of the saints." He would further agree that the primary purpose of sacred biography is *instructio*—not to condition the human being to a "cringing punctiliousness that is actually insulting to God, but to perfect truthfulness in deeds and thought, which is a way of realizing a certain unity for the sake of the One and Only."[92] This profoundly anti-relativistic way of looking at sacred biography has much in common with the way in which it is viewed by Moroccan Sufis themselves. When informed that I was writing "a book about Imam al-Jazūlī," a venerable mystic in the city of Salé told his companion, "Yes, but what can he *say* about him?"

I can only reply that one must say something. Schuon and his followers have reminded us that it is necessary to view the Moroccan saint as both the recipient and the transmitter of a long-standing mystical tradition.[93] But a *walī Allāh* is more than a spiritual trope, just as he or she is more than a figment of the narrative imagination. The *walī Allāh* is also a human being who acts, like other human beings, in several dimensions at once. At one moment the *walī* is a teacher, at another a philosopher, at other times a pure charismatic, at others a politician. There must be a way to express the many-sided reality of Moroccan sainthood without reducing the *walī Allāh* to any single essence. There must also be a way to make the "inside" view of Moroccan sainthood intelligible to those who experience reality outside of both the Islamic and the Sufi traditions.

To accomplish these goals, the historian of sainthood must be concerned with what Aviad Kleinberg has called "saving the text."[94] It is not to be forgotten that all history, whether oral or written, expresses a variety of *topoi*. However, as historians who assess the stories told by others, we must assume that our informants tell us the truth as they see it. This is not to say that we cannot interpret this information in our own way and even reconceptualize our informants' appraisal of the truth as a product of social conditioning or rhetoric. But we must maintain the integrity of their beliefs in what we write about them. To say that premodern people believed in saintly miracles is to acknowledge that such miracles indeed existed—to premodern people. Whether or not we believe that miracles exist today is irrelevant to our understanding of what they meant to human beings in the past. Faith claims, such as the belief in miracles and paranormal phenomena, are inherently unprovable. On the other hand, they are also undeniable assertions and thus fall under the rubric of what phenomenologists of religion call *epoché,* the suspension of judgment.[95] Historians of religion should never forget that the Moroccan Muslim of past ages—both the *walī Allāh* and his audience, whether educated or uneducated, scholar or soldier—lived in a sacralized cosmos in which the transcendent, not the material, represented the greater reality. Whatever our modern or postmodern assumptions may be, remaining true to our subjects' cultural space and time requires that we acknowledge the *walī Allāh* as both a transmitter of spiritual wisdom and an agent of the miraculous.

PART I

Sainthood and Authority in Morocco: The Origins and Development of a Paradigm

CHAPTER ONE

Sainthood in an Urban Context: Ṣulaḥā', *Scholars, and "Anchors of the Earth"*

The Sāliḥ, *A Social Paradigm for Moroccan Sainthood*

According to Richard Bulliet, the history of Islam as viewed "from the edge" (i.e., as a product of individuals, local communities, and cultures) is a history of the religious scholars, the ulama.[1] These arbiters of tradition are important to Islam because they mediate the interpretation of religion and ensure the continuity of legal, educational, and administrative institutions despite the vicissitudes of time and politics. As a corporate group, they identify themselves with urban institutions, have an urban-based education, and memorialize themselves in a tradition of collective biography that reflects an urban ethos.

In premodern Morocco, the symbolic universe of Muslim sainthood was similarly interpreted by the ulama.[2] By imposing a "normative homogeneity" on the definition of sainthood, these scholars promoted an image of holiness that reflected their own values and concerns.[3] This is not to say that rural sainthood could not, at times, present a different aspect from its urban counterpart. It does mean, however, that any differences that might have existed between urban and rural forms of sainthood were not absolute, for the actions and sayings of Moroccan saints were recorded in a genre of sacred biography that was modeled on what the ulama wrote for themselves. Early Moroccan hagiography was thus different from "ulamology" primarily in regard to its subject matter, not in its authorship or use of rhetoric.[4] It was written by ulama for other ulama (or potential ulama), and sought to define sainthood in ways that the ulama could understand and accept. The advantage of this tradition was that it legitimized the Muslim saint by typologizing his roles in ways that were both extralocal and pan-Islamic. Its disadvantage was that it often sacrificed the distinctiveness of local interpretations of sainthood on the altar of universalism.

Sufism was a latecomer to Morocco, not appearing in the historical record until the beginning of the eleventh century C.E.—about two hundred and fifty years after it first appeared in the Muslim East and nearly a century after it was introduced in Muslim Spain. For the most part, the earliest traditions of Moroccan Sufism were doctrinally conservative in nature: the models of Sufism depicted in doctrinal and hagiographical works reflected an early emphasis on piety and asceticism well into the Islamic Middle Period. This was in part due to the ethical perspective of the Maliki school of Islamic law, which emphasized a strict complementarity between inner belief and outer practice. This "show me" attitude of Maliki credalism is clearly apparent in the works of the earliest Moroccan hagiographers, who conceived of Sufism more as a type of heroic pietism than as a form of metaphysics. It was similarly visible in the long-standing popularity of early pietistic works such as ʿAbdallāh ibn al-Mubārak's (d. 181/797) *Kitāb az-zuhd wa'r-raqāʾiq* (Book of asceticism and exemplary acts of worship), a treatise on spiritual discipline that was written by a student of the so-called jurist of the Sufis, Sufyān ath-Thawrī (d. 161/778).[5]

The first impression that one gets of Moroccan Sufism in the earliest works of hagiography is thus of a no-nonsense pietism, in which a person's privately held doctrines mattered less than did the visible example of his behavior.[6] For orthodox mystics[7] such as the influential Moroccan jurist and hagiographer Abū Yaʿqūb Yūsuf ibn az-Zayyāt at-Tādilī (d. 628/1230–1),[8] a "Sufi" was no more (or less) than a sincere Muslim who dedicated himself to the highest ideals of his faith. What separated the Sufi from his fellow believers was not his mystical doctrine but the extent of his piety. At-Tādilī saw no necessary connection between Sufism and mysticism, nor did he show much interest in metaphysics. Instead, his concern was to memorialize regional exemplars of piety and virtue whose defining attribute was their adherence to the behavioral example (*sunna*) of the Prophet Muḥammad, his Companions (*aṣ-ṣaḥāba*), and their Successors (*at-tābiʿūn*).

No work has had more influence on the Moroccan view of sainthood than at-Tādilī's *Kitāb at-tashawwuf ilā rijāl at-taṣawwuf* (Book of insight into the tradition bearers of sufism). For this reason, it is significant that at-Tādilī's view of Muslim sainthood was not based on Maliki precedent alone, but also on Sufi doctrines that came from outside of the Maghrib. Rather than relying on purely local definitions of sainthood, he based his models on ideal types that originated as far away as the eastern Iranian province of Khurasan. His most important sources of Sufi doctrine were the hagiographical works of Buyid- and Seljuq-era Sufis such as Abū ʿAbd ar-Raḥmān as-Sulamī (d. 412/1021),[9] Abū Nuʿaym al-Iṣfahānī (d. 430/1038–9),[10] and Abū'l-Qāsim al-Qushayrī (d. 467/1074).[11] At-Tādilī's debt to al-Qushayrī in particular was so great that his entire discussion of Sufism as a distinctive methodology (*madhhab*) in Islam is lifted nearly verbatim from the latter's *Risāla fī ʿilm at-taṣawwuf* (Treatise on the discipline of Sufism). This work was made known to him by a mystic of Iranian origin who visited Marrakesh in the year 597/1200–1.[12] At-Tādilī's appropriation of al-Qushayrī's definition of Sufism should not be taken to mean, however, that Moroccan Sufism was merely a copy of a Persian original. Quite the contrary. One of At-Tādilī's main purposes in writing *at-Tashawwuf* was to promote a specifically Moroccan fellowship of the holy.

At-Tādilī's "tradition bearers of Sufism" are a collectivity of men (plus a few women) whose rhetorical purpose is to exemplify the Sunna of the Prophet Muḥammad. As guarantors and transmitters of normative tradition (*rijāl al-ʿilm*), they display a detailed understanding of the requirements of faith that confirms the trust that God has put in them.[13] In return for their sincerity and devotion, God confirms His closeness to them by causing them to produce miracles (*karāma,* pl. *karāmāt*). Further confirmation of their status comes from the ulama—their fellow *rijāl al ʿilm*—who pass on accounts about their lives, thus allowing hagiographers such as at-Tādilī to typify and memorialize their example in works that arrange them in ranks and categories (*ṭabaqāt*). Thus validated by God and revalidated by their peers, at-Tādilī's "Sunni–Sufi" saints are protégés of God who pay back His favors by bestowing blessings on their fellow believers.[14] Indeed, says at-Tādilī, "No era will lack a *walī* from among the *awliyāʾ* of God Most High, through whom Allah will protect the land and bestow mercy on [His] worshippers."[15]

This statement tells us that for at-Tādilī, the *awliyāʾ Allāh* are responsible to God and humankind in equal measure. With respect to God, this responsibility is expressed as *ʿibāda,* devoted servitude; with respect to their fellow believers, it is expressed as *ṣalāḥ,* socially conscious virtue. This praxis-oriented interpretation of sainthood is derived from a statement of God in the Qur'an. According to the Qur'an, the best Muslims reside "in the company of those whom Allah has favored: the prophets (*anbiyāʾ*), the truthful (*ṣiddīqīn*), the martyrs (*shuhadāʾ*), and the virtuous (*ṣāliḥīn*). What a beautiful fellowship they are!"[16] The greatest honor a person can thus attain is to be known as a "slave of God" (*ʿabd Allāh*) and a "virtuous man" (*rajul ṣālih*) at the same time. This is why at-Tādilī uses the term *ʿabd ṣāliḥ* as a synonym for *walī Allāh.*[17]

As a member of society, the *ṣāliḥ* is a morally upstanding and socially constructive individual who performs visible acts of piety and works for the betterment (*iṣlāḥ*) of himself and his fellow believers. By upholding the example of the Prophet's Sunna, he stands in direct contrast to the *fāsid,* the irresponsible individualist, who jeopardizes the Muslim community by undermining the standards of faith and virtue that the *ṣāliḥ* seeks to establish. In at-Tādilī's day, this moral distinction between socially conscious virtue (*ṣalāḥ*) and asocial individualism (*fasād*) reflected the juridical dichotomy of faith (*īmān*) versus unbelief (*kufr*) that separated Muslims from those who refused to accept Islam.[18] Because the Maliki school of law deemed it inappropriate for a Muslim to deny the faith of a fellow believer under all but the most extreme circumstances, the mere disobedience of God's laws would almost never cause a person to be accused of unbelief. Instead, the *ṣalāḥ* versus *fasād* distinction provided a means of dealing with deviancy that still gave room for the sinner to return to the fold.

Holy Jurists in Fez: The Ṣāliḥ as an "Anchor of the Earth"

For at-Tādilī, the primary function of the *ṣāliḥ* was to personify the values of Sunni Islam. This he did by scrupulously adhering to the tenets of God's Law (*ash-sharīʿa*). It is therefore not surprising to find that many of the saints in *at-Tashawwuf* and other early hagiographical works are people who follow the prescriptions of Islamic law to a degree far surpassing that of the ordinary believer. Often, these individuals act as dissemenators of Islam in the countryside or as partisans of Maliki jurisprudence in the cities.

It is still believed in North Africa that many of the Muslim warriors (*mujāhidūn*) who came to the Maghrib with the Arab armies of conquest settled in this region and devoted themselves to disseminating the Islamic faith. In the foothills between Tetuan and Shafshāwan in northern Morocco are mosques that are said to have been built (ca. 74–7/711–14) by the Muslim commanders Ṭāriq ibn Ziyād and Mūsā ibn Nuṣayr. In this same region are tombs dedicated to the eponyms of local tribes, who are believed to have arrived in Morocco as companions of these early leaders. These venerated ancestors, whose cults have more to do with the cultural effects of Arabization than with the recollection of actual deeds, include Yalṣū al-ʿUthmānī al-Qurashī, putative ancestor of the Banū Yalṣū tribal segment of Ghumāra; Ḥabīb ibn Yūsuf al-Fihrī, ancestor of the tribe of Jabal Ḥabīb; and Muḥammad ibn Zajal al-Qurashī, ancestor of the Banū Zajal of Ghumāra.[19]

Apart from holy warriors and tribal eponyms, the most important saints of early Moroccan Sufism were legal specialists (sing. *faqīh,* pl. *fuqahāʾ*). Indeed, the legal scholar comes up so often in the hagiographical record that one is led to doubt the validity of the widely accepted dichotomy between juridical Islam and Sufism. Before jumping to the opposite extreme, however, and concluding that opposition to Sufism was the exception rather than the rule, it must be recalled that not everybody who was designated as a "Sufi" in works such as at-Tādilī's *at-Tashawwuf* actually thought of himself as such. It has long been common among Sufi hagiographers to lend credibility to their tradition by including both Sufi and non-Sufi *awliyāʾ* under the same cover. Those who employed this strategy, such as the influential Iranian hagiographer Abū Nuʿaym al-Iṣfahānī, hoped to convince their readers that the paradigmatic figures of early Islam were also the forerunners of Sufism. In their works, these saints are depicted as proto-Sufis whose teachings foreshadow later Sufi doctrines.

In addition, the term *walī Allāh* might at times be used by authors who were non-Sufi or even anti-Sufi. In his *Risāla,* a treatise on Maliki law, the Tunisian jurist Abū Muḥammad ibn Abī Zayd al-Qayrawānī (d. 386/996) makes the following statement: "God, may He be glorified, has created heaven as an eternal resting place for His *awliyāʾ,* whom He honors with the light of His noble countenance."[20] Far from being a Sufi, Ibn Abī Zayd was a staunch supporter of exoteric Malikism against the Fatimid Shiʿism of tenth-century Ifrīqīya. Since the Ismāʿīlī Fatimids set themselves apart from the majority of Muslims by virtue of their esoterism, Ibn Abī Zayd opposed all esoteric forms of Islam, including Sufism.[21] Nevertheless, he was forced to accept the concept of the *walī Allāh* in principle because this term appears in the Qur'an.[22] Ibn Abī Zayd's example is an important reminder that the mere use of a term associated with Muslim sainthood does not necessarily imply an acceptance of its Sufi meaning.

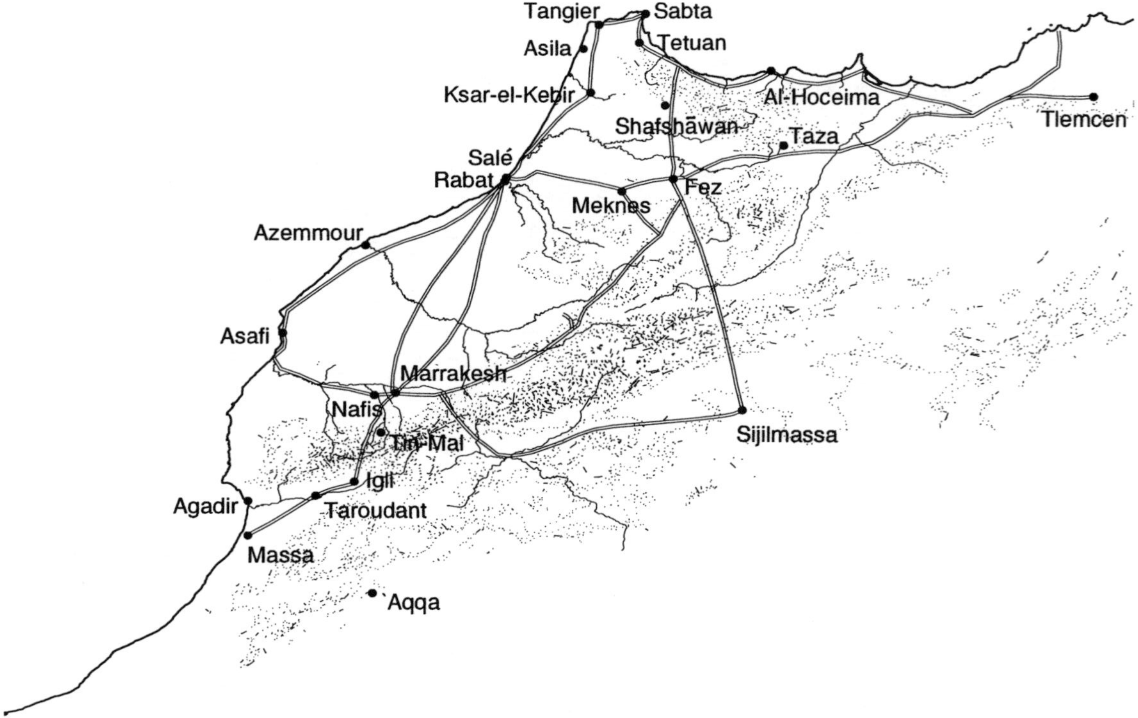

MAP THREE

Urban Areas in Premodern Morocco

However, the practice of including jurists and other non-Sufis in Sufi hagiographical literature might be more than just a ploy. All *ṣulaḥāʾ* (sing. *ṣāliḥ*), Sufi or otherwise, are potentially worthy of inclusion among the ranks of the *awliyāʾ* because they uphold the normative values of Islam. The idea that virtue (*ṣalāḥ*) and piety (*ʿibāda*) were necessary (although not sufficient) conditions for sainthood made it possible for at-Tādilī and his successors to include jurists and other non-Sufi ulama among the ranks of the earliest Moroccan saints. Given the urban orientation of Islamic intellectual life, one would also expect to find these scholars associated with the few cities that existed in the Far Maghrib at that time. Of these cities, Fez (Ar. *Fās*) was the most important because it served as the economic hub for the entire western Maghrib.

An often overlooked characteristic of Fez is that most of its inhabitants were originally from rural or Berber backgrounds. After only a few generations of city life, the Arab cultural milieu of Fez would transform these rural immigrants into Arabic-speaking urbanites. Now identifying themselves as "people of Fez" (*ahl Fās*), they exchanged their original Berber culture for Arabo-Islamic civilization.[23] This pattern of cultural change was established early on in the city's history, when Andalusian refugees from the suburbs of Córdoba and Seville settled on the downhill side of the Fez river from the city's original Idrisid center of al-ʿAliyya.[24] These Arabized immigrants played a major role in the enculturation of those who came after them. In time, the *ahl Fās* came to comprise two distinct subcultures: that of the more insular and purely Arab "Qayrawānīs" on the upper side of the city, and that of the more heterogeneous "Andalusians" downhill. Since rural immigrants tended to settle downriver on the "Andalusian" side of Fez, it was in that area that most cultural change took place. Eventually, the Arabizing influence of Fez penetrated the surrounding countryside. By the early twelfth century the city was encircled by a constellation of Arabized Berber tribes (Banū Yūsuf, Fandalāwa, Banū Bahālīl, Zawāwa, Majāsa, Ghiyātha, and Salāljūn) who retained a memory of their Berber roots but had long since adopted Arabic speech and customs.[25]

The earliest *awliyāʾ* of Fez were a group of juridically trained ascetics and legal experts who were known as "anchors of the earth" (*awtād al-arḍ*). They were given this appellation because they acted metaphorically as tent pegs (*watad*, pl. *awtād*) in "holding down" or maintaining the Sharīʿa in their locality (*arḍ*). One of the most significant of these *awtād* was the Maliki legist Darrās ibn Ismāʿīl (d. 357/968). Although Maliki law was introduced into Morocco as early as the ninth century,[26] in Darrās' time it had not yet become the official legal school (*madhhab*) of the Far Maghrib.[27] The ulama of Fez still practiced Hanafi or "Kufan" jurisprudence, which was favored by the original Idrisid rulers of the city.[28] Darrās aided in the triumph of Malikism by introducing *Al-Mudawwana al-kubrā* (The Greater Compendium), the compendium of juridical practice by Saḥnūn ʿAbd as-Salām at-Tanūkhī (d. 240/854).[29] As an advanced scholar, Darrās studied under the greatest Maliki legists of his age and was a teacher of Ibn Abī Zayd al-Qayrawānī.[30] In his travels in search of knowledge, he journeyed from Muslim Spain, where he fought against the Christians, to points as far east as Alexandria and Mecca.[31]

Upon returning from the Mashriq, Darrās built a private mosque on the Andalusian side of Fez, where he taught Maliki jurisprudence to all comers, including those who could not afford the fees normally paid to a *faqīh* for individual study. The fact that a scholar of Darrās' stature did not teach in the major congregational mosques in the city, such as al-Qarawiyyīn, ash-Shurafāʾ, or al-Andalus, is evidence of the disputes that must have raged between this Maliki activist and Fez's pro-Idrisid ulama, who resented his criticisms of their ʿAlid politics and Kufan methodology. Unfortunately for the modern scholar, the details of these disputes are ignored in local histories of Fez. Instead, the authors of these works prefer to treat Darrās' conflict with the ulama of Fez obliquely, mentioning only that the direction of prayer (*qibla*) in his mosque was more accurate than that of the Masjid al-Qarawiyyīn.[32]

The practice in Islam of using private mosques for the teaching of alternative approaches to the religious sciences goes back to the late eighth century, when it became associated with juridical reformers such as Aḥmad ibn Idrīs ash-Shāfiʿī (d. 204/820).[33] Apart from rural hermitages (*ribāṭ*, pl. *ribāṭāt*), which will be discussed in Chapter Two, private mosques of the type created by Darrās ibn Ismāʿīl were the most important institutions of higher learning in early Middle Period Morocco.[34] Independent scholars preferred them over endowed religious schools (*madrasa*, pl. *madāris*) because Maliki restrictions on the personal control of endowments (*waqf*, pl. *awqāf*) made the creation of family-run endowments all but impossible.[35] Under Maliki law, the founder of an endowment was prohibited from serving as his own beneficiary. In addition, he was required to hand over the control of his endowment to the state upon completion of the deed.[36] A scholar such as Darrās who built a mosque on his own initiative could remain free from governmental interference only so long as the building was his own property and was supported by his own funds. If he wanted a descendant or another beneficiary to administer the mosque after his death, he could not leave it behind as a *waqf,* but instead would have to transfer its title to the new owner as an outright gift (*hadīya*).[37]

Historical and biographical sources tell us that Darrās was so fond of the Prophetic Sunna that his contemporaries called him "Abū Maymūna *al-Muḥaddith*" (the hadith scholar)—an uncommon and rather suspect epithet at a time when an emphasis on hadith study had yet to take root in the Maghrib. He is also credited with knowing all of the works of Mālik ibn Anas (d. 179/795) and his disciples by heart. This reputation was more than sufficient for him to be regarded as a *mujtahid,* a specialist in juridical reasoning. Accounts portray him as a "knower of God" (*ʿārif bi'llāh*), a devoted worshiper (*ʿābid*), an ascetic (*zāhid*), and a God-conscious *ṣāliḥ* who practiced extreme caution (*waraʿ*) in his behavior. It was also rumored that he was clairvoyant and could divine the sincerity or hypocrisy of anyone who spoke to him.[38]

There is little question that Darrās was venerated as a saint in his lifetime. He was especially revered as a protector of Fez—a position he shared with others in the *awtād al-arḍ* category. Equally important was the fact that his *baraka* retained its potency after his death. At the moment of his interment, we are told, the iron gate leading to the cemetery in which he was buried fell off of its hinges and never opened again, thus symbolizing the closing of the "gate of independent reasoning" (*ijtihād*) in Moroccan jurisprudence. Until recently, the most efficacious time for visiting Darrās' tomb was around sunset on Thursday evening, when the spirit of the Prophet Muḥammad was thought to intercede before God on behalf of those who sought the saint's aid.[39]

Fez's "anchor of the earth" in the next generation was Abū Jayda ibn Aḥmad al-Yazghī (or al-Yazghatnī; d. after 369/978), who came from the Arabized Berber tribe of Banū Yazghā about thirty kilometers southeast of the city. As a transmitter of hadith, a commentator on the Qur'an, and a specialist in Maliki law, the figure known popularly as "Sīdī Bū Jīda" was, like his predecessor Darrās, a powerful protector of Fez against its enemies. This latter ability was first noticed when his presence prevented the Fatimid commander Jawhar "the Sicilian" (the eventual conqueror of Egypt) from sacking Fez in 349/960.[40] This anti-Shiʿite intervention did not mean, however, that Abū Jayda was any better disposed toward the Fatimids' rivals, the Umayyads of Spain. Twenty years later, when Fez fell under the control of the Andalusian regent al-Manṣūr ibn Abī ʿĀmir (r. 369–92/978–1002), the saint was again called upon for protection. Upon taking office, al-Manṣūr's governor asked the ulama of Fez to decide whether their city had been taken willingly (*ṣulḥan*) or by force (*ʿanwatan*). Unwilling to show support for either the Umayyads or the Fatimids, the ulama summoned Abū Jayda to solve their problems for them. Displaying impeccable tact, he both preserved the fiction of his city's independence and avoided the imposition of punitive taxes by answering, "Neither willingly nor by force. Her inhabitants are simply resigned to it."[41]

The Andalusian Connection: The Sufi as Uṣūlī

Given the economic and intellectual ties that bound North Africa to the Iberian peninsula in pre-Islamic times, it is logical to expect that these two regions of the Muslim West would influence each other in the development of Islamic doctrines and institutions as well. As long as al-Andalus remained part of the Islamic world, the path of learning for scholars and mystics from Morocco regularly passed through the cities of Iberia. Intellectual contacts between the Far Maghrib and Muslim Spain were especially close in the eleventh and twelfth centuries, when the absorption of the Ṭāʾifa (factional) states of al-Andalus into the Almoravid and Almohad empires caused many Iberians to seek their fortunes on the opposite side of the Strait of Gibraltar.[42] This southward migration of the Muslim intelligentsia went hand-in-hand with a broad expansion of cultural and intellectual life in the Islamic West as a whole. It was thus no surprise that in this intellectually fertile period many of the Andalusian legists and theologians who visited North Africa also had an interest in Sufism.

These Andalusian scholars lived in an era of social and political upheaval which witnessed, in the course of less than a century, the conquest of the cities of Toledo and Saragossa by the newly invigorated Crusader states of northern Iberia; a demographic reorientation toward the southern and eastern parts of the Iberian peninsula as thousands of refugees fled toward the Ṭāʾifa states of Seville, Granada, and the Iberian Levant; the rise of North African hegemony under the Almoravids and Almohads, which heralded the end of urban autonomy in al-Andalus; a populist and Sufi-led revolt in the Algarve of present-day Portugal; and the Almohad revolution of Muḥammad ibn Tūmart (d. 524/1130), which mitigated the region's previous ethnic stratification and opened the way for the integration of the indigenous peoples of North Africa and Iberia into a community where every believer was entitled to equal status under God.[43]

Although the issue is open to dispute, there is more reason to view pre-Almohad Andalusian society as a collectivity of "communal contenders" than as a culturally unified entity.[44] Despite a nostalgic "lost paradise" image of al-Andalus that is popular in both Spanish and Arab nationalist circles today, textual evidence suggests that many of the Ṭāʾifa states were in fact inegalitarian and tension-ridden societies that continued to display vestiges of their original, ethnically stratified Umayyad social structure. According to an extended passage in the anonymous *Mashāhīr Fās fīʾl-qadīm* (The Notables of Fez in ancient times),[45] most religious, administrative, and military sinecures in Muslim Spain belonged to the descendants of Arab immigrants, who traced their lineages to the tribes of Banū Hāshim, Quraysh, Banū Ismāʿīl, or Qaḥtān. Those who did not belong to these privileged clans, such as Berbers and indigenous Iberians (whether Christian, Jewish, or Muslim convert), comprised distinct "ethnoclasses" that were subjected to political and economic discrimination.[46]

Most of the Berbers of Umayyad and ʿAmirid Spain practiced menial or low-skilled occupations. Those living in rural areas herded cattle, harvested grain, cut wood, gathered salt, and prepared butter, olive oil, honey, and wool. Urban Berbers produced household and farm implements, such as mats, blankets, baskets, rope, plows, saddle blankets, brooms, and mops. Others served as manual laborers, carrying grain or produce in local markets, or worked as water carriers, construction laborers, and plaster preparers.[47]

New converts to Islam fared the same or even worse than their Berber neighbors. A symbol of their low status was their designation by the Arabs of al-Andalus as *muwalladūn* ("half-breeds"), a term used in pre-Islamic Arabia for the offspring of slaves.[48] If they lived on the plains, *muwalladūn* were likely to be cattle and sheep herders, small farmers, or honey gatherers. Those living in the mountains worked as gardeners or tended the orchards of Arab landowners, while others served as woodcutters and charcoal makers. Converted Christians along the coast were often fishermen or boat builders. Converted Jews in Muslim Spain seem to have shared a similar status to that of converted Christians, although their occupations were more urban-centered. These included sewing clothing and fabrics, tentmaking, the spinning of trimming and braiding, hatmaking, dyeing, barbering, locksmithing, peddling, and shoe repairing.[49]

In the middle of the social spectrum was a separate class consisting of the clients (*mawālī*) of prominent Arab families. Many of these people were either Christians or recent converts to Islam. The *mawālī* of Muslim Spain were mainly urbanites who specialized in the handicrafts most valued by their Arab patrons: weaving, shoemaking, milling, lathing, woodworking, carpentry, saddle making, tailoring, pottery making, metalworking, weapons crafting, and copper working. Others served as doctors, musicians, barbers, butchers, caravan agents, and hostel (*funduq*) operators. *Mawālī* among the Jews of al-Andalus appear to have been small entrepreneurs or craftsmen, specializing in the production and sale of high-value items such as books, ornamented wood, tile, brass, jewelry, pearls, and musical instruments.[50]

The division of Andalusian society into ethnoclasses and communal contenders created tension and hostility among the disadvantaged Berbers and Iberian *muwalladūn*.[51] A number of ethnically based uprisings arose periodically against the Arab-dominated Umayyad state, starting with the revolt of the Berber Shaqya ibn ʿAbd al-Wāḥid against ʿAbd ar-Raḥmān I in the late eighth century.[52] This Berber dissidence was later augmented by several *muwallad* rebellions, which culminated in the nativist revolt of ʿUmar ibn Ḥafsūn in 267/879.

In early eleventh century C.E., the collapse of the Umayyad caliphate and its replacement by the Ṭāʾifa system of independent city-states marked a change in the structure of Andalusian society. The importation of Zanāta Berber cavalry from central Morocco, and the gradual assimilation of *muwalladūn* and *mawālī* into the upper classes of Muslim society through clientship and intermarriage, affected certain regions to the point where the old Arab elites felt their hold on power threatened by newly Arabized "helpers" (*anṣār*) who competed with them for positions of authority.[53] This unexpected challenge, coming from a people who had only recently been dismissed as second-class, caused the elites of cities such as Córdoba and Seville to respond by perpetuating restrictive Umayyad legal codes and patterns of social differentiation throughout the Ṭāʾifa and Almoravid periods.[54]

In the fields of religion and jurisprudence, the reactionary spirit of post-Umayyad Arabism was expressed as a stubborn adherence to insular forms of pre-Ashʿarite theology and Maliki legal methodology. The legists maintaining these doctrines, who were assailed by their opponents as "Maliki anthropomorphists" (*malakiyya ḥashwiyya*) or legal particularists (*ahl al-furūʿ*), sought to perpetuate the status quo ante by resisting any attempt to promote a true meritocracy or to make Andalusian intellectual life conform to the ethos of "Sunni internationalism" that had become the standard in the east.[55]

Symbolic of this opposition was the repudiation by Andalusian jurists of the Shafiʿi doctrine of *uṣūl al-fiqh* ("the sources of jurisprudence"). The aim of the *uṣūl* approach was to unify Islamic practice by making legal reasoning dependent on standardized sources and methods. These standards included the Qur'an, authorized collections of hadith, the use of syllogistic analogy (*qiyās*) in legal decision making, and the concept of binding consensus (*ijmāʿ*).[56] In its original form, the *uṣūl* method challenged the legitimacy of Maliki practice, which relied more on its own body of juridical precedent than on Prophetic hadith. For this reason, Maliki legal scholars were often less proficient than their eastern counterparts in the field of hadith studies. In addition, they showed little interest in the development of a more comprehensive approach to the religious sciences that would combine Qur'anic hermeneutics, hadith studies, and the law in a single, unified discipline.[57]

The *uṣūl* method was frequently championed in al-Andalus by specialists in hadith, who were more likely than other religious scholars to have been influenced by Shafiʿi doctrines. Significantly, many of these hadith scholars came from Berber or *muwallad* backgrounds. The Shafiʿi school of law recruited its first followers in al-Andalus as early as the reign of the caliph Muḥammad I (d. 253/866), and by the beginning of the Ṭāʾifa period had earned a positive reputation for the clarity of its doctrines. An important advocate of Shafiʿism at this time was ʿAbdallāh al-Bushkulārī (d. 461/1068–9) of Córdoba.[58] Another was Aḥmad "Ibn ad-Dilāʾī" (d. 478/1086), a hadith specialist who studied under the most renowned traditionists of Syria, Iraq, and Khurasan. Upon returning from the Mashriq, Ibn ad-Dilāʾī settled in his native Almería, where his teachings influenced the mystical tradition that would later be represented by the Sufi Ibn al-ʿArīf (d. 536/1141).[59]

Allied with the Shafiʿi scholars of al-Andalus were a significant number of Maliki legists and Sufis who sought to reform the intellectual traditions of Muslim Spain by integrating *uṣūl* methodology into the fields of religious dogmatics and jurisprudence. One of the first of these "Maliki internationalists" was Aḥmad ibn Muḥammad b. Qarlumān aṭ-Ṭalamankī (d. 429/1037). A scholar and Sufi of possible Christian background (his grandfather may have been named after Charlemagne), aṭ-Ṭalamankī received his education in Córdoba during the final years of the ʿAmirid regency. While there, he attached himself to the well-known Sufi and hadith transmitter Abū Jaʿfar ibn ʿAwn Allāh. Later, he spent time in Medina with the Egyptian Sufi Abūʾl-Qāsim al-Jawharī, who (as we shall see in Chapter Two) was a major influence on the Nūriyya mystical tradition of Morocco. After finishing his studies in the east, aṭ-Ṭalamankī returned to his native region of Madrid and made a name for himself by teaching the doctrines of *uṣūl.* Eventually, he became one of the most influential dogmatists in Muslim Spain.[60]

A contemporary of aṭ-Ṭalamankī and another apparent adherent of both Sufism and *ʿilm al-uṣūl* was Aḥmad al-Ilbīrī "al-Uṣūlī" (d. 429/1037–8). Although he was born in the town of Elvira, al-Ilbīrī spent most of his life in Granada, where he was a poet, a theologian, and a demagogue who promoted himself as a spokesman for the lower classes. Despite the fact that subsequent historians have condemned him for inciting a bloody pogrom against the Jews of Granada, he gained a more honorable reputation for himself by introducing al-Ḥārith ibn Asad al-Muḥāsibī's (d. 243/857) *Kitāb ar-riʿāya li-ḥuqūq Allāh* (Book of the observance of the rights due to God) into the Iberian peninsula.[61]

The most important uṣūlī theologian of Muslim Spain during the Ṭāʾifa period was Muḥammad ibn Saʿdūn al-Qayrawānī (d. 485/1092). This native of Ifrīqīya came to the western Maghrib after studying under the Maliki reformer Abū ʿImrān al-Fāsī (d. 430/1039) in the Tunisian city of al-Qayrawān. During his long sojourn in al-Andalus, Muḥmmad ibn Saʿdūn was known for his attempts to reform Islamic law by making the regional corpus of juridical precedent conform to the tenets of *uṣūl al-fiqh.* Occupying a succession of teaching positions in Córdoba, Valencia, and Almería, he was instrumental in promoting uṣūl methodology in the Andalusian Levant.[62]

These examples demonstrate that a new doctrinal consensus was emerging in Ṭāʾifa Spain that was based on the contributions of uṣūl-oriented legists, Sufis, and hadith scholars. The "international" and universalistic orientation of this movement posed a direct challenge to the ethnically based sectarianism of post-Umayyad society. In addition, the decline of Córdoba and the growing political power of the southern and eastern Ṭāʾifa states created a more decentralized environment that fostered alternative approaches to law and religion. The loss of Córdoba's intellectual preeminence allowed Seville to supplant the former capital as a center for the study of the Qur'an, Arabic grammar, and jurisprudence. In later years, the cities of the Spanish Levant (particularly Valencia and Almería) would become centers for the study of hadith. A similar process of decentralization was at work in the Far Maghrib as well. First Aghmāt and later Marrakesh, Ceuta, and Tlemcen began to vie with Fez as regional centers of learning. On both sides of the Strait of Gibraltar, uṣūlī approaches to the interpretation of religious texts were introduced through the efforts of hadith scholars who had been trained under Shafiʿi ulama in the Mashriq.

The desire of uṣūlī scholars for a more universalistic interpretation of Islamic doctrines led to a renewed interest in the opinions and activities of the Companions of the Prophet and their Successors. The publication of biographical works which detailed the categories (*ṭabaqāt*) of these early exemplars helped foster the ideal of a God-fearing, socially conscious, and theologically pristine Muslim community that was defined according to the example of its "ṣāliḥ-forebears" (*as-salaf aṣ-ṣāliḥ*).[63] The widespread popularity of *as-salaf aṣ-ṣāliḥ* as a paradigm among uṣūlī scholars in Muslim Spain and North Africa also helped create an ascetic, praxis-oriented, and jurisprudentially validated form of mysticism. This new tradition of "juridical Sufism" owed a considerable debt to the integrative works of the Iranian mystic and theologian Abū Ḥāmid al-Ghazālī (d. 505/1111).[64]

An important aspect of the juridical Sufi perspective was a non-sectarian attitude toward the four Sunni schools of Islamic law. Although they were influenced by Shafiʿi methodology, most orthodox mystics in the Maghrib tended to avoid making explicit criticisms of the Maliki school and preferred instead to retain a sort of cultural allegiance to their traditional *madhhab*. Much like their eastern counterparts, western Sufis were attracted to Shafiʿism not because its legal decisions were intrinsically better, but because it was more rigorous in its application of the Sunna. In the words of the Iranian Sufi Abū Saʿīd Abū'l-Khayr (d. 440/1049): "If Sufis adopt the doctrine of ash-Shāfiʿī, it is because this doctrine imposes more restrictions and exacts a greater rigor in the practice of religious obligations. It is thus for the purpose of mortifying desires that they have made their choice for Shafiʿi doctrine and not because they have found a difference between [different] doctrines or wished to signal a preference for [any] one of the [Sunni] imams."[65]

The uṣūlī approach to Sufism furthered the agenda of Sunni internationalists by drawing mysticism into the fold of normative Islam. By tying

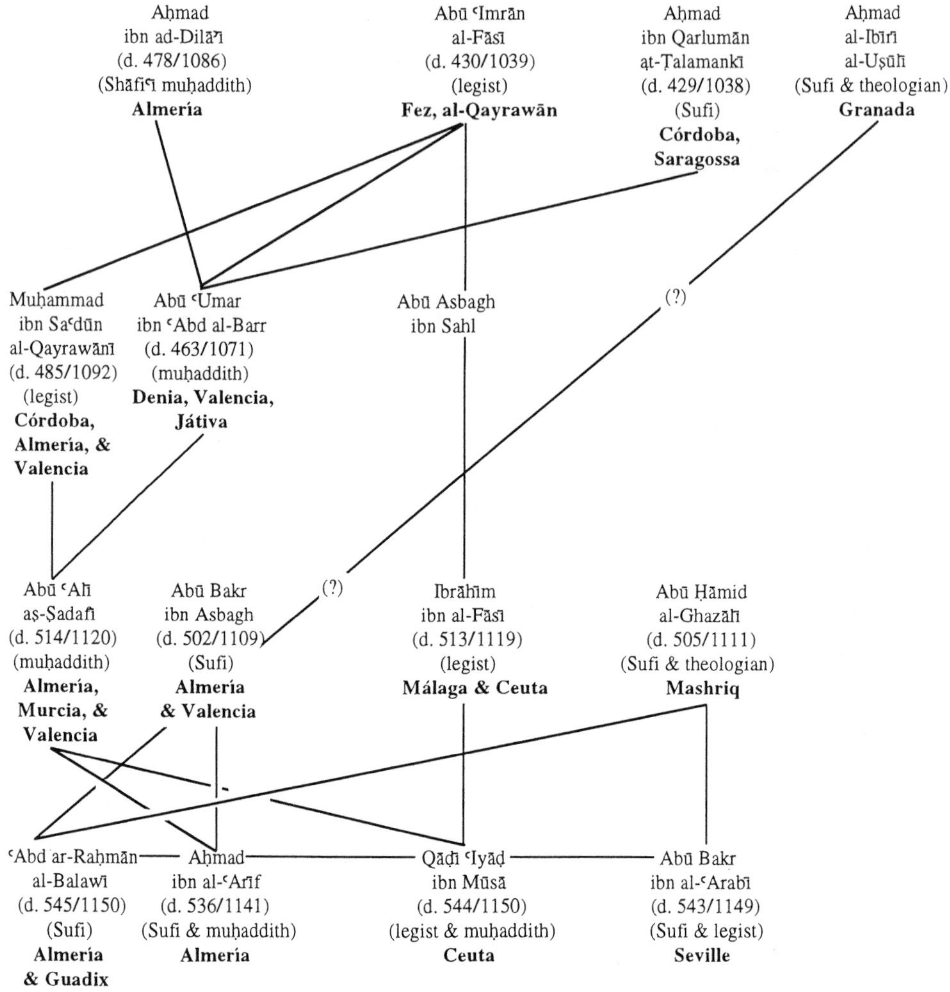

FIGURE ONE
Uṣūlī Sufi Relations in the Western Maghrib

the practices of mystics to those of the Prophet Muḥammad and *as-salaf aṣ-ṣāliḥ* (who were the original *rijāl,* the transmitters of Sunni tradition), hagiographers such as at-Tādilī found it easier to defend Sufi practices from the criticisms of Maliki legists. By demonstrating that it was their insular Maliki detractors and not the Sufis who were out of step with the Sunna, these scholars went a long way toward establishing Sufism as a juridically acceptable form of Islam.

Figure 1 depicts intellectual links between uṣūlī scholars and Sufis in the

Far Maghrib and al-Andalus during the Ṭāʾifa and Almoravid eras. The first thing to be noticed about this chart is that, as previously asserted, hadith transmitters were integral to the development of the orthodox-mystical tradition. Second, the central position of Abū ʿImrān al-Fāsī and Muḥammad ibn Saʿdūn al-Qayrawānī demonstrates that the process of doctrinal transmission was not one-way (from Spain to the Maghrib), as many Western scholars have supposed, but was instead bidirectional—the result of long-established connections between the European and African shores of the Mediterranean. The importance of the Maghrib to the intellectual life of Muslim Spain is also reflected in the concentration of uṣūlīs in the southern and eastern portions of the Iberian peninsula—in cities such as Granada, Málaga, Valencia, Almería, Guadix, and Murcia—which provided easy access to western North Africa and Ifrīqīya. Last but not least, this chart portrays a strikingly different image of Andalusian Sufism from that proposed by the Spanish orientalist Miguel Asín Palacios, who assumed, on the basis of circumstantial and ultimately faulty evidence, that the Sufi tradition of Muslim Spain had little to do with mainstream Islam but was instead heir to the doctrines of the mystical philosopher Ibn Masarra (d. 319/931).[66] Contrary to Asín Palacios' hypothesis, the data presented here leads to the conclusion that the scripturally based and anti-philosophical traditions that were the hallmark of orthodox mysticism were firmly established in Muslim Spain and North Africa.

Ibn al-ʿArīf: An Uṣūlī Mystic of Almería

One of the most prominent examples of an uṣūl-oriented mystic and Sunni internationalist in post-Ṭāʾifa Spain was Aḥmad ibn Muḥammad b. Mūsā b. ʿAṭāʾillāh aṣ-Ṣanhājī, better known to posterity as Ibn al-ʿArīf. Although his origins were from Tangier in northern Morocco, Ibn al-ʿArīf was born and raised in Almería, where his father had moved in order to become a platoon leader (*ʿarīf*) in the local guard.[67] As a student, he was attracted to the circles of Qur'an and hadith studies that had made Almería a major center of uṣūl-based education. In fact, it was not as a Sufi, but as a reciter of the Qur'an and a transmitter of hadith, that he was best known to his biographers in al-Andalus. The biographer Ibn Bashkuwāl (d. 578/1183), for example, makes no mention at all of Ibn al-ʿArif's interest in Sufism, recalling only that worshipers of God (*ʿubbād*) and ascetics (*zuhhād*) would attend his lectures.[68]

Ibn al-ʿArīf's notoriety in the hadith sciences is confirmed by the West

African legist and Maliki memorialist Aḥmad Bābā (d. 1036/1627), who mentions that Ibn al-ʿArīf attained mastery in *fiqh,* hadith, and Qur'an recitation while studying under the most renowned scholars of Almería and Córdoba.[69] The thirteenth-century Valencian biographer Ibn al-Abbār notes that Ibn al-ʿArīf was one of the prize pupils of Abū ʿAlī aṣ-Ṣadafī (d. 514/1120), the doyen of hadith sciences in the Andalusian Levant.[70] After teaching Qur'anic recitation for a time in Almería and Saragossa, he took the position of inspector of markets and public censor (*wālī al-ḥisba*) for the city of Valencia.[71] It was here that he was introduced to the Khurasani practices of asceticism (*zuhd*), scrupulousness (*waraʿ*), and altruism (*īthār*) that proved his status as a Sufi "man of perfection" (*rajul al-kamāl*).[72]

There is more than a hint in biographical sources that Ibn al-ʿArīf's predilection for Sufi chivalry (*futuwwa*)[73] signaled a taste for populist or nativist politics. It is reported that he maintained a solicitous regard for the poor, who, like the Sufis, were known in al-Andalus as *fuqarā'*. It is additionally claimed that he enjoyed the support of politically active Sufis, whose social consciousness led them to oppose the ethnoclassism of the Ṣanhāja Berber Almoravids after their occupation of Islamic Spain.[74] Significantly, among his disciples were large numbers of both Berbers and *muwalladūn.* This presence may reflect nothing more than the ethnic heterogeneity of the southern and eastern portions of the Iberian peninsula. On the other hand, Ibn al-ʿArīf's attractiveness to Berbers and Iberian converts may also indicate that he had more than just a passing interest in the *damnés de la terre* of Andalusian society.

In support of a possible connection between Ibn al-ʿArīf and Iberian nativism, Paul Nwyia has pointed out that the shaykh was in regular contact with the mystic and political activist Abū'l-Ḥakam ibn Barrajān of Seville (d. 536/1141). Citing as evidence fragments of correspondence between Ibn al-ʿArīf and Ibn Barrajān that he discovered in Morocco, Nwyia asserts that Ibn al-ʿArīf thought of Ibn Barrajān as his spiritual superior. In one letter, Ibn al-ʿArīf addresses Ibn Barrajān as the "Supreme Guide of those who lead souls to the ways of salvation [and] the Imam who possesses the benediction of Muḥammad as his legitimate representative."[75] His use of the term *imām* in this correspondence, an apparent double entendre alluding to the question of caliphal authority, is highly significant, given the disputes over political legitimacy that then beset Ṭā'ifa and Almoravid Spain.

According to the sixteenth-century Egyptian Sufi and hagiographer ʿAbd al-Wahhāb ash-Shaʿrānī, more than 130 villages in the Andalusian sierra recognized Ibn Barrajān as their imam.[76]

Ibn al-ʿArīf's conception of the imamate may also have had a bearing on his equivocal relationship with the self-styled messiah of the Algarve, Abū'l-Qāsim ibn Qasī (d. 546/1151). This controversial mystic was the instigator of an anti-Almoravid revolt of Sufi adepts in the western part of al-Andalus, which was spearheaded by a militia based at Ribāṭ Rayḥāna near Silves in southern Portugal. The political ideology of Ibn Qasī's movement was premised on the belief that after the Prophet Muḥammad, God continues to bestow divine authority on certain individuals. This idea was to reappear in a more metaphysical guise a generation later in the writings of the great Andalusian mystic Ibn al-ʿArabī.[77] For Ibn Qasī, both political and spiritual authority were embodied in a divinely ordained imamate that was passed on from generation to generation until the end of time. This imamate could be incarnated in the direct descendants of the Prophet—as in Idrisid or Zaydi Shiʿism—or through the Prophet's collateral relatives (such as the ʿAbbasids) via Muḥammad's grandfather ʿAbd al-Muṭṭalib. After the year 500 A.H., Ibn Qasī claimed, the succession of imams would end with the advent of "Muḥammad al-Mahdī," a divinely guided leader who was also known as the Seal of Authority (*khātim al-wilāya*).[78]

Despite Ibn Qasī's claim to have been a disciple of Ibn al-ʿArīf, there is no evidence that the shaykh of Almería had any formal connection with either the Mahdī of the Algarve or his *murīdiyya* movement. It is apparent, however, that Ibn al-ʿArīf stressed the authoritative nature of sainthood in ways that might be construed as implying an acceptance of Ibn Qasī's view of the imamate. Furthermore, it is well established that he corresponded with Ibn Qasī and some of his followers. A heretofore overlooked collection of Ibn al-ʿArīf's lessons and writings entitled *Miftāḥ as-saʿāda wa taḥqīq ṭarīq al-irāda* (The Key to salvation and the realization of the way of divine desire)[79] contains transcripts of letters written to one Abū'l-Walīd ibn al-Mundhir, who may have been related to Muḥammad ibn Mundhir, the commander of Ibn Qasī's militia.[80] The same volume also reproduces a letter from Ibn al-ʿArīf to "Imam Abū'l-Qāsim ibn Qasī," in which the shaykh remarks: "[Someone] . . . has told me that you know me by name. I do not understand what you mean (*fa-shaghalanī farāghī ʿan maʿnāka*)."[81]

This passage, if genuine, indicates that Ibn Qasī's portrayal of himself as Ibn al-ʿArīf's disciple was made under false pretenses. It also implies that the shaykh, perhaps wishing to avoid the wrath of the Almoravid authorities, objected to having such claims broadcast. At other times, however, Ibn al-ʿArīf reacts more favorably to Ibn Qasī. Elsewhere in *Miftāḥ as-saʿāda* he states that after having read one of Ibn Qasī's works he became convinced of the latter's "complete understanding" of Sufi doctrine. This praise should not be taken to mean, however, that Ibn al-ʿArīf also believed in Ibn Qasī's claims of infallibility. Later on in the same letter, he relates the following anecdote: "At the age of twenty-six I asked a man who was well-versed in the Qur'an, the *Muwaṭṭāʾ* [of Mālik ibn Anas] and travel [for the sake of learning]: 'How is it with those who have cut short their knowledge?' 'Exertion (*ijtihād*) and effort (*ʿamal*) have conquered them,' he replied, 'thereby lessening for them knowledge (*ʿilm*) and inquiry (*baḥth*).'"[82] This statement seems to indicate that Ibn al-ʿArīf doubted Ibn Qasī's ability in the very fields that would have legitimated his self-proclaimed status as the Seal of Authority.

Regardless of the ties that may or may not have existed between Ibn al-ʿArīf and Ibn Barrajān or Ibn Qasī, the Almoravid rulers of Muslim Spain suspected that an ulterior political motive lay behind his activities. These fears were exacerbated when a spirited defense of uṣūl methodology sprang up among Sufis and hadith scholars in the southern part of the Iberian peninsula. Rather than viewing this critique of insular Malikism as part of an ongoing debate within the ulama class, the Almoravid emirs viewed the uṣūl movement as an attack upon the legitimacy of their state. These concerns were heightened after a former Mufti of Almería, Abū'l-Ḥasan al-Barjī (d. 509/1115–16) issued a juridical opinion (*fatwā*) condemning the pro-Almoravid chief justice (*qāḍī al-jamāʿa*) of Córdoba for ordering the confiscation and destruction of al-Ghazālī's magisterial work on the Islamic sciences, *Iḥyāʾ ʿulūm ad-dīn* (Revivification of the religious sciences).[83] In the decades following the promulgation of this decree, accusations of sedition were directed against most of al-Barjī's students, including Ibn al-ʿArīf. These accusations plus the revolt of the shaykh's purported "disciple" Ibn Qasī caused other anti-Almoravid activists in the western Maghrib to consider Ibn al-ʿArīf an ally. He was eventually arrested and brought in chains to the Almoravid capital of Marrakesh, where he died of poisoning in 536/1141. Immediately after his death, he was hailed as a martyr by the Almohads and other opponents of the Ṣanhāja state. In the succeeding generation, Ibn al-ʿArīf's posthumous "political correctness" helped to spread his doctrines from Muslim Spain to as far away as Ifrīqīya.

Ibn Ḥirzihim and the Ghazalians of Fez

Despite the rise of Sunni internationalism in al-Andalus and North Africa, the twelfth century of the common era (the sixth century A.H.) dawned on a Maghrib that was still dominated by ethnoclassism, theological literalism, and isolationist legal practice. Although the spiritual grandfather of the Almoravid movement, Abū ʿImrān al-Fāsī, appears to have been a proponent of uṣūl methodology through the influence of his teacher, the theologian Abū Bakr al-Bāqillānī (d. 403/1013), this open-mindedness did not last beyond the death of the Almoravid sultan Yūsuf ibn Tāshfīn in the year 500/1106. Ibn Tāshfīn's son ʿAlī ibn Yūsuf (d. 538/1143), his successor as ruler of the Almoravid state, was strongly attracted to the sophisticated culture of Muslim Spain and adopted Andalusian customs, administrative practices, and intellectual trends throughout his empire. Viewed from North Africa, however, this newly instituted Hispanization of the Maghrib was no improvement. Almoravid internationalism simply meant that the Arab dominance that had heretofore characterized Andalusian society was now replaced on both sides of the Mediterranean by an equally exclusivistic Arab–Ṣanhāja entente. Rather than facilitating the increased access by non-Arab peoples to positions of political and intellectual influence, the Almoravids monopolized the highest positions of military and political authority for themselves, leaving religious and diplomatic affairs to their advisers, the Arab elites of Muslim Spain.

Once Andalusian Malikism became state policy in Marrakesh and Fez, as well as in Córdoba and Seville, Arab jurists acting under the authority of Almoravid governors set out to suppress dissenting opinions. As part of their crackdown, all copies of al-Ghazali's *Iḥyāʾ ʿulūm ad-dīn* were ordered confiscated and publicly burned. According to most historians, the banning of this work was due to al-Ghazālī's Shafiʿi-inspired critiques of non-uṣūlī legal traditions. Another reason, perhaps, was al-Ghazālī's belief, following his teacher Abūʾl-Maʿālī ʿAbd al-Malik al-Juwaynī (d. 499/1105), that all knowledgeable Muslims—and not just the official ulama—could act as representatives of the Muslim community.[84] According to this theory, all learned men had a right to be considered as "those who loosen and bind" (*ahl al-ḥall waʾl-ʿaqd*) and could have a voice in the confirmation or rejection of claimants to the throne. Since this wider group of ulama included both uṣūlī dissidents and juridically oriented Sufis, such views would not have been popular at the Almoravid court.[85]

An immediate result of the suppression of al-Ghazālī's works was the spread of uṣūlī dissidence throughout the western Maghrib. The most significant exponent of this movement was the Maṣmūda Berber Muḥammad ibn Tūmart, the founder of the Almohad (*al-muwaḥḥid*—"unitarian") movement.[86] Ibn Tūmart was joined in his opposition to the Almoravids by a number of Andalusian and North African Sufis, whose journeys to the Muslim East had brought them into contact with Shafiʿi jurists, Ashʿari theologians, and other representatives of Sunni internationalism. As had earlier been the case in the days of Darrās ibn Ismāʿīl, scholars from the city of Fez were instrumental in furthering this latest attempt at reform.

A major center for the dissemination of uṣūlī doctrines in Fez was the *rābiṭa,* Sufi hermitage, of Abū Muḥammad Ṣāliḥ ibn Ḥirzihim (d. after 505/1111–12).[87] The Ibn Ḥirzihim (or Aḥrāzem) family, who traced their ancestry to ʿUthmān ibn ʿAffān, the third caliph of Islam, had been prominent in Fasi scholarly circles for more than a century. They first distinguished themselves in the early eleventh century by supporting the anti-Idrisid policies of the Maghrāwa Berbers, who governed Fez as surrogates for the Umayyads of Spain. As the scion of this family of religious notables, Abū Muḥammad Ṣāliḥ had the financial means to travel as far away as Syria for his education, where he is said to have studied *Iḥyāʾ ʿulūm ad-dīn* under al-Ghazālī himself.[88]

Abū Muḥammad Ṣāliḥ was succeeded as head of the Ibn Ḥirzihim *rābiṭa* by his nephew Abūʾl-Ḥasan ʿAlī (d. 559/1164), the famous "Sīdī Ḥarāzem" of Fez.[89] Despite his uncle's passionate adherence to al-Ghazālī's teachings, the younger Ibn Ḥirzihim initially disapproved of *Iḥyāʾ ʿulūm ad-dīn* and even agreed with its banning, until his opinions were changed by a dream in which the Prophet Muḥammad whipped him for his mistaken beliefs. Henceforward, he became one of the most outspoken defenders of al-Ghazālī in the Far Maghrib and devoted the rest of his life to teaching the *Iḥyāʾ* to his students, who had to copy the full text of the book every year.[90]

Largely because of his role in disseminating the works of al-Ghazālī, ʿAlī ibn Ḥirzihim was one of the most influential Moroccan Sufis of the formative period. Biographical sources reveal him to have been a highly complex individual. He was an accomplished legal scholar and studied under the renowned Andalusian jurist Abū Bakr ibn al-ʿArabī al-Muʿāfirī (d. 543/1148).[91] He was also well-versed in the sciences of hadith and Qur'anic exegesis and had a fondness for *Kitab ar-riʿāya li-ḥuqūq Allāh,* al-Muḥāsibī's treatise on Sufi psychology and ethics. This work, along with al-Ghazālī's *Iḥyā'*, was a required text for Ibn Ḥirzihim's disciples. In his personal comportment, he was the quintessential *ʿabd ṣāliḥ:* pious and ascetic, modest in dress, morally virtuous, of an open demeanor, and pleasant in nature. All who met him were moved to affection for him. He found time for young and old alike and answered all who called upon him. Upon inheriting a considerable sum of money from his father, he gave all of it to the poor. He also respected learning of all kinds and strove to improve the quality of education in Fez, where he was born, and in Marrakesh, where he was eventually exiled.[92]

Despite his reputation as a ṣāliḥ, Ibn Ḥirzihim was also the founder of the Moroccan Path of Blame (*ṭarīq al-malāma*). In Ibn Ḥirzihim's case, however, *malāmatī* behavior did not imply the open contravention of the Sharīʿa that earned antinomian extremists the censure of ulama throughout the Muslim world.[93] What prompted the Almoravid elite to disapprove of him were rather his politically motivated disregard for the prerogatives of rank, his apparent pretentiousness in referring to himself as the Axis of the Maghribis (*quṭb al-Maghāriba*), and his outspoken criticism of the Almoravids for their ethnoclassism and prejudice.[94] Apart from seeing the role of the ṣāliḥ as one of political activism, Ibn Ḥirzihim did little more than heed the advice of Ḥamdūn al-Qaṣṣār an-Nīṣabūrī (d. 271/884–5), the reputed "father" of the *malāmatiyya:* "Avoid impressing human beings at all times and avoid seeking their pleasure in any type of characteristic or behavior. If you do not, you will soon be blamed for what God's agency has caused you to possess."[95]

Even the forced closing of the Ibn Ḥirzihim *rābiṭa* and Sīdī Ḥarāzem's exile to Marrakesh could not still this saint's acerbic tongue. The most detailed account of his sojourn in Marrakesh appears in at-Tādilī's *at-Tashawwuf* and forms a postscript to the arrest and execution of the Andalusian Sufi Ibn Barrajān in 536/1141.[96] No anecdote more clearly illustrates Ibn Ḥirzihim's opposition to the Almoravid regime and his contempt for its policies. In the following passage, the saint's success in occupying the moral high ground causes Sultan ʿAlī ibn Yūsuf to back down from a confrontation over Ibn Barrajān's burial. It is easy to imagine how the sultan's equivocal response to Sīdī Ḥarāzem's challenge played into the hands of the opponents of the Almoravids in their ongoing attempt to undermine the legitimacy of Ṣanhāja rule:

> When Abū'l-Ḥakam ibn Barrajān was ordered to be brought from Córdoba to Marrakesh, he was asked about the matters causing his censure and brought them forth, commenting on their implications and differentiating [his beliefs] from those for which he was accused. Abū'l-Ḥakam said, "By God, I will not live, and the one who brought me here [ie., the sultan] will not live after my death!" Then Abū'l-Ḥakam died [ie., was executed] and the sultan commanded that he be thrown onto the city garbage heap and that no one make the funeral prayer for him. This [command] was authorized by the jurists who were his accusers.
>
> A black man who worked for ʿAlī ibn Ḥirzihim and attended his lessons went to [the shaykh] and told him what the sultan had ordered concerning Abū'l-Ḥakam. Then Ibn Ḥirzihim said to him, "If you wish to sell your soul to God, do what I tell you."
>
> "Command what you wish and I will do it," the man replied. [The shaykh] said, "Proclaim in the streets and markets of Marrakesh: 'Ibn Ḥirzihim orders you to be present at the funeral of the shaykh, the legist, the exalted ascetic Abū'l-Ḥakam ibn Barrajān. May the curse of God be upon him who is able to come and does not!'"
>
> The man did as he was commanded and when [Ibn Ḥirzihim's challenge] was made known to the sultan, he said, "He who is aware of [Ibn Barrajān's] excellence and is not present will be cursed by God."[97]

An important associate of Sīdī Ḥarāzem in Fez was a legist and teacher of *uṣūl al-fiqh* named Abū'l-Faḍl ibn an-Naḥwī. Originally from the Ṣanhāja city-state of Qalʿat Banī Ḥammād in western Algeria, Ibn an-Naḥwī lived for a time in the caravan center of Sijilmasa and then moved to Fez, from which he was eventually expelled by the city's Almoravid governor. After being exiled from his adopted home, he returned once again to Qalʿat Banī Ḥammād, where he died in 513/1115.[98] Ibn an-Naḥwī advocated an uṣūl-based prioritization of the texts that formed the basis for juridical decision making. According to this method, each *mujtahid*, an interpreter of Islamic law, had to search for the answer to a juridical problem (*masʾala*) in the Qur'an or the hadith. If these sources were not sufficient, he could then consult the traditions of the Prophet's Companions and others among *as-salaf aṣ-ṣāliḥ*. Only when these primary sources failed to provide guidance could the *mujtahid* resort to the traditional guidance of his legal school or his own reasoning.

Because of his fondness for the uṣūl method, Ibn an-Naḥwī shared with Ibn Ḥirzihim a preference for al-Ghazālī's *Iḥyā᾽ ulūm ad-dīn.* His devotion to this work was so great that he had it copied, like the Qur'an, in thirty sections of equal length, so that he could read a section each evening in the month of Ramadan. He particularly agreed with al-Ghazālī's emphasis on the Qur'anic verse commanding Muslims to "enjoin the good and forbid evil" (*amr bi'l-ma῾rūf wa nahy ῾an al-munkar*), an attitude that allied him with the Almohad Ibn Tūmart, who was similarly expelled from Fez for preaching this doctrine.[99] At-Tādilī reports that Ibn an-Naḥwī even went so far as to write a letter to the sultan disputing the order to burn the *Iḥyā᾽*. When sympathetic jurists in Fez informed him that ῾Alī ibn Yūsuf had ordered the Sufis to publicly swear that they did not possess any copies of the condemned book, he issued a *fatwā* in which he claimed that the sultan's command was not legally binding.[100] By asserting that ῾Alī ibn Yūsuf's order did not reflect the unanimous opinion (*ijmā῾*) of the ulama, he was treading on dangerous ground, for his *fatwā* implied that the sultan's decree was *fāsid,* illegitimate.

The isolation felt by Ibn an-Naḥwī as the proponent of an innovative doctrine in an unreceptive environment is poignantly evoked in the following lines of poetry:

> I have fallen among those who have religion without manners,
> And those who have manners [but are] devoid of religion.
>
> I have fallen among them—an isolated species—alone,
> Like the verse of Ḥassān in the compendium of Saḥnūn.[101]

Ibn an-Naḥwī was not content, however, with writing bitter lines of poetry. He actively promoted the teaching of uṣūl throughout the western Maghrib and spoke out against the injustices that, in his opinion, arose from a lack of concern for the Prophetic Sunna. Even his opponents accorded him a grudging respect for his persistence and stubbornly held convictions. A common saying in twelfth-century Fez was: "I seek refuge in God from the curse of Ibn an-Naḥwī!"[102] To illustrate the truth of this saying, at-Tādilī reports that when Ibn an-Naḥwī lived in Sijilmasa he stayed at a certain mosque, where he taught *uṣūl al-fiqh.* One day, an official notary (*῾ādil*) passed by the door to the mosque and asked, "What is the discipline that this person is teaching?" When told that Ibn an-Naḥwī was conducting lessons on the scripturally based sources of jurisprudence, the notary, who followed only the Maliki tradition, replied derisively, "How is this one allowed to teach us subjects we do not know of?" and ordered the shaykh to be thrown out of the mosque. Before leaving, Ibn an-Naḥwī rose to his feet and said to his tormentor, "You have killed knowledge. Now God will kill you in this very place!" The next day, when the man went to the mosque in order to notarize a marriage contract, he was killed by a tribesman whose clan was feuding with his own.[103]

Another advocate of uṣūl in late Almoravid Fez was the scholastic theologian (*mutakallim*) Abū ʿAmr as-Salāljī, who was nicknamed "al-Uṣūlī" (d. 564/1167). The son of a prominent family of Arabized Berbers from Jabal Salīljū near Fez, as-Salāljī was a disciple of Ibn Ḥirzihim and studied *Kitāb al-irshād* (The Book of guidance), the theological treatise of al-Ghazālī's teacher al-Juwaynī, under the tutelage of an uṣūlī scholar in Seville. Later generations of scholars would praise as-Salāljī as "the savior of the people of Fez from anthropomorphism" (*munqidh ahl Fās min at-tajsīm*) and he rose under the Almohads to become the foremost expert on philosophical theology in all of Morocco. His best-known work is a credal manifesto (*ʿaqīda*) entitled *Al-ʿAqīda al-burhāniyya.* This he dedicated to a female Sufi named Khayrūna al-Andalusiyya.[104]

Also allied with the Ibn Ḥirzihim *rābiṭa* of Fez were a heterogeneous group of Sufis from Sijilmasa on the edge of the Sahara desert. During the Almoravid era Sijilmasa was the northern terminus for two important African gold trails: the Ṭarīq Lamtūnī, which hugged the western Saharan coastline before turning inland to the entrepôt of Waddan, and another, more ancient route, going to the Niger Bend via the salt-pans of Taghaza. Because of its economically strategic location, Sijilmasa was second only to Fez as a source of revenue for the Almoravid state. At the onset of Ibn Tūmart's Almohad revolt in the Atlas mountains (which seems to have precipitated Ibn Ḥirzihim's forced removal to Marrakesh), the Sufi shaykhs of Sijilmasa were exiled to Fez at the order of Tāshfīn ibn ʿAlī, governor of Fez and heir to the Almoravid throne.[105] Once there, they were thrown into prison and interrogated, often under torture. Under these trying circumstances, some recanted their opposition to the Almoravids. At-Tādilī tells the story of one Abū'l-Faḍl ibn Aḥmad (d. 542/1147), whose renunciation of dissidence allowed him to be sent back to his homeland. Once there, he assisted the Almoravids by equating the concept of religious ethics with political quietism and feared that God would punish him for telling a "lie" that had caused the sultan's anger.[106]

More characteristic of this group was Muḥammad ibn ʿUmar al-Aṣamm, a Sufi whose nickname could be taken to mean either "deaf" or "stubborn." Noted as much for his indomitable will as for the miracles he was said to perform, Muḥammad al-Aṣamm was constrained by nothing, even prison walls. While incarcerated in Fez, he would matter-of-factly remove the shackles from his feet before each call to prayer, leave the dungeon where he was held, pray at a nearby mosque, and then calmly return to his place of confinement. Eventually, Tashfīn ibn ʿAlī allowed al-Aṣamm and the other Sufis of Sijilmasa to leave prison, but he ordered them to remain under surveillance in Fez. Shortly after his release, al-Aṣamm was assassinated while making his devotions. Fearing the desecration of his corpse, his companions interred him among some houses until they could place him in a proper cemetery. Upon returning to retrieve the body a few days later, they found that it had vanished.[107]

The most notorious of the Sufi activists of Almoravid Sijilmasa was Abū ʿAbdallāh ad-Daqqāq. Like Ibn Ḥirzihim, he appears to have followed the doctrines of the *malāmatiyya,* for his statements provoked criticism from official ulama and Sufis alike. Some of these utterances, like Sīdī Ḥarāzem's, included the open proclamation of his sanctity. Unlike Ibn Ḥirzihim, however, whose "path of blame" was based on a reputation for political activism, ad-Daqqāq's *malāmatī* behavior more often recalls that of such familiar eastern figures as Abū Yazīd al-Bisṭāmī (d. 261/874) and Ḥusayn ibn Manṣūr al-Ḥallāj (d. 309/912). This impression is reinforced by the fact that ad-Daqqāq's defenders judged his statements as permissible only because they were made under the influence of ecstatic spiritual states (*ḥāl,* pl. *aḥwāl*).

Although he was supported by Ibn al-ʿArīf and Ibn Barrajān, ad-Daqqāq was at times criticized by other mystics. This can be seen in the following satirical poem, which was written against ad-Daqqāq by one of his Sufi contemporaries:

Say to the little man among the powerful,
"Poverty is the most excellent trait of the free."

Oh complainer to men about the poverty granted by his Lord,
Can you not complain about a [truly] heavy load?

Oh, what vestments of piety you profess to wear!
If your Lord had only wished, you would come before Him naked![108]

Despite this rebuke, which accuses ad-Daqqāq of the very un-Sufi practice of denying poverty, later hagiographers claimed that his status as a holy man was confirmed in repeated dreams of the Prophet Muḥammad. Although neither the date nor the circumstances of his death have been recorded, it is likely that ad-Daqqāq also met his end at the hands of the Almoravid authorities. His tomb outside of Bāb al-Gīsa on the Andalusian side of Fez was venerated for many centuries, partly because of the reputation of his most important disciple, the Andalusian "Shaykh of Shaykhs" Abū Madyan.[109]

This chapter has introduced the ṣāliḥ, a Qur'anic *topos* that is used in hagiographical literature to designate the Muslim saint of premodern Morocco. Whether a *walī Allāh* was best known as a martyr, a holy warrior, a mystic, a miracle worker, or an urban scholar, he or she was seen to personify *ṣalāḥ,* a multifaceted concept that represented the social, or active, dimension of the Islamic ideal. In contrast to most of the models of Muslim sainthood discussed in the Introduction, which have highlighted the metaphysical or structural aspects of this phenomenon, the *ṣāliḥ/ṣalāḥ* paradigm brings into focus the ethical and praxis-oriented understanding of holiness in the Islamic West. As we have just seen in the example of Abū ʿAbdallāh ad-Daqqāq, a person's knowledge of mystical doctrine mattered little if his or her behavior did not correspond to the ideal of the *ʿabd ṣāliḥ,* the socially conscious slave of God.

We have also seen that the typical Moroccan ṣāliḥ was an urban figure: either an "anchor of the earth," who protected the homeland and introduced paradigms of pan-Islamic import such as the Maliki school of law, or a Sufi-cum-scholar who set the standards for later interpretations of doctrine, as Ibn Ḥirzihim did by propagating the teachings of al-Ghazālī and founding the Moroccan *malāmatiyya.* During the Almoravid and Almohad eras, many *ṣulaḥāʾ* were advocates of the Shafiʿi-inspired doctrine of uṣūl and sought to integrate the regional Islamic practice of the Maghrib into the wider world of Sunni Islam. They were aided in this effort by juridically oriented Sufis and hadith scholars from al-Andalus, such as Ibn al-ʿArīf, who found common cause with their brethren on the opposite shore of the Mediterranean.

This chapter also confirms a point that was first made in the Introduction: since Morocco was not the intellectual backwater that many have taken it to be, the study of its religious and social institutions must be linked to the history of Islamic civilization in general. Moroccan Sufism, while distinctive, was not entirely separate from its eastern counterpart. For example, the Sufi traditions of Morocco were closely related to those of Khurasan, in eastern Iran, and paradoxically had less to do with the Arab Middle East, which was nearer and easier of access for Moroccan pietists and mystics. This datum underscores the cosmopolitan nature of premodern Muslim society and supports Richard Bulliet's contention that the "view from the edge" is as important to the study of Islam as is the view from the center. When one adds to this point the evidence of long-standing intellectual ties between the Far Maghrib and Muslim Spain, it becomes impossible to think of Morocco—even in this early period—as a marginalized region that was out of step with the mainstream of Islamic civilization. This point will be revisited in the next chapter, where the rural traditions of Moroccan Sufism will be seen to share in the same urban and "Sunni international" traditions as does Sufism elsewhere.

CHAPTER TWO

Arbiters of the Holy in the Countryside: Rural Legists, Spiritual Masters, and Murābiṭūn

We have seen in the previous chapter that the ṣāliḥ first appears in Morocco as a product of urban society. Although this observation was made by Alfred Bel more than fifty years ago, the saint of the Far Maghrib is still most often typified as a rural figure. From the exploratory inquiries of Edward Westermarck to the studies of Dermenghem, Gellner, and Geertz, a pervasive pastoral ideal has come to dominate the study of sainthood in this region.[1] This predilection for the rural—and, by implication, the peripheral—has caused Western scholars to highlight culturally circumscribed paradigms such as maraboutism to the exclusion of other, more universal constructs such as the ṣāliḥ/ṣalāḥ model just introduced.

The reader who is familiar with the study of sainthood in Christianity may already have come to suspect that the neglect of the ṣāliḥ/ṣalāḥ paradigm and other scripturally based "foundation metaphors" in Islam has led to a serious deracination of the concept of the *walī Allāh* in Maghrib Studies.[2] This suspicion is largely correct. Instead of being seen as a symbolic nexus of textually mediated ideologies of piety, power, and ethics, the holy person is most often cast in an off-Broadway play of restricted roles, parochial interests, and localized social categories.[3] This is not to say that sociologically oriented studies have been of no use in furthering our understanding of the Moroccan saint. It is to say, however, that the models used by most social historians and anthropologists, including the transaction approach taken by Geertz, fail to account for the fact that the person whom Western scholars call a marabout inhabits an ideological terrain that goes beyond merely local arenas of discourse. In its scope, the epistemological world of such an individual is often as broad as the Islamic world itself.[4]

Urban Islam in the Countryside: The School of Abū ʿImrān al-Fāsī

Within a generation after the death of Darrās ibn Ismāʿīl in 357/968, Maliki jurists, working in conjunction with the ulama of al-Andalus, began systematically to introduce their school of law in the Moroccan countryside. This activity was part of a concerted effort by the ulama of North Africa to Islamize areas that were beyond the reach of the state and hence outside of the practical limits of the Sharīʿa. Major destinations for these Maliki missionaries included: Tāmesnā, homeland of the Barghwāṭa tribe of Berber pastoralists, who retained a unique and syncretistic form of Islam that may have been related to early Kharijism;[5] Ghumāra, which, despite adhering officially to orthodox theology, remained susceptible to the heretical doctrines of the Berber prophet Ḥāʾ Mīm;[6] the caravan center of Sijilmasa, which continued to be influenced by Kharijism, even though it had officially turned Sunni under its Miḍrārid ruler, ash-Shākir Bi'llāh (d. 347/958);[7] and the central Sūs valley, whose two tribal moieties practiced a ritualized form of feuding that was expressed in sectarian terms: the tribal segment based at Taroudant adhered to a crudely anthropomorphic version of Malikism, while its rival in the neighboring caravan center of Tīwīwīn venerated Mūsā al-Kāẓim, the seventh imam of today's Ithnāʾ ʿAsharī (Twelver) Shiʿites.[8]

This mission to the countryside was carried out through rural mosques and centers of instruction (Ar. *ribāṭ* or *rābiṭa*), which were created to provide Qur'an-based literacy and religious education to sedentary and pastoralist peoples alike. These institutions promoted the praxis-oriented Islam of early Malikism, as well as a more contemporary emphasis on uṣūl. As we have seen in the previous chapter, this conformed very closely to what was happening at the same time in Muslim Spain, where Maliki hadith specialists and Sufis were hard at work disseminating uṣūlī doctrines in the Iberian Levant.[9]

The most important proponent of institutionalized Malikism in this period was the Arabized Berber legist from Fez, Abū ʿImrān al-Fāsī. Born

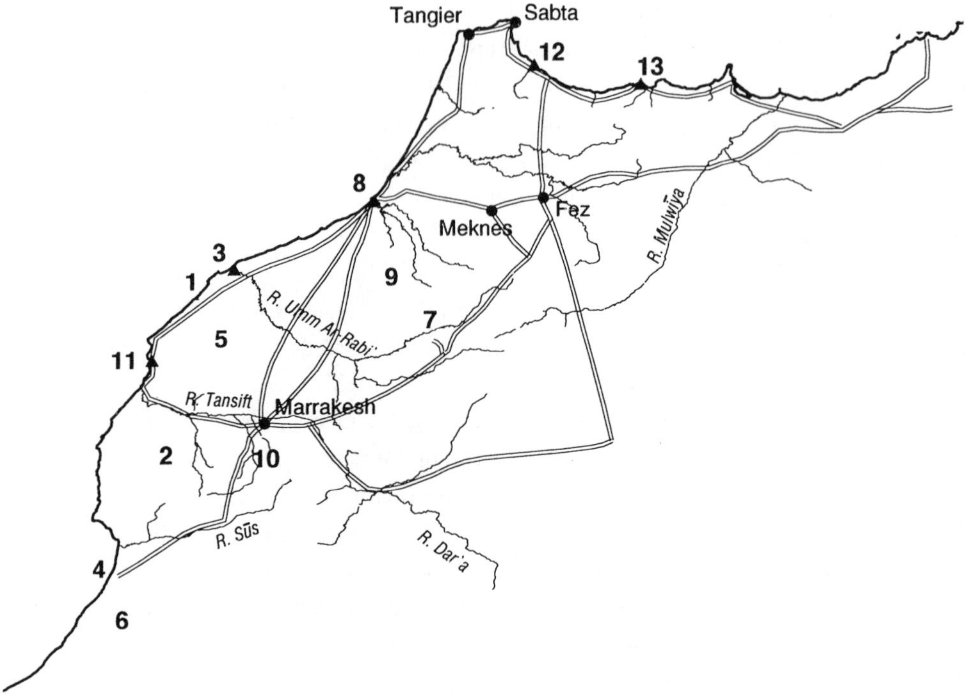

MAP FOUR
Early Ribats in Morocco

1. Ribāṭ Tīṭ-n-Fiṭr (Banū Amghār)
2. Ribāṭ Shākir (Ragrāga saints)
3. Ribāṭ Āzammūr (Abū Shuʿayb)
4. Ribāṭ Māssa
5. Ribāṭ Iliskāwan (Abū Innūr)
6. Dār al-Murābiṭīn (Aglu)
7. Ḥiṣn Dayy (Middle Atlas saints)
8. Ribāṭ al-Fatḥ (Rabat)
9. Tāghīyā (Abū Yiʿzzā)
10. Aghmāt Ūrīka
11. Ribāṭ Āsafī (Abū Muḥammad Ṣāliḥ al-Māgirī)
12. Ribāṭ of Abū Dāwūd Muzāhim
    (Major Sufi center of the Rif mountains ca. 560/1163)
13. Al-Mazimma (Ribāṭ Nakūr)

between the years 365/975 and 368/978–9 in his family quarter of Darb ibn Abī Ḥājj on the Qarawiyyīn side of Fez, al-Fāsī took advantage of his family's wealth and high social position to study under some of the greatest scholars in the Muslim world. He first traveled to Umayyad Córdoba, then in the final years of its glory under the regent al-Manṣūr ibn Abī ʿĀmir. There, he attended the lectures of noted scholars in the fields of hadith, Qur'anic studies, and jurisprudence.[10] After traveling to Ifrīqīya and staying for a few years in al-Qayrawān, he journeyed to Baghdad, where his most important teacher was the theologian, jurist, and political theorist Abū Bakr al-Bāqillānī. Under al-Bāqillānī, al-Fāsī was introduced to the then-revolutionary idea that Ashʿarite theology and the Shafiʿite doctrine of uṣūl might be harmoniously combined in a Maliki environment.[11] Upon returning from Baghdad to Fez, he attempted to teach these doctrines in the major mosques of his native city and was exiled for his trouble.[12] Leaving Fez for a second time, al-Fāsī again traveled to al-Qayrawān, where he taught his uṣūl-based version of Maliki jurisprudence and Ashʿarite theology for the remainder of his life.[13]

By the time of his death, Abū ʿImrān al-Fāsī had arguably become the most influential authority on Malikism in all of North Africa. Because of his Berber background, he encouraged students from the rural and desert regions of the Maghrib to attend his study circle in al-Qayrawān. Circumstantial evidence indicates that al-Fāsī's solicitousness toward his own ethnic group was part of a wider plan to empower Berbers through religious education. He is best remembered in the historical record as the person who encouraged Yaḥyā ibn Ibrāhīm, chief of the Gudāla Ṣanhāja pastoralists of the Sahara desert, to seek a teacher among his students in the Far Maghrib.[14] Eventually, this desert chieftain was put in touch with the Sūsī scholar ʿAbdallāh ibn Yāsīn al-Jazūlī (d. 451/1059), who was to become the spiritual leader of the Almoravid movement. Whatever al-Fāsī's overall plan may have been, he was convinced of the need to purify the rural Maghrib from heresy and desired the reinclusion of the Muslim West under the authority of the ʿAbbasid caliph in Baghdad.[15]

One of the most important disciples of Abū ʿImrān al-Fāsī was Waggāg (u-Aggāg) ibn Zallū al-Lamṭī (d. 445/1053–4).[16] A member of the Lamṭa (Oryx) tribe of Ṣanhāja Berbers from the Wādī Nūn region of southern Morocco, Waggāg presided over a network of mosques and educational centers on the mountainous fringes of the pre-Saharan desert. The most famous of these educational centers was his headquarters, Dār al-Murābiṭīn, which he established at the coastal hamlet of Aglū, near modern-day Tiznit.[17] Waggāg achieved supremacy in religious matters in the regions south of the Atlas mountains and remained in close contact with Abū ʿImrān al-Fāsī in al-Qayrawān until his teacher's death. It was he who instructed ʿAbdallāh ibn Yāsīn al-Jazūlī to teach Islamic dogma and Maliki doctrine to Yaḥyā ibn Ibrāhīm's Veiled Ṣanhāja warriors. The ties that bound the Almoravids to Waggāg appear to have been as close as those between the disciples of Abū ʿImrān al-Fāsī and their master in al-Qayrawān. The brothers Sulaymān and Abū'l-Qāsim ibn ʿAddū, the eventual successors to Ibn Yāsīn as Almoravid imams, were also students of Waggāg and continued to maintain close contact with Dār al-Murābiṭin even after their teacher's death.[18]

The success of Waggāg ibn Zallū al-Lamṭī's religious activism depended on the social and economic ties maintained by Ṣanhāja pastoralists in the desert regions of the western Maghrib. Like any successful pairing of dissimilar entities, this marriage of convenience between Maliki reformism and tribal social mores involved compromise on both sides. Sources document the frustration felt by Waggāg and his disciples at the reluctance of their pastoralist followers to give up long-held practices and beliefs. In the following passage from *at-Tashawwuf,* the Berbers of the Nafīs valley ignore Waggāg's attempt to portray himself as little more than a teacher of the Sharīʿa and the Prophetic Sunna. Instead, maintaining a stubborn (and ultimately well-justified) belief in his ability to work miracles, they treat him as a broker or a middleman who is well-positioned to plead their case before God:

> I heard Abū Mūsā ʿĪsā ibn ʿAbd al-ʿAzīz al-Jazūlī say: A drought occurred among the people living along the river Nafīs. So they went to Waggāg ibn Zallū al-Lamṭī in the Sūs. When they reached him he asked, "What has happened to you?" They replied, "We have suffered drought and have come so that you might ask God to provide rain for us." "Verily," he exclaimed, "you are like a group of people who see a honeycomb and assume that it contains honey! However, stay with me, for you are my guests." So he was their host for three days [the term mandated by the Sunna]. When they had resolved to leave and came to him to ask his permission to return to their lands he said to them, "Be careful not to take the road that you came on, but take another instead, so you can take

refuge from the rain in hollows and caves." When they left him God sent them clouds full of rain, which fell so copiously upon them that they did not arrive at their homes for six months.[19]

Similar misunderstandings, this time with the Maṣmūda Berbers of the High Atlas mountains, were experienced by another disciple of Abū ʿImrān al-Fāsī, an urban scholar from Ifrīqīya named ʿAbd al-ʿAzīz at-Tūnisī (d. 486/1088). Unlike Waggāg, who founded mosques and other centers of learning in sparsely populated rural areas, at-Tūnisī established a *rābiṭa* at Aghmāt Ūrīka, then the premier urban center of the Nafīs valley, just south of the new Almoravid capital of Marrakesh. In the twelfth century C.E. the geographer al-Idrīsī depicted Aghmāt as a town hidden in the shadow of the new imperial city but still prospering from the profits earned by its merchants. He tells us that during Aghmāt's heyday in the early eleventh century the merchants of the town traded copper, brass, glass buttons and beads, turban cloth, woven textiles, spices, and iron tools for the gold, skins, and slaves of the Middle Niger region. He also reports that their caravans could comprise as many as 187 camels, and that the wealthy of Aghmāt advertised their riches on carved columns erected by the doors of their houses.[20]

ʿAbd al-ʿAzīz at-Tūnisī was so vexed by the mercantile ethics of highland Maṣmūda culture that he once exclaimed: "By giving them knowledge we have become like one who sells weapons to a thief!"[21] A particularly irritating characteristic of these Berber merchants was their desire to turn any advantage, including their knowledge of religion, into a profit—a detail which is remarked upon by at-Tādilī in *at-Tashawwuf:*

> It is said about ʿAbd al-ʿAzīz that the Maṣmūda learned jurisprudence from him and then returned to their homelands, [where they] went about among their people with what they had learned, becoming judges, notaries, preachers, and other occupations. [Once] ʿAbd al-ʿAzīz went on one of his journeys to the farthest Maghrib, and whenever he passed by a [group of] people they came out to meet him. He found that his students had used what they had learned from him to gain authority and high positions. So he discontinued his teaching of jurisprudence and ordered his students to read the *Riʿāya* of al-Muḥāsibī and others of its type among the books of Sufism, until he found that, out of ignorance of jurisprudence, some of his students had begun to practice usury. "Glory

be to God!" he said. "I disapproved of teaching jurisprudence out of fear that you would attain the material world with it, but you have [instead] lost the knowledge of right and wrong (*al-ḥalāl wa'l-ḥarām*)!"[22]

Through the efforts of teachers such as Waggāg ibn Zallū al-Lamṭī and ʿAbd al-ʿAzīz at-Tūnisī, the disciples of Abū ʿImrān al-Fāsī were able to assert doctrinal authority over the rural inhabitants of the Far Maghrib south of the Atlas mountains. This was particularly the case with regard to the Veiled Ṣanhāja Almoravids, who had recently come to dominate the caravan trade across the Sahara desert. The *ṣulaḥāʾ* who taught Maliki doctrine to these aloof and aristocratic *imashaghen* ("free" camel nomads) retained the loyalty and veneration of their disciples until the fall of the Almoravid dynasty in 541/1146. ʿAbd as-Salām at-Tūnisī, a nephew of the abovementioned shaykh of Aghmāt, was a favored advisor to the Almoravid ruling elite, despite his rude behavior and disregard for social pretensions. Famous for both his scrupulousness and his violent temper in defense of moral principles, the younger at-Tūnisī once refused an inheritance of 1,000 dinars brought to him by his sister, saying, "[Why] have you come to me with these devils? I have no need of them!" When she insisted that he at least take the share allotted to him in the Qur'an he replied, "It is yours because it is in your hands. As for me, I have no idea what it is and will not take it from you!"[23]

The mosques and educational centers established by the students of Abū ʿImrān al-Fāsī were widely distributed throughout the western Maghrib. When the father of ʿAbd as-Salām at-Tūnisī died in Tlemcen, the latter immediately left Marrakesh in order to take his place and devoted the remainder of his life to providing spiritual advice for the Almoravid elites of that Algerian city. ʿAbd as-Salām's association with the politically powerful, however, did not mean that he considered himself subservient to them. It is related that while the shaykh was tending his garden near Tlemcen, the amir Mazdalī ibn Tiliggān, a noted companion of the Almoravid ruler Yūsuf ibn Tāshfīn, rode up to him. After only the most perfunctory of greetings, the amir dismounted from his horse, put his burnous on the ground, and sat on it, expecting words of wisdom. Noting his student's lack of respect, at-Tūnisī rebuked him, saying: "What are these actions, oh Mazdalī? And where will you find a burnous to sit upon tomorrow?"[24]

A similar story is told about Abū Zakariyya ibn Yughān (d. 537/1139), another "amir of the Ṣanhāja" and disciple of ʿAbd as-Salām at-Tūnisī. When he first met this shaykh, the Ṣanhāja notable was told that to prove his sincerity he would have to go to the countryside beyond the walls of Tlemcen, gather a load of wood, and carry it on his back into the middle of the government house, the Dār al-Imāra, where he could be observed by all the members of his matrilineal clan. After Abū Zakariyya complied with these demeaning requirements, ʿAbd as-Salām was so pleased with his new disciple that he honored him by calling him *malik az-zuhd* (King of Asceticism).[25]

The Ribāṭ and the Institutionalization of Rural Sufism

As mentioned in the Introduction to this book, no figure in the field of Maghrib Studies has received more attention from Western scholars than has the marabout. It may thus surprise the reader to discover that the term *murābiṭ* was not widely employed in Morocco prior to the sixteenth century C.E. The situation was somewhat different in Muslim Spain, where *al-murābiṭ* appears as a nickname (*laqab*) as far back as the Umayyad period. In Andalusian parlance *murābiṭ* did not usually mean a rural Sufi or a holy man, as it did on the North African side of the Strait of Gibraltar. Instead, the term was used as a jihad-related honorific, describing *ṣulaḥā*ʾ who defended the fortified outposts of central Iberia against the Crusader kingdoms of Castile and Aragon.[26]

Although the term *murābiṭ,* as presently understood in Morocco, is of comparatively recent vintage, the ribāṭ as an institution is much older. Textual evidence suggests that the ribāṭ was conceived as a formal institution in the Far Maghrib as early as the middle of the ninth century. An account of one of the earliest ribāṭs in Morocco can be found in *Kitāb al-masālik wa'l-mamālik* by the Andalusian geographer al-Bakrī (d. 487/1094). This work details the history of the ribāṭ and city-state of Nakūr, which lasted for two centuries at al-Mazimma (near modern El Hoceima) in the Rif mountains. The origins of Nakūr may date as far back as the first century of Islam, when, during the reign of the Umayyad caliph al-Walīd ibn ʿAbd al-Malik (r. 86–96/705–15), a South Arabian holy warrior known as al-ʿAbd aṣ-Ṣāliḥ ibn Manṣūr al-Ḥimyarī began to call the Ṣanhāja and Ghumāra peoples of northern Morocco to the Islamic faith.[27]

In the year 240/854–5, al-ʿAbd aṣ-Ṣāliḥ's grandson, Saʿīd ibn Idrīs b. Ṣāliḥ al-Ḥimyarī, founded both Ribāṭ Nakūr and the town that shared its name. Al-Bakrī informs us that this ribāṭ was built as a rural mosque, and that its design and supporting endowments were modeled after the initial mosque of Alexandria in Egypt.[28] By the time Saʿīd ibn Idrīs was succeeded by his son ʿAbd ar-Raḥmān ash-Shahīd (d. before 305/917), Nakūr had grown into a modest city-state. To counteract the growing influence of their political rivals, the Idrisid sharifs of Fez and the nearby region of Ghumāra, the Banū Ṣāliḥ intermarried with the Banū Sulaymān clan of Tlemcen, who, like the Idrisids, claimed to be descendants of the Prophet Muḥammad. This matrimonial policy helped the Banū Ṣāliḥ maintain a religiously legitimated principality, allied with the Umayyads of Spain, that was similar in administrative organization to the mini-states founded by the Idrisids themselves.

Unlike the Idrisids, however, whose well-established ʿAlid origins enabled them to enjoy the fruits of an ascribed nobility, the Banū Ṣāliḥ had to depend on a more unstable form of acquired status that demanded continual reaffirmation. Throughout his turbulent career, ʿAbd ar-Raḥmān ash-Shahīd, despite his training as a jurist and the completion of no fewer than four pilgrimages to Mecca, had to deal with numerous Berber uprisings and reassert his claim to legitimacy by conducting jihads against a variety of enemies. Unfortunately, as his nickname, *ash-Shahīd* (the Martyr) implies, the only uncontested nobility he was ever able to attain was that of a heroic death, for he was killed in al-Andalus while aiding his Umayyad patrons in their suppression of the *muwallad* revolt of ʿUmar Ibn Ḥafṣūn.[29]

THE ṢANHĀJA APPROACH: RIBĀṬ TĪṬ-N-FIṬR

Although Nakūr appears in the historical record mainly as a buffer for Umayyad Spain, one can nonetheless observe in its ribāṭ the outlines of what was to become a pivotal religious and sociopolitical institution. Like Ribāṭ Nakūr, most Moroccan ribāṭs of the tenth through the thirteenth centuries C.E. were privately built and locally maintained.[30] Contrary to the case in al-Andalus and Ifrīqīya, where ribāṭs were built for military purposes, the ribāṭs of Morocco were primarily centers of instruction in Islamic dogma (*iʿtiqādāt*) and practice (*muʿāmalāt*). Ribāṭs also served an important secondary role as communication hubs, facilitating interaction between economic and political networks in rural areas. For this reason, they were often located where their founders could most effectively exploit the physical and human resources of the surrounding region. Not surprisingly, many of these sites had been meeting places in pre-Islamic times, such as tribal markets and former religious sites.

The history of one of the earliest and most important ribāṭs of the Far

Maghrib—Tīṭ-n-Fiṭr, located on the Atlantic coast of Morocco some eight kilometers south of the modern city of El Jedida—is detailed in a fourteenth-century manuscript entitled *Bahjat an-nāẓirīn wa uns al-ʿārifīn wa wasīlat Rabb al-ʿĀlamīn fī manāqib rijāl Amghār aṣ-ṣāliḥīn* (The Delight of observers, the intimacy of the gnostics, and the agency of the Lord of the Worlds in the exploits of the exemplary Amghār Ṣāliḥīn).[31] This hagiographical monograph, made up of collected *manāqib* (exploit narratives), is useful for modern historians because its compiler, Muḥammad az-Zammūrī, a judge from the town of Azemmour who was also a member of the Banū Amghār family, includes transcriptions of documents that provide important information about the ribāṭ's social functions and political relations. These texts, which include correspondence between the Banū Amghār and the rulers of their day, offer a rare glimpse into the activities of rural Moroccan Sufis during the Almoravid and Almohad eras.[32]

According to az-Zammūrī, the Banū Amghār were descendants of the Prophet Muḥammad by way of a chieftain (Ber. *amghār*) whose full name was Abū ʿUthmān Saʿīd ibn Abī Zakariyya Yaḥyā b. Abī Shākir Ḥammād b. Abī Sulaymān Dāwūd b. Abī Zakariyya al-Ḥunayf.[33] Whether or not this family was purely North African, as the name "Banū Amghār" implies, or from the Hijaz, as is stated in the manuscript, they used their status as descendants of the Prophet to claim both religious and political authority over the Ṣanhāja pastoralists of the Atlantic coastal region of Dukkāla. Indeed, their very name implies a political role. In Morocco, the Berber word *amghār* is roughly equivalent in meaning to the Arabic term *shaykh.* Unlike *shaykh,* however, which may refer to a Sufi master or religious notable as well as a tribal leader, *amghār* carries the exclusive connotation of political leadership.

The traditions reproduced in *Bahjat an-nāẓirīn* place the founder of Ribāṭ Tīṭ, Abū Ibrāhīm Ismāʿīl, in Medina at the end of the tenth century C.E., where he is portrayed as an ascetic and a firm adherent of the example of *as-salaf aṣ-ṣāliḥ.* After living for a time in the Red Sea port of Jeddah, he hears a voice that tells him to go to the Maghrib, where his baraka and private formula of invocation (*wird*) will be of benefit. In time, this hidden voice gives him specific instructions: "Oh Ismāʿīl, go to the Maghrib and follow the light that you see before you. Wherever that light settles in the Maghrib, there should you stay, for it will be a place of ṣāliḥīn."[34]

Accompanied by two of his brothers, Ismāʿīl follows what is referred to in the text as "the Hashimite light" (*an-nūr al-Hāshimī*) until they come to an island just off the Atlantic coast of Morocco. Crossing over to the island at low tide, they discover a cluster of bushes, a spring of pure water, and a hive of honeybees. Because their basic necessities are provided for by this spring and its surroundings, they call the place ʿAyn al-Fiṭr, "Spring of Sustenance" (Ber. *Tīṭ-n-Fiṭr*).

Az-Zammūrī goes on to explain that the region of Dukkāla was then covered with low scrub and inhabited by lions. These beasts would surround Ismāʿīl when he prayed and rub their bodies against his clothes when he performed his invocations. This behavior was observed from afar by herdsmen from the nearby Ṣanhāja tribe of Azammūr, who reported it to their chief, ʿAbd al-ʿAzīz ibn Baṭṭān. Going immediately to the place where his men had seen the miracle, Ibn Baṭṭān found Ismāʿīl Amghār standing in a field, surrounded by a pride of lions. However, when he asked the saint to join his tribe the latter refused, protesting that an *ʿabd ṣālih* could not leave the place where God had commanded him to settle. When Ibn Baṭṭān tried to compel the saint to go with him by force, the ground opened up beneath the tribal leader's feet and held him captive until he apologized. Several months later, after Ismāʿīl Amghār mediated an intratribal dispute over the use of a well and successfully petitioned God to provide rain during a drought, the leaders of the Ṣanhāja Azammūr held a council, at which they decided that just having such a saint in their vicinity would give them a distinct advantage over their rivals.[35]

The second master of Ribāṭ Tīṭ-n-Fiṭr, Abū Jaʿfar Isḥāq ibn Ismāʿīl, is the first about whom the text of *Bahjat an-nāẓirīn* contains transcribed documents. The earliest of these is an edict promulgated by the Maghrāwī sultan of Fez, Tamīm ibn Zīrī b. ʿAṭiyya, in the year 409/1018. This decree, which was probably issued soon after Abū Jaʿfar succeeded his father as head of Ribāṭ Tīṭ, authorizes the murābiṭ and his descendants to take a share of the produce tax (*kharāj*) claimed by the state from the Ṣanhāja Azammūr as upkeep for their family, servants, and clients. This is to last as long as the murābiṭūn of Tīṭ-n-Fiṭr maintain their spiritual rank and do not relocate to another region.[36] The formal and contractual nature of the relationship between the Banū Amghār and their clients is reconfirmed in another edict from the Marinid period (ca. 696/1297), in which Abū Mūsā ʿĪsā Amghār is allotted ten gold dinars per month in return for serving as a judge and official witness (*ʿādil*) for the Ṣanhāja Azammūr—again with the proviso that the murābiṭ neither leave Tīṭ-n-Fiṭr for another location nor change his saintly status, and so long as he and his descendants maintain a sufficient level of expertise in the religious sciences.[37] The importance of the Banū Amghār to the Marinid state is underscored by the fact that this second edict was renewed no fewer than three times (in 729/1328, 821/1418, and 850/1446).[38]

Also attributed to Abū Jaʿfar Amghār is the earliest creed (*ʿaqīda*) by a rural religious figure in the Far Maghrib. This document was written in 412/1021 in response to questions posed by a scholar from the Tunisian city of Sfax. In the premodern Maghrib, an *ʿaqīda* was a doctrinal position paper or statement of principles that was meant to prove the orthodoxy of its author's beliefs.[39] The portion of Abū Jaʿfar's *ʿaqīda* that is reproduced in *Bahjat an-nāẓirīn* is similar in content to the *ʿaqīda* that is found in the opening chapter of the *Risāla* of Ibn Abī Zayd al-Qayrawānī.[40] This tells us that the Banū Amghār's interpretation of Islam was probably little different from that of mainstream Maliki reformers such as Abū ʿImrān al-Fāsī.[41]

Abū Jaʿfar Amghār is further credited by az-Zammūrī with laying out the physical complex of Tīṭ-n-Fiṭr and turning the ribāṭ into a formal institution. At first the murābiṭ, along with his family and entourage, lived in simple huts clustered about his father's grave. In 419/1027–8, the effects of a famine caused by fighting between the Ṣanhāja Azammūr and the Barghwāṭa tribe of Tāmesnā compelled Abū Jaʿfar to move south along the Atlantic coast, to a fortified settlement known as Iyīr (Tashelhit Ber. *iyir:* rock, boulder).[42] Here, he taught Qur'anic studies and Maliki jurisprudence to the Maṣmūda inhabitants of highland Dukkāla.[43]

Although some of the inhabitants of Iyīr accepted Abū Jaʿfar as their imam, most opposed him, thus forcing him to give up his mission to the Maṣmūda and return to his clients the Ṣanhāja Azammūr. It was at this juncture that he decided to develop and fortify the site of Tīṭ-n-Fiṭr. After clearing away the low scrub that covered the coastal area across from the island and its holy spring, Abū Jaʿfar built a small mosque and a permanent dwelling. Seeing that several families of Ṣanhāja pastoralists wanted to settle near him in order to partake of his baraka, he provided for their needs by digging a well, later known as Tīn Gīdūt (Tashelhit Ber. *tīn gi.ggūt:* Well of Abundance), that was fed by the spring of ʿAyn al-Fiṭr.[44] Later, he constructed a congregational mosque next to the well. The main structure of this mosque, which was originally built of driftwood, has long since collapsed, but its cut-stone minaret, the oldest privately built religious structure still extant in Morocco, stands today.[45]

Sometime around the year 475/1083, Abū ʿAbdallāh ("Mūlāy ʿAbdallāh")

Amghār succeeded his father Abū Jaʿfar as head of Ribāṭ Tīṭ-n-Fiṭr. Acknowledged throughout the Far Maghrib as one of the most influential religious figures of his day, he was particularly noted as a specialist in the Qur'an. Along with his son and successor, Abū ʿAbd al-Khāliq (d. ca. 614/1217), this long-lived murābiṭ is credited with founding *aṭ-Ṭāʾifa aṣ-Ṣanhājiyya,* the earliest recorded example of an institutionalized Sufi order in the western Maghrib.[46] In the latter half of the fourteenth century C.E., the Algerian jurist and hagiographer Ibn Qunfudh cited aṭ-Ṭāʾifa aṣ-Ṣanhājiyya as one of the most important rural Sufi orders in all of North Africa.[47] As its name implies, the Ṣanhājiyya Sufi order was an ethnically oriented institution whose membership was limited to Ṣanhāja Berbers. Its members, however, did not only come from the Ṣanhāja Azammūr of Dukkāla. Rather, aṭ-Ṭāʾifa aṣ-Ṣanhājiyya was multiregional in scope and claimed the allegiance of virtually every Sufi of Ṣanhāja stock between Dukkāla and the Western Sahara.

The Almoravid sultans of Morocco appear to have regarded Abū ʿAbdallāh Amghār as a semiofficial spokesman for all of the Ṣanhāja Berbers of Morocco. Az-Zammūrī reports that prior to the year 522/1128, ʿAlī ibn Yūsuf b. Tāshfīn and his vizier Abū'l-Walīd ibn Rushd (the noted Maliki jurist and grandfather of the famous Andalusian philosopher) solicited the blessings of the murābiṭ for the construction of new defensive walls for their capital of Marrakesh.[48] Another letter, dated 527/1133 and also written in the name of ʿAlī ibn Yūsuf, is the earliest to officially acknowledge "Mūlāy ʿAbdallāh" Amghār as a descendant of the Prophet. This time the Almoravid ruler appears to solicit the murābiṭ's support against the Almohad revolt, which had just broken out in the High Atlas mountains. In light of this communication, it is significant that when the Sufi shaykhs and ṣulaḥāʾ of the Far Maghrib were summoned to Marrakesh to reconfirm their oath of allegiance to ʿAlī ibn Yūsuf, Mūlāy ʿAbdallāh demurred, citing as his reason an "extreme lack of care for the world."[49] His son and successor, Abū ʿAbd al-Khāliq, enjoyed a close relationship with the Almohad caliph Yaʿqūb al-Manṣūr (d. 595/1199), who supported Ribāṭ Tīṭ-n-Fiṭr financially and allowed the murabiṭ to intercede at court on behalf of the Ṣanhāja Azammūr.[50] It is thus likely that the Banū Amghār joined other prominent Sufis of Morocco in supporting the Almohad movement against the Almoravids.[51]

Although it is presently impossible to reconstruct the complete spiritual method of aṭ-Ṭāʾifa aṣ-Ṣanhājiyya, its outlines can be gleaned from *Bahjat an-nāẓirīn* and other sources. Hagiographers agree in portraying the murābiṭūn of Tīṭ-n-Fiṭr as firm adherents of the Muḥammadan Sunna. In *at-Tashawwuf,* for example, at-Tādilī depicts Abū ʿAbd al-Khāliq Amghār as saying to his sons: "Do you know how your ancestor surpassed the other ṣāliḥīn of the Maghrib? He did not surpass them because of the frequency of [his] prayers or fasting. He surpassed them in his adherence to the Sunna."[52]

The sources also maintain that Mūlāy ʿAbdallāh Amghār, like other Sunni internationalists in Muslim Spain and North Africa, was devoted in equal measure to the Maliki school of law and the uṣūlī approach that was championed by most Sufis of his generation. He would dictate selected passages from Saḥnūn's *Mudawwana* to his students and instruct them in the example of as-Salaf aṣ-Ṣāliḥ. At the same time, he was so fond of al-Ghazālī's writings that he miraculously transported himself to the latter's funeral.[53]

The Sufi doctrines of aṭ-Ṭāʾifa aṣ-Ṣanhājiyya appear to have been short on metaphysical principles but long on *ṣalāḥ* and asceticism. Abū ʿAbdallāh Amghār was particularly noted for his love of spiritual retreat (*khalwa*) and bodily mortification (Mor. Ar. *al-jidd wa'l-ijtihād*). This latter practice involved frequent fasting and extreme sensitivity in regard to the amount, type, or origin of whatever one ate or drank. Abū ʿAbdallāh's scrupulousness was so intense that he refused to eat food that other people produced, lest it be polluted by the traces of their sins. For this reason, he restricted his diet to the leaves of trees, "allowable plants of the earth," and fish from the sea.[54]

In the way of practice, Abū ʿAbdallāh Amghār required his disciples to follow ten Rules of Companionship (*shurūṭ aṣ-suḥba*) that were similar in nature to the rules of the early *futuwwa* groups of Khurasan. These ten principles were: (1) the avoidance of disputes, (2) the pursuit of justice, (3) generosity, (4) contentment with whatever God provides, (5) forbearance, (6) concealment of esoteric teachings from the uninitiated (*ḥifẓ al-ghuyūb*), (7) concealment of the sins of others, (8) conceding the final word in an argument, (9) satisfaction with one's lot in life, and (10) refusing to exert oneself for worldly goods.[55]

Commandments similar to these can be found in *Kitāb al-futuwwa* (Book of Sufi chivalry) by Abū ʿAbd ar-Raḥmān as-Sulamī, whose writings were well-known in the Maghrib by the Almoravid period. One cannot but recall the pastoral ethos of Moroccan maraboutism when as-Sulamī writes: "*Futuwwa* involves the movement toward God (*al-hijra ilā Allāh*) in one's heart and soul . . . [following the way of Lot] . . . who turned away from his city and moved toward his Lord."[56] Traces of Abū ʿAbdallāh Amghār's commandments can also be discerned in the following sayings: "*Futuwwa* . . . is awareness of the rights of one who is above you, other than you, or alike to you; and that you do not turn away from your brethren because of a fault, a quarrel, or knowledge of a lie. He who loves his brother should see his [brother's] obstinacy as loyalty and his rejection as acceptance and must not hate him in any state or moral condition" (Abū ʿAmr ad-Dimashqī [d. 320/932]).[57] "[*Futuwwa*] means putting morality (*akhlāq*) into practice" (Shāh ibn Shujāʿ al-Kirmānī [d. before 300/912–13]).[58] "Be honest, loyal, and dependable; be generous; maintain a noble character; be satisfied with little; do not make fun of your friends, and live with them in harmony; do not listen to slander; desire to do good; be a good neighbor; speak well and be loyal to your word; treat your household and those who are dependent upon you well; treat those who serve you well; educate the young and teach them good behavior; respect your elders and superiors; refrain from holding grudges and seeking vengeance; do not cheat or manipulate people, or criticize or talk against them" (as-Sulamī).[59]

The Banū Amghār of Tīṭ-n-Fiṭr enjoyed a preeminent position among the rural Sufis of Morocco throughout the Almoravid and Almohad periods. Mūlāy ʿAbdallāh Amghār in particular maintained friendly relations with many of the most important religious figures of his day. These included the Andalusian jurist Abū Bakr ibn al-ʿArabī, a student of al-Ghazālī and teacher of Sīdī Ḥarāzem, who wrote a work dedicated to the murābiṭ entitled *Sirāj al-muhtadīn fī ādāb aṣ-ṣāliḥīn* (Lamp for the guided in the conduct of the ṣāliḥīn). Another correspondent was Qāḍī ʿIyāḍ ibn Mūsā al-Yaḥsubī (d. 544/1149–50), a noted jurist and hadith specialist from Sabta, who was the author of *Kitāb ash-shifāʾ bi-taʿrīf ḥuqūq al-Muṣṭafā* (The Antidote in knowing the rights of the Chosen Prophet), a highly influential work on the veneration of the Prophet Muḥammad.[60] Az-Zammūrī also claims that Mūlāy ʿAbdallāh Amghār exchanged letters with Sufis in Iraq, and that after his death a delegation of ṣulaḥāʾ from Yemen came to visit his tomb.[61]

Clearly, Tīṭ-n-Fiṭr served as a model for other ribāṭs in Morocco and its shaykhs were considered paradigmatic murābiṭūn. Abū ʿAbdallāh Amghār's *laqab* ("Abū'l-Budalāʾ") is indicative of this family's central importance to Moroccan Sufism. According to traditions still current in Dukkāla, no fewer than ten leaders of the Banū Amghār held the rank of "substitute" (sing. *badīl,* pl. *budalā', abdāl*), a candidate for the title of Axis of the Age (*quṭb az-Zamān*).[62] Today, poetic odes are still sung in Dukkāla which recount the glories of the Banū Amghār and lament the downfall and dispersion of this eminent maraboutic family.

The Banū Amghār were recognized as authorities on Islam and were legitimate members of the ulama class. However, not unlike the less sophisticated saints of the Atlas studied by Ernest Gellner,[63] it was equally part of their role to maintain a local political presence as tribal brokers.[64] Because they assumed the role of official witnesses (*ʿādil,* pl. *ʿudūl*) among the Ṣanhāja Azemmour, and maintained their position as neutral outsiders by choosing their wives from al-Andalus and other regions external to Dukkāla, the murābiṭūn of Tīṭ-n-Fiṭr were trusted by their clients to act as just arbitrators and mediators. The eventual creation, under the Marinids, of the post of judge (*qāḍī*) at Tīṭ-n-Fiṭr formally institutionalized this mediating role.

The acknowledgment by the Marinids that a competent jurist could be found at Ribāṭ Tīṭ demonstrates that rather than administering an unsophisticated and arbitrary form of "qadi-justice,"[65] the Banū Amghār functioned, like the students of Abū ʿImrān al-Fāsī, as bearers of the urban traditions of Maliki jurisprudence. Both *Bahjat an-nāẓirīn* and other, more contemporaneous sources, such as at-Tādilī's *at-Tashawwuf* and Muḥammad ibn Qasim at-Tamīmī's (d. 604/1207–8) *Kitāb al-mustafād fī dhikr aṣ-ṣāliḥīn wa'l-ʿubbād bi-madīnat Fās wa mā yalīhā min al-bilād* (Compendium of the recollection of the ṣāliḥīn and the pious of the city of Fez and adjoining lands), attest to the fact that the Banū Amghār were anything but the marginally educated opportunists so often depicted in modern studies of maraboutism.[66] Such a peripheralized model of the rural ṣāliḥ obscures the fact that many were legitimate scholars in their own right and could even be included among the most important ulama of their day.

Another aspect of maraboutism that is clarified by the example of Tīṭ-n-Fiṭr concerns the relative valuation of ascribed versus acquired forms of status. The idea that descent from the Prophet Muḥammad is a necessary and sufficient proof of religious or political authority was not widely accepted in the Maghrib during the Almoravid and Almohad periods. Despite the precedent of sharifian rule set by the Idrisid imams, descendants of the Prophet do not begin to proliferate in Morocco until the thirteenth century of the Common Era. Even the question of whether the Banū Amghār were in fact the sharifs they claimed to be does not appear as a major issue until the publication of *Bahjat an-nāẓirīn* in the fourteenth century. Neither at-Tādilī nor at-Tamīmī, writing almost two hundred years before az-Zummūrī, mentions anything about a Prophetic lineage for the murābiṭūn of Tīṭ-n-Fiṭr. Instead, at-Tādilī merely states that Abū ʿAbdallāh Amghār was "Ṣanhājī" by origin, while at-Tamīmī lists him as "Zammūrī," after his approximate place of residence, Azemmour. This lack of a sharifian genealogy did not, however, diminish the status of this family in the pages of either *at-Tashawwuf* or *al-Mustafād.*[67]

It will be seen in Chapter Four that the most significant indicators of sainthood in the formative period of Moroccan Sufism were miracles and socially conscious virtue, ṣalāḥ. Ṣalāḥ is similarly significant in the hagiographic record of the Banū Amghār. Examples of this type of spirituality include the *futuwwa*-inspired Commandments of Companionship set down by Abū ʿAbdallāh Amghār for aṭ-Ṭāʾifa aṣ-Ṣanhājiyya, as well as more universal indicators of piety and virtue, such as knowledge of the Qur'an, expertise in Islamic law, and inner purity. In regard to the Banū Amghār's sociopolitical role, the most important example of institutionalized ṣalāḥ can be found in the eleventh-century edict of the sultan Tamīm ibn Zīrī. This edict confirms the murābiṭ's role as both a tribal arbitrator and an Islamic imam, and it intimates that virtue above all meant using one's knowledge to establish and maintain justice in a local context.

Transaction theorists in the field of Symbolic Anthropology have long stressed the responsibility of social brokers "to construct and purvey meanings concerning a variety of relationships and interactions."[68] This means that when the murābiṭūn of Tīṭ-n-Fiṭr applied Qur'anic and Islamic legal precepts among the Ṣanhāja Azammūr, their success depended on their ability to translate the elaborated code of universal Arabo-Islamic discourse into the more restricted code of their pastoralist clients.[69] The murābiṭ's ability to practice his vocation was predicated on his skill in bridging the "privatization of meaning" that divided the urban-based world of normative Islam from the rural world of tribal relations in which he lived.[70] To do so, it was necessary for him to keep a foot in both environments—the local as well as the universal. Although his political role kept him tied to a specific locality, his pedagogical role demanded a relatively thorough knowledge of Islamic theology and jurisprudence.

It was because he acted as a social broker, and not because of some idealized etymology of the word *murābiṭ,* that the marabout was "bound" (*marbūṭ*) to a particular locality or tribe. For the Banū Amghār, these ties were affirmed in the form of a social contract that was modeled after the covenant struck between the Prophet Muḥammad and the people of Medina following the Hijra. According to the terms of this contract, the murābiṭ of Tīṭ-n-Fiṭr undertook to act as an imam for the Ṣanhāja Azammūr and to mediate their disputes in return for a formalized "gift" (*hiba*) that was paid to him either in specie or in kind. Eventually, the "actional formalism"[71] of this transaction was recognized by the state and institutionalized in a series of written edicts.[72] When this relationship was further institutionalized by the creation of an ethnically based Sufi order that included all of the Ṣanhāja Berbers of Morocco, the very possibility of the Banū Amghār transcending their "Ṣanhājī" identity became moot. It was virtually unthinkable for an institution that defined itself in terms of Ṣanhāja tribal membership to divorce itself from its main source of support. In the end, rather than being "bound" only to God, as the etymology of the term *murābiṭ* has most often been understood, the murābiṭūn of Tīṭ-n-Fiṭr were equally bound to an ethnic subculture that defined their sainthood in its own parochial terms.

THE MAṢMŪDA APPROACH: RIBĀṬ SHĀKIR

Although the Banū Amghār of Tīṭ-n-Fiṭr may have established the paradigm for subsequent generations of murābiṭūn in rural Morocco, evidence provided in the works of geographers, biographers, and local historians makes it clear that the ribāṭ as a center for Sufi instruction existed well beyond the confines of Dukkāla. The geographer al-Bakrī, for example, mentions Ribāṭ Māssa, south of the present-day city of Agadir, as a "retreat for those given to pious devotions."[73] Even more to the point is his mention of "Madīnat Niffīs," a middle-sized town dating from pre-Islamic times that was located a day's journey inland from the mouth of the Tansīft river between modern Asafi and Essaouira. According to al-Bakrī, the Muslim conqueror ʿUqba ibn Nāfiʿ defeated a combined force of Byzantines and Christian Berbers at this site in the year 62/681–2. After this victory, he is said to have ordered the construction of a congregational mosque for the propagation of Islam in the Far Sūs.[74]

Further upstream, in the region of Ragrāga, a companion of ʿUqba known as Sīdī Shākir was instrumental in the conversion of Maṣmūda Berbers living in the Atlas foothills. Around the end of the tenth century C.E., a ribāṭ was built on the site of Shākir's tomb by a Berber *mujāhid* named Yaʿlā u-Mṣlīn. This ribāṭ, unlike Tīṭ-n-Fiṭr, was initially founded as a defensive outpost against the Barghwāṭa, who were then making regular incursions into Dukkāla and Ragrāga.[75] Ribāṭ Shākir ("Sidi Chiker" on modern maps) served for more than three centuries as a center for the propagation of Islam and Sufism among the Maṣmūda Berbers of Ragrāga and Dukkāla, as well as for the inhabitants of the entire western portion of the High Atlas mountains. In this way, it provided the same type of support for the sedentary and transhumant populations of the southern Moroccan highlands as Ribāṭ Tīṭ did for the pastoralist Ṣanhāja who competed with them for land along the Atlantic littoral.[76]

Although much of the history of Ribāṭ Shākir remains shrouded in mystery, circumstantial evidence indicates that from the Almoravid period it functioned as the headquarters of a Maṣmūda Sufi tradition that grew up in response to the Ṣanhāja Sufism of Ribāṭ Tīṭ-n-Fiṭr. In the three centuries following the Muslim conquest of the Far Maghrib, social relations in the regions of Ḥāḥā, Shyāẓma, Ragrāga, and Dukkāla were drastically transformed by in-migrations of Ṣanhāja pastoralists moving north from their original homelands in the Anti-Atlas mountains. This Ṣanhāja encroachment on lands previously occupied by Maṣmūda farmers resulted in the displacement of most of the sedentary communities of Maṣmūda Berbers who lived in the lowlands along the Atlantic coast. Those who were left, such as the Banū Māgir in the hinterlands of Asafi, were forced to withdraw into fortified villages in the more easily defensible highlands.

Significantly, the earliest Maṣmūda saints to be mentioned in the hagiographical record date from the time of the Ṣanhāja migrations. By the early Almoravid period, folk tales about the so-called Seven Saints (*ar-rijāl as-sabʿa*) of Ragrāga had begun to be circulated as a means of promoting the Maṣmūda tradition. These seven *awliyāʾ*—forerunners of the more famous Seven Saints (*sabʿatu rijāl*) of Marrakesh—were said to be Berber companions of the Prophet Muḥammad who introduced Islam into Morocco long before the arrival of the Arab armies of ʿUqba ibn Nāfiʿ and Mūsā ibn Nuṣayr. Modern historians, however, can find no evidence that any of these saints—Sīdī Wāsmīn (buried at Jabal Ḥadīd, north of Essaouira), Abū Bakr Ashmās (buried at Zāwiyat Qarmūd, now the village of Akermoud), ʿAlī ibn Abī Bakr Ashmās, ʿAbdallāh Adnās, ʿĪsā Bū Khābiyya, Saʿīd ibn Yabqā as-Sābiq, and Sīdī Yaʿlā (the founder of Ribāṭ Shākir)—predated the Barghwāṭa polity in Tāmesnā, which was founded in 124/741–2. In fact, Sīdī Yaʿlā was supposedly martyred while defending his homeland against the Barghwāṭa during one of their raids south of the Umm ar-Rabīʿ river.[77] This indicates that he may have been a contemporary of Abū Jaʿfar Amghār, who fled Tīṭ-n-Fiṭr in 419/1027–8 ahead of a similar raid across the Umm ar-Rabīʿ.

One of the earliest bearers of the Maṣmūda tradition at Ribāṭ Shākir was Abū ʿAbdallāh ar-Ragrāgī (fl. ca. 480/1087–8) from the potter's village of Tālaght.[78] Although biographical sources preserve neither the date of his birth nor of his death, ar-Ragrāgī is known to have been an associate of ʿAbd al-ʿAzīz at-Tūnisī, the student of Abū ʿImrān al-Fāsī who taught Maliki jurisprudence at Aghmāt. Despite the fact that at-Tūnisī criticized ar-Ragrāgī's indulgence toward the Maṣmūda tribesmen who came to him for blessings, he learned to appreciate his rural contemporary after the latter was commended to him by the Prophet Muḥammad in a vision.[79] It is difficult to avoid the impression that Abū ʿAbdallāh ar-Ragrāgī was more of a miracle worker than an actual Sufi mystic. This impression is reinforced by the fact that he was most remembered in at-Tādilī's day for walking along the arc of a rainbow.[80]

A more intellectual representative of the Maṣmūda tradition can be found in Abū Zakariyya al-Malīgī, who presided over a mosque in his home village of Malīga (Ber. *al.iggī:* the Pines), near present-day Chichaoua, before becoming the head of Ribāṭ Shākir.[81] Because his reputation as a "substitute" (*badīl*) required a greater level of legitimation than was the case for a miracle worker such as Abū ʿAbdallāh ar-Ragrāgī, the exploits attributed to al-Malīgī are more in conformity with the tradition of juridical Sufism, as discussed in Chapter One. He is said, for example, to have been extremely scrupulous in his religious observances and would say all of his prayers at the earliest possible time. When told by his disciples that an echo from nearby hills prevented them from hearing the call to prayer, he obligingly asked God to remove it for them.[82] He is also said to have made the pilgrimage to Mecca every year.[83]

Pilgrimages such as these, although arduous, were not impossible. The Almoravid conquest of the western Maghrib at the end of the eleventh century C.E. facilitated travel by both land and sea to the point where larger numbers of Moroccans than ever before were able to fulfill this obligation. The real miracle in al-Malīgī's case (given adequate finances, of course) was that of time. Performing regular journeys to Mecca meant traveling at least nine months out of every year, leaving a shaykh little time to instruct disciples.[84] However, this fact alone should not cause one to dismiss such claims out of hand. As we shall see in Chapter Five, the Maṣmūda Berbers of southern Morocco gave unusual importance to the Ḥajj pilgrimage throughout the premodern era and even established an agency to aid pilgrims on their journeys.

Al-Malīgī was succeeded as head of Ribāṭ Shākir by the noted Sufi and scholar ʿAbd al-Khāliq ibn Yāsīn ad-Daghūghī (d. 571/1174). Characterized in the sources by such titles as *imām* and *shaykh al-Islām wa'd-dīn* (master of Islamic dogma and the religious sciences), he shared an abiding interest in Qur'anic studies with his friend and contemporary Abū ʿAbdallāh Amghār of Tīṭ-n-Fiṭr.[85] After his death, his tomb complex at Sabt Banī Daghūgh, outside of Marrakesh, served both as a pilgrimage site and a school for many centuries. It was also used as a food distribution center during times of famine or political unrest. In fact, one of ad-Daghūghī's most well-known sayings was: "We have long sought divine approval (*tawfīq*), but have erred. Verily, it is in the provision of food (*fa-idhā huwa iṭʿam aṭ-ṭaʿm*)."[86]

Ribāṭ Shākir was unique among the ribāṭs of Morocco because of the large number of women who visited the complex—either year-round as full-time *ṣāliḥāt* or as seasonal visitors who came for the yearly festival (*mawsim*) of Sīdī Shākir on the twenty-seventh day of Ramaḍān.[87] One of these women, who was important enough to be included among the *rijāl* of at-Tādilī's *at-Tashawwuf*, was Munya (or Manīna) bint Maymūn (d. 595/1199). Munya appears to have been a Banū Hilāl Arab who lived out her widowhood in Marrakesh, from whence she made periodic visits to Ribāṭ Shākir.[88] Known by the residents of Marrakesh as "Mīmūna Tagnawt" (Ber. Maymūna the Black) because of her dark and shriveled skin, this specialist in mortification of the flesh was highly respected by her male contemporaries.[89] Her biography provides important evidence of the wide (and heretofore ignored) extent of female participation in early Moroccan Sufism.

When visiting Ribāṭ Shākir, Mīmūna would pray alongside her male counterparts, a practice that is normally allowed for women only in the precincts of the Sacred Mosque in Mecca. She also reported that a thousand female *awliyāʾ* once visited the ribāṭ in a single year.[90] It is evident, however, that Munya's reputation could not have been so easily maintained had she not presented herself in gender-neutral terms. This image was based on her position as an *ʿajūza*, a widow of advanced age, as well as on her severe practice of bodily mortification, which reduced her appearance to skin and bones.[91] Besides purifying her internally, these exercises sharpened her powers of insight (*baṣīra*), an ability that was seen as a major proof of her acceptance by God. Her particular gift was discerning through visionary means whether or not food came from an unlawful source:

> A merchant invited me for dinner and I accepted reluctantly. When he placed the platter of food before me, it spoke to me and said, "Do not eat me, for I am forbidden!" Because I was concerned not to offend my host, I put a small piece of meat to my lips and then put it down. After that, I was prevented from making invocations and superorogatory prayers for three days and voices spoke to me from my right and left, saying, "This is how it is with dogs whose stomachs cause them to wander!"[92]

Perhaps the most interesting figure associated with Ribāṭ Shākir was Abū Ibrāhīm Ismāʿīl u-Gmāten (d. 595/1198–9), a Maṣmūda Berber from the market town of Addār in Ragrāga.[93] A scholar of considerable repute, Abū Ibrāhīm was venerated, much like Darrās ibn Ismāʿīl in Fez, as an "anchor of the earth," despite the fact that his *malāmatī* proclivities led him to feign ignorance in the presence of those who were unaware of his true state. His official sinecure was that of imam of the congregational mosque at Agawz (Ribāṭ Jawz, the present Souira Kédima), the seaport for Aghmāt, which was situated upriver from the mouth of the Tansīft.[94]

Besides being a *malāmatī,* Abū Ibrāhīm was also divinely "attracted" or possessed (*majdhūb*) and was subject to sudden and uncontrollable spiritual states (*ḥāl,* pl. *aḥwāl*). When a *ḥāl* came upon him, he would fall into a stupor and then awaken, intoxicated, to enunciate the first thing that came to his mind in the purest Classical Arabic.[95] Because of the unpredictability of these states, he shunned the company of others. He would only emerge from his seclusion—at times in fine clothing and at times in sackcloth—to officiate at Friday prayers. At the onset of a state he would shout: "Beware not to harm the saints of God! Beware not to harm the saints of God! Beware not to harm the saints of God! Verily upon the saints of God shall be no harm, nor shall they grieve!"[96]

As part of his Sufi training, Abū Ibrāhīm lived for twenty years in Medina as a devotee of the Prophet's mosque. Before going there, he spent time in Syria, where he was the disciple of a female Sufi from Morocco called Sayyidat an-Nās. This name was the feminine version of Sayyid an-Nās (Lord of Mankind), a popular honorific of the Prophet Muḥammad. Abū Ibrāhīm further perfected his "Muḥammadan" approach to Sufism by studying *Qūt al-qulūb* (Sustenance of hearts), the famous tradition-based manual of Sufism by Abū Ṭālib al-Makkī (d. 386/996). Like his female contemporary Munya bint Maymūn, Abū Ibrāhīm was known for his extreme scrupulousness and seldom ate meat. Instead, he subsisted almost entirely on plants, the bulbs and seeds of which he brought with him from the Muslim East and tended in his own garden.[97]

The inhabitants of Agawz often called on Abū Ibrāhīm to protect them from abuses of power. Upon hearing of the commission of a sin or the tyranny of a local official, he would become so enraged that he frothed at the mouth. Once, after giving a sermon critical of Almohad fiscal policies, he was imprisoned by the local governor. After three days in jail, the saint gathered the other prisoners around him and said, "Repent to God Most High." "We repent," they replied. After making his companions repent a second time he asked, "Do you want to be freed from your prison?" "Yes," they said. Suddenly, the wall of the jail collapsed and the prisoners escaped to freedom. Significantly, all of these unfortunates had been jailed for nonpayment of taxes.[98]

On another occasion, Abū Ibrāhīm was giving the Friday sermon at Agawz when he exclaimed, "Do you want me to bite you?" Thereupon he admonished the Almohad governor of the town in terms so severe that the entire congregation feared for their lives. Infuriated at having to listen to such impertinence, the governor had Abū Ibrāhīm imprisoned and thrown into a deep dungeon. He then resolved to send a report detailing Abū Ibrāhīm's seditious comments to the Almohad caliph in Marrakesh. After less than an hour had passed, however, the spiritually intoxicated imam was seen wandering about in the streets of the town, exclaiming, "Would you kill a man who says, 'God is my Lord?' "[99] At this the governor became even more enraged and supervised Abū Ibrāhīm's second arrest himself. To make sure that he could not escape again, he attached heavy iron balls and chains to the saint's legs and commanded his soldiers to watch over him. No sooner had the governor's secretary put pen to paper in order to write his report then Abū Ibrāhīm got up and left the prison, saying, "Would you kill a man who says, 'God is my Lord?' " Upon witnessing this second miracle with his own eyes, the governor quickly forgot about both the offending sermon and the report he had intended to write to the caliph.[100]

A Merging of Horizons: The Nūriyya *Tradition of Rural Moroccan Sufism*

It is fitting that the trading center of Aghmāt would eventually become the locus of a "merging of horizons" between Ṣanhāja and Maṣmūda Sufism.[101]

The inhabitants of this town, Maṣmūda Berbers from the High Atlas mountains, made a profitable living by managing caravan traffic between the Sahara desert and the markets of the Nafīs valley. This arrangement made it necessary for them to conclude alliances and safe-conduct agreements with the pastoralists through whose lands their caravans passed. Many of these peoples, such as the Gazūla of the Sūs valley and the Lamtūna and Massūfa of the Western Sahara and Mauritania, were Ṣanhāja in origin. Thus, the Maṣmūda merchants of Aghmāt were compelled, out of their own self-interest, to learn the cultural and linguistic codes of their Ṣanhāja partners.

A similar multiculturalism can be seen in the early doctrines of the Almohad movement, whose founder, Muḥammad ibn Tūmart, sought to unite the diverse peoples of the Maghrib against the Almoravids and their Arab advisers.[102] In addition, the extensive social networks maintained by the Sufis of southern Morocco, as well as the homogenizing effects of the uṣūl-oriented Islamic universalism taught at ribāṭs such as Tīṭ-n-Fiṭr and Ribāṭ Shākir, helped to promote a sense of supra-tribal identity that was similar to the regionalism then developing among the *muwalladūn* and Berbers of al-Andalus. For the first time in the history of the Far Maghrib, Almohad nativism and the universalism of Sunni internationalism combined to transcend the tribal segmentation that had heretofore characterized social and political relations in the region.

Many of the doctrines that supported this supra-tribalism were not indigenous, but were transmitted by uṣūli scholars and juridical Sufis who had learned them in the east. An important advocate of eastern Sufi traditions in Morocco was a Maṣmūda Berber from Dukkāla named ʿAbd al-Jalīl ibn Wayḥlān (d. 541/1143), who founded the Nūriyya mystical tradition at Aghmāt. His teacher, an Egyptian Sufi named Abū'l-Faḍl al-Jawharī, traced his spiritual lineage (*nasab*) to Abū'l-Ḥasan (or Abū'l-Ḥusayn) an-Nūrī (d. 295/907–8), a Baghdad native of Khurasani origins who taught a spiritual method similar to that of his more famous friend and companion, Abū'l-Qāsim al-Junayd (d. 297/909–10).[103]

Although North African writers have characterized the spiritual method of ʿAbd al-Jalīl ibn Wayḥlān as "Junaydī," the concept of light (*nūr*), the root of an-Nūrī's name, was of great importance to his doctrine. In fact, several of the most important masters of the Moroccan Nūriyya even went so far as to incorporate the word *nūr* into their own names. However, it is not entirely incorrect to characterize the Nūriyya tradition as Junaydī. This is because Sarī as-Saqaṭī (d. 253/867), al-Junayd's teacher and maternal uncle, was the master of Abū'l-Ḥasan an-Nūrī as well. Because of this shared discipleship, both an-Nūrī and al-Junayd followed the same rules of conduct and gave similar weight to the doctrines of sincerity (*ṣidq*), poverty (*faqr*), and altruism (*īthār*).[104]

Unlike the more theologically oriented al-Junayd, who gained lasting fame for defining the Sufi concept of divine unity (*tawḥīd*), an-Nūrī stressed moral conduct (*akhlāq*) and is most often remembered as a master of *futuwwa*. According to the biographer as-Sulamī, one of an-Nūrī's favorite hadiths was: "He who fulfills the needs of his Muslim brother has the reward of one who has served God all of his life."[105] The altruism expressed in this tradition is referred to as *īthār* in Sufi treatises and was one of the hallmarks of futuwwa. It was also congruent with the concept of ṣalāḥ, which, as we have seen, was central to the Moroccan concept of sainthood.

An-Nūrī also gave great importance to proving inner states through outward actions. This made his doctrine attractive to Sufis who were educated in the ethical environment of North African Malikism, which shared a similar ethos. The importance of moral conduct and sincerity in an-Nūrī's spiritual method is clearly visible in as-Sulamī's *Ṭabaqāt aṣ-ṣūfiyya* (Categories of the Sufis), which contains the following aphorisms of this shaykh: "Sufism does not consist of formalistic behavior or memorized knowledge; rather, it is moral conduct"; "The most valuable things in our age are two: a scholar who acts upon his knowledge and a gnostic who speaks through his spiritual insight"; "The true Sufi is one who does not importune God the Exalted for his means of livelihood, but relies upon Him in every state."[106] It is also related that when an-Nūrī was brought before the ʿAbbasid caliph for questioning, he was asked, "From whence do you get your sustenance?" To which he replied, "We know of no means through which to obtain our recompense. We are a people who fend for ourselves."[107]

True to the altruistic principles of the Nūriyya tradition that he had learned in Egypt, the Moroccan saint ʿAbd al-Jalīl ibn Wayḥlān lived a life of extreme poverty and taught *uṣūl al-fiqh* without asking for anything in return. Eventually, his poverty and asceticism became so extreme that he was forced to divorce his wife because of his inability to provide for her. Realizing that he was obliged to make a property settlement as part of the divorce, he gave her half of the garment he was wearing—his only possession—and kept the other half for himself.[108]

Although ʿAbd al-Jalīl was trained as a jurist, his relations with other legal scholars were strained. Before visiting an exoteric legist, he would say to his companions: "Come. We will take knowledge from fire."[109] Much of the disapproval to which he was subjected by the ulama was due to his popularity among the lower classes. Because of this acclaim, he was forced to spend almost all of his time at home, leaving only to attend Friday prayers. Upon departing from the mosque, so many people would crowd around him, presenting petitions and trying to touch his clothes for blessings, that he would not be able to reach his house until the time for the afternoon prayer.[110]

Like other jurisprudentially trained scholars who were noted for both ṣalāḥ and the working of miracles (such as Abū Ibrāhīm u-Gmaten and Darrās ibn Ismāʿīl), ʿAbd al-Jalīl ibn Wayḥlān was revered as an "anchor of the earth" and patron-protector of Aghmāt. As such, he was called upon to mediate local disputes and to act as a semiofficial ombudsman. Often, he represented the vox populi before government officials, who were outsiders appointed from Marrakesh. The last occasion on which he performed these services was during the Almohad siege of Marrakesh in the year 541/1143. Desiring to commandeer the houses of Aghmāt for his troops, the Almohad caliph ʿAbd al-Muʾmin sent a crier through the streets of the town, proclaiming that all the residents had to evacuate, with the exception of ʿAbd al-Jalīl. The unfairness of this order so disturbed the shaykh that he, too, prepared to move out of Aghmāt. When it was reported to ʿAbd al-Muʾmin that ʿAbd al-Jalīl was leaving, he sent his crier to inform the people that they were permitted to return to their homes. A short time later, an order came that the shaykh should present himself at the caliphal headquarters at Jabal Igīllīz, just outside of Marrakesh. He first tried to excuse himself on the grounds that he was ill, to which the caliph's messenger replied, "You must go there, even if we have to carry you in a litter!" He then obtained permission to delay his departure until the time of the afternoon prayer. By the time the muezzin called the prayer, ʿAbd al-Jalīl had died and his funeral procession was winding its way through the streets. True to his clients to the end, he had preserved by his death in Aghmāt the protection that would have been denied his town had he followed the caliph's messenger to Igīllīz.[111]

The saint who actually "merged the horizons" of Ṣanhāja and Maṣmūda Sufism within the Nūriyya tradition was Abū Shuʿayb ("Mūlāy Būshʿayb") ibn Saʿīd as-Ṣanhājī (d. 561/1166). Although he was born to a prominent family of Ṣanhāja Azammūr pastoralists on the banks of the Umm ar-Rabīʿ river, Abū Shuʿayb avoided the Ṣanhāja spiritual center of Ribāṭ Tīṭ-n-Fiṭr until late in life, preferring instead to study at the feet of Maṣmūda spiritual masters who were associated with Ribāṭ Shākir.

The first of Abū Shuʿayb's Maṣmūda teachers was a disciple of ʿAbd al-Jalīl ibn Wayḥlān named Abū Innūr (Ber. the Illuminated One; d. before 550/1155–6) ibn Wakrīs al-Mashanzāʾī. Known today as Sīdī Bennūr, he is still revered as one of the most important saints of Dukkāla. His tomb at Ribāṭ Ilīskāwen, the present-day town of Sidi Bennour, continues to draw pilgrims from throughout Morocco.[112] The tales recounted about this murābiṭ are redolent with the themes of power and authority. His main function was to protect the Maṣmūda farmers and merchants of northern Dukkāla, who, after being caught between Barghwāṭa raids from the north and Ṣanhāja migrations from the south, found their livelihoods threatened.[113] Hagiographical anthologies such as at-Tādilī's *at-Tashawwuf* reveal that the Maṣmūda saints of Dukkāla played an important role in their sedentarist clients' strategy for survival, since their supernatural powers could be used to compensate for the military and political weakness of the sedentarists themselves. The protection afforded by men of power from their own ethnic group gave the Maṣmūda an enhanced status in the eyes of their Ṣanhāja rivals and allowed them to find alternative niches in the changing socioeconomic structure of the region.

The themes of patronage, protection, and "broker–client intersubjectivity,"[114] all of which are well-known concepts to transaction theorists in the field of Social Anthropology, are clearly discernible in the hagiographical accounts of Abū Innūr's activities. Ibn Qunfudh, for example, reports that Abū Innūr survived the Almoravid conquest of the Far Maghrib and continued to protect his people well into the reign of the second Almoravid sultan, ʿAlī ibn Yūsuf. During this period the Almoravids, who displayed a clear ethnic bias in the pattern of their conquests and subsequent rule, sent a force of Veiled Ṣanhāja to punish Ilīskāwen for nonpayment of the *kharāj* tax that had been levied on the Mashanzāya as a conquered people. Abū Innūr went before the inhabitants of Ilīskāwen as the raiding party approached and announced, "God has expelled them from you!" At a distance of only half a Roman mile from the town the commander of the expedition suddenly fell ill and died, and the raid was called off.[115]

At-Tādilī also recounts a story about one of Abū Innūr's successors, Abū Ḥafṣ ʿUmar ibn Tṣūlī u-Abūskat al-Mashanzāʾī (d. 595/1198–9), who played a similar role by protecting Ribāṭ Ilīskāwen from the predations of Banū Hilāl Arabs:

> A group of Arabs entered the land of Dukkāla. One of them went to the garden of Abū Ḥafṣ and took some grapes from it. When he put them into his mouth, he was stricken by cramps that nearly killed him. He went to Abū Ḥafṣ to tell him about it. Abū Ḥafṣ rubbed the [Arab's] throat and that which had stricken him left him. Then he asked, "What made you enter my garden?" "I used to eat [at will] from the gardens of the people of Tāmesnā," [the Arab] replied, "and nothing happened to me, so I thought that your garden was like those others."[116]

It was perhaps because of Abū Innūr's reputation for baraka that Abū Shuʿayb sought guidance from this Maṣmūda saint instead of the Ṣanhāja murābiṭ of Tīṭ-n-Fiṭr. Abū Shuʿayb spent most of his youth at Ilīskāwen, where he could be seen leaning on his walking stick and teaching the Qur'an to the children of the ribāṭ. Because he would remain in one place for hours at a time, his colleagues called him *as-Sāriya* (the Support, Pillar), an appellation that was to become even more meaningful when he was called upon to represent the people of Azemmour before government officials.[117]

While at Ilīskāwen Abū Shuʿayb displayed the ethical hypersensitivity that was a hallmark of the Nūriyya tradition. Upon finding his cow eating from a neighbor's garden, he ran toward it, stuck his hands into its mouth, and forcibly pulled out all of the undigested material that he found inside. In order to make symbolic restitution for what his cow had eaten, he kept the animal at home for three days (until all of its food had been digested) and gave its milk to the poor.[118] On another occasion, he told ʿAbd al-Khāliq ibn Yāsīn ad-Daghūghī that he would never eat raisins grown on vines that were watered by a shared canal, since if the land over which the water flowed had been obtained unlawfully, it would pollute lawfully acquired land downstream.[119]

After the death of Abū Innūr, Abū Shuʿayb moved to Aghmāt, where he completed his discipleship under ʿAbd al-Jalīl ibn Wayḥlān. In confirmation of his role as a bridge between the traditions of Ṣanhāja and Maṣmūda Sufism, he presided over rābiṭāt in both Azemmour (a Ṣanhāja town) and Aghmāt (a Maṣmūda town) after ʿAbd al-Jalīl passed away. His position as the patron saint of both localities is confirmed by Ibn Qunfudh, who reports that Abū Shuʿayb once led the *ʿĪd al-Aḍḥā*ʾ prayer (celebrating the end of the pilgrimage to Mecca) at Aghmāt and then returned to Azemmour four days later to find its inhabitants still waiting for him to officiate at their own prayer and sacrifice.[120] It is also reported that while supervising the *ʿĪd* ritual at Azemmour in later years, he would feel the people of Aghmāt praying behind him.[121]

Like his teachers, Abū Shuʿayb was noted for his social activism. His initial opponents were the Almoravids, whose religious leaders disapproved of Sufism and subjected the pastoralists and merchants of Dukkāla to unpopular and onerous taxes. According to a widely reported account, when the Almoravid governor of Azemmour wanted to execute a group of tax rebels Abū Shuʿayb went to him in order to plead their case. When the haughty Saharan *imashagh* noticed the shaykh's dark-brown complexion, he considered him to be of low status and rebuffed him. After roughly ordering Abū Shuʿayb to leave his presence, the governor was stricken by severe stomach cramps. "The man you have just sent away is Abū Shuʿayb," someone told him. "He is one of the *awliyāʾ* and he is angry at you for rebuffing him." The governor quickly apologized to the shaykh and allowed him to intercede for those he had condemned to death. Henceforth, whenever this particular governor heard that Abū Shuʿayb was coming, he would release all of his Ṣanhāja prisoners before the shaykh arrived.[122]

Despite his dislike for the Almoravids, Abū Shuʿayb never forgot his sense of justice. This caused him to speak out against the massacres of the Veiled Ṣanhāja that were carried out by the Almohads after their conquest of Marrakesh. The shaykh's interference resulted in his arrest at the order of the Almohad caliph ʿAbd al-Muʾmin. Rather than defending his actions, Abū Shuʿayb boldly used his trial as a pretext to intercede for the wives and concubines of the Almoravid ruling family:

> [Abū Shuʿayb] went to Marrakesh in the year 541, brought there at the order of ʿAbd al-Muʾmin ibn ʿAlī. But when [the Almohad caliph] saw his colorless countenance, he took pity upon him. He wanted to interrogate him, but feared him because of the powers of clairvoyance that he perceived in him. So he delegated the questioning to a merchant who was a companion of Imām al-Mahdī [Ibn Tūmart]. He first asked the shaykh about the doctrine of divine unity (*tawḥīd*), which had a particular definition among [the Almohads]. The shaykh answered [the questions] with the answers of the as-Salaf aṣ-Ṣāliḥ, using verses from the Qur'an.
>
> It is related that when he was asked [about *tawḥīd*] Abū Shuʿayb answered [with the Qur'anic verse]: "God. There is no god but He, the

> Living, the Eternal . . ." to the end of the verse.[123] Then [Ibn Tūmart's companion] u-Aṣnār (Waṣnār) asked again, "What is *tawḥīd*?" and Abū Shuʿayb answered: "[I hope that] God will not cause him to die because of this!" ʿAbd al-Muʾmin was shocked by this response and knew that Abū Shuʿayb's curse would certainly strike [u-Aṣnār]. After some time he questioned him [again], saying, "What is *tawḥīd,* oh shaykh?" So [Abū Shuʿayb] said to him: "God bears witness that there is no god but He and the angels and the foremost in knowledge. . . ." until "the Glorious, the most Wise."[124] Then the shaykh repeated the curse against him and sought protection in God. After some time he said [again], "What is *tawḥīd,* oh shaykh?" and Abū Shuʿayb said to him: "God, the Exalted, the Almighty, said: 'Say: He is Allāh the One, Allāh the Incomparable'. . . ." to the end of the *sūra.*[125] He repeated the first answer, and the shaykh reaffirmed his curse.
>
> Suddenly, a great tremor shook ʿAbd al-Muʾmin's palace. He blanched at this and knew that it could not have taken place except for the shaykh. So he praised [Abū Shuʿayb] profusely and commanded that he be the object of *ziyāra* [ritual visiting] and that all of his needs be fulfilled. But [the shaykh] said, "I have no need for anything, except that you allow me to intercede for the wives of ʿAlī ibn Yūsuf [b. Tāshfīn] and the wives of his sons, and [that you] allow them to go wherever they wish."[126]

The career of Abū Shuʿayb marks a turning point in the history of Moroccan Sufism. Although Sufism was introduced into rural Morocco by urban-based mystics and ṣulaḥāʾ from abroad such as the Banū Amghār of Tīṭ-n-Fiṭr, it soon took on a local color that superficially separated it from its urban roots. Even Abū ʿImrān al-Fāsī's attempt to introduce Maliki doctrine in the tribal homelands, which was directed by urban-educated legists such as Waggāg ibn Zallū al-Lamṭī, had to incorporate minor doctrinal adjustments in order to achieve its goals. In the case of Waggāg's pupil ʿAbdallāh ibn Yāsīn, the cultural concessions that had to be made in the Islamization of the Veiled Ṣanhāja caused the Andalusian geographer al-Bakrī to forget that the traditions of Malikism taught by this Berber reformer were essentially the same as his own.[127]

The problem of cultural intersubjectivity that is raised by the local coloration of rural Sufism is particularly relevant with regard to the ribāṭ. Even a formally institutionalized entity such as aṭ-Ṭāʾifa aṣ-Ṣanhājiyya, possibly the first Sufi order to arise out of Morocco, could not escape being bound to a specific ethnic, and hence social-structural, identity. Abū ʿAbdallāh Amghār, the founder of the Ṣanhājiyya Sufi order and greatest murābiṭ of Ribāṭ Tīṭ-n-Fiṭr, was never able to escape the "Ṣanhājī" appellation. Despite his undeniable erudition and spiritual authority, he was known to following generations as the Ṣanhāja Axis (*al-quṭb aṣ-Ṣanhājī*), and never the Axis of the Age (*quṭb az-zamān*).

With the introduction of the Nūriyya tradition of Sufism under ʿAbd al-Jalīl ibn Wayḥlān, an important shift in emphasis occurred. Through the influence of the pilgrimage to Mecca and the "journey in search of knowledge" (*riḥla li-ṭalab al-ʿilm*), Sufi doctrines whose origins lay in the east began to penetrate the rural west. As the doctrines of *uṣūl ad-dīn* and *uṣūl al-fiqh* began to take hold in the mosques and ribāṭs of the rural Far Maghrib, the influence of eastern intellectual trends prompted a renewed interest in scriptural sources and a turn toward Sunni internationalism among Moroccan ulama.

It was widely accepted in the Muslim East by this time that the most authoritative approach to epistemology, theology, and the law was to be found in the writings of al-Ghazālī. Because of the influence of his magisterial work *Iḥyāʾ ʿulūm ad-dīn,* many North African Sufis tried to trace their own uṣūlī roots to either al-Ghazālī or his doctrinal forebears. In Morocco, this tendency was epitomized by an adherence to the so-called School of Baghdad and its two most famous exponents, Abū'l-Ḥasan an-Nūrī and Abū'l-Qāsim al-Junayd. Once the Nūriyya tradition and the doctrines of Junaydī Sufism had been introduced into this region, the previously localized traditions of rural Sufism could now be harmonized with the dominant intellectual currents of the Muslim world as a whole. By "merging the horizons" of the ethnically oriented Ṣanhāja and Maṣmūda approaches to institutional Sufism, Abū Shuʿayb and his successors prepared the way for hagiographers to set the doctrinal paradigms of Moroccan Sufism and to define sainthood in ways that accorded with perspectives that were current in the east.

CHAPTER THREE

Knowledge, Power, and Authority in Monographic Biography

"The conventional is that upon which the majority agree."
(*al-Mashhūr alladhī ʿalayhi al-jumhūr.*)

—ABŪ'L-ʿABBĀS AḤMAD AL-ʿAZAFĪ
(WRITTEN CA. 613–20/1216–23)[1]

Sainthood is a matter of discourse. It can be nothing else. Whether the other who bestows legitimacy on the saint is divine or human, learned or unlearned, a process of negotiation is invariably involved. Despite the occasional mention of "hidden" (*makhfī*) or "unknown" (*majhūl*) saints in Sufi treatises and hagiographies, sainthood needs to be recognized by another to exist. In order to be recognized, the prospective saint must manifest certain outward signs: exceptional piety, ecstatic states, intercession, evidentiary miracles, unusual modes of behavior, and the like. Whether this initiative is taken by the prospective saint himself or herself or is imposed by others, the parameters of sanctity and even the question of sainthood itself are open to debate. Yet even when sainthood is accepted in principle, other questions remain to be asked: Does the potential saint manifest a virtuous life? Can the community benefit from the saint's powers? Can the saint's actions be used as examples for others?[2]

Sometimes, a written record is part of the negotiating process. When this occurs, the saint is on the way to becoming what

Michel Foucault has termed a "discursive formation," a sort of literary monument that imposes an artificial coherence on the saint's life.[3] This constructedness explains why it is not enough to conceive of the saint as simply a jigsaw puzzle of holy traits, composed of bits and pieces of collective recollection. Instead, one must think of the saint who has been "constructed" by sacred biography as an ongoing work, an *oeuvre* whose "meaning" is continually re-expressed in the languages of social discourse and rhetoric.[4]

In Morocco, the *oeuvre* that defines a *walī Allāh* for his or her audience may be composed of a variety of texts: autobiographical fragments, doctrinal works, poems, aphorisms, eyewitness accounts, notices in *rijāl* collections, transcribed letters, and exploit narratives or monographic biographies.[5] Since each of these texts is itself embedded in a set of discursive formations, what Foucault has termed the "enunciative modalities" of discourse must be defined before assessing the "meaning" of a saint's life: Who is speaking in the text? What are the author's qualifications for speaking? Who (or what) bestows authority on the hagiographer? What is the institutional locus from which the hagiographer speaks? How does this site give the discourse its legitimacy? What is the "library" or documentary field of the discourse? Where is the hagiographer located in the information networks of the day?[6]

Epistemological questions such as these should be asked in any critical investigation of sainthood. In the field of Islamic Studies, however, such an effort has rarely been made. Instead, the discursive environment of the "official" sacred biography, whether the *manāqib* of a single individual or the *rijāl* collection of many saints, receives only cursory analysis. In most cases, the modern reader is presented with little more than a biography of the biographer, which is itself extrapolated from other works in the same genre. Once in a while, mention might be made of a *fihris* or *fahrasa* (a sort of premodern curriculum vitae) in which the hagiographer's teachers, diplomas, and books studied and written are listed as proof of his grounding in authentic tradition. What the issue of rhetoric means to the overall presentation of sainthood, however, is seldom addressed.[7]

In Latin Christianity, sacred biography was a conservative genre that adhered closely to the rhetorical conventions of Aristotle's theory of narrative. According to this model, the behavior portrayed within the narrative was more important to the meaning of a hagiographical work than the argument of the narrative itself. Because the stories of saints were often made to be recited to an illiterate public, the language of the *vitae* had to be polysemic. Through the rhetorical use of the dramatic act and the *imitatio Christi,* these works proved the existence of divine agency in the world through typified lives that were meaningful to several audiences at once.

The polysemic nature of hagiography meant that the composition of this genre required a continual process of dialogue between author and audience. This requirement, in turn, led to the paradox of what Thomas Heffernan has called the "biographical dualism" of sacred biography. In the hagiographer's construction of the saint, overemphasizing the supernatural might cause one to lose sight of the person. On the other hand, overemphasizing the ordinary might cause one to lose sight of the saint. To arrive at a happy medium, the hagiographer had to employ his rhetorical skills to convey how he wanted the saint to be perceived. If the resulting image accorded with the collective recollection of his community and met ecclesiastical expectations, it might be incorporated into the body of tradition. Within this hermeneutical circle, rhetoric, church politics, and local opinion all played an important role in constructing the image of a saint.[8]

A similar process can be found at work in Moroccan sacred biography. In the first place, the *imitatio Christi* that was a defining characteristic of Christian sainthood was paralleled by a sort of *imitatio Muhammadi* that helped set the paradigm for sainthood in the Muslim world in general.[9] This situation was made possible in part because the classical rhetorical dichotomy of *imitatio* (exemplification) versus *elocutio* (argument) was employed in both Christendom and Islamdom.[10] Also common to both the Christian and Islamic worlds was the fact that the raw data of hagiography consisted of verbal messages that originated within the community of belief. It was through such accounts, which preserved the living voice of tradition, that ordinary people participated in the "authorship" of hagiographical works.

The authenticity of a saintly reputation could be demonstrated in a number of ways. Firsthand or eyewitness accounts might be passed on as testimony. Other information might be transmitted as reminiscence or hearsay. Most commonly, however, the data of sacred biography were recorded as oral tradition.[11] For verbal messages to be accepted as tradition, it was necessary that their performance be replicated over more than one generation. For this reason, the veracity of the transmitter was vitally important in assessing the truth or falsehood of an account. This is also why so much of sacred biography was devoted to turning oral tradition into evidence—the kind of information that might be accepted in a court of law. In medieval Europe, the experts who turned tradition into evidence and composed the *vitae* that confirmed a prospective saint's sanctity were Church clerics trained in Canon law.[12] In Middle Period Morocco, the same function was often performed by a judge (*qāḍī*) or a specialist in legal reasoning (*faqīh*).

The art of hermeneutics was fundamental to the *uṣūl al-fiqh* method. The responsibility of a *faqīh* was: (1) to derive a legal ruling from a textual source such as the Qur'an or hadith; (2) to distinguish a speculative proof from one that is definitive; (3) to differentiate the general application of a rule from a limited and specific case; (4) to know what weight to give the literal versus the metaphorical meaning of a text; and (5) to identify all of the legal implications of a text or other type of evidence.[13] To carry out these tasks, the *faqīh* had to be proficient in formal logic, because he was called upon to employ analogical reasoning in deciding questions of juristic preference, social utility, or appropriate custom. This process of reasoning was never haphazard. On the contrary, the *faqīh* did his best to ensure that his solution of a problem would be accepted by his peers and upheld in future generations. It takes little imagination to understand how influential the "expert testimony" of such a person could be when applied to a controversial issue such as sainthood.

The false dichotomy between "doctor" and "saint" in Moroccan Islam has been laid to rest in Chapter One. It is well-established that practitioners of *uṣūl al-fiqh*[14] were instrumental in the development and spread of Sufism in both Morocco and al-Andalus. This blurring of the epistemological lines of conflict, however, should not cause the student of Islam to ignore the very real differences that continued to exist between the world views of the jurist and the mystic. The medieval upholders of formal monotheism—whether Christian, Jewish, or Muslim—sought to maintain an externally bounded and internally regulated community of belief by defining orthodoxy and orthopraxy on the basis of normative consensus. Mystics, on the other hand, sought to transcend these limits by aspiring to a higher level where questions of belief and practice were posed differently. This disagreement over the nature and use of divinely inspired knowledge meant that the history of Islam was replete with doctrinal disputes between Sufis and legists, as well as occasional persecutions of esoterists by exoterists. One need only recall the banning of al-Ghazālī's *Iḥyā' ʿulūm ad-dīn* by the Andalusian jurists who supported the Almoravid state to realize that mystics walked a narrow line.

Yet a middle ground always existed. One could always find exoterists, such as the Hanbali jurist Ibn Taymiyya (d. 728/1328), who criticized "hard-hearted ulama" for making blanket condemnations of all forms of Sufism.[15] Conversely, one could also find Sufis, such as Ibn Taymiyya's Moroccan contemporary ʿAbd al-Ḥaqq al-Bādisī (d. after 722/1322), who criticized less-orthodox mystics for exceeding established norms. Such was the case, for example, when al-Bādisī condemned the Andalusian Hermetist Ibn Sabʿīn of Murcia (d. 669/1270) for using the neologism "faqīr-ism" (*al-faqīriyya*) when discussing the Sufi way.[16]

Al-Bādisī's pious caution epitomizes what has variously been termed "Sunni Sufism," "orthodox mysticism," or "Sharīʿah-minded Sufism,"[17] but which I call "juridical Sufism." Juridical Sufism is a type of mysticism that is epistemologically subservient to the authority of religious law. This praxis-oriented approach, which is based on the jurisprudence of interpersonal behavior (*fiqh al-muʿāmalāt*), conceives of Sufism more as a methodology than as a school of metaphysical doctrine. For this reason, it tends to downplay metaphysical issues and reverses the normal polarity of belief and practice.

While it maintained rigorous standards with regard to ritual, morals, ethics, and the legitimation of tradition, juridical Sufism could still allow for different and even contradictory approaches to mystical doctrine. This variation ranged from the nomocentric, such as that of Abū Ḥāmid al-Ghazālī, to the logocentric, like that of Ibn al-ʿArabī and his followers. It should not be forgotten, however, that as far as sainthood was concerned, it was the nomocentrists, and not the logocentrists, who composed most of the *rijāl* and *manāqib* works that defined the *walī Allāh* in the Maghrib. Even more, many of these authors (such as at-Tādilī and Ibn Qunfudh) were practicing jurists who made their case for sainthood in the language of the courtroom and books of juridical precedent.[18] Since consensus had already confirmed these legists as the guardians of Islam's doctrinal frontiers, their arguments were bound to have an impact on public opinion that metaphysicians could seldom equal.

"Knowledge From Our Presence": Al-ʿAzafī's Admiranda *of Abū Yiʿzzā*

One of the most important apologists for popular religion in premodern North Africa was a legist from Sabta (modern Ceuta) named Aḥmad al-ʿAzafī (d. 633/1236).[19] The son of the chief jurist of Sabta and a respected member of the Banū al-ʿAzafī clan of legal scholars who were to rule the city throughout the thirteenth century, Aḥmad al-ʿAzafī made his reputation as an expert in the analysis of oral tradition (*riwāya wa dirāya*).[20] His most significant works were *Ad-Durr al-munaẓẓam fī mawlid an-nabī al-muʿaẓẓam* (The Properly strung pearl in the festival of the most glorious prophet), which almost single-handedly legitimized the Prophet's birthday as a holiday in the Far Maghrib,[21] and *Diʿāmat al-yaqīn fī ziʿāmat al-muttaqīn* (The Pillar of certainty in the leadership of the God-conscious), a sacred biography of the Berber saint Abū Yiʿzzā (d. 572/1177).

The subject of *Diʿāmat al-yaqīn,* the widely venerated "Mūlāy Būʿazzā" of the Middle Atlas mountains, is one of the great enigmas of western Islamic spirituality. Nearly everything about this saint, including his genealogy and the vocalization of his name, is open to dispute.[22] Most traditionists agree, however, that he was an illiterate and monolingual Maṣmūda Berber from the mountainous region of Haskūra. His tomb now stands on the site of the mosque he built at Adrār-n-Irūggān near the Middle Atlas village of Tāghiyā, between the present-day towns of Rommani and Oulmès. To his Sufi contemporaries, Abū Yiʿzzā was "Shaykh of the Shaykhs of the Maghrib." To the masses who came to partake of his baraka, however, he was the wonder of his age in the working of miracles.[23] When he died of an epidemic at over one hundred years of age, he enjoyed the veneration of all classes of Moroccan society, with the partial exception of some ulama from Fez. As late as the sixteenth century, it was not unusual for pilgrims to prove their devotion to Abū Yiʿzzā by walking barefoot the eighty kilometers from Meknès to his mountaintop tomb.[24]

The themes that appear most often as the foundations of Abū Yiʿzzā's spiritual method are the *futuwwa* doctrines of humility and service to others. These he combined with a strict vegetarianism and a hypercautious concern for purity that prevented him from eating anything grown by another. Traditions related by at-Tādilī in *at-Tashawwuf,* as well as the first-hand testimony of Abū Yiʿzzā's contemporary, the hagiographer Muḥammad ibn al-Qāsim at-Tamīmī, show that this cautiousness was part of a systematic asceticism and not a mere idiosyncrasy. At-Tādilī, for example, reports: "I heard Muḥammad ibn ʿAlī say that he heard Abū ʿAbdallāh al-Bājī[25] say: "I saw Shaykh Abū Yiʿzzā gather mallow (*khubbāza*) and cook it, dry it, and winnow it. When he wanted to eat some of it he would divide it into portions, take a handful or two, and roar like a tyrant to himself, saying to his ego (*nafs*), 'Nothing of you belongs to me but this!'"[26] Similarly, at-Tamīmī, who once visited Abū Yiʿzzā at his mountaintop retreat on

Adrār-n-Irūggān, testifies that the shaykh refused to take more for a meal than the portion of a small child.[27]

In a later biography of Abū Yiʿzzā, the Jazūlite Sufi Aḥmad aṣ-Ṣūmaʿī (d. 1013/1604–5) reports that for more than a quarter of a century the saint wandered about the uninhabited regions of Morocco, where he subsisted on wild plants and was befriended by lions, birds, and other beasts of the forest.[28] At one point in his career, he may have been a partisan of the Almohad cause, for at-Tādilī tells us that for another twenty years Abū Yiʿzzā lived on the high peaks of the Atlas mountains above Tīn Māl, where the mosque and former tomb of Ibn Tūmart, the founder of Almohadism, can still be found. During this period Abu Yiʿzzā was known as Bū Agartīl (Ber. The One With the Prayer Mat), because he used a woven reed mat to cover his nakedness.[29]

Later in his life, Abū Yiʿzzā went down to the Dukkāla coast, where he stayed for another eighteen years. During this phase, he was nicknamed Bū Wanalgūṭ, after a plant he would eat that grew out of trash and compost heaps.[30] For a time, he subsisted on nothing but the edible hearts of oleander and wild acorn mash, which he would make into flat breads and carry in a small pouch on his belt.[31] During his sojourn in Dukkāla, Abū Yiʿzzā became a disciple of Abū Shuʿayb aṣ-Ṣanhājī, patron of the town of Azemmour and master of the Nūriyya tradition. By this time Abū Yiʿzzā had begun to practice a form of *malāmatiyya*-inspired role playing which scandalized the exoteric ulama of Fez. At least once, this led him to engage in cross-dressing and the reversal of gender roles:

> One of the companions of Abū Yiʿzzā got married. His wife asked him for a female slave, but he did not have one. So Abū Yiʿzzā said to him, "I will substitute myself for the female slave," for he was black and had no hair on his face. He dressed himself in the clothes of a female slave and served the man and his wife for an entire year. He ground wheat, kneaded dough, made bread, and poured the water—all at night—while in the day he performed his devotions in the mosque. After a year had gone by, the wife said to her husband, "I have never seen anyone like this slave! She does all that is [normally] done during the day at night, and never appears in the daytime." Her husband turned away from her and neglected to answer, but she continued to ask him until he said, "No one works for you but Abū Wanalgūṭ, and he is no female slave!" Then she knew it was Abū Yiʿzzā and said, "By God, this one will never work for

me again, and I swear that I will do my work myself!" From that time on, she did her work herself.[32]

As a disciple of Abū Shuʿayb, Abū Yiʿzzā was instructed in the Nūriyya Sufi tradition that was traced in the previous chapter to ʿAbd al-Jalīl ibn Wayḥlān of Aghmāt. Evidence of this can be found in the frequent use of light symbolism in the names and doctrines of this saint and his teachers. Abū'l-Ḥasan an-Nūrī, the founder of this tradition, was said to have received his nickname because of the light that illuminated the room when he instructed his disciples.[33] The Maṣmūda murābiṭ Abū Innūr (the Illuminated One), the teacher of Abū Shuʿayb, was also noted for this phenomenon, and Abū Yiʿzzā himself is reported to have had a countenance so bright that those who looked at him were often blinded.[34] Last but not least is the example of Abū Yiʿzzā's own given name, "Yalannūr," which is explained by the Moroccan historian Ahmed Toufiq as an Arabization of the Berber *ilā.innūr*, "Possessor of Light."[35]

Another connection between Abū Yiʿzzā and the Nūriyya tradition was the saint's emphasis on *īthār*, altruism or the practice of giving preference to others over oneself. Abū'l-Ḥasan an-Nūrī also made solicitousness for all human beings an important pillar of his spiritual method.[36] Given this fact, it seems no coincidence that Abū Yiʿzzā ended his period of reclusiveness only after meeting Abū Shuʿayb, who would have taught him this aspect of an-Nūrī's doctrine. Although in later years Abū Yiʿzzā lived alone with his family atop Adrār-n-Irūggān, at-Tamīmī informs us that he would give public audiences at the mosque he built further down the hill. This visitor to Abū Yiʿzzā paints a vivid picture of the shaykh sitting motionless at these sessions, patiently hearing the petitions of the hundreds of people who sought his baraka. His forbearance was so great, we are told, that he would give up pieces of his turban, the food on his plate, and even the hairs on his head to those who desired them.[37] At times, however, Abū Yiʿzzā's altruistic behavior smacked of irony. The nineteenth-century biographer al-Kattānī notes that when ulama from Fez came to visit him, Abū Yiʿzzā would drop to his knees, kiss their feet, and exclaim: "Welcome, my lords! Welcome, oh lamps of the material world!"[38]

In 541/1146–7, Abū Yiʿzzā was summoned with his master Abū Shuʿayb to Marrakesh at the order of the Almohad caliph ʿAbd al-Muʾmin, who had just wrested the capital city from the last of its Almoravid rulers. Although the pastoralist tribes of Dukkāla at this time were Ṣanhāja in origin, they had never fully supported their Almoravid "cousins" and used the situation of weakened central authority during the Almohad revolution to attain a high degree of autonomy. This state of affairs was advantageous to the region's murābiṭūn, whose role as tribal brokers and intermediaries allowed them to assume defacto political roles. One of the most prominent of these saintly leaders was Abū Shuʿayb, whose Ṣanhāja followers were among the most independent in all of Dukkāla.[39] When the pastoralists of northern Dukkāla refused to pay the *kharāj* tax to the newly established Almohad state, ʿAbd al-Muʾmin sent a massive force of cavalry and foot soldiers to punish them. This campaign culminated in a surprise attack on the Ṣanhāja near Abū Shuʿayb's hometown of Azemmour, in which the tribesmen were driven into the sea and drowned by the better-trained Almohad forces. Ibn as-Sammāk, the author of the fourteenth-century chronicle *Al-Ḥulal al-mawshiyya,* claims that after this debacle so many prisoners were taken that a woman could be bought for as little as one dirham and a boy fetched half of that price.[40]

To be fully understood, the inquisition of Abū Shuʿayb and Abū Yiʿzzā must be seen in the context of the Dukkāla tax revolt and in light of the fact that Abū Shuʿayb's own shaykh, ʿAbd al-Jalīl ibn Wayḥlān, had resisted the Almohads during their siege of Marrakesh. While under arrest, Abū Yiʿzzā was kept apart from his master in the minaret of the Kutubiyya mosque.[41] However, during his trial, he followed the same strategy as Abū Shuʿayb by answering all of the questions that were put to him with quotations from the Qur'an. Although the details of his interrogation are not available, a mutual understanding appears to have been reached between Abū Yiʿzzā and the Almohad caliph, for upon his release he ordered his followers to cease their criticisms of ʿAbd al-Muʾmin, saying: "Leave him alone. You have no recourse against him."[42]

After being released from Marrakesh, Abū Yiʿzzā moved to Fez, where he established a rābiṭa at Ḥūmat al-Blīda.[43] After an unspecified amount of time, he relocated again, this time to his final home at Tāghiyā in the Middle Atlas mountains.[44] Here, Abū Yiʿzzā lived in seclusion with his family on the forested peak of Adrār-n-Irūggān, descending from the mountain only to greet visitors, teach his disciples, and lead communal prayers. Exactly why he chose Tāghiyā as a place to live is not mentioned in the sources. By doing so, however, he remained faithful to one of the oldest religious customs, that of building sanctuaries at former cult centers. Soon after their occupation of Morocco in 1912, French investigators reported finding a circle of megaliths near this village, indicating that Tāghiyā had been revered as a holy place long before the advent of Islam.[45]

It is curious how little of the above information—especially concerning Abū Yiʿzzā's association with Sufism—appears in al-ʿAzafī's monographic biography of this saint. Indeed, the reader is not even told that Abū Yiʿzzā was a Sufi shaykh. Instead, al-ʿAzafī describes an illiterate holy man and miracle worker, whose idiosyncratic practices require a semiofficial exegesis to make them acceptable. Unlike al-Tamīmī, al-ʿAzafī never met Abū Yiʿzzā. He is no wide-eyed believer in miracles, nor does he accept the commonly held doctrine of the infallibility of the saints. Instead, he is a prudent and cautious man, as befits his position in life, and struggles to come to terms with this highly unorthodox Berber whose reputation has spread like wildfire from the wilds of the Moroccan mountains to his native city.

The theme of wildness comes up frequently in *Diʿāmat al-yaqīn.* In al-ʿAzafī 's book, Abū Yiʿzzā seems to associate with beasts as often as with human beings. Like the lions and serpents who befriend, inform, and protect him, this saint is depicted as a wild creature of mountain (Ber. *adrār*) and forest (Ber. *lghabt*)—a liminal being, impervious to domestication, whose potency is accentuated by the fact that his abode lies beyond the bounds of civilization.[46]

Abū Yiʿzzā's wildness and miraculous abilities challenge al-ʿAzafī with a paradox that demands resolution. Surely, he opines, if God has blessed such a person, there must be a reason for His divine favor. Too many sober and reputable witnesses have testified to Abū Yiʿzzā's miracles for his actions to be ignored. What is one to make of such a unique man of power? Is there a particular need for him in these unstable times, when the Almohad state is crumbling and the Banū Marīn fight over its remains like scavengers over carrion?[47] The answer to these questions, al-ʿAzafī concludes, lies in the divinely guided authority that Abū Yiʿzzā epitomizes, an idea that he enshrines in the very title of his book: The Pillar of certainty in the leadership of the God-conscious.[48]

In preparing the case for Abū Yiʿzzā's authority, al-ʿAzafī first discusses the nature of oral tradition. This is of two types: *tawātur* and *aḥād. Tawātur,* the type of tradition most often cited in *Diʿāmat al-yaqīn,* consists of "all accounts related orally by [plural] transmitters, for whom the truthfulness of their account is known as a matter of necessity."[49] *Aḥād,* on the other hand, refers to "every account whose truth has not been established beyond the preponderance of speculation (*ghalabat aẓ-ẓann*), irregardless of whether it is [transmitted] by one or more [persons]."[50]

What is significant about these definitions is that they do not correspond to the rules of *tawātur* and *aḥād* that one finds in books of hadith. For hadith specialists, what differentiates the two types of tradition is simply the number of transmitters involved: at least one transmitter for each link in an unbroken chain of *aḥād* accounts and more than one for each link of *tawātur*.[51] In neither case is the veracity of the transmitter nor the accuracy of the tradition itself called into question. For al-ʿAzafī, however, an *aḥād* account is qualitatively different from its *tawātur* counterpart, since the differentiating factor is the believability of the tradition, not the number of transmitters involved.

This point is important because it tells us that *Diʿāmat al-yaqīn* is not just a work of "hadith-oriented Sufism."[52] Rather than locating his discourse in the field of hadith studies, al-ʿAzafī instead operates in the more concrete world of human behavior and perception. This is an epistemologically real world of juridical practice and the determination of fact, where the jurist's knowledge of society, the veracity of witnesses, and the preponderance of the evidence all combine to determine the truth or falsehood of testimony.[53]

The metaphor of the courtroom and its rules of evidence are brought into an even sharper focus by al-ʿAzafī's discussion of *tawātur* traditions. Those that make the best evidence are traditions that are transmitted verbatim (*tawātur lafẓī*). To be accorded such a distinction, four conditions must be met: (1) that the reports be acquired through certain knowledge (*ʿilm*) and not through speculation (*ẓann*); (2) that each report go back, person-to-person, to an individual who apprehended the information through his or her own senses; (3) that each link in the chain of transmission conform independently to the above rules, without regard to previous conclusions (this is crucial, says al-ʿAzafī, because "the information that is known to the people of every era is independent, in and of itself, [of what comes before or after it]");[54] and (4) that the number of transmitters at each stage of transmission be as large as possible ("if a man were killed in the marketplace, and a group of people went from the scene of the killing and came to us, informing us of his murder, the first statement would stimulate an opinion [about the veracity of the report], the second and third statements would confirm it, and confirmation would continue until we were forced to conclude that it is impossible to deny it").[55]

Because verbatim traditions are seldom available, the hagiographer must frequently use reports that are *tawātur maʿnawī,* accounts for which "the majority or a great number may not agree on every particular, but agree on many particulars when [they are] taken together."[56] In this case as well, the most important criterion for ascertaining the truth-value of a tradition is the preponderance of the evidence, once all possible ambiguities have been taken into account.

After discussing oral tradition, al-ʿAzafī next argues the case for miracles (*karāmāt*) as proofs of the Muslim saint's status before God. This argument is presented in a way that confirms his training as a legist in the uṣūlī tradition. First, the legal admissibility (*jawāz*) of miracles is established by recourse to hadiths from the Prophet Muḥammad and traditions from the as-Salaf aṣ-Ṣāliḥ. Sources used by al-ʿAzafī include the *Ṣaḥīḥ* of al-Bukhārī, the *Sunan* of at-Tirmidhī, and accounts from Abu Nuʿaym al-Iṣfahānī's *Ḥilyat al-awliyāʾ wa ṭabaqāt al-aṣfiyāʾ* (Adornment of the saints and categories of the pure). To further bolster his conclusions, two additional authorities are added to this list: the Maliki legist Ibn Abī Zayd al-Qayrawānī and al-Ghazālī's mentor in uṣūl methodology, the Shafiʿi theologian ʿAbd al-Malik al-Juwaynī (d. 478/1085–6).[57]

Next, al-ʿAzafī defines the miracle itself. This is "a paranormal act (*fiʿlun khāriqun li'l-ʿāda*) which appears at the hands of a slave for whom ṣalāḥ is manifest in his religion, who is obedient to God in all of his states, and who adheres to the [Sufi] Way in his conduct."[58] For the Ashʿarite theologian Abū Bakr al-Bāqillānī, the appearance of miracles demonstrates that the person who manifests them has attained salvation.[59] Although al-ʿAzafī rejects this opinion on theological grounds, he agrees with al-Bāqillānī on the negative point that miracles do not necessarily prove a saint's infallibility.[60]

The textual core of *Diʿāmat al-yaqīn* consists of *manāqib,* narratives of exemplary acts that are attributed to Abū Yiʿzzā on the basis of *tawātur* transmission. It is clear that al-ʿAzafī wishes to portray his subject as a socially conscious ṣāliḥ who cares deeply about the common folk. The reader of *Diʿāmat al-yaqīn* thus finds himself in the presence of a saint for whom divinely bestowed power is counterbalanced by a sense of intimacy and accessibility. This accessibility is reinforced by the simplicity of Abū Yiʿzzā's discourse and the inclusion of Berber vocabulary in al-ʿAzafī's text. Both of these devices are illustrated in the following account, which was related to al-ʿAzafī as direct testimony from his most believable witness, the Sufi shaykh, holy warrior, and martyr Abū Ṣabr Ayyūb al-Fihrī (d. 609/1212):[61]

> I once traveled to [Abū Yiʿzzā] riding on a donkey that belonged to me. One day, after I had put it out to pasture, some people came to me while I was in the mosque and said: "Look after your donkey, for it is dying!" I ran to it and found it kicking its legs and hoofs and foaming at the mouth. I understood the reason for this when someone said to me: "It ate the grain of the Shaykh while it was stacked in a bundle and this happened at once." So I went directly to the Shaykh and said: "*Yā Daddā Abā Yiʿzzā* (which means, 'Oh my father!' in the language of the West [*sic*]), *īmmūt aghyūl.īnū* [my donkey has died]!" "*Warīmmūt* [He is not dead]," he replied. I said: "He can be nothing but dead, for he has eaten your provisions." Then he said: "*Warīmmūt!* I am your provision, the grain is your provision, and the donkey is your provision!" Then he went with me to [the donkey], opened its mouth, and spat into it. It stood up immediately, and no harm had befallen it. This is indeed a wondrous miracle![62]

Evidence of Abū Yiʿzzā's sense of social responsibility includes the reconciliation of newlyweds who were about to divorce, the mediation of tribal conflicts, the suppression of vengeance feuding (*thaʿr*), "good citizenship" expressions of loyalty to the state, and demonstrations of respect for the ulama.[63] His best-known act of ṣalāḥ, however, was healing the sick. It is possible to speculate, although difficult to prove, that this miracle was associated culturally with the darkness of Abū Yiʿzzā's skin.[64] Several accounts in at-Tādilī's *at-Tashawwuf* demonstrate that the status of sub-Saharan Africans was low among premodern Moroccan Berbers—so much so, in fact, that marriage to a black African was even forbidden by certain tribes.[65] One honorable occupation that sub-Saharan Africans could perform, however, was healing. At-Tādilī provides a number of examples of black healer-saints who flourished in the decades before the Almohad revolution.[66] Abū Yiʿzzā's particular style of healing troubled the ulama because it allowed him to touch the bare breasts of women. When told that the ulama accused him of fondling women and gazing at them in a lecherous manner, he replied: "Do they not allow a doctor to look at that place and touch it out of necessity? Has even one of their doctors become my enemy? I touch only diseased bodies in order to heal them."[67]

Many of Abū Yiʿzzā's miracles were epistemological in nature, since they involved transcendent forms of knowledge, such as mind reading or the prediction of events to come. This type of *karāma* is commonly referred to as "prophecy" in the Judeo-Christian tradition, but is known as *firāsa* (clairvoyance) in Morocco. One of the most striking of such cases in *Diʿāmat al-yaqīn* involves the saint's use of a serpent as an oracle:

> One day, [my father] and his companions went down to the river that ran by his house to wash their clothes. When the shaykh lay down to sleep in the shade of a tree, a great serpent, with a hood ("mane"—Ar. *ʿurf*) the size of a colt's (*muhr*) or thereabouts, approached the river, drank from it, and went to where Shaykh Abū Yiʿzzā [was lying]. Everyone was afraid of it. When it reached the shaykh, it licked his feet and went underneath his clothes until its head emerged from his sleeve. At this [the shaykh] said: "Do not be afraid! Verily, [the serpent] is a messenger (*rasūl*) who has come to tell me that forty riders will arrive here tonight. They will be *Qāʾid* Abū ʿAbdallāh ibn Ṣanādīd and his companions." Then he ordered his companions to look after their women and prepare food.[68]

Al-ʿAzafī's inclusion of such dramatic miracles in *Diʿāmat al-yaqīn* implies that Abū Yiʿzzā's powers were unique to himself and hence irreproducible by others. According to the Granadan jurist Ibn ʿAṭiyya (d. 541/1146–7), the author of one of the most influential Almohad-era Qur'anic commentaries,[69] the chief characteristic of the "God-conscious" (*al-muttaqīn*)—the very people referred to in the title of *Diʿāmat al-yaqīn*—is the ability to strike observers with awe and wonderment.[70] It is this sense of the *mysterium tremendum* that makes a unique saint like Abū Yiʿzzā worthy of notice in the first place. Al-ʿAzafī points out, however, that it is not the saint whom people really fear. Instead, it is the power of God, the divine patron and ultimate source of the saint's knowledge and authority, that they sense in the saint's presence. For this reason, says al-ʿAzafī, miracle workers such as Abū Yiʿzzā are the quintessential *awliyāʾ Allāh:* "[They] are brought near to [Allah] through obedience, and [Allah] reciprocates by giving them miracles."[71]

The idea that power and authority are related to one's closeness to God lies behind all of the epistemological miracles of saints in Moroccan hagiographies. *Awliyāʾ Allāh* such as Abū Yiʿzzā acquire knowledge (which al-ʿAzafī describes as *ʿilm,* rather than the Sufi term *maʿrifa*) directly from God Himself and then broadcast it to others illuminatively, "as if they were pulpits of light."[72] The following account, taken from at-Tādilī's *at-Tashawwuf,* illustrates the didactic nature of this type of miracle:

> Abū ʿAlī ibn Tamāgrūt said: "I used to carry a load of raisins for Abū Yiʿzzā every year from Nafīs to Jabal Irūggān. One year, I went to him with a load of raisins, and gave them to his muezzin, who left them in a room. I sat down to talk with [the muezzin] and he said: 'Would that the words of Shaykh Abū Yiʿzzā hide the faults of humankind rather than disclose them! For the man is ignorant and without knowledge. He says to those who come to him, "You have stolen from someone, you so-and-so! You have committed adultery, you so-and-so! You have done such-and-such, you so-and-so!" And he tells everyone what he has done.'
>
> Suddenly, his words were cut off. I examined him and [found that] he had been prevented from speaking. When I addressed him, he did not answer me. I had been with him like this for some time when Abū Yiʿzzā approached, staff in hand. He greeted me and asked about my situation and that of my family. Then he went to his muezzin, placed his hand on [the man's] throat, rubbed it, and said: 'My son, you have spoken the truth. Indeed, I am ignorant. I have no knowledge other than what my Lord has made known to me.'
>
> A drop of blood fell from [the muezzin's] throat so that he spoke, and he started to say: 'I seek the forgiveness of God the Exalted!' But Abū Yiʿzzā said to him: 'Why are you remorseful, my son, since you have spoken the truth? I am ignorant. I know nothing but what my Lord has made known to me (*ʿarrafanī mawlāya*).' "[73]

The key to the meaning of this account can be found in Abū Yiʿzzā's statement: "I know nothing but what my Lord has made known to me." This is a paraphrasis of a divine command to the Prophet Muḥammad in the Qur'an: "Say . . . I follow naught but what is revealed unto me" (X [*Yūnus*], 15). It is also similar to a hadith in the *Sunan* of Aḥmad ibn Ḥanbal (d. 241/855), a source that was well known to twelfth-century Moroccans: "I am a man who remembers nothing but what God has made known to me (*ʿallamanī Allāh*)."[74] Statements such as these were made by the Prophet Muḥammad in order to show that his personal opinions were in agreement with the word of God.[75] Since Abū Yiʿzzā was not only illiterate like the Prophet but also spoke no Arabic, he thus intimates, by using a similar figure of speech, that his own inspiration comes from the same divine source.[76]

The trope of an immediate and quasi-prophetic knowledge from God—exemplified in the Qur'an by the phrase, *ʿallamnāhu min ladunnā ʿilman* ("We taught him knowledge from Our own presence"—XVIII [*al-Kahf*], 65)—is tailor-made for an illiterate man of power such as Abū Yiʿzzā.[77] To make use of this rhetorical device, however, al-ʿAzafī must first deal with objections about Abū Yiʿzzā's supposed ignorance, especially with regard to his inability to quote hadith or even recite more than a handful of verses from the Qur'an. He counters these objections by arguing that Abū Yiʿzzā was not so much "ignorant" (*jāhil*) as "unlettered" or intellectually innocent (*ummī*),[78] an image that further reinforces the saint's identification with Muḥammad, the Unlettered Prophet (*an-Nabī al-Ummī*):

> How can an ignorant person (*jāhil*) be a *walī*—who comes near to his Lord (*yatawalā sayyidahu*) and is empowered by Him (*yatawallāhu*)? How can he neither keep the covenant of the Law of his Lord nor follow the pattern of conduct set down by his Master when our Lord has made it clear to us that He has chosen him and glorified him? . . . How can one be ignorant when brilliant signs and dazzling paranormal phenomena are manifested through him? How can one who is mentally competent (*ʿāqil*) tolerate such [doubts] in his belief? For the *jāhil*, if he is not an unbeliever, must be a sinner. We [jurists] do not mean by *jāhil* a person who knows his [prayer] requirements for both day and night, and who maintains his obligations of faith, [such as] knowledge of God and His Messenger and what Islam requires of him in the way of prayer, fasting, and *zakāt*. This is the opinion of the majority of ulama.[79]

This passage is replete with terminology that would be familiar to any Muslim jurist. Most important are the semantically antithetical terms *jāhil* and *ʿāqil*, which, in the context of Islamic law, refer to a person's suitability as a witness. The testimony of the *jāhil* is rejected because the ignorant person's lack of knowledge implies an inability to differentiate right from wrong, a deficit of moral judgment that is detrimental to justice. The *ʿāqil*, on the other hand, is mature and in full command of his or her faculties, including that of moral discrimination. In the text of *Diʿāmat al-yaqīn*, al-ʿAzafī uses the legal meaning of these terms to deny that Abū Yiʿzzā is *jāhil*. Instead, he argues that the saint should be considered a *rajul ʿāqil*, a man who gives truthful and accurate testimony on all matters, whether they be worldly or extramundane.

But what, his opponents might respond, can one say in defense of Abū

Yiʿzzā's ignorance of the Qur'an, or his lack of knowledge of Prophetic traditions? Al-ʿAzafī 's unexpected response is that eastern masters of uṣūl did not consider memorization of either Qur'an or hadith to be a condition of religious leadership (*imāma*). In fact, he asserts, many of the Mashriqi ulama who understood the word of God the most actually memorized the Qur'an the least, whereas in the Maghrib the popularity of rote and unthinking memorization led even uneducated people to commit the Qur'an to heart without understanding anything of what they recite.

To prove his point, al-ʿAzafī cites the example of Abū ʿUbayda ibn al-Muthannā (d. 209/824–5), a precursor of the uṣūlī method and author of one of the earliest Qur'anic commentaries. Abū ʿUbayda, he claims, not only never learned the Qur'an by heart, but even made mistakes in its recitation.[80] As for Abū Yiʿzzā's inability to speak Arabic, why should this be an issue when eastern schools of law, such as the Hanafi, do not even require Arabic for saying one's prayers? Surely, al-ʿAzafī concludes, it is the quality of a person's knowledge, not the number of verses or traditions recited, that counts the most.[81]

The Power of Compassion: The Imitanda *of Abū'l-ʿAbbās as-Sabtī*

The final section of *Diʿāmat al-yaqīn* deals with three problematical figures in Islamic sacred history—the esoteric teacher al-Khiḍr and the prophets Ilyās (Elijah) and al-Yasaʿ (Isaiah)—each of whom is associated with the same type of divinely bestowed knowledge (*ʿilm ladunnī*) as is Abū Yiʿzzā. The al-Khiḍr legend has long been popular in Morocco, if for no other reason than because the Strait of Gibraltar lies at the confluence of two seas similar to that mentioned in the story of al-Khiḍr in the Qur'an. A more pertinent reason for including the al-Khiḍr myth in al-ʿAzafī 's book, however, is that this legendary purveyor of perennial wisdom, although denied the status of prophet by the majority of Muslim opinion, was nonetheless able, as a *walī Allāh,* to surpass the Prophet Moses in his understanding of the mysteries that lie beyond mundane perception.

Although the name "al-Khiḍr" is not mentioned in the Qur'an, it can be traced at least as far back as the ninth century C.E., for the term appears in both the *Ṣaḥīḥ* of al-Bukhārī (d. 256/870) and the highly respected Qur'anic commentary of aṭ-Ṭabarī (d. 311/923).[82] According to al-ʿAzafī, al-Khiḍr's ultimate origin is anybody's guess. No fewer than ten "original" names and genealogies are cited in *Diʿāmat al-yaqīn,* ranging geographically from Iran to Pharaonic Egypt, and even to Rome.[83] Perhaps the most suggestive aspect of these genealogies is the fact that most of them are non-Arab, an attribute that is also shared by the Berber saint Abū Yiʿzzā.

Whatever al-Khiḍr's origin may have been, the most important thing about him for al-ʿAzafī was that he could surpass a prophet in his own, separate domain of knowledge. This achievement implies that the knowledge by which God honors His saints is complementary to, rather than dependent on, the message of prophethood.[84] The corollary which al-ʿAzafī draws from this is that the vocation of the saints in Islam is both epistemological and social in nature: to make use of their knowledge of the orders of existence (*al-kāʾināt*) and hidden destinies (*al-ʿawāqib al-mughībāt*) to improve the lives of others.[85]

Al-ʿAzafī's comparison of Abū Yiʿzzā to al-Khiḍr once again implies that the example of this Berber saint cannot be duplicated. As depicted in *Diʿāmat al-yaqīn,* "Sīdī Būʿazzā" is a monument to be marveled at rather than an example to be imitated. In medieval European hagiography, the vita of such a saint would fall under the category of *admiranda,* "things to be wondered at." In the twelfth century, this emphasis on holy people as objects of wonderment was replaced by a new emphasis on *imitanda* ("things to be imitated"). This change, in turn, led to saints being regarded as behavioral exemplars whose precedent could influence others to change their ways.[86]

Similar exemplars can be found in Moroccan hagiography from the same period. At-Tādilī's *at-Tashawwuf,* for example, with its strong emphasis on the concept of ṣalāḥ, is a veritable encyclopedia of *imitanda.* But at-Tādilī, like al-ʿAzafī, also finds occasion to discuss al-Khiḍr.[87] Does this mean that *admiranda* and *imitanda* might be found in the same person? Could a divinely guided "knower of hidden destinies" also serve as an example for the common person? At-Tādilī answers these questions by devoting the Appendix of his book to a uniquely powerful saint who was also a well-known exemplar in his own city of Marrakesh. Coincidentally, the subject of this monograph, Abū'l-ʿAbbās as-Sabtī (d. 601/1204), was born in al-ʿAzafī's city of Sabta.

To the French Islamicist Adolphe Faure, who was deeply moved by as-Sabtī's compassion, this saint's life reflected a "passionate soul, oriented toward the good, yet open to a horizon of extreme privation."[88] What Faure neglects to tell us, however, is that, as was the case with his Christian contemporary St. Francis of Assisi,[89] as-Sabtī's hagiography was in part composed by as-Sabtī himself. Although most of what we know about as-Sabtī comes from at-Tādilī's *Akhbār Abī'l-ʿAbbās as-Sabtī,*[90] much of this work relies either on direct testimony from the saint himself or on oral tradition passed on according to as-Sabtī's personal wishes. The presence of the saint's guiding hand confirms the didactic and exemplary nature of at-Tādilī's discourse by drawing the reader's attention to the meaning that lies behind each paranormal act. This was because as-Sabtī's spiritual method, based as it was on the ethics of charity (*ṣadaqa*) and good works (*iḥsān*), was social in nature and expressed values that demanded replicability.

Although both at-Tādilī and al-ʿAzafī, as legitimizers of sainthood, could be called "professional agents of collective memory,"[91] there is a clear difference between *Akhbār Abī'l-ʿAbbās as-Sabtī* and *Diʿāmat al-yaqīn.* While al-ʿAzafī has to draw on his legal knowledge and religious imagination to redefine the sainthood of Abū Yiʿzzā and legitimize a pre-existing cult that grew up spontaneously, at-Tādilī is more of a publicist than an apologist. Although as-Sabtī, like Abū Yiʿzzā, was an object of suspicion for the Almohad ulama, unlike the latter he was a highly educated and intellectual Sufi who adhered to the well-known *futuwwa* doctrines of Khurasan. Because there was therefore less need to justify the legitimacy of his actions, at-Tādilī could devote more time to making a moral rather than a legal argument for his authority.

Social consciousness was so important to as-Sabtī's model of sainthood that he even defined the pillars of Islam (normally a religious obligation alone) according to this principle:

> *Tawḥīd:* The meaning of *tawḥīd* is the absolute oneness of God Most High without the creation of any god other than Him from among the goods of the material world. For verily, everything that masters a person is his god.
>
> *Ṣalāt:* He who does not understand the meaning of prayer has not prayed. The beginning of prayer is the Magnification of Consecration (*takbīr al-iḥrām*), which involves raising your hands and saying, "God is Most Great." The meaning of "God is Most Great" is that you do not begrudge [Allah] anything. Therefore, when one considers a particular aspect of the material world to be most important for him, he has not consecrated himself and has not magnified God in his prayers. The meaning of raising one's hands to magnify God signifies that you have been emptied of everything and are saying, "I possess neither much nor a little."

Ṣawm: The secret of fasting is that you are hungry. When you are hungry you remember the one who is always hungry and know the strength of the fire of hunger that afflicts him, so that you become charitable toward him. Thus, if you are in the act of denying yourself food and have no compassion for the hungry and your fasting does not cause this idea to occur to you, you have not [truly] fasted and have not understood the intended meaning of the fast.

Zakāt: As for the alms tax, it is made obligatory for you every year so that you become accustomed to spending and giving of yourself.

Ḥajj: The essence of pilgrimage is that you appear in the dress of the poor, with a shaved head, unkempt, and wearing sandals, [after] having divested yourself of fine clothing, expending your efforts for the sake of God Most High, and showing worshipfulness [toward Him].

Jihād: The essence of *jihād* is the expenditure of self for the pleasure of God Most High, emptying oneself of everything for His sake, and divesting oneself of reliance on the material world.[92]

The close link between as-Sabtī's spiritual method and the way of futuwwa was well known to his hagiographers. In the sixteenth century C.E., Aḥmad aṣ-Ṣūmaʿi drew an explicit comparison between futuwwa and as-Sabtī's method in his commentary on the shaykh's famous dictum: "Hesitation at the first thought is miserliness" (*at-taraddud fī'l-khāṭir al-awwal bukhlun*). This saying, which on the surface means that a person should not withhold charity just because one is short of cash, is traced by aṣ-Ṣūmaʿī to Abū'l-Ḥasan al-Bushanjī (d. 348/959–60), an early Khurasani master of futuwwa.[93]

In *Ṭabaqāt aṣ-ṣūfiyya,* as-Sulamī tells us that al-Bushanjī was noted for his high moral standards and refined sense of justice. He is said to have characterized Sufism as "Freedom and *futuwwa;* the abandonment of ostentation in one's generosity and grace in one's moral behavior."[94] Of the related concept of ethical dignity (*muruwwa*), al-Bushanjī remarked: "[It is] the practice of goodness in one's inner and outer self."[95] In the work entitled *Kitāb al-futuwwa,* as-Sulamī discusses al-Bushanjī's concept of social consciousness in terms that are reminiscent of the Golden Rule of the Christian tradition: "[Futuwwa] is the goodness of one's innermost being in the presence of God, which means that you desire for your brothers that which you desire for yourself; indeed, that you prefer them over yourself. . . . For the Prophet has said: 'None of you has believed until he desires for his brother that which he desires for himself.' One who has combined these two attributes in himself correctly practices futuwwa and follows the Way."[96]

As-Sabtī was equally devoted to these principles. His sessions of invocation in Marrakesh (which at-Tādilī attended) were noted for their atmosphere of mutual respect, and none of his disciples was subjected to open criticism. The same consideration led to his refusal to allow poems of praise to be recited in his honor, for he feared that others might take umbrage at not being praised as well.[97] In addition, an overriding concern for the socially disadvantaged underlay nearly all of as-Sabtī's public acts, just as had been the case for many eastern masters of futuwwa. "Do you not know," he once told his followers, "that the power of God lies in service to the weak?"[98] On another occasion he remarked: "The Companions of the Messenger of God did not attain [their honored status] except by generosity of spirit, openness of heart, charity, and service to others."[99]

Using a topos common to sacred biography in both Christianity and Islam, as-Sabtī portrayed himself as having a mystical ambition (*himma*) from the earliest years of his life: "In the beginning I was an orphan in the city of Sabta and my mother would take me to the shoemakers [to learn their trade]. But I would run away from them to study in the circle of Abū ʿAbdallāh al-Fakhkhār. She would beat me for this until Abū ʿAbdallāh al-Fakhkhār said to her, 'Why do you beat this child?' 'He is an orphan,' she said, 'and refuses to work at his trade while I have nothing.' So he said to me, 'My son, why do you not do what your mother has ordered?' 'Because I love the words that I hear from you,' I answered. Then he said to her, 'Leave him and I will pay you the amount of his earnings and will also pay for an instructor who will teach him to read.'"[100]

Within only six years, as-Sabtī had memorized the Qur'an, the *Risāla* of Ibn Abī Zayd al-Qayrawānī, and the fundamentals of Arabic language and literature. He chose goodness and charity as his personal path to God after reflecting on the Qur'anic verse: "Verily, Allah commands justice and the doing of good" (XVI [*an-Naḥl*], 90). After listening to his pupil's commentary on this verse, al-Fakhkhār told him: "My son, I possess several disciplines of the followers of *futuwwa,* but no one has yet asked me about the path of sharing in proportionate measure (*mushāṭara*), even though it is the highest attainment of the human being."[101] As al-Fakhkhār had predicted, as-Sabtī was to make *mushāṭara,* the ritualistic sharing of goods in proportionate measure, the hallmark of his spiritual praxis:

I found a verse in the Book of God that had a great effect on both my heart and my tongue. It was, "Verily, God commands justice and the doing of good." I pondered this and said [to myself], "Perhaps [finding] this is no coincidence and I am the one who is meant by this verse." I continued to examine its meaning in the books of exegesis until I found *Gharīb at-tafsīr,* which stated that [the verse] was revealed when the Prophet established brotherhood between the Emigrants (*muhājirūn*) and the Helpers (*anṣār*). They had asked the Prophet to establish a pact of brotherhood between them, so he commanded them to share among themselves. In this way, they learned that the justice commanded [by God] was through sharing. Then I looked into the saying of the Prophet: "My community will be divided into seventy-two sects, all of which will be in the Fire except the one followed by me and my companions,"[102] and found that he said this on the morning of the day that he had ordered the pact of brotherhood [to be established] between the Emigrants and the Helpers. . . . So I understood that what he and his companions adhered to were the practices of *mushāṭara* and *īthār.* Then I swore to God Most High that when anything came to me I would share it with my believing brethren among the poor. I followed this practice for twenty years, and this rule affected my ideas to the point where nothing dominated my thoughts more than uncompromising honesty (*ṣidq*).

After I had reached forty years of age, another idea occurred to me, so I returned to the [original] verse and meditated upon it, and discovered that justice was in sharing but that true goodness (*iḥsān*) went beyond that. So I thought about it a third time and swore a vow to God that if anything, small or large, came to me, I would keep one-third and expend two-thirds for the sake of God Most High. I followed this [practice] for twenty years, and the result of that decision among humankind was [both] sainthood (*wilāya*) and rejection; I would be venerated by some and rejected by others.

After twenty [more] years, I meditated on the first obligation of the station of goodness (*iḥsān*) required by God Most High for His worshipers, and found it to be gratitude for His bounty. This is proven by the emergence of the instinct toward good at birth, before the acquisition of either understanding or intellect. I then found that eight grades of behavior were required for charity and that seven other grades [were required] for *iḥsān* in addition to [those required for] justice. This is because for oneself is a portion (*ḥaqq*), for the wife a portion, a portion for what is in the womb, for the orphan a portion, and a portion for the guest. . . . Once I arrived at this degree, I swore an oath to God that whatever came to me, whether it be little or much, I would keep two-sevenths of it for myself and my wife and [give up] five-sevenths to the one for whom it was due.[103]

In later years, after he had become a widely venerated saint and enjoyed the patronage of the Almohad caliph in Marrakesh, as-Sabtī refined the practice of *mushāṭara* even further:

I divide everything that comes to me into seven portions. I take one-seventh for myself and the second seventh for that which I am required to spend on my wife and the small children under her care, as well as the slaves and slave girls [in our household], all of whom number thirty-two individuals. Then I look after those who have lost their sustenance; they are the neglected orphans who have neither mother nor father. I take them in as my own family and see to it that not one of them lacks a [proper] marriage or a burial, unless someone else provides it for them. Then I look after my kinfolk, who number eighty-four individuals. They have two portions: their right as family members and their right of residence. Then come those who have been deprived of their support as mentioned in the Book of God Most High. They are the poor who have fallen into hardship on the Way of God: those who are unable to work the land and are thought of as ignorant, but who are [actually] rich in patience and restraint; they are the ones unable to manage their own affairs. I found [some of] them even to be of the family of ʿAlī ibn Yūsuf ibn Tāshfīn [the Almoravid ruler, whose descendants were killed or dispossessed after the Almohad conquest] and the Banū ʿAzīz, who used to be kings but have now become poor. I took them in as if they were my own relatives, and when one of them died I replaced him with another. I carried out these obligations for fourteen years without respite.[104]

Somewhere between the age of sixteen and twenty, as-Sabtī left Sabta for Ajdīr on the Rifian coast, where he taught mathematics and grammar while living on stipends provided by the local treasury. Anything not needed for his own sustenance he gave to students who were preparing to become Almohad missionaries.[105] Further proof of as-Sabtī's support for the Almohad cause can be found in a report claiming that while in Ajdīr the young Sufi, following the example of the Almohad *Ḥizb Allāh* (Party of God) futuwwa organization, would take a whip with him whenever he went to the marketplace in order to punish those who neglected their prayers.[106]

As-Sabtī moved to Marrakesh in 540/1145–6, during the final weeks of the Almohad siege of the city. For a number of years he lived in a cave on the hill of Igillīz outside of Marrakesh, only coming into town on Fridays in order to perform the obligatory communal prayer. At-Tādilī reports that the shaykh first gained official notice when one of his disciples went to collect the wages that were due to him for helping to build a house. When the owner of the house refused to pay him, the house collapsed, and its owner was told that it could only be restored by as-Sabtī. When the man apologized to the shaykh, paid the disciple's back wages, and gave a large donation to the city's homeless, the house was miraculously restored to its former condition. The news of this miracle spread rapidly through the streets and alleys of Marrakesh, until a delegation led by no less a personage than the Almohad caliph ʿAbd al-Muʾmin paid their respects to as-Sabtī at his hillside cave.[107] This official recognition was a far cry from the persecution suffered by Sufis who were not recognized as Almohad supporters, such as Abū Shuʿayb and Abū Yiʿzzā.

As-Sabtī was particularly noted for his fluency in classical Arabic. This was due in part to his education in Sabta, which at the time was an important center for the study of grammar and rhetoric. Biographers mention that he enjoyed debating and would respond with passages from the Qur'an or proofs based on logic whenever someone objected to his reasoning. As demonstrated by the autobiographical sections of *Akhbār Abī'l-ʿAbbās as-Sabtī,* the shaykh took pleasure in being a man of the people and tailored his lessons to suit the educational level of his audience. Once his retreat at Igillīz was discovered, he began to go down to Marrakesh at regular intervals, where he conducted question-and-answer sessions in public markets or in open places along widely traveled thoroughfares. During these sessions he would urge his listeners to practice charity, illustrating his points with selections from the Qur'an or hadith. If donations were given to him, he would divide them among the poor at the end of his lecture and abruptly leave.[108]

Because of as-Sabtī's popularity among the lower classes, the elites of Marrakesh often regarded him as a threat. Apologists called him a *malāmatī* Sufi because of his self-abnegating demeanor and the profane utterances he sometimes made during moments of spiritual intoxication; his disciples called him *quṭb,* a spiritual axis; and a few (usually Almohad ulama) went so far as to accuse him of being, at turns, a heretic, an unwarranted innovator, a magician, and a sorcerer.[109] Some Almohad officials even accused him of "bewitching the masses" with the fluency of his tongue, a clear indication that they were discomfited by his potential as a political dissident.[110] Adding fuel to their fire was the fact that as-Sabtī, like his predecessor ʿAlī ibn Ḥirzihim of Fez, was prone to proclaiming his sanctity openly, saying "I am a guide toward *iḥsān* and an intermediary between humankind and their Creator."[111] He also said "I am a merchant of God among His creatures" (*anā tājir Allāh bayna khalqihi*).[112]

The official approval enjoyed by as-Sabtī under ʿAbd al-Muʾmin changed to hostility under the next caliph, the philosophically inclined Abū Yaʿqūb Yūsuf (r. 558–80/1163–84). A crisis was instigated when a group of official notaries signed a petition claiming that the shaykh was a heretic. The qāḍī al-jamāʿa of Marrakesh, who either issued the charge in the first place or was unable to deny the claims of as-Sabtī's accusers because they were "just witnesses" under Islamic law, brought the petition to the ruler and sent for the shaykh in order to test his beliefs. When as-Sabtī arrived at the palace, Abū Yaʿqūb gave him a gift of one-fourth of a dinar, a gesture of extreme disrespect from a ruler who was known for his openhandedness toward favorites. "What do you desire, oh Commander of the Faithful?" asked Sīdī Bel ʿAbbās. "Oh Sīdī," said the caliph, "these legal scholars have written a document and I want it to be read in your presence because the *qāḍī* has approved of what is in it." "In the Name of God, let him who has written it read it," said the shaykh. So the document was read in the presence of everyone who was in attendance. "And by the Grace of Him who says, 'Be,' and it is" (claims at-Tādilī), everything bad that was written about the shaykh was changed to good and every negative claim was changed to its opposite. *Zindīq* (heretic) was changed to *ṣiddīq* (one who testifies to the Truth) and *ṭāliḥ* (wicked or villainous) was changed to *ṣāliḥ.* The *qāḍī* was greatly ashamed at what had happened and knew that it was a sign from God. Then as-Sabtī said to the caliph, "Oh Commander of the Faithful, since these men have spoken so well of us, may God reward them with good!" Upon leaving the palace, he turned to his servant and remarked, "Did you see how one-fourth of a dinar made a liar out of everyone?"[113]

Another reason for the opposition to as-Sabtī during this period was his habit of raising the consciousness of the rich by engaging in a form of *mushāṭara* that is best described as "bargaining for the future."[114] To his opponents, this practice amounted to little more than a spiritual form of extortion. The growth of Marrakesh, in the space of less than seventy-five years, from a virtual nonentity into the capital of a major empire caused disparities in living standards that were exacerbated by the price inflation that accompanied imperial expansion. Like its commercial rival Fez, Marrakesh was a magnet for large numbers of the rural poor, who flocked to the city in search of a better life through military service or the trade-oriented "service industries" that supported the Almohad ruling classes. This boom-town economy provided an opportunity for some but bitter disappointment for many others. Those who could not compete joined the masses of the destitute, who were abandoned by a regime that (according to the testimony of as-Sabtī's supporters) relegated the Islamic pillar of charity to a secondary or even tertiary level of importance.

When a person came to as-Sabtī requesting his intercession, the shaykh would ask, "Where is the release (*ayna al-fatḥ*)?" At this point, the petitioner would give up all of the hard currency he possessed for distribution to the poor. In one account a poor woman came to as-Sabtī, complaining that her only son had contracted leprosy. "Where is the release?" asked the shaykh, and she brought forth one dirham, all of the money that she possessed. He then told her to buy cucumbers with the dirham and give them to the poor, saving only the last, which she should feed to her son. The woman did as the shaykh commanded, and when the youth ate the cucumber his stomach swelled and he began to sweat profusely. Then he fell into a long, deep sleep. When he awoke, he found that his leprosy had peeled off of him like the skin of a snake.[115]

On another occasion as-Sabtī went to the governor of Marrakesh, accompanied by a large number of the city's homeless. "Bring forth the release for these people!" he demanded. "What is the release?" asked the governor. "Honesty," replied the shaykh. "And what is that?" "Alms," said as-Sabtī. "For whom?" "For the sake of God Most High," replied the shaykh. "Indeed, God has no need of that!" the governor haughtily retorted. At this, the shaykh turned toward the governor's servant and said, "This governor is demoted. He has demoted himself!" According to at-Tādilī, who transmitted this account as firsthand testimony, the governor lost his post only twenty-five days later when the caliph returned from Córdoba.[116]

As-Sabtī's most endearing quality to the poor of Marrakesh was his willingness to make his own sacrifices when circumstances warranted. In one of the most poignant accounts of altruism to be found anywhere in Sufi literature, at-Tādilī relates how the shaykh "gave up" the life of his own daughter for that of the caliph's granddaughter:

> One day the daughter of the Amir [Yaʿqūb al-Manṣūr] entered, weeping, and stood before the shaykh. "What makes you weep, oh Lady?" he asked. "Oh Sīdī," she said, "I have [only] one girl and God has not given me more than her. I have left her at death's door. If she dies, then I will die from losing her." "Where is the release?" asked the shaykh. "Oh Sīdī," she said, "here are one thousand gold dinars for the sake of God," and she threw a hundred [ten-dinar] coins into his lap. Now the shaykh had both young and old daughters, so he said to her, "Oh Lady, what is the age of your daughter from among these?" "The same as this one," she said, pointing to one of the daughters of the shaykh. Then the shaykh called to his wife and said, "Oh slave girl of God, will you sell me this daughter of yours for one thousand dinars, so that with her we might ransom the daughter of this lady?"
>
> "Oh Sīdī," she said, "who can bear separation from a loved one?" Then he said, "Give this thousand in the Way of God to one whose back is unclothed, whose stomach is hungry, and whose eyes are sleepless from debt." His younger daughter made herself ready for him while the shaykh consoled his wife until she relented. Then the shaykh told his daughter to bid farewell to her mother, and her mother took her and kissed her. The shaykh took her, placed her in his lap, and kissed her, while tears welled in his eyes. Then her soul departed by the Will of God Most High. "Arise, oh Lady, and go to your house," said the shaykh. She went home and found her daughter sitting up, as if she had never been ill.[117]

For the hagiographer at-Tādilī, as-Sabtī, like al-ʿAzafī's Abū Yiʿzzā, was one of those rare individuals who possessed the knowledge of hidden destinies. An understanding of this epistemological miracle is dependent on a thorough knowledge of the concept of fate, which is most often expressed in Islamic theology by the complementary terms *qaḍāʾ* and *qadar*.[118] In his treatise *Fuṣūṣ al-ḥikam* (The Ring settings of wisdom), the Andalusian Sufi Ibn al-ʿArabī, who as a young man actually met as-Sabtī[119] and shared some of the latter's mystical doctrines, differentiates these terms by defining *qaḍā'* as comprehensive predetermination. As for *qadar,* it is "the specification of the appointed time at which each [predetermined] thing should actually occur."[120] For Ibn al-ʿArabī, foreknowledge of *qadar*—the point at which a thing conceived by the divine will is actually brought into existence—was the most sublime state of knowledge a Sufi could attain. However, it was also the most painful state of knowledge, for, as Toshihiko Izutsu remarks:

> *Qadar* is an extremely delicate state in which an archetype is about to actualize itself in the form of a concretely existent thing. To know *qadar,* therefore, is to peep into the ineffable mystery of Being, for the whole secret of Being extending from God to the world is disclosed therein. Ibn ʿArabī remarks that "the mystery of *qadar* is one of the highest knowledges, which God grants only to (a small number of) men who are privileged with a perfect mystical intuition." If a man happens to obtain the true knowledge of *qadar,* the knowledge surely brings him a perfect peace of mind and an intolerable pain at the same time. The unusual peace of mind arises from the consciousness that everything in the world occurs as it has been determined from eternity. And whatever may happen to himself or others, he will be perfectly content with it. Instead of struggling in vain for obtaining what is not in his capacity, he will be happy with anything that is given him. He must be tormented, on the other hand, by an intense pain at the sight of all the so-called "injustices", "evils", and "sufferings" that reign rampant around him, being keenly conscious that it is not in his "preparedness" to remove them from the world.[121]

According to the theodicy of "preparedness" described by Izutsu in this passage, as-Sabtī did not "cause" his daughter to die in place of the granddaughter of Yaʿqūb al-Manṣūr. Rather, he was acutely aware that her fate was to serve as a sacrifice to God by giving up her life at the same instant that the reflux of universal manifestation was ready to take in the soul of a young girl. By perceiving this window of opportunity, the shaykh could, in a sense, insert the *qadar* of his daughter into the opening provided by the *qaḍā'* of the princess. In this way, he was able to serve as a "master of time" (*ṣāḥib al-waqt*) and a "master of charity" (*ṣāḥib aṣ-ṣadaqa*) in a single dramatic moment.

Also related to the concept of "preparedness" is the belief that a relationship of reciprocity exists between God and the world. Without such a concept, the "spiritual extortion" for which as-Sabtī was so feared by the rich of Marrakesh could not have been conceived. To as-Sabtī, every act of human mercy (*raḥma*) evoked a merciful response from the All-merciful God (*ar-Raḥīm*): "The root of all good in this world and the Hereafter is doing good unto others, and the root of all evil in this world and the Hereafter is miserliness. God Most High has said: 'So for the one who gives out of the fear of God and testifies to the best, We will indeed make smooth for him the path to salvation. But he who is a greedy miser and thinks himself self-sufficient, and gives the lie to the best, We will indeed make smooth for him the path to damnation (Qur'ān XCII [*al-Layl*], 5–10).'"[122]

As-Sabtī summed up his theory of reciprocity with the maxim: "[Divine] Being is actualized by generosity" (*al-wujūd yanfaʿilu bi'l-jūd*). This statement is a variation on the well-known Arabic proverb, "Existence is bettered by generosity" (*al-wujūd yantafiʿu bi'l-jūd*).[123] The Andalusian philosopher Ibn Rushd (Averroës, d. 595/1199), who visited as-Sabtī several times during his service as a caliphal physician in Marrakesh, assumed that the saint had learned this doctrine from the Greeks.[124] If so, his inspiration would most likely have been *sympathaeia*. This doctrine, which was borrowed by the Neoplatonists from the Stoics, postulated a set of "sympathies" or reciprocal relations that linked God to the material universe.[125] Others have seen in as-Sabtī's doctrine of reciprocity a reflection of the Christian concept of *agapé*, the "gratuitous love" that God bestows on all of humankind, regardless of merit.[126]

Whether or not he was acquainted with late-antique theodicies, the doctrine of *sympathaeia* was pertinent to as-Sabtī's understanding of God's mercy in the world. The idea that creation "constrains" God to behave in a predictable manner is logically prior to the belief that the divine archetype of mercy is present in each merciful act. Because of the reciprocity that pertains between God and the world, every act of human mercy evokes a merciful response from God. To restate this doctrine in more Qur'anic terms: each act of *raḥma* (human mercy) calls forth a response from ar-Raḥīm (God as the All-merciful), who rewards the believer in proportion to his expenditure of self.

About two decades before his death, as-Sabtī regained the official approval that he had formerly enjoyed under the caliph ʿAbd al-Mu'min. In 584/1188, at the end of his campaign against the Banū Ghānīyya (a particularly troublesome group of Almoravid holdouts in Ifrīqīya), the newly installed Almohad caliph Yaʿqūb al-Manṣūr was forced to execute his uncle for refusing to surrender the city of Tlemcen to his authority. A short time later, the same fate befell his brother, the governor of Murcia, who had concluded a treasonous alliance with Alfonso VIII of Castile.[127] The caliph was paralyzed with remorse at having to carry out these executions. In consolation, he turned to the Sufis of the western Maghrib for both personal solace and political support.

The recognition accorded as-Sabtī by Yaʿqūb al-Manṣūr was part of this policy. Amid great fanfare, the caliph brought the saint down from his cave on the hill of Igillīz and installed him in a large house that had been constructed near the Kutubiyya mosque. Later, he provided a hostel for as-Sabtī's disciples as well as a *madrasa* for study and teaching that was maintained by the caliph's own funds.[128] Whenever Yaʿqūb al-Manṣūr visited as-Sabtī he made a point of behaving in a humble manner and acted "as a servant" in the saint's presence.[129]

When al-Sabtī died in 601/1204, he was laid to rest in a grave that had originally been reserved for the philosopher Ibn Rushd, who preferred to be buried in his native city of Córdoba instead.[130] The humility that was such an important part of as-Sabtī's example was recalled in the saint's deathbed wish that his grave not be covered by a dome, so that it could be exposed to the open air like that of any other believer. Despite the fact that the tomb of Sīdī Bel ʿAbbās in Marrakesh is now surmounted by a large *qubba* built by the ʿAlawite rulers of present-day Morocco, his wishes are still respected to the extent that his resting place is marked, not by the usual catafalque, but by an unobtrusive gravestone that memorializes the studied simplicity of his life.

CHAPTER FOUR

Qualifying the Ineffable: Sainthood in the Hagiographical Anthology

In the previous chapters, I traced the development of Moroccan Sufism in its formative period, concentrating on the fifth and sixth centuries A.H. (the eleventh and twelfth centuries C.E.). As part of this process, I proposed four correctives to long-held assumptions about the nature of Islam in North Africa. First, contrary to the assumptions of Alfred Bel, Ernest Gellner, and Clifford Geertz, I suggested that Moroccan Sufism (like Sufism everywhere) has an urban ethos, even when it is found in the countryside. This means that Moroccan sainthood, insofar as it is expressed in terms of Sufi doctrine, is defined in terms of an urban-oriented "symbolic universe."

Second, I asserted that the murābiṭ, that quintessentially rural paradigm of Moroccan sainthood in ethnographic literature, was a more complex figure than the "marabout" of French colonial scholarship. In the first place, not every rural holy man could be called a murābiṭ. In early Moroccan Sufism, *murābiṭ* was a technical term that denoted an actionally formal relationship between the head of a socioreligious institution (the ribāṭ) and a particular tribe or group of tribes. In addition, the murābiṭ was a much more nuanced figure than Bel's "human fetish." Often, he was an urban-educated intellectual who translated the norms of "orthodox" Islam into terms that his pastoralist clients could understand and accept. Even the saint who had little or no contact with towns or cities could not escape the influence of urban culture. In the case of Abū Yiʿzzā, urban paradigms were at the heart of the Sufism that he taught to his disciples. Furthermore, since urban legists such as al-ʿAzafī recorded Abū Yiʿzzā's miracles and decided which of his teachings would be passed on to future generations, the image of his sainthood remained congruent with models that were formulated in an urban context.

This point brings up my third corrective to previous views of Moroccan sainthood: that the veneration of saints, whether living or dead, was not a heterodox phenomenon. Because this practice was validated by mainstream Sufism and revalidated by most jurists, it should be seen as a "normal" aspect of premodern Islam. This does not mean, of course, that everyone accepted the Sufi interpretation of sainthood. Some exoteric scholars opposed the veneration of *awliyāʾ* as a matter of principle. But the fact that juridically trained ulama dominated the writing of sacred biography meant that the onus of dissent was on those who sought to deny the reality of sainthood, not the other way around.

Finally, in opposition to the views of some modern scholars of Sufism who define Muslim sainthood solely according to the theoretical arguments found in Sufi texts, I asserted that living sainthood is a social phenomenon. This means that a walī Allāh's public image must conform to consensually validated standards before his or her holiness is acknowledged. Only later is the saint's example typified in terms of Sufi doctrine. This point is proven by the fact that textual arguments for sainthood have little or no predictive value. One is hard put to find a Sufi treatise that tells the reader—in practical terms—how to identify a walī Allāh when he or she sees one. Theoretical analyses of sainthood are certainly important, but the decision as to whether a person stands before a real saint or a counterfeit is, in the final analysis, subjective. If, as the Qur'an claims, every prophet in Islam had naysayers, why should sainthood be self-evident?[1]

Once it is acknowledged that living sainthood is social, one must conclude that the "unknown" (*majhūl*) saints who sometimes appear in Moroccan hagiographies are typifications or doctrinal topoi, not objectively real people.[2] The Muslim author of sacred biography, like his Christian counterpart, was not only a celebrant of people and events but also a theoretician who assessed the evidence of tradition from a variety of perspectives—social, doctrinal, and even political. When an arbiter of tradition such as Abū Nuʿaym al-Iṣfahānī says, in *Ḥilyat al-awliyāʾ*, that "the servants whom God loves the most are the . . . hidden," the meaning of this statement has more to do with the nuances of Sufi doctrine than with the observed lives of saints in Muslim society.[3] When used as a rhetorical device, being "hidden" might be a euphemism for saying that a person "makes things happen" for no apparent reason. Conversely, the trope of unknown saints might be a way of "filling in the blanks" by establishing symmetry between theoretical hierarchies. Whatever the case, even the most stubborn textualist has to admit that every saint who is mentioned in sacred biography is not really unknown, but has been noticed by somebody. If the saint is real at all, there must be a name, or at least a nickname, by which to make the identification.

It is also important to remember that the saint (a person of extraordinary ability) and the sage (a person of extraordinary knowledge) are not necessarily the same person. Although an individual may be a saint and a sage at the same time, he or she is just as likely to be one or the other separately. The fact that an extraordinary figure like Abū Yiʿzzā can be depicted in contrary hagiographical perspectives reminds us that even when a saint and a sage are one and the same, two different audiences respond, each in its own way. Abū Yiʿzzā's Sufi followers looked upon him as a teacher of wisdom (a shaykh or *ustādh*) more than as a miracle worker. However, it is clear from hagiographical accounts that his miracles were much more widely appreciated than his mystical teachings—a detail which points to another, more numerous audience that was largely unreceptive to the lessons and proverbs so highly valued by the authors of Sufi treatises. This second group, the devotees of the charismatic "Daddā Būʿazzā," who sought Abū Yiʿzzā's healing touch and after his death walked barefoot from Meknès to Adrār-n-Irūggān to share in the baraka emanating from his tomb, revered a man of power rather than a teacher. There can be no doubt that for such an audience, a "hidden" or "unknown" saint is no saint at all.

It is for this reason that I have chosen the ṣāliḥ as the leitmotif of this book. Being a Qur'anic topos that figures prominently in the hagiographical literature of Morocco, the ṣāliḥ is more than just an artificial construct imposed from the outside. Instead, it is both the product of rhetoric and a socially validated ideal type. As an ideal type, it provides a common measure by which every potential walī Allāh of the Far Maghrib—whether miracle worker, sage, mystic, or martyr—can be assessed. This is possible because the concept of ṣalāḥ, which defines the ṣāliḥ for the Muslim public, is not ineffable. Its parameters are clearly known from Qur'an, hadith, and treatises on Sufi practice. In addition, it conforms to the praxis-oriented, universalistic model of Islam advocated by the uṣūlī authors of sacred biography.

Since ṣalāḥ is a visible concept, the ṣāliḥ must be a visible person. Each ṣāliḥ or *ṣāliḥa* lives out his or her life in the view of others and is judged by his or her peers. This being so, it should be possible to interpret the ṣāliḥ's role in distinct social and historical contexts. Since information about ṣulaḥā' can often be found in hagiographical works that are nearly contemporaneous with the subjects they describe, it should also be possible to submit Moroccan sainthood to sociological analysis, following the lead of Pierre Delooz, Weinstein and Bell, and others in the *Annales* tradition. This is the goal of the present chapter, in which hagiographical anthologies of the Almohad era will be used to assess the significance of sainthood in the formative period of Moroccan Sufism.

The Typification of Sainthood in Almohad Morocco

The height of the Almohad era, which spanned the years between the caliph ʿAbd al-Mu'min's conquest of Marrakesh in 541/1146 and the death of his great-grandson Muḥammad an-Nāṣir in 611/1214, is considered to be the period in which the peoples of the Maghrib first became conscious of a common identity.[4] For the first time since the advent of the Fatimids in the tenth century, the regime that ruled North Africa purported to represent more than just the interests of a single group. Although the Almohad caliphs soon adopted a political ideology that was more ethnically Berber than purely Islamic, the polity that they governed continued to be defined in religious and millenarian terms throughout the period under discussion. The founder of Almohadism, Muḥammad ibn Tūmart, was officially a *mahdī* for all Muslims, not just the "*mahdī* of the Ṭargha tribe," as Marinid historians would later refer to him. Furthermore, the network of preachers and administrators that Ibn Tūmart and his successors set up across the Maghrib was still powerful enough to thwart any innovations that might be contemplated by a particular ruler.

Within a quarter of a century after the Almohad conquest, the city of Marrakesh became the capital of a western Islamic empire that stretched from central Spain to Cyrenaica. As such, it was uniquely poised to take advantage of the cosmopolitanism that its new geopolitical status allowed. With the capital and a few other cities of the western Maghrib, such as Sabta, Tlemcen, and Salé (Salā), now beginning to vie with Fez as centers of intellectual and cultural life, the perquisites of imperial power helped foster a climate of literary sophistication and intellectual inquiry never before experienced outside of al-Andalus. A significant factor in this development was the patronage of scholars by the Almohad caliphs—especially Abū Yaʿqūb Yūsuf and Abū Yūsuf Yaʿqūb al-Manṣūr. Both caliphs attracted intellectuals to their court from across the Maghrib and even from as far away as Egypt, Syria, and the Hijaz. In return for living quarters, stipends, and gifts, these scholars were assigned to teach at state-funded institutions, such as the school built by ʿAbd-al-Muʾmin in Marrakesh for the formation of Almohad cadres. Many of these immigrants also taught at congregational mosques in the main administrative centers of the empire, whose endowments and programs of study were modeled after those of the Masjid al-Qarawiyyīn in Fez.[5]

The intellectual awakening of the western Maghrib was also stimulated by a literacy campaign.[6] The Almohad promotion of education bore its greatest fruit in the Moroccan Sūs, the home of Ibn Tūmart and a major center of Almohadism. For the first time in its history, the Sūs became a source of notable scholars, particularly of the nativist (*shuʿūbī*) variety. This new tradition is exemplified by the figure of Sālim ibn Salama as-Sūsī (d. 589/1193), who translated major works on Islamic jurisprudence into the Tashelhit Berber dialect.[7]

Sālim ibn Salama's efforts notwithstanding, the Muslim belief in the divine origin of the Qur'an and the lack of an acceptable Berber script helped ensure that literacy would still be defined in terms of a person's knowledge of Arabic. This limitation led to an increase in grammatical and lexicographical studies of the Arabic language throughout the Almohad empire. Most centers of linguistic education were concentrated along or near the shores of the Mediterranean, where scholars in such cities as Tangier, Sabta, and al-Qaṣr ʿAbd al-Karīm (the present El Ksar El Kebir) taught the methodologies of the grammarians of Baṣra in Iraq and corresponded regularly with their Andalusian counterparts in Seville and Almería.[8]

Despite the rise of provincial centers of education, the city of Fez, long the economic hub of the western Maghrib, continued to dominate intellectual life in this period. Especially important was the role of its ulama (detailed in Chapter One) in introducing Ashʿarite theology and the new methodology of uṣūl. This process was taken even further in the Almohad era by Fāsī scholars such as Abū'l-Ḥasan "Ibn al-Ishbīlī" (d. 567/1171–2), who attempted to create a synthesis between *ʿilm al-uṣūl* and philosophical theology (*ʿilm al-kalām*).[9] In the first quarter of the thirteenth century, similar experiments in the application of uṣūl were made by Abū'l-Ḥasan at-Tujībī of Marrakesh (d. 637/1239–40), who proposed the outlines of a new "science of the fundamentals of hermeneutics" (*ʿilm uṣūl at-tafsīr*).[10]

We have seen in Chapter One how the struggle for Islamic universalism that culminated in the Almohad revolution and the rise of Sunni internationalism was present in Sufism as well. This consensus was reflected in the development of a Western variant of orthodox mysticism that drew heavily on the works of the great Eastern systematizers of Sufism, such as as-Sulamī, al-Qushayrī, and al-Ghazālī. Just as in the Mashriq, the most important publicists for this uṣūl-oriented Sufism were the composers of sacred biography, who sought to link the mystics and saints of their own region to the ṣulaḥāʾ of universal Islamic history. Of these writers, the most influential were the authors of hagiographical anthologies, who conceived of the awliyāʾ as quintessential *rijāl,* transmitters of Islamic tradition.[11] Although composers of the related genre of *manāqib* literature, such as al-ʿAzafī, could make an impact by promoting the example of a single famous saint, it was the *rijāl* collections with their tens or even hundreds of notices that established the paradigm for sainthood in the western Maghrib as a whole.

In Almohad and early Marinid Morocco, three *rijāl* works stand out for their impact on later generations. The reader has already been introduced to *Kitāb at-tashawwuf ilā rijāl at-taṣawwuf* by Abū Yaʿqūb at-Tādilī. Completed in 617/1220, this collection of 279 hagiographical notices was to become the most influential work of its kind in the Muslim West. Borrowing methodologically from the hadith-oriented Medina school of historiography,[12] and stylistically from the *Maqāmāt* of al-Qasim ibn ʿAli al-Ḥarīrī (d. 516/1122), at-Tādilī sought to promote a typified "theology of behavior"[13] that would establish a normative paradigm for sainthood in the region of southern Morocco, just as al-Qushayrī had done for Khurasan and the Muslim East.

In his study of sacred biography in Europe, Thomas Heffernan has pointed out that the vitae of saints in medieval Latin Christendom reflected a rhetorical dichotomy between an idealized and perfect "city of God" (*civitas Dei*) versus a worldly and corrupt "city of man" (*civitas hominis*).[14] This dichotomy, whose origins can be traced to the writings of Saint Augustine and the philosophical schools of Hellenism, was eventually mediated by the other-worldly paradigm of the "community of saints" (*communio sanctorum*), which exemplified the "city of God" in heaven. Since the same Greco-Roman rhetorical models influenced Islamic thought, it is tempting to conjecture that the Sufi community as an ideal type might also be conceived as a "city of God." This impression is reinforced by the fact that a distinct sense of the Sufis as a separate community of believers can be found in the writings of at-Tādilī and his contemporaries. These Moroccan *rijāl,* however, did not constitute a community that resided only in heaven. Rather, they are portrayed as living exemplars who reaffirm the values of Muḥammad's original community of Medina.

Thus, the Moroccan *communio sanctorum,* unlike its Christian counterpart, was more than just a heavenly ideal. Instead of merely reaffirming the corruptibility of human society, it hinted at its redemption by pointing toward an ideal community that was theoretically replicable because it had already existed on earth. This same motivation, and not just a desire for the accurate transmission of tradition, led the jurists of the Maliki school to base their legal methodology on the practice of the "people of Medina" (*ahl al-Madīna*) rather than that of the imperial centers of Syria or Iraq. Given the uṣūlī background of Almohad-era hagiographers, it comes as no surprise that they too sought to replicate this original "city of God" in their own place and time.[15]

Despite his widespread influence, at-Tādilī was not the originator of the Moroccan *rijāl* tradition of sacred biography. This distinction belongs instead to Muḥammad ibn Qāsim at-Tamīmī (d. 604/1207–8) of Fez.[16] Recently, eighty notices from at-Tamīmī's Kitāb *al-mustafād* were discovered in a manuscript dating to the year 813/1410.[17] An examination of this work reveals the extent to which at-Tādilī was indebted to at-Tamīmī in writing *at-Tashawwuf.* Both collections are organized similarly and include a liberal dose of elegiac and edifying poetry. The two books differ from each other mainly to the extent that *al-Mustafād* concentrates on the region of Fez rather than Marrakesh and is more often told in the first person. At-Tamīmī reveals himself to be a learned and well-traveled Sufi of the mercantile class who performed the pilgrimage to Mecca. He was also a disciple of the "Shaykh of Shaykhs" Abū Madyan and visited Abū Yiʿzzā at Adrār-n-Irūggān. Like at-Tādilī, he was heavily influenced by al-Qushayrī's *Risāla.* In a first-person anecdote at the end of his notice on Abū Madyan, at-Tamīmī brings this work to the Andalusian shaykh for a lesson, only to be told that he is too immature to appreciate its contents.[18]

Some of the notices that are missing from the extant manuscript of *al-Mustafād* can be found in a later compilation, *Jadhwat al-iqtibās fī dhikr man ḥalla min aʿlām madīnat Fās* (The Torch of learning in the recollection of the most influential notables of the city of Fez), by the Saʿdian-era courtier Aḥmad ibn al-Qāḍī al-Miknāsī (d. 1025/1616). Although this work is more of a local history and dictionary of famous personages than a true hagiography, it remains useful for the study of early Moroccan sainthood because its author made use of a complete manuscript of *al-Mustafād* then available to him in the library of the Qarawiyyīn mosque. It is particularly valuable for accounts about Fez's earliest saints, such as Darrās ibn Ismāʿīl and Abū Jayda al-Yazghī.

The third collection to contain information on the early saints of Morocco is *Al-Maqṣad ash-sharīf wa'l-manzaʿ al-laṭīf fī't-taʿrīf bi-ṣulaḥāʾ ar-Rīf* (The Noble objective and admirable goal in knowing about the ṣulaḥāʾ of the Rif), by ʿAbd al-Ḥaqq al-Bādisī.[19] Written in 711/1311, some forty years after the establishment of Marinid rule in the Far Maghrib, this work provides information on the saints of the Rif mountains between the time of Abū Madyan and the beginning of the eighth century A.H. (the late twelfth to early fourteenth century C.E.).[20] Al-Bādisī conceived of *al-Maqṣad* as a supplement to at-Tādilī's *at-Tashawwuf* and saw himself as continuing along the path of juridical Sufism laid out by eastern doctrinal specialists such as al-Qushayrī, al-Iṣfahānī, and Abū Ṭālib al-Makkī.[21]

The hagiographical anthologies of at-Tamīmī, at-Tādilī, and al-Bādisī contain 316 distinct notices about awliyāʾ Allāh who lived prior to the death of the Almohad caliph Muḥammad an-Nāṣir in 611/1214. Despite the problems inherent in such a "rexocentric" approach to historiography,[22] this date is a convenient cutoff point from which to assess the development of the paradigm of sainthood in premodern Morocco. Since a large majority (but not all) of these saints were Sufis, the information contained in these notices also enables the modern researcher to create a socioeconomic profile of Sufism in this period. In general, the study of sainthood as depicted in *al-Mustafād*, *at-Tashawwuf*, and *al-Maqṣad* opens a window onto the idea of holiness in one of the most exciting periods of Moroccan history. In these works, one can perceive a uniquely "Western" community of Muslim saints whose example reveals a distinctive blend of doctrine and practice.

Sainthood and Sufism in the Anthologies

In order to come up with a sociological profile of sainthood in the formative period of Moroccan Sufism, the data of the 316 hagiographical notices were entered into a computer-generated spreadsheet. This, in turn, was used to create several interrelated databases, following the example of Pierre Delooz in *Sociologie et canonisations* and Weinstein and Bell in *Saints and Society.* As a first step, the notices were examined for information detailing the individual life histories, approximate social class, and spiritual rank of their subjects. Other categories included dates of birth and death, patterns of residence, the extent of urbanism, ethnicity, or literacy, educational level, and occupation.

After the biographical portion of the survey was completed, a second set of categories was generated from this first set of data. These secondary categories, which often proved important to the conclusions of the survey, covered a variety of subjects, including (to name but a few) extent of travel, location of education and residence, types of miracles, and varieties of spiritual practices. Since much of the information in the anthologies was too standardized to give more than just a general outline of emerging trends, the categories were compared with each other as percentages of the total sample. Also, certain measures of statistical analysis, such as standard deviation, were left out because of the prior selectivity of the anthologies. The results of the comparisons are displayed as histograms, pie charts, and line charts in order to provide the clearest presentation of their contents.

The quantitative approach that is used in this chapter is based on the assumption that the most frequently cited categories in the anthologies are the most important to the perception of sainthood as conceived by the authors of the anthologies themselves. While few would dispute the validity of a quantitative approach to subjects such as education, urbanism, or socioeconomic background, objections might be raised when this method is applied to less "objective" categories such as miracles or spiritual practices. According to some modern esoterists and doctrinal purists, a sociological analysis of Muslim sainthood is futile because it fails to capture the "real" meaning of this phenomenon as expressed in Sufi texts. To this I would respond that the intent of the present exercise is to qualify Moroccan sainthood, not to quantify it. It is legitimate to fear that quantitative analysis, when applied uncritically, might overlook the depiction of complete persons and mistake statistical results for the whole reality. But no one who has read the previous chapters of this book should fear such reductionism. My desire is to bridge the gap between social and doctrinal interpretations of Moroccan sainthood, not to widen it further. Those who long for a more traditional approach should turn to Part II, where the doctrines of the Jazūliyya Sufi order are examined using Sufi treatises.

The historical social sciences possess many tools that are of value to the student of Muslim sainthood.[23] In the first place, quantitative analysis has been used for nearly half a century for the study of collective history. What are the *rijāl* collections, if not sources of collective history? Second, computer-based studies are predicated on the systematic comparison of standard units, both with respect to the phenomena to be explained and to the explanations proposed for them. Such standard units can also be found in hagiographical anthologies. These are the terms and concepts, whether tropological or otherwise, that appear repeatedly in the notices. Third, historical social science was originally intended to test theories against hard data. Sufi doctrinal treatises, while not "scientific" in a modern sense, are clearly expositions of theory. If the "hard data" that one finds in the *rijāl* collections prove to be different from what one is led to expect in Sufi treatises, this is significant because it would imply an epistemological break between what sainthood is "supposed to be" in doctrinal terms and "what it is" as a social phenomenon. Finally, although the sociological study of Moroccan sainthood might be criticized for proving the obvious, what appears obvious in retrospect is not always obvious in prospect. Unless one tests Sufi models of sainthood against the data at hand, how can one be sure that such models, created as they were by an educated mystical elite, have much bearing on the "popular" interpretation of Moroccan sainthood? This issue is relevant and deserves to be investigated.

The first impression that one gets from a survey of the three hagiographical anthologies is of the strong Arab flavor of Moroccan Sufism—a striking development at a time in which the demographic profile of the Far Maghrib was overwhelmingly Berber. The large proportion of Berbers in the sample, comprising a majority of 50.6% (160 cases), is no surprise, given the fact that during this period Arabs comprised a relatively small minority of the Moroccan population. What is surprising, however, is that the Arab or Arabized portion of the sample is so large—making up nearly 41% (129 cases) of the 316 hagiographical notices, a figure that is much greater than the actual percentage of Arabized peoples in the Far Maghrib at that time.[24]

This unusually high level of Arab influence may in part be due to the fact that Islamization transmits a significant Arabic cultural component.[25] Even in the absence of immigration from Muslim Spain or an influx of Arab tribes, Arab cultural traditions and values could still be transmitted to indigenous peoples through the teachings of hadith and the traditions of

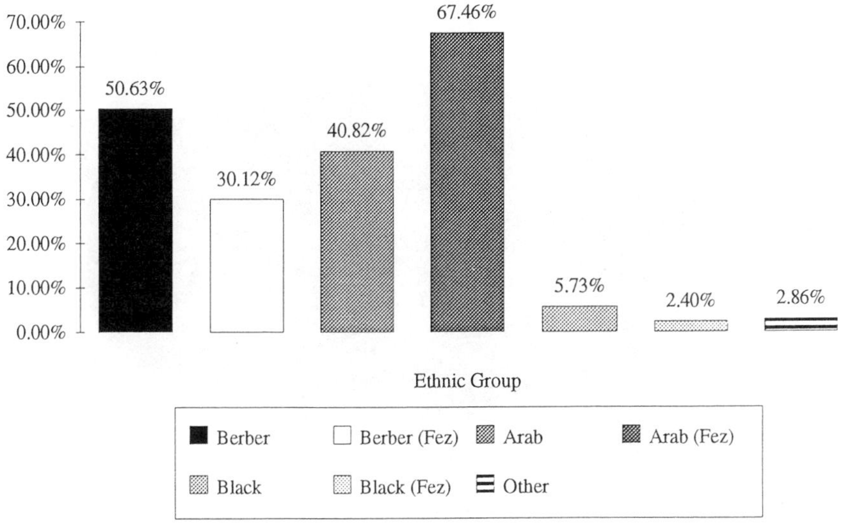

FIGURE TWO
Ethnicity of Moroccan Awliyā᾽

Muḥammad's Companions, which often had as much to do with the social customs of Arabia as they did with religious behavior per se. Pressure to conform to the entire complex of practices outlined in the Sunna would have been particularly strong after the introduction of the uṣūl method, which relied heavily on the traditions of the Prophet and as-Salaf aṣ-Ṣāliḥ as sources of precedent. During the Almoravid and Almohad eras, the emphasis on the hadith collections of al-Bukhārī, Muslim, at-Tirmidhī, and Ibn Ḥanbal—not to mention the *Muwaṭṭā᾽* of Mālik ibn Anas—provided an indirect yet potent means by which the ulama of the region could introduce the Berbers of Morocco to the cultural traditions of the Arab world.[26]

The importance of towns and cities to the acquisition of Arabo-Islamic culture is revealed in Figure 2, which compares the overall ethnic profile of the 316 notices with a sample taken from the city of Fez alone. The process of linguistic and cultural Arabization that occurs when a family changes its residence from the countryside to a North African city is illustrated by the fact that the Arab/Berber ratio is reversed for the *ahl Fās* when compared with the subjects of the anthologies in general. More than two-thirds (67.5%) of the native-born Fāsīs in these sources can be counted as "Arab" or Arabized, as opposed to only 30% who are Berber. Also interesting is the sharp decrease in the small yet noticeable number of people designated as

(n=177)

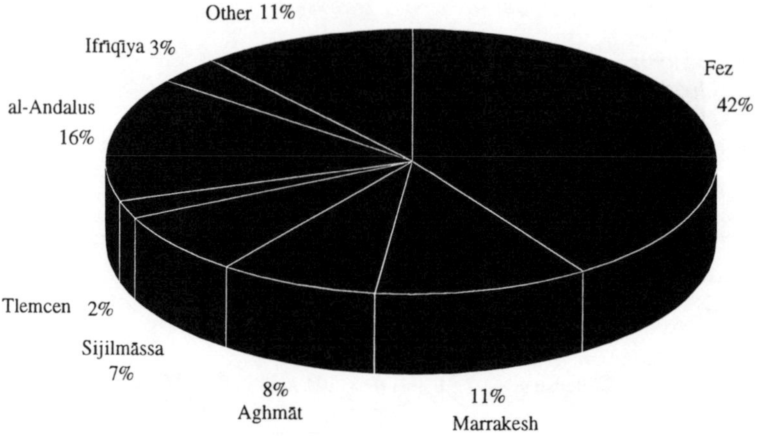

FIGURE THREE
Urban Origins of Moroccan Awliyāʾ

"black" (*ḥabashī* or *aswad*), a finding which is perhaps indicative of Fez's distance from the trans-Saharan trade routes and the slave-based oasis economies that supported them.

Fully 86% of the subjects in the anthologies (271 individuals) had some degree of sustained contact with a city or major town. A breakdown of full-time urban dwellers (177 individuals or 56% of the overall sample)[27] according to their place of origin can be seen in Figure 3, which further highlights the importance of Fez in setting the standards for intellectual and religious life.

More than half of the urban awliyāʾ in the notices were residents of either Fez or the cities of Muslim Spain, the twin poles of urban culture in this era. If one adds the new Almoravid and Almohad capital of Marrakesh to this picture, the total comes to 69%, or more than two-thirds of the sample. This data provides strong evidence that the Sufi traditions of Morocco were not only urban in origin, but were also linked to the cosmopolitanism of the main political and commercial centers of the western Maghrib. Also worthy of note are the caravan centers of Aghmāt and Sijilmāsa, which together provided 15% of the urbanites in these works.

Easy access to information and its means of transmission is crucial to the development of common paradigms. In order to disseminate a model of sainthood that was consistent with the teachings of Sunni Islam, juridical Sufis and ulama needed to locate themselves in places where they could easily pass on information about doctrinal developments in the East. The most logical solution to this problem was to build mosques and ribāṭs at sites where pre-established economic networks could be used as vehicles for information exchange.

Also relevant to the hypothesis of an urban ethos for both Sufism and sainthood is evidence that the rural ribāṭ played only a minor role in the training and education of most awliyā'. Surprisingly, less than 8% of the total sample (twenty-four subjects) were associated with a ribāṭ during their careers. Since the rest of the subjects of the anthologies—those who were educated outside of either urban centers or ribāṭs—had to acquire their learning somewhere, it must be assumed that their educational requirements were met by rural mosques, where instruction in religious fundamentals was the responsibility of local imams or preachers. This conclusion is consistent with patterns that are known to have existed in the Mashriq prior to the eleventh century C.E., where the imams of independent mosques were also the main teachers of Islam in rural areas.[28]

The significance of formal education to the Moroccan Sufi tradition is illustrated by Figure 4, which details the extent of learning acquired by Moroccan awliyā' prior to 611/1214. Seven out of every ten subjects (70.5%) in

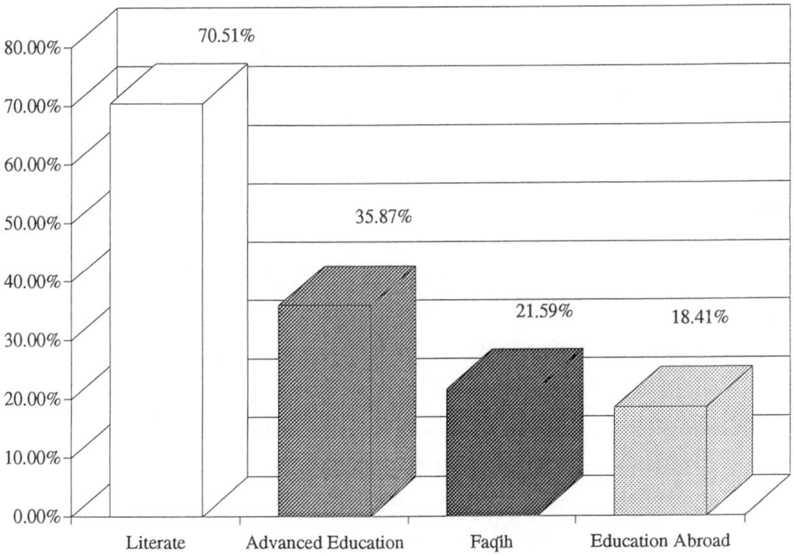

FIGURE FOUR
Educational Profile of Moroccan Awliyā'

these works can be classified as literate—a detail inferred from references to knowledge of the Qur'an, the acquisition of formal sciences such as fiqh, the authorship of books or poems, specific mention of written correspondence, and anecdotal references to reading itself. The most important point to note at the present juncture is that the high percentage of literates in these sources is, if anything, understated. In fact, literacy is so taken for granted by the authors of the anthologies that the subject is scarcely mentioned. Instead, illiterate saints such as Abū Yiʿzzā receive special notice because they are the exceptions that prove the general rule.

Also noteworthy is the fact that more than one-third of Moroccan awliyāʾ (35.9%) were the beneficiaries of an advanced education. This means that they acquired at least one of the Islamic sciences from an acknowledged teacher. Although scholarship in the premodern Islamic world often involved learning by rote, a high degree of literacy and a thorough understanding of doctrine were essential for entry into advanced courses. Students would have to be proficient in writing in order to make exact copies of their instructors' lectures. They also needed formal training in logic and rhetoric in order to participate in the debates (*munāẓarāt*) that were an important part of a scholar's education in the Almohad era.

The "orthodox" nature of Sufism and sainthood in premodern Morocco is confirmed by the finding that nearly 22% of the subjects of the anthologies (68 individuals) were *fuqahāʾ*. To some observers, this might seem misleading, since *faqīh* is an ambiguous term in the Maghrib, where it can mean anything from a fully trained jurisprudent to a practitioner of divination. A closer examination of the biographies of these *fuqahāʾ*, however, reveals that they were indeed jurisprudentially trained, a detail that disproves Ernest Gellner's thesis that the typical North African legist or "doctor" was hostile to the concept of sainthood.[29]

Gellner's position becomes even harder to maintain when one sees how frequently Moroccan saints sought a formal education abroad. As illustrated in Figure 4, fifty-eight of the 316 subjects of the notices (18.4% of the total) sought an advanced education beyond their home region.[30] Those who undertook a "journey for the sake of knowledge" (*riḥla li-ṭalab al-ʿilm*) in the Mashriq or Ifrīqīya were particularly influential in the spread of Sunni internationalism, since they were in closest contact with the intellectual currents of the central Islamic lands.[31] Equally significant is the fact that a small but significant percentage of Moroccan saints can be linked to uṣūlī doctrines. Twenty-five of these individuals (7.9% of the total) are mentioned as defenders of al-Ghazālī and his *Iḥyāʾ ʿulūm ad-dīn.* Another twenty-three (7.3%) were noted for their opposition to either local custom (*ʿāda*) or insular Malikism (*ʿilm al-furūʿ*), and fourteen (4.4%) promoted the rationalistic and hadith-based Sufism of al-Muḥāsibī. Taken together, these figures support the hypothesis, advanced in Chapter One, that scholars trained in *ʿilm al-uṣūl* were especially sympathetic to the doctrines of Sufism.

The importance of the pilgrimage to Mecca as both a religious obligation and a means of information exchange is reflected by the fact that sixty-seven subjects (21.3%) performed the Ḥajj even before the creation of an official Moroccan pilgrimage caravan in the thirteenth century. An even greater percentage (32.1%) traveled to Mecca from the city of Fez, a figure which may reflect the higher living standards of Sufis in this major commercial and industrial center. Travel for pilgrimage increases markedly after the Almoravid conquest of the western Maghrib in the late eleventh century. This change might reflect increased security within the boundaries of the new imperial state or a loosening of travel restrictions once the Almoravids pledged their allegiance to the ʿAbbasid caliph in Baghdad. The incidence of awliyāʾ Allāh making the Ḥajj drops off again between the years 519/1125 and 570/1174. This finding is consistent with an overall lack of security during the Almohad revolution. The incidence of travel picks up again after 575/1179–80, when the Almohad caliph Yaʿqūb al-Manṣūr put an end to the Almoravid-inspired Banū Hilāl and Banū Ghāniyya rebellions in the eastern Maghrib.

Long-distance travel for education or pilgrimage required considerable resources. Therefore, it is not surprising to discover in Figure 5 that a significant minority (13.7%) of Moroccan saints belonged to the upper classes of society. These are defined as urban and rural political elites, the scholarly elites of cities (such as the Ibn Ḥirzihim and Banū al-ʿAzafī families), and merchants who specialized in seaborne or long-distance trade. Overall, however, it is apparent from the 284 entries in which status could be identified that Sufism in premodern Morocco was what today would be called a "middle-class" phenomenon. Nearly half of Moroccan awliyāʾ Allāh (48% or 137 individuals) supported themselves as urban craftspeople, professional scholars, shopkeepers, or rural landowners. In other words, they maintained adequate livelihoods but did not enjoy large surpluses of

(n=284)

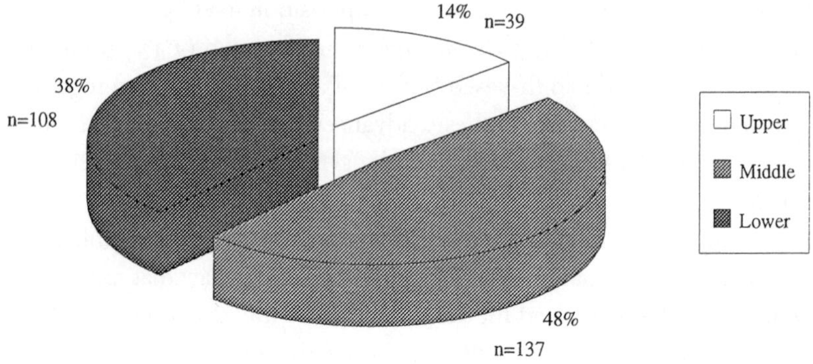

FIGURE FIVE
Occupational Status of Moroccan Awliyāʾ

wealth. On the other side of the coin, members of the lower classes—poor urban laborers, peasants, and pastoralists—made up slightly more than one-third, or 38% of the sample (108 subjects).

It is a truism of quantitative analysis that the devil in such figures is in their interpretation. Using the "middle-class" designation as a benchmark, it is possible to combine the above categories in two different ways and find clear majorities in either the "middle-upper" (62%) or the "middle-lower" (86%) class range. Where, then, should one place the "typical" saint and Sufi of the Almoravid and Almohad eras: in the upper or the lower end of the socioeconomic spectrum? The safest way to answer this question is to calculate at the arithmetical mean of the status sample of 284 subjects. When numerical values are assigned to each class (1 for "low," 2 for "middle," and 3 for "upper"), the mean of the sample comes to 1.76, which tells us that the "typical" Sufi of this period was a member of what could roughly be called the "lower-middle class."[32]

Exactly one-third of upper-class Moroccan saints (thirteen individuals) became interested in Sufism after experiencing a crisis of self-blame (*lawma*) or repentance (*tawba*). A few even went so far as to symbolically lower their status, such as the Almoravid amir who became a servant and financial supporter of ʿAlī ibn Ḥirzihim (see Chapter One), and Abū Ibrāhīm al-Khazrajī (d. 581/1185–6), a wealthy Arab merchant from Marrakesh who ended his days ministering to orphans. After hearing the "voice of God" commanding him to "lift up with a generous hand all who stumble," this ascetic freed his slaves, gave away all of his money, and devoted the rest of his life to the service of abandoned children and the poor.[33] The argument for a pietistic reaction against material excess in price-inflated Almohad Marrakesh is supported by the finding that these thirteen upper-class individuals represent fully one-half of all conversion cases mentioned in the anthologies.

A tendency toward social leveling can also be discerned in the pages of *at-Tashawwuf, al-Mustafād,* and *al-Maqṣad.* This can be seen in the downward declassment of certain wealthy individuals through the practices of asceticism and repentance and an upward movement from the lower levels of society via an advanced education and institutional connections. These reciprocal processes convey the impression that the social values of Moroccan sainthood reflected the "middle-class" mores of those who had the most to gain from the ideal of a meritocracy based on piety, good works, and education. Because most centers of advanced education were in urban areas, the less-affluent residents of cities such as Fez and Marrakesh were better placed than their rural counterparts to enjoy the advantages such a system had to offer. To make the most of the same opportunities, aspiring Sufis who lived in the countryside required outside support to maintain themselves during their years of study. Except for the lucky few who were born in the vicinity of a major ribāṭ, prerogatives such as these were available only to the rural elites. Significantly, apart from a few major exceptions such as Abū Yiʿzzā and Abū Madyan, one finds no evidence that the rural poor played a major role in Moroccan Sufism during this period.

It is also possible to conclude from the occupations mentioned in the anthologies that most Moroccan saints possessed relatively stable sources of income. This finding should not be taken to imply, however, that participation in Sufism or inclusion in an intellectual study circle was defined occupationally, as it appears to have been in later periods of Moroccan history.[34] On the contrary, the range of occupations originally performed by the subjects of these works runs the gamut from pimp to prince, and includes nearly everything in between.

According to the results of the survey, one would expect that the spiritual disciplines associated with Moroccan sainthood (see Figure 6) would reflect the ethical and pietistic values of juridical Sufism. It would be odd, in fact, if this were not the case, since one of the purposes of the hagiographical anthology was to provide a "theology of behavior" that was consistent with the values of uṣūlī activists and Sunni internationalists. The

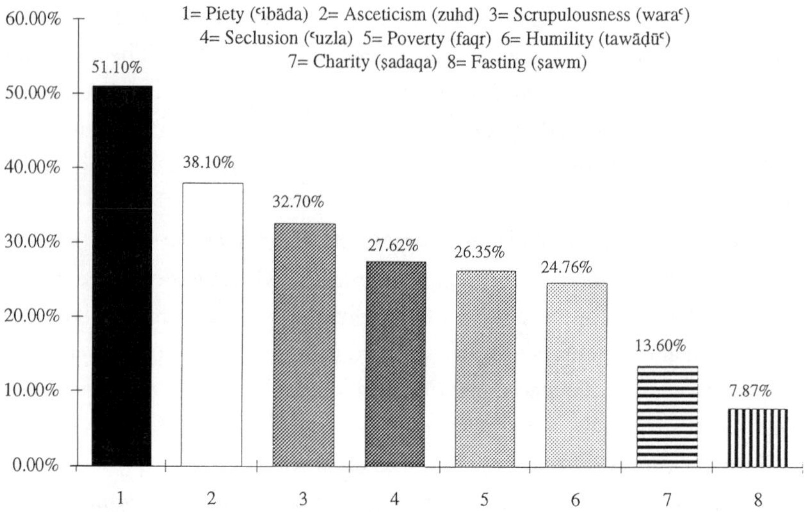

FIGURE SIX

Spiritual Practices of Moroccan Awliyāʾ

rhetorical character of this paradigm, however, should not mislead the reader into assuming that the spiritual practices outlined in Moroccan hagiographical literature were mere tropes and nothing more. Because they were real behaviors practiced by real people (including the non-uṣūlī), they can tell us much about the ethical and religious values of Moroccan Muslims in general. Indeed, such data might even provide a useful benchmark from which to assess spiritual practices elsewhere in the Muslim world.

Consistent with Weinstein and Bell's findings for medieval Europe, the sine qua non of Sufi praxis in premodern Morocco was piety (*ʿibāda*), the quintessential Qur'anic criterion of merit. What distinguished the subjects of the anthologies from ordinary Muslims, however, was the degree to which piety became part of their daily lives. The pious acts performed by Moroccan awliyāʾ Allāh involved much more than just the daily maintenance of prayers and invocations. Instead, saintly piety was a genuine vocation, through which the holy person's devotional practices reached levels that the ordinary believer could seldom, if ever, attain. The *ʿabd ṣāliḥ* of the western Maghrib did not merely recite the five canonical prayers; instead, he or she spent hours standing, lost in invocation and supplication. Concerned lest the unconsciousness of sleep should lead to the forgetfulness of God, the *ʿabd ṣāliḥ* would spend entire nights standing and reciting the Qur'an, leaving only the period between dawn and midmorning for rest.

Piety and the reverential fear of God also fostered asceticism (*zuhd*), which led the saint of Middle Period Morocco to disdain material comforts. These ascetic practices, however, were pragmatic in nature, and they usually did not involve the extreme repudiation of the flesh that was medieval Europe's legacy from late antiquity.[35] While asceticism was important to the Sufi concept of praxis in Morocco, economic privation (*faqr*) was relatively rare, coming only fifth on the list of mentioned spiritual practices. Overall, poverty was a by-product of world-transcendence rather than an end in itself. The main issue was again pragmatic: if salvation is the goal of the spiritual life, it makes little sense to waste one's time in worldly pursuits, which mean little in the sight of God and do nothing to advance the Sufi on his spiritual journey. It is in this sense that the traveler on the road to God can be called a *faqīr,* a "poor one." However, disinterest and denial are not the same thing. In order to liberate oneself from earthly concerns, the *ʿabd ṣāliḥ* of this period found it necessary to avoid all world- or body-oriented activities, even those that would lead to a preoccupation with self-denial. Whether a person spends one's time acquiring the world or casting it away, in either case this obsession with earthly matters would be a diversion from the goal of inner peace and salvation.

More characteristic of the ascetic life than economic privation was scrupulousness or pious caution (*waraʿ*). The quest for ethical purity was one of the hallmarks of western Islamic mysticism, and has been illustrated in detail in the previous chapters. Here, it is sufficient to note that scrupulousness seems to correlate positively with seclusion (*ʿuzla*). Once again, the motivation for this practice was pragmatic: if one is to avoid the sins of humanity, it is easiest to make one's abode a retreat where the sources of temptation can be kept at bay. However, seclusion from the world did not necessarily imply the avoidance of social concerns. We have seen in Chapter Three how Abū'l-ʿAbbās as-Sabtī came down from his cave outside of Marrakesh and tended to the poor who needed his protection. Even Abū Yiʿzzā, who hid himself away in the wilds of the Middle Atlas mountains, could not refuse the multitude who followed him to his mountaintop and demanded the services that requited them for their devotion.

The *via negativa* of asceticism and seclusion, combined with a strategy of world-avoidance that promoted ethical purity, were constants of Moroccan Sufism until the early modern period. Such pietistic individualism was far removed from the group-oriented and hierarchized "*ṭarīqa* Sufism" that characterized Moroccan Sufism after the sixteenth century. Rather, it evokes the example of the early Muslim ascetics who are the protagonists of al-Qushayrī's *Risāla* or al-Iṣfahānī's *Ḥilyat al-awliyā*ʾ. This seemingly paradoxical attempt to move ahead spiritually by looking back to the past is a reflection of the uṣūlī approach to tradition. Activist Sufis, uṣūlī ulama, and their allies sought to overcome an ethnically based and rigidly stratified Almoravid power structure by appealing to the more idealistic and egalitarian ethos of earlier days. The ultimate outcome of this movement (which was at times prone to excess, like most social dramas) provides yet another example of the periodicity which observers since Ibn Khaldūn have seen as a hallmark of North African history. Just as the Almoravids once consigned uṣūlī works such as al-Ghazālī's *Iḥyā*ʾ *ʿulūm ad-dīn* to the flames at the beginning of the twelfth century, so the Almohad caliph Yaʿqūb al-Manṣūr, by the end of his life an ardent supporter of both Sufism and sainthood, ordered the burning of anti-uṣūlī and anti-Sufi works at the end of the same century.[36]

The criteria by which the inhabitants of premodern Morocco judged potential saints to belong to a special (*khāṣṣ*) category of human beings (Figure 7) confirms the hypothesis that an important part of the saint's role in Moroccan society was to serve as a broker or intermediary. As one might expect, the most important criterion of whether a person merited the status of sainthood was the manifestation of evidentiary miracles, a sign long considered in both Latin Christendom and North African Islam as the ultimate proof of divine favor. Specific mention of paranormal phenomena (*khawāriq al-ʿādāt*) occurs in 163 (51.6%) of the individual notices. Another proof of divine favor was the occurrence of altered behavioral states (*aḥwāl*), which comes third on the list of special signs and is mentioned in seventy-one (slightly more than 22%) of the notices. These data make it clear that behaving religiously as an orthoprax Muslim, but in ways that went far beyond the norm, was likely to cause a person to be noticed as a potential saint. If paranormal phenomena were not yet part of one's repertoire, then an attitude of extreme otherworldliness might suffice as a proof of grace.

It was not enough, however, for a prospective saint to be merely different. Divine favor also had to be translated into proactive behavior for sainthood to be acknowledged. This point is illustrated by the finding that acting as a patron or intermediary, as Abū Shuʿayb did for the people of Azemmour, ranks second in importance among the signs of special status, occurring in ninety-nine (31.3%) of the notices. The remaining indicators

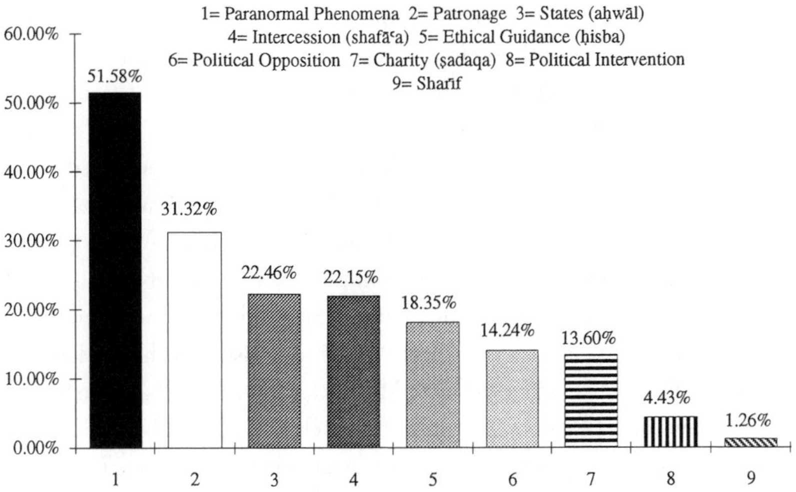

FIGURE SEVEN
Criteria of Special Status

of special status shown in Figure 7 also confirm the impression that divine favor in the Almoravid and Almohad periods was conceptualized as a concrete and visible form of power that could meet practical needs. These activities might include the walī Allāh's intercession before God through prayers and invocations (seventy-one cases, 22.2% of the total) or political intervention on behalf of clients (fourteen cases, 4.3% of the total). Combining both types of intercession (that before God and that before human authorities) into a single category yields a figure of 26.5%, thus moving intercessory activities ahead of altered states into third place on the chart. These findings confirm the hypothesis that success as a patron was important to the development of a saintly reputation.

In forty-five cases (14.2% of the total), Moroccan saints opposed the policies of political figures. As we have seen in the case of ʿAlī ibn Ḥirzihim, such intervention was often justified by the need to restore lapsed ethical standards or religious norms. The importance of socioreligious activism to the Moroccan image of sainthood is further confirmed in Figure 7 by the relatively high incidence of *ḥisba,* the correction of deviant behavior, which occurs in fifty-eight notices, 18.4% of the sample. Another aspect of ṣalāḥ, proactive social virtue, is nurturance or beneficence (*ighātha*). The importance of this characteristic to the Moroccan image of sainthood is illustrated by the incidence of charity (*ṣadaqa*) in the sample. This latter category comprises forty-three cases, 13.6% of the total.

One criterion of distinction that appears to have had little impact on the overall paradigm of sainthood in the formative period of Moroccan Sufism was descent from the Prophet Muḥammad. Only four of the 316 individuals mentioned in the anthologies can be classified as sharifs. Two of these are Banū Amghār murābiṭūn from Dukkāla, who were not mentioned as descendants of the Prophet by either at-Tamīmī or at-Tādilī and thus had a tenuous claim to a Prophetic lineage at best. Once the Banū Amghār are removed from the sharifian ranks, the sample is left with only two people, who make up a statistically insignificant 0.6% of subjects in the anthologies.

This last finding is enough by itself to demonstrate that the tendency of many social scientists to essentialize Moroccan sainthood is seriously mistaken. How can a paradigm of sainthood (such as that used by Gellner and Geertz) which is dependent on sharifian status have much heuristic value when descent from the Prophet is statistically insignificant in the very period in which the paradigms of Moroccan sainthood were formulated? It will be shown in Part II that the rise of sharifism, which began in earnest after the fifteenth century, was not inherent to Moroccan Islam, but was due to a combination of social and political factors. These included the increased Arabization of rural society following the Banū Hilāl and Banū Maᶜqil migrations at the end of the Almohad period, the pro-sharifian propaganda of the Idrisids, and an attempt by the Marinid dynasty to co-opt the sharifs of Morocco into their own circle.

On the other hand, it is indeed clear that the walī Allāh of Morocco served as an intermediary between ordinary Muslims and two antithetical poles of authority: the divine and the human. As we have seen in Chapter One, the Moroccan saint's connection with God was accepted by most religious authorities, including non-Sufis. This was because the walī Allāh's relationship with God was both sanctioned by the Qur'an and confirmed by a broadly based consensus of opinion.

Claiming that divine favor implied authority in the material world, however, was another matter. This aspect of the saint's role threatened the power elites of the time and thus had to be justified by pundits such as al-ᶜAzafī. Yet whether or not worldly power figures acknowledged the authority of the walī Allāh, the ordinary Moroccan was aware that by occupying an intermediate position between himself and those who controlled his destiny, the saint was well-positioned to act as a broker in several directions at once. In terms of Victor Turner's "anti-structural" model of sainthood, one could say that the Moroccan holy person created a renewed sense of "com-

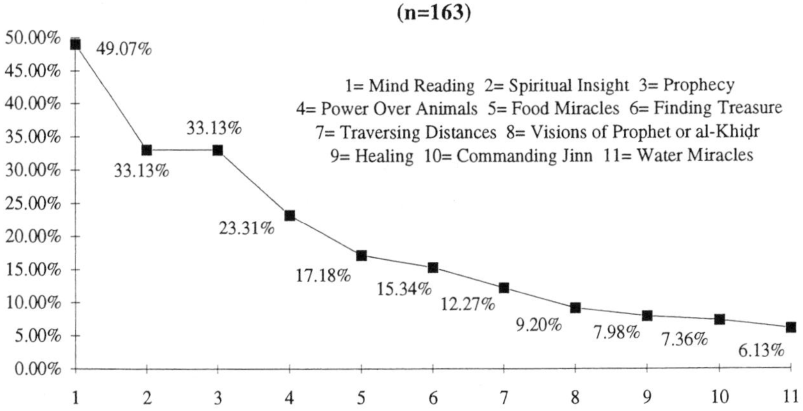

FIGURE EIGHT
Types of Miracles

munitas" by evoking a universal Muslim *umma* that transcended the distinctions of hierarchy and status.[37] This communitas is represented in the anthologies by the Sufi "community of saints" discussed above.

Since the Moroccan walī Allāh functioned as a broker or intermediary, it is not surprising to find that the most frequent miracles performed by the subjects of the anthologies have to do with what might be termed "epistemological capital" (Figure 8).[38] In the 163 notices where *karāmāt* are mentioned, nearly one-half (80 cases, 49.1%) involve the ability to read thoughts, a miracle which is described in the sources as *mukāshafat adh-dhikr*. This ability is followed by the similarly epistemological miracles of foretelling the future (*firāsa*) and uncovering hidden secrets (*baṣīra*), each of which makes up fifty-four cases, 33.1% of the sample. Surprisingly, one epistemological miracle that figures prominently in Sufi theoretical treatises, the reception of visionary guidance from either the Prophet Muḥammad or al-Khiḍr, appears much less often in the hagiographical anthologies, occurring in only fifteen (9.2%) of the notices.

What about the most well-known evidentiary miracles, those that impact the physical environment, such as the ability to tame wild beasts, traverse long distances, locate hidden treasure, provide food, heal the sick, subdue spirits, or find water?[39] Overall, these appear much less frequently than do epistemological miracles. When the occurrences of both kinds of miracles are compared, one finds that paranormal abilities having to do with knowledge are mentioned nearly three times as often as are those having to do with power over nature.

On the basis of this latest information, it is possible to conclude that in the formative period of Moroccan Sufism it was more important for a saint to be a person of knowledge than a person of power. Knowledge itself was power—the epistemological capital of the Moroccan saint was the source of the power that he or she exercised. Such holy "people in the know," whose esoteric knowledge allowed them to possess information beyond the grasp of ordinary human beings, could make things happen in the world around them in the same way that a stockbroker, being privy to market trends unknown to his or her clients, can profit from transactions in ways that might seem miraculous to the uninitiated. According to this brokerage or information-management analogy, the Moroccan saint, like any other broker, functioned in the social environment as if it were an epistemological marketplace where knowledge was the medium of exchange.[40] The holy broker ensured his reputation by maintaining a posture of indispensability—either by virtue of the information he possessed or by virtue of the networks (both divine and human) that could be activated. This meant that to be a "real" or effective saint (i.e., one who met the needs of one's clients) the walī Allāh had to know how and where to invest the "symbolic capital" of knowledge most successfully.[41]

The miracles that are mentioned in *al-Mustafād, at-Tashawwuf,* and *al-Maqṣad* can be separated conceptually into two categories. Epistemological miracles (such as mind reading, insight, and visionary guidance) seem to have been most relevant to the Sharīʿa-minded authors of the hagiographical anthologies and their Sufi readers. In general, the disciples of a sage tend to be more interested in the esoteric knowledge that gives rise to miracles than in the miracles themselves. On the other hand, the "power miracles" that are mentioned in these works, such as subduing wild animals, food miracles, finding treasure, traversing great distances, healing, controlling spirits (*jinn*), and finding water, are more relevant to the concerns of everyday life than to Sufi doctrine.

Life in premodern Morocco was both difficult and dangerous. Rainfall was unpredictable, and drought and famine were commonplace. One would thus expect to find frequent mention of food and water miracles in the anthologies. In the countryside, the precariousness of existence was magnified by isolation, the threat of wild or carnivorous beasts, the inability to supplement a subsistence livelihood with commodities that could be traded for food or tools, and unexplained occurrences of disease or madness. For those who suffered from such dangers, protection demanded the manifestation of raw power more than the reflection of metaphysical realities.

To better understand these two "worlds" of Moroccan sainthood, a second set of databases was created, this time focusing only on the thirty-three individuals designated by at-Tādilī as "great shaykhs and awliyā'" (*kibār al-mashā'ikh wa'l-awliyā'*). Because of their widespread renown as sources of baraka, it was assumed that these saints would more consistently reflect the popular image of holiness than would the sample in general. As expected, significant differences between the "great shaykhs" and the other 283 awliyā' Allāh were apparent from the outset. First of all, the ethnicity of this second group was overwhelmingly Berber, comprising 84.9% of the total (twenty-eight individuals), rather than 51% for the anthologies in general. Arab ethnicity correspondingly drops to only five individuals (15.1% of the total), a figure much more in tune with the demographic reality of the western Maghrib at that time. Equally suggestive is the fact that sub-Saharan Africans disappear from the sample entirely. This finding may indicate that their low status in Berber society prevented them from becoming major saints.

The incidence of urbanism also declines significantly when the great shaykhs are examined separately. While more than half of the subjects in the anthologies were urbanites, in this new group rural inhabitants make up 70% of the total (23 individuals). The rural background of the great shaykhs can also be seen in the sources of their education. Eleven subjects, or 33.3% of the total, sought their education in a ribāṭ, a number which makes up nearly half of the twenty-four individuals who were ribāṭ-educated in these works overall. This suggests that the ribāṭ's notoriety as a religious institution in Morocco may have been due to the fact that it produced a disproportionate percentage of well-known shaykhs. With this additional information, it is now easier to understand the persistence of Bel's "popular" or "maraboutic Sufism" paradigm. Without the contradictory evidence of a systematic survey, it might appear to the observer as if rural institutions were more important to the development of Moroccan Sufism than was actually the case.

The socioeconomic status profile of the great saints remains true to the picture provided by the anthologies in general. If anything, these latest figures are even more explicit in demonstrating that premodern Moroccan Sufism was a "middle-class" phenomenon. In the present sample, the "upper-class" category drops away to the point where it is represented by only a single individual: Abū ʿAbdallāh Amghār of Tīṭ-n-Fiṭr. The remainder of the elite is now replaced by members of the "middle class," who comprise over half of the great shaykhs and awliyāʾ (51.5%, seventeen individuals). As for lower-class saints, their percentage proves to be only slightly higher than it was before, comprising fifteen individuals, about 45% of the greatest awliyāʾ Allāh.

Although the spiritual practices of the great saints differ little from those of Moroccan Sufis overall, the voice of the people can again be heard when one reexamines signs of special status. The incidence of evidentiary miracles now rises from 52% to 91% (30 out of 33 cases), while intercession more than doubles in frequency, going from 22% to 54.5% (eighteen cases). In addition, charity replaces altered states in third place, now appearing as an important indicator of sainthood in 39.4% of the cases (thirteen individuals).

Clearly, the reputation of the great saints of premodern Morocco depended to a large extent on how much they could do for others. Although epistemological miracles remain important, their incidence declines perceptibly, losing approximately five percentage points in every category. More significantly, miracles having to do with the transcendence of nature (flying through the air, walking on water, or traversing great distances) now rise to second place, occurring in 36% of the biographies of the great saints (twelve cases). Thus, in contrast to the "people of knowledge" who typify premodern Moroccan sainthood in general, the greatest awliyāʾ Allāh were most often "people of power" whose potency was demonstrated in dramatic and visible ways.

Given the results of this survey, is it possible to conclude this chapter by proposing a modal profile of the "typical" walī Allāh in the formative period of Moroccan Sufism? While it is important to take into account the limitations of hagiographical anthologies as sources of data, one can, I think, answer this question in the affirmative. According to the information contained in *al-Mustafād, at-Tashawwuf,* and *al-Maqṣad,* the "typical" saint of premodern Morocco was a male[42] from an Arab or Arabized Berber background who spent much of his life in an urban environment, where Arabo-Islamic civilization played a major role in his education and moral development. As a result of this urban influence he was able to read and write in Arabic and was more inclined than was the general public to seek advanced schooling.

Since a significant minority of the saints in the anthologies are legal scholars, one can also infer that many of the ulama in this era had little or no objection to either Sufism or the Sufi definition of sainthood. This relatively liberal stance was reinforced by the fact that Moroccan Sufis and ulama belonged to intersecting social and intellectual networks and played similar roles in the importation and dissemination of knowledge. For this reason, the typical Sufi, like the typical scholar, had a cosmopolitan outlook on life, as well as a more than cursory awareness of the theological, philosophical, and juridical trends of his time.

In social status the typical Moroccan saint was a member of the "lower-middle class." He would have been born into a family of minor tradesmen, craftsmen, or small-scale rural landowners and, like the Jewish authors of the Geniza records of Egypt, would have religious beliefs that were characterized by an "undiluted, sober monotheism with a strong ethical coloring."[43] He would be exceedingly scrupulous with regard to what passed through his hands or into his mouth and lived simply and unostentatiously, practicing the virtues of poverty, humility, and charity. He was also likely to temper his religious devotions with contemplation, and often secluded himself from the hubbub of human society. He would particularly avoid involvement with officials of the state, both to preserve his reputation as an impartial broker and also to stress his ethical view of politics as intrinsically immoral.

The Moroccan saint was overwhelmed by an all-embracing awareness of the divine presence—"nearer than his jugular vein"[44]—which manifested itself through the granting of miracles and the power of intercession to those who were worthy enough to receive them. The most important of the saint's miracles were epistemological in nature. Although paranormal knowledge was a gift from God, making the most of it depended on an advanced spiritual training that was available only to a limited number of adepts. This type of epistemological capital was highly valued, since to make use of it one had to be a Sufi—an initiated member of a semi-institutionalized spiritual elite.

In contrast, the greatest saints presented an image that was significantly different from the model just described. In the first place, they were ethnically Berber and rural in origin, sharing much more than other Moroccan saints the culture and worldview of the people who venerated them. Also, they were less likely than were their peers to have been influenced by Arab culture. Once born in the countryside they usually remained there, often acquiring their education in rural mosques or ribāṭs. Their widespread popularity, however, did not mean that the socioeconomic status of these saints was any lower than that of their urban brethren. In fact, they were even more "middle class" than other awliyāʾ Allāh and their approach to religious doctrine was equally "orthodox."

The nature of the miracles granted the great saints by God was what primarily set them apart from their peers. Whereas the miracles of most awliyāʾ Allāh were epistemological, those of the greatest saints were more power-oriented and attuned to commonplace needs. These individuals were more likely than their peers to walk on water, ride rainbows, end droughts, subdue wild beasts, ensure bountiful harvests, and heal the sick. By serving their clients' needs and demonstrating that all believers had access to divine mercy, these holy men (no women were included among them) earned the trust of the masses and were venerated as sources of consolation and protection. They were thus ideally suited to provide an alternative source of authority in the absence of a strong central government and could disseminate their views to the widest possible audience.

PART II

The Paradigm Institutionalized

CHAPTER FIVE

Moroccan Sufism in the Marinid Period

The seventh through the ninth centuries A.H. (the thirteenth to fifteenth centuries C.E.), which witnessed the institutionalization of Moroccan sainthood in the context of the corporately organized Sufi order (*ṭāʾifa*, pl. *ṭawāʾif*), is a period that resists categorization. Modern scholars tend to view this so-called Marinid period of Moroccan history as a time of gilded decadence, in which the spirit of innovation that characterized the Almohad period was replaced by a tribally oriented realpolitik tailored to the needs of the Banū Marīn clan of Zanāta Berbers who ruled Morocco from their capital of Fez.[1] A semifeudal oligarchy of Berber warriors (the "shaykhs of the Banū Marīn") divided up the Far Maghrib as a patrimony in which land, tax revenues, and political influence were both alienable and concessible. This spoils system was maintained by an uneasy alliance of three major interest groups: Zanāta tribesmen related by kinship to the Banū Marīn ruling family, Arab and Berber associates whose loyalty was ensured through marriage or the prospect of legalized plunder, and the region's religious and mercantile elites, who acquiesced to Marinid rule in return for political and economic security.[2]

According to the Moroccan historian Mohamed Kably, the establishment of Marinid rule meant that an "ideological void" now replaced Almohadism. In return for protection, the Banū

Marīn appropriated the resources of Morocco through grants of tribal usufruct (*iqṭāʿ*) and an increasingly onerous system of taxation.[3] Their justification for these imposts, the defense of the House of Islam (*dār al-Islām*), was merely an excuse for cutthroat competition between themselves, the Nasrids of Granada, the Zayyanids (Banū ʿAbd al-Wād) of Tlemcen, and the Hafsids of Tunis. Jihad consisted of little more than ineffective counterattacks against Castilian and Aragonese incursions in Muslim Spain. Islamic law lost its vitality after the ulama of Morocco were co-opted into the Marinid system, and the rise of "maraboutic" or "popular" Islam eroded much of the authority that urban religious institutions still commanded.[4] Within this slowly decaying structure, the common people of Morocco lived out their lives as a "flock" that was cared for only to be exploited.[5]

When one views this period from the point of view of the ulama, however, things look a little better. Rather than viewing the Marinid political ethos as decadent, one might better characterize it as neoconservative. Although Maliki jurists were once again the arbiters of religious and social life, theirs was a Malikism that had been forever transformed by the methodology of uṣūl al-fiqh. The Sunni internationalism that gave rise to the eclecticism of the Almohad era continued to be maintained through the reestablishment of relations with the Muslim East, which had lapsed in the previous century because of the ideological and political threats posed by Almohadism itself. Although Almohad doctrine was now a dead letter, Ibn Tūmart's vision of an ethnically diverse Islamic society was still reflected in the increased access by non-Arabs to high positions in the religious establishment and the central government. Most importantly, a new religious orthodoxy was promoted in the Marinid era through measures that (for Morocco, at least) were innovative: the creation of state-sponsored study centers (*madrasa,* pl. *madāris*) and the implementation in them of educational programs that were based on standardized abridgments of theological, grammatical, and juridical classics.

The epistemological outlook of this period was formed in what the Moroccan historian Muḥammad al-Manūnī has called the "First Marinid Age," which spanned six decades from 667/1268 to 731/1330.[6] This was a time of peril for Islam in general and for North Africa in particular. In 656/1258 came word of the conquest of Baghdad by the Ilkhan Hülägü and the execution of the ʿAbbasid caliph al-Mustaʿṣim.[7] Compounding this calamity were the occupation by Crusaders of the Egyptian city of Damietta and the depredations of Castilian and Aragonese raiding parties in Muslim Spain. Christian armies roamed at will throughout al-Andalus as the Almohad state unraveled, eventually retaking Córdoba, Seville, and Valencia, the region's most important political and intellectual centers. These attacks struck uncomfortably close to home in 659/1260, when Castilian raiders sacked and burned the Moroccan city of Salé, taking more than 3000 women and children captive.[8]

The raid on Salé made it clear to the ulama that the Far Maghrib was even more isolated and open to attack than was the rest of North Africa. Well into the fourteenth century C.E., the inhabitants of the region maintained their livelihoods under constant threat—if not from armies or fleets of Christians from beyond their borders, then from heretics or predatory pastoralists within. The legist Muḥammad al-ʿAbdarī at-Tilimsānī, who performed the pilgrimage to Mecca in 688/1289, reports in his travel memoir (*riḥla*) that the formerly prosperous hinterlands of Tlemcen in western Algeria were so overrun by Arab pastoralists that pilgrims had to pay protection fees and journey with an armed escort if they wanted to pass through this region safely. Further to the east, the interdiction of seaborne commerce by Christian corsairs and bedouin raids on overland caravans reduced the port of Bijāya to a shadow of its former self.[9] Even the Banū Marīn, who tried to pose as defenders of Islam after their relief of Salé, were part of the problem. Historians of the period allude to severe food shortages caused by Marinid raids in the Rif mountains and on the Saïs plain of Morocco. The oleoculture of this region, which in Almohad times provided a harvest worth as much as 85,000 gold dinars, took decades to recover from the destruction of olive groves by Banū Marīn predators.[10]

To make matters worse, anti-Maliki sentiment and antinomianism were rampant in rural Morocco, despite the elimination of the Almohad state in 667/1268. In the High Atlas mountains southwest of the former capital of Marrakesh, the independent Maṣmūda amirate of Saksyūwa was to maintain itself in the region of Imī-n-Tānūt for more than two centuries. In the late thirteenth century, it provided a refuge for Abū Zayd ibn ʿUmar al-Murtaḍā (d. 712/1313), the only surviving son of the last Almohad caliph, who supported himself as a copyist of books.[11] The most important ruler of Imī-n-Tānūt, ʿAbdallāh ibn ʿAbd al-Wāḥid as-Saksyūwī (d. 762/1360–1), was a freethinking intellectual who was suspected of dabbling in philosophy, alchemy, and other forms of esoterism. Most scandalous to his juridical opponents was the rumor that he associated regularly with Jewish rabbis, from whom he learned the arts of magic and divination.[12]

The amirs of Saksyūwa were not alone in undermining the authority of Malikism. Near the Tizi-n-Test pass that linked the High Atlas mountains to the Sūs valley, the Maṣmūda tribes of Tīn Māl continued to venerate the tomb of the Almohad mahdī Ibn Tūmart, safe in the knowledge that their rocky stronghold could protect them from all but the most determined assault. The importance of Tīn Māl as a pilgrimage center increased in the thirteenth century as the Berbers of the High Atlas came to realize that the fall of the Almohads marked the end of their influence in regional affairs. Throughout the Marinid era, calls for a mahdist revival continued unabated in the Atlas mountains. The doctrines of this post-Almohad nativism were spread by wandering preachers called *ʿakākiza* (staff bearers), so named for the walking sick (*ʿukkāz*) that they carried on their peregrinations. According to the Algerian jurisconsult Aḥmad al-Wansharīsī (d. 914/1508), these Berber missionaries taught that Ibn Tūmart's abstract interpretation of the unity of God was incumbent upon every Muslim, that eating the food of non-mahdists or praying in their company was a major sin, and that one need not bathe after sexual intercourse.[13]

Also worrisome to the Maliki ulama were outbreaks of Shiʿite messianism in al-Andalus and Morocco.[14] In 666/1267–8, an Andalusian named Ibrāhīm al-Fāzārī proclaimed the millenium at Málaga. According to a noted Sufi of the time, al-Fāzārī rose in his pretensions from the rank of walī Allāh to that of al-Muntaẓar (the Expected One), and ended his life claiming to be a prophet with a new revelation.[15] By the time his revolt collapsed, large numbers of Maliki ulama in southern Spain had been imprisoned, tortured, or killed by his followers. Two decades later, on the festival of ʿAshūrāʾ in 686/1287, a Berber called al-Ḥājj al-ʿAbbās ibn Ṣāliḥ from the aṣ-Ṣanhāja aṣ-Ṣaghīr tribe of the Moroccan Rif arose and proclaimed himself Rasūl al-Fāṭimī (Messenger of the Fatimid). His rebellion in northern Morocco succeeded in capturing the port of Bādis and caused widespread destruction before being put down by Marinid troops.[16]

To combat these centrifugal forces, the Moroccan ulama sought the help of the Marinids as protectors of Sunni Islam. Rather than being co-opted by force, as Kably suggests, they instead traded their political support in exchange for the Maliki domination of institutional religion. From the time of Sultan Abū Yūsuf al-Marīnī (d. 685/1286), an "official," state-sponsored version of Malikism was promoted as a major ideological component of the Marinid regime.[17] Abū Yūsuf embellished this policy by rejecting the caliphal title of *Amīr al-Muʾminīn* used by the Almohads in favor of the less pretentious *Amīr al-Muslimīn* favored by the earlier Almoravids. This change of title symbolized the fact that Morocco had returned to the fold of Sunni Islam, and that its rulers once again recognized the ʿAbbasid caliph (now a mere figurehead in Egypt) as their titular sovereign. A second symbolic move was the establishment of relations with the Mamluks of Egypt, who had proclaimed themselves the guardians of Islam after Sultan Baybars defeated the Mongols at ʿAyn Jālūt in 658/1260. Contacts between Abū Yūsuf and the Mamluk sultan al-Mālik an-Nāṣir Qalāwūn (r. 678–89/1280–90) brought benefits to both sides: the Marinids recognized the Mamluks as protectors of the caliphate, while the Mamluks used the Marinids as intermediaries between Egypt and Castile.[18]

Under Abū Yūsuf's successor, Abū Yaʿqūb Yūsuf an-Nāṣir (d. 706/1307), cultural and political relations between Morocco and Egypt revolved around the organization of an official pilgrimage caravan to Mecca. The first of these caravans was an elaborate affair, which carried a brocaded cover for the Kaʿba and an illuminated Qur'an for the sharif of Mecca. In addition to five hundred of the best Zanāta cavalry, "protection" was provided by four Banū Amghār murābiṭūn.[19] On their return, the Marinid delegation took advantage of Mamluk hospitality by allowing the son of the deposed sharif of Mecca to seek asylum in Fez. This Moroccan interference in Arabian affairs prompted the current sharif to assert his independence from Egypt by pledging his allegiance to the Marinid sultan. Although this act infuriated the Mamluks, their hands were tied. They could neither punish the Marinids militarily nor attack Mecca, a holy city that had allied itself with a fraternal Sunni state. On the Moroccan side, this initiative enhanced the Marinids' prestige as protectors of the family of the Prophet and innaugurated more than four centuries of close relations between Morocco and the Hijaz.[20]

One of the most important cultural by-products of close relations between Morocco and Egypt in the Marinid period was the adoption of Eastern pedagogical techniques. The most visible symbol of this innovation was a reliance on abridgments (*mukhtaṣar,* pl. *mukhtaṣarāt*) in teaching grammar, theology, and law. The use of these abridgments increased rapidly after the introduction of the *Mukhtaṣar ibn al-Ḥājib,* an abridged manual of uṣūl al-fiqh, around the year 720/1320–1.[21] Although this practice was denounced by the Sufi poet and mathematician Ibn al-Bannāʾ al-Marrākushī (d. 721/1321),[22] who understood that a reliance on abridgments would lead to an overall decline in religious and legal expertise, the popularity of these works in rural areas rendered his objections moot. First used in Morocco by Maṣmūda ulama from the Sūs, abridgments were widely employed in the mosques and other centers of learning that had sprung up in smaller semi-independent polities such as Imī-n-Tānūt, Sabta, Tīṭ-n-Fiṭr, Bādis, and Asafi.[23]

Abridgment is the handmaiden of standardization. Thus, the use of abridgments was readily approved by the ulama, whose chief interest was to standardize the sources of religious and legal knowledge. It was not long before the abridgments that were used in rural Morocco made their way into the state-controlled *madāris* of Fez.[24] No fewer than eight of these boarding schools, all linked to the mosque-university of al-Qarawiyyīn, were built in the Marinid capital. By the end of the reign of Sultan Abū'l-Ḥasan (r. 731–49/1331–48), at least one madrasa had also been built in each of the provincial cities of Meknès, Marrakesh, Taza, Salé, Tangier, Anfa, Asafi, and Azemmour.[25]

The Maliki madrasa was different from its counterpart elsewhere in the Muslim world, in that it could not be maintained as a private endowment and thus could not be used to provide sinecures for specific individuals or families. For this reason, the Moroccan madrasa was almost always a state-run institution. The *waqf* that supported it was overseen by an administrator (*naẓīr*) appointed by the qāḍī al-jamāʿa of the city in which it was built. This arrangement made it easy for the Marinid rulers and their associates to maintain control over all aspects of the madrasa's operation, including the appointment of teachers.

Since the aim of the Marinid educational system was the promotion of a common epistemology based on legal reasoning, the study of jurisprudence was obligatory for all students who progressed beyond the elementary level. One can hardly underestimate the importance of this discipline to the formation of Moroccan intellectuals. Whether they were poets, historians, geographers, judges, government officials, or mathematicians, all were trained in juridical methodology. At times, they would even go so far as to apply jurisprudential logic to non-juridical subjects.[26] Although a certain flexibility of subject matter continued to exist in the absence of a fully uniform curriculum, most advanced students, regardless of their ultimate educational goals, studied and memorized the same introductory and middle-level works on law and the religious sciences. Inevitable offerings in law included the *Risāla* of Ibn Abī Zayd al-Qayrawānī, the *Mukhtaṣar* of Ibn al-Ḥājib, the *Mukhtaṣar* of Khalīl ibn Isḥāq (fl. after 805/1402–3), and (the only unabridged text) the *Mudawwana* of Saḥnūn.[27]

A result of the Marinid emphasis on jurisprudential education was a revival of juridical arguments against Sufism. Anti-Sufi polemics in the Marinid era tended to take two forms. The first, which was most prevalent in al-Andalus, involved the revival of Almoravid-era refutations of al-Ghazālī's *Iḥyāʾ ʿulūm ad-dīn.* In his memoir of court life under Sultan Abū'l-Ḥasan al-Marīnī, the Algerian governmental secretary Muḥammad ibn Marzūq at-Tilimsānī (d. 781/1379) documents the frustration of the uṣūlī ulama of Fez at having to listen to these outdated diatribes. In particular, he cites with relish a nightmare "sent by God" to punish the sultan of Granada after he had allowed himself to be convinced of al-Ghazālī's heresies by narrow-minded scholars at the Nasrid court.[28]

A more effective form of anti-Sufi polemic was directed against the mystical dimension of Islam in general. This movement was stimulated by the teachings of the theologian and jurist of the Hanbali school of law Ibn Taymiyya, whose students were influential at the Marinid court in the fourteenth century.[29] A principal target of their critiques was the phenomenon of rural Sufism, which proliferated during the unrest that accompanied the disintegration of the Almohad state. One of the earliest opponents of rural Sufis was the scholar Abū Muḥammad al-Fishtālī (d. 660/1261), who accused them of being "hypocrites who use religion to extort the goods of simple and credulous people, thus satisfying their thinly disguised cupidity."[30] A more politically focused opinion was voiced by the Fasi legist ʿAbd al-ʿAzīz al-Qayrawānī (d. 750/1349–50), who saw the Sufis of rural Morocco as a threat to the official ulama. Even pietistic and socially conscious Sufis could not escape his wrath. Indeed, their very excellence made such Sufis the most dangerous of all, because "their innovation, which consists of corrupting the beliefs of the commoners, is quicker than the coursing of poison through the body and is more harmful to religion than sexual promiscuity, theft, or any other transgression or sin."[31]

These criticisms should not cause the modern observer to conclude that Sufism was any less popular in the Marinid era than it had been under the Almohads, or that it had lost the support of the state. On the contrary, from the very beginning of their reign, the Banū Marīn sought to legitimize themselves by promoting popular as well as elite forms of piety. Umm al-Yumin, the mother of Sultan Abū Yūsuf, is portrayed by Marinid-era historians as a ṣāliḥa in her own right and was the disciple of a Rifian Sufi named Abū ʿUthmān al-Waryaghlī.[32] According to the hagiographer al-Bādisī, the Sufis of Baqqūya in the Rif mountains would gather three times a year at the rābiṭa endowed by this pious woman, who was the daughter of a tribal leader from the same region.[33]

Sufism also proliferated among the ulama during the two and a half centuries of Marinid rule. As in previous generations, a pro-Sufi stance correlated positively with support for the doctrines of uṣūl ad-dīn and uṣūl al-fiqh. The roster of uṣūlī scholars who combined their theological or legal vocations with Sufism included several prominent figures. One was the noted hadith specialist Muḥammad ibn Rushayd as-Sabtī (d. 721/1321), who served as an imam and Friday preacher in both Morocco and al-Andalus.[34] The courtier Ibn Marzūq (at-Tilimsānī), who was himself an adherent of the Suhrawardiyya Sufi order, mentions that Muḥammad ibn ʿAlī b. ʿAbd ar-Razzāq al-Jazūlī (d. 749/1348), a grandson of one of the most important disciples of Abū Madyan, served as a judge, an instructor in uṣūl methodology, and a preacher for no less than three Marinid rulers.[35] Finally, one finds in the annotated "curriculum vitae" (*fihris*) of the legist and historian Muḥammad ibn Ghāzī (fl. 896/1491) that this highly respected scholar saw no problem in admitting his attachment to a Khiḍrian Sufi tradition, whose chain of initiation bypassed not only the early masters of Sufism but also the Prophet Muḥammad himself.[36]

Many of the tensions that existed between Sufis and their exoteric opponents were mirrored in the ambiguous relations between urban Sufis, known collectively as *aṣ-ṣūfiyya,* and rural Sufis, called *fuqarāʾ*. Imbued with a desire for order and discipline derived from their legal training, the urban Sufis of Morocco were highly skeptical of doctrines and practices that developed beyond their control. This attitude can be observed in the writings of Ibn Marzūq, who grumbles about the failure of rural Sufis to adhere to the ways of the "people of knowledge."[37] This courtier also provides one of the earliest examples of the word *murābiṭ* being used as a term for rural Sufis. When describing an audience held by Abū'l-Ḥasan al-Marīnī after his conquest of Tlemcen, Ibn Marzūq notes the arrival of a delegation of *murābiṭūn* from the mountains of Chélif in Algeria, who scandalize the assembly by kissing the sultan on the head. When the sultan's retainers try to stop the leader of the murābiṭūn from repeating this breach of protocol, Abū'l-Ḥasan signals them to desist, saying: "Do not forbid him.

Rather, let him do as he will so that he may derive a blessing from it. His eagerness comes from his good intentions, and he will not spoil his religion."[38]

Despite the fears of jurists and urban Sufis, not all of rural Morocco was given over to ignorance. Several schools of advanced study were established in the countryside during the thirteenth century. At Nūl Lamṭa in the Sūs, a ribāṭ specializing in uṣūl ad-dīn and mathematics was created around a teacher named Abū Sulaymān al-Ḥāḥī (fl. 663/1264–5).[39] Other centers of learning included a school for Qur'anic exegesis in the Darʿa oases and another in the Haskūra region of the High Atlas mountains, which was founded by ʿAlī ibn Tarūmīt (Ber. "Son of the European Woman" [fl. ca. 721/1321]).[40] At Ribāṭ Tīṭ-n-Fiṭr, Abū'l-Ḥasan ʿAlī Amghār (fl. late seventh/thirteenth century), now called *raʾīs* (chief) because of his temporal authority as the master of northern Dukkāla, continued his ancestors' custom of instructing students in the Qur'an and Maliki law.[41] Other educationally oriented ribāṭs, specializing primarily in Sufism but also giving instruction in uṣūl-oriented subjects, included Ribāṭ Āsafī, founded by Abū Muḥammad Ṣāliḥ al-Māgirī (d. 631/1234) and Ribāṭ Aghmāt, headed by Abū Zayd al-Hazmīrī (d. 706/1306–7).[42]

The Mediterranean coast of Morocco was a particularly important source of intellectual activity. The expanding influence of Sabta, its regional capital and scholarly hub, under the independent rule of the Banū al-ʿAzafī family of ulama[43] stimulated an increase in Sufi activity in the Jabāla foothills and the Rif mountains. These northern regions, benefiting at the time from the latest scholarly trends in Fez and al-Andalus, seem for a time to have supplanted the previously dominant central and southern portions of the Far Maghrib as centers for the transmission of new ideas.[44] Most importantly, northern Morocco was the site of the earliest manifestation of so-called *ṭarīqa* Sufism in the western Maghrib. The first textual evidence of this arrival can be found in al-Bādisī's notice of the Rifian shaykh al-Ḥājj Ḥassūn al-Baqqūwī (d. first quarter of the seventh/thirteenth century), who sought to link the way of Abū Madyan with that of the Iraqi master Aḥmad ar-Rifāʿī (d. 578/1183).[45]

The Tradition of Abū Madyan

Although the Rifāʿiyya were present in Morocco as early as the beginning of the thirteenth century C.E., the dominant Sufi traditions of the Far Maghrib remained mostly regional throughout the Marinid period. This regionalism was to remain an important characteristic of Moroccan Sufism until the end of the Islamic Middle Period. As late as 787/1385, a list of rural Sufi orders drawn up by the Algerian Sufi and jurist Ibn Qunfudh mentions not a single "international" confraternity, but instead includes such long-established Maghribi institutions as aṭ-Ṭā'ifa aṣ-Ṣanhājiyya of Dukkāla.[46] Among the Sufis mentioned by Ibn Qunfudh, those who based their doctrines on the way of Abū Madyan were the most influential. As proof of Abū Madyan's importance, one might add that of the forty-six Rifian saints profiled by al-Bādisī in *Al-Maqṣad,* nearly one-third (fifteen subjects) were students of the "Shaykh of Shaykhs" or his disciples.

Abū Madyan Shuʿayb ibn al-Ḥusayn al-Anṣārī was born into a lower-class family of possible *muwallad* origins in the suburban town of Cantillana near Seville around the year 509/1115–16.[47] According to autobiographical traditions transmitted by at-Tādilī and Ibn Qunfudh, he was orphaned early in life and worked for his brothers as a shepherd until an overwhelming desire for religion drove him to study the Islamic sciences in Morocco. Stopping first in Marrakesh, he enrolled himself in the regiment of Andalusian soldiers assigned to guard the Almoravid capital during the reign of ʿAlī ibn Yūsuf ibn Tāshfīn. After completing this contract, he took the money he had earned and traveled to Fez, where he joined the study circle of ʿAlī ibn Ḥirzihim. Here he received the mantle of initiation (*khirqa*) into the Ghazalian tradition of orthodox mysticism and spent a number of years studying the works of al-Ghazālī, al-Muḥāsibī, and al-Qushayrī. While in Fez, he also studied under Abū'l-Ḥasan ibn Ghālib al-Qurashī (d. 568/1172–3),[48] a disciple of the Almerían shaykh Ibn al-ʿArīf, and the notorious *malāmatī* from Sijilmāsa, Abū ʿAbdallāh ad-Daqqāq.[49]

Although Abū Madyan received his formal initiation into Sufism at the hands of Ibn Ḥirzihim, there is little doubt that the greatest influence on his spiritual development came from the Berber shaykh Abū Yiʿzzā, whose rābiṭa he headed in Fez.[50] More problematical are later reports that he performed the pilgrimage to Mecca and there became a disciple of the famous Sufi of Baghdad, ʿAbd al-Qādir al-Jīlānī (d. 563/1166).[51] Despite the fact that Abū Madyan's teachings have been linked to those of al-Jīlānī since at least the fourteenth century C.E., none of the earliest sources on his life gives any indication that these two shaykhs ever met, or even that Abū Madyan made the pilgrimage to Mecca in the first place. According to Ibn Qunfudh, Abū Madyan attempted to travel to the Mashriq, but conditions prevented him from going beyond Ifrīqīya.[52] The earliest account claiming a connection between Abū Madyan and al-Jīlānī comes from a tradition transmitted by Abū Muḥammad Ṣāliḥ al-Māgirī. In this account, Abū Madyan says to his disciples: "I saw al-Khiḍr and asked him about the shaykhs of the East and the West in our time. Then I asked him about Shaykh ʿAbd al-Qādir and he said: 'He is the imam of the truthful and the proof of the gnostics. He is the inspiration behind gnosis, but his destiny is not to be physically present among the saints. I arrange the ranks of saints according to his direction.'"[53] This rhetorical use of al-Khiḍr to link Abū Madyan to ʿAbd al-Qādir al-Jīlānī may explain how he was considered a "disciple" of al-Jīlānī without actually having met him.[54]

By the time he founded his own center for sufi instruction, Rābiṭat az-Zayyāt (Hermitage of the Oil Seller)[55] in the Algerian city of Bijāya, Abū Madyan had assimilated all of the major traditions of western Maghribi mysticism. Under ʿAlī ibn Ḥirzihim he learned the ways of orthodox mysticism through the writings of al-Muḥāsibī, al-Qushayrī, and al-Ghazālī. The uṣūl-based methodologies of Andalusian juridical Sufism were also part of his training from Ibn Ghālib, via the latter's master, Ibn al-ʿArīf. The rural Sufism of the ribāṭs of Dukkāla was made known to him through the doctrines of futuwwa and the Nūriyya tradition, which he learned from his Berber master, Abū Yiʿzzā. The activism of the Moroccan *malāmatiyya* was also part of his background, via both Ibn Ḥirzihim and the enigmatic Abū ʿAbdallāh ad-Daqqāq. Both the biographical and the doctrinal record reveal that no other shaykh in this period had a more eclectic spiritual and intellectual formation than did Abū Madyan. More than any other mystic of his time, he stands as the axial figure of early Maghribi Sufism—an assertion proven by the popularity of his written works, the large number of his disciples, and a doctrinal influence that can be felt even today.

A factor contributing to Abū Madyan's fame was his accessibility to all types of people, from scholars to common laborers. This openness may have been a reason why the collective recollection of this saint became associated with the populism of the Qādiriyya Sufi order. Biographical sources reveal that during his lifetime Abū Madyan, like ʿAbd al-Qādir al-Jīlānī, was as well known for his public discourses as he was for his private teachings. During these public "sessions of admonition" (*majālis al-waʿẓ*), petitioners would ask him questions about mysticism, the Sharīʿa, or the religious sciences in general. In answering their queries, he would tailor his responses to his audience's needs, often coming up with aphoristic answers that were later assembled into a collection titled *Uns al-waḥīd wa nuzhat al-murīd* (The Intimacy of the recluse and the pastime of the seeker).[56] Abū

Madyan was also renowned for composing poetic odes on various aspects of Sufi doctrine. Many of these poems were recited in "audition" (*samāʿ*) sessions attended by the shaykh and his disciples.[57] Several of his more famous odes, such as *Al-Qaṣīda an-nūniyya* (The Ode in [the letter] *nūn*), are regarded as literary masterpieces and are still recited in the Maghrib.[58]

Abū Madyan's widespread notoriety and high level of social engagement did not sit well with the Almohad authorities in Bijāya, who viewed his activities with suspicion. When accusations of sedition by the shaykh's enemies proved too strident to ignore, the Almohad caliph Yaʿqūb al-Manṣūr summoned the now aged Sufi master to his capital for questioning. It was on this forced journey to Marrakesh in 594/1198 that Abū Madyan died in the western Algerian city of Tlemcen and was buried in the nearby cemetery of Rābiṭat al-ʿUbbād. In the following generations, his tomb became a major stop on the overland pilgrimage route from the Far Maghrib and was a symbolic bone of contention between the Marinid and Zayyanid states. The ornate mosque of Sīdī Bū Madyan, constructed next to the tomb by the Marinid sultan Abū'l-Ḥasan in 739/1339, stands today as one of the finest examples of Hispano-Maghribi architecture in North Africa.[59]

The way of Abū Madyan, as depicted in the shaykh's extant writings, owes an unmistakable debt to the mystical traditions of Khurasan. Particularly important was the ethical fraternalism of futuwwa, which was as central to Moroccan Sufism as it was in Khurasan itself. *Bidāyat al-murīd* (Basic principles of the Sufi path), a handbook for novices that reproduces Abū Madyan's teachings, contains numerous references to early masters of futuwwa such as al-Fuḍayl ibn ʿIyāḍ (d. 187/803) and Shāh ibn Shujāʿ al-Kirmānī.[60] Consistent with Abū Madyan's accent on fraternal ethics was his emphasis on social engagement. This outward orientation of ethico-religious expression is significant because it suggests that the "intensive interiorization" of the spiritual life, so often regarded as essential to the formal definition of Sufism, comprised only part of the ʿ*amal* (work) of a Maghribi saint.[61]

For Abū Madyan, the distinction between the outer (*ẓāhir*) and inner (*bāṭin*) aspects of reality was not understood to mean that interiority, being more "real" than quotidian concerns, was the sole criterion of meaningfulness. Instead, his way followed an Islamic "middle path"[62] between the sacred and the profane: a spiritual method in which all aspects of a person's life (outer and inner, public and private, worldly and spiritual) complemented each other as part of a single reality. Abū Madyan regarded the *ẓāhir/bāṭin* dichotomy as both a rhetorical device and a metaphysical truth. If Sufism is the essence of Islam, and if Islam is a way of life, then outer practice, *ʿamal,* must complement, and not oppose, inner knowledge, *ʿilm.* Giving too much weight to either outer practice or inner knowledge might upset the balance required for spiritual progress.

Abū Madyan's emphasis on balance contains an important lesson for Sufis in Europe and America today, who often stress the metaphysical at the expense of the practical. When metaphysical concepts from the pre-Islamic world, such as the outer/inner or world/non-world dichotomies, show up in an Islamic context, they do not necessarily reflect the esoteric perspectives of classical Neoplatonism or Hermetism. More often, their meanings can be found to have changed in response to the different epistemological and cultural environment of Islam. While a doctrinal parallelism might indeed suggest the existence of a primordial tradition, its appearance more often affirms the commonality of human experience rather than a true *philosophia perennis.*

A Moroccan Sufi's self-image in comparison with his coreligionists was different from that of his pre-Islamic predecessors. Hellenistic and late-antique intellectual circles tended to be highly esoteric and elitist, and the dominant ethos was a sense of alienation from common humanity:

> The pious are few, the wicked many; and this is a state of affairs divinely ordained, for God gave reason (*logos*) to all, but intellect (*nous*) only to some, and those who lack it are like the animals. To thirst after knowledge of God is to become alien to this world and to the opinion of the many, who will react in the best case by turning one to scorn, and in the worst by bloody persecution. So to keep the doctrine secret is a matter of self-protection as well as of piety: the circle of adepts must be small, and its members will certainly all be well-known to one another.[63]

Although similar sentiments have been attributed to Sufism, the above passage summarizes the world view of late-antique Egyptian Hermetists, not of Middle Period Muslims. In Islam, the concept of an elite collectivity of adepts conflicts with the egalitarian ethos of a universal confessional community based on a shared faith. Although Muslim society in North Africa was undeniably educationally and class-stratified, the normativeness of extreme social differentiation was not as universally accepted as it was in classical or late antiquity.[64] Instead, the paradigm of the *umma* as a community based on faith ensured that the ideal of egalitarianism would always be promoted—an ideal in which religious merit rather than intellectual sophistication was the most meaningful criterion of status.[65]

Differing concepts of self and other can also produce subtle but important changes in the referential use of language. When dealing with philosophers and mystics like al-Farābī (d. 339/950) and Ibn Sabʿīn, who accepted the epistemological premises of late antiquity, it is appropriate to translate the Arabic terms *khāṣṣ* and *ʿāmm* as "elite" and "common" respectively. We have seen in Chapter Three, however, that a distinguishing characteristic of Moroccan Sufism was the primacy of Sunna-based paradigms and the language of fiqh. In juridical discourse, *khāṣṣ* and *ʿāmm* do not mean "elite" and "common." Instead, they mean "specific" and "general." Although they clearly point to a division of labor, they do not necessarily imply a difference in status.[66]

The reinterpretation of concepts that occurs when one moves from the field of philosophy to that of law makes it problematical to characterize Sufis as "elites" in the commonly understood sense of the word. In the context of fiqh, the Sufi appears as one who is "singled out," but not because of any innate value as a member of the intellectual class. Instead, the Sufi is "special" because he or she has a specialized role to play among other human beings. It is in this sense that an activist Sufi such as Ibn Ḥirzihim or Ibn al-ʿArīf can be an esoterist and a populist at the same time. Since the God of the Qur'an judges all Muslims by the same criteria, the mere fact of being a Sufi does not, in and of itself, raise one above one's fellow believers or absolve one of responsibility to the community.

For Abū Madyan, the behavioral example of the Sufi shaykh was a matter of paramount importance. The spiritual master's relationship to his disciples was comparable to that of a sultan among his subjects or a doctor among his patients. The value of the true "knower of God" was that such a person could intervene in human lives and teach others the way to eternal bliss (*saʿāda*). However, a false or misguided shaykh might cause his followers to be lost in eternal sorrow (*shaqāwa*). Because of the shaykh's potential to cause harm, Abū Madyan insisted that all who claimed this rank be free of vanity or pretense. "Beware," he said, "of one whom you see advocating in the name of God a state which is not outwardly visible," for "the most harmful of things is companionship with a heedless scholar, an ignorant Sufi, or an insincere preacher."[67]

Like the ninth-century Sufi al-Muḥāsibī, Abū Madyan saw the ego (*nafs*) as the main obstacle to self-awareness. Because the *nafs* thrives on desire, the most effective weapon against it is hunger, for hunger weakens the desire for eternal existence that gives rise to the ego's stratagems. Essential to the systematic practice of hunger was fasting. Fasts performed by Abū Madyan and his followers included (in addition to the obligatory fast of Ramaḍān) abstaining from food during the months of Rajab and Shaʿbān, the hadith-based Fast of David, and a supplementary fast of three days per month that was done at an individual seeker's discretion. The most distinctive regime practiced by Abū Madyan was the *ṣawm al-wiṣāl,* the "fast of intimate union," a forty-day fast modeled on the austerities of Moses in the Egyptian desert and those of the Prophet Muḥammad in the cave of Ḥirāʾ prior to revelation.[68] The Sufi who performed the *ṣawm al-wiṣāl* would first repent all sins, take a bath, and pray two prostrations. The Sufi would then go into seclusion for forty days, abstaining from all food (including what was normally taken at night) and subsisting only on water. Constantly repeating the first part of the profession of faith (*Lā ilāha illāʾllāh* "There is no god but Allāh"), the Sufi would leave the retreat only to answer the call of nature, attend Friday prayers, and sleep whenever forced by exhaustion to do so.[69]

The purpose of the *ṣawm al-wiṣāl* was to instill in the disciple a firm reliance on the will of God (*tawakkul*). In later generations, Abū Madyan was to be memorialized by North African Sufis as the master of *tawakkul* par excellence. Among the more than 160 of his aphorisms that have survived to the present day, those dealing with *tawakkul* are second in number only to those having to do with asceticism. Closely linked to *tawakkul* were the related concepts of quiescence (*khumūl*) and acquiescence (*sukūn*). Attaining complete quiescence meant the cessation of all ego-motivated thoughts and desires, so that the heart would open itself up to divine inspiration: "The heart has no more than one aspect at a time, such that when it is occupied with a certain thing, it is veiled from another. Take care that you are not attracted to anything but God, lest He deprive you of the delights of intimate converse with Him."[70]

Abū Madyan's characterization of his disciples as "sultans," "amirs,"[71] and the "Party of God" (*ḥizb Allāh*)[72] firmly situates his doctrines within the tradition of futuwwa as practiced by his North African teachers and contemporaries. It also explains why his activities were viewed with suspicion by the Almohads. Since Ibn Tūmart also referred to his followers as the Party of God, the Mahdī's successors could hardly have been comfortable with a Sufi rival.[73] Ironically, these fears may have been exacerbated because the social doctrines of Ibn Tūmart and Abū Madyan were so much alike. For Abū Madyan, an aspirant's spiritual progress could never be separated from his social responsibility: "Sufism is not the [mere] observance of rules, nor does it consist of degrees or stages. Instead, Sufism consists of personal integrity, generosity of spirit, the emulation of what has been revealed, knowledge of the [divine] Message, and adhering to the way of the prophets. He who deviates from these sources finds himself grazing in the gardens of Satan, submerged in the ocean of lusts, and wandering in the darkness of ignorance."[74]

The mystic who embarked on the way of Abū Madyan was no withdrawn ascetic, lost in the contemplation of God while ignoring the injustices that beset the Muslim community. Instead, the mystic was a full participant in social life, who used discipline and detachment from the world to maintain a constant vigilance over oneself and one's neighbors: "The true Sufi must be neither jealous, egotistical, nor arrogant with his knowledge nor miserly with his money. Rather, he must act as a guide: not confused, but merciful of heart and compassionate with all of creation. To him, every person is as [useful as] one of his hands. He is an ascetic: everything is equal to him, whether it be praise or blame, receiving or giving, acceptance or rejection, wealth or poverty. He is neither joyful about what comes to him nor sad about what has been lost."[75]

ABŪ MUḤAMMAD ṢĀLIḤ AND THE INSTITUTIONALIZATION OF THE ḤAJJ

Few of Abū Madyan's disciples were doctrinal innovators. Instead, most were content to provide training for their students and to spread their master's brand of socially conscious mysticism from al-Andalus to Egypt. An exception was a Maṣmūda Berber shaykh from southern Morocco named Abū Muḥammad Ṣāliḥ ibn Yanṣāren al-Māgirī.[76] Although Abū Muḥammad Ṣāliḥ's tomb in the Moroccan city of Asafi remains one of the most important pilgrimage sites in the Dukkāla and Ragrāga regions, his historical significance lies in the creation of a yearly, Sufi-led pilgrimage caravan known as *ar-Rakb aṣ-Ṣāliḥī.* When his sons transformed this caravan into a full-fledged pilgrimage society, they created the most important institutional innovation in Moroccan Sufism since the Banū Amghār's establishment of aṭ-Ṭā'ifa aṣ-Ṣanhājiyya in the sixth century A.H. (the twelfth century C.E.).

Born into a prominent family of Banū Māgir Berbers from the hill country of southern Dukkāla, Abū Muḥammad Ṣāliḥ spent nearly twenty years in the Egyptian city of Alexandria, which he used as a home base for his travels in search of knowledge. While in Alexandria, he was a disciple of ʿAbd ar-Razzāq al-Jazūlī (d. ca. 592/1196), a prominent student of Abū Madyan and one of the first Moroccan Sufis to attract a following in Egypt.[77] The most interesting aspect of al-Jazūlī's teachings was his doctrine of the "first impression" (*al-khāṭir al-awwal*), a tenet that was similar to the *tenuia simulacra* of Epicurianism. The philosopher Epicurus (341–271 B.C.E.) taught that mental images bypassed the sense organs and penetrated directly into the mind. These "clear sense-impressions" provided a touchstone for reality by confirming the truth or falsehood of experience. In order to attain an advanced level of understanding, the man of wisdom trained himself to relate his thoughts to the "first mental image" that arose in his mind.[78] Although information about Abd ar-Razzāq al-Jazūlī's version of this method is missing from extant sources, its preparatory stages included fasting, seclusion, and meditation, disciplines which figure prominently in Abū Madyan's treatise, *Bidāyat al-murīd.*[79]

Toward the end of his stay in Alexandria, Abū Muḥammad Ṣāliḥ was struck by the possibility of using the institution of the pilgrimage as a means of increasing his people's knowledge of Islam. Since the yearly Ḥajj pilgrimage to Mecca gathered together believers from all parts of the Muslim world, it offered a unique opportunity for Muslims to interact with and learn from one another. This situation was doubly advantageous. It not only brought peoples from the periphery of the Islamic world into contact with the Muslim heartland, but it also fostered the standardization of interpretation that the ulama of the period so ardently desired.

Upon returning to Morocco at the beginning of the thirteenth century C.E., Abū Muḥammad Ṣāliḥ founded a ribāṭ on the coast of southern Dukkāla at Asafi, an ancient fishing village that had recently begun to be used as a port for the Sūs.[80] Shortly thereafter, he made this ribāṭ the headquarters of an ethnically based Sufi order which he named *aṭ-Ṭāʾifa al-Māgiriyya* after his own tribe, the Banū Māgir. Little explicit information survives about the doctrines of the Māgiriyya, except that its members conformed to Abū Madyan's teachings on *tawakkul* and that its disciplines were based on repentance and the remembrance of God.[81] Abū Muḥammad Ṣāliḥ's doctrines were apparently so similar to those of his Andalusian predecessor that his disciples considered him the principal successor to Abū Madyan in the Far Maghrib, even to the extent of minimizing the role of his actual master, ʿAbd ar-Razzāq al-Jazūlī.[82]

Although his followers regarded Abū Muḥammad Ṣāliḥ as a second Abū Madyan, officials of the Almohad state were concerned about the political significance of the Māgiriyya as a formal institution. Particularly worrisome was the order's use of symbolic signs of group solidarity, such as shaving the head and wearing distinctive clothing. This Māgiriyya "uniform" included a number of articles that were adopted from eastern Sufism, such as the patched cloak (*muraqqaʿa*), staff (*ʿaṣā*), pouch (*rakwa*), and soft felt cap (*shāshiyya*) of the Khurasani tradition. An item that appears to have been introduced by Abū Muḥammad Ṣāliḥ himself was a large rosary (*tasbīḥ*) of a thousand beads that was carried around the neck when not in use.[83]

While these symbols of institutionalization aroused the suspicion of the Almohad authorities, they had no objection to Abū Muḥammad Ṣāliḥ's creation of a Sufi-led pilgrimage to Mecca and Medina.[84] In organizing and maintaining this yearly caravan, the shaykh relied on the widespread North African network of Abū Madyan's followers and their disciples, who supplied and protected Sufi pilgrims in regions beyond the range of governmental authority. All aspirants to the Māgiriyya were required to perform the Ḥajj before being initiated as fuqarāʾ. As the number of his disciples grew, Abū Muḥammad Ṣāliḥ sent the more able of them to the towns and cities of the central and eastern Maghrib, where they joined Sufis from related groups and created support networks that provisioned and provided shelter for pilgrims traveling on their own. Aspirants to the Māgiriyya who did not have the money to finance their own pilgrimage were supplied with provisions by Ribāṭ Āsafī and traveled to the Mashriq in groups, spending the night in friendly bedouin encampments or in hostels that had been established for this purpose.[85]

According to *Al-Minhāj al-wāḍiḥ,* a memorial to Abū Muḥammad Ṣāliḥ written by the shaykh's great-grandson (ca. 696/1297),[86] the fuqarāʾ of the Māgiriyya wasted no opportunity to publicize their order. Forming a procession upon reaching the outskirts of a settlement, they would chant, "*Yā Allāh, ya'r-Raḥmān, ya'r-Raḥīm* (Oh God, oh Beneficent, oh Merciful)!" until they arrived at their lodgings for the night.[87] Often, groups of local boys or young men would follow the pilgrims, attracted by the commotion that they caused or by their displays of Sufi fellowship. These hangers-on would be invited to eat supper with the fuqarāʾ, at which time they would be introduced to the teachings of Abū Muḥammad Ṣāliḥ and Abū Madyan. Whenever possible, new recruits were encouraged to continue on to the

Mashriq as pilgrims. Upon arriving in Alexandria, Cairo, or the holy cities of Mecca, Medina, and Jerusalem, the Māgiriyya pilgrims would stay at *fanādiq al-Maghāriba* or *buyūt al-Maghāriba* (hostels or houses of the Westerners), which were founded by Abū Muḥammad Ṣāliḥ's son Aḥmad (d. 660/1262) during his eleven journeys to the East.[88] As chief administrator of the *funduq al-Maghāriba* in Alexandria, Aḥmad al-Māgirī appointed his own son Ibrāhīm (the father of Abū Muḥammad Ṣāliḥ's biographer), whose descendants managed the Egyptian terminus of the pilgrimage for several generations.[89]

By the time of Abū Muḥammad Ṣāliḥ's death in 631/1234, ar-Rakb aṣ-Ṣāliḥī had developed to such an extent that the shaykh's sons decided to open it up to pilgrims who lived beyond the confines of Dukkāla and Ragrāga. This strategy appears to have been conceived by Abū Muḥammad Ṣāliḥ's eldest son and heir, ʿAbdallāh (d. 651/1253), who directed his brother Aḥmad to set up centers for the assembly and instruction of pilgrims at Dādes, Haskūra, Sijilmāsa, Aghmāt, Hintāta, and northern Dukkāla.[90] After succeeding to the leadership of the ribāṭ in his own right, Aḥmad ibn Abī Muḥammad Ṣāliḥ decoupled ar-Rakb aṣ-Ṣāliḥī from the Māgiriyya Sufi order and created a separate organization called *aṭ-Ṭāʾifa al-Ḥujjājiyya* (the Pilgrims' Society). To oversee it, he appointed a separate network of officials, whose primary function was to facilitate the flow of pilgrims back and forth from the Mashriq rather than to guide disciples in Sufism.

By the time that Aḥmad al-Māgirī passed away in 660/1262, the Māgiriyya Sufi order and the Ḥujjājiyya pilgrimage society had become so fully integrated into the social life of rural southern Morocco that Ribāṭ Āsafī became the defacto capital of this region. This prominence caused several members of the Banū Abī Muḥammad Ṣāliḥ family to suffer imprisonment or destitution at the hands of the Almohad rulers of Marrakesh, who feared them as rivals for the allegiance of the Maṣmūda Berbers who made up the majority of Ḥujjājiyya pilgrims. However, the Marinid dynasty reaffirmed the status of this family after their conquest of Marrakesh in 667/1268. In this year, Sultan Abū Yūsuf al-Marīnī appointed ʿĪsā (d. 698/1299), the last and youngest of Abū Muḥammad Ṣāliḥ's sons, as governor of Asafi and its surrounding region. As for aṭ-Ṭāʾifa al-Māgiriyya itself, the recognition of its preeminence by the Banū Amghār murābiṭūn of Tīṭ-n-Fiṭr ensured that it would remain the most influential ribāṭ-based organization in southern Morocco.[91]

THE ḤĀḤIYYŪN OF CENTRAL MOROCCO

Apart from the Māgiriyya, one other Moroccan Sufi order in the tradition of Abū Madyan deserves mention. This brotherhood, which was called *aṭ-Ṭāʾifa al-Ḥāḥiyya* after its founder, Abū Zakarīyā al-Ḥāḥī (d. end of the seventh/thirteenth century), was based in the High Atlas mountains south of Marrakesh. Although the fuqarāʾ of the Ḥāḥiyya applied themselves to the study of Sunni dogma, commentaries on Maliki jurisprudence, and mathematics, their institutional exclusivism and fanatical allegiance to their shaykh earned them the censure of most ulama. Particularly worrisome was the fact that al-Ḥāḥī enjoyed "the complete allegiance of the masses" (*wa lahu ʿinda'l-jumhūr qubūlun tāmmun*) and that many of his followers believed in his ability to supernaturally punish those who criticized him or left his order to follow other masters.[92] Even the normally indulgent jurist and Sufi Ibn Qunfudh, who allowed that "good ṣulaḥāʾ" could still be found among the Ḥāḥiyyūn, felt it necessary to add the caveat: "But do not believe that all [Ḥāḥiyyūn] are alike!"[93]

Ironically, it was a member of this much-criticized group who was to inherit the mantle of Ghazālian Sufism that had been worn nearly two centuries earlier by Abū Madyan's first shaykh, ʿAlī ibn Ḥirzihim. This person was Aḥmad ibn ʿĀshir al-Anṣārī (d. 764/1362), a native of the town of Jimena in southern Spain who was to become the patron saint of the Moroccan city of Salé.[94] Despite the fact that the present-day cult surrounding Ibn ʿĀshir's tomb recalls the unorthodox reputation of the Ḥāḥiyyūn by attracting devotees from among the mentally ill and the lowest strata of Moroccan society, the actual "Sīdī Ben ʿĀshir" was a reclusive and intellectual figure who earned his living as a copyist of books.[95]

Ibn ʿĀshir spent much of his youth in the Spanish port of Algeciras (al-Jazīra al-Khaḍrāʾ), where he taught Qur'an recitation and followed a *malāmatī* Sufi known as Abū Sirḥān al-Ablah (the Simpleton).[96] Being warned by al-Ablah about the imminent Christian occupation of Algeciras (ca. 744/1343), he took the opportunity provided by this threat to perform the pilgrimage to Mecca. Upon returning from the East, he joined his sister in Morocco, where the two lived for a time among the Andalusian émigré community of Meknès. After seeing to his sister's marriage, Ibn ʿĀshir left Meknès and became a disciple of ʿAbdallāh al-Yābūrī (an Andalusian refugee from the town of Evora), who was the master of a state-funded *zāwiya* in the Marinid necropolis of Chella (Shālla) near modern Rabat.[97] Foregoing the support that the state provided for students at such institutions, Ibn ʿĀshir earned his own upkeep by teaching the Qur'an to young children and spent his spare time doing spiritual exercises and studying Sufi classics. When al-Yābūrī died, Ibn ʿĀshir moved across the Bou Regreg river to Salé, where he attached himself to the local rābiṭa of aṭ-Ṭā'ifa al-Ḥāḥiyya. The shaykh of this rābiṭa, Muḥammad ibn ʿĪsā, was a prominent disciple of Abū Zakarīyā al-Ḥāḥī himself.[98]

Once settled in Salé, Ibn ʿĀshir assembled a like-minded group of disciples and embarked upon the study of Sufi texts. To support their efforts, the shaykh and his students copied and sold many of the works that influenced their spiritual development. These included *Kitāb an-naṣā'iḥ* (Book of admonitions) and *Kitāb ar-riʿāya li-ḥuqūq Allāh* of al-Muḥāsibī, *Qūt al-qulūb* by Abū Ṭālib al-Makkī, and *Iḥyā' ʿulūm ad-dīn* by al-Ghazālī.[99] The sessions at which these books were discussed were informal affairs and Ibn ʿĀshir often downplayed his own level of expertise: "I am neither your shaykh nor your teacher of the books of the ulama. . . . So let none of you follow my example in anything that you do not first find in them. I am neither an exemplar nor an imam, but a Muslim."[100] Ibn ʿĀshir spent each morning commenting on the texts that his companions read to him. After these sessions, he would pass the remainder of the day in retreat, either in a garden near Salé's Sabta gate or at a spot behind the city's congregational mosque, where he would face Mecca and meditate.[101]

According to the biographer Abū ʿAbdallāh al-Ḥaḍramī, who became a disciple of Ibn ʿĀshir in 763/1361–2, the way of this shaykh was based on ten principles that were derived from the doctrines of al-Muḥāsibī. These included: (1) pious caution (*waraʿ*), (2) asceticism (*zuhd*), (3) God-consciousness (*taqwā*), (4) obedience to divine commands and prohibitions, (5) desire for the afterlife, (6) moderation in one's earnings, (7) observance of the rights due to God (*ar-riʿāya li-ḥuqūq Allāh*), (8) the avoidance of slander and backbiting, (9) scholarship in religion, and (10) the practice of ethics.[102] So great was Ibn ʿĀshir's emphasis on combining theoretical knowledge with ethical practice that he used to say, "Knowledge (*ʿilm*) without practice (*ʿamal*) is like a tree without fruit."[103]

To those who were not his disciples, Ibn ʿĀshir was a reclusive saint who was paradoxically sought out as an object of pilgrimage because it was so difficult to find him. Ibn Qunfudh testifies that the shaykh fled from his presence when they first met in 763/1361–2.[104] Since Ibn Qunfudh was then employed as a judge for the Marinids, Ibn ʿĀshir's reaction may have been due to his fear of exposing himself to the sins of one who passed judgment over others. When the Marinid sultan Abū ʿInān Fāris, who had come to power by deposing and eventually murdering his father, sought Ibn ʿĀshir's counsel in 757/1356, the shaykh went to extraordinary lengths to avoid meeting him.[105]

Ibn ʿĀshir's reclusiveness, however, did not prevent him from speaking out on matters of principle. Soon after Abū ʿInān's aborted visit, the shaykh wrote a brutally frank letter to the sultan, in which he criticized the deposition of Abū ʿInān's father, Abū'l-Ḥasan al-Marīnī, and condemned Abū ʿInān's lack of social justice. After disavowing any political motives of his own, Ibn ʿĀshir admonished the sultan with this warning: "Know that God watches over you at every moment in time, at every hour, at every breath, and at every blink of the eye. [Know that] you must encounter Him, that He will ask you about what you have done, and that His justice will envelop you. He will also ask you about the affairs of your subjects and what you have done for them."[106]

To prevent Abū ʿInān from falling further into error, Ibn ʿĀshir advised him to study al-Muḥāsibī's *Kitāb-ar-riʿāya li-ḥuqūq Allāh,* so that "perhaps through the baraka of this [book] God will enable you to acquire the fear of God and mercy, which will be the means of your deliverance." Finally, the shaykh gave the sultan some parting advice: "The Commander of the Faithful must remember that neither his servants nor his bodyguard will save him. Instead, they will flee from him on the Day of Judgment as he will flee from them. God will not grant you anything unless you maintain Him in your heart and act according to what He has commanded and forbidden you to do."[107] In a reply to Ibn ʿĀshir reproduced by the Moroccan historian Mohamed B. A. Benchekroun, Abū ʿInān accepts the shaykh's criticisms but offers the excuse that "all who hold power are unjust and despotic, are deceived by their confidants, and allow their intimates to carry them away with their passions."[108] Less than two years later, in 759/1358, the sultan would be assassinated by these very intimates, the "shaykhs of the Banū Marīn," who feared his attempts to replace the Marinid system with an Almohad-style centralized state.[109]

"Ṭarīqa Sufism" and the Establishment of the Shādhiliyya

Perhaps the most important innovation of the Islamic world in the twelfth and thirteenth centuries was the institutionalized Sufi order. Between 1150 and 1250 C.E., communities of mystics that had heretofore consisted of loosely organized groups of disciples following individual spiritual masters were transformed into corporate and increasingly hierarchical entities. In the Far Maghrib, this innovation first appeared in the form of ethnically oriented *ṭawāʾif* that were centered around important rural institutions, such as Ribāṭ Tīṭ-n-Fiṭr and Ribāṭ Āsafī. This increase in complexity correlated with the expansion of each ribāṭ's influence beyond its home region. Such was the case, for example, with the creation of aṭ-Ṭāʾifa aṣ-Ṣanhājiyya in the late twelfth century. What started as a parochial institution dependent on the support of a single Ṣanhāja subgroup ended as the center of a transregional Sufi order that recruited mystics on an ethnic basis from all over the Far Maghrib. A slightly different situation occurred with Ribāṭ Āsafī and aṭ-Ṭaʾifa al-Māgiriyya in the thirteenth century. Only a generation after the death of Abū Muḥammad Ṣāliḥ, the Māgiriyya's primary role as a localized vehicle for Sufi doctrine began to conflict with its secondary role as the institutional center for a trans-Maghribi pilgrimage organization. This discrepancy led at first to a formal division of labor and later to the creation of two separate institutions: aṭ-Ṭāʾifa al-Māgiriyya for Sufis and aṭ-Ṭāʾifa al-Ḥujjājiyya for pilgrims.

These developments are in general agreement with the model of institutional Sufism proposed by J. Spencer Trimingham in *The Sufi Orders in Islam* (1971). For Trimingham, the Arabic word *ṭarīqa* (pl. *ṭuruq*) referred to a hagiographically validated mystical tradition or "school" (*madhhab*), while *ṭāʾifa* referred to a hierarchically organized corporate institution that developed in a later period of Islamic history.[110] In Morocco, *ṭāʾifa* was the most common term used for the institutionalized Sufi order until the modern period, when the word *ṭarīqa* took its place. The problem with Trimingham's evolutionary schema, however, is that the use of *ṭarīqa* and *ṭāʾifa* elsewhere in the Muslim world was not as systematic as it was in Morocco. Often, the word *ṭarīqa* was also associated with institutional Sufism and denoted an "internationalized" network *ṭawīʾif* within a single, eponymously named tradition. It is in this latter sense that I will use the terms *ṭarīqa* and "*ṭarīqa* Sufism" in the discussion that follows.

Although the exact origins of ṭarīqa Sufism are unknown, the region of southern Iraq was important to its development. This was particularly true of Baghdad and its environs, which, in the century preceding its destruction by the Mongols in 656/1258, was a major source of social and doctrinal ferment. From out of this chaotic but generative environment grew three mystical orders that were to influence Sufism throughout the Muslim world:

the Qādiriyya, founded by the Hasanid sharif ʿAbd al-Qādir al-Jīlānī; the Rifāʿiyya, founded by the Hasanid sharif Aḥmad ar-Rifāʿī; and the Suhrawardiyya, eponymously linked to Abū Najīb as-Suhrawardī (d. 563/1168) but founded by his nephew, the futuwwa master Shihāb ad-Dīn ʿUmar as-Suhrawardī (d. 632/1234).[111]

At present no one knows exactly what caused these orders to institutionalize to a greater extent than did the majority of their predecessors. That this transformation was linked to the increasing institutionalization of futuwwa is probable.[112] That it was a direct outgrowth of the attempt by the ʿAbbasid caliph an-Nāṣir li Dīn Allāh (r. 575–622/1180–1225) to bureaucratize (and hence control) the futuwwa organizations of Iraq is less likely, because ʿAbd al-Qādir al-Jīlānī's successors had already turned the Qādiriyya into an "international" Sufi order before an-Nāṣir ascended the throne.[113] In addition, as early as the beginning of the thirteenth century C.E., adherents of the Rifāʿiyya ṭarīqa were propagating their doctrines in regions as far removed from Iraq as the Rif mountains of northern Morocco.

Yet despite the presence of Rifāʿī Sufis in the Rif, no organization called "aṭ-Ṭāʾifa ar-Rifāʿiyya" or "aṭ-Ṭāʾifa al-Aḥmadiyya" appears in Moroccan historical or hagiographical sources from this period. A lacuna of this magnitude is too important to ignore and leads one to suspect that the Eastern innovation of the "international" Sufi ṭarīqa had yet to take root in Moroccan soil. This insularity of Moroccan Sufism may have been due to the fact that the Sufi way had already been institutionalized by homegrown *ṭawāʾif* such as the Ṣanhājiyya and the Māgiriyya. It was therefore in conformity with previous patterns that when the "international" ṭarīqa first came to the Far Maghrib, it did so in the name of a Sufi from Morocco itself.

Aṭ-Ṭarīqa ash-Shādhiliyya, the institution named after the Moroccan sharif Abū'l-Ḥasan ʿAlī ibn ʿAbdallāh b. ʿAbd al-Jabbār "ash-Shādhilī" (d. 656/1258), was the vehicle for this innovation.[114] Since the death of Abū Madyan in 594/1198, no subsequent body of Sufi doctrines had been able to exert a dominant influence in either North Africa or Muslim Spain.[115] Even the Māgiriyya of Abū Muḥammad Ṣāliḥ, whose pilgrimage society provided a framework for the expansion of Sufi contacts throughout the Muslim West, remained a regionally localized institution that failed to gain many adherents beyond the confines of Morocco and al-Andalus. This was not the case, however, with the Shādhiliyya. Apart from the Qādiriyya and

Naqshbāndiyya Sufi orders, it is hard to find any other ṭarīqa that was to have such a widespread influence. By the end of the fourteenth century C.E., the network of Shādhiliyya *zawāya* extended from Iran to the Atlantic Ocean. In modern times, Shādhilī Sufis can be found in Europe, America, and Southeast Asia as well.

Despite his importance as the founder of a major Sufi order, Abū'l-Ḥasan ash-Shādhilī has still not been studied in adequate detail. In a way similar to that of his predecessor ʿAbd al-Qādir al-Jīlānī, whose writings sometimes seem at odds with the Qādirī way as expressed by his more recent followers, the record of ash-Shādhilī's life and teachings has been preserved in different and sometimes contradictory traditions, each claiming to represent the true "Shādhilī way." Much of this discrepancy can be traced to two competing versions of the shaykh's life and works that appeared in the generations after his death. The earlier and (paradoxically) more stereotypical of the two, which I will call the Egyptian tradition, is exemplified by *Laṭāʾif al-minan* (The Subtleties of grace), a hagiographic monograph that is primarily devoted to ash-Shādhilī's successor, Abū'l-ʿAbbās al-Mursī (d. 684/1285). This work was written by the noted doctrinal specialist and second successor to ash-Shādhilī in Egypt, Aḥmad ibn ʿAṭāʾillāh al-Iskandarī (d. 709/1309).[116] In response to the publication of *Laṭāʾif al-minan,* there arose in Tunisia a separate North African tradition of sacred biography that was focused more specifically on Abū'l-Ḥasan ash-Shādhilī himself. This sense is represented by the equally influential *Durrat al-asrār* (The Pearl of secrets) of Muḥammad ibn Abī'l-Qāsim al-Ḥimyarī, more commonly known as Ibn aṣ-Ṣabbāgh (fl. 720/1320).[117]

Although it appeared after *Laṭāʾif al-minan,* Ibn aṣ-Ṣabbāgh's book is the more reliable as a historical source. The value of *Laṭāʾif al-minan* as an unbiased source of data is mitigated by the fact that it was written as an apologia for the Egyptian branch of the Shādhiliyya. Its primary purpose was to legitimize the leadership of Abū'l-ʿAbbās al-Mursī (and, by extension, his successor, Ibn ʿAṭāʾillāh) by showing that al-Mursī's teachings were in agreement with those of ash-Shādhilī himself. Ash-Shādhilī thus appears in *Laṭāʾif al-minan* more as a trope than as a living saint, and his biography is devoid of most historical detail. For Ibn aṣ-Ṣabbāgh, however, who follows a more anecdotal style based on the North African *manāqib* tradition, ash-Shādhilī is both an active spiritual master and a political leader. In *Durrat al-asrār* he appears as a strong-willed and decisive patron, dangerous to his enemies yet protective of his clients. Perhaps most importantly, he shows intense pride in the nobility of his Prophetic ancestry and employs it to great effect in the antithetical worlds of politics and the spirit.

The problem of linking ash-Shādhilī to the historically verifiable record of Sufism in late-Almohad Morocco can be solved by comparing *Laṭāʾif al-minan* and *Durrat al-asrār* against a hitherto unnoticed work: *Shajarat al-irshād* (The Tree of guidance) by Ḥasan ibn ʿAlī Wafāʾ (d. mid-ninth/fifteenth century). The author of this annotated spiritual genealogy (*nasab*) was a member of the Egyptian Wafāʾiyya branch of the Shādhiliyya who additionally maintained long-standing familial ties to the Rifāʿiyya Sufi order.[118] Both *Laṭāʾif al-minan* and *Durrat al-asrār* claim that as a youth ash-Shādhilī set out from Tunis in order to find the axial saint (*quṭb*) of his age. During this journey, he is said to have joined the circle of students around Abū'l-Fatḥ al-Wāsiṭī (d. ca. 642/1244–5), who is credited with establishing the Rifāʿiyya Sufi order as an important institutional presence in Egypt. Although most authors place ash-Shādhilī's encounter with al-Wāsiṭī in Iraq, it is more likely that this occurred in Alexandria, where a so-called Ribāṭ al-Wāsiṭī exists to this day.[119] Among Western scholars of Sufism, only Trimingham has remarked on a possible doctrinal connection between the Rifāʿiyya and Shādhiliyya orders.[120] In *Shajarat al-irshād* Ibn ʿAli Wafāʾ claims that al-Wasiṭī encouraged ash-Shādhilī to return to the Far Maghrib and to learn from Rifāʿī Sufis there. One of these was a sharif from ash-Shādhilī's home region of Ghumāra named ʿAbd as-Salām ibn Mashīsh (d. ca. 625/1228). Today the patron saint of Moroccan Sufism, "Mūlāy ʿAbd as-Salām" was to earn lasting fame as ash-Shādhilī's master of spiritual awakening (*shaykh al-fatḥ*).[121]

Ibn ʿAli Wafāʾ illustrates Ibn Mashīsh's links to the Rifāʿiyya by adding information about the latter's Sufi *nasab* not found in other sources. Most accounts maintain that ʿAbd as-Salām was the disciple of a fellow Moroccan sharif known as ʿAbd ar-Raḥmān al-ʿAṭṭār al-Madanī, a spice merchant from the city of Sabta.[122] Al-Madanī's spiritual master was Taqī ad-Dīn al-Fuqayyir, who hailed from the Iranian city of Nahrawān but lived near Wāsiṭ in Iraq, the home city of Abū'l-Fatḥ al-Wāsiṭī. Taqī ad-Dīn apparently had two spiritual lineages: one involving an Iraqi line that is commonly cited as his main *nasab* in the Maghrib, and another, now forgotten, leading to Aḥmad ar-Rifāʿī himself.[123] Another of al-Madanī's spiritual masters, the Andalusian Sufi Jaʿfar ibn ʿAbdallāh al-Khuzāʿī, is also mentioned by Ibn Wafāʾ as a shaykh of Rifāʿiyya.[124]

In Ibn aṣ-Ṣabbāgh's *Durrat al-asrār,* ash-Shādhilī, like his predecessor Aḥmad ar-Rifāʿī, uses his status as a descendant of the Prophet Muḥammad to establish an aura of power and authority for himself. Other means that he uses to stress his authority include composing prayers on behalf of the Prophet, whom he pointedly refers to as "my ancestor" (*jaddī*). He also relies on proofs of intimacy with God, such as quasi-prophetic conversations (*munājāt*) with the divinity.[125] In a typical account, ash-Shādhilī's right of spiritual authority is confirmed by Ibn Mashīsh's eldest son Muḥammad, who tells him: "Oh ʿAlī, you wanted to ask the shaykh about the greatest name of God, yet it is not your affair to ask about the greatest name. It is rather your affair to *be* the greatest name of God!"[126]

Ash-Shādhilī also used his status as a descendant of the Prophet to gain the upper hand over political opponents. In an account that does not appear in Ibn ʿAṭāʾillāh's *Laṭāʾif al-minan,* Ibn aṣ-Ṣabbāgh relates that the shaykh established close relations with the leaders of the Banū Hilāl bedouins of Egypt's Western Desert. Putting his baraka to the test, these Arab shaykhs asked ash-Shādhilī to intercede for them in a tax dispute with the Ayyubid sultan. When the shaykh went to Alexandria, a letter arrived from his nemesis Ibn al-Barrāʾ, the qāḍī al-jamāʿa of Tunis, who accused him of being a Fatimid pretender. Fearing for his throne, the sultan ordered ash-Shādhilī to be confined in Alexandria until he could be brought to Cairo for questioning. Rather than submitting to this injunction, the shaykh proceeded directly to the Cairo citadel. After an acrimonious audience in which the sultan repeated Ibn al-Barrāʾ's charges, ash-Shādhilī stalked out of the audience chamber, uttering the ominous imprecation, "The tribes, you, and I are all in the hands of God!" Upon hearing these words, the sultan was struck speechless and begged the shaykh's pardon. From this point forward, ash-Shādhilī was treated with the utmost respect by the sultan and his Banū Hilāl clients were exempted from their taxes. Later, the sultan gave the shaykh the use of spacious quarters in a guard tower on Alexandria's defensive wall. This ribāṭ, which included a mosque as well as living quarters for ash-Shādhilī's family and disciples, was to remain his headquarters for the rest of his life.[127]

The outlines of ash-Shādhilī's career have been detailed before and need not be repeated at this time.[128] What is important, however, is to recall the links between the order he founded and the wider tradition of Moroccan Sufism. An important step in establishing the Shādhiliyya in the Far Maghrib was taken when the shaykh inherited the title of Axis of the Age (*quṭb az-zamān*) from the Egyptian Sufi Abū'l-Ḥajjāj al-Uqṣūrī (d. 642/1244). Abū'l-Ḥajjāj, who presided over a ribāṭ inside of the ancient temple of Amon at Luxor, had (like his Moroccan contemporary Abū Muḥammad Ṣāliḥ) learned the doctrines of Abū Madyan from ʿAbd ar-Razzāq al-Jazūlī.[129] This highly popular shaykh was an influential teacher of North African and Andalusian mystics, who would visit him on their way to Mecca and Medina.[130] By assuming the mantle of Abū'l-Ḥajjāj in a ceremony of the "investiture of axis-hood" (*bayʿat al-quṭba*) attended by many of the latter's disciples, ash-Shādhilī identified himself with Abū Madyan's legacy and replaced al-Uqṣūrī as a resource for Moroccan and Andalusian pilgrims making their way to the Mashriq.[131]

Ash-Shādhilī's appropriation of the so-called Midianite Mantle (*al-khirqa al-Madyaniyya*), the legacy of Abū Madyan, from Abū'l-Ḥajjāj al-Uqṣūrī was more than just symbolic. By doing so, he assumed responsibility for North African Sufi pilgrims on their journey from Cairo to Mecca. His institutional role thus complemented that of the Ḥujjājiyya pilgrimage society of Morocco, which guaranteed the safety of Maghribi pilgrims as far as Egypt. Inheriting al-Uqṣūrī's axis-hood also meant that ash-Shādhilī took on all of the other obligations that wearing *al-khirqa al-Madyaniyya* implied. These included responsibility for the followers of the way of Abū Madyan who visited or resided in Egypt.

Ash-Shādhilī performed the pilgrimage to Mecca every two years, with an entourage that often numbered several hundred people.[132] Claiming that his "hand was over his disciples wherever they may be," he extended his protection to anyone who wished to travel with him.[133] For ash-Shādhilī, the Sufi shaykhs exercised comprehensive authority over their followers as "kings in the guise of the poor." They also commanded their own "armies" of Sufi adepts (*ʿasākir awliyāʾ Allāh*) and non-Sufi allies (*anṣār*).[134] Also like a worldly ruler, ash-Shādhilī saw himself as duty-bound to recompense his followers by assisting them with the "wealth in God" (*al-ghināʾ bi'llāh*) that came into his hands. It was for this reason that he protected the pilgrimage caravan to Mecca and met regularly with the sultan of Egypt to arrange logistical details.

During his early years in Tunis, ash-Shādhilī sought to ensure the survival of his nascent order by recruiting well-connected citizens as disciples. These included a brother of the Hafsid sultan Abū Zakarīyā (d. 647/1249), the secretary of the qāḍī al-jamāʿa of Tunis, and the administrators of the Hafsid treasury.[135] Formal relations were also established between ash-

Shādhilī and the leaders of at least two Berber villages, as well as with other Sufis in the environs of the Hafsid capital.[136] The shaykh continued this policy even after moving to Egypt. First, to protect himself against attacks from exoteric jurists, he proclaimed a state of "brotherhood" between himself and the grand mufti of Egypt. Later, he arranged for his daughter ʿArīfat al-Khayr to marry the noted Egyptian Sufi ʿAlī ad-Damanhūrī.[137] This practice of arranging politically useful marriages was continued by ash-Shādhilī's successors after his death and served the ṭarīqa well, since powerful in-laws could help neutralize potential opposition. In Tunis, marriages between the sons and daughters of Shādhilī Sufis and the children of prominent ulama were so common that the leading scholars of the city soon came from the same families as the Shādhilī Sufis. The connection helped the order secure an influential position at the Hafsid court.

Upon ash-Shādhilī's departure for Egypt, the direction of the Tunisian branch of the Shādhiliyya was taken over by one of the shaykh's closest friends and earliest disciples, the sharif Abū'l-Ḥasan aṣ-Ṣiqillī (d. 657/1258–9). Ibn ʿAṭāʾillāh intimates in *Laṭāʾif al-minan* that had aṣ-Ṣiqillī not died soon after ash-Shādhilī, the shaykh's successor, Abū'l-ʿAbbās al-Mursī, would have had difficulty proving that he was ash-Shādhilī's legitimate heir.[138] In addition to the ribāṭ in Tunis, another center was maintained in al-Qayrawān by Abū Yaḥyā al-Ḥabībī. This person may have been related to ash-Shādhilī's meditation partner from Jabal Zaghwān, Abū Muḥammad ibn Salāma al-Ḥabībī, who also remained in Ifrīqīya.[139]

Upon the death of aṣ-Ṣiqillī, the leadership of the Shādhiliyya in Tunis was passed on to Muḥammad ibn Sulṭān al-Masrūqī (d. after 700/1301), the younger brother of Māḍī ibn Sulṭān al-Masrūqī (d. 718/1318), a long-lived companion of ash-Shādhilī who was the main informant for Ibn aṣ-Ṣabbāgh. According to Ibn aṣ-Ṣabbāgh, ash-Shādhilī took such an interest in Muḥammad ibn Sulṭān that he "adopted" him as a young boy and groomed him as a possible successor.[140] When Ibn Sulṭān reached maturity, Abū ʿAbdallāh al-Qurṭubī, another of ash-Shādhilī's early disciples, was sent from Egypt to instruct him. Al-Qurṭubī took al-Masrūqī from his natal village of al-Masrūqiyyīn to Tunis, where he trained him under aṣ-Ṣiqillī's supervision.[141]

During his tenure as head of the Shādhiliyya in Tunis, Muḥammad ibn Sulṭān, who was known locally as "Sīdī Abū ʿAbdallāh ar-Raʾīs," was an energetic leader who devoted himself to propagating ash-Shādhilī's doctrine among the elites of the Hafsid capital. Following a policy similar to that of Abū'l-ʿAbbās al-Mursī in Alexandria, whose authority he ostensibly recognized,[142] Ibn Sulṭān cultivated close ties with prominent Sufis and ulama. The most important of these was ʿAbdallāh al-Marjānī (d. 699/1300), a confidant of the new qāḍī al-jamāʿa of Tunis and an adviser to the Hafsid sultan.[143] In order to secure a permanent place for the Shādhiliyya in the Hafsid hierarchy, Muḥammad ibn Sulṭān arranged for his sons to marry the daughters of al-Marjānī's favorite students. The children born from these unions were to become instrumental in the Shādhiliyya's eventual displacement of the Suhrawardiyya as the semiofficial Sufi order of the Hafsid court. This new status was confirmed a half-century later, when Shādhilī Sufis took teaching positions at the Jāmiʿ az-Zaytūna mosque-university. According to the Moroccan historian Muḥammad al-Manūnī, the identification of the Shādhiliyya with this prestigious center of learning was crucial in establishing the order in other centers of Islamic scholarship in the Maghrib, such as Tlemcen and Fez.[144]

Some time after Abū'l-ʿAbbās al-Mursī's death in 684/1285, a dispute appears to have arisen between the Egyptian and Tunisian branches of the Shādhiliyya. This rupture was signaled by the return to Tunis of Māḍī ibn Sulṭān al-Masrūqī, the elder brother of Muḥammad ibn Sulṭān. Although neither Ibn aṣ-Ṣabbāgh nor Ibn ʿAṭāʾillāh discusses this rift openly, circumstantial evidence indicates that it was precipitated by a disagreement over who—Aḥmad ibn ʿAṭāʾillāh al-Iskandarī or Muḥammad ibn Sulṭān al-Masrūqī—was more qualified to lead the Shādhiliyya in its third generation. It can hardly be a coincidence that Ibn ʿAṭāʾillāh, whom the Egyptian fuqarāʾ recognized as al-Mursī's successor, does not mention Muḥammad ibn Sulṭān in the pages of *Laṭāʾif al-minan.* This is a significant omission, since the latter had long been acknowledged as the head of the Shādhiliyya's western branch.[145]

At the present time, it is impossible to determine how much this split between the Shādhiliyya's eastern and western branches was due to a doctrinal dispute or whether it was the result of personal politics. There is little doubt, however, that a separate North African Shādhilī tradition, whose roots were different from those of the Egyptian branch of the order, developed in the century and a half following this rupture. As it turned out, it was more than half a century before the influence of Egyptian Shādhilism was felt in the Far Maghrib. In the year 745/1344, one Abū ʿUthmān al-Ḥasanī, a Shādhilī Sufi and sharif who had studied in Egypt, was reported to be in attendance at the court of Abū'l-Ḥasan al-Marīnī. This person was a disciple of ʿAbdallāh ibn Dāwūd ash-Shādhilī, whose father, Dāwūd ibn ʿUmar al-Bākhilī (d. 733/1333), had been a prominent disciple of Ibn ʿAṭāʾillāh. Another disciple of Dāwūd al-Bākhilī, Muḥammad Wafāʾ (d. 765/1364), was the grandfather of the author of *Shajarat al-irshād.*[146]

Some time after the year 700/1301, Muḥammad al-Masrūqī died in Tunis and was succeeded by his elder brother Māḍī ibn Sulṭān, who directed the western branch of the Shādhiliyya until his own death in 718/1318.[147] Because he had been famous as one of the earliest disciples of ash-Shādhilī and because his death at the advanced age of 116 caused him to outlive even Ibn ʿAṭāʾillāh, Shādhilī Sufis in the eastern and central Maghrib came to regard Māḍī ibn Sulṭān as their main source for traditions about the order. One chain of transmission linked to Māḍī ibn Sulṭān leads to a major lineage of Sufi ulama: the Ibn Marzūq family of Tlemcen. This family included the descendants of Muḥammad ibn Marzūq at-Tilimsānī, the Marinid courtier who was mentioned at the beginning of this chapter as a member of the Suhrawardiyya Sufi order.[148]

The doctrines of Egyptian Shādhilism appear to have first entered Morocco through the influence of the Andalusian Sufi Muḥammad ibn ʿAbbād ar-Rundī (d. 792/1390). This noted ascetic served as the imam of the al-Qarawīyyīn mosque in Fez and wrote the first commentary in the Far Maghrib on Ibn ʿAṭāʾillāh's *Kitāb al-ḥikam* (The Book of aphorisms).[149] Three of Ibn ʿAṭāʾillāh's works could be found in the Maghrib by the middle of the fourteenth century: *Laṭāʾif al-minan,* a work on *tawakkul* entitled *Kitāb at-tanwīr fī isqāṭ at-tadbīr* (The Book of illumination in the cessation of self-determination), and *Kitāb al-ḥikam.*[150] These works, along with the invocations of ash-Shādhilī, were probably introduced to Ibn ʿAbbād by his teacher in Ronda, Ibrāhīm Shandarukh. This Andalusian Sufi and jurist served as imam of the congregational mosque of Ronda between the years 750–1/1349–50 and ended his days in the Moroccan city of Salé.[151] He was trained in the use of ash-Shādhilī's *Ḥizb al-baḥr* (Invocation of the sea) by an Egyptian Sufi named Sirāj ad-Dīn ad-Damanhūrī, who had learned it from Sharaf ad-Dīn Muḥammad ibn Abīʾl-Ḥasan, one of the sons of ash-Shādhilī himself.[152]

Despite Ibn ʿAbbād's importance in transmitting the teachings of Ibn ʿAṭāʾillāh, he appears not to have been formally connected with the Egyptian branch of the Shādhiliyya.[153] This situation is not as paradoxical as it seems. In the fourteenth century C.E., the Shādhiliyya claimed numerous adherents among the ulama of Fez and Tlemcen. Most of these Sufis, however, were linked to the Tunis branch of the order rather than to that of Egypt. As late as the eighteenth century, one could still find members of the North African Shādhiliyya tracing their lineages to figures other than Ibn ʿAṭāʾillāh. In fact, one of the earliest Moroccan mystics to be linked unequivocally to this Egyptian shaykh was the late fifteenth-century Sufi Aḥmad Zarrūq (d. 899/1493). Had Zarrūq not been forced to relocate from his native city of Fez to Cairo, even he might not have learned Ibn ʿAṭāʾillāh's doctrines.[154]

At the beginning of the fifteenth century, the Shādhiliyya was closely associated with the political and intellectual elites of North Africa. This was to be expected, since ash-Shādhilī, al-Mursī, and Muḥammad ibn Sulṭān all made a point of recruiting followers from the upper classes of urban society. Almost without exception, the Shādhilī Sufis who appear in the biographies of the later Marinid period are ulama, courtiers, or sharifs. In the rare cases where one finds an exception to this rule, the person in question is most likely to be a skilled craftsperson or a purveyor of luxury goods.[155] This absence of a lower-class following indicates that the leaders of the Shādhiliyya in Tunis, Tlemcen, and Fez were primarily concerned with presenting their order as an alternative to the other elite confraternities of North Africa, such as the Suhrawardiyya. To become fully integrated into the social life of the region, the Shādhiliyya needed a doctrinal orientation that would appeal to people from all levels of society and enable it to transcend its patrician origins. This would be provided by a sharif and scholar from the Moroccan Sūs named Muḥammad ibn Sulaymān al-Jazūlī.

CHAPTER SIX

An Emplotment of a Paradigmatic Saint: The Career of Muḥammad ibn Sulaymān al-Jazūlī

As we have seen in the previous chapters, sainthood must be viewed from more than just a single perspective if it is to be fully understood. A saint in any religious tradition expresses a set of values that is both religious and social in nature, yet the mere fact that sainthood has a social dimension does not mean that the saint portrays a "sampling" of the ethical norms of society and nothing more.[1] In Morocco, for example, the walī Allāh affirms the values of society by transcending them, not just in measuring up to them as does the ordinary believer. Because of this ability to both meet and exceed communal expectations, simply identifying the traits that are listed in hagiographical anthologies is not sufficient to understand what a Moroccan saint is all about. Especially when the saint's audience is socially, educationally, and doctrinally heterogeneous, as in many of the cases discussed above, the interpretation of the saint's example may differ widely according to each group of spectators.

The empiricist paradigm of modern social science has proven inadequate in addressing either the doctrinal or the rhetorical dimension of Muslim sainthood. Because the claims expressed in Sufi treatises and hagiographies are excluded from the realm of presumably "objective" fact, most anthropologists and social historians ignore these writings and approach the Muslim saint from one of three methodological perspectives: Weberian scholars such as Ernest Gellner work from the hypothesis that the meaning of sainthood is to be found in the structure of social relations; Durkheimians such as Clifford Geertz start from the assumption that the symbolism of the sacred reflects the hidden logic of the cultural system in which the sacred is perceived; Marxists such as Pierre Bourdieu seek to explain the ideology of sainthood in terms of class structure and the competition for material resources. Although all of these approaches are relevant, each precludes the possibility of finding heuristic value in either the hermeneutics of scripture or the metaphysics of the sacred. Only a small number of social scientists—who, for the most part, work outside of the field of Islamic Studies—have given the literary tradition of sainthood its proper due.[2] Certain of these scholars, such as the anthropologists Victor Turner and S. J. Tambiah, have noted that the behavior of holy persons in literate societies is understood through the mediation of "root metaphors."[3] Since these metaphors enter public discourse through the medium of written texts, a hermeneutical approach is crucial for their understanding.

Many of the root metaphors that lie behind the interpretation of sainthood in Muslim societies can be found in the writings of the great systematizers, reformers, and interpreters of the mystical tradition. These individuals—of whom al-Ḥakīm at-Tirmidhī, al-Junayd, al-Ghazālī, and Ibn al-ʿArabī are among the most influential—perform the important function of defining sainthood in the language of Sufi doctrine. In doing so, their works highlight the structures of formal and symbolic logic upon which a more broadly based understanding of sainthood is constructed. In Morocco, the sharif and Sufi shaykh Muḥammad ibn Sulaymān al-Jazūlī was similarly important in defining the root metaphors of Muslim sainthood. In the decades following his death in 869/1465, his views on the power and authority of the walī Allāh were used to justify an increased participation by Sufis in local and dynastic politics. In more recent times, such disparate figures as the French colonial historian Alfred Bel and the Moroccan independence activist ʿAllāl al-Fāsī saw al-Jazūlī as a key figure in the development of popular religion in North Africa.[4]

According to the culture critic and historiographer Hayden White, the "organic" inclusiveness of hindsight causes biographers to "emplot" the careers of their subjects in such a way that their impact on later generations is seen as paradigmatic.[5] This propensity for tying up the loose ends of tradition means that any after-the-fact study of a historically significant person will tend to idealize and universalize its subject by assuming his or her centrality to the future course of events. This is an important point to remember when dealing with a half-legendary figure such as al-Jazūlī, about whom little is known for certain. In theory, any of al-Jazūlī's doctrines or actions might be essentialized and incorporated into a new version of the Jazūlite tradition.

Moroccan authors of sacred biography did, in fact, portray al-Jazūlī in organicist terms. First of all, he was the paradigm of choice for several generations of politically active mystics. Secondly, the Moroccan hagiographical tradition has credited him with revivifying Sufism by transforming the multifarious and often competing mystical traditions of the Far Maghrib into a single, universalistic spiritual path in which the authority of the Sufi shaykh was based on an explicit analogy between the saint and the Prophet Muḥammad. This approach was termed the "Muḥammadan way" (*aṭ-ṭarīqa al-Muḥammadiyya*) by the second-generation Jazūlite shaykh ʿAbdallāh al-Ghazwānī. Aided by the wide popularity of *Dalāʾil al-khayrāt wa shawāriq al-anwār fī dhikr aṣ-ṣalāt ʿalā an-nabī al-mukhtār* (Tokens of blessings and advents of illumination in the invocation of prayers on behalf of the chosen prophet), al-Jazūlī's well-known book of prayers on behalf of the Prophet Muḥammad, this method eventually transcended its western origins and influenced Sufis in regions as far removed from Morocco as India and Southeast Asia.[6] Given the geographical scope of the "Muḥammadan Way" and its transmission via multiple institutional vehicles, one might well correct Hayden White's thesis and ask instead: Might not the organicist tendency of hagiography serve as a mirror for actual developments as much as a script for future "emplotments"?

Al-Jazūlī's present-day reputation is based primarily on a work that was written more than two hundred years after his death: *Mumtiʿ al-asmāʿ fī dhikr al-Jazūlī wa at-Tabbāʿ wa mā lahumā min al-atbāʿ* (The Delight of the Hearing in the Recollection of al-Jazūlī, at-Tabbāʿ, and Their Followers), by Muḥammad al-Mahdī al-Fāsī (d. 1109/1698). The author of this hagiographical anthology was born to an Andalusian family from Málaga that emigrated to Fez in the late fifteenth century C.E. After establishing themselves as purveyors of the decorative candles that were used for religious holidays or left as offerings at saints' shrines, a portion of the family moved to the northwestern Moroccan city of Qaṣr Kutāma (present-day El Ksar El Kesir), where they adopted the name "al-Fāsī." At Qaṣr Kutāma they made a comfortable living trading the products of Fez for firearms and other goods of European manufacture that entered Morocco through the Portuguese-held ports of Tangier, Asila, and Larache.[7] It was in Qaṣr Kutāma that Muḥammad al-Mahdī al-Fāsī's great-grandfather, Abū'l-Maḥāsin Yūsuf al-Fāsī (d. 1013/1605), founded the "Fāsiyya" Sufi order that gave the family a suitable pretext for returning to Fez when trade across the Muslim–Christian frontier became impossible.[8]

Unlike the Almohad-era hagiographers discussed in the first part of this book, Muḥammad al-Mahdī al-Fāsī was not a jurist. Instead, he belonged to a wealthy and well-connected Sufi clan for whom mysticism was as much a part of the family business as was the import–export trade. This situation allowed him to specialize in subjects that were more an aspect of noblesse oblige than an actual profession: Sufism, traditions about the prophets of Islam, the history of the Fāsiyya Sufi order, and the biographies of saints and rulers. As a prominent member of the mercantile class, al-Fāsī also maintained friendly relations with the ʿAlawite sharifs of Morocco and supported their political agenda. Part of this agenda was to neutralize the influence of powerful murābiṭūn, such as the shaykhs of the zāwiya of Dilāʾ in the Middle Atlas mountains, whom the ʿAlawites had to defeat in order to gain power.[9] The ulama of Fez supported the ʿAlawites by advocating a model of authority that was pro-sharifian and politically quietistic in equal measure.[10] Hagiographers such as al-Fāsī cooperated in this endeavor by demonstrating through their works that although Sufi reformers such as al-Jazūlī may have seen themselves as the moral beacons of the Far Maghrib, they had no intention of taking political power themselves.

It was thus in the context of an ideological confrontation between official and non-official models of authority that *Mumtiʿ al-asmāʿ* was written in the second half of the seventeenth century C.E. Although there is no evidence that al-Fāsī wrote this book at the behest of the ʿAlawite sultans, he might as well have. His work tends to highlight the juridically validated and pro-sharifian aspects of al-Jazūlī's personal doctrines, while apologetically explaining away the Jazūliyya Sufi order's interference in dynastic politics. Paradoxically, this attempt to sanitize the institutional history of the Jazūliyya is at least partly undermined by the accounts that al-Fāsī himself transmits. In the following chapter we shall see that the politically problematic nature of Jazūlite doctrine is confirmed by the writings of al-Jazūlī's immediate successors, whose works, like those of al-Jazūlī himself, had begun to slip into obscurity by the time *Mumtiʿ al-asmāʿ* was written.

Another paradox of al-Fāsī's book is that this purportedly definitive study of al-Jazūlī and the Jazūlite tradition was written by a Sufi who was not really a member of the Jazūliyya at all. According to *Mirʾāt al-maḥāsin* (The Mirror of exemplary qualities), a hagiographical monograph written two generations prior to *Mumtiʿ al-asmāʿ* by al-Fāsī's great-uncle Muḥammad al-ʿArabī al-Fāsī (d. 1052/1642–3), the Fāsiyya Sufi order was linked to the Jazūliyya only by means of a tenuous and informal "way of blessing and influence" (*ṭarīq at-tabarruk wa'l-istifāda*). Its real doctrinal connection (*ṭarīq al-irāda*) went instead to a rival Sufi order, the Zarrūqiyya.[11] The Zarrūqiyya had close ties to the Ottoman Empire and opposed the Saʿdian dynasty of sharifs whom the Jazūlite shaykhs helped to power. Although they professed to revere al-Jazūlī as an important Sufi and imam, the leaders of the Zarrūqiyya, including the ṭāʾifa's founder, Aḥmad al-Burnusī al-Fāsī, called "Aḥmad Zarrūq," condemned the shaykhs of the Jazūliyya as quasi-heretical innovators.[12] This criticism served the interests of not only the Ottomans, who resented doctrinal as well as political expressions of Moroccan independence, but also the ʿAlawite dynasty of Morocco itself, for it indirectly cast their predecessors, the Saʿdians, in an unfavorable light.

Thus, although *Mumtiʿ al-asmāʿ* provides the most complete account of the teachings and activities of the shaykhs of aṭ-Ṭāʾifa al-Jazūliyya, al-Fāsī's treatment of this order may have more to say about political correctness in the early ʿAlawite period than about the Jazūliyya's actual doctrines. The reader of this work thus traverses the same ambiguous rhetorical terrain that Hayden White discusses in *Tropics of Discourse.* When the teachings of a paradigmatic saint and his followers are recorded for posterity by a self-proclaimed "admirer" who in fact owes allegiance to his subjects' rivals, the reader should approach the author's conclusions with caution and keep in mind White's caveats about the "fictions of factual representation."

For this reason, the discussion of al-Jazūlī and his doctrines in this chapter will often depart from the text of *Mumtiʿ al-asmāʿ* and will rely as much as possible on the writings of al-Jazūlī himself. Exposure to these primary sources should enable the reader to go beyond the semiofficial interpretation of the Jazūliyya as it was conceived in the early ʿAlawite period and instead see how it appeared in its original, post-Marinid form. This distancing of the narrative from the text of *Mumtiʿ al-asmāʿ* should not be taken to imply, however, that the information in al-Fāsī's book is false. Quite the contrary. Al-Fāsī was actually a relatively careful transmitter of tradition. His problem lies more in his interpretation of Jazūlite doctrine than in his description of actions, sayings, and events. On an analytical level, *Mumtiʿ*

al-asmāʿ is best seen as an attempt by a servant of the ʿAlawite regime to reconceptualize the doctrines of al-Jazūlī and his successors so that their revolutionary ideology of saintly authority could no longer threaten sharifian interests. Al-Fāsī's need for political correctness does not apply to ourselves, however. As modern investigators, we are free to view the Jazūlite experiment as one of the great "what-ifs" of Islamic history—a drama of triumph and tragedy in which the final, ironic twist of fate was the co-optation of a revolutionary ideology of saintly power and authority by a political establishment that had little or no intention of using it as it was originally intended.

Background to a Life: Morocco in the Fifteenth Century

By the year 1450, three developments had occurred which were to be decisive in Moroccan social and political life for the next two centuries. The first was the Arabization of rural society, which began in earnest after the Almohad caliph Yaʿqūb al-Manṣūr forced the Riyāḥ and Jusham segments of the Banū Hilāl tribe to settle in the Dukkāla and Habṭ regions of Morocco after their defeat near al-Qayrawān in 583/1187.[13] Although large numbers of Arabs had already been present in the Far Maghrib before this event, most were urbanites who exerted only an indirect influence over their rural neighbors. This situation changed rapidly after the middle of the thirteenth century, when groups of Arab pastoralists began to establish themselves in the Atlantic lowlands. Most of these immigrants supported the anti-Almohad Banū Marīn, who were also moving into Morocco through the Rif mountains. Motivated by a desire for the lands being vacated by Berber pastoralists as the Banū Marīn moved toward Fez and the foothills north of the Taza gap, these Hilālī and later-arriving Banū Maʿqil tribal groups were eager to assist in the dismemberment of the Almohad state. In 643/1245, the Banū Sufyān segment of the Banū Hilāl rose in support of the Marinids in the region of Taza and in 656/1258 a revolt among the Banū Jābir and Khuluṭ tribes of Tāmesnā broke the back of Almohad power in the central Moroccan plains.[14]

Once in power, the Berber Marinids proved to be eager Arabophiles. They incorporated Arab cultural practices into their court and family traditions and even claimed descent from the North Arabian tribe of Muḍar. The Banū Marīn also sought to Arabize their bloodlines by marrying the daughters of prominent sharifs and bedouin leaders. Middle Period and early modern chroniclers document frequent marriages between the Marinid ruling family and "noble" clans of the Banū Hilāl, such as the Banū Muhalhal segment of the Khuluṭ tribe.[15] In the early 16th century, the Granadan refugee and ambassador Leo Africanus (ca. 935/1529), whose *Description of Africa* provides the clearest depiction of social life in post-Marinid North Africa, documented similar arrangements between the Dhawī Manṣūr segment of the Banū Maʿqil and the successors of the Marinids, the Banū Waṭṭās.[16]

Further to the east, the Banū ʿAbd al-Wād clan of Zanāta Berbers who governed the Algerian city of Tlemcen had a subclan, the Banū al-Qāsim, who claimed descent from a son of Mūlāy Idrīs II, the founder of Fez. Like their rivals the Marinids, the sultans of Tlemcen also made a point of marrying the daughters of sharifs and Arab notables.[17] Especially important were the alliances that the Banū ʿAbd al-Wād maintained with the Banū Maʿqil Arabs, who took over the trans-Saharan trade routes that had previously been controlled by Ṣanhāja Berbers. Maʿqil tribal segments first appeared in southern Morocco around the beginning of the thirteenth century C.E. By the beginning of the fifteenth century, they were in control of the desert between Tlemcen and Taourirt in the central Maghrib as well as a vast section of the Far Maghrib, extending from the Mūlwīya watershed between Oujda and Figuig through Taza, Sijilmāsa, Darʿa, and Gazūla, and as far as Nūl Lamṭa on the Atlantic coast south of the Anti-Atlas mountains.[18] Their political influence was so pervasive that Mohamed Kably has characterized the entire fifteenth century of the common era as the "Maʿqil era" of Moroccan history. This was because Banū Maʿqil control of the mountain passes leading to the Sahara desert made tribal segments such as the Dhawī Ḥassān, Awlād Ḥuṣayn, and Dhawī ʿUbayd Allāh key players in the conflicts that led to the establishment of the Saʿdian state.[19]

The second development that came to a head in the fifteenth century was the popularization of sharifism, an ideology based on early Shiʿism, in which religious and political authority were predicated on descent from the Prophet Muḥammad. Coincident with the arrival of the Banū Hilāl, a veritable rash of ʿAlid and mahdist insurgencies broke out all over North Africa.[20] Although most of these revolts took place in Ifrīqīya and the central Maghrib, where the Banū Hilāl were most numerous, several uprisings occurred in Morocco as well. Particularly important was the revolt of ʿAbd ar-Raḥīm ibn ʿAbd ar-Raḥmān al-Mahr, who arose in al-Jazūlī's homeland of Gazūla in 599/1203. This self-styled "al-Mahdī al-Qaḥṭānī" exploited the resentment felt by the Ṣanhāja Berbers and Banū Maʿqil Arabs of Gazūla at being dominated by the Maṣmūda Berber Almohads.[21]

Also significant was the rising of Muḥammad ibn ʿAbdallāh b. al-ʿAḍīḍ, a possible grandson of the last Fatimid caliph of Egypt, who led a revolt in the Jabal Warghla region north of Fez between the years 600 and 610 (1204 to 1213 C.E.). The core of Ibn al-ʿAḍīḍ's followers were Fatimid refugees from Egypt who had settled in Morocco after the fall of their dynasty to the Ayyubids in 567/1171. These Ismāʿīlī Shiʿites allied themselves with the Idrisid sharifs of Fez, who saw an opportunity to regain their former influence. After Ibn al-ʿAḍīḍ was defeated by a Maṣmūda army sent by the Almohad caliph Muḥammad an-Nāṣir, his banner was taken up by other self-proclaimed Fatimids in southern Morocco, who relied on the support of Banū Maʿqil contingents migrating west from Ifrīqīya. The most successful of these pretenders was the so-called al-Mahdī al-ʿUbaydī, who arose in Gazūla in the year 612/1215. An Arab from the Banū ʿUbayd Allāh segment of the Banū Maʿqil who claimed to be a relative of Ibn al-ʿAḍīḍ, al-ʿUbaydī secured the allegiance of large numbers of Arab pastoralists and even managed to threaten Fez before being bought off by the city's governor.[22]

An important side effect of these revolts was an increase in sharifian involvement in rural politics. This was particularly true after the beginning of the eighth/fourteenth century, when the Idrisids, along with other, later-arriving sharifs coming on the heels of Banū Hilāl and Banū Maʿqil migrations, regained an honored status not enjoyed since the fall of the Idrisid dynasty more than three centuries later. Throughout the Marinid era, sharifian families insinuated themselves into the social fabric of Arab tribes, often assuming conflict-management positions such as that of *farīḍ al-qabīla,* a sort of ombudsman used by the Khuluṭ confederation.[23]

Part of what Kably calls the "sharifian policy" of the Marinid state was to maintain close relations with the Banū Amghār of Ribāṭ Tīṭ-n-Fiṭr, whom they appointed as judges for northern Dukkāla. An edict promulgated by the Marinid sultan Abū ʿInān in 755/1354, which officially recognized the Prophetic lineage of the Banū Amghār, may have been intended to solidify their political position in a region that was now occupied by the Banū Ṣabīḥ segment of the Banū Hilāl.[24] To further solidify their position, the Banū Amghār married their daughters to the sons of Banū Ṣabīḥ leaders who lived in and around the town of Azemmour.

The influence of the sharifs in tribal and regional affairs became even more pronounced in the fifteenth century C.E., when they took an active role in the jihad against the Iberian Reconquista. In 841/1437, sharifs from the Sūs and Tāfilalt regions led contingents of Berbers and Berberized (*mustaʿjam*)[25] Arabs to Tangier, which was being threatened by a Portuguese invasion force.[26] Here they joined up with the vizier and regent of the Marinid state, Abū Zakarīyā al-Waṭṭāsī (d. 852/1448), who had already aided the sharifian cause by establishing the cult of Mūlāy Idrīs II in Fez.[27] This successful defense of Tangier (in which Muḥammad ibn Sulaymān al-Jazūlī may have participated) proved to be a watershed in the history of Morocco, for it both highlighted the sharifian potential for political leadership and demonstrated that the descendants of the Prophet could be able defenders of Islam.

The jihad of the fifteenth century recalls the third development to affect Morocco during the lifetime of al-Jazūlī: the political and economic penetration of the Far Maghrib by Christian Europe. The blame for this development was laid by Moroccan chroniclers at the feet of the later Marinids, who were accused of "busying themselves with abandon in [the pursuit of] pleasures and a disregard for affairs of importance."[28] Although much of this criticism was undoubtedly the result of anti-Marinid propaganda spread by sharifs who hoped to undermine the state to their own advantage, there is little question that the combination of Arab pastoralist hegemony in the countryside and divisive harem politics in Fez lessened the ability of the Marinids to maintain control over their possessions. As early as 760/1359, the former Almohad capital of Marrakesh was taken over by Hintāta Berbers from the High Atlas mountains, whose chiefs governed the city independently from Fez.[29] This weakening of Marinid authority in Marrakesh was followed in 774/1372 by the defacto secession of Azemmour. This important seaport on the Dukkāla coast was now controlled by an oligarchy of merchants and Banū Ṣabīḥ tribal leaders.[30]

It was against this background of rivalry between Marinid codominants that the twenty-one-year-old Dom Henrique of Portugal called for the conquest of Sabta. This audacious move into Africa, the first expedition organized by the future Prince Henry the Navigator, revealed even at this early date the twin pillars of subsequent Portuguese policy in Morocco: Catholic imperialism and aggressive mercantilism. First, the conquest of Sabta would contribute to the unification of the Iberian peninsula by cutting off the Muslim kingdom of Granada from its last source of supplies and reinforcements. Second, it was hoped that the capture of the city would secure a major entrepôt for the gold of the Western Sudan and the spices of Asia.

Although this latter promise came to nothing when Muslim merchants boycotted the new Christian enclave, Henrique's plan was highly attractive to a royal court that was desperate for sources of hard currency.

In August 1415, a fleet of galleys, barges, and tall ships lent by the states of northern Europe arrived before the walls of Sabta, which was governed independently from Fez by a family of wealthy merchants.[31] Taken completely by surprise, the defenders had no time to summon help. Within a week, the city's ramparts were breached by an overwhelming assault. The last stand of Sabta's inhabitants was as hopeless as it was valiant. The Portuguese chronicler Gomes Eannes de Azurara, writing in 1448, reports that many Christian soldiers were killed by civilians, who ambushed them in their homes as they attempted to loot their possessions. Progress through the city's streets was slow and costly as the defenders retreated step by step, resisting to the last. The citizens of Sabta continued fighting until their weapons broke, whereupon they retreated to the rooftops, hurling pieces of masonry at their attackers. Finally, lacking any weapons at all with which to fight, the Muslim defenders threw themselves unarmed against the Portuguese, fighting with fists, teeth, and fingernails. The final battle near the castle (*qaṣba*) in the city's center was especially bloody, as the last remaining contingent of indigenous troops fired indiscriminately upon Christian invaders and Muslims alike, who swarmed below the walls in a frenzied melée of hand-to-hand combat.[32]

One cannot overemphasize the impact of the conquest and subsequent depopulation of Sabta on the inhabitants of the Far Maghrib. Even the fall of Granada in 1492 failed to provoke the same level of outrage and despair as the loss of this mercantile and intellectual center on the formerly secure southern shore of the Dār al-Islām. This despair became even more acute after 1418, when a force of 100,000 irregulars from such disparate locations as Granada, Fez, Tunis, Marrakesh, and Bijāya failed to retake the city from its garrison of only 2,700 soldiers and knights outfitted with firearms.[33] Even the defeat of the Portuguese expedition to Tangier in 1437 put little more than a temporary brake on the inexorable Christian march along the North African coast. In 1458 al-Qaṣr aṣ-Ṣaghīr, the second major stronghold on the Mediterranean shore of Morocco, fell to the Portuguese. This loss was followed by the occupation of Anfa (modern Casablanca) in 1469 and the successful invasion of Asila and Tangier in 1471.

Within the next forty-five years, all of the major ports of Morocco—with the exception of Salé—were to fall into Portuguese hands. Asafi was occupied in 1508, followed by Tīṭ-n-Fiṭr in 1510 and Azemmour in 1513. During this period the Portuguese reinforced their positions by building strongholds and trading posts (*fortalezas e feitorias*) in the coastal regions of Dukkāla, Shyāẓma, and the Sūs. These outposts served the dual function of extending Portuguese influence into the interior of Morocco and providing handy supply bases for their fleets of caravels, which traveled regularly between Lisbon and the gold fields of West Africa. These *feitorias* and the towns that grew up around them—Santa Cruz do Cabo de Gué (the present city of Agadir, founded in 1505), Mogador (modern Essaouira [aṣ-Ṣawīra], founded in 1506), and Mazagan (present-day El Jedida [Mazīghan al-Jadīda], founded in 1514)—were to become major objectives of the Moroccan jihad in the sixteenth century C.E.[34]

The erosion of political autonomy in Morocco was accompanied by a nearly total European monopoly of overseas trade. From Dukkāla to Santa Cruz do Cabo de Gué at the mouth of the Sūs river, merchants from as far away as England and Flanders risked capture by Portuguese naval patrols to carry on a profitable trade in cloth and contraband firearms. After the Banū Waṭṭās subclan of the Banū Marīn seized control of northern Morocco in 875/1470, restrictions were lifted on trade with Europe and Christian merchants flooded into the coastal emporia of Larache (al-ʿArāʾish) and Salé. This "open-door" policy was justified by the Wattasids as an extension of earlier trade agreements concluded by the Marinids, who for years had allowed their domains to be used as a commercial preserve by the Genoese. As early as 1438, just after the defeat of the first Portuguese invasion of Tangier, Italian merchants could be found throughout Marinid territory, where they underwrote the activities of their Muslim counterparts by serving as bankers and moneylenders.[35] The port of Asila was used by the Genoese as an outlet for tanned hides, an arrangement which continued even after the town's conquest by the Portuguese. More positively, Italians aided in the acquisition of up-to-date military technologies by the rulers of Fez, who used Italian experts for designing fortifications and constructing galleys of war. For a time, Italian influence in the Wattasid state was so pervasive that a single Genoese merchant, Luis de Presenda, became the sole agent for all of Fez's import-export trade.[36]

The presence of large numbers of Europeans in Moroccan markets and the increasing political strength of Arab pastoralists alarmed the ulama of the Far Maghrib, who feared that their land would succumb to the same loss of autonomy and Islamic values that threatened al-Andalus. Most of the time, this concern was expressed as a blanket condemnation of immorality and governmental corruption or a jingoistic rejection of Christian-inspired practices. Leo Africanus, for example, notes that houses of prostitution and wine shops on the Andalusian side of Fez were protected by the city's governor and chief of police and that several hostels (*fanādiq*) had become gathering places for transvestites. Especially disturbing to this Granadan refugee was the fact that such a "deplorable way of life" was openly tolerated by the Wattasid state, which employed homosexuals as cooks for the army.[37]

Fifteenth- and sixteenth-century social critics were also concerned about rural society, which, if accounts are to be believed, was not only as morally bankrupt as its urban counterpart but was mired in ignorance as well. Leo Africanus claims that the ulama of the Banū Masgilda Berbers of the Middle Atlas mountains drank wine in secret and argued openly for the permissibility of alcohol.[38] In his *ʿAqīda,* which can be found at the Bibliothèque Hassania in Rabat, al-Jazūlī indirectly alludes to public debauches being held in the region of Ḥāḥā on the Atlantic coast.[39] In a later work entitled *Al-Alfiyya as-saniyya* (The Exalted poem in one thousand verses), the third-generation Jazūlite shaykh ʿAbdallāh al-Habṭī (d. 963/1556) blames the prevalence of transvestitism, drunkenness, and sexual infidelity in the northern region of Shafshāwan on the irresponsibility of family patriarchs, who fail to prevent their wives and children from learning "what the enemy has to teach."[40]

Clearly, Morocco was ripe for change. For Sufis and exoteric legists alike, something had to be done, and quickly, to improve the moral standards of the region and to encourage the Muslim masses to act collectively in their own defense. Unfortunately, most urban advocates of social reform, lacking an adequate ideology to shape their efforts, were unable to transcend traditional patterns of response. Instead of coming up with new ideas, they continued to fall back on ad hoc modifications of earlier models. This resulted in an abundance of hand-wringing complaints about rural depravity and the denigration of moral values, coupled with calls for the revivification of Islamic legal institutions and jihad. Such heartfelt but largely ineffective jeremiads typified Moroccan social criticism from the 1350s to the end of the fifteenth century C.E. The failure of the urban elites to do more than simply complain about a bad situation left the field free for Sufis such as al-Jazūlī, whose links to the countryside allowed him to transcend urban–rural differences, to propose new strategies of reform.

The Enigmatic Imam

Like ʿAbdallāh ibn Yāsīn, Muḥammad ibn Tūmart, and other reformers who preceded him, Abū ʿAbdallāh Muḥammad[41] ibn ʿAbd ar-Raḥmān b. Abī Bakr b. Sulaymān al-Jazūlī is better remembered as a character of legend than as a real human being. Having spent the majority of his life in rural Morocco, and sojourning only briefly in the urban centers where his biographers were to live, al-Jazūlī was known to the generations following his death more for his charismatic reputation than for his Sufi teachings. Even more, because so many of the traditions that detailed his life were transcribed at a much later date from secondary sources or hearsay, none of his biographies can be considered definitive.

Such ambiguity is, in fact, common to paradigmatic saints in the Muslim world. In an article on Sufi hagiography in the sultanate of Delhi, Bruce Lawrence notes that a paradox often arises in which a spiritual master whose writings and biographical notices are sparse becomes more important than other, more historically well-known Sufis in later generations.[42] The reasons for this paradox are twofold. First, as Delooz predicted in his theory of collective recollection, the idealized memory of what a saint ought to have been replaces the actual memory of what he or she was. Second, each shaykh, in the role of teacher, reshapes the way in which his followers think about their doctrinal forbears.[43] The hieratic conception of authority that characterizes institutional Sufism implies that a contemporary Sufi can seldom equal the rank of his spiritual master, since the latter is the source of the wisdom he has attained. This is extended syllogistically to include the shaykh of one's own shaykh, who is considered to be better than the both of them, until the chain reaches the founder of the order to which all belong. It is this individual who is most often referred to as the *quṭb,* the axial saint of the age. In such a way, a figure like Muʿīn ad-Dīn Chishtī of Ajmer (d. 634/1236), whose reputation may have been "constructed" out of a Rajasthani tomb cult, is seen by Chishtī Sufis to be incomparably greater than his successors, whose literary legacy was far more significant.[44] The same can also be said of Mūlāy ʿAbd as-Salām ibn Mashīsh, the teacher of ash-Shādhilī, who, despite the absence of any written legacy except a short prayer called *Aṣ-Ṣalāt al-Mashīshiyya* (The Prayer of Ibn Mashīsh), has risen to the status of patron saint for all of Moroccan Sufism.[45]

This reconfiguration of collective memory also affects the narrative tradition by causing a blurring to occur along the epistemological divide between fiction and history.[46] The structural continuity that links historical narrative to fiction makes history appear as a story whose flow is pulled forward by the mechanics of plot development. I have already described such an emplotment in al-Fāsī's depiction of al-Jazūlī in *Mumtiʿ al-asmāʿ*. In this work, the fragmentary and sometimes contradictory accounts of events in al-Jazūlī's life are "read back" by al-Fāsī in a way that resembles what Paul Ricoeur has termed the "discordant concordance" of classical tragedy. Although they retain the flavor of oral tradition by being presented in a piecemeal manner, these historical "remains" (Ar. *āthār*) are reassembled in a way that transforms them into the elements of a classic Aristotelian plot: suffering (*pathos*), recognition (*anagnōrisis*), and reversal of fortune (*peripeteia*).[47] As if this were not enough, the sudden and unexpected death of al-Jazūlī at the height of his career brings about unforeseen effects that extend the theme of reversal beyond the point where the story would normally have ended. Was this posthumous reversal of fortune meant to demonstrate that al-Jazūlī had a tragic flaw? Such a query begs the question, raised in Chapter Three, of whether or not North African hagiography was influenced by Aristotle's *Poetics*. Whatever the case, the tropes of triumph and tragedy that appear in al-Fāsī's rendition of al-Jazūlī's life are enough to prove that this "history" is a product of conscious artistry.

Although the date of al-Jazūlī's birth is not known, enough information exists to provide a rough outline of his origins and background. His *nisba* (attributional name) tells us that he came from the Simlāla (Idā-u-Simlāl) tribe, one of the most important Ṣanhāja Berber groups in Gazūla. In the fifteenth century, the homeland of the Idā-u-Simlāl was in the coastal plains of the Sūs river between the High Atlas and Anti-Atlas mountains, just north of the modern town of Tiznit. This region had long been important to the religious history of Morocco, since it lay between the early ribāṭs of Māssa and Dār al-Murābiṭīn and was a former center of Fatimid irridentism.[48]

According to traditions that are still current in the Sūs, al-Jazūlī was born in the village of Tānkarat, along a river of the same name.[49] These accounts also claim that his family were sharifs, although there is some question as to which lineage of sharifs they belonged. The most widely circulated genealogies trace al-Jazūlī's ancestry to either Jaʿfar or Sulaymān ibn ʿAbdallāh al-Kāmil, supposed "brothers" of Mūlāy Idrīs I (d. 177/793), the founder of the Moroccan state.[50] Neither of these names appears in any authenticated genealogy of Hasanid sharifs, although Sulaymān has long been thought of in the Maghrib as the ancestor of the sharifs of Tlemcen. A possible solution is proposed by al-Fāsī, who conjectures that the "Jaʿfar" in al-Jazūlī's genealogy might have been a grandson (via the daughter) of ʿAlī Zayn al-ʿĀbidīn, the son of al-Ḥusayn and the fourth Shiʿite imam. This hypothesis, although it is just as unprovable as any other, is at least consistent with the pattern of Fatimid revolts in Gazūla, which were precipitated by pretenders claiming sharifian descent through the Husaynid line.[51]

In his *Description of Africa,* Leo Africanus says that the inhabitants of Gazūla lived a transhumant or semipastoral existence. Migrating seasonally between highland and lowland grazing areas that were centered on regional markets, they were prone to blood feuds and relied on an institutionalized schedule of truces to maintain their economic activities:

> The inhabitants of these lands are rough and without money, but have many flocks and large amounts of barley. In this region are many copper and iron mines, and they make many types of copper utensils which they carry to different lands, exchanging them for cloth, spices, horses, or anything else that they need. In all of this mountain [i.e., the Anti-Atlas] there exists no city or castle—only large villages comprising one thousand hearths, more or less. The inhabitants of this region have no lord. Instead, they govern themselves well enough, although they are always divided into warring factions. Their truces do not last for more than three days out of the week. During these truces enemies are able to trade with each other and can move from one locality to another. But outside of these days, they kill each other like beasts.[52]

This description of life in Gazūla confirms al-Fāsī's assertion that al-Jazūlī was forced to leave his homeland because its culture of violence made serious scholarship impossible. As it turned out, the young sharif had to travel all the way to Fez to get an education, since the meagre intellectual resources of Marrakesh, the usual destination for students from southern Morocco, made study in that city impossible as well.[53] While in Fez, al-Jazūlī lived at Madrasat al-Ḥalfawiyyīn (the present Madrasat aṣ-Ṣaffārīn), the oldest of the Marinid *madāris,* whose rooms were reserved for students from the Sūs. While there, he studied the *Mukhtaṣar* of Ibn al-Ḥājib, the standard introductory work on uṣūl al-fiqh. He also studied *Al-Mudawwana al-kubrā,* Saḥnūn's ninth-century compendium of Maliki law.[54] Al-Jazūlī's room in this madrasa is still known, and can be shown to the visitor by the madrasa's caretaker.

A widely repeated account of al-Jazūlī's student days conveys an image of extreme introspection. During his sojourn at Madrasat al-Ḥalfawiyyīn he would spend long periods alone in his room, leaving it only to attend class. While in his room, he would lock the door and allow no one to enter. Because of this antisocial behavior, word began to spread that al-Jazūlī was concealing money. When news of these suspicions reached his father in Gazūla, the latter hurried to Fez to see what was happening. Upon arriving at the madrasa, ʿAbd ar-Raḥmān al-Jazūlī demanded to enter his son's room. When he opened the door, he saw the word "death" (*al-mawt*) written over and over again on the walls. Understanding that his son was in a deep state of spiritual contraction (*qabḍ*), he remarked to the madrasa's caretaker, "Do you see where this one is and where we are?"[55]

Tracing al-Jazūlī's career after the completion of his studies in Fez is problematized by sparse and conflicting information. Most sources claim that he composed *Dalāʾil al-khayrāt,* his book of prayers on behalf of the Prophet Muḥammad, in Fez, relying on manuscripts that were available in the library of the Qarawiyyīn mosque.[56] His biographers disagree, however, about the exact stage of his life in which this occurred. It is unlikely that al-Jazūlī could have written his world-famous collection of devotions as a marginally educated faqīh. Instead, this more probably occurred only after he had gained a reputation for piety and erudition. Assuming this hypothesis to be correct, and given the dates of other, better-known periods of the shaykh's life, it is most likely that al-Jazūlī wrote *Dalāʾil al-khayrāt* sometime after his participation in the defense of Tangier in 841/1437. This latter conclusion is supported by a tradition recorded by the Jazūlite Sufi Aḥmad ibn Abīʾl-Qāsim aṣ-Ṣūmaʿī, who claims that al-Jazūlī was told to return to Fez by a female ṣāliḥ (*marʾa ṣāliḥa*) whom he encountered in Tangier.[57] When he stated that fighting Christians was more praiseworthy than scholarship, she retorted: "Oh Muḥammad, where are you going? The people of the Maghrib need you!"[58]

The figure of an inspirational holy woman appears over and over again in al-Jazūlī's biography.[59] This presence may have been a reason for the openness of his successors toward women's participation in Sufi rituals and activities.[60] In al-Fāsī's description of al-Jazūlī's encounter with this female saint, the shaykh is portrayed as being astounded by her paranormal insight, which, he learns, is God's reward for her prayers on the Prophet Muḥammad.[61] Another version of this story, this time from Marrakesh rather than Fez, increases the dramatic impact of the narrative by suggesting that al-Jazūlī's inspiration came not from a grown woman but from a young girl:

> The reason for [al-Jazūlī's] writing [*Dalāʾil al-khayrāt*] . . . was that one day he was late for his prayers, even though it was his custom to seek the approval of God the Exalted by not delaying a prayer beyond the earliest possible time for its performance. When he arose to make his ablution, however, he was unable to find anything with which to take water out of the well. This preoccupied him greatly and he was very annoyed. While he was in this state a young girl caught sight of him from a high place and said, "Who are you, uncle?"
>
> [The shaykh] then told her about himself, hoping that she would give him a bucket and thus ease his cares and worries. Instead [the girl] exclaimed, "You are the one whom people praise greatly, yet you are unable to take water from a well in order to purify yourself!" Then she came down from that high place and spat into the well while reciting the Name of the Lord of Creation. No sooner had she done so than water tasting as sweet as the sweetest sugar poured forth from [the well] until it spilled over the face of the earth as a miracle from the One who rolls up the scroll of time.
>
> The shaykh made his ablution and marveled at this splendid miracle. When he finished, he swore by God the Almighty that [the girl] should reveal to him how she had acquired this great rank. "By making constant prayers on the Best of Creation (may God bless and preserve him) to the number of breaths and heartbeats (*bi-ʿadad al-anfās wa'd-daqāʾiq*)," she replied. So [al-Jazūlī] resolved at that moment to write a book about the excellence of prayers on behalf of the Chosen Prophet and to include in it many transmitted texts from the mine of prophecy and from those who have drowned in the sea of the effusion of [God's] abundant generosity. All of this (which was due to what he perceived in this great miracle) would not have been possible had it not been for this girl, who was devoted to reciting prayers on the Adornment of the Last Day (*zayn al-qiyāma*).[62]

According to *Mirʾāt al-maḥāsin,* al-Jazūlī joined aṭ-Ṭāʾifa aṣ-Ṣanhājiyya—the venerable, ethnically oriented Sufi order founded by the Banū Amghār murābiṭūn of Ribāṭ Tīṭ-n-Fiṭr—after completing *Dalāʾil al-khayrāt.*[63] Long-standing ties of discipleship between the Banū Amghār and the Ṣanhāja pastoralists of southern Morocco helped ensure that these murābiṭūn would be sought by aspiring Sufis from the tribes of Gazūla, who comprised the largest group of Ṣanhāja Berbers north of the Sahara desert. Al-Jazūlī may have met the shaykh of the Ṣanhājiyya, Abū ʿAbdallāh

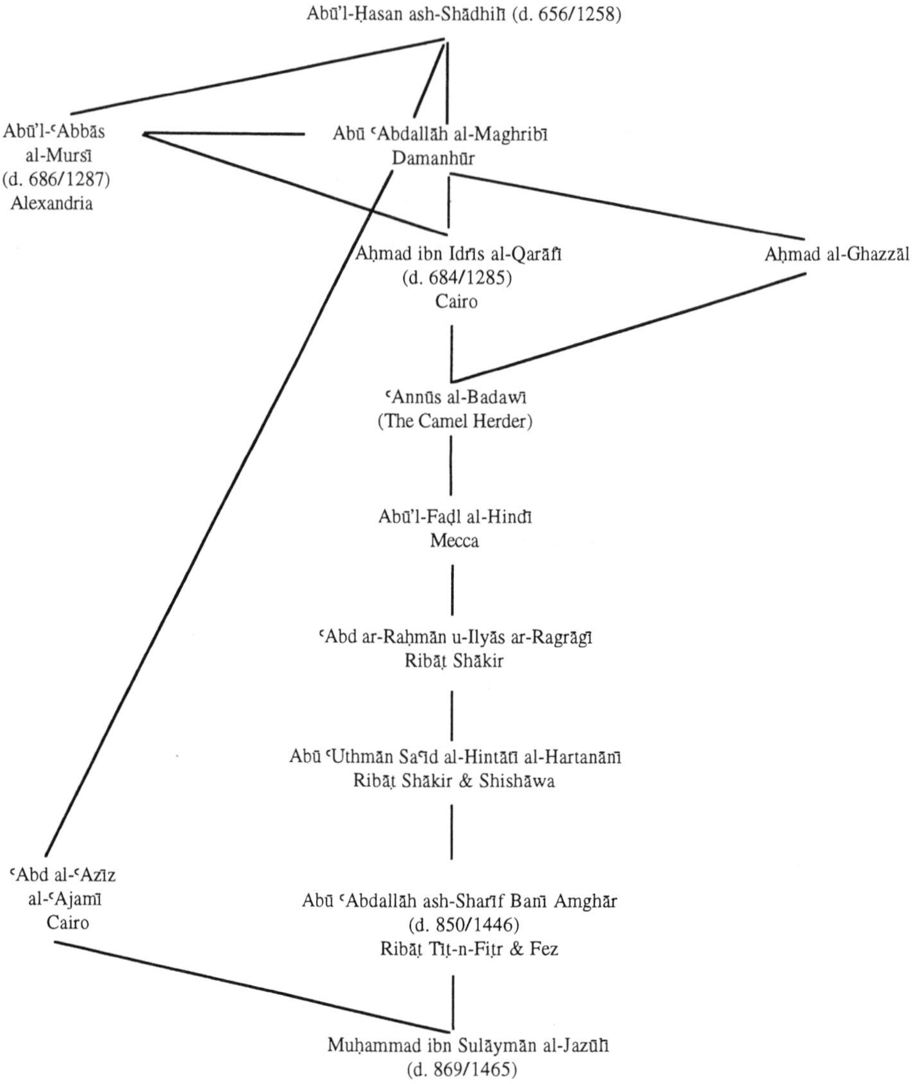

FIGURE NINE

The *Silsila* of Muḥammad ibn Sulaymān al-Jazūlī to Abūʾl-Ḥasan ash-Shādhilī

Muḥammad Amghār aṣ-Ṣaghīr (d. ca. 850/1446), while a student in Fez, for the latter was a *sāʾiḥ* (peripatetic Sufi), who wandered among the towns and cities of Morocco seeking followers.[64] This itinerant saint, who also recruited warriors for the anti-Portuguese jihad, initiated his disciples into a rural variant of the Shādhiliyya order whose spiritual lineage was traced through the shaykhs of another ribāṭ-based Berber group, aṭ-Ṭāʾifa ar-Ragrāgiyya of Ribāṭ Shākir.

Although most sources agree with *Mirʾāt al-maḥāsin* that al-Jazūlī was initiated into the Ṣanhājiyya only after he had completed *Dalāʾil al-khayrāt,* the spiritual maturity of this latter work, as well as the known doctrinal orientations of Ribāṭ Tīṭ-n-Fiṭr and Ribāṭ Shākir, cast doubt upon this assertion. We have seen in Chapter Two that Sufis from both ribāṭs practiced spiritual methods that stressed, like al-Jazūlī's, the veneration of the Prophet Muḥammad. Further evidence of a "Muḥammadan" perspective at Ribaṭ Tīṭ-n-Fiṭr and Ribāṭ Shākir can be found in reports that in the later Marinid period the leading families of these institutions recognized the doctrinal supremacy of the Māgiriyya Sufi order at Ribāṭ Āsafī. The shaykhs of the Māgiriyya, who maintained links with the Qādiriyya Sufi tradition, required aspiring disciples to pass extended periods of time at the Prophet's mosque in Medina. Al-Jazūlī himself held Ribāṭ Āsafī in such high esteem that he built his own zāwiya on its ruins and appropriated Abū Muḥammad Ṣāliḥ's rules of Sufi practice for his ṭāʾifa.

Despite the conclusions of al-Fāsī and others, it is doubtful that al-Jazūlī would have found it necessary to join the Ṣanhājiyya after having written an influential book of Prophetic devotions. A Sufi who is spiritually advanced enough to produce a work like *Dalāʾil al-khayrāt* is more likely to attract his own disciples than to search for a master. It is thus more plausible to assume that al-Jazūlī composed *Dalāʾil al-khayrāt* after becoming a disciple of Abū ʿAbdallāh Amghār, and not the other way around. If this is correct, then one might date his association with the Ṣanhājiyya to the period immediately prior to his participation in the relief of Tangier in 841/1437. It is even possible that al-Jazūlī fought at Tangier in the company of Ṣanhājiyya, for the Banū Amghār were strong supporters of jihad and their base in northern Dukkāla abutted the territory of the ash-Shāwīya Arabs, who also participated in the Tangier campaign.

A further problem about the composition of *Dalāʾil al-khayrāt* involves a lacuna in the narrative of al-Jazūlī's hagiography. This is a "lost period" of the shaykh's life in which no activities are recorded for an interval of from seven to fourteen years. According to al-Fāsī, this period, which could not have begun any earlier than 842/1438, was given over to a regime of pious retreat (*khalwa*) and invocation (*dhikr*) at either Ribāṭ Tīṭ-n-Fiṭr or another site on the Dukkāla coast.[65] Other accounts, however, claim that al-Jazūlī spent at least seven years in the Muslim East, and that during this time he performed invocations and recited the daily litanies (*ḥizb,* pl. *aḥzāb*) of *Dalāʾil al-khayrāt* before the Prophet's tomb in Medina.[66] Another tradition, originating with ʿAbdallāh al-Ghazwānī, the third paramount shaykh (*shaykh al-jamāʿa*) of the Jazūliyya, asserts that al-Jazūlī studied at the al-Azhar mosque in Cairo under a mystic named ʿAbd al-ʿAzīz al-ʿAjamī.[67] In addition, the eighteenth-century Yemenite Sufi and traditionist Muḥammad al-Murtaḍā az-Zabīdī (d. 1207/1791), in his commentary on al-Ghazālī's *Iḥyāʾ ʿulūm ad-dīn,* maintains that in the fifteenth century C.E. a Sufi from the Iranian city of Shiraz wrote a manual of prayers on the Prophet that was nearly identical to *Dalāʾil al-khayrāt,* "except that Allah, may He be praised and exalted, granted [a measure of] acceptance and fame to al-Jazūlī's book that was given to none other."[68]

Are we to infer from the above account that al-Jazūlī's purported authorship of *Dalāʾil al-khayrāt* was false and that his most famous work was plagiarized from an unknown Iranian source? At present, it is impossible to answer this question definitively. Moroccan commentators maintain that the worldwide popularity of *Dalāʾil al-khayrāt* is proof enough of the work's uniqueness.[69] Although this argument is teleological, it does make an important point. Scholars in the premodern Maghrib were often inspired by books that they read in the Mashriq. The influence of these works might even, at times, be symbolized by the appropriation of titles.[70] This appropriation of titles, however, only rarely extended to the contents of the works themselves and would have made no sense in the case of a popular book of invocations such as *Dalāʾil al-khayrāt,* whose plagiarisms could easily have been exposed after it had circulated for a while in the East. The fact that this did not happen can be taken as circumstantial evidence (along with the manifestly Maghribi style of its text) that whatever the source of *Dalāʾil al-al-khayrāt*'s title may have been, its contents and organization were al-Jazūlī's alone.

Although az-Zabīdī's claim of a Shirazi origin for *Dalāʾil al-khayrāt* is probably erroneous, al-Jazūlī's Sufi doctrines were clearly influenced by non-Maghribi teachings. According to al-Ghazwānī, the source of this influence was ʿAbd al-ʿAzīz al-ʿAjamī, al-Jazūlī's teacher at al-Azhar, whose *nisba* suggests an Iranian or possibly Iraqi background. Also according to Al-Ghazwānī, al-ʿAjamī had been initiated into the Shādhiliyya Sufi order "without an intermediary" (*bilā wāṣita*) by Abū'l-Ḥasan ash-Shādhilī himself.[71] This practice of attaching oneself without an intermediary to a long-dead Sufi shaykh was common in early-modern Egypt, where it often symbolized a secondary ṭarīqa affiliation.[72] As we shall see, circumstantial evidence provided by al-Ghazwānī, as well as the text of *Dalāʾil al-khayrāt,* suggests that al-ʿAjamī's primary affiliation may not have been with the Shādhiliyya Sufi order, but with the Egyptian branch of the Qādiriyya.

The source for al-Ghazwānī's information on al-ʿAjamī was his own shaykh, ʿAbd al-ʿAzīz at-Tabbāʿ (d. 914/1508–9). At-Tabbāʿ believed that the shaykh who could claim lineal descent from the Prophet Muḥammad exercised spiritual authority over his followers by virtue of divine right. This sharifian interpretation of authority was an important hallmark of the Jazūliyya. It was also important among the North African Qādiriyya, whose hagiographers claimed that ʿAbd al-Qādir al-Jīlānī's status as the Axis of the Age was a matter of birthright as well.[73] Throughout the sixteenth century C.E., the ranks of the Jazūliyya included both Shādhilī and Qādirī Sufis. It would have been highly unusual for Qādirīs to have been initiated into this order if there had not been a connection between the Jazūliyya and the Qādiriyya in the first place. At-Tabbāʿ provides evidence of such a connection in a poem which traces his spiritual genealogy. This poem, entitled *Salāʾil al-anwār wa tuḥfat manāqib al-akhyār* (Offsprings of light and fruits of the exploits of the virtuous), includes the following verse:

> My banner covers the Spiritual Axes and is raised above them,
> And Sīdī ʿAbd al-Qādir [al-Jīlānī] is a heaven in my firmament![74]

At-Tabbāʿ's attempt to link himself doctrinally to ʿAbd al-Qādir al-Jīlānī is significant, since it comes from a strong partisan of the Shādhiliyya. But this is not all. Further evidence of a doctrinal connection between the Jazūliyya and the Qādiriyya can be found in the text of al-Jazūlī's *Dalāʾil al-khayrāt,* which reproduces verbatim ʿAbd al-Qādir al-Jīlānī's "Minor Prayer" (*Aṣ-Ṣalāt aṣ-ṣughrā*) on behalf of the Prophet Muḥammad:

> Oh God, bless our lord Muḥammad, whose light precedes creation and whose appearance is a mercy to the worlds, to the number of Your creatures who have gone before and who remain and [to the number of] those

> among them who are saved and damned; a blessing beyond number that exceeds all bounds; a blessing without limitation, end, or conclusion; an eternal blessing through Your eternal nature; and protect his family and Companions for all time (*Allāhumma ṣallī ʿalā sayyidinā Muḥammad as-sābiq li'l-khalqi nūruhu wa raḥmatun li'l-ʿālamīna ẓuhūruhu ʿadada man maḍā min khalqika wa man baqiya wa man saʿida minhum wa man shaqiya ṣalātan tastaghriqu al-ʿadda wa tuḥīṭu bi'l-ḥaddi ṣalātan lā ghāyata lahā wa lā muntahā wa lā inqiḍāʾa ṣalātan dāʾimatan bi-dawāmika wa ʿalā ālihi wa ṣaḥbihi wa sallim taslīman*).[75]

This invocation, which can be found in the Wednesday litany of *Dalāʾil al-khayrāt,* is well-known to Qādirī Sufis and was even the subject of a commentary.[76] Al-Jazūlī could easily have learned it while studying in Egypt, for a "mosque of the Qādirī saints" (*jāmiʿ as-sādāt al-Qādiriyya*) had been built in the Qarāfa section of Cairo at the end of the thirteenth century C.E. This Qādirī center was founded by the descendants of ʿAdī ibn Musāfir al-Hakkārī (d. 558/1163), an early Iraqi disciple of ʿAbd al-Qādir al-Jīlānī.[77] According to a Tunisian commentary on *Aṣ-Ṣalāt aṣ-ṣughrā,* the version of this prayer that is included in *Dalāʾil al-khayrāt* is identical to one transmitted by the Egyptian biographer and hadith specialist Muḥammad as-Sakhāwī (d. 902/1497), who flourished in the generation after al-Jazūlī.[78]

A possible original source for the transmission of *Aṣ-Ṣalāt aṣ-ṣughrā* is provided by as-Sakhāwī in the person of a juridical Sufi named ʿAbd al-ʿAzīz as-Sunbāṭī (d. 879/1475).[79] This resident of Cairo came from a family of Tunisian origin, was trained in Maliki law, and had an educational background very similar to that of al-Jazūlī. Even more, he knew as-Sakhāwī personally and was particularly fond of invoking prayers on the Prophet Muḥammad. Most tantalizing, however, is the fact that as-Sunbāṭī's spiritual master was a Sufi named Yūsuf al-ʿAjamī. Could this ʿAbd al-ʿAzīz as-Sunbāṭī, who knew as-Sakhāwī and was of the same generation as al-Jazūlī, have been called "ʿAbd al-ʿAzīz al-ʿAjamī" after his shaykh? Although this cannot be proven, it is possible, for it was relatively common for Egyptian Sufis to name themselves after their ṭarīqa affiliations. When one adds to this the fact that "al-ʿAjamī" was a common *nisba* among Egyptian Sufis in the fifteenth century C.E., ʿAbd al-ʿAzīz as-Sunbāṭī at least becomes a plausible link between al-Jazūlī and the Qādiriyya.

Whatever the case, the very fact that an Egyptian variant of a Qādirī prayer is included in *Dalāʾil al-khayrāt* makes it highly unlikely that this work was completed before al-Jazūlī's trip to the East. If the traditions claiming that the shaykh studied in the Mashriq for seven years are in fact accurate, one can reconcile the reports about the "lost period" of his life in the following way: Al-Jazūlī spent the years between 843/1439–40 and 850/1446 in Morocco, where he was based at Ribāṭ Tīt-ṇ-Fiṭr and was the disciple of Abū ʿAbdallāh Amghār aṣ-Ṣaghīr. The latter's death in Fez around 850/1446 would have freed al-Jazūlī to travel to the Mashriq, where he performed the pilgrimage to Mecca and visited the Prophet Muḥammad's mosque and tomb in Medina. He next traveled to Cairo, where he may have paid his respects at the tomb of (his ancestor?) al-Ḥusayn, studied under ʿAbd al-ʿAzīz al-ʿAjamī at the al-Azhar mosque nearby, and associated with Qādirī Sufis in Qarāfa. He probably returned to Morocco around the year 857/1453.

According to an authoritative manuscript of *Dalāʾil al-khayrāt* at the Bibliothèque Ben Youssef in Marrakesh, al-Jazūlī presented the final version of this work to his disciple Muḥammad aṣ-Ṣughayyir as-Sahlī (d. 917/1511–12) in 862/1457–8.[80] This so-called Sahlī copy (*an-nuṣkha as-Sahliyya*) is the standard upon which all other copies of *Dalāʾil al-khayrāt* are based. Since al-Jazūlī presented the definitive version of his most famous work to as-Sahlī a mere seven years before his death, it is hard to believe that he could have written it as early as the 840s A.H. (1436–45 C.E.) and then carried it around the Arab world in rough-draft form for nearly two decades. A more plausible scenario is that al-Jazūlī began the compilation of *Dalāʾil al-khayrāt* upon his return to Morocco in 857/1453 and then revised it during the period in which he organized the Jazūliyya Sufi order. Besides being more in agreement with the evidence at hand, this hypothesis also assumes, as one would normally expect, that *Dalāʾil al-khayrāt* was less a miracle of doctrinal precociousness than the product of long-term Sufi training.

Other examples of Eastern influence on al-Jazūlī's doctrines can be found in the fragments of his treatise on Sufism, *An-Nuṣḥ at-tāmm li-man qāla rabbī Allāh thumma istaqām* (Complete advice for one who says, "My Lord is God" and follows the straight path).[81] One of the more interesting sections of this work is an essay on love mysticism (*maḥabba*) that is preserved in a Saʿdian-era collection of Sufi writings from the Bāb Dukkāla mosque in Marrakesh.[82] What sets al-Jazūlī's *Risāla fīʾl-maḥabba* apart from others of its type in the Islamic West is that its version of the story of Joseph (Yūsuf) and Potiphar's wife Zulaykhā is highly atypical. Rather than adhering closely to the Qur'anic text of *Sūrat Yūsuf,* as is usually done in the Maghrib, al-Jazūlī presents this romance in a way that recalls the Persian classic *Yūsuf u Zulaykhā* by the Naqshbāndī Sufi ʿAbd ar-Raḥmān al-Jāmī of Herat (d. 898/1492). In al-Jazūlī's version, as in Jāmī's, Zulaykhā embraces the religion of Islam out of love for the handsome prophet. After realizing, however, that she can attain the full consummation of her desires only by loving God alone, she abandons her desire for Yūsuf and says: "Oh Yūsuf, I used to love you before knowing God the Exalted. But once I had come to know the One-and-Only Conqueror (*al-Wāḥid al-Qahhār*), love for anything apart from Him could not remain with [my] love for Him. Now I desire nothing but Him!"[83]

Zulaykhā's conversion to Islam, a leitmotif that is common to the Joseph romance after Jāmī, is uncharacteristic of most earlier works on love mysticism. Farīd ad-Dīn al-ʿAṭṭār (d. ca. 618/1221), one of the most influential Persian masters of this genre, does little more than recapitulate the Qur'anic narrative of Yūsuf, which he sees as an allegory of the divine name *al-Jamīl* (the Beautiful).[84] Jalāl ad-Dīn ar-Rūmī (d. 672/1273), another Persian master of love mysticism, barely mentions the story of Joseph in his famous *Mathnāwī,* preferring instead to use the romances of Majnūn and Laylā and Solomon and Bilqīs as vehicles for his teachings.[85] The only major exception is the twelfth-century Khurasani Sufi Abū'l-Faḍl al-Mībūdī (fl. 520/1126), who discusses the aftermath of Zulaykhā's conversion in his exegesis of the Qur'an. In al-Mībūdī's version of this romance, a blind, poor, and unsightly Zulaykhā encounters the prophet Yūsuf after having lost her family and all of her possessions. Informing Yūsuf that she has embraced Islam, she begs him to intercede with God to restore her eyesight and beauty. Upon regaining the bloom of youth, she next asks Yūsuf to marry her. After discovering, to his surprise, that Zulaykhā is still a virgin, the prophet marries her and fathers two sons, one of whom is the grandfather of Moses.[86]

Among the Qur'anic exegetes who were well-known in the Arab world, only Ibn al-ʿArabī's commentator ʿAbd ar-Razzāq al-Kāshānī (d. 730/1330), in his *Tafsīr al-Qurʾān al-Karīm* (Commentary on the Noble Qur'an), alludes to Zulaykhā's conversion. Al-Kāshānī suggests that Zulaykhā was attracted to the light of God that was reflected in Yūsuf's beauty. Unconsciously, her desire to unite with God was sublimated into the desire to physically unite with Yūsuf, whose countenance reflected the divine attribute of beauty. Being careful not to invent a conclusion that went against the text of the Qur'an itself, al-Kāshānī leaves it to the reader to decide whether Zulaykhā's desire for Yūsuf might have changed once she understood the true nature of her love.[87]

Zulaykhā's conversion is not the only motif in al-Jazūlī's treatise on love to suggest the possibility of Persian influence. This work also includes a discourse on the stations (*maqāmāt*) of love whose ultimate source may have been the Sufi Ibn Khafīf of Shiraz (d. 371/981).[88] Made famous in the works of Abū'l-Ḥasan ad-Daylamī (fl. ca. 390/1000) and Rūzbihān al-Baqlī ash-Shirāzī (d. 606/1209), Ibn Khafīf's doctrine of love relies on a rhetorical use of etymologies that was derived from the disciplines of Arabic belles lettres and philosophy.[89] Al-Jazūlī cites neither Ibn Khafīf nor Rūzbihān but instead refers to unnamed "masters of the [Arabic] language" (*arbāb al-lugha*) as his sources of information. However, his hierarchical model of the stations of love closely resembles that of Rūzbihān, differing from the latter only with respect to some of the terms employed. These stations are as follows: desire (*hawā*), attachment (*ʿalāqa*), care (*kulf*), passion (*ʿishq*), infatuation (*shaghaf*), love-sickness (*tabl*), craving (*walūʿ*), ardent desire (*gharām*), enchantment (*huyām*), intimate companionship (*khulla*), self-effacement (*iṣṭilām*), and consummation (*tatyīm*).[90]

Also like that of Rūzbihān, al-Jazūlī's treatise on love postulates a thirteenth station, which represents the supreme goal of the Sufi path. For Rūzbihān, this station is universal love, *ʿishq-i kullī*. For al-Jazūlī, however, it is the root principle of love itself, *maḥabba*.[91] Al-Jazūlī uses this latter term because the word *maḥabba* in Arabic is related to *ḥabb* (seed), which carries within itself the archetypal essence of the plant it is to become. Thus, by the rule of semantic correspondence, *maḥabba* connotes both the essence of love and—by analogy—the essence of Sufism. The ultimate value of *maḥabba* is proven by the fact that, as a spiritual station, its rank is higher than that of gnosis (*maʿrifa*), which is usually thought of as the acme of esoteric knowledge.[92]

Upon his return to Morocco in 857/1453, al-Jazūlī's innovative doctrines and charismatic personality caused a stir in Sufi circles.[93] His doctrine of *maḥabba* in particular was so powerful that it was believed that he occupied a unique station at the feet of the Prophet Muḥammad. It was also rumored that during his absence from Morocco al-Jazūlī met "with many of the prophets, angels, and saints (*al-asfiyāʾ al-kirām*), who taught him esoteric sciences (*ʿulūm ghaybiyya*) and God-given secrets (*asrār wahbiyya*)."[94]

Al-Jazūlī most likely spent the first year after his return to Morocco in Fez, where he composed the initial draft of *Dalāʾil al-Khayrāt* and reassessed the social and political situation of his country. Then he traveled via Ribāṭ Tīṭ-n-Fiṭr to his natal village of Tānkarat in Gazūla, where he may have left a wife and a child.[95] After recruiting his first disciples among the Awlād ʿAmr and other Banū Maʿqil Arab tribes in the Sūs, he moved to the city of Asafi (which had by then grown in importance to become the port of Marrakesh) and established a zāwiya on the site of the thirteenth-century ribāṭ of Abū Muḥammad Ṣāliḥ.[96] Al-Jazūlī clearly thought of this founder of aṭ-Ṭāʾifa al-Māgiriyya as the inspiration for his own model of institutional Sufism. In another fragment from *An-Nuṣḥ at-tāmm* he encourages his readers to use Abū Muḥammad Ṣāliḥ's treatise *Maʿdin al-jawāhir* (The Mine of jewels) as a manual of Sufi practice.[97]

Al-Jazūlī borrowed heavily from the institutional repertoire of the Māgiriyya Sufi order and required his disciples to adopt the staff, pouch, and distinctive clothing of Māgirī fuqarāʾ. An important difference between the Jazūliyya and the Māgiriyya, however, was that the peripatetic mystics (*sāʾiḥūn*) of the Jazūliyya were encouraged to visit other Sufis in the Maghrib instead of performing the Ḥajj pilgrimage to the holy cities of Mecca and Medina.[98] This emphasis on visits to living shaykhs and the shrines of local saints was in part due to the fact that the pilgrimage centers of the Mashriq were often inaccessible to fifteenth-century Moroccans. The fall of Sabta to the Portuguese, the dissolution of governmental authority in the central and western Maghrib, and increased corsair activity in the western Mediterranean all conspired to cut off most of the sea and land routes used by North African pilgrims on their journeys to the East. One cannot help but suspect, however, that al-Jazūlī also had a more instrumental purpose in ordering his followers to stay at home. His emphasis on visiting local religious leaders prepared an already-established Sufi network for political mobilization and promoted a distinct, regional identity for the Jazūliyya that set it apart from other Sufi orders in the Maghrib.

Al-Jazūlī also appropriated Abū Muḥammad Ṣāliḥ's three doctrinal pillars of repentance (*tawba*), remembrance (*dhikr*), and virtue (ṣalāḥ).[99] These principles ultimately go back to Abū Madyan and, as we have seen, were outlined in *Bidāyat al-murīd,* a synopsis of the Andalusian shaykh's rules for novices that may have been compiled by Abū Muḥammad Ṣāliḥ himself. The male aspirant who wished to join the Jazūliyya first had to demonstrate his repentance by shaving off his "hair of unbelief" (*shaʿr al-*

kufr)—in the manner of a Meccan pilgrim—as a symbol of his desire to break with the past. This custom, which was based on the Prophet's practice of cutting off the coiled locks of Arabs who converted to Islam from polytheism, was used by al-Jazūlī as both a rite of passage and as a symbol of initiation into aṭ-Ṭāʾifa al-Jazūliyya as an institution.[100]

Once tonsured, the Jazūlite penitent (*tāʾib*) next had to perform the difficult, forty-day regime of fasting and seclusion known as *ṣawm al-wiṣāl*, a practice which was borrowed from Abū Madyan.[101] After completing these austerities, the *tāʾib* became a full member of the order and swore an oath of allegiance (*bayʿa*) to al-Jazūlī as his personal imam. Simply becoming a member of the Jazūliyya, however, was not enough for one to become a full-fledged Sufi. It was still necessary for the *faqīr* to acquire personal discipline, eliminate discord (both within the individual and between the individual and others), and establish brotherhood (*ukhuwwa*). To help in the accomplishment of these goals, al-Jazūlī required the faqīr to follow a fourteen-step program, which he called his "Rules of Repentance" (*shurūṭ at-tawba*):

1. Follow spiritual masters who are knowledgeable in both the exoteric and the esoteric aspects of religion. This rule sets the epistemological parameters of the faqīr's knowledge.
2. Avoid places where prohibited things are done. This lessens the urge to sin.
3. Practice self-discipline. This combats the laziness of the soul.
4. Avoid the immoral, love the good, follow the Sunna of the Prophet, befriend the friends of God, and be an enemy to the enemies of God. This defines ṣalāḥ.
5. Practice constant remembrance of God (*dhikr Allāh*) and prayers on behalf of the Prophet (*aṣ-ṣalāt ʿalā an-Nabī*). This takes the faqīr outside of the individual self.
6. Never hate those with faith (*ahl al-īmān*). This fosters unity by encouraging love for all Muslims.
7. Perform the five daily prayers at their proper times. This upholds the Sharīʿa.
8. Never sully spiritual practice (*ʿamal*) with egoism, arrogance, tyranny, or self-love in act, word, or deed. This builds character.
9. Make your speech wisdom (*ḥikma*), your silence contemplation (*tafakkur*), and your vision deliberation (*iʿtibār*). This fosters spiritual maturity (*muruwwa*).

10. Know that salvation is in God, His saints, and the prophets of God, and that perdition is in the ego (*nafs*) and what arises from it. This establishes the hierarchy of spiritual authority.
11. Avoid backbiting, gossip, and slander. This eliminates dissension and disharmony in the Muslim community.
12. Do not love the mighty, but love the doers of good (*ahl al-khayr*) and be their companion. This combats elitism and worldly ambition.
13. Avoid evildoers and love the poor (*masākīn*) and the Sufis (*fuqarāʾ*) and be one of them. This maintains the link between spiritual poverty and social consciousness.
14. Learn the knowledge that brings one closer to God. This reinforces the understanding that the only true ambition for the Sufi is *himma,* the ambition to find God.[102]

After following the Rules of Repentance for a sufficient amount of time, the Jazūlite initiate, who has now advanced to the stage of the "sincere disciple" (*murīd ṣādiq*), must complete his training by acquiring ten attributes that summarize the essence of the Jazūlite way. To eliminate any feeling of self-importance that might remain in the faqīr, these attributes are specifically related to the example of a dog:

> In the dog are ten praiseworthy attributes that are found in the sincere disciple: (1) he sleeps only a little at night; this is a sign of the lovers of God (*muḥibbīn*); (2) he complains of neither heat nor cold; this is a sign of the patient (*ṣābirīn*); (3) when he dies, he leaves nothing behind which can be inherited from him; this is a sign of the ascetics (*zāhidīn*); (4) he is neither angry nor hateful; this is a sign of the faithful (*muʾminīn*); (5) he is not sorrowful at the loss of a close relative, nor does he accept assistance; this is a sign of the secure (*muqīnīn*); (6) if he is given something, he consumes it and is content; this is a sign of the contented (*qāniʿīn*); (7) he has no known place of refuge; this is a sign of the wanderers (*sāʾiḥīn*); (8) he sleeps in any place that he finds; this is a sign of the satisfied (*rāḍīyīn*); (9) once he knows his master, he never hates him, even if he beats him or starves him; this is a sign of the knowers (*ʿārifīn*); (10) he is always hungry; this is a sign of the virtuous (*ṣāliḥīn*).[103]

The cornerstone of Jazūlite praxis was the daily recitation of prayers on behalf of the Prophet Muḥammad from *Dalāʾil al-khayrāt* and the morning and noon recitation of al-Jazūlī's *Ḥizb al-falāḥ* (Litany of good fortune).[104]

To these were added Abū'l-Ḥasan ash-Shādhilī's *Ḥizb al-barr* (Litany of the land)[105] and *Al-Musabbaʿāt al-ʿashr* (The Ten sevens), a collection of Qur'anic invocations compiled by Abū Ṭālib al-Makkī but attributed to al-Khiḍr.[106] Al-Jazūlī also composed another litany, *Ḥizb al-Jazūlī* (Litany of al-Jazūlī) or *Ḥizb subḥāna ad-Dāʾim* (The "Glory Be to the Eternal" litany), which was reserved for the use of his family.[107] In the generation after his death, this litany was appropriated by the ʿĪsāwiyya Sufi order of Morocco, and now forms the basis of their own invocation.[108] The preferred manner of performing these litanies was to recite them out loud (*jahran*) in circles of fuqarāʾ who chanted them in harmony (*bi-aṣwāt mawzūna*) or in a round (*biʾl-munāwaba*).[109] According to al-Fāsī, this was done to "lift the veil of the heart" and allow the invocations to work their alchemy upon the soul.[110] The recitation of these litanies did not, however, supplant the prescribed Islamic devotions; instead, they supplemented and complemented them.

The authority of the spiritual master in the Jazūliyya Sufi order was absolute. Al-Jazūlī and his successors expected unquestioning obedience from their followers, and they were looked upon as inerrant sources of divine knowledge. One must cleave to spiritual masters, said al-Jazūlī, "even if they are in Baghdad, for going to them brings illumination, mercy, and the Secret to hearts."[111] The fully actualized Jazūlite shaykh (*ash-shaykh al-wāṣil*) "has arrived at the station of direct perception (*maqām al-mushāhada*) and has disappeared into the lights of perfection, such that he is concerned with nothing but the King of Truth. When he returns among humankind, he returns with illumination (*anwār*), knowledge (*ʿulūm*), and laws (*aḥkām*). He who follows him is educated and inspired, and understands what those who are cut off from him will never understand."[112]

But this was not all. *Ash-shaykh al-wāṣil* was indispensable to the disciple because he drew his wisdom from the divine source of prophecy itself: "Write down what you hear from me, for I am an intermediary between yourselves and the Truth. The Truth illuminates and the slave understands. He who is inspired toward the right (*aṣ-ṣawāb*) has an obligation to speak, and [his guidance] is a benefit to others."[113] The fact that *ash-shaykh al-wāṣil* possessed such quasi-prophetic knowledge made obeying him a near-canonical obligation: "He who follows the example of his shaykh follows the example of his Lord. For the sacredness (*ḥurma*) of the shaykh before his disciples is like the sacredness of the Prophet before the Companions."[114]

Because of his charismatic personality and penchant for uttering ecstatic statements (*shaṭaḥāt*) that pushed the envelope of orthodoxy, few of those who came into contact with al-Jazūlī were able to remain neutral. Instead, each potential disciple had to decide whether the shaykh was a man of unique epistemological gifts or a misguided and dangerous heretic. Al-Jazūlī justified his ecstatic statements by claiming that he was the Mujaddid, the Renewer of his age, whose prerogatives included a sort of poetic license in regard to divinely inspired utterances.[115]

The tradition of the Renewer in Islam is based on a hadith from the *Sunan* of Abū Dāwūd which states: "God will send to this community at the turn of every century someone who will restore religion."[116] This person is most often described in Muslim sources as a scholar who will restore the original purity of Islam by returning Muslims to the Prophetic Sunna.[117] It was not difficult for the juridically trained al-Jazūlī to portray himself as a mujaddid. By composing *Dalāʾil al-khayrāt* and thus focusing attention on the specifically "Muḥammadan" aspects of divine inspiration, he was in a favorable position to cast himself as a reviver of the Sunna. It was also to al-Jazūlī's advantage that he came from the region of Ribāṭ Māssa in Gazūla, where the Mahdī, the ultimate *Mujaddid* of Islamic eschatology, was expected to appear at the end of time.

The fact that al-Jazūlī portrayed himself as a spiritual leader with social and political responsibilities meant that his doctrine of sainthood was more attuned to the theme of authority (*wilāya*) than that of closeness to God (*walāya*). However, he made no attempt to minimize the doctrinal importance of *walāya.* Indeed, al-Jazūlī considered intimacy with God to be the quintessential fruit of gnosis. In the doctrinal perspective of Shādhilī Sufism, the *via contemplativa,* which leads to the vision of the divine (and hence *walāya* sainthood), is superior to the *via activa,* which is characterized by outward discipline and self-mortification. For al-Jazūlī, this meant that a sainthood based on intimacy with God was fundamental to all Muslim saints, from the God-addicted lover (*majdhūb*) to the spiritual warrior (*mujāhid*). In fact, this very point, which the shaykh often expressed in his writings through the metaphor of divine attraction (*jadhba*), is one of the main lessons to be learned from his exegesis of the romance of Yūsuf and Zulaykhā. A similar argument is made in the following passage, where al-Jazūlī intimates that every "active" worker of righteousness (ṣāliḥ) is at the same time a "contemplative" knower of God (*ʿārif*):

> The knowers of God (*al-ʿārifūn*) are a folk who work righteousness (*aṣlaḥū*). By working righteousness, they are freed [from material constraints]; when they are freed, they come near [to God]; when they come near, they enter [the divine presence]; when they enter, they remain and are established [in God's presence]; when they are established, they become secure and seek [God's knowledge]; when they seek, they find, and when they find, they witness (*shāhadū*); when they witness, they are overcome and weakened; when they are weakened, they die; when they die, they come back [to God] and live [again]; when they live, they speak with the Living who never dies; when they speak, they become intimate (*astāʾnasū*). These are the attributes of the knowers of God, the drinkers of love and unveiling, those brought near on the carpet of intimacy and direct perception, the *sālik* (traveler to God), and the *majdhūb*.[118]

Al-Jazūlī demonstrated his closeness to Allah and the Prophet Muḥammad through divine inspirations (*ilhāmāt*), divine addresses (*muḥādathāt*), and quasi-prophetic conversations with God (*mukālamāt*).[119] These attestations of divine favor also served as proofs of his *wilāya* sainthood by confirming his exalted rank as the paradigmatic saint, the Axis of the Age (*quṭb az-zamān*). Many of al-Jazūlī's statements consist of bold declarations of unparalleled spiritual supremacy, both among his contemporaries and in comparison with earlier generations of Sufis. More than a few of these, which include assertions that he occupied the rank of successor to the Prophet (*khalīfa*), are reminiscent of the claims made by mahdist pretenders in earlier eras. Also like the millenarian leaders of past generations, al-Jazūlī's doctrines were attractive to the poor and socially disadvantaged. Eventually, the political potential of this clientele was to provoke the Marinid sultan ʿAbd al-Ḥaqq II (d. 869/1465) into opposition against the shaykh and his supporters.

Several of al-Jazūlī's conversations with God (*muḥādathāt*) call for the revival of Islam under a divinely guided imam. These discourses are replete with double meaning and make use of ambiguous and highly provocative vocabulary. For example, in the *muḥādathāt* reproduced below, are the *mujtahidūn* those who strive to carry out the commands of God or an institutionalized collectivity of scholars? Are the *mujāhidūn* those who struggle to better themselves on the path of God or holy warriors? Is al-Jazūlī's vision of a community of *mujtahidūn* and *mujāhidūn*, which he calls "our state" or "our polity" (*dawlatunā*), a metaphorical depiction of his Sufi order or an actual state with an official judiciary and a standing army? If the latter, then who rules it? What about al-Jazūlī's claim that nobility (*sharaf*) lies in descent from the Prophet Muḥammad? To the later Jazūlite shaykh al-Ghazwānī, this statement meant that spiritual authority (*taṣrīf*) belongs to the shaykh who partakes most fully of the Prophetic Inheritance (*al-wirātha an-nabawiyya*).[120] Does this mean that the leader of every Muslim state must be a descendant of the Prophet as well? The following selections beg all of these questions and more:

> Reputation is not gained through possessions or sons. Instead, reputation comes from one's repute before the Lord of Lords. One is not great because of the glory of wealth and children. Rather, one is great because of the glory of God and His attributes. One is not great because of the greatness of his tribe or his love of high rank. Instead, one is great because of the greatness of nobility (*sharaf*) and lineage (*nasab*). I am noble in lineage (*Anā sharīfun fī'n-nasab*). My ancestor is the Messenger of God (may God bless and preserve him) and I am nearer to him than all of God's creation. My reputation is eternal, dyed in gold and silver. Oh you who desire gold and silver, follow us, for he who follows us dwells in the heights of *ʿIliyyīn* in this world and the Hereafter![121]
>
> Past nations (*umam*) have asked to be included in our polity (*dawlatunā*). Yet no one can be included in it unless he has already attained salvation (*saʿāda*). Our polity is the state (*dawla*) of those who strive (*mujtahidīn*) and struggle (*mujāhidīn*) in the path of Allah—fighters against the enemies of Allah. The kings of the Earth are in my hands and under my feet![122]
>
> Oh assembly of Muslims! Do you not know that the Chosen One (may God bless and preserve him) is near to me (*qarībun minnī*) and that his authority (*ḥukmuhu*) is in my hands? He who follows me is his follower, but he who does not follow me will never be his follower. I have heard [the Prophet] say (may God bless and preserve him): "You are the Mahdī! He who desires to be saved (*man arāda an yusʿada*) must come to you!"
>
> Oh assembly of Muslims! Cleave to the community of the Chosen One (may God bless and preserve him) and do not cleave to his enemies because of your rejection of the faith, disputes, cheating, or treason! Oh assembly of Muslims! God has created one to guide you at the end of time,

> so praise him! Oh assembly of Muslims! No one hates us for our covenant with God except the one who possesses neither this world nor the hereafter, and no one is jealous of our obedience to God (the Glorious and Mighty) except the one who has no future with God (the Gorious and Mighty)![123]

It is not difficult to imagine the fear that such proclamations, coming from a man who attracted more than 12,000 followers in less than thirteen years, provoked in the ruler of a Marinid state that was disintegrating from within. To dampen the fires of mahdism that his statements aroused, al-Jazūlī was careful to distinguish his own brand of millenarian discourse from the Fatimid paradigm that inspired some of his more literal-minded disciples.[124] According to al-Fāsī, when told on the night before his death that some of his followers persisted in calling him "al-Fāṭimī," al-Jazūlī became angry and predicted that they would be destroyed by "one who will cut their throats."[125]

Al-Fāsī's attempt to mitigate the Fatimid overtones of al-Jazūlī's teachings cannot hide the fact that these doctrines scandalized the ulama of Fez and even some of al-Jazūlī's fellow Sufis. Since the shaykh's opponents were particularly concerned about his use of institutional symbology, such as shaving the head, wearing the distinctive garments of the Māgiriyya brotherhood, and reaffirming the ethos of Moroccan Sufism through the practice of visiting spiritual masters, it is clear that what was most threatening to vested interests was the idea of Jazūlite corporateness. Al-Jazūlī was little concerned with these fears, however, and even condemned the ulama of Morocco for their hypocrisy and irrelevance, especially with regard to their failure to arouse the Muslim masses in defense of their religion. "Say to the ulama," he told his disciples, "'How happy you would be if only you were sincere!'"[126]

The shaykh reserved his most bitter invectives for those scholars who, while criticizing rural Sufis for their lack of religious knowledge, allowed the masses of the Far Maghrib to slip into ever deeper levels of ignorance and corruption. By living off the wealth of their sinecures and doing little to spread their knowledge to others, these ulama shared responsibility for the rise of Christian-inspired customs and social deviance in the Moroccan countryside. In his *ʿAqīda,* al-Jazūlī lays such problems as hooliganism, the indiscriminate mixing of the sexes, and full-body tattooing squarely at the feet of the scholarly establishment.[127] Rather than wasting their time making pronouncements about the permissibility of minor variations in Islamic practice, the ulama should instead teach the fundamental values of Islam to everyone: "Teach . . . the women and the children, the Sufis and the masses, whether free or slave, especially if they are closely tied [to you] by contract or personal relationship, such as family members or others. The Prophet (may God bless and preserve him) said: 'God has not charged anyone with a sin greater than the ignorance of his people.'"[128]

By the end of 863/1459, al-Jazūlī and his followers had begun to wear out their welcome in the city of Asafi. The year had already been one of the worst in recent memory. It began with the Portuguese conquest of the Mediterranean stronghold of al-Qaṣr aṣ-Ṣaghīr, which removed the last hope of reinforcing the kingdom of Granada in Spain and marked the resumption of the Christian Reconquista that had temporarily been blocked at Tangier in 1437. If this disaster were not enough, the same year witnessed an orgy of political intrigue and bloodshed in the Marinid capital of Fez. The regent Abū Zakarīyā al-Waṭṭāsī, the commander of the relief expedition to Tangier and symbolic leader of the Moroccan jihad, was long absent from the scene, having been captured and executed by Banū Maʿqil Arabs in 852/1448.[129] He was succeeded as vizier by a pious and honest cousin named ʿAlī ibn Yūsuf, who administered what was left of Marinid Morocco in a competent manner. Immediately after the fall of al-Qaṣr aṣ-Ṣaghīr, however, ʿAlī ibn Yūsuf himself fell victim to the Banū Maʿqil. He was succeeded in turn by Abū Zakarīyā's son, Yaḥyā al-Waṭṭāsī, who proved to be as corrupt as his predecessor was honest. Once installed in office, he sought to use the post of vizier as a launchpad for his own ambitions. Hoping to gain the sultanate for himself, he confined the Marinid ruler ʿAbd al-Ḥaqq II to his palace and gravely weakened the army of Fez by demobilizing its best troops and stripping them of their weapons.[130]

Yaḥyā al-Waṭṭāsī's day in the sun was not to last long, however. ʿAbd al-Ḥaqq II, a distrustful and vindictive man who had been raised in the cutthroat world of harem politics, lost no time in conspiring with the commander of the Fez garrison to arrest and execute his vizier on the pretext of self-defense. This royalist coup de main, which took place before Yaḥyā al-Waṭṭāsī had been able to complete even a single year in office, was followed by a purge that eliminated nearly all of the Banū Waṭṭās clan then residing in the Marinid capital.[131] The clamor that was aroused by the slaughter of a highly respected family for the deeds of one rotten apple reached a crescendo when the sultan abolished the post of vizier altogether and put the financial and police affairs of Fez in the hands of two Jewish merchants from the city of Meknès.[132] This affront to the prerogatives of the Muslim elite provoked an immediate outcry from the ulama. Many of these scholars rallied to the banner of Muḥammad ash-Shaykh, Yaḥyā al-Waṭṭāsī's brother and sole remaining heir to the Banū Waṭṭās line, who had escaped the carnage in Fez and found refuge among the Awlād Ḥuṣayn Arabs in Asila.

News of the unrest in Fez must certainly have reached Asafi, where al-Jazūlī had been calling for jihad since his arrival. The merchants of the city, who at the time numbered as many as six hundred individuals, were loath to abandon the profits they were earning from the Portuguese, who used Asafi as a source of the trade items that they exchanged for gold on the West African coast.[133] These dealings were severely criticized by al-Jazūlī and his disciples, who resided in a great circle of tents around Abū Muḥammad Ṣāliḥ's ribāṭ. This restive mass of Sufis and Arab tribesmen, who at the time numbered half of the population of Asafi itself, posed an unacceptable threat to the city's elites.[134] Cognizant of the fact that they could not assert their independence with impunity, the merchants forced the Marinid governor of Asafi to summon al-Jazūlī to an audience, "fearing him because of the number of people (*abnā' ad-dunyā*) around him and fearing that [the shaykh's followers] might push them out of their world."[135] The governor challenged al-Jazūlī with an ultimatum: "If you do not get away from me, I will rid myself of you!" To this the shaykh replied: "I am the one who will get away from you, but you will follow me as well!" This prediction came true only two years later, when the merchants of Asafi, now in league with the Portuguese, proclaimed their city's independence from Fez and forced the hapless governor to flee for his life.[136]

After being expelled from Asafi, al-Jazūlī and his entourage moved south to Ḥāḥā, a foothill region of the High Atlas mountains midway between Dukkāla and the Sūs. Although the sources do not specify why he chose Ḥāḥā as the site for his headquarters instead of his homeland of Gazūla, possible reasons are not hard to find. In the first place, Ribāṭ Māssa, just north of al-Jazūlī's home village of Tānkarat, had already fallen under Portuguese control. Second, although Ḥāḥā was pastoral and largely undeveloped, it supported a sizable population and, according to Leo Africanus, could provide as many as 32,000 warriors for a jihad.[137] Third, Ḥāḥā would not have seemed foreign to a person from Gazūla, since both regions shared similar patterns of culture, trade, and sociopolitical organization. Even more, the tribes of Ḥāḥā were linked to those of Gazūla by a network of alliances that could be activated in times of conflict. These so-called *liff* (pl. *alfūf*) alliances tied together non-neighboring tribes and markets that would normally have been cut off from each other because of distance or politics.[138] By making use of *alfūf* as supply and communications networks, the merchants of Ḥāḥā made a profitable living trading copper and luxury items from Aqqā, on the edge of the Sahara desert, for European cloth and weapons.[139] Finally, since it was located midway between the economically important regions of Dukkāla and the Sūs, Ḥāḥā was crucial to the defense of southern Morocco. A military force based in this region could serve as a buffer against Christian incursions by threatening the Portuguese at both Asafi to the north and Ribāṭ Māssa to the south.

Al-Jazūlī established his new ribāṭ at Āfūghāl, in the Aït Dāwūd tribal region east of the present town of Tāmānār. According to Leo Africanus, the Aït Dāwūd (Ber. People of David) were a tribe of former Jewish agriculturalists and petty merchants who had converted to Islam and developed a reputation for legal knowledge.[140] Because of this specialty, the settlement that they built on the site of their regional market (the present-day town of Sabt Aït Daoud) served as a defacto administrative center for much of Ḥāḥā. The exact location of al-Jazūlī's ribāṭ remains a matter of conjecture. The inhabitants of Sabt Aït Daoud and the administrator (*muqaddam*) of al-Jazūlī's shrine in Marrakesh now believe that it was in the vicinity of the shrine known today as Sīdī M'ḥand u-Slīmān, the Berber version of the name Muḥammad ibn Sulaymān. Others disagree, however, and claim that Sīdī M'ḥand-u-Slīmān is actually the site of premodern Tāṣrūt, where al-Jazūlī was buried in 890/1485, after the defeat of the rebellion started by his disciple ʿAmr ibn as-Sayyāf al-Mughīṭī. This tradition, following Leo Africanus, asserts that Āfūghāl was actually located further to the north, near a fortress called Qulīʿat al-Murīdīn (Small Stronghold of the Disciples), which served as the rebels' headquarters.[141]

The Moroccan historian ʿAbd al-Karīm Krīm, basing his theories on patterns of transhumance in colonial-era Ḥāḥā, believes that al-Jazūlī maintained two ribāṭs in this region: one for use in the summer and one for use in the winter.[142] According to this hypothesis, the shaykh's summer ribāṭ would have been near the pass (Ber. *tīzī*) of Sīdī ʿAlī Maʿshū in the Jabal Igrān region, where the High Atlas mountains rise to an altitude of over 6,000 feet. His winter ribāṭ, by contrast, would have been located nearer the coast—below Jabal Amsitten near the present town of Smimou—where the Atlas foothills reach no more than 3,000 feet in elevation. Although

Krīm's hypothesis makes anthropological sense, the market town of Sabt Aït Daoud with its nearby shrine of Sīdī M'ḥand u-Slīmān is also located at a moderate altitude, and it has the additional advantage of occupying a position midway between the migration termini of Tīzī Maʿshū and Smimou. Anthropologists who specialize in the study of transhumance have long noted that political advantages accrue to saints who locate themselves at market centers, boundaries between tribal territories, or strategic points along seasonal migration routes.[143] These findings, coupled with the fact that ribāṭs in the Far Maghrib were usually built at sites that could provide a stable livelihood for their occupants, support the conclusion that al-Jazūlī's Āfūghāl was most probably near Sabt Aït Daoud as local traditions maintain.

As it turned out, al-Jazūlī was to spend no more than six years at Āfūghāl. According to the testimony of his closest disciples, on the fourth day of Dhū'l-Qaʿada 869 (28 June 1465), he collapsed and died while making his morning prayers.[144] Because of the suddenness of his death and the fact that he gave no sign of illness beforehand, it was immediately assumed that someone had poisoned him. Almost as soon as al-Jazūlī's body was wrapped in its burial shroud, a dispute arose between the Sufi adepts in the shaykh's entourage and his pastoralist followers, who revered him not as a teacher and mystic but as a divinely appointed leader and man of power. This confrontation was lost by the Sufi adepts, who were forced to leave Āfūghāl and take up residence elsewhere in Morocco. The departure of al-Jazūlī's most learned companions now meant that both his ribāṭ and his mortal remains were under the control of unlettered Banū Maʿqil bedouins. On the advice of the marginally educated ʿAmr ibn as-Sayyāf al-Mughīṭī, al-Jazūlī's body was placed in a movable ark (*tābūt*) rather than being buried in the ground.

The sudden death of the shaykh and the revolt of Ibn as-Sayyāf (Son of the Sword Maker) in the regions of Ḥāḥā and Shyāẓma are the most significant plot reversals in the narrative of al-Jazūlī's life. This uprising also serves as an instructive example of what Jack Goody has termed the "feedback effect" of written traditions on oral societies.[145] Goody and other anthropologists working in West Africa have remarked that former illiterates or semiliterates play an important role in transmitting literary epistemologies in societies where literacy itself is rare. Although most of al-Jazūlī's Banū Maʿqil followers were either completely or partially illiterate, they nonetheless were believers in Islam, the quintessential "Religion of the

Book." Furthermore, they shared with the shaykh and his disciples a universe of discourse that was permeated with mystical vocabulary. We know from the *Kunnāsh* (Autobiographical notebook) of Aḥmad Zarrūq, the only contemporary source to have left a detailed account of these events, that ʿAmr ibn as-Sayyāf had once been a student of the Muftī of Fez, ʿAbdallāh al-Qawrī (d. 872/1467). As Goody might have predicted, this bedouin from Shyāẓma was far from a perfect student and often misunderstood his lessons. Al-Qawrī once described his former pupil as having "a Sufi hat (*qalansuwa*) on his head, a rosary (*taṣbīḥ*) around his neck, a sword in his hand, *dhikr* on his tongue, and heresy in his actions."[146]

Ibn as-Sayyāf was notorious for taking al-Jazūlī's teachings out of context and distorting their meanings. For example, he based his claim to be the messianic Heir to Prophethood (*Wārith an-Nubuwwa*) on a crudely literalistic interpretation of the famous hadith: "The scholars are the heirs to the prophets" (*al-ʿulamāʾ warathat al-anbiyāʾ*).[147] Despite the absurdity of this logic to one who has been trained in what Goody calls the "creative" art of metaphor, it was perfectly rational for tribesmen who had not yet "learned to learn" the thought processes of the literary-minded: Al-Jazūlī was a scholar; therefore, he was an heir to the prophets. If he was an heir to the prophets, he must have been like a prophet in his knowledge. Ibn as-Sayyāf is the heir to al-Jazūlī; therefore, he must be an heir to the prophets as well.[148]

Zarrūq also claims that Ibn as-Sayyāf displayed an inordinate interest in the doctrines that al-Jazūlī attributed to al-Khiḍr. He would copy these teachings on wooden tablets in a ritualistic manner and then congratulate his master with the words: "God has given us a great gift in you."[149] After al-Jazūlī died, Ibn as-Sayyāf asserted that these doctrines were "revelations" from al-Khiḍr and that the latter had now chosen to speak to Ibn as-Sayyāf directly. As we have seen in Chapter Three, al-Khiḍr is a famous hermetic figure of Islamic folklore who is believed to return in every age to reaffirm the truth of divine inspiration. To Ibn-as-Sayyāf, this meant that al-Khiḍr occupied the same rank as the prophets of Islam. Even more, since al-Khiḍr was believed to have revealed hidden truths to Moses and still communicated with living saints such as al-Jazūlī, he shared with the Prophet Muḥammad the role of "messenger of God." Since Ibn as-Sayyāf also received communications from al-Khiḍr, he thus felt justified in interpreting and even abrogating Qur'anic verses on his own authority.[150] His apparent belief in the "magic" or inherent esoterism of inspirational texts also agrees with Goody's hypotheses about the unique epistemology of "restricted literacy."[151]

Ibn as-Sayyāf referred to himself as "ʿAmr ibn Sulaymān as-Sayyāf" to show that he was a "brother" of al-Jazūlī who had been kept from his rightful inheritance by jealous Sufis in the shaykh's entourage.[152] He also called his followers *murīdūn* in order to show that they alone were the true followers of al-Jazūlī, whom he eventually equated with Moses in comparison with himself as al-Khiḍr. According to some accounts, he even forced al-Jazūlī's widow and teenage daughter to marry him, purporting to follow the pre-Islamic Arab and Moroccan Jewish custom of levirate marriage.[153]

After establishing himself as the head of a messianic community, Ibn as-Sayyāf's most pressing task was to eliminate potential opposition by avenging himself on those who could be blamed for al-Jazūlī's death. Conveniently, his wrath fell first upon those who were nearest at hand and best placed to unmask the changes he had made to al-Jazūlī's doctrines—the shaykh's remaining Sufi disciples and the scholars of Aït Dāwūd.[154] Taking advantage of the Aït Dāwūd's minoritarian status and Jewish background, he claimed that the "jealousy" of this tribe's ulama had caused them to poison al-Jazūlī. After putting the scholars of Aït Dāwūd to death and forcing the shaykh's remaining Sufi disciples to flee for their lives, Ibn as-Sayyāf began his own mission to the inhabitants of Ḥāḥā, urging them to maintain their prayers and unleashing his Arab followers on anyone who refused to obey his commands.[155]

Until the end of the fourteenth century, Ḥāḥā had been part of the Berber amirate of Saksyūwa, whose capital was the stronghold of Imī-n-Tānūt, a short distance (as the crow flies) to the east of Aït Dāwūd. It will be recalled from the previous chapter that the amirs of Saksyūwa were thought to be esoterists who conversed with Jewish rabbis. Could the ulama of Aït Dāwūd have been the descendants of these rabbis?[156] Imī-n-Tānūt also served as a refuge for the last claimant to the Almohad throne and had long been associated with heresy and millenarianism. This brings to mind other millenarists—the followers of the Almohad mahdī Ibn Tūmart—who also frequented this region. Both post-Almohad messianism and the Murīdiyya revolt of Ibn as-Sayyāf were tribally based movements that espoused mahdist beliefs and relied for legitimacy on inspirational or "revealed" texts. In addition, their followers were similarly uncompromising in their dealings with mainstream Muslims and regarded Maliki ulama as unbelievers.

Perhaps the most important similarity between the followers of Ibn as-Sayyāf and Ibn Tūmart involves their treatment of their leaders' remains. Just before Marinid armies sacked Ibn Tūmart's mortuary mosque at Tīn Māl, his followers disinterred the Mahdī's body and reburied it in a secret location. They continued to venerate this now unknown site for more than three centuries. Accounts detailing Ibn as-Sayyāf's revolt tell us that al-Jazūlī's body was similarly treated. Rather than being buried, it was left in an ark so that it could be taken on campaigns as a talisman of victory.[157] When not in the field, the ark that held the shaykh's remains was placed in an open-air ribāṭ on the summit of a hill near Qulīʿat al-Murīdīn, where it was guarded around the clock and illuminated at night by large torches. Al-Jazūlī's Sufi biographers, who wished to avoid tainting his reputation while at the same time blackening that of Ibn as-Sayyāf, are unanimous in asserting that this rebel never lost a battle while the ark containing the shaykh's body was with him. They further claim that the fear of another uprising, in which al-Jazūlī's body would once again be dug up by restive tribespeople, was the main reason why the Saʿdian sharif Aḥmad al-Aʿraj moved the shaykh's remains to Marrakesh in the year 940/1533–4.[158]

The emplotment of al-Jazūlī's career as a saint comes to an end in 890/1485, with the murder of ʿAmr ibn as-Sayyāf at the hands of his wife. According to Leo Africanus, who visited Qulīʿat al-Murīdīn in 1514 and recorded the then-current version of local tradition, this woman, who may originally have been al-Jazūlī's own wife, killed the self-styled Heir to the Prophets after finding him in bed with her daughter, who may have been al-Jazūlī's child as well.[159]

Some twenty years previously, in Ramaḍān 869 (May 1465), the Marinid dynasty, which had represented governmental authority in Morocco for more than two centuries, had also come to an ignominious end.[160] ʿAbd al-Ḥaqq II, who despised the elites of Fez for their pro-Wattasid sympathies, instructed his Jewish ministers to collect taxes from the previously exempt categories of the ulama and the sharifs. Infuriated at this revocation of their prerogatives, a preacher from the Qarawiyyīn mosque named ʿAbd al-ʿAzīz al-Waryāghlī (d. 880/1475–6) incited the inhabitants of Fez against the sultan, who had his throat cut like a sheep by a gang of thugs.[161] Next, al-Waryāghlī unleashed a pogrom against the Jewish quarter (*mallāḥ*) of the city. This action was opposed by the jurist ʿAbdallāh al-Qawrī and his Sufi student, Aḥmad Zarrūq. Unfortunately, the objections of these scholars did little to quell the blood lust of the mob, who slaughtered many of the Jews of the *mallāḥ* and distributed their possessions among the poor.[162] Sufficient revenge having been taken, al-Waryāghlī selected a new sultan—the leader of Fez's community of sharifs, the Idrisid Muḥammad al-Ḥafīd al-ʿImrānī al-Jūṭī.

In yet another of the many ironies of Moroccan history, a new political entity was born amidst reactionary violence and religious bigotry. For the first time since the downfall of the Idrisids in the tenth century, a descendant of the Prophet Muḥammad assumed power in Fez. This time, however, he was chosen by an alliance of urban notables and other interest groups and was not beholden to any tribally based power behind the throne. Although the sharifian state of Muḥammad al-Ḥafīd was to last for only six years, his assumption of power marked the beginning of the end for tribally based rule in the Far Maghrib. In the following century, under the influence of the Jazūliyya Sufi order and allied mystics, the former paradigms of political authority in this region would be replaced by a sharifian doctrine that created a distinct identity for Morocco and laid the ideological foundations for the country's present monarchy.

CHAPTER SEVEN

The Ideology of Paradigmatic Sainthood: The Jazūlite Doctrine of the "Muḥammadan Way"

"This is the way of illumination; it will continue
and persist as long as life exists."
(*Hādhihi ṭarīqat al-ishrāq, dāmat wa tabqā mā'l-wujūdu bāq*)

—AḤMAD IBN AL-BANNĀ' AL-MARRĀKUSHĪ[1]

One of the most enduring, but least helpful, concepts in Islamic Studies is "popular Sufism." This idea first appeared in Maghrib Studies as a corollary to Alfred Bel's paradigm of "maraboutic Sufism," an ideal type that Bel believed to be exemplified by the Jazūliyya Sufi order.[2] Today, the term "popular Sufism" is often used as a catchall for anything that does not fit the orthodox–mystical norm. As such, it might include the rural faqīrism of post-Almohad Morocco as well as *malāmatī* Sufism and antinomian varieties of mysticism. "Popular" Sufism is assumed to differ from "philosophical" Sufism insofar as it is more concerned with praxis than with doctrine. This tendency to downplay the intellectual side of the mysticism of the common person[3] is apparent in a recent book about the Moroccan poet and *malāmatī* mystic ʿAbd ar-Raḥmān al-Majdhūb (d. 976/1579). In this work, we are told that for this "popular Sufi" and folk hero of the Gharb, the Sufi way "consists in concrete terms of a practical ascetic teaching with a view to the disciple's acquiring attitudes of humility and submission . . . more than an intellectual consideration of theologically elaborated spiritual themes."[4]

It is certainly appropriate to distinguish a Sufi demagogue such as ʿAmr ibn as-Sayyāf al-Mughīṭī from a sober and juridically minded *shaykh aṭ-ṭarīqa* like Aḥmad Zarrūq, who was fond of citing the maxim: "Be a legist first and a Sufi second, not a Sufi first and a legist second" (*kun faqīhan ṣūfīyan, lā takun ṣūfīyan faqīhan*).[5] This does not mean, however, that one is justified in drawing a sharp distinction between "philosophical Sufism" as a doctrinal norm and "popular Sufism" as its antithesis. If the doctrines of Sufi populists have yet to be studied in detail, how can present-day historians make accurate comparisons between "philosophical" and "popular" ideal types? Are there in fact any objective criteria by which one can conclude that "popular" Sufism is less sophisticated or intellectual than its "philosophical" counterpart?

The mere fact that a term like "popular Sufism" is commonly used does not make it correct. On the contrary, it can be shown that the uncritical use of this concept has led to misleading conclusions. Without relying on empirical evidence to back up his understanding of popular Sufism, the Moroccan historian Mohamed Kably attempted to contrast the "intellectual" mysticism of northern Moroccan Shadhilism with an anti-intellectual and antinomian southern counterpart whose existence he did not even bother to prove.[6] His was a pseudocontrast, leading to confusion rather than clarification of his subject. Without considering the full range of primary sources, the Spanish historian Mercedes García-Arenal concluded that the "popular mysticism" of al-Jazūlī was the source of the "Fatimism" that Aḥmad Zarrūq criticized in his *Ar-Radd ʿalā ahl al-bidʿa* (Refutation of the heretics), despite the fact that Zarrūq never made such an accusation himself.[7]

The concept of "popular Sufism" might be of some use in contrasting different conceptions of mysticism within a single, mass-based Sufi order. For example, it might be used to distinguish the beliefs of untutored enthusiasts (commonly referred to in Morocco as *muḥibbīn*) from those of formally initiated disciples. Nevertheless, this usefulness does not give one license to reduce the entire phenomenon of Sufi populism to its lowest common denominator. Although the concept of "popular Sufism" is often seen as comparable to "popular religion," the two terms are not as alike as they may appear on the surface. A religion is a complex system of beliefs and practices that can manifest itself in many guises, from ritual to doctrine and in both literate and nonliterate forms of expression. When popular religion is depicted as "nonformal religion," this is possible because formal and nonformal varieties of religious expression exist at the same time, thus defying a common definition of orthodoxy. Such is not the case, however, for a premodern science such as Sufism, which is based on a specific interpretive method within a single belief system. Sufism can be understood as a science because, to use the broad definition of science developed by Thomas Kuhn, it constitutes an "implicit body of intertwined theoretical and methodological belief that permits selection, evaluation, and criticism."[8]

Once Sufism is seen as a science, the term "popular Sufism" becomes analogous to "popular psychology." One can use terms such as "popular science" or "popular mysticism" when discussing general approaches to knowledge, but when applied to a formal discipline, as in "popular psychology" or "popular Sufism," such broad concepts become almost meaningless. Just as knowing a few terms from Freud does not make one a psychiatrist, participating in occasional *dhikr* ceremonies or visiting a saint such as Abū Yiʿzzā does not make one a Sufi. Popularizing a discipline is not the same as saying that it has popularity. Popularization entails simplification, which entails the elimination of much of the "intertwined theoretical and methodological belief" that makes a science what it is. In short, the premise of "popular Sufism" contradicts the very nature of Sufism as an Islamic science. Just because al-Jazūlī had thousands of followers (i.e., he enjoyed popularity), we cannot necessarily assume that his doctrines were "popular" and not scientific. Also, the mere fact that ʿAmr ibn as-Sayyāf al-Mughīṭī was a disciple of al-Jazūlī does not necessarily mean that his crude brand of messianism was directly linked to al-Jazūlī's doctrines.

I will demonstrate in this chapter that the ideology of the Jazūliyya Sufi order was far from "popular" in the sense described above. Rather, it was the result of a formal attempt to harmonize two different concepts of saintly authority. The first, which I shall call the "paradigmatic" concept of saintly authority, was derived from what some scholars have called the "imitatio Muhammadi" and the prophetological writings of jurists and mystics. The second, or "sharifian" concept of saintly authority, was an outgrowth of the Idrisid interpretation of Hasanid Shiʿism. This model of authority entered Moroccan Sufism through the mediation of the Shādhiliyya and Qādiriyya Sufi orders, whose founders were lineal descendants of the Prophet Muḥammad and put a high premium on prophetic descent as a possible sign of sainthood. Despite the fact that both models gained wide appeal, neither had much in common with the concept of "popular Sufism" as understood in modern academic literature. Instead, they were fully developed ideologies that converged at a critical moment in Moroccan history and eventually diverged again under the centrifugal pull of competing interests. For a brief moment in time and in the guise of the so-called *aṭ-Ṭarīqa al-Muḥammadiyya,* this ideological synthesis became the catalyst for profound changes in the political and intellectual configuration of Moroccan Islam.

The Imitatio Muhammadi *and Moroccan Sharifism*

What Annemarie Schimmel has called the "*imitatio Muhammadi,*" or assimilation of the character of the Prophet Muḥammad, has a long history in Islam.[9] Imitating the Prophet as a "beautiful example" (*uswa ḥasana*) is enjoined on all Muslims in the Qur'an and is the principle reason for the study of hadith.[10] By the third century A.H. (the ninth century C.E.), this had come to involve the complete emulation of the Prophetic Sunna—a practice which included Muḥammad's actions, words, and judgments, as well as the divinely inspired consciousness that gave rise to them. So conceived, the *imitatio Muhammadi* was different from the *imitatio Christi* of Christianity, in that all aspects of the Prophet's perfected yet still human personality were included in the paradigm instead of the more limited attributes of forbearance, suffering, and forgiveness that provided the model for Christian piety.[11]

In Sufism, assimilating Muḥammad's "beautiful example" was an important means to spiritual advancement. Many Sufis were noted for following the Prophetic Sunna to a degree far exceeding that of other believers. This fervor is reflected in the writings of a number of early mystics. For example, the Iranian Sufi Abū Naṣr as-Sarrāj (d. 378/988) includes a "Book of the Example and Imitation of the Messenger of God" (*Kitāb al-uswa wa'l-iqtidā' bi-Rasūl Allāh*) in his influential *Kitāb al-luma'* (Book of radiances).[12] In this treatise, as-Sarrāj depicts the Prophet Muḥammad as a spiritual archetype for all of humankind. The Sufi who wishes to assimilate the Muḥammadan paradigm must imitate the Prophet as completely as possible—a task which entails not only patterning one's behavior on the ritualistic aspects of the Sunna but also adhering to the Prophet's etiquette, his moral and spiritual states, and, whenever possible, his inner realities.[13] In fact, says as-Sarrāj, it is only by virtue of modeling themselves on the *uswa ḥasana* that Sufis stand out as special in the sight of God and can claim to be successors to the Prophet's Companions.[14]

In the twelfth century C.E., the Sufi version of the *imitatio Muhammadi* became identified with a regional cult of the Prophet's family in northern Morocco. This cult was built on a tradition of veneration for the descendants of Muḥammad (Mor. Ar. *sharīf,* pl. *shurafā*ʾ) that had grown up in the Far Maghrib more than two hundred years previously. This practice did not arise by itself but was the result of a promotional campaign conducted by the Idrisids, the descendants of the first ruler of a united Moroccan state, "Mūlāy" Idrīs ibn ʿAbdallāh.

Mūlāy Idrīs and his successors were descendants of the Prophet's grandson al-Ḥasan (d. ca. 49/669). Upon leaving the Arabian peninsula, they carried with them a form of archaic Shiʿism that was similar in many respects to Zaydism.[15] These sharifs rejected the Husaynid imamate advocated by later Ithnāʾ ʿAsharī and Ismāʿīlī Shiʿites in favor of a specifically Hasanid form of leadership. The birth of Hasanid Shiʿism can be traced to an uprising of al-Ḥasan's descendants after the death in an ʿAbbasid prison of Mūlāy Idrīs's father, ʿAbdallāh al-Kāmil in 143/760–61.[16] The exclusivity of the Idrisid claim to the imamate can be seen in the admonition of Idrīs II to the Berbers of Morocco when they pledged their allegiance to him at Walīlī (the ancient Roman capital of Volubilis) in 188/804: "Do not submit to anyone other than ourselves, for the establishment of [God's] truth (*iqāmat al-ḥaqq*) that you seek is only to be found in us."[17]

The authority of the Idrisids is linked to a specifically "Muḥammadan" tradition of leadership in accounts detailing the imamate of Idrīs II (d. 213/829), the son of Mūlāy Idrīs and founder of the city of Fez. This is not to say that Mūlāy Idrīs did not also believe that his status as a descendant of the Prophet was important to his own claim of political legitimacy. However, Idrīs II is more closely associated in the hagiographical and historical record with the innate and personal aspects of the Prophet's *uswa ḥasana.*

The theme of an inherited Muḥammadan baraka, which was to become an important aspect of the concept of sharifism, appears prominently in works of Idrisid hagiography, such as *Naẓm ad-durr wa'l-ʿiqyān* by the Algerian chronicler Abū ʿAbdallāh at-Tanasī (d. 899/1494). In the following passage from this work, a companion of Idrīs II named Dāwūd ibn al-Qāsim is informed about the qualities which led his master to victory over the Kharijites:

> I was amazed by what I saw of [Idrīs II's] bravery, strength, and firmness of resolve. Then he turned toward me and said, "Oh Dāwūd, why is it

that I see you staring at me so much?" I said, "Oh Imam, I am amazed at the qualities in you that I have seen in no one else." "What are they?" he asked. "Your goodness, your beauty, the firmness of your intellect, the openness of your demeanor, and your determination in fighting the enemy," I answered. Then he said, "Oh Dāwūd, what you have seen is what we have inherited from the baraka of our ancestor the Messenger (may God bless and preserve him) and from his prayers for us and blessings upon us. This [the Prophet] has passed on as a legacy to our father, the Imam ʿAlī (may God honor his countenance)."[18]

Upon his death Idrīs II left twelve sons, who were sent throughout Morocco by their grandmother, the Berber concubine Kanza an-Nafziyya, to propagate Hasanid Shiʿism. The history of the Idrisid state is well-known to students of Moroccan Studies and does not need to be repeated here.[19] One Idrisid imam, however, became through his descendants an important figure in the development of the sharifian paradigm of sainthood. ʿAlī Ḥaydara, a grandson of Idrīs II, received the *bayʿa* as Imam and ruler of Fez in 221/836. When he failed to designate his infant son Aḥmad Mizwār as his successor before his own death in 234/849, the Idrisid imamate passed into the hands of his cousins, the descendants of ʿUmar ibn Idrīs II, who lived in the regions of Habṭ and Ghumāra in northern Morocco. After being passed over for the imamate, Aḥmad Mizwār became disenchanted with politics and devoted himself to a life of worship and asceticism. Sometime before the turn of the tenth century, or just before the Idrisid state became a bone of contention between the Fatimids of Ifrīqīya and the Umayyads of Spain, he moved from Fez to northern Morocco and established himself at Ḥajar an-Nasr (Escarpment of the Eagle), a fortress situated in the Habṭ region among the Ṣanhāja Berber tribes of Ahl Sarīf, Banū Yūsuf, and Sumāta.[20]

As his nickname, *mizwār* (Ber. leader or spokesman) implies, this great-grandson of Idrīs II was adopted as a spiritual leader by the tribes who lived near his mountaintop stronghold. According to local tradition, when the chiefs of these tribes asked Aḥmad Mizwār to delegate a member of his family to join them and favor them with the baraka of the Prophet Muḥammad, he chose his son ʿAbd as-Salām (known locally as "Sīdī Sellām"). As a means of honoring the young sharif, who had recently married, the tribesmen renamed themselves "Banū ʿArūs" (Sons of the Bridegroom), the appelation by which they are known today.[21]

For the next seven generations, the descendants of Sīdī Sellām established themselves among the Berbers of Banū ʿArūs while maintaining a reputation for holiness that was based almost exclusively on their Hasanid descent. Around the year 530/1135–6, a child named Sulaymān, but later nicknamed "Mashīsh" (Ber. Little Cat), was born to a sharif of the Banū ʿArūs known as Abū Bakr ibn ʿAlī. Upon reaching maturity, Sulaymān Mashīsh withdrew from the world as an ascetic and built a hermitage that still stands among the ruins of his natal village of Aghyul.[22] In either 559/1164 or 563/1168, he sired a son named ʿAbd al-Salām, who would become the patron saint of Moroccan Sufism.[23]

ʿAbd as-Salām ibn Mashīsh lived for sixty-three years, the same lifespan as that of the Prophet Muḥammad. During this period, his career passed through three distinct phases. First, he was a scholar and studied the Qur'an and Maliki jurisprudence under the Idrisid sharifs of Banū ʿArūs. Later, he was a *mujāhid,* a defender of the faith, and lived in Sabta, where he supported himself by teaching Qur'anic recitation to children and fought with the Almohad army in Spain. Finally, after embracing Sufism, he devoted the last twenty years of his life to worship and contemplation on the heights of Jabal al-ʿAlam (Flag Mountain), a period which culminated in his encounter with his only disciple, the fellow Idrisid and founder of the Shādhiliyya Sufi order, Abū'l-Ḥasan ash-Shādhilī.[24]

As we have seen in Chapter Five, the question of sharifism in the doctrines of Ibn Mashīsh and ash-Shādhilī was passed over by Ibn ʿAṭā'illāh and his followers among the Egyptian branch of the Shādhiliyya, who sought to minimize the importance of genealogical ties to their ṭarīqa's founder. There is little doubt, however, that both shaykhs gave great importance to their Hasanid origins. It has already been noted that at least one Egyptian source traces the origins of the Shādhiliyya to the Rifāʿiyya Sufi order, whose founder Aḥmad ar-Rifāʿī was also a Hasanid sharif. Accounts from northern Morocco additionally claim that ash-Shādhilī first discovered Mūlāy ʿAbd as-Salām through the mediation of a local sharif named Aḥmad al-ʿAsalānī.[25] As for Ibn Mashīsh's own master in Sufism, he too was an Idrisid sharif, ʿAbd ar-Raḥmān al-ʿAṭṭār from Sabta, who was called "az-Zayyāt" or "al-Madanī" because he resided in the oil sellers' quarter of Medina while devoting himself to worship at the Prophet's mosque.[26] The "Muḥammadan" focus of al-Madanī's spirituality was passed on by Ibn Mashīsh to ash-Shādhilī, who once stated: "Were the Prophet to be veiled from me for but the blink of an eye, I would not count myself among the Muslims."[27]

Supporting the Idrisids in creating a sharifian paradigm for sainthood and religious authority in Morocco were the legists of Sabta, who used the celebration of Muḥammad's birthday (*al-mawlid an-nabawī*) as a means of promoting the cult of the Prophet and his family. Although the origins of this festival go back to the Shiʿite Fatimids, who celebrated the birthdays of the "Five Impeccable Ones" (*al-khamsa al-maʿṣūmīn*)—the Prophet Muḥammad, ʿAlī, Fāṭima, al-Ḥasan and al-Ḥusayn—the *mawlid* was supported by Sabta's Sunni elite because they thought it would lessen the influence of Christianity on uneducated Muslims and new converts. The most influential proponent of this holiday was Aḥmad al-ʿAzafī, whom we have met in Chapter Three as the biographer of Abū Yiʿzzā. In *Ad-Durr al-munaẓẓam fī mawlid an-nabī al-muʿaẓẓam,*[28] al-ʿAzafī advocates the celebration of the Prophet's birthday as an antidote to the Andalusian practice of observing non-Muslim holidays such as Christmas, Nawrūz, and Mehrejān.[29] Using the Maliki concept of *maṣlaḥa* (public interest) as a justification for this innovation, he primarily viewed the *mawlid* as an opportunity for spiritual consciousness raising. Its central ritual in Sabta was a procession of parents, who would visit all of the Qur'anic schools of the city in turn, singing songs in praise of the Prophet and bearing gifts for their children.[30]

In 648/1250, the *mawlid* was made an official holiday in Sabta by al-ʿAzafī's son, the "Supreme Jurist" (*al-faqīh al-aʿẓam*) Abū'l-Qāsim al-ʿAzafī.[31] To promote it further, he sent a copy of his father's book to the Almohad caliph ʿUmar al-Murtaḍā (d. 665/1266), who ordered the *mawlid* to be celebrated in Marrakesh as well.[32] These efforts were supported by another scholar from Sabta, Abū ʿAlī ar-Rahūnī, who composed a poem of 6,300 verses, *Naẓm ad-durar bi-āy Aḥmad ajall al-bashar* (The Arrangement of pearls in the [Qur'anic] verses about Aḥmad, the greatest of human beings). This work received its first public recitation at the Marrakesh *mawlid* in 661/1263.[33] In 691/1292, Abū'l-Qāsim al-ʿAzafī's son Abū Ṭālib decreed that the *mawlid* be celebrated throughout the Rif region. He also convinced the Marinid sultan Abū Yaʿqūb Yūsuf an-Nāṣir to order its celebration in Fez.[34]

The *mawlid* was particularly popular among members of Abū Muḥammad Ṣāliḥ's Māgiriyya Sufi order, who spread it along the pilgrimage routes between the Far Maghrib and Egypt in the second half of the thirteenth century C.E. A member of this order, Abū Marwān al-Yuḥānisī (d. 667/1268–9), introduced the celebration in Muslim Spain. Al-Yuḥānisī's biographer Aḥmad al-Qashtālī reports that by the time this shaykh left his native city of Guadix to take up residence in Sabta, the *mawlid* at his rābiṭa attracted more than 10,000 participants.[35] By the fourteenth century, *al-mawlid an-nabawī* had become an institution among North African Sufis in general. In 769/1368, the Algerian hagiographer Ibn Qunfudh was present at a *mawlid* in Dukkāla that was sponsored by the Banū Amghār murābiṭūn of Ribāṭ Tīṭ-n-Fiṭr. Saying that so many Sufis attended this celebration that his eyes "went out of focus," Ibn Qunfudh claims that just the grapes provided for the fuqarāʾ filled ninety large baskets and cost thirty gold dinars.[36]

Another influential advocate of the cult of the Prophet was Qāḍī ʿIyāḍ ibn Mūsā al-Yaḥṣubī, the premier hadith scholar of the late Almoravid period and qāḍī al-jamāʿa of the cities of Granada and Sabta.[37] His most famous work, *Kitāb ash-shifāʾ*, is a tradition-based treatise that promotes the veneration of Muḥammad as the universal archetype of humanity. As an antidote to Christian traditions about the divine nature of Jesus, Qāḍī ʿIyāḍ portrays the Prophet as a mortal man who was blessed with superhuman qualities.[38] Although he acknowledges that Muḥammad had human limitations, he restricts these to the Prophet's outward or bodily aspect alone. With respect to his inner qualities, the Prophet had more in common with angels than with others of his species. This is proven for Qāḍī ʿIyāḍ by the Prophet's enjoyment of divine protection and his freedom from major sins and weaknesses.[39]

For Qāḍī ʿIyāḍ, Muḥammad's *uswa ḥasana* is a paradigm for religious and nonreligious behavior alike. Thus, the Prophet's actions exemplify the best of human undertakings: the best manner of living, the most efficacious teaching, the most useful knowledge, and the finest of personal attributes. Since many of these qualities pertain to the Prophet's inborn nature and cannot be duplicated by other human beings, Qāḍī ʿIyāḍ urges his readers to instead emulate Muḥammad's acquired virtues, such as his generosity, forbearance, bravery, good fellowship, moral standards, justice, asceticism, and God-consciousness.[40]

Qāḍī ʿIyāḍ also asserts that perfection in the imitation of the Prophet is proven by the appearance of miracles (*karāmāt*), especially those that replicate Muḥammad's own miracles (*muʿjizāt*). These include speaking about the unseen, enjoying divine protection, exercising exceptional judgment, and possessing an intuitive sense of propriety and ethics.[41] These attributes have already been discussed in Chapter Four as important indicators of sainthood in premodern Morocco. Those holy persons who most closely conform to the Prophetic example are extolled by Qāḍī ʿIyāḍ as "God-conscious saints" (*awliyāʾ Allāh al-muttaqīn*): "those on whom Allah confers honor through the bestowal of His holiness, who are estranged from mankind because of [their] intimacy [with Allah], and who are set apart by means of [Allah's] knowledge, the vision of His earthly dominion, and the effects of His power."[42] On this point, Qāḍī ʿIyāḍ is in agreement with Aḥmad al-ʿAzafī, who saw these same "God-conscious saints" as the true leaders of the Muslim community.

From the Muḥammadan Reality to the Muḥammadan Image

The relationship between prophethood and sainthood that is implied by Qāḍī ʿIyāḍ in *Kitāb ash-shifāʾ* had already been discussed in explicit terms by the third-century A.H. Sufi al-Ḥakīm at-Tirmidhī. In his treatise *Sīrat awliyāʾ Allāh* (Biography of the friends of God), at-Tirmidhī depicts the Prophet Muḥammad as an intercessor for three kinds of individuals: the prophets, the saints, and anyone who follows the prophets and saints.[43] This intercessory quality of the Prophet is continued in the postprophetic age through a figure whom at-Tirmidhī calls the "Seal of Sainthood" (*khātim al-walāya*). This paradigmatic saint, who takes on a different identity in each generation, is the person "upon whom the leadership (*imāma*) of the Friends of God is incumbent, who bears in his hand the Banner of the Friends of God, and whose intercession all the Friends of God have need of, just as the prophets have need of Muḥammad."[44] The authority of the Seal of Sainthood even extends to the eschatological realm. On the Day of Judgment he will come forth as the proof of the saints just as Muḥammad will come forth as the proof of the prophets. Because he is characterized by the complete assimilation of the Muḥammadan paradigm, the Seal of Sainthood acts as a deputy (*khalīfa*) of the Prophet Muḥammad and symbolically takes his place during the time allotted to him on earth.[45]

At-Tirmidhī's doctrine of the Seal of Sainthood was revived by the thirteenth century C.E. by the Andalusian mystic Muḥyīʾ ad-Dīn ibn al-ʿArabī. In his treatise *Fuṣūṣ al-ḥikam*, Ibn al-ʿArabī conceives of the human being as having both a terrestrial and a cosmic significance. On the cosmic level, the human being is the epitome of divine self-disclosure: "the very spirit of the whole world of Being, a being summing up and gathering together in himself all the elements that are manifested in the universe."[46] Ibn al-ʿArabī calls this cosmic archetype of humanity the "Perfect Human Being" (*al-insān al-kāmil*). Because all human beings are made to act as a mirror for the Absolute, the Perfect Human Being, as their archetype, reflects all of the divine attributes except divinity itself. Thus, the Perfect Human Being is uniquely qualified to claim the rank of Vicegerent of God on Earth (*khalīfat Allāh fī'l-arḍ*): "No one is suited for the vicegerency but *al-insān al-kāmil,* for Allah has created his outward image out of the realities of the world and its forms, while creating his inward image out of [Allah] the Exalted's own image. For this reason [Allah] says about him, 'I am his hearing and his sight.'"[47]

Ibn al-ʿArabī further states that the Perfect Human Being is the expression of the divine word or Logos (*kalima*), through which God manifests Himself in the universe. As an expression of the divine word, all of the potentialities of existence are actualized in him. For this reason, the symbol of the Perfect Human Being is the bezel of a signet ring (*faṣṣ al-khātam*), which holds the jewel of creation and protects God's earthly treasures:

> He is the eternally creative person (*al-insān al-ḥādith al-azalī*), the endlessly renewed creation (*an-nashʾ ad-dāʾim al-abadī*), and the decisive and all-comprehensive Logos (*al-kalima al-fāṣila al-jāmiʿa*). The existence of the world depends on his existence, for he is to the world what the bezel of a signet ring is to the ring itself. He is the locus of embellishment and the symbol (*ʿalāma*) by which the King seals His treasury. He is called Vicegerent (*khalīfa*) by virtue of this, for through him [Allah] the Exalted protects His creation just as the seal protects the treasuries; so long as the King's seal is upon it, no one will break it to open them except the one who has His permission and is delegated to protect the kingdom. Therefore, the world will remain protected as long as *al-insān al-kāmil* exists.[48]

For Ibn al-ʿArabī, the essence (*sirr*) of the Perfect Human Being is the "Muḥammadan Reality" (*al-ḥaqīqa al-Muḥammadiyya* or *ḥaqīqat Muḥammad*), a concept that finds its genesis in a hadith which states that Muḥammad was prefigured as an archetype before being sent to earth as God's Messenger.[49] For Ibn al-ʿArabī, this preexistent Muḥammad represents the "Immutable Entities" (*al-aʿyān ath-thābita*), which occupy an intermediate stage between the Absolute and the created cosmos.[50] Although this archetype may seem divine because it is a product of the divine imagination, is in fact part of mundane existence and its meaning can only be understood in the context of created forms.[51]

In historical time, the Muḥammadan Reality is expressed through the messengers (*rusul*), the prophets (*anbiyāʾ*), and the saints (*awliyāʾ*). Each of these individuals has the right to be called Vicegerent of God because he (and sometimes she, in the case of saints) is the most visible proof of the Absolute living at the time. Despite their essential identity, however, the messengers, prophets, and saints are not equal in every respect but are ranked according to the comprehensiveness of their natures. Ibn al-ʿArabī uses a tripartite model to describe this hierarchy. First, the concept of vicegerency itself derives from the archetype of *al-insān al-kāmil.* The Perfect Human Being is the "Vicegerent of God on Earth" because archetypal human nature comprehensively mirrors the Immutable Entities. In his historical form as a prophet or a messenger, however, the Perfect Human Being is more narrowly conceived as a "Vicegerent on Behalf of God" (*khalīfa ʿan Allāh*). In this second-level, prophetic manifestation, the Perfect Human Being acts as an executive for the divine authority by bringing forth revealed laws and putting them into effect. Because the Prophet Muḥammad was the final bearer of the divine Law, the leaders of the Muslim community who came after him (and who appropriated the title of *khalīfa* (caliph) for themselves) were not really the vicegerents of God that they claimed to be. Rather, they were "Vicegerents on Behalf of the Messenger" (*khulafāʾ ʿan ar-Rasūl*), because their role was to follow the Prophet's example and govern the Muslims according to his directives. On this third level of manifestation, the only exception to the Vicegerent on Behalf of the Messenger is that rarest of saints who partakes of the vicegerency (*khilāfa*) from the Prophet and from God at the same time. This individual, the final manifestation of *al-insān al-kāmil,* is what Jazūlite Sufis would later call the axial saint (*quṭb*) or the "Bell" (*jaras*):

> Belonging to God on earth are "Vicegerents on Behalf of God," who are the messengers. As for the vicegerency of today, it is on behalf of the Messenger, not on behalf of God. This is because [the vicegerents of today] do not rule except by means of the laws that the Messenger has mandated and do not go beyond them. . . . The "Vicegerent on Behalf of the Messenger" is one who derives his authority directly from [the Prophet] or through independent reasoning (*ijtihād*), whose source is also in what is transmitted from [him].

> Among us, however, is one who takes his authority directly from God and is a "Vicegerent on Behalf of God" via the essence of that authority. His substance derives from the same source as the substance of [Allah's] Messenger. Outwardly, he is a follower [of the Prophet] because of his lack of disagreement with [the divine] judgment—like Jesus, who judged on the basis of what was revealed to him, or the Prophet Muḥammad (may God bless and preserve him) according to [Allah's] statement: "These are the men whom Allah has given guidance, and through them is an example [for others]" [Qur'ān, VI (*al-Anʿām*), 90]. But in reality, what he knows is based on that which is specific to him and is in accordance with [what has been revealed to previous prophets]. He occupies a station that was [first] established by the Prophet by agreeing with what other Messengers have decided on the basis of precedent. We follow him by virtue of [Muḥammad's] example, not because of what someone else has decreed before him.
>
> Thus, following the Vicegerent on Behalf of God is the same as following the Messenger. In the language of disclosure or insight we call him the "Vicegerent of God," while in outward language we call him the "Vicegerent of the messenger of God." This is why when the Messenger of God died he did not designate anyone as his successor. He appointed no one because he knew that from his community would come a person who would take the vicegerency directly from his Lord and would be the Vicegerent on Behalf of God while conforming to the rules of the Sharīʿa.[52]

Ibn al-ʿArabī's concept of *al-insān al-kāmil* was further elaborated in the fourteenth century C.E. by ʿAbd al-Karīm al-Jīlī (d. 805/1402–3), a Sufi from the suburbs of Baghdad who studied under a Qādirī master in the Yemeni city of Zabīd.[53] In a treatise titled *Al-Insān al-kāmil fī maʿrifat al-awākhir wa'l-awā'il* (The Perfect Human Being through the understanding of the endings and beginnings), al-Jīlī explains how the Perfect Human Being is made manifest in the Sufi saint. In doing so, he brings Ibn al-ʿArabī's metaphysics a little closer to earth by showing how terrestrial forms emanate from the Immutable Entities. First, al-Jīlī separates the Entities into four categories of divine names: (1) names of essentiality (*asmā' adh-dhāt*), (2) names of perfection (*asmā' al-kamāl*), (3) names of majesty (*asmā' al-jalāl*), and (4) names of beauty (*asmā' al-jamāl*). Within these categories, each divine name is an archetype for a particular subset of earthly creation. Because the Perfect Human Being is the only creature who knows the divine names in their totality, this individual stands alone as God's "Perfect Slave" (*al-ʿabd al-kāmil*) and mediates divine self-expression.[54] In doing so, the Perfect Human Being stands in an analogous position to the Qur'an, since both the Perfect Human Being and the Qur'an are expressions of the Divine Logos. To illustrate this point, al-Jīlī cites the following hadith: "The Qur'an was sent down to me in a single sentence" (*unzila ʿalayya al-Qurʾānu jumlatan wāḥidatan*).[55] For al-Jīlī, this tradition meant that Muḥammad, as the final historical manifestation of *al-insān al-kāmil* in the form of a prophet, was infused with the Qur'an in a single instant and became the embodiment of revelation itself. As such, he epitomizes God's desire to maintain His creation and is symbolically linked to the divine name *ar-Raḥmān*.[56]

In the age after Muḥammad, saints or sages may also become Perfect Slaves by taking on what al-Jīlī calls the "Muḥammadan Image" (*aṣ-ṣūra al-Muḥammadiyya*).[57] Although this aspect of the Perfect Human Being is given a separate name, the "Muḥammadan Image" is in reality little different from Ibn al-ʿArabī's "Muḥammadan Reality." For Ibn al-ʿArabī, only one Perfect Human Being expresses the Muḥammadan Reality in each generation; likewise, only one person expresses *aṣ-ṣūra al-Muḥammadiyya* in each generation. Al-Jīlī calls this individual the "Axis of the Age" (*quṭb az-zamān*) or "One of a Kind" (*wāḥid al-awān*).[58]

Before the Muḥammadan Image can appear in a human being, it is first prefigured by an entity known as the Spirit of Muḥammad (*nafs Muḥammad*). As the following passage demonstrates, it is the presence of this spirit in every human form that imparts to a person his or her divine nature:

> When God the Exalted created Muḥammad from His perfection and made of him an example of His beauty and majesty, He also created every reality within Muḥammad from the realities of His names and attributes. Then He created the Spirit of Muḥammad from His own, [divine] Spirit. . . . [Likewise] Allah . . . created the spirit (*nafs*) of Adam as a copy of (*nuskhatun min*) the Spirit of Muḥammad. It was because of this mystery that when [Adam] was forbidden from eating the fruit [of knowledge] in heaven he still did so, because it had [also] been created from the essence of Lordship (*dhāt ar-rubūbiyya*).[59]

To recapitulate: the Muḥammadan Reality, which is a product of the divine imagination, is transformed before creation into the Spirit of Muḥammad. The Spirit of Muḥammad, in turn, is "breathed" into human beings.

The presence of this spirit in each person reveals the essential "Muḥammadan Image" that is imprinted on every human form. Because of this preexistent act of imprinting, the Muḥammadan Image serves as an archetype or paradigm for all humankind. It can only be expressed to its fullest extent, however, by *al-insān al-kāmil,* who appears on earth as a prophet, a messenger, or a saint. Since each of these types bears the same Muḥammadan Image, each "is a copy of the other in his perfection. No one loses what the other possesses except by way of accident, such as when one has his hands or legs cut off, or is accidentally born blind in his mother's womb."[60]

Over time, the persona of the Muslim saint is progressively replaced by that of Muḥammad. This convergence of the saint's identity and the Muḥammadan Image is completed when the saint is fully transformed into the Perfect Human Being. The walī Allāh who attains this sublime station has now arrived at the pinnacle of sanctity and at the very door of prophecy. Because the individual persona of the saint is now fully conjoined with that of Muḥammad, the saint's disciples may confuse their teacher's earthly form with that of the Prophet himself. When this happens, the saint becomes a veritable personification of the Messenger of God:

> Know, may God preserve you, that the Perfect Human Being is the axis (*quṭb*) around which revolve the manifestations of being (*aflāk al-wujūd*) from the beginning to the end. Although he is one [in essence] from the beginning of existence until the end of time, he varies according to the image he occupies and appears in human bodies (*kanāʾis*). He is only named, however, according to a single image and is not named according to any other image. His original name is Muḥammad, his *kunya* is Abū'l-Qāsim (the Consecrated), his description is ʿAbdallāh (Slave of God), and his nickname (*laqab*) is Shams ad-Dīn (Sun of the Religion). He has other names with respect to other images and in every age possesses a name associated with his image at that particular time.
>
> I discovered [Muḥammad] (may God bless and preserve him) in the image of my master, Shaykh Sharaf ad-Dīn Ismāʾīl al-Jabartī, although I did not know [then] that he was the Prophet. I only knew that he was a shaykh. This is one of the visions that was granted to me in Zabīd in the year 796/1394. The secret of this matter is that [the Prophet's] image can appear in every image, so that when the disciple (*adīb*) sees him in one of the Muḥammadan Images that characterize him in [daily] life, he calls him by the name in which he [normally] sees him. But when he sees him

> in a particular image among others and knows that he is [in reality] Muḥammad, he cannot name him except by the name of that [Muḥammadan] image. Indeed, the name would not occur to him [in the first place] except by means of the Muḥammadan Reality.
>
> Did you not see [Muḥammad] (may God bless and preserve him) when he appeared in the image of [the Sufi Abū Bakr] ash-Shiblī?[61] Ash-Shiblī told his disciple: "I bear witness that I am the Messenger of Allah!" Because his disciple was a master of spiritual insight (*ṣāḥib kashf*), he knew him [in his Muḥammadan image] and said: "I bear witness that you are the Messenger of Allah! . . ."
>
> Beware, lest you imagine my statements to be based on the doctrine of metempsychosis (*tanāsūkh*)! May God and the Messenger of God forbid that this was ever my intention! Rather, the Messenger of God is latent in every human image until he becomes manifest in that image, and his habit (*sunna*) is to be depicted in every age in the image of [humanity's] most perfect forms so that he may exalt them and cause others to be attracted to them. They are his successors (*khulafāʾuhu*) on the outside and he is their reality on the inside.[62]

Al-Jīlī's theory of the Perfect Human Being is based on several premises that would later be incorporated into the doctrines of the Jazūliyya Sufi order. The most important of these is the idea that the Prophet Muḥammad is not just the deceased founder of a religion but a living reality who reappears to guide Muslims toward the pinnacle of human achievement. These appearances are not physical, however, and do not involve the transmigration of souls or the resurrection of Muḥammad as a flesh-and-blood human being. Rather, they occur on the level of analogy. This is what al-Jīlī means when he says that the Muḥammadan Reality is the "secret" (*sirr*) of *al-insān al-kāmil*. This secret is latent in all human beings, but it is only actualized in the person whose qualities best match those of the Prophet himself. This Perfect Human Being, whose image is reconfigured by the Muḥammadan attributes he has taken on, is revealed in his true form as the paradigmatic saint and the successor (*khalīfa*) to the Prophet in his time.

The Jazūlite Doctrine of the Muḥammadan Way

The doctrine of the Perfect Human Being lies behind many of the invocations in Muḥammad ibn Sulaymān al-Jazūlī's book of prayers on behalf of the Prophet, *Dalāʾil al-khayrāt*. In terms of genre alone, this work was not unusual for its time, for a considerable amount of devotional literature in praise of the Prophet had existed in the Maghrib since the first half of the fourteenth century.[63] Most of these works were commentaries on a panegyric poem by the Egyptian Sufi Sharaf ad-Dīn al-Būṣīrī (d. 697/1298), *Al-Kawākib ad-durriyya fī madḥ khayr al-bariyya* (The Spheres which glitter in praise of the best of humankind), better known as *Al-Burda* (The Mantle).[64] *Al-Burda* was particularly popular in Dukkāla, where al-Jazūlī received much of his Sufi training. One commentary on this work, Abū'l-Qāsim al-Māgirī's *Uns al-waḥda fī sharḥ al-Burda* (The Intimacy of union in the exegesis of *al-Burda*), was written in the fourteenth century C.E. and could have been used by al-Jazūlī at Ribāṭ Tīṭ-n-Fiṭr.[65]

Also relevant to al-Jazūlī's compilation of *Dalāʾil al-khayrāt* was a collection of invocations entitled *Maqṣūra nabawiyya ʿalā madḥ khayr al-bariyya* (A Prophetic sanctuary for praise of the best of humankind), by Abū Zayd al-Maqūdī (d. 807/1404–5).[66] A friend and companion of the Andalusian Shādhilī master Ibn ʿAbbād ar-Rundī, al-Maqūdī spent the latter part of his life in Fez, where al-Jazūlī was to study a few decades later. Ibn ʿAbbād also added to the corpus of prophetological literature by writing *Fatḥ at-tuḥfa wa idāʿat aṣ-ṣadafa li-taqaʿ al-muwāfaqa* (Revealing the gem and setting the mother-of-pearl in preparation for divine acceptance). In this treatise, the noted Sufi and preacher at the Qarawiyyīn mosque advocated an approach to Islamic practice that was based on the spiritual aspects of the Prophet's Sunna. Such an approach was particularly necessary, he felt, in his own time, when religious and political leaders adhered to the Sunna in public, but routinely deviated from it in private.[67]

Most of the invocations in *Dalāʾil al-khayrāt* were drawn from well-known hadith collections and devotional works such as Abū Ṭālib al-Makkī's *Qūt al-qulūb.* This reliance on traditional sources does not mean, however, that al-Jazūlī was unfamiliar with the doctrines of Ibn al-ʿArabī or al-Jīlī. On the contrary, he often describes the Prophet in ways that clearly recall the concept of *al-insān al-kāmil.* This can be seen, for example, when he refers to Muḥammad as "the person who is the quintessence of existence and the cause for all that exists" (*insān ʿayn al-wujūd wa's-sabab fī kull al-mawjūd*).[68] Elsewhere, al-Jazūlī evokes Ibn al-ʿArabī's concept of the Muḥammadan Reality when he deconstructs the Arabic root of the Prophet's name (*ḥmd*) as: "the *ḥāʾ* of [divine] mercy (*raḥma*), the *mīm* of creation (*mulk*), and the *dāl* of everlastingness (*dawām*)."[69]

Even better evidence of al-Jazūlī's acquaintance with the concept of the

Perfect Human Being can be found in his inspirational sayings, which were written down by his disciples and preserved in hagiographical anthologies such al-Fasī's *Mumtiʿ al-asmāʿ*. These divine addresses (*muḥadathāt*) and conversations with God (*mukalāmāt*) demonstrate that al-Jazūlī saw himself as *al-insān al-kāmil.* He even went so far as to claim that the greatest Muslim saints shared in the station of prophethood:

> Assembly of *murīdīn!* Look at your Master, for He is with me! I have no perception (*naẓar*) except through Him. His perfection has encompassed my breast and my life. Indeed, it has encompassed me for all of my life! His perfection has annihilated me from everything other than Him.
>
> Oh you who would see me on earth! See me instead in Heaven, on the Throne, and even above it! Do you not know that the axial saints are needed by every created being? They are in the station of prophethood (*maqām an-nubuwwa*), revealing the divine secret (*yafshūna as-sirr*)! Oh you who would attain salvation! Go to them, even if they are in Baghdad! For going to them brings illumination, mercy, and the [divine] secret to hearts.[70]
>
> Oh My slave! Do not begrudge what I have given you of My speech (*ḥadīthī*) and My words (*kalāmī*). For I have spoken to you in preeternity before your existence. I have renewed your understanding after your creation and illuminated your heart before your existence. I have illuminated your essence after your creation, I have made known to you the details of My knowledge, and I have honored you among the best of My creation. I have inspired you to hearken unto Me, I have given you authority over the finest of My creatures, and I have bestowed on you the greatest secret. Oh My slave, all of the ulama are in your grasp![71]

Apart from a few treatises and inspirational sayings such as these, little of al-Jazūlī's doctrinal output has survived to the present. For this reason, the legacy of Ibn al-ʿArabī and al-Jīlī in the doctrines of the Jazūliyya must be traced through the students of al-Jazūlī's successor, ʿAbd al-ʿAzīz at-Tabbāʿ. The writings of these second-generation Jazūlite shaykhs rely heavily on Ibn al-ʿArabī's model of sainthood and provide an image of *aṭ-Ṭarīqa al-Muḥammadiyya* that is strikingly different from the stark and sober reformism most often depicted in academic literature.

The first Jazūlite Sufi to explicitly base his model of sainthood on the doctrines of Ibn al-ʿArabī and al-Jīlī was ʿAlī Ṣāliḥ al-Andalusī. This merchant-scholar and refugee from Granada was a disciple of at-Tabbāʿ and headed the Jazūliyya zāwiya in Fez.[72] In a work entitled *Sharḥ Raḥbat al-amān* (Commentary on the "Terrain of Safety"), he uses al-Jīlī's concept of the Muḥammadan Image as the basis for his own theory of paradigmatic sainthood (*quṭbiyya*). This theory develops out of a commentary on a wisdom saying (*ḥikma*) of al-Jazūlī that was known to Jazūlite Sufis after the words of its opening sentence: *Raḥbat al-amān ṭarīq al-aqṭāb* ("The terrain of safety is the way of the axial saints."):

> The Terrain of Safety is the way of the axial saints. The Terrain of Safety—above it are the Gardens, the gardens of miracles (*rawḍāt al-karāmāt*). Above these are the Fields (*al-mayādīn*), the fields of those who have arrived. Above this is the Musk, the musk of those who have attained (*misk al-wāṣilīn*). Above this is the Ambergris, the ambergris of those who are are brought near (*ʿanbar al-mutaqarrabīn*). Above this is the Moon, the moon of [Allah's] intimates (*qamar al-mustaʾnisīn*). Above this are the Rewards (*majālib*), the spoils (*ghanāʾim*) of those who are protected (*li-ahl al-ʿināya*).[73]

For al-Andalusī, al-Jazūlī's aphorism details the paranormal gifts that are the "rewards" or "spoils" of mystics who have experienced supernal intoxication (*al-ḥaḍra al-ʿaliyya*). Such rewards are only granted to those who follow the Sufi path with "humility and submissiveness, accompanied by the ultimate in asceticism, contentment, and an unwavering belief in orthodoxy" (*iʿtiqād al-khafq fīʾl-jamāʿa*).[74] Their very existence refutes the assertions of jurists and theologians who claim that sainthood belongs only to past ages and act as a rebuke to anti-Sufi exoterists who deny that sainthood exists at all. Saints produce miracles, says al-Andalusī, to prove that the source of their knowledge is the Prophet himself. To deny that miracles and sainthood exist, therefore, is to deny the *sunna* of both God and His Messenger: "He who is ignorant of Allah's acts of grace (*laṭāʾif*) is ignorant of Allah. He who is ignorant of Allah is ignorant of divine guidance and the laws (*aḥkām*) of Allah. He who is ignorant of Allah and the laws of Allah has nearly become an unbeliever" (*fa-qad kāda yakūn kāfiran*).[75]

To admit the validity of sainthood and miracles, however, is not to deny the authority of exoteric religion. For al-Andalusī, esoterism does not oppose exoterism; it complements it. The difference between the two perspectives lies mainly in their initial assumptions. The legalistic perspective of exoterism assumes a weakness or inadequacy on the part of the human being that requires discipline and indoctrination to overcome. For this reason, it stresses sincerity and effort and depends on outward conformity with the divine command. Its epistemology is based on knowledge of the laws of God (*al-ʿilm bi-aḥkām Allāh*) and is summarized by the phrase, "We have heard" (*samiʿnā*). Esotericism honors the same virtues, but starts from the premise that the human being is prepared to fulfill his role as God's vicegerent. For this reason, it stresses love and perfection rather than discipline and depends on inward conformity with the divine command. Its epistemology is based on unmediated knowledge from God (*al-ʿilm bi'llāh*) and is summarized by the phrase, "We have witnessed" (*shahidnā*).[76]

Were it not for exoterism, esoterism would have no meaning. Divine illumination (*nūr*) is found everywhere, whether it be in God's laws (*sharīʿa*) or in His reality (*ḥaqīqa*). For this reason, the fully actualized Jazūlite shaykh (*ash-shaykh al-wāṣil*) must be a master in both epistemological worlds—that of the Law and of transcendent reality alike:

> The shaykh is not a shaykh until he has attained the acme of both exoteric and esoteric knowledge—whether through his own efforts or granted by Allah through the Ḥaqīqa or the Sharīʿa, on the basis of [his knowledge of] the obligatory (*wājib*), the justifiable (*jā'iz*), and the impossible (*mustaḥīl*)—and has attained the ultimate in practice and sincerity for the sake of Allah alone. Here he finds the reality of divine favor, divine guidance, and divine protection both within himself and at the hands of his shaykh. He obtains the authorization (*idhn*) of his shaykh according to the Sharīʿa, but finds the reality of this authorization to have come from his Lord by virtue of the Ḥaqīqa. In other words, he is absolved from personal responsibility to the extent that his desire is the same as his Lord's. By virtue of the Sharīʿa, he guides those who follow him to sufficiency in the Book of Allah and the Sunna of the Messenger of Allah. By virtue of the Ḥaqīqa, he becomes a leader of men, who assent [to his guidance] by carrying out what he asks them to do. This is the sign of the truthfulness of the shaykh who guides himself and his followers according to the Sharīʿa and who, by virtue of the Ḥaqīqa, is protected from the whisperings of his ego. . . . Thus, he who wishes Allah to guide him by means of the Ḥaqīqa is guided to the shaykh by means of the Sharīʿa.[77]

Once the seeker has found a shaykh who understands the essential reciprocity between Sharīʿa and *ḥaqīqa,* the sincere disciple (*al-murīd aṣ-ṣādiq*) entrusts himself to the shaykh's guidance and begins the quest for spiritual enlightenment. This journey, says al-Andalusī, will consume the seeker's entire life, for knowledge of the Absolute is "an ocean without a shore."[78] To embark upon this ocean, the seeker needs a boat, which are the exoteric, transmitted sciences of Islam (*al-ʿulūm an-naqliyya*). This knowledge is necessary because the provisions required for the journey are the exoteric disciplines of obedience, repentance, and awareness of one's obligations toward oneself. To acquire these the seeker must turn toward God in prayer, fasting, and invocation, and must lessen the power of the ego through prayers on behalf of the Prophet. In time, the seeker will progress to the stage of responsibility (*taklīf*) in the Sufi path and will receive the invocation (*wird*) that he will use for the rest of his life. At this point, the seeker acquires the disciplines that are specific to Sufism, such as retreat, the mortification of desires, self-criticism (*muḥāsaba*), and self-awareness (*murāqaba*). To perfect these disciplines the sincere disciple travels frequently, befriending the members of his brotherhood and visiting other Sufi shaykhs. If these shaykhs are living, the seeker sits at their feet and learns from them. If they are dead, the seeker honors them with the ritual of visiting (*ziyāra*).

Upon seeing the "face of God" in the extinction of his personal attributes, the seeker is now ready to advance beyond formal learning to the stations of the supernal. The sincere disciple passes through these stations one-by-one until his selfhood is extinguished in the divine presence through the obliteration of all "essence and attributes, his names, acts, thoughts, ability, choice, determination, desires, and cares—what comes from him and through him, including his speech." The sincere disciple has now attained the sainthood of intimacy (*walāya*), which is characterized by God's direct maintenance of the saint's existence (*baqāʾ*). Here the seeker merges with the divine essence, his attributes conjoin with the divine attributes, his names are one with the divine names, and his actions are determined by the divine will. This is also the station of miracles, for paranormal phenomena now issue forth from the seeker by necessity rather than choice. These miracles act as proofs of the seeker's attainment of *walāya* and are a by-product of the specialized role (*takhṣīṣ*) through which the sainthood of *walāya* is manifested on earth.

From the station of *walāya*, the seeker next ascends through even greater levels of exaltation, starting with the loss of physical consciousness (*ghayba*), and continuing through intoxication in the divine presence (*al-ḥaḍra al-*

ulūhiyya), the awareness of divine singularity (*waḥdāniyya*), knowledge of the secrets of the divine names, and the complete understanding of the Supreme Name (*fahm al-ism al-ʿaẓīm*).[79] At this point, the newly minted saint attains the acme of his quest—a station that is beyond physical description and which can only be described metaphorically. Now fully actualized as *ash-shaykh al-wāṣil,* the former disciple is entirely maintained by the Light of Muḥammad (*nūr Muḥammad*): "[Muḥammad] is their lord, their imam, their means to their Master, and the epitome of [Allah's] favor upon them. Were it not for [Muḥammad], they would not be themselves or other than themselves. The totality of their existence is by virtue of [Muḥammad's] existence and all are illuminated by his radiance. Allah sanctifies them with the holiness of [Muḥammad's] light."[80]

This highest level of spiritual attainment is what al-Jazūlī calls the "Terrain of Safety." Here the saint becomes *al-insān al-kāmil.* As such, he and his fellow *awliyāʾ Allāh* are exalted over other men as substitutes for God's messengers (*abdāl ar-rusul*). This is because (as first explained by Ibn al-ʿArabī) they possess a portion of the Muḥammadan Reality in proportion to their role as exemplars of specific prophetic messages.[81] Like their predecessors, the historical prophets and messengers, they are the vicegerents of God on earth and the agents that God uses to govern His dominion:

> Allah makes [the axial saints] His vicegerents in managing the affairs (*taṣrīf*) of His dominion because of His concern for [mankind] and in order that they take refuge in them. He grants them knowledge from His own presence (*ʿilman min ladunihi*) and by means of His support and design directs them toward the preservation of His religion. He makes them guides (*adillāʾ*) to His presence and oneness and to His commands and prohibitions, and makes them visible in the world so that through them He may demonstrate the proof [of Himself] to His worshippers and so relate them to His names and attributes. In the material world (*al-wujūd*) they are the objects of His self-awareness: [they express] His will, His desire, His laws, His actions, His choices, and His management of affairs, according to the principles of justice (*ʿadl*) and virtue (*iḥsān*).[82]

In this greatest of all stations, *wilāya,* the sainthood of authority, takes precedence over *walāya,* the sainthood of intimacy. Because God has given *ash-shaykh al-wāṣil* the authority to dispose of the affairs of other human beings, the Jazūlite shaykh now has the right to inherit the states of Muḥammad, Messenger of God (*mīrāth aḥwāl an-nabī*). As a perfected saint, the shaykh's persona mirrors the Muḥammadan Image and the shaykh becomes, analogically speaking, the "Muḥammad" of his time:

> When Allah, in His Glory and Majesty, desires to create His worshippers and all of His creation . . . He concentrates in pre-eternity (*fī'l-azal*) on the radiance of the purity of His glory and beauty and ignites (*qadhafa*) from it the glory and beauty of our Prophet Muḥammad (may God bless and preserve him). Then, He makes of [the Prophet] a pure, illuminating, beautiful, perfect, and great light and makes from that light a mirror and an eye for knowledge. . . . Then Allah displays [Himself] before [the mirror] through His attributes and active names and imprints (*inṭabaʿa*) the images of His actions, attributes, and names on the mirror of perception before its creation. [This is done] so that His names and attributes will be linked to [the human archetype] so that [mankind] can know the first of them as well as the last. . . . Then Allah creates heirs (*waratha*) to [the Prophet Muḥammad] from his community, who inherit from him one-by-one and learn from him in each generation.[83]

Al-Andalusī concludes his commentary by stating that the Terrain of Safety is the "point of complete knowledge" (*nuqṭat al-ʿilm al-kamālī*) that legitimizes the sainthood of authority, *wilāya*. The "city" (*madīna*) of this dominion is Muḥammad, the "gate" (*bāb*) of the city is the Prophet's cousin and son-in-law ʿAlī, the founder of the Sufi Way, and the "key" (*miftāḥ*) to the gate is the Generative Saint (*al-ghawth*) or Axis of the Age (*quṭb az-zamān*). This person stands alone and unique as the successor to the Prophet and "heir to the supernal station" (*wārith al-maqām al-aʿlā*).[84]

The use of light imagery in *Sharḥ Raḥbat al-amān* recalls the "Light of Muḥammad" (*nūr Muḥammad*) metaphor that has been a part of both Sunni and Shiʿite mysticism since the ninth century C.E.[85] In one part of this work al-Andalusī interprets the famous "Verse of Light" of the Qur'an (XXIV [*an-Nūr*], 35) as alluding to the Light of Muḥammad—an exegesis which appears to be based on that of the Iraqi Sufi Sahl at-Tustarī (d. 283/896).[86] Here the axial saint is seen as a lamp lit by the oil of gnosis, which is set in the niche of Muḥammad's eternal light. As a way of highlighting Jazūlite Sufism's dependence on the Prophetic archetype, al-Andalusī remarks that this light would not have been passed down to succeeding generations if it had not been for the family of the Prophet. He traces its line of transmission from ʿAlī to ʿAbd al-Qādir al-Jīlānī, and thence via Abū'l-Ḥasan ash-Shādhilī to al-Jazūlī.[87]

ʿAlid symbology is even more explicit in the writings of al-Andalusī's student ʿAbdallāh al-Ghazwānī (d. 935/1528–9), the successor to ʿAbd al-ʿAzīz at-Tabbāʿ as shaykh al-jamāʿa of the Jazūliyya and the apparent originator of the term *aṭ-ṭarīqa al-Muḥammadiyya.* The career of al-Ghazwānī will be discussed in detail in the following chapter. However, it is important to note at the present juncture that this Bedouin Arab shaykh from the ash-Shāwiya region near the modern Moroccan capital of Rabat maintained a zāwiya for several years among the Banū Fazankār tribe in northern Morocco, whose homeland was near the Idrisid center of Jabal al-ʿAlam. Al-Ghazwānī was strongly influenced by the traditions of both Shādhilī Sufism and Idrisid sharifism, and he tended to downplay other influences on Jazūlite doctrine. Al-Ghazwānī was also to become central to the development of the sharifian state, for it was he who gave crucial support to sharifian political aspirations and institutionalized the annual pilgrimage to the open-air tomb (*rawḍa*) of ʿAbd as-Salām ibn Mashīsh on Jabal al-ʿAlam.[88] By making the tomb of ash-Shādhilī's teacher an object of pilgrimage for Jazūlite Sufis, al-Ghazwānī helped to ensure the primacy of the Shādhilī perspective in Jazūlite Sufism and linked the political agenda of aṭ-Ṭāʾifa al-Jazūliyya to that of the sharifs.

Al-Ghazwānī's writings were compiled after his death into a volume titled *An-Nuqṭa al-azaliyya fī sirr adh-dhāt al-Muḥammadiyya* (The Eternal point in the secret of the Muḥammadan essence).[89] The overriding theme of this eclectic collection of essays, letters, poems, and aphorisms was the explication of the "point of complete knowledge"—a term first coined by al-Jazūlī and later used by al-Andalusī to describe the epistemological basis of the Muslim saint's authority.[90] Although his writings can thus be seen as complementary to *Sharḥ Raḥbat al-amān,* al-Ghazwānī does more than merely restate al-Andalusī's premises. Instead, he proposes his own theory of sainthood that takes al-Andalusī's model more fully into the sociopolitical arena. The centerpiece of this more engaged theory of sainthood is the concept of *aṭ-Ṭarīqa al-Muḥammadiyya,* which al-Ghazwānī also called the "Method of the Muḥammadan Sunna" (*madhhab as-sunna al-Muḥammadiyya*), the "Way of the Muḥammadan Sunna" (*ṭarīqat as-sunna al-Muḥammadiyya*), and the "Technique of Archetypal Perception" (*sulūk an-naẓra al-azaliyya*).[91]

Clearly, al-Ghazwānī saw himself as a doctrinal innovator. This is proven by the first treatise in *An-Nuqṭa al-azaliyya,* which is called by its redactor "The Religious Manifesto (*ḥizb millī*) of Sīdī ʿAbdallāh al-Ghazwānī."

This essay was written in response to questions from two scholars in Cairo who were popular teachers of North African Sufis at the end of the fifteenth century C.E.: the Moroccan Aḥmad ibn ʿAbd ar-Raḥmān al-Hintātī, whom al-Ghazwānī calls the "exemplar of Maliki futuwwa at al-Azhar mosque," and the Egyptian *muftī,* Sufi, and Qur'anic exegete Muḥammad al-Laqānī (d. 935/1528–9).[92] Perhaps reflecting criticisms of the Jazūliyya Sufi order that were then being voiced by the disciples of al-Laqānī's master Aḥmad Zarrūq, al-Hintātī questions al-Ghazwānī about the nature of spiritual insight (*kashf*) and asks him to explain the doctrines of his followers, who call themselves the "Folk of Reverberation" (*ahl al-jursiyya*).

These queries provide an excuse for al-Ghazwānī to give a detailed explanation of his theory of the "Bell" (*jaras*), a term he uses for the axial saint, in place of the more widely employed *quṭb az-zamān.* Finding a new way of describing the axial saint was necessary at this time because the interpretive circularity of the concept of the Perfect Human Being allowed multiple claimants to ultimate spiritual mastership to appear at the same time in different places—sometimes even within the same country. Because of this development, the paradigm of *al-insān al-kāmil,* like that of the *khalīfa* after the tenth century C.E., was reduced in practice to a model of regional rather than pan-Islamic applicability. A way had to be found to make the idea of paradigmatic sainthood regain its original uniqueness and universality.

Although al-Ghazwānī's use of the bell as a symbol for paradigmatic sainthood appears unusual for a Muslim, it was in fact in complete agreement with Islamic tradition. This seemingly "Christian" metaphor was legitimized by a well-substantiated hadith in which the Prophet Muḥammad describes revelation as coming to him like the "clanging of a bell" (*ṣalṣalat al-jaras*).[93] The metaphor of the bell was also used in *Al-Insān al-kāmil* by al-Jīlī, who interpreted the phrase *ṣalṣalat al-jaras* as referring to the divine attribute of potency (*aṣ-ṣifa al-qādiriyya*). Making a pun on the name of his own Sufi order (the Qādiriyya), al-Jīlī describes this reverberation as part of the "potent" (*qādirī*) manifestation of the divine names in the guise of the axial saint, who gives proof of his station through the worldly attributes of power and prestige (*al-hiba al-qādiriyya*).[94]

Al-Jīlī was not the first mystic, however, to use the bell as a metaphor for divine self-disclosure. In earlier generations, it had been linked to Ibn al-ʿArabī's theory of the Muḥammadan Reality through the doctrines of letter divination. In his latter tradition, which existed on the margins of North African Sufism, the Arabic letter *mīm*—which symbolized the name Muḥammad—was visualized as the clapper of a bell, whose "rope" (the downward-hanging tail of the *mīm*) represented the isthmus (*barzakh*) between the material world and the divine archetypes. According to *Shams al-maʿārif al-kubrā* (The Sun of the greatest forms of knowledge), a widely read work on divination by Ibn al-ʿArabī's North African contemporary Aḥmad al-Būnī (d. 622/1225): "The bell tolls for each man. He who listens to it is elevated and is taken from the world for union with Allah, which is the goal of prayer."[95]

For al-Ghazwānī, this preexistent bell is the Logos, which "peals out" (*ajrasa*) the Muḥammadan Reality to the world: "The Axial Saint (*al-quṭb*) is light, the Generative Saint (*al-ghawth*) is a secret, and the Bell (*al-jaras*) is a piercing sound (*ṣarāṣir*)."[96] This piercing sound, the "pealing" or reverberation of the divine archetypes on the verge of their actualization, creates a subtle music or harmonic that is heard by each Muslim saint according to his or her rank and ability. The "melody" of this harmonic is understood most fully by the Jazūlite *ash-shaykh al-wāṣil,* who uses its music to guide disciples toward *aṭ-Ṭarīqa al-Muḥammadiyya.* At its culmination, this path leads to what al-Ghazwānī calls the "Sovereignty of Saintly Authority" (*siyādat al-imāma*). Here the saint inherits the authority of the prophets through his assumption of the "Prophetic Inheritance" (*al-wirātha an-Nabawiyya*).[97] "If you knew the truth of what lies deep within you," al-Ghazwānī asserts, "you would be a messenger (*rasūl*) to your peers and a leader (*qāʾim*) because of the rights you possess over the one who seeks you out. . . . The people of your time would appoint you caliph (*istakhlafūka*) . . . and you would attain the perfection of the Muḥammadan Sunna."[98]

The terminology employed by al-Ghazwānī in *An-Nuqṭa al-azaliyya* suggests that this bedouin shaykh may have been responsible for what García-Arenal and others have called the "Fatimid" aspects of Jazūlite doctrine. This hypothesis is confirmed in passages where al-Ghazwānī describes the Bell in ways that are clearly reminiscent of the Shiʿite doctrine of the imamate. Depending on the role that the axial saint performs in his community, he may be called King (*malik*), Exemplar of His Time (*qudwat ahl zamānihi*), Viceregent of God on Earth (*khalīfat Allāh fī'l-arḍ*), Lord Imam (*as-sayyid al-imām*), the One Who Has Arisen (*al-qāʾim*), the Commander (*al-amīr*), Disposer of Affairs (*ṣāḥib at-taṣrīf*), the Supreme Paradigm (*al-mathal al-aʿlā*), or the Mirror of God (*mirʾāt Allāh*).[99] In addition, the Bell is granted the following prerogatives:

1. He is protected (*maʿṣūm*) from the faults of tyranny or sin.
2. His abilities are beyond those of ordinary human beings.
3. His understanding and perception are greater than those of his contemporaries.
4. Everything on earth invokes his name, either intentionally or otherwise.
5. When he attains his ambition (*himma*), it is through his own agency alone.
6. Everything depends on him, whereas he is dependent on nothing and no one but God.[100]

Since the chief responsibility of the Bell saint is to uphold the Muḥammadan paradigm in lieu of the Prophet, he must actively participate in worldly affairs and guide others according to what al-Ghazwānī calls the saint's "inspirational dictate" (*ḥukm al-anbāʾ*). The axial saint is thus a "messenger" and a "witness" for his peers (*wa yakūnu ar-rasūlu ʿalaykum shahīdan*)[101] and is confirmed by God as a worker of miracles and a leader of men (*ṣāḥib at-taṣrīf*).[102] He exercises authority directly and on his own behalf, without needing to justify his actions by analogy (*qiyās*) and without authorization from the ulama.[103] God alone is the guarantor of the Bell saint's judgments and makes His wishes known through divine addresses (*mukhāṭabāt*) and inspirational revelations (*waḥy al-ilhām*).[104]

Because of the Bell saint's divine election (*iṣṭifāʾiyya*), he is the hope (*amān*) of every seeker and the imam of every saint. He is the proof of God's salvation (*saʿādat Allāh*) on earth, the proof of God's guidance (*hidāyat Allāh*) in heaven, the proof of God's favor (*riḍāʾ Allāh*) toward His dominion, and the proof of God's glory (*ʿizz Allāh*) in his knowledge. The knowledge of the Bell saint legitimizes his authority over his fellow human beings and encompasses both the exoteric and the esoteric aspects of the Muḥammadan Sunna. Following him is thus obligatory (*wājib*), and his disciples are bound to him by an oath of loyalty that ensures ultimate salvation (*bayʿat as-saʿāda*).[105]

Apart from the rule of formal appointment (*naṣṣ*) by one's predecessor and the transmission of the Prophetic Inheritance through the bloodline, there is little to distinguish al-Ghazwānī's Bell saint from the Shiʿite Imam.

For example, a list of the prerogatives of the Imam that is very similar to al-Ghazwānī's prerogatives of the Bell saint was written down in the early eleventh century C.E. by the Ithnā' ʿAsharī theologian ash-Shaykh al-Mufīd (d. 413/1022):

1. The Imam takes the place of the prophets in enforcing judgments, safeguarding the Sharīʿa, and educating mankind.
2. He is protected from sin and error.
3. He is the recipient of extraordinary knowledge, including the knowledge of people's thoughts and the ability to learn every science and language.
4. He can perform miracles and receive signs (*ayāt*) from God.
5. After death he is transported from his tomb to God's Paradise (*jannat Allāh*) and intercedes for supplicants until the Day of Resurrection.
6. His status on earth is similar to that of the prophets in respect to the honor, reverence, and obedience that are due to him.[106]

The question of possible Shiʿite influence on the Jazūlite conception of authority is problematized by the fact that many of the characteristics of the Shiʿite Imam were appropriated by Sunni mystics as early as the ninth century C.E. After all, what was al-Ḥakīm at-Tirmidhī's concept of the "Seal of Sainthood" if not a Sufi gloss on the Hidden Imam? Even though al-Ghazwānī uses terminology that appears to have Shiʿite origins, one should not take this to mean that this sixteenth-century Moroccan shaykh was a crypto-Shiʿite. However, neither was he typically Sunni. This is proven by the accusations of Fatimism that were leveled at al-Ghazwānī and his disciples by the Moroccan ulama and certain juridical Sufis. It is equally as inaccurate to say that his model of sainthood was "Sunni" as it is to say that it was "Shiʿite." The real truth lies somewhere in the middle. Clearly, al-Ghazwānī's ideas were based on Sufi traditions that were formulated in the context of Sunni Islam. In particular, they show little evidence of the specific types of Neoplatonism (such as the doctrine of *al-ʿaql al-kullī,* the Universal Intellect) that are usually associated with Fatimid Shiʿism. It is similarly unlikely that al-Ghazwānī was exposed to Ithnā' ʿAsharī teachings. No members of this sect were to be found in Morocco in the fifteenth and sixteenth centuries C.E. and al-Ghazwānī himself never traveled outside of Morocco. If the modern researcher wants to look for Shiʿite influences on his doctrine of the paradigmatic saint, it is best to start closer to home—

with the traditions of Idrisid sharifism that were discussed at the beginning of this chapter.

Apart from the Moroccan historian Abdallah Laroui, few modern scholars have taken the Shiʿism of the Idrisids very seriously.[107] This has resulted in part because sharifian Morocco has taken pains to depict itself as a Sunni country that follows the Maliki school of law and upholds the majoritarian tenets of the *Ahl as-Sunna wa'l-Jamāʿa*. According to this stance, there is nothing to link either the Moroccan state or its religious institutions to the doctrines that now divide Shiʿites and Sunnis. This is certainly correct. However, those who accept this position uncritically forget that the Hasanid traditions that came to Morocco with Mūlāy Idrīs in the late eighth century C.E. had little to do with either Ismāʿīlī or Ithnāʾ ʿAsharī Shiʿism. Hasanid Shiʿism, like its half-sibling Zaydism, was a set of political doctrines that saw authority as vested in the ʿAlid *qāʾim* who first "stands up" against injustice or unbelief. There is nothing in these doctrines to prevent a potential Hasanid imam from being a Maliki jurist, an Ashʿarite theologian, or even a Sufi shaykh—roles that in fact were played simultaneously by the patron saint of Moroccan Sufism, Mūlāy ʿAbd as-Salām ibn Mashīsh. We have already seen how Mūlāy ʿAbd as-Salām's reputation was based as much on his Hasanid origins as it was on his knowledge of Sufism. Equally significant is the fact that he is portrayed in his native Ghumāra as a *qāʾim* who was martyred while opposing heresy and injustice.[108]

To say that al-Ghazwānī drew from the doctrinal well of Idrisid Shiʿism is not to say that he was a crypto-Shiʿite, or even that he always agreed with the political agenda of the Idrisid sharifs. On the contrary, it will be shown in the following chapter that relations between al-Ghazwānī and the Idrisids were mixed at best. What is more, the text of *An-Nuqṭa al-azaliyya* makes it clear that the Bell saint does not have to be a blood relation of the Prophet Muḥammad. This was not the case for al-Jazūlī, however, whose claim of sharifian descent was an important argument for his authority. The importance of a Prophetic genealogy was also acknowledged by al-Ghazwānī's shaykh, ʿAbd al-ʿAzīz at-Tabbāʿ, even though the latter was not generally acknowledged as a sharif. These views are reflected in the following lines of poetry, where at-Tabbāʿ appears uncomfortable with his given name, al-Ḥarrār (the Silk Weaver), and asserts that, in reality, he too belongs to the Prophet's family by attribution if not by descent:

Verily, I am a slave of God and the Follower (*at-tābiʿ*) [of the Prophet],
Exalted in praise through [my] perfection and qualities.

Yet ʿAbd al-ʿAzīz the Silk Weaver is my name,
Turning my filth into potters' clay (*yuṭānu ṭamathī*) and leading me to guidance.

If my ancestor the Messenger of God were alive [today],
I would say that this, too, is part of my reality![109]

For al-Ghazwānī, who was of bedouin origin and thus could not realistically claim to be a genealogical descendant of Muḥammad, at-Tabbāʿ's assertion of sharifian status was metaphorical rather than literal. Although al-Ghazwānī accepts the ʿAlid maxim that "whoever is not related to the Messenger of God cannot uphold the rights of God," he qualifies this assertion of sharifian authority by claiming that according to the "most exalted imams" (*khuṣūs al-āʾimma*), Muslims are ennobled not only through their birth but also through their piety, words, and deeds. In the end, al-Ghazwānī's final position on nobility is decidedly non-ʿAlid: "Those who are ennobled by reputation are better than those who are ennobled by birth" (*Shurafāʾ al-ḥasab afḍal min shurafāʾ an-nasab*).[110]

It is here that al-Ghazwānī's doctrine of the Prophetic Inheritance departs most conclusively from the ʿAlid doctrines that provided so much of its terminology. Although sharifs were well represented among the Sufis of the Ghazwāniyya branch of the Jazūliyya, they were intrinsically no better than anyone else. For al-Ghazwānī, the nobility of Prophetic descent was a potential that could only be proven by visible acts of piety and virtue. Indeed, he asserted, anyone who fully assimilated the Muḥammadan archetype has the right to call himself a "sharif" and aspire to the highest spiritual rank: "We have earned the right to act as witnesses for the Messenger of God because we took the oath of righteousness (*al-ʿahd al-mustaqīm*) as part of the pre-eternal covenant (*al-ʿahd al-qadīm*). . . . [We] took as our means to this end the manifest wisdom and eternal life of the Muḥammadan Sunna and, independently of our own choice, found it to be all-inclusive. [We] make the Sharīʿa obligatory for ourselves, but add the refinement (*adab*) that comes from the complete assimilation of the Sunna."[111]

A problem that is left unresolved by al-Ghazwānī's approach to sainthood, however, is that the "complete assimilation of the Sunna" to which he refers gives rise to revelatory states that are usually considered to be the prerogative of the prophets alone. This is because the Bell saint, in fulfilling his role as *al-insān al-kāmil* and heir to the prophets, attains his rank through "absolute fusion" (*jamʿ muṭlaq*) with the Muḥammadan Image. As Qāḍī ʿIyāḍ had remarked nearly four centuries previously, the assimilation of this archetype is heralded by miracles that mimic the Prophet's own. These miracles may include divine inspiration (*ilhām*), the direct perception of God (*mushāhada*), or even revelation itself (*waḥy*).[112] Although al-Ghazwānī is careful to point out that the revelation of God's word (*waḥy al-kalām*) has ended with the death of Muḥammad, he nonetheless maintains that inspirational revelation (*waḥy al-ilhām*) has not ceased but continues in the postprophetic era. This latter type of revelation is most clearly manifested in the illuminative states (*ishrāq*) of the God-intoxicated saint (*majdhūb*) and is a direct consequence of the walī Allāh's identification with the Muḥammadan Image. This convergence of Prophet and saint is illustrated by al-Ghazwānī in the following poem:

> First, we came together at the fountainhead of reality.
> Second, we separated at the appearance of sainthood.
>
> Third, all came together in the act of fusion
> For a specific purpose, including the prophethood of humankind.
>
> Fourth, another fusion, the glory of our mission,
> In every locality proclaiming and interpreting every sign.
>
> Fifth, a truth, a right of our fusion,
> "Those of inflexible resolve" (*ūluw al-ʿazm*) in the night of my
> sublimity.[113]
>
> This was the mission for which the Lord of Humanity was delegated,
> Muḥammad the imitated, the exemplar of my exemplarity![114]

For the student of Sufism who is used to the metaphysical discourses of Ibn al-ʿArabī or al-Jīlī, al-Ghazwānī's writings may at times seem uncomfortably political. His model of "Muḥammadan" sainthood was not only theoretical but was meant to be actualized in practice as well. His detours into worldly matters anticipate the so-called neo-Sufism of later generations and bring up the question of whether aṭ-Ṭāʾifa al-Jazūliyya was in fact the first "neo-Sufi" order in the Maghrib. Since al-Ghazwānī's concept of the "Muḥammadan Way" is often linked to neo-Sufism in Western scholarship, one might even feel justified in characterizing the shaykhs of the Jazūliyya as neo-Sufis.[115]

The problem with this assumption is that there is little other than the term *aṭ-ṭarīqa al-Muḥammadiyya* itself to link al-Ghazwānī to the concept of neo-Sufism as originally conceived by Fazlur Rahman and J. Spencer Trimingham.[116] As R. S. O'Fahey has pointed out in his study of the "neo-Sufi" shaykh Aḥmad ibn Idrīs al-Fāsī (d. 1253/1837), the North African tradition of the Muḥammadan Way had almost nothing to do with neo-Sufism as defined in academic literature. The same can be said for al-Ghazwānī's definition of this concept. Although his paradigm of the Bell saint was predicated on al-Jīlī's doctrine of the extinction of the Muslim saint in the Muḥammadan Image, he never intended this to replace the mainstream Sufi concept of extinction in God. Also contrary to the assumptions of Rahman and Trimingham, neither al-Ghazwānī nor his Sufi critics such as Aḥmad Zarrūq were sympathetic with the exoteric approach of the Hanbalite jurist Ibn Taymiyya.[117] In the final analysis, the only aspects of neo-Sufism that apply to al-Ghazwānī are his fascination with spiritual hierarchies and his fondness for bureaucratic organization, attitudes that were common to sixteenth-century institutional Sufism in general. If it is necessary to continually qualify neo-Sufism by explaining away exceptions such as these, one must ask whether this concept has any validity whatsoever—at least in the context of early-modern North Africa.

Perhaps the most "modern" aspect of al-Ghazwānī's Sufism was the view that sainthood is as much a social reality as it is a metaphysical concept. In *An-Nuqṭa al-azaliyya* the sainthood of authority (*wilāya*) is dependent on other people's knowledge (or recognition) of the saint, not on the saint's own knowledge.[118] According to al-Ghazwānī's theory of sainthood—which would have pleased the likes of modern scholars such as Pierre Delooz and Ernest Gellner—a candidate for sainthood first stakes a claim to be a walī Allāh on the basis of public attention. However, contrary to Gellner's model and more like that of Delooz, sainthood is confirmed only when the prospective saint is recognized as such by his Sufi peers. But the process of legitimation does not end here. Only when the greatest Sufis of one's generation (*al-khuṣūṣ al-khāṣṣa*) acknowledge the prospective saint does the saint attain the state in which authority on earth (*wilāya*) is confirmed by closeness to God (*walāya*).

In strictly doctrinal terms, however, the extent to which the saint can wield power over others depends on his closeness to God and his ability to receive and transmit divine knowledge. The authority of the saint is not only validated by one's peers, but it must also be validated by God Himself. This is illustrated in al-Ghazwānī's writings by a hierarchy of signs of intimacy with God, which reveal the nature of the saint's *walāya.* The lowest level of *walāya* is heralded by the onset of divine inspirations (*walāyat al-ilhām*). Next, the saint acquires the ability to interpret these inspirations (*walāyat al-fahm*). Third, he is imbued with the divine Logos and speaks with the words of God Himself (*walāyat al-kalim*). Finally, after arriving at the stage of the "sainthood of the people of the Logos" (*walāyat ahl al-kalim*), the walī Allāh perceives Reality without the need to extinguish his sense of self (*walāyat an-naẓr bilā fanāʾ*). He hears the "reverberation" of the divine discourse at all times (*walāyat as-samʿ bilā taḥdīd*), and answers the needs of his petitioners with miracles that are bestowed on him as divine tokens of intimacy (*walāyat al-istijāb wa'l-istihāb*).

After reaching the level of *walāyat al-istijāb wa'l-istihāb,* the saint is now empowered to exercise authority on Earth (*wilāya*). This is first expressed as the authority to interpret the laws of God (*wilāyat al-ḥukm*). Next, the saint is granted the authority to issue his own commands (*wilāyat al-amr*). Finally, he is given the authority to dispose of the affairs of others (*wilāyat at-taṣrīf*). This penultimate level of *wilāya* sainthood is manifested in every dimension at once: outwardly, in the world of visible reality (*aẓ-ẓāhir*); inwardly, in the world of invisible reality (*al-bāṭin*); and subtly, in the essence of reality itself (*bāṭin al-bāṭin*). Here, authority is a function of the saint's role as a spiritual and behavioral paradigm. Paradoxically, however, the penultimate stage of *wilāya* is called by al-Ghazwānī the "Sainthood of Contingency" (*wilāyat at-tamkīn*). This is because the powers of the saint are not universal, but remain qualified by time (*tamkīn al-waqt*) and limited by space (*tamkīn maḥdūd*). The saint whose "contingency" is unlimited or universal (*tamkīn munazzah*) is at a still higher level: that of the *jaras,* the Bell saint. This truly paradigmatic figure is characterized by infallibility (*ʿiṣma*) and his authority over others is comparable to that of the Prophet himself.

The Bell saint of the Jazūliyya-Ghazwāniyya was the most potent manifestation of sainthood in Moroccan Sufism. Combining the Idrisid concept of the imamate with the *imitatio Muhammadi* as expressed through Ibn al-ʿArabī's theory of the Muḥammadan Reality and al-Jīlī's corollary of the Muḥammadan Image, this supreme shaykh and paradigmatic saint was tailor-made to assume the role of both political leader and savior in a region that had fallen into a state of economic dependency, social turmoil, and political prostration. According to the model of sainthood that was formulated by al-Andalusī and al-Ghazwānī, all popularly legitimated holy persons, from the educated *shaykh aṭ-ṭāʾifa* to the ecstatic and even illiterate *majdhūb,* could claim a significant share of the Muḥammadan paradigm. By actualizing a portion of the Muḥammadan Inheritance that was latent in every human being, each saint could be compared by analogy with the Prophet Muḥammad, the Messenger of God.

The widespread acceptance of this model in early-modern Morocco made it difficult for the ulama to oppose the political agenda of the Jazūliyya Sufi order. This was especially the case because most of these scholars shared the Jazūlite shaykhs' desire for reform and jihad against the Portuguese. More than at any other time since the late Almoravid period, the Sufis of this era involved themselves politically as *mujāhidūn,* moral censors, and agents of the collective will. It is to this "worldly" aspect of Jazūlite Sufism that we will turn in the final chapter of this book.

CHAPTER EIGHT

Paradigmatic Sainthood in the Material World: The Jazūliyya and the Rise of the Sharifian State

Reconsidering Sufi Populism

At the end of the fifteenth century C.E., Aḥmad Zarrūq, the juridical Sufi from Fez who was forced into exile because of his opposition to a pogrom against the Jews of his native city, wrote the following critique of Moroccan Sufism in *Ar-Radd ʿalā ahl al-bidʿa:*

> Our concern is with a particular clique which overran and spread throughout this our Maghrib in both rural and urban areas, and much more in the rural areas. This was invented by certain people to benefit from the rulers of this world. They started gathering the ignorant and vulgar, male and female, whose hearts are blank and whose minds are immature. They instilled into them from a religious point of view the belief that repentance is to be had by shaving the head, gobbling up food, gathering for banquets, invoking by turn, utterances and cries, using the mantles and beads, making a show of themselves, and holding that so-and-so is their master and that there is no other master save him. They tour the country, and whenever they arrive at a populated area they start invoking by turn, as sheep and cattle are slaughtered for them. They move from one place to another with their servants. Some of them on their horses. They assert that by this they revive and display religion, while persuading the vulgar to believe that

> the ulama are obstructing the way to God, and warn the ignorant against them. So they became enemies of the learned and learning. Yet they are disunited because of the plenitude of their Shaikhs, and ramified into different groups, each group drawn up behind its Shaikh, speaking ill of the other group and its Shaikh. Thus enmity and hatred occurred among the Shaikhs to the degree that each of them wishes to drink the blood of the other. That is because of the rulers of this world. They have sold the Hereafter for this world and led astray many of God's creatures and corrupted their faith. God said: "Those who cancel what God has revealed of the Book and sell it for a paltry price—they shall eat naught but fire in their bellies. God shall not speak to them on the Day of Resurrection nor purify them and there awaits them a painful chastisement" [Qur'ān II (*al-Baqara*), 174].[1]

This polemic, which is repeated in greater detail in Zarrūq's *ʿUddat al-murīd aṣ-ṣādiq* (The Equipment of the sincere disciple),[2] is directed at the excesses of what Mohamed Kably has called "Sufisme en action" or "Sufisme engagé."[3] There is little doubt that the object of Zarrūq's reproach is aṭ-Ṭā'ifa at-Tabbāʿiyya, the institutional name given to the followers of ʿAbd al-ʿAzīz at-Tabbāʿ, the successor to al-Jazūlī as leader of the Jazūliyya Sufi order. But is this description really accurate? Are we justified in taking Zarrūq's critique of Sufi populism at face value? Before coming to a conclusion about Sufi populism, it might first be prudent to take a look at the complainant himself.

As we have seen in Chapter Six, Aḥmad Zarrūq was deeply scarred by his experiences in Morocco. This legist and Shādhilī shaykh was an eyewitness to the cruelty and injustice that could arise from a populism which gave free rein to its prejudices without the restraint of the law. For this reason, he valued stability above all else and advocated a centralized state that was buttressed by a strong military and a highly trained ulama. In the generation after his death, his disciples maintained his legacy by opposing nearly every form of popular dissent. For them, the restraints of order and tradition were the only sure protection against *fitna,* social unrest.[4] Consequently, they opposed the involvement of the Jazūliyya in dynastic politics and cast their lot with the Ottoman Empire and its Moroccan protégé, the Wattasid "Kingdom of Fez."

Given Zarrūq's background and experiences, it is best to take his critique of the Tabbāʿiyya with a grain of salt. Did he in fact witness the beginnings of a "maraboutic crisis"? Or might there be another, less-alarmist way of interpreting Sufi activism in the fifteenth and sixteenth centuries C.E.? The rich yet largely unexamined contents of the Moroccan archives should shed some light on these questions. To take but one example, a hagiographical monograph on the life of ʿAbdallāh al-Khayyāṭ (d. 939/1533), a politically influential Sufi from Algeria who founded a zāwiya[5] on the Zerhoun massif near the city of Meknès, provides a strikingly different perspective:

> At the zāwiya of [al-Khayyāṭ] there were about a thousand people who had memorized the Qur'an (*ḥamalat al-Qurʾān*), such that on every tree and rock in the forest near his house one could find two or three students reciting the Qur'an. Formal teaching (*tadrīs al-ʿilm*) went on non-stop at his zāwiya every day. Usually, the shaykh taught the *Risāla* of Ibn Abī Zayd [al-Qayrawānī] and the *Ḥikam* of Ibn ʿAṭāʾillāh [al-Iskandarī]. However, the students had to rely on [other instructors] at the zāwiya for [most of] their studies because the shaykh would often rise [from his lectures] in a spiritual state (*ḥāl*) and go off into seclusion.[6]

In this description of Sufi populism one can find none of Zarrūq's "enemies of the learned and learning." Yet according to Zarrūq's critique of Moroccan Sufism, this should not have been the case. Viewed superficially, ʿAbdallāh al-Khayyāṭ seems to have been the very type of mystic that Zarrūq feared the most. First of all, he was an ecstatic, a detail that is proven by his habit of cutting short his lectures and abandoning his students in a state of *ḥāl*. Second, he was connected to two politically active Sufi orders that often received the censure of sixteenth-century ulama: the Jazūliyya Sufi order, through an Arab disciple of al-Jazūlī called "Sīdī Ḥasan Ajāna," and the Rhāshidiyya-Milyāniyya Sufi order, via the noted Algerian ecstatic Aḥmad ibn Yūsuf al-Milyānī (d. 929/1523).[7]

But ecstatic Sufism and populism were only part of ʿAbdallāh al-Khayyāṭ's profile. He was also acquainted with eastern Sufi traditions and had been initiated into the Rifāʿiyya Sufi order by his father, who spent thirty years in Egypt and even studied under Aḥmad Zarrūq.[8] In addition, his most important shaykh, Aḥmad ibn Yūsuf al-Milyānī, was also a disciple of Zarrūq. Even more, far from being an opponent of the status quo, al-Khayyāṭ remained loyal to the Wattasid state and sought to make peace between the rulers of Fez and their rivals, the Saʿdians. He even went so far as to counsel his Sufi brethren to stay out of politics, saying, "Brothers, disagreement causes enmity and enmity brings misfortune; so leave the power over worldly affairs to the princes."[9]

The example of ʿAbdallāh al-Khayyāṭ tells us that there was more to Sufi populism than Zarrūq cared to admit. This should come as no surprise, since a major premise of this book has been that social activism is integral to the traditions of Moroccan Sufism. As we have seen in the previous chapters, many Moroccan saints saw themselves not only as teachers of disciples, but also as major players in local and regional politics. This "worldly" side of saintly authority is sometimes linked in sacred biography to the saint's role as an exemplar (*qudwa*). In most Sufi theoretical treatises, however, the political aspect of the spiritual master's role is not stressed. More often than not, the shaykh is an exemplar only for his disciples and not for society at large.

Once again, the role of the saint appears to be of a different order than that of the sage or spiritual master. As both imam and ṣāliḥ, the Moroccan saint of the early-modern period was more than just a teacher or a mystic. Instead, he symbolized all aspects of the Muḥammadan paradigm. As a spiritual master, he imitated the Prophet Muḥammad as an interpreter of religion and a model of piety; as a ṣāliḥ, he imitated Muḥammad as a social critic and friend of the poor; as an imam, he imitated Muḥammad as a leader of people. In the Jazūlite model of sainthood as summarized in the doctrine of *aṭ-ṭarīqa al-Muḥammadiyya,* Moroccan shaykhs found a means to manifest both the social and the religious dimension of the Prophetic archetype in a single persona. This is what made them so influential in political affairs. For the shaykhs of the Jazūliyya, the involvement of saints and Sufis in the political conflicts of the time was no "maraboutic crisis" motivated by a desire for personal gain. Instead, these exemplars of the Prophetic Inheritance stepped into a preexisting leadership vacuum and did their best to preserve the integrity of Muslim society according to the dictates of their calling.

The Beginnings of Jazūlite Activism

For Muḥammad ibn Sulaymān al-Jazūlī, social consciousness was part of the very essence of Sufism. For this reason, he promoted social activism in his *ʿAqīda,* a genre of religious literature that is usually devoted to doctrinal matters alone. In this short treatise, he calls on his followers to do everything possible to improve the moral standards of their communities.

Addressing the Arab pastoralists who resided near his ribāṭ at Āfughāl, he condemns their drunkenness, licentiousness, and body tattooing, and he castigates those who engage in such behaviors as "madmen (*majānīn*), enemies of God, the Messenger, and religion, and enemies of those God-fearing souls who call [people] to Him."[10] As a remedy for their sins, he suggests that they give up their nomadic lifestyle and take up farming (*ḥirātha*).[11] This prescription indicates that al-Jazūlī wanted his pastoralist followers to abandon their predatory ways for a livelihood that fostered creation and nurturance rather than destruction and theft. It may also indicate that he sought to institute a policy of sedentarization, since the stability of a fixed abode made Sufi training and socialization easier to accomplish.

Sedentarization was in fact to become a formal aspect of Jazūlite doctrine two generations later under ʿAbdallāh al-Ghazwānī. This second-generation leader of the Jazūliyya required his pastoralist followers to abandon their wandering and to engage in four productive activities: farming, planting orchards, devoting themselves to the service of others, and commanding the good and forbidding evil.[12] Each of these activities went against the traditional bedouin lifestyle and required its practitioner to maintain a fixed abode. Al-Ghazwānī also encouraged his disciples to become economically self-sufficient by growing their own food and avoiding that sold by bedouins. Besides ensuring that what they consumed was ethically unpolluted, this rule made it harder for al-Ghazwānī's pastoralist followers to establish bonds of tribal solidarity that would undercut their Sufi ties. Finally, as a way of enticing pastoralists to limit their wandering and settle down near Jazūlite centers, al-Ghazwānī made them dependent on his zāwiya by distributing free food on market days.[13]

Extant sources give no definitive information as to whether al-Jazūlī's own companions practiced such a systematic policy of sedentarization. It is clear, however, that when they dispersed throughout the Far Maghrib following the assumption of power at Āfughāl by ʿAmr ibn as-Sayyāf al-Mughīṭī, many of them settled among nomadic Arab tribes. One of these shaykhs was Muḥammad al-ʿAmrī (d. 918/1512), otherwise known as "Sīdī aṣ-Ṣughayyir as-Sahlī." This member of the Banū Maʿqil tribe of Awlād ʿAmr chose not to return to his homeland in the Sūs but instead went north to Fez, where he informed the Sufis of the Marinid capital about the events surrounding al-Jazūlī's death.[14] From Fez he went north again to the region of Aḥyāyna, where he settled among fellow Banū Maʿqil Arabs at a site called Khandaq az-Zaytūn (Canal of the Olive) on Wādī al-Laban.[15]

Another disciple of al-Jazūlī and emigrant to Aḥyāyna was the initial master of ʿAbdallāh al-Khayyāṭ, al-Ḥasan ibn ʿUmar Ajāna. "Sīdī Ḥasan Ajāna" was an Arab from the Western Sahara who became popular as a teacher of Sufis in the region of Meknès.[16] This northward move by a shaykh whose origins lay at the southernmost extremity of the Far Maghrib provides strong evidence that the activities of the Jazūliyya in this period were focused on Fez, the political and economic hub of Morocco, and on the homelands of the Arab tribes to the north and west of the capital city. This conclusion is supported by the presence in the same region of another disciple of al-Jazūlī, Aḥmad al-Ḥārithī as-Sufyānī (d. before 910/1504–5).[17] Al-Ḥārithī was the teacher of Muḥammad ibn ʿĪsā al-Fahdī (d. 933/1526–7), the founder of the ʿĪsāwiyya Sufi order, which initially recruited its members among Arabs living in the Saïs plain between Fez and the Atlantic Ocean.[18] The fact that al-Ḥārithī and Ibn ʿĪsā came from the Banū Hilāl tribe, and not from the Banū Maʿqil, provides a corrective to the theories of Mohamed Kably, who assumes that the Jazūliyya recruited exclusively among the Banū Maʿqil.[19]

Accompanying Sīdī aṣ-Ṣughayyir as-Sahlī to Aḥyāyna was ʿAbd al-ʿAzīz at-Tabbāʿ, who became the first shaykh al-jamāʿa of the Jazūliyya after al-Jazūlī's death. Singled out by al-Jazūlī himself for his "alchemy of hearts," an intuitive knowledge of the human psyche, at-Tabbāʿ was entrusted by the shaykh to as-Sahlī, who put him to work herding sheep and cutting wood at Khandaq az-Zaytūn until he could instruct disciples on his own.[20] Around the year 880/1475, at-Tabbāʿ left Aḥyāyna for Marrakesh, where he founded the first urban zāwiya of the Jazūliyya Sufi order. Never forgetting his working-class origins (he was a silk weaver in Marrakesh before joining the order), he saw himself as a spokesman for the common people. At-Tabbāʿ is also credited with uniting the Jazūliyya after the collapse of ʿAmr ibn as-Sayyāf's revolt in 890/1485 and ending the doctrinal disputes that divided its members.[21]

As leader of the Jazūliyya, at-Tabbāʿ's career was similar to that of Abū'l-ʿAbbās al-Mursī, the successor to Abū'l-Ḥasan ash-Shādhilī in Egypt. Like al-Mursī, he left little behind as a written legacy, preferring instead to act as an instructor for his disciples and to turn the ṭāʾifa into a corporate institution. Also like al-Mursī, he extended the scope of his order both geographically and intellectually. This involved traveling to Fez, where he gave lectures on Sufism and led recitations of *Dalāʾil al-khayrāt* at Madrasat al-ʿAṭṭārīn. In Fez, he recruited the Granadan refugee and author of *Sharḥ*

Raḥbat al-āmān, ʿAlī Ṣāliḥ al-Andalusī, who founded the second urban zāwiya of the Jazūliyya in the Wattasid capital.[22]

Like al-Jazūlī himself, at-Tabbāʿ was regarded by his followers as the possessor of great spiritual knowledge and baraka. Hagiographical accounts claim that his face glowed with a "light" or radiance, and that merely looking at him could cause a person to become rich.[23] The colonial-era biographer Ibn al-Muwaqqit reports that a large crowd once gathered outside of at-Tabbāʿ's zāwiya in Marrakesh while the shaykh was in retreat. When he appeared into the sunlight, his countenance was so radiant that it "gave birth" to five hundred saints.[24] Traditions such a these are taken seriously in Marrakesh even today. It is still believed that a visit to at-Tabbāʿ's tomb can cure both physical and psychological ailments. Within its precincts can be found large numbers of the physically and mentally handicapped, who seek relief by touching at-Tabbāʿ's catafalque or by drinking water from a fountain in the tomb's courtyard.[25]

While at-Tabbāʿ and other members of the Jazūliyya were establishing *zawāya* in Marrakesh and Fez and disseminating their doctrines among the Arabs of northern Morocco, a greater political role for Sufis was being advocated by members of the Qādiriyya Sufi order, who had also been influenced by al-Jazūlī's doctrines. Although non-Maghribi ṭarīqa affiliations are seldom mentioned in sources from this period, Sufis whom one would today identify as Qādirī can be recognized by their devotion to the Almohad-era saints Abū Madyan and Abū Yiʿzzā. These shaykhs, it will be recalled, were assimilated into the Qādirī tradition as early as the thirteenth century C.E. It is also likely that a connection between the Shādhilī and Qādirī brotherhoods of Morocco was established by al-Jazūlī himself, for, as we have seen, much of Jazūlite ritual borrows from Qādirī precedent. In addition, al-Jazūlī was a close friend of a Qādirī Sufi from Meknès named Muḥammad al-Amīn al-ʿAṭṭār (or "az-Zarhūnī"; d. 860/1456).[26]

The most influential Qādirī zāwiya in late fifteenth-century Fez was Zāwiyat Bū Quṭūṭ (Zāwiya of the Owner of Cats), headed by Muḥammad az-Zaytūnī (d. after 900/1494–5).[27] Nicknamed the "Blind Viper" because of the powerful "bite" of his curses,[28] az-Zaytūnī was the principal exponent of the way of Abū Madyan in the western Maghrib.[29] According to the historian Muḥammad ibn aṭ-Ṭayyib al-Qādirī (d. 1187/1773), several descendants of ʿAbd al-Qādir al-Jīlānī left al-Andalus for Fez in the mid-fifteenth century C.E.[30] Once there, they expanded Qādirī networks that had already been established in the Marinid capital. They also allied themselves with the Idrisid sharifs of Fez, whom they supported in the rebellion against the Marinid sultan ʿAbd al-Ḥaqq II in 869/1465. Az-Zaytūnī used his ties with these groups to establish a reputation as the saintly protector of the Moroccan Ḥajj caravan. In this way he was able to link his zāwiya to other Qādirī orders in the central and eastern Maghrib. Much like the shaykhs of the Māgiriyya Sufi order in the thirteenth century (who were also linked to the Qādiriyya through their connections in Egypt), az-Zaytūnī concluded safe-conduct agreements with Arab tribes in the countryside between Morocco and Ifrīqīya.[31]

One of the most important of az-Zaytūnī's disciples was a Berber scholar named Muḥammad ibn Yaggabsh at-Tāzī (d. 920/1514).[32] A juridical Sufi and associate of the legist Muḥammad ibn Yūsuf as-Sanūsī (d. 899/1493), at-Tāzī was noted as a social reformer and advocate of jihad. He was also known for his poetry, which stimulated an entire genre of socially conscious didactic verse among the Sufis of Morocco and western Algeria. Although at-Tāzī appears never to have been a disciple of al-Jazūlī, his writings show unmistakable Jazūlite influence. This is apparent in the introduction to his most important work, *Kitāb al-jihād,* which celebrates "all of those who say, 'My Lord is God' and follow the Straight Path" (*kullu man qāla Rabbī Allāh thumma istaqām*). This is a clear reference to al-Jazūlī's now-lost treatise on Sufism, *An-Nuṣḥ at-tāmm li-man qāla rabbī Allāh thumma istaqām.*[33]

Kitāb al-jihād is an overtly political work that was inspired by the fall of the Atlantic port of Asila to the Portuguese in 876/1471.[34] It was written to exhort the ulama of the Far Maghrib to awaken to the social and political crises that plagued their region and to undertake the reforms that were necessary to unite the Muslim community in its defense. The beginning of this work is written in the style of a *khuṭba,* a Friday sermon, and evokes a stark image of impending doom:

> Worshipers of God, what is this great heedlessness that has fixed itself in your hearts, upon which the ego relies, and which has negated proper guidance and God's favor? Are you not aware that your enemies are investigating you and are employing every stratagem in order to get at you? They have gathered together in numbers too large to count and have sent their spies and scouts to every land in order to inform them of what your numbers are, as well as your strength and convictions. They have told [their leaders] of your foolishness and heedlessness, and that

> your numbers, compared to theirs, are as insignificant and as weak as can be. For you are divided against your Muslim brethren and care nothing about debasing the religion of the Lord of Messengers and taking [as captives] the believing worshipers of God.
>
> Once they have known everything about your condition, your lack of care, and preoccupations, they will crave . . . to attain their goals. Then they will gather . . . and go out into these lands. But they will be satisfied neither with possessing it nor with obtaining wealth and slaves. Instead, they will cause glory and happiness to be transformed into debasement and sorrow. They will cause despair and expulsion to prevail, both in feeling and in fact. [The people of this land] will be shackled with chains and irons and every day they will suffer grievous torment; they will become like chattel and slaves and those who only yesterday were rich and secure will tomorrow be poor and afraid. They will be robbed of their possessions, their material conditions will be upset, their women will be separated from them, their daughters will be taken from them, and the unbelievers will compete over the prices at which they will purchase them. Then they will be separated from each other and sent to every land and [the unbelievers] will seduce them away from their religion and will undermine the strength of their convictions.
>
> So what is this heedlessness about your brethren, oh Muslims? Even now, [the unbelievers] are watching you at every moment in time. They are not satisfied with food, nor do they find rest in sleep. What is the condition of one who lies fettered in chains or shackles and under arrest? These [unfortunates] only serve [their masters] beneath reprimands and blows, with abuse, slaps, and insults; they will find neither pity nor mercy; they cannot imagine the sorrow and affliction that they undergo; their tears will pour down their cheeks and they will be overcome by a sadness that knows no relief![35]

"Is there anyone," at-Tāzī laments, "who can cool these embers? Where is the compassion of the people of Islam? Where is the mercy of Muḥammad's *umma,* who are characterized by the noblest of qualities—the devotees of the one who is famous for his excellence and the instrument of attainment to God?"[36] The only course of action is to rise up in defense of Islam: "The herald has announced: 'Heaven is under the shade of [drawn] swords!' Verily, for the martyr, stabbing and thrusting are more pleasurable than a drink of cool water!"[37]

Like al-Jazūlī before him, at-Tāzī believed that true Islam could be found among those who dared to put their lives on the line as holy warriors. Best of all were the lovers of God who sought union with their Creator through the loss of life or limb: "Where are the lovers? Where are those in whom the fire of love has burned their hearts? Where is the one who desires salvation in this beauty? Where is the one who hungers to attain his desire in the sweetness of union? By the grace of God you have attained your hopes, oh seeker! You have reached your desires, oh lover! The One you have longed for will not cause you to be frightened at the coming of death, nor will He deny you the eternal happiness that you so passionately desire by ending what is merely ephemeral!"[38]

After calling believers to the common defense, at-Tāzī next turns to the social and moral conditions of Moroccan society. To introduce this theme, he relates a tradition in which Satan identifies his friends and enemies. The friends of Satan are those whom at-Tāzī blames for the debased condition of Moroccan society in his day: the tyrannical ruler (*sulṭān jāʾir*), the arrogant man of wealth, the dishonest merchant, the wine drinker, the usurer, the adulterer, the murderer, the trustee who steals the inheritance of orphans, the miser, and the lover of the material world. By contrast, Satan's enemies are those who provide the answer to Morocco's problems: the just leader (*imām ʿādil*), the humble man of wealth, the honest merchant, the chaste slaveboy, the trustworthy believer, the sincere repenter, the man who is merciful, abstains from women, and is generous, the almsgiver, the bearer of the Qur'an, the God-fearing legist (*al-mujtahid fī Allāh*), and the holy warrior (*al-mujāhid fī sabīl Allāh*).[39]

From at-Tāzī's point of view, the friends of Satan are the cause of the discord that has beset the Far Maghrib since the beginning of the fifteenth century C.E. The insecurity that this discord has engendered has led to the loosening of social bonds and the erosion of trust and solidarity. Now that this affliction has infected the elites, the result is internal strife and political weakness. If something is not done to halt this slide into chaos, the Muslims of Morocco will be cursed by God with expulsion and dispersion like the children of Israel (*yalʿanukum kamā laʿana Banī Isrāʾīl*).[40] Indeed, at-Tāzī claims, Islam itself might fall into a decline from which it can never recover, for religion now means so little in Morocco that even its most basic tenets are ignored: "You have transgressed the bounds of the Sharīʿa for the sake of that which is repugnant, as if the [Qur'an] had never been revealed to you and as if the Lord of Lords had never taught you the difference between right and wrong. . . . You have sold your religion for the world and for the dirham. The outcome of the first is the Fire and the outcome of the second is perdition!"[41]

To rescue Morocco from its decline, at-Tāzī calls for a leader who is proficient in both religion and the sword—an imām and amīr whose religious expertise is acknowledged by the ulama and who, like the Rightly Guided Caliphs of old, can guide Muslims in battle as a true successor to the Prophet. This leader will "take care of the Muslims and arrange them in ranks for battle as has been mentioned by the ulama in many volumes. If he finds weakness or fear in them, he will urge them to be patient and take refuge in God's forgiveness and in making numerous prayers to the Conquering King, Who alone possesses power and victory."[42]

It was no coincidence that during this same period, the sharifs of Morocco began to promote themselves as the "just imams" called for by at-Tāzī and other Sufi activists. Although their stance was opportunistic, Mohamed Kably goes too far in claiming that the sharifian *conditteri* who led the anti-Portuguese jihad to power in the sixteenth century had no ideology.[43] Instead, it is more accurate to say that the ideology they adopted was not entirely of their own making. The institutional advantages the sharifs enjoyed as a by-product of their genealogy were not enough in and of themselves to justify their political ambitions. At times in fact, these advantages could even work against them. In the first half of the fifteenth century, the Idrisids of Fez suffered a diminution of their prerogatives because their arrogation of special privileges caused widespread resentment.[44] Even the "rediscovery" of Mūlāy Idrīs II's tomb in 841/1437 was not enough to restore their former position. For this reason, the attempt by the sharifs to reestablish the Idrisid state after the Fez revolt of 869/1465 ultimately failed and ended with a revival of the Marinid ancien régime under Muḥammad ash-Shaykh al-Waṭṭāsī. If the sharifs of Morocco were ever to gain power for good, they had to find a better argument (Kably prefers "pretext") for their aspirations. In the end, this argument was to be found in the obligation of jihad, while the ideology that they needed was waiting for them in the Jazūlite concept of *aṭ-ṭariqa al-Muḥamadiyya.*[45]

Al-Ghazwānī and the Revival of Sharifism

ʿAbdallāh al-Ghazwānī, the successor to at-Tabbāʿ as shaykh al-jamāʿa of the Jazūliyya, was born among the Banū Ghazwān tribal segment of the ash-

Shāwīya Arabs who occupied the lands between the coastal plains of central Morocco and the city of Fez. He inherited a taste for mysticism from his father, Abū'l-Barakāt ʿAjāl al-Ghazwānī (d. after 910/1504–5), a *malāmatī* Sufi and holy warrior who preached jihad and religious revival at tribal markets.[46] The younger al-Ghazwānī joined aṭ-Ṭāʾifa al-Jazūliyya in Fez, where his father had sent him to acquire a legal education at Madrasat al-Wādī on the Andalusian side of the city.[47] While there, he was recruited by a group of Jazūlite Sufis who stopped by the madrasa and invited its students to hear the words of their master, ʿAlī Ṣāliḥ al-Andalusī. To encourage the students to join them, the Sufis allowed them to take part in their invocations and gave them all the couscous they could eat.[48] That very night, al-Ghazwānī "placed himself between the hands" of al-Andalusī and asked to be accepted as his disciple. After receiving the assent of the other Sufis, al-Andalusī agreed to al-Ghazwānī's request and clasped the young man's hands in his own, saying, "This is a powerful bedouin!"[49]

Soon afterward, al-Ghazwānī went to Marrakesh and joined ʿAbd al-ʿAzīz at-Tabbāʿ, who put him to work cultivating crops and tending his orchard. Extant sources tell us little about the so-called prophetic training (*tarbiyya nabawiyya*)[50] that at-Tabbāʿ provided for his pupil. Instead, these sources tell us about the outward aspects of al-Ghazwānī's education, such as cutting wood and watering at-Tabbāʿ's flocks.[51] These activities were designed to foster a sense of discipline in the headstrong young bedouin and to curb an overdeveloped attitude of self-confidence.

Muḥammad al-ʿArabī al-Fāsī, the author of *Mirʾāt al-maḥāsin,* hints that at-Tabbāʿ's consolidation of the activities of the Jazūliyya under his direction was motivated by a desire to involve the order in regional politics. After training al-Ghazwānī for ten years, at-Tabbāʿ told his pupil to go to Muḥammad ibn Dāwūd (d. before 940/1533–4),[52] the leader of the ash-Shāwīya Arabs, and deliver the message, "We need some fat (*idām*)."[53] The tribes of ash-Shāwīya were bitter enemies of the Wattasid ruler Muḥammad ash-Shaykh (d. 910/1505), who had seized Fez from the Idrisids in 876/1471. After establishing himself in Fez, Muḥammad ash-Shaykh saw his most important task to be the punishment of the Arab tribes who had refused to support his accession to power. The nearest of these tribes to Fez was the ash-Shāwīya confederation. This group of Banū Hilāl Arabs was hounded mercilessly by Wattasid troops and their Banū Maʿqil allies and forced to flee westward to Tāmesnā, inland from present-day Rabat. The aftermath of this campaign was vividly described by Muḥammad al-Kurrāsī (fl. 950/1534), the official chronicler of the Wattasid regime:

> [Muḥammad ash-Shaykh] assaulted and scourged them ceaselessly,
> Until they drank from the cup of humiliation and bitterness,
>
> And what remained of them crept off to Tāmesnā,
> Like ants crawling softly in the darkness.
>
> They watched [the sultan fearfully] morning and evening,
> Making flight permissible for them without an excuse.[54]

When al-Ghazwānī delivered at-Tabbāᶜ's summons to Muḥammad ibn Dāwūd, the Arab chieftain exchanged his rich clothes for the simple garb of a Sufi, turned his lance point downward as a sign of submission, and went to Marrakesh, where he pledged his loyalty to the leader of the Jazūliyya. Ibn Dāwūd was welcomed with great respect by at-Tabbāᶜ, who told him to return to Tāmesnā and create a ribāṭ for the Jazūliyya in that region. A short time later, al-Ghazwānī was again called to his master's presence and was ordered to recruit disciples among his own tribe of Banū Ghazwān.[55]

At first glance, at-Tabbāᶜ's opposition to the Wattasids seems illogical, given Muḥammad ash-Shaykh's stated intention to wage jihad against the Portuguese. The ruler of Fez had ample reason to be concerned about the Iberian threat, for his wives, daughters, and son had all been captured by the Portuguese and held for ransom after the conquest of Asila. For at-Tabbāᶜ, however, this course of events merely confirmed his belief that Muḥammad ash-Shaykh was so power-hungry that he was even unwilling to protect his own family, for it was widely held that Asila (and later that same year, Tangier) had fallen only because the sultan had been more concerned with securing the throne than with defending Islam. This trade-off of Asila and Tangier for Fez was seen by the shaykhs of the Jazūliyya as the lowest example of adventurism and self-indulgence. Even worse, immediately after assuming power Muḥammad ash-Shaykh had concluded a twenty-year truce with his Christian enemies. Although this pact was promoted as a way of providing breathing space for the preparation of a new offensive, it was widely suspected that its real purpose was to buy time for the Wattisid ruler to consolidate his power. Muḥammad ash-Shaykh's subsequent campaign against the Arabs of Dukkāla did nothing to dispel this notion. Although hagiographical accounts do not mention the year in which at-Tabbāᶜ made his overtures to the ash-Shāwīya Arabs, it is likely that this took place around 896/1490–1, when the sultan extended his treaty with the Portuguese for another five years.[56]

Whether it was intentional or not, Muḥammad ash-Shaykh's truce with Lisbon did give the *mujāhidūn* of northern Morocco time to organize themselves. During this period, four bases were created for a counterattack against the Portuguese forts at Asila, Tangier, and al-Qaṣr aṣ-Ṣaghīr. These four were: Shafshāwan, founded in 876/1471–2 by the Banū Rāshid family of Idrisid sharifs from Jabal al-ʿAlam; Tetuan (Ber. *tīṭāwīn,* "springs"), an abandoned town that was reoccupied in 888/1483 by Andalusian refugees under the Granadan amir Muḥammad al-Manẓarī; al-Kharrūb, located in the Jabal Ḥabīb region midway between Tetuan and Larache and occupied by a collectivity of tribes that were loyal to the Banū Rāshid; and Targha, located east of Tetuan on the Mediterranean coast, which guarded the region between Shafshāwan and Bādis.[57]

Shafshāwan was the most important of these garrisons, since its strategic location made it the most suitable site for a base of operations. The town was built near the village of Ghurūzīm, which, in the latter half of the fifteenth century C.E. was home to several families of legists who claimed descent from Mūlāy ʿAbd as-Salām ibn Mashīsh.[58] In 876/1471–2, the most senior of these scholars, al-Ḥasan ibn Jumuʿa al-ʿAlamī, resolved to build a command and supply center for a future offensive against Portuguese-held Tangier. However, no sooner had he begun to assemble groups of Banū Zajal Berbers and Andalusian refugees than the Portuguese, who were aware of the threat that he posed to their interests, contrived to have him assassinated. He was succeeded by his nephew, ʿAlī ibn Rāshid (d. 917/1511–12), who actually built the town of Shafshāwan and founded its dynasty of Banū Rāshid amirs.

As ruler of Shafshāwan, ʿAlī ibn Rāshid demonstrated such political and military acumen that conflict with the Wattasids became inevitable. During his reign the population of the town grew to over 10,000 inhabitants, including 6,000 Moroccan Muslims, 3,000 Andalusian Muslims, and 1,000 Jews.[59] He was lionized as Morocco's most successful fighter against the Portuguese and in the popular imagination was hailed as the just ruler that was sought by at-Tāzī in *Kitāb al-jihād.* He was particularly successful in recruiting military contingents from al-Andalus to help his cause, a policy that led to the repopulation of Tetuan in 888/1483.[60] He enhanced the prestige of the ʿAlamī sharifs by promoting the cult of Mūlāy ʿAbd as-Salām ibn Mashīsh and appointing members of the clan of al-ʿAlamī as local imams and judges. In addition, he secured for himself important symbols of political autonomy, such as a flag, distinctive court traditions, a bureaucracy, and a tax administration. In short, ʿAlī ibn Rāshid was developing into the Wattasids' worst nightmare: a just ruler whose virtues as a defender of the faith were well-proven and whose potential for making trouble could not be ignored.

In the end, however, Ibn Rāshid was undone by his own ambition. The anticipated conflict between the Banū Rāshid and Wattasids came about at the end of the year 900 A.H. (July–August 1495), when the sharif of Shafshāwan, egged on by the Idrisids of Fez, proclaimed himself the Renewer (*mujaddid*) of the tenth Islamic century.[61] Fearing for his throne, the sultan of Fez sent an emissary to the Portuguese captain of Ceuta, who, in exchange for unspecified concessions and the delivery of one of Muḥammad ash-Shaykh's sons as a hostage, agreed to assist him in a joint attack against Shafshāwan.[62] Seeing that he was not powerful enough to fight two enemies at once, ʿAlī ibn Rāshid fled into the Rif mountains and saved his neck by recognizing the Wattasid sultan as his sovereign.

Thus, at the dawn of the tenth century A.H., neither sharifian alternative in northern Morocco—the Idrisids of Fez nor the Banū Rāshid of Shafshāwan—posed much of a threat to the Wattasids. This must have come as a great disappointment to ʿAbd al-ʿAzīz at-Tabbāʿ, who looked upon the family of the Prophet as prime candidates for religious and political leadership. The rapprochement between the Banū Rāshid and the Wattasids took an even more troubling turn after 917/1511–12, when Ibrāhīm ibn ʿAlī ibn Rāshid (d. 947/1539) succeeded his father as the ruler of Shafshāwan and married the daughter of the Wattasid sultan Muḥammad al-Burtughālī (d. 931/1524).[63] Wattasid interests in northern Morocco were also protected at this time by a third group of Idrisid sharifs, the Banū ʿArūs of Qaṣr Kutāma (present-day El Ksar El Kebir), who kept an eye on the activities of Sufis and holy warriors at al-Kharrūb and their original homeland, the Idrisid tomb center of Jabal al-ʿAlam.[64]

In 910/1505, the Wattasid sultan Muḥammad ash-Shaykh died and was succeeded by his son Muḥammad al-Burtughālī, who was given his unusual nickname (the Portuguese) because he had spent seven years as a hostage in Lisbon. The good news for the Jazūliyya was that the new sultan had no taste for the accomodationist policies of his father. Within the first four years of his reign, al-Burtughālī conducted several offensives against the Portuguese in the Gharb and Dukkāla regions. These actions were in response to earlier offensives by the Portuguese themselves, who had moved south from their bases in Tangier and Asila in order to eliminate Muslim resistance at al-Kharrūb. The unfortunate result of these raids and counter-raids was the nearly total depopulation of the Atlantic coastal region between Asila and Qaṣr Kutāma, whose Banū ʿArūs rulers now found themselves responsible for large numbers of refugees.[65]

Unfortunately, Muḥammad al-Burtughālī was by nature an uncompromising autocrat, whose love for jihad was mitigated by a tendency to ruthlessly suppress any hint of dissent. The weapon he used to punish his opponents was his brother Mūlāy an-Nāṣir (d. 930/1523), who was called *al-Gaddīd* (Old Dried Meat), because of his cruelty toward his victims. As governor of Meknès, Mūlāy an-Nāṣir's main task was to keep a watchful eye on the Arab tribes who lived along the caravan routes linking Fez to the port city of Salé.[66]

The year of al-Burtughālī's accession found ʿAbdallāh al-Ghazwānī in northern Morocco, although conflicting reports make it difficult to determine exactly where he was at any given time. According to Muḥammad al-ʿArabī al-Fāsī, when at-Tabbāʿ died in 914/1508–9 al-Ghazwānī was still among the Banū Ghazwān, for this author of *Mirʾāt al-maḥāsin* claims that al-Ghazwānī traveled to Marrakesh to pay his last respects to at-Tabbāʿ with a group of ash-Shāwīya Arabs.[67] After returning to his homeland, he was visited by a group of Jazūlite Sufis who informed him that, while making their invocations, they had heard his voice leading their assembly. From this they surmised that al-Ghazwānī had been chosen by God to be at-Tabbāʿ's successor. Upon receiving this news, al-Ghazwānī sent one of his disciples to the leaders of the northern Arabs to see whether they would support him. Upon receiving a favorable response, he moved north to the region of al-Habṭ. Although it was nominally within the borders of what Spanish and Portuguese writers called the "Kingdom of Fez," al-Habṭ was beyond direct Wattasid control and was ruled independently by local tribal leaders. One of these leaders, the head of the Banū Fazankār clan near Jabal al-ʿAlam, donated land outside of the village of Taṣrūt for the shaykh's zāwiya. Ever coy about what was clearly a political decision to live within the saintly penumbra of Mūlāy ʿAbd as-Salām ibn Mashīsh, al-Fāsī states that after moving to Taṣrūt al-Ghazwānī's fortunes "increased greatly."[68]

It is difficult to get a complete picture of al-Ghazwānī's activities in al-Habṭ. Some information can be obtained from oral tradition, while a little more can be found in letters reproduced in *An-Nuqṭa al-azaliyya* and other sources. Local traditions in the Jabal al-ʿAlam region claim that al-Ghazwānī was instrumental in popularizing the cult of Mūlāy ʿAbd as-Salām ibn Mashīsh and institutionalizing the pilgrimage that now culminates in the yearly *mawsim* (festival of the saint) on the fifteenth day of the Islamic month of Shaʿbān. As part of these efforts, al-Ghazwānī established ribāṭs along the route from Marrakesh to Jabal al-ʿAlam and encouraged his disciples to use the *mawsim* of Mūlāy ʿAbd as-Salām as a substitute for the pilgrimage to Mecca.[69] According to the present *muqaddam* of the tomb complex of Mūlāy ʿAbd as-Salām ibn Mashīsh, al-Ghazwānī made repeated visits to Jabal al-ʿAlam, determined the exact location of the saint's grave, and constructed the open-air *rawḍa* that now crowns the hill where ash-Shādhilī's teacher is buried.[70] Although tradition also asserts that al-Ghazwānī was the first to institute the annual pilgrimage to this site, it is known from written sources that the *mawsim* of Mūlāy ʿAbd as-Salām actually dates from the fourteenth century C.E., soon after the Shādhiliyya Sufi order was introduced into Morocco from al-Andalus.[71]

Al-Ghazwānī's promotion of the pilgrimage to Mūlāy ʿAbd as-Salām was part of a wider plan to integrate the ideology of sharifism with the doctrines of the Jazūliyya. The time was ripe for such a move because the most important sharifian families of Jabal al-ʿAlam, the Banū Rāshid and Banū ʿArūs, had lost face by siding with the Wattasids. The text of *An-Nuqṭa al-azaliyya* contains an interesting exchange of letters between al-Ghazwānī and his disciples ʿAbdallāh al-Habṭī, ʿAbd ar-Raḥmān ibn Raysūn (d. 951/1544–5), and Muḥammad ibn Khajjū (d. 956/1550), who ask the shaykh to support the amir of Shafshāwan, Ibrāhīm ibn ʿAlī b. Rāshid. In his reply, al-Ghazwānī is openly skeptical about the motives of the Banū Rāshid. It is the duty of the sharifs, he says, to support the Jazūliyya, not the duty of the Jazūliyya to support the sharifs:

> Tell our lords the sharifs, as well as their legal scholars and fuqarāʾ: We love you with all of our heart and soul, and desire to look upon your faces. But we have smelled the scent of unbelief (Mor. Ar. *shammīnā rāʾiḥat al-kufr*) overcoming and impairing [your] faith. The ambition of the ṣāliḥīn is to dispel its oppression so that you may magnify the exalted word of God and attain the baraka of the Messenger of God (may God bless and preserve him). Verily, the word of God is exalted, while that of the unbelievers is lowly!

> We have not seen any counsel given [by the sharifs] to the people of Tāmesnā or [about] conditions in Marrakesh that is not of benefit to the [Wattasid] rulers of this Maghrib of ours (May God maintain it and guide it to uphold the authority of the Sunna!). Yet we have not, God willing, altered our regard for you despite what we have mentioned. We and all of our brothers the fuqarā᾿ are happy about your dedication to invocation, friendship, self-sacrifice, and generosity. May God maintain ourselves and you in the manifest way of His saints—through the axial sainthood (*quṭbāniyya*) that is the legacy of your ancestor Sīdī ʿAbd as-Salām ibn Mashīsh, the path of honor (*ṭarīqat al-ikrām*) of Abū'l-Ḥasan ash-Shādhilī, who chose it for our lord (*sayyidinā*) and source of grace (*barakatinā*) Sīdī Muḥammad al-Jazūlī, out of all the Sufi paths. He inspired us with the truth and passed it on to us as a legacy from the lord of the God-fearing and the people of his age, the force of truth in all of God's manifestations, Sīdī ʿAbd al-ʿAzīz at-Tabbāʿ. These [shaykhs] are our [true] means to God and our exemplars in loving the Messenger of God, our Prophet Muḥammad (may God bless and preserve him), both outwardly (*ẓāhiran*) and inwardly (*bāṭinan*).[72]

The submission of the Banū Rāshid to Wattasid authority precipitated a conflict among the Idrisids of northern Morocco. Those who were opposed to a rapprochement between Shafshāwan and Fez either became disciples of al-Ghazwānī or allied themselves with the shaykh's successors in resisting the accommodationism of Ibrāhīm ibn ʿAlī. Idrisid sharifs from this region who were disciples of al-Ghazwānī included ʿUmar ibn ʿAbd al-Wahhāb al-ʿAlamī (d. 958/1551) and the Ibn Raysūn brothers: the celibate ʿAbd ar-Raḥmān, one of the recipients of the letter quoted above, and his more politically active sibling, ʿAlī (d. 963/1555–6).[73]

The evidence of both sacred biography and al-Ghazwānī's own words in *An-Nuqṭa al-azaliyya* suggest that he aspired to be both the paramount shaykh of Moroccan Sufism and the axial saint of the Far Maghrib in general. This conclusion is supported by numerous statements in which al-Ghazwānī makes it clear that the Imamate of Justice (*imāmat al-ʿadl*), which reformers such as at-Tāzī desired, was to be found in him alone. On one occasion, while in Fez, after hearing a woman make the distinctive "yoo-yoo" cry of greeting (Mor. Ar. *tazghrīḍ*) for Sultan Muḥammad al-Burtughālī, al-Ghazwānī reprimanded her, saying, "I am the Sultan of this world and the next!"[74] Also, during his sojourn among the Banū Fazankār, his disciples were instructed to respond to the question, "Who is your sultan?" by saying: "Sīdī ʿAbdallāh al-Ghazwānī."[75]

Al-Ghazwānī's understanding of Sufi praxis, like that of most Moroccan mystics, was based on the principles of futuwwa. As explained in Part I, the themes of brotherhood and social consciousness that made up this doctrine gave Moroccan Sufism the activist complexion that set it apart from other regional varieties of Islamic mysticism. The central motif of al-Ghazwānī's futuwwa-based populism was the rejection of all forms of elitism. This is expressed in the following aphorism: "Oh fuqarāʾ [i.e., Sufis], choose the fuqarāʾ [i.e., the poor] from among the fuqarāʾ!"[76] Association with the so-called sons of the world (*abnāʾ ad-dunyā*)—the ulama, amirs, and others who held posts in government—was to be avoided at all costs. This was done so that the Sufis of the Jazūliyya would not become the "apostles" (*ḥawāyīr*) of their patrons and forget the common people whose interests they were duty-bound to protect.[77]

More than any other issue, it was this defacto repudiation of the official ulama that aroused the ire of juridical Sufis such as Aḥmad Zarrūq. However, there was more than one side to this argument. To al-Ghazwānī, the real issue was not whether one should respect the ulama, but rather which ulama one should respect. Given the low standard of ethics and accommodation toward its enemies that characterized the Marinid–Wattasid state in its final years, it is no surprise that the shaykhs of the Jazūliyya would be skeptical of those on the government payroll. From the Jazūlite perspective, al-Ghazwānī's arrogation of leadership to himself was no more than an expedient way of preserving the integrity of Islamic values and institutions.

As part of the Jazūlite attempt to take on the responsibilities of the ulama, a number of centers of religious education were established in the Moroccan countryside in the first decades of the sixteenth century. This policy filled an educational vacuum in the rural areas and at the same time created an alternative to urban centers of learning, such as the mosques and madāris of Fez, whose instructional standards were thought to be in decline. If the right kind of scholar could not be found in the cities, then such a person would have to be produced in the countryside. The fruits of this Jazūlite educational program would eventually be seen in the administration of the Saʿdian state, which was staffed with locally trained scholars from Ḥāḥā, the Sūs, and the caravan centers of southern Morocco.[78]

One of the more "modern" aspects of al-Ghazwānī's approach to Sufi reform was his insistence that membership in the Jazūliyya not be restricted to men alone. Because of this policy, the first half of the sixteenth century stands as a high-water mark of women's participation in the religious life of Morocco. Jazūlite hagiographers mention several women who distinguished themselves as authorities on Sufism. One of these was ʿĀʾisha bint Aḥmad al-Idrīsiyya (d. 696/1563), a disciple of al-Ghazwānī who was the mother of the hagiographer Ibn ʿAskar (d. 986/1578). True to the activist example of her shaykh, ʿĀʾisha al-Idrīsiyya was to play an important role in the Saʿdian takeover of Shafshāwan.[79] On at least one occasion, al-Ghazwānī also inducted all of the women of a single village into the Jazūliyya. This act precipitated a flurry of missives from the official ulama decrying the dangers of men and women mixing during sessions of invocation. In the following generation, two of al-Ghazwānī's most important disciples, ʿAbdallāh al-Habṭī and Yūsuf at-Tlīdī (d. 950/1543–4), maintained separate zawāya for their female disciples. These were identical in form and function to the zawāya used by men, and differed from the latter only in the gender of their *muqaddamāt,* who were women trained in the methodology of uṣūl al-fiqh.[80]

Al-Ghazwānī was able to introduce such innovations because, as a Bell saint and possessor of the Muḥammadan Inheritance, his interpretations of Islamic doctrine were divinely legitimated. To further demonstrate his worthiness for this station, he displayed a passionate love for the Prophet Muḥammad, whom he called the "Bridegroom of the Universe" (*ʿarūs al-akwān*).[81] Like his predecessor al-Jazūlī, he spoke of himself in superlatives and allowed himself to be addressed by such politically charged titles as "Exemplar of Our Salvation" (*qudwat saʿādatinā*), "Possessor of Solicitude and Power" (*dhuw ʿināya wa salṭāna*), "Possessor of Justice and Authority" (*dhuw ʿadl wa ḥukm*), and "Symbol of [divine] Inspiration" (*āyat an-nūr*).[82] Also like al-Jazūlī, he was the recipient of divine addresses (*mukhāṭabāt*), which he attributed to the "purification of his mind, conscience, insight, inspiration, secrets, and innermost being."[83] Many of these discourses expressed states that on the surface were just as exalted as those of al-Jazūlī himself and at times came perilously close to the proscribed doctrine of *ittiḥād,* identity between the mystic and his Creator:

> Oh My slave, you are My essence and I am your essence without distinction or fusion; were it not for My essence, you would not exist.

Oh My slave, you are the Name and I am the one named; your essence is Mine and My essence is yours.

Oh My slave, if you searched for Me, you would find only yourself.

Oh My slave, I have made for every saint an ocean from which to ladle, and every ocean that I make for him is a power through which he may repel evil. But I repel evil from your ocean Myself, for the sake of your privileged calling and even greater intimacy. One who is not established by means of your confirmation will never escape the oppression of the body and be purified from the appetites of the senses.

Oh My slave, be as I am so that I may be as you are. Oh My slave, be as I was so that I may be as you were. Oh my slave, return to your source so that I may return to My source. If you are in need of Me, I will fulfill your needs. But if you feel independent of Me, I will make sure that you need Me.

Oh My slave, I have manifested My essence through My essence, so that you may see your essence in My essence; and I am the Most High!

Oh My slave, I have made you a slave in the Lord and a lord among slaves. If one of [My slaves] acts as a lord toward you, then be as a slave toward him; and if one of them acts as a slave toward you, then be as a lord toward him; for I am the All-Powerful Lord!

Oh My slave, all that exists is from your existence, all that lives is from your life, everything everlasting is from your everlastingness, everything persistent is from your persistence, all glory is from your glory, all wealth is from your wealth, every miracle (*karāma*) is from your generosity (*karamika*), every act of mercy is from your mercy, all knowledge is from your knowledge, every secret is from your secret, all light is from your light, all speech is from your speech, every vision is from your vision, all hearing is from your hearing, all glory is from your glory, all beauty is from your beauty, all perfection is from your perfection, everything desired is from your wish, and everything possible is from your ability!

Oh My slave, I am the All-Merciful (*ar-Raḥmān*), and mercy (*raḥma*) belongs to the All-Merciful. Therefore, you must be that mercy and I will be a bestower of mercy (*raḥīman*) on [human beings] through you.[84]

The doctrine of Muḥammadan sainthood that was disseminated by the shaykhs of aṭ-Ṭāʾifa al-Jazūliyya stimulated an Islamic revival throughout

Morocco in the sixteenth century C.E. It is easy to imagine how threatening the ideology of saintly authority that these shaykhs advocated (especially given the millenarian terms in which it was expressed) must have appeared to the rulers of the time. At the end of the sixteenth century, the popular image of the Sufi master that grew out of the Jazūlite model of sainthood was expressed by Riḍwān ibn ʿAbdallāh al-Januwī (d. 991/1583), who served al-Ghazwānī in the latter's final years and recorded some of the earliest accounts of his activities. Remarking on his first impression of al-Ghazwānī, he said: "There was a splendor and a radiance about him, as if I had seen a man with an enormous body. His complexion was ruddy, as if it were made of light. When I looked at him, I said [to myself], 'He is he!'"[85]

After approximately five years among the Banū Fazankār, while traveling beyond the protection of his tribal allies, al-Ghazwānī was arrested by Ṭalḥa al-ʿArūsī, the Idrisid ruler of Qaṣr Kutāma, who delivered the shaykh to Sultan Muḥammad al-Burtughālī. Reflecting a topos that is frequently found in North African hagiographical literature, the blame for al-Ghazwānī's arrest has been laid by historians at the feet of a jealous faqīh named ʿAbd al-Kabīr as-Sufyānī.[86] According to the most commonly accepted version of this story, the shaykh responded meekly to this turn of events, saying, "Obedience to the Sultan is obligatory." To his companions, however, he exulted, "My desire has come to pass!"[87]

The most detailed account of al-Ghazwānī's incarceration and interrogation in Fez is provided on the authority of ʿAbd al-Wārith al-Yalṣūtī (d. after 960/1554), a disciple of Sīdī as-Ṣughayyir as-Sahlī who acted as al-Ghazwānī's advocate. According to this tradition, which is reproduced in *Mirʾāt al-maḥāsin,*[88] al-Ghazwānī was first thrown into prison in the old Amoravid fort near present-day Bāb Bū Julūd. Because of public pressure on his behalf, he was moved a few days later to a mosque in the Darb as-Suʿūd quarter in the Idrisid city of Fās al-Bālī. Here he was questioned by a qāḍī who is identified by al-Fāsī as "Abū ʿAbdallāh al-Miknāsī." When the qāḍī asked al-Ghazwānī, "What is this that people say about you?" al-Yalṣūtī answered for him: "This man settled in a land of great evil; indeed, it is one of the most evil of all. Then this man started to forbid people from doing evil. God has allowed him to guide whomever he wills and punishes those who reject him!"

The next day, the qāḍī escorted al-Ghazwānī to the palace, where he was interrogated before Muḥammad al-Burtughālī and his son Aḥmad, who was then governor of Taza. When questioned by the Sultan's secretary, the shaykh refused to answer and replied disdainfully, "Do not speak to me until you have cleansed yourself of your sexual impurities (*janābatika*)!" At this, the amir Aḥmad al-Waṭṭāsī intervened: "What these people mean by *janāba* is different from what is understood by the rest of us." When the Sultan asked his son how he had come to know this, Aḥmad replied, "From Sīdī Muḥammad ibn Yaggabsh at-Tāzī." Upon hearing this information, Muḥammad al-Burtughālī immediately called off the interrogation. Although the reason for this decision is not given by al-Yalṣūtī, Aḥmad al-Waṭṭāsī's mention of at-Tāzī's name suggests that the doctrines of Sufi populism had already penetrated the Sultan's entourage. To be on the safe side, al-Burtughālī ordered al-Ghazwānī to remain in Fez, where the shaykh's activities could be monitored by his officers.

The problem with al-Yalṣūtī's account of al-Ghazwānī's arrest and interrogation is that his "eyewitness" testimony disagrees in several important details with that of his near-contemporary, Muḥammad ibn ʿAskar. The most significant disagreement between the two accounts concerns the date of al-Ghazwānī's arrest and hinges on whether the shaykh was interrogated by the qāḍī al-jamāʿa of Fez, Abū ʿAbdallāh Muḥammad al-Miknāsī (d. 915/1509–10), or someone else. According to Ibn ʿAskar, al-Ghazwānī was not met by the qāḍī al-jamāʿa but by the shaykh al-jamāʿa and muftī of Fez, who was also named Abū ʿAbdallāh al-Miknāsī. This latter person was the noted legist and historian Muḥammad ibn Ghāzī al-Miknāsī, whose death is known to have occurred in 919/1513. In Ibn ʿAskar's version of the story, Ibn Ghāzī accompanies the previous ruler, Muḥammad ash-Shaykh al-Waṭṭāsī, on a military expedition against the Portuguese at Asila, after which al-Ghazwānī is arrested and brought to Fez in chains. Now in his final illness, the aged muftī is brought back to Fez in a litter and feels excruciating pain as he passes by the city's prison. Believing this to be the result of baraka emanating from someone inside the prison, Ibn Ghāzī orders his bearers to investigate and receives the news that al-Ghazwānī has been incarcerated. After receiving the blessing of al-Ghazwānī, Ibn Ghāzī announces to his companions that he will die the following day. When they object to his prediction, he says, "God has promised me that He would not take my soul until I had seen one of His saints. He has just shown me one of them."[89]

Both of these accounts are problematical. In the first place, Ibn Ghāzī could not have accompanied Muḥammad ash-Shaykh in the year proposed by Ibn ʿAskar, since the founder of the Wattasid state died in 910/1505, a full nine years before Ibn Ghāzī himself. However, it is equally unlikely that al-

Ghazwānī was brought to Fez in 915/1509–10, when the qāḍī al-jamāʿa died, because he visited the grave of at-Tabbāʿ in Marrakesh in 914/1508–9, while living among the ash-Shāwīya Arabs. Dating his arrest to 915 means that al-Ghazwānī would have spent less than a year at Jabal al-ʿAlam, which is highly improbable, given the extent of his involvement in developing the cult of Mūlāy ʿAbd as-Salām ibn Mashīsh.

The key to this problem, I believe, can be found in the letter, quoted earlier, to al-Ghazwānī's disciples al-Habṭī, Ibn Raysūn, and Ibn Khajjū. This document could not have been written before 917/1511–12, the year in which Ibrāhīm ibn ʿAlī ibn Rāshid succeeded his father as amir of Shafshāwan. It is apparent from the text of the letter that al-Ghazwānī was in full liberty at the time and probably living at Jabal al-ʿAlam. It is difficult to believe that the shaykh would have felt free to criticize both the Banū Rāshid and the Wattasids if he had been under house arrest in Fez. Thus, it seems most probable that al-Ghazwānī was arrested and brought to Fez sometime after 917, and perhaps in the year 919, as Ibn ʿAskar suggests. Does this mean that ʿAbd al-Wārith al-Yalṣūtī had as faulty a memory for names as Ibn ʿAskar apparently had for the details of dynastic succession? Not necessarily. The most likely scenario is that Muḥammad al-ʿArabī al-Fāsī, the hagiographer who transmitted al-Yalṣūtī's more up-to-date account, was confused about the two Abū ʿAbdallāhs from Meknès: the qāḍī al-jamāʿa and the shaykh al-jamāʿa. Since al-Fāsī died in 1052/1642, more than a century after the events he describes, it is reasonable to conclude that he stumbled into one of the aporias of tradition by confusing one Abu ʿAbdallāh al-Miknāsi with the other.[90]

Upon being confined to Fez, al-Ghazwānī ordered his students to join him and established a zāwiya inside of Bāb Futūḥ at a place called Bāb al-Qalīʿa.[91] One of his disciples was the Fez native Muḥammad al-Harwī aṭ-Ṭālib (d. 964/1557), whose *Waẓīfat al-Jazūliyya al-Ghazwāniyya* (The Required invocation of the Jazūliyya-Ghazwāniyya) appears to be the only original version of a Jazūlite litany still in existence. The manuscript of this work, which was copied in the year 1011/1600, can be found at the Bibliothèque Nationale in Paris. Its opening passages, translated below, provide a rare, firsthand glimpse of the exalted terms in which Jazūlite Sufis conceived of themselves and their place in Moroccan society:

> Beneath the Banner of Praise with our Prophet and noble master Muḥammad (may the most excellent blessings and purest greetings be

upon him)! Allah elevates whomever He wills through His mercy, for Allah's is the greatest excellence. All praise be to the Planner, the All-Wise, the Conqueror, the All-Knowing, the opener of the hearts of His saints to the knowledge of His grace and blessings! [The saints] are happy in His blessings upon them and bear witness to none but Him alone, putting all of their aspirations in Him (*ʿākifīna himamahum ʿalā bābihi*), devoting themselves to praising and glorifying Him, and happily awaiting the day when they will depart from the world by meeting Him on the carpet of His goodness and in His heaven, calling and urging humankind to listen to them and accept them.

[Allah's saints] are the Crowns of the Kingdom (*tījān al-mamlaka*) and the Moons of Existence (*aqmār al-wujūd*), illuminating [the earth] with the light of their inheritance from and adherence to the honest and trustworthy Messenger. They are the followers of [Allah's] Straight Path and guides to the Most Noble Master. He who agrees to follow and serve them will attain the full recompense of the One who gives birth to no sons; but he who rejects them and falls from their way has fallen into a great ocean and a bottomless pit and has brought upon himself a grievous punishment and a terrible calamity!

Allah has made us immune to both outward and inward strife (*ʿaṣamanā Allāhu min fitnati mā ẓahara wa mā baṭana*), has rewarded us with the most beautiful of doctrines, and has made us impervious to the depravity of our egos and the evil of arguments and criticisms through His beneficence, generosity, excellence, compassion, power, and might; for He is the master of everything and the All-Powerful who does as He wills. He is the protector of the believers, the recourse of the fearful, the goal of the seekers, and the answer of those who call upon Him. . . . The souls of those who know Him take on the attribute of lowliness and maintain the station of supplication with reverence and self-abnegation, placing themselves between the hands of the Mysterious, the Unique, the Conquering, the Glorious, the All-Powerful, the Compelling. They take pleasure in the different varieties of invocations and supplications for forgiveness (*istighfār*), and use as their means to Him the Pure, the Purified, the Intercessor, the Chosen [Prophet Muḥammad] (may God bless him and his family).[92]

Al-Ghazwānī probably spent only five or six years in Fez, for a late sixteenth-century *manāqib* work, *Shams al-maʿrifa fī sīrat ghawth al-*

mutaṣawwifa (The Sun of gnosis in the biography of the nurturer of the Sufis), by Aḥmad al-Ḥalfawī (d. after 1000/1590), puts him in Marrakesh in 921/1515, where he prevents the conquest of the city by the Wattasid amir Mūlāy an-Nāṣir. In consolation for the Wattasid defeat at Marrakesh, he is said to have "given" Muḥammad al-Burtughālī, the Sultan of Fez, victory over the Portuguese at Maʿmūra Sabū (present-day Mahdiyya), a fort on the Atlantic coast of Morocco between the regions of ash-Shāwīya and al-Gharb. This tradition is transmitted by Abū ʿAmr al-Qasṭallī (d. 974/1566–7), a third-generation Jazūlite shaykh and the subject of the above-mentioned work, whose own teacher (and al-Ghazwānī's principal Jazūlite rival) ʿAbd al-Karīm al-Fallāḥ (d. 933/1527), also claimed some of the credit for this miraculous trade-off.[93]

Both of the events mentioned in *Shams al-maʿrifa*—Mūlāy an-Nāṣir's abortive siege of Marrakesh and the subsequent Wattasid victory over the Portuguese at Maʿmūra—are well-known and can be dated with precision. Mūlāy an-Nāṣir's expedition to Dukkāla and the Sūs, of which the siege of Marrakesh was but a sideshow, is confirmed by the Wattasid chronicler al-Kurrāsī as occurring in 921/1515.[94] Apparently, Mūlāy an-Nāṣir believed that the defenders of the Marrakesh would give up without a fight, for the previous year a Portuguese raiding party had been able to approach the city's gates at will.[95] The defeat of the Portuguese at Maʿmūra, which was hailed as the greatest Moroccan victory since the relief of Tangier in 841/1437, also occurred in 921/1515, and resulted in the capture of more than fifty cannons and hundreds of Christian prisoners.[96]

The dates of these battles also agree with the most widely accepted account of al-Ghazwānī's departure from Fez, which is said to have occurred in a year of severe drought. Such a drought did, in fact, occur in 921/1515 and precipitated one of the two major famines that Morocco would undergo in the first half of the sixteenth century.[97] According to Muḥammad al-Mahdī al-Fāsī, al-Ghazwānī used a canal that drew water to the outskirts of Fez from Wādī al-Laban, whose Banū Maʿqil inhabitants had supported the Jazūlite cause a generation earlier. Seeing that the shaykh's canal always flowed with water while the others in the area had dried up, Mūlāy an-Nāṣir (the perennial nemesis of al-Ghazwānī in hagiographical literature) sought to commandeer it for the state. In the bargaining that followed, Sultan Muḥammad al-Burtughālī consented to the shaykh's departure from Fez in exchange for this canal. As al-Ghazwānī and his companions left the Marinid–Wattasid capital for the last time, the shaykh took his burnous

(Ber. *akhnīf*) in his right hand and pointed it first toward Fez and then toward the south, saying solemnly: "Go with me, oh sultanate, to Marrakesh!" (*Ayyā yā salṭāna, ilā Marrākush*).[98]

Upon leaving Fez, al-Ghazwānī burned all of his bridges to the Wattasids and the Idrisids and cast his lot once and for all with the lesser-known Saʿdian sharifs of the Darʿa valley in southern Morocco. Unlike northern Morocco, which had long suffered from the depredations of Arab pastoralists and Christian invaders, the lands south of the Atlas mountains still maintained stable social and economic structures. As explained in Chapter Six, the strategically important regions of Ḥāḥā, Sūs, Gazūla, Haskūra, and Darʿa had been independent from the Marinids since the end of the thirteenth century C.E. and shared similar patterns of culture, trade, and social organization. The original inhabitants of these regions consisted of both sedentary and transhumant tribes of Berbers and their Jewish or sub-Saharan African clients. In the fifteenth and sixteenth centuries, these groups paid tribute to Banū Maʿqil Arabs who inhabited the riverine and coastal lowlands. According to Mohamed Kably, the Banū Maʿqil, especially the Shabānāt tribe who allied themselves with the Portuguese, upset the economic balance of southern Morocco to such an extent that resistance to them became an economic necessity. For this reason, Kably views the subsequent Saʿdian jihad in the Sūs as an economically motivated "anti-Maʿqilism" rather than an ideologically based movement.[99] Although there is some truth to this assertion, Kably's economically deterministic model of Saʿdian origins is problematized by the fact that the Banū Maʿqil disciples of al-Jazūlī, such as Sīdī aṣ-Ṣughayyir as-Sahlī, were as much in favor of jihad as were their Banū Hilāl and non-Arab brethren. Indeed, given the new information about Jazūlite ideology that has been brought to light in the previous chapters, one must ask if it is any longer credible to suggest, as Kably has done, that the ideological orientation of the Jazūliyya and their Saʿdian allies was nothing more than a mystification of socioeconomic "realities."

Because of the segmentary and "acephalous" social organization of the tribes of southern Morocco, local murābiṭūn had long played an important role in the maintenance of social and economic life. These saintly leaders were particularly concerned with maintaining the trans-Saharan trade, which tied the oases of the Sūs and Darʿa valleys to markets as far away as Tlemcen in western Algeria. When the regional balance of power was upset by the creation in 911/1505 of the Portuguese stronghold and *feitoria* of Santa Cruz do Cabo de Gué (now the modern city of Agadir), the Berbers of these regions looked to their saintly patrons to help them deal with this new threat. By the first decade of the sixteenth century, four Sufi *zawāya,* all located in towns or tribal homelands that were associated with the trans-Saharan trade, had become centers of anti-Portuguese activity.

The easternmost of these centers was Zāwiyat M'ḍaghra, which was located in the region of Tāfīlalt, not far from the old mercantile city of Sijilmāsa. Its founding shaykh, ʿAbdallāh ibn ʿUmar al-M'ḍaghrī (d. 927/1521), allied himself with the senior sharifian family of southern Morocco, the "Sijilmāsīs" (today's ʿAlawites), whose influence extended from Haskūra in the west to Figuig near the present Moroccan-Algerian border.[100] Zāwiyat M'ḍaghra was also allied with the sharifs of Zāwiyat Tāgmadert in the middle Darʿa valley, which had begun to expand its influence under the leadership of Muḥammad ibn ʿAbd ar-Raḥmān az-Zaydānī (d. 923/1517).[101] Although the sharifs of Sijilmāsa and Tagmadert were said to be distantly related, they were by no means equal. On the contrary, the more senior Sijilmāsīs not only looked down on their Banū Zaydān "cousins," but even claimed that they had falsified their Prophetic genealogy.[102]

The most important religious center of the Sūs valley proper was Zāwiyat Tidsī, located south of the city of Taroudant in a town that served as a source of sugar and indigo for the Saharan trade.[103] Its paramount shaykh, Barakāt ibn Muḥammad at-Tidasī (d. 917/1511), had gained considerable prestige as a holy warrior who skirmished with the Portuguese near the *feitorias* of Māssa and Santa Cruz. Along with his prosecution of jihad, he also ransomed prisoners and kept the peace between feuding tribes. Despite his local reputation as a murābiṭ who could get things done, he was unable to convince the Portuguese to enter into relations with him. To their mind, a *morabito* such as Sīdī Barakāt did not have royal status and thus could not validate a treaty.[104] This tendency of the Portuguese to confuse Moroccan social structure with their own brand of feudalism and to equate murābiṭūn with minor officials of the Catholic church caused them to misinterpret indigenous structures of authority and hence to miss important political opportunities.[105]

Perhaps the greatest murābiṭ in the lands south of the Atlas mountains was Am'ḥammad u-M'bārak al-Āqqawī (d. 924/1518), a Berber from the emporium and mining center of Āqqā in the lower Darʿa valley. This shaykh ensured the economic stability of the region of Gazūla in the lower Sūs by instituting a commercial truce of three consecutive days per week called the "Days of Sīdī M'bārak" (*ayyām Sīdī M'barāk*). On these days tribespeople were forbidden from feuding, bearing arms, or harming any living creature. According to Ibn ʿAskar, one could even witness the unheard-of sight of a man trading with the person who had killed his father or his son.[106] The sixteenth-century Jazūlite Sufi and biographer Muḥammad al-Baʿqīlī reports that the fear of Sīdī M'barak was so great that the Arabs of Gazūla even policed themselves, lest the actions of one of their kin bring misfortune upon the entire tribe: "It was God's will that a bedouin caught a jerboa [a type of squirrel] on one of those days. A friend of his said, 'Let it go, for today is one of the Days of Forgiveness (*ayyām al-ʿāfiya*) and it belongs to the murābiṭ!' Then his friends set upon him because of his action and accused him of breaking the rules."[107] Al-Baʿqīlī also informs us that the staff (*ʿukkāz*) that Sīdī M'barak used to punish truce breakers was so laden with baraka that after his death the merchants of Gazūla would place it in front of their treasures to protect them from thieves.

When the Berbers of the Sūs and Darʿa regions turned to Sīdī M'bārak and Sīdī Barakāt for help against the Portuguese, Sīdī M'bārak suggested that they rally instead behind Sharif Muḥammad ibn ʿAbd ar-Raḥmān of Tāgmadert, who had already sent his sons Aḥmad and M'ḥammad to Fez to gain official authorization for a jihad.[108] According to the eighteenth-century historian Muḥammad al-Ifrānī, in the year 915/1509 the sharif of Tagmadert, who now adopted the mahdist title of *al-qāʾim bi-amri'llāh* (He Who Has Arisen by the Command of God), was instructed by Sīdī M'bārak in the tradition of the just ruler. In 916/1510, at the zāwiya of Sīdī Barakāt at Tidsī, Muḥammad al-Qāʾim received the submission of the Berber tribes of the Sūs and promised to lead them in an attack against the Portuguese *feitoria* of Fonti (Tafatant).[109]

Thus was born the "Saʿdian" dynasty of Morocco, which, in a little over forty years, was to politically unify the Far Maghrib for the first time since the Almohads. Much speculation, none of it very satisfactory, has been devoted to the origin of this name, which differs from the family's actual *nisba,* "az-Zaydānī." The historian al-Ifrānī, an apologist for the Saʿdians, discusses the controversy about their sharifian origins in considerable detail and cites the ʿAlawite assertion that they were of the tribe of the Prophet's wet nurse, the Banū Saʿd ibn Bakr, rather than of the Prophet's family; hence the designation "Saʿdī." By way of rebuttal, he also cites the Jazūlite shaykh Aḥmad ibn Mūsā as-Simlālī ("Sīdī Aḥmad u-Mūsā"; d. 971/1563–

4), who believed in the sharifian origins of the Saʿdians and called his disciple, the Saʿdian sultan Abū ʿAbdallāh al-Ghālib Bi'llāh (d. 981/1574), the "Ruby of the Sharifs" (*yaqūtat al-ashrāf*). On another occasion, Aḥmad ibn Mūsā declared that his royal protégé was more of a ṣāliḥ than a sultan—a strong testament, as al-Ghazwānī might have said, to the Saʿdians' nobility by *ḥasab* if not by *nasab*.[110]

If the Saʿdians were indeed sharifs, as Aḥmad ibn Mūsā claimed, and not from the tribe of Banū Saʿd, as asserted by their ʿAlawite opponents, what might have accounted for the term "Saʿdian"? A possible answer can be found in the Saʿdian dynasty's use of millenarian discourse.[111] One of their favorite terms was *saʿāda,* which can be translated into English as "happiness," "bliss," or "salvation." This term appears often in Saʿdian-era texts, and it can also be found in such appellations as Dār as-Saʿāda (House of Bliss), which, following Ottoman usage, was the official name for the royal palace of the Saʿdian rulers in Marrakesh.

Significantly, *saʿāda* also figures prominently in the writings and sayings of Muḥammad ibn Sulaymān al-Jazūlī. An important example of such usage can be found in a statement of al-Jazūlī that was quoted in Chapter Six: "Past nations have asked to be included in our polity. Yet no one can be included in it unless he has already attained salvation (*saʿāda*). Our polity is the state (*dawla*) of those who strive and struggle in the path of Allah—fighters against the enemies of Allah."[112] Muḥammad al-Qāʾim, the founder of the Saʿdian polity, used the region of Ḥāḥā as his base for jihad against the Portuguese. This was the same region that provided a base for al-Jazūlī in the final years of his life. As a leader of the anti-Portuguese jihad, Muḥammad al-Qāʾim associated himself so closely with the memory of al-Jazūlī that he ordered himself to be interred next to the shaykh upon his death in 923/1517.[113] Could it be that he saw himself as the founder of the state of salvation that al-Jazūlī advocated?

For the greater part of its history, the Saʿdian state could arguably be called a jihad state of the type sought by al-Jazūlī, since the official reason for its existence was the liberation of the Dār al-Islām (specifically the Far Maghrib) from foreign domination.[114] As a jihad state, the Saʿdian state would have been by definition a salvation-oriented polity (Ar. *dawlat as-saʿāda*); first, because its goal was the salvation of Morocco as a political entity, and second, because those who fought in its armies were absolved from their sins by participating in a holy war.

Although this brings us a step closer to a possible solution for the origin of the name "Saʿdī," the phrase *dawlat as-saʿāda* (State of Salvation) is still not the same as *ad-dawla as-saʿdiyya* (The Saʿdian State). However, if the Arabic noun *saʿāda* is made into an adjective on the pattern of the English word "salvific," an interesting possibility arises. One form that this adjective might take is the neologism *saʿādī,* which is all but unheard-of in the Arabic language. Another alternative, however, is *saʿdī,* which is in fact how the Saʿdians referred to themselves. If this latter term were used, the phrase *dawlat as-saʿāda* (State of Salvation) would become semantically equivalent to *ad-dawla as-saʿdiyya* (The Salvific State), which is the name by which the Saʿdian dynasty appears in Moroccan history. Those who lived in such a state, both rulers and ruled alike, would be known as *as-saʿdiyūn* (The "Saʿdians," or Those Who Are Saved).

The significance of this exercise in philology is that it links the political ideology of the Saʿdian dynasty to the religiopolitical ideology of the Jazūliyya Sufi order. Insofar as it reflected popular aspirations for a new order of faith and justice, the Saʿdian state might also be seen as a *civitas dei,* a "city (or polity) of God," a concept that was discussed in Part One as part of the ethos of the Moroccan community of saints. The fact that the Saʿdians were descendants of the Prophet Muḥammad made their claim to be the leaders of such a polity all the more logical. We have seen how closely the Jazūlite doctrine of *aṭ-ṭarīqa al-Muḥammadiyya* approximated Shiʿite models of authority and how al-Ghazwānī's concept of the Sovereignty of Saintly Authority (*siyādat al-imāma*) was as close to political Shiʿism as one could come in the context of Sunni Islam. If Sufi shaykhs could enjoy the fruits of the Prophetic Inheritance, how much more worthy of this honor were the Saʿdian sharifs, who had the advantage of being holy by birth as well as by attribution?

The Saʿdian attempt to establish an ideology of royal authority by divine right is best illustrated by the example of Muḥammad al-Qāʾim's younger son, Muḥammad (M'ḥammad) ash-Shaykh "al-Mahdī" (d. 964/1557), the man who finally unified Morocco under the white and gold Saʿdian banner. According to the sixteenth-century Portuguese *Chronicle of Santa-Cruz,* this sharif was venerated by his followers as "a great sorcerer" who could perceive hidden realities and whose presence in battle was crucial to the morale of his troops.[115] If this testimony were not enough, the inscription engraved on Muḥammad ash-Shaykh's tomb in Marrakesh leaves little doubt as to the aura of divine legitimation that surrounded his public persona:

Pay your respects to a tomb enveloped in mercy,
And whose sides are shaded by clouds.

From it, I have inhaled the breath of sanctity,
Which comes to me on zephyr's wings from the eternal.

His death has eclipsed the sun of guidance and has clothed,
Thusly, the seven spheres in darkness.

Oh heart overtaken by the ghoul of death decreed,
And whose arrow of fate is fixed firmly within,

Your death has spitefully laid low the highest peaks,
And your funeral has shaken the seven heavens!

Your bier of alloy has been carried toward Eden
By the melodies and voices of angels.

The Pleiades rise above it, and
You are enthroned in pearls beneath the earth.

Oh mercy of God, let him taste the wine of divine pleasure,
Whose cups are regularly filled on his behalf!

So be it! He will be vindicated by history, for through him was made manifest
The house of the Imam of Guidance and the garden of the Mahdī![116]

Muḥammad ash-Shaykh as-Saʿdī could not have become the unifier of the Far Maghrib, however, if al-Ghazwānī and his followers had not helped him. But before he could become a power behind the Saʿdian throne, al-Ghazwānī first had to assert his authority over the other shaykhs of the Jazūliyya in Marrakesh. Since none of these were clearly superior to the others in terms of doctrinal or spiritual knowledge, they were undecided as to who best exemplified the Prophetic Inheritance. This problem was particularly acute at the time of al-Ghazwānī's arrival in Marrakesh because ʿAbd al-Karīm al-Fallāḥ, who had managed at-Tabbāʿ's zāwiya and supervised its kitchen, had begun to promote himself as the next shaykh al-jamāʿa of the Jazūliyya.[117] To bolster his case, al-Fallāḥ claimed that at-Tabbāʿ had predicted that the next shaykh al-jamāʿa would come from among the latter's disciples in Marrakesh. Believing that this prediction referred to himself, al-Fallāḥ summoned the shaykhs of the Jazūliyya to a meeting at at-Tabbāʿ's tomb. After dinner, he announced: "You will not leave here until you have told us about yourselves. The shaykh has sworn that his successor will be one of us and that his secret is among us, yet we will not recognize him. Therefore, we will bestow the authority of the shaykh on the one whose attributes most closely resemble those of [at-Tabbāʿ] and [can prove to be] his heir. He should make himself known to us, for the shaykh has said: 'Neither a secret that is hidden nor wealth that is divided shall separate the fuqarāʾ from one another.'"

The first to speak up was Saʿīd ibn ʿAbd al-Munʿim al-Ḥāḥī (d. 953/1546),[118] the founder of the controversial Ḥāḥiyya branch of the Jazūliyya, who recounted the paranormal states that he shared with at-Tabbāʿ and the consideration he had been given during at-Tabbāʿ's lifetime. The second to make a claim was the *malāmatī* Sufi Abū'l-ʿAzm Raḥḥāl al-Kūsh (d. after 945/1538–9),[119] who announced: "I am the vehicle of bridegrooms (*rikāb al-ʿarāʾis*). He who has not ridden his bridegroom is not meant to ride. Verily I am the Nurturer (*ṣāḥib al-ighātha*) on land and sea!" Then ʿAlī ibn Ibrāhīm al-Būzīdī (d. 956/1549)[120] said: "I am the most worshipful among you; I pray all night and fast all day." At this al-Ḥāḥī spoke again: "I am the scholar among you; he who desires knowledge of both outward and inward states should come to me, for I have mastered them." Finally al-Fallāḥ spoke, and said, "I am your provision (*māʾidatukum*); he who desires nourishment should come to me, for neither the sharecropper (*khammās*) nor the common laborer (*marrās*) is excluded from my blessing!"

Throughout all of these speeches al-Ghazwānī remained silent. "Each of you has said what he possesses," al-Fallāḥ stated, "but you, Sīdī ʿAbdallāh, what do you possess and what do you have to say?" Al-Ghazwānī replied, "I am your sultan and the ruler of your silence (*ṣāḥib saktikum*); with me alone you are minted. He who stamps his own dirham or dinar will succeed; if not, he will not (*wa man lā fa-lā*)!" The assembled shaykhs were stunned by the apparent arrogance of al-Ghazwānī's statement. "Why are you silent?" he asked. "Do you dislike my words?" "Yes," they replied. Then al-Ghazwānī stretched out his hand and said, "God is directing this!" and grasped the empty air. Next he balled his fingers into a fist. "What do you say?" he asked, "and what does each of you [now] possess?"[121] After al-Ghazwānī's dramatic assertion of divine legitimation, most of those who were present accepted him as the heir to at-Tabbāʿ. The main exception was Sīdī Raḥḥāl, who protested so insistently that al-Ghazwānī said: "Either you leave this to me or I will leave it to you. Two serpents cannot live together in the same hole!" Realizing that he could count on little support for his leadership, Sīdī Raḥḥāl gathered his disciples and left for Anmāy, a day's ride east of Marrakesh, where he remained for the rest of his life.[122]

Al-Ghazwānī spent the final years of his life in Marrakesh, where he used his authority and reputation to lend credibility to the Saʿdian cause. This effort was particularly necessary after the Saʿdian takeover of Marrakesh in 930/1524, which resulted in the murder of the city's Hintātī amir. The less than noble circumstances of this coup cost the sharifs dearly in terms of lost prestige, and the leaders of the Saʿdian movement, the brothers Aḥmad al-Aʿraj (d. 964/1557) and Muḥammad ash-Shaykh, needed an ally whose reputation was unassailable. As it turned out, the final and most dramatic of al-Ghazwānī's miracles also took place in 930/1524 and involved his intercession on behalf of the Saʿdians when their occupation of Marrakesh was contested by the Wattasid sultan Muḥammad al-Burtughālī.[123] According to Ibn ʿAskar, the Wattasid forces laying siege to Marrakesh were so successful in bombarding the city's walls with their cannons that the inhabitants of the city began to fear for their lives. Seeing that the situation was critical, al-Ghazwānī and his most senior disciples rode out of the Abū'l-ʿAbbās as-Sabtī Gate (named after the patron saint of Marrakesh) in order to arrange a truce. Stopping at a point midway between the opposing forces, the shaykh found himself targeted by Wattasid arquebusiers. One of the balls that they fired struck al-Ghazwānī just above the heart and tore a hole in his woolen tunic. Miraculously, it flattened itself against his chest without penetrating the skin and left no more than a minor burn. Taking the hot fragment of lead between his fingers, al-Ghazwānī exclaimed, "This is the end of their war!" and turned back toward the city. The next day, Muḥammad al-Burtughālī received word that his nephews had risen against him in Fez. Fearing for his throne, he turned his army back toward his capital and never threatened Marrakesh again.[124]

Jazūlite Activism After al-Ghazwānī

Al-Ghazwānī's death in 935/1528–9 marks a watershed in the history of Jazūlite Sufism. Although subsequent Jazūlite shaykhs, such as Abū ʿAmr al-Qasṭallī, would embellish the concept of *aṭ-ṭarīqa al-Muḥammadiyya* by adding such innovations as a hierarchy of Prophetic visions, there were no major changes in the central doctrines of the Muḥammadan Way or in the paradigm of religiopolitical authority that went with it. This does not mean, however, that third-generation Jazūlite shaykhs were in agreement on all doctrinal matters. On the contrary, al-Ghazwānī's rival ʿAbd al-Karīm al-Fallāḥ took pains to distance his more charismatic and politically neutral "Tabbāʿiyya" approach from the pro-Saʿdian activism of the Ghazwāniyya. When one adds to these two factions the ʿĪsāwiyya Sufi order of Muḥammad ibn ʿĪsā al-Fahdī, whose followers also regarded their shaykh as the rightful heir to at-Tabbāʿ, it becomes easy to understand Aḥmad Zarrūq's contention that competition among the shaykhs of the Jazūliyya had led them to "drink each other's blood."

The existence of intra-Jazūlite factionalism also problematizes the notion of a common Jazūlite political agenda. In the first half of the sixteenth century one can find Jazūlite shaykhs supporting both the Saʿdians and their enemies, the Wattasids. Such was the case, for example, in 940/1533–4, when two Jazūlite shaykhs from the region of Meknès, ʿUmar al-Khaṭṭāb of the Tabbāʿiyya (d. ca. 943/1536)[125] and Abū Ruwāyīn of the ʿĪsāwiyya (d. before 960/1553), brokered the treaty that formally divided Morocco between the Wattasid "Kingdom of Fez" in the north and the Saʿdian "Kingdom of Marrakesh" in the south. While Abū Ruwāyīn remained a supporter of the Saʿdians throughout his life, ʿUmar al-Khaṭṭāb was so angered by the sharifs' arrogance and naked ambition that he vowed to prevent them from entering Fez "as long as he was on the face of the earth."[126]

Although it is beyond the scope of the present work, a study of the dissolution of aṭ-Ṭāʾifa al-Jazūliyya in the post-Saʿdian era would be of great help in understanding the phenomenon of popular mysticism in the Far Maghrib. A particularly interesting chapter could be written about the ʿĪsāwiyya Sufi order, which is usually dismissed as a marginal and heterodox institution. Although the ʿĪsāwī saint Abū Ruwāyīn has been discussed at some length by de Prémare, who cites him as an example of a *malāmatī* social activist,[127] no one has yet remarked on the fact that Abū Ruwāyīn's attempt to extort concessions from the rich and powerful was a near carbon copy of the *mushāṭara* of his more famous predecessor, Abū'l-ʿAbbās as-Sabtī. A more thorough study of the ʿĪsāwīyya might help scholars trace the distinctive elements of Moroccan Sufism into the modern period and flesh out some of the hypotheses proposed in this book.

In the decades after al-Ghazwānī's death, the doctrinal perspective of the Ghazwāniyya faction of the Jazūliyya was most often expressed in terms of two different yet complementary strategies: the reform of political and social life in Morocco and the reform of Sufi practice. One of the most influential proponents of the latter approach was ʿAbd al-Wārith al-Yalṣūtī, whom we have already met as al-Ghazwānī's advocate at the latter's interrogation in Fez. Al-Yalṣūtī's most important work, the didactic poem *Sullam al-murīd* (Ladder of the Aspirant), addresses some of the same issues that were raised by Aḥmad Zarrūq and his followers in their critiques of Jazūlite Sufism. It thus constitutes a refutation of the less doctrinally sophisticated and charismatic approach to sainthood advocated by ʿAbd al-Karīm al-Fallāḥ and the shaykhs of the Tabbāʿiyya faction of the Jazūliyya, and substitutes in its place the orthodox–mystical Ghazwāniyya emphasis on mass education and respect for the Law. These themes are present in the following passage from *Sullam al-murīd,* where al-Yalṣūtī decries the low moral and intellectual standards of Sufis in his day and proposes a greater integration of the Sharīʿa into Sufi practice:

The [true] spiritual master is known by his signs,
But not the signs of the people of this age!

When he is known by his miracles (*karāma*),
He is a symbol for us of the Imamate (*imāma*).

But the Imamate belongs only to those with knowledge
Among the keepers of tradition (*rijāl*) on the Sufi way.

When you find a person promoting himself,
And following his own rules and nothing else,

Cut yourself off from him for your own protection,
If you desire to gain a lasting reward!

Avoid mixing with Sufis who are ignorant,
And do not lose yourself in love for them.

Even if you see one of them flying through the air,
Or if you see him walking on the water,

He is but a false prophet (*dajjālun min ad-dajājil*)
Who tries to get by on his own devices!

When the scholars of the community have died off,
The people take the ignorant for leaders

And pass judgment on the Sharīʿa without precedent to guide them.
Indeed, one even looks to himself for guidance!

Thusly they deceive others, and the people are misled,
But in this they see no harm to themselves![128]

Among al-Ghazwānī's students, ʿAbdallāh al-Habṭī was clearly the most successful at combining social activism and Sufi reformism in a single career.[129] Born near Tangier and orphaned early in life, he spent his childhood in the care of his elder brother, who had suffered twenty years of privation and torture in Portuguese prisons.[130] After being ransomed from the Portuguese, the elder al-Habṭī moved to Shafshāwan, where he joined the holy warriors gathered around the sharif ʿAlī ibn Rāshid. Previous Jazūlite efforts to raise the level of education in rural areas allowed ʿAbdallāh al-Habṭī to master the sciences of fiqh and Qur'anic exegesis within the region of Shafshāwan itself. Upon reaching maturity, he moved to Fez, where he completed his formal studies under the theologian Abū Aḥmad at-Tilimsānī (d. 931/1524–5) and the legist Aḥmad az-Zaqqāq (d. 939/1532–3).[131]

According to Ibn ʿAskar, al-Habṭī spent his youth studying under Sufi shaykhs in both northern Morocco and the region of Marrakesh. Besides al-Ghazwānī, these included the poet and polemicist Muḥammad ibn Yaggabsh at-Tāzī and Abū ʿAmr al-Qasṭallī, a prominent disciple of ʿAbd al-Karīm al-Fallāḥ.[132] Studying under these shaykhs gave al-Habṭī the opportunity to draw from the most important sources of Sufi doctrine then available in the Far Maghrib: the Tabbāʿiyya approach to Jazūlite Sufism via al-Qasṭallī, the Ghazwāniyya approach via al-Ghazwānī himself, and the Zaytūnī–Qādirī method via at-Tāzī. Of these three individuals, al-Ghazwānī was by far the most important to al-Habṭī's formation as an intellectual. References to al-Habṭī in the pages of *An-Nuqṭa al-azaliyya* reveal that al-Ghazwānī was so fond of his young pupil that he treated him as a son.

Upon returning to Shafshāwan, al-Habṭī sought out his old friend and classmate, Muḥammad ibn Khajjū (d. 956/1550), who served as a judge for the sharifian clan of Banū Ḥassān. At first, Ibn Khajjū was horrified that al-Habṭī had embraced Sufism and exclaimed, "I would rather see you a Jew or a Christian before seeing you attach yourself to the errors of that folk!"[133] In time, however, he too became disciple of al-Ghazwānī and even went so far as to write a treatise defending the Jazūlite doctrines he once opposed.

Sometime after 917/1511, al-Habṭī and Ibn Khajjū sat down together and mapped out a program of social and religious reform for the lands under the control of the Banū Rāshid sharifs. This unique team was assisted by al-Habṭī's wife Āmina, who was Ibn Khajjū's sister. As a fully trained legist in her own right, Āmina bint Khajjū presided over a zāwiya next to that of her husband, where she taught the fundamentals of Islam and Sufism to the women of Shafshāwan.

Al-Habṭī's critiques of Moroccan society are preserved in a remarkable didactic poem entitled *Al-Alfiyya as-saniyya fī tanbīh al-ʿāmma wa'l-khāṣṣa ʿalā mā awqaʿa min at-taghyīr fī'l-milla al-Islāmiyya* (The Exalted Poem in one thousand verses awakening the masses and the elites to the deviations that have occurred in the Islamic community).[134] The thousand-verse (*alfiyya*) format that al-Habṭī employed in this work had long been used in the Far Maghrib as a method for teaching grammar, and was first introduced as a way of disseminating the doctrines of reformist Sufism by Muḥammad ibn Yaggabsh at-Tāzī. In al-Habṭī's hands, the *alfiyya* form was used as a propagandistic device that recalled the pamphlets and missives then being printed by Protestant activists in Europe. This propagandistic use of the *alfiyya* form was facilitated by the repetitive nature of the genre's *rajaz* rhyme pattern, which eased memorization and hence dissemination in a society that had not yet discovered the printing press.

Like his teachers, al-Habṭī believed that the main cause of the social ills besetting Morocco was the loss of faith. This was exacerbated by ignorance and illiteracy, contact with Portuguese soldiers and merchants, and excessive loyalty to custom (Ar. *taqlīd* or *ʿāda*). In particular, al-Habṭī castigates the religious and political elites of Shafshāwan for their lack of concern about the moral decay surrounding them. The worst of these offenders were the official ulama, whom al-Habṭī calls "rabbis" (*aḥbār*) because of their concern for the letter rather than the spirit of the law.[135]

Al-Habṭī fully agreed with al-Ghazwānī's emphasis on women's education. He was concerned that mothers, as the initial teachers of their children, were unprepared to instill a knowledge of Islam in their offspring. Rather than blaming these women for their ignorance, however, he instead focused on their husbands and fathers, accusing them of abandoning their responsibility to teach. According to al-Habṭī, each married man bore responsibility for the moral and intellectual upbringing of his family. This was part of his role as imām of the family, which constitutes an Islamic *umma* in miniature. Uneducated women raise ignorant children, and ignorant children become sinful adults. This sinfulness undermines the moral basis of society. To ensure that mothers were equipped to teach their children the proper values, certain of al-Habṭī's disciples, such as the sharif Mūsā ibn ʿAlī al-Wazzānī (d. 870/1562–3), even went so far as to make prospective brides pass tests in Islamic dogma before witnessing their marriage contracts.[136]

Al-Habṭī's educational program emphasized instruction in the Sharīʿa and the development of a reading knowledge of the Arabic language. As a first step, he and Ibn Khajjū would go to a village or tribal encampment and convince its leaders of the need for change. Next they would assemble the inhabitants of the village and quiz them on what they knew about the teachings of Islam. Subjects that were stressed in these sessions included Islamic history, the concept of monotheism, the Five Pillars of Islam, bodily hygiene and purification, and the rules pertaining to the monthly periods of women and the taboo period (*ʿidda*) after the death of a woman's husband. Al-Habṭī and Ibn Khajjū would remain in the village until its leaders signed a contract, swearing that they would forbid usury, encourage daily prayers, and follow the Sunna.[137] If a mosque did not exist in the village, al-Habṭī would supervise its construction himself and stay long enough to see that it was properly maintained. If alcohol were sold, he would convince its purveyors to leave the locality or go into another line of business. He was more severe with tattoo artists, however; these were ostracized and expelled from the region of Shafshāwan altogether.[138]

Although al-Habṭī focused most of his attention on social reform, he did not overlook the obligation of jihad against the Portuguese. He and Ibn Khajjū traveled widely around northern Morocco, calling for Muslim unity in the face of the Christian threat. They also sent admonitory letters to the rulers, jurists, students of the law, and official notaries of the region. Al-Habṭī was especially concerned that the authorities resist the conversion of Muslims to Christianity, which had begun to occur in the border areas near the Portuguese enclaves of Tangier and al-Qaṣr aṣ-Ṣaghīr. Like at-Tāzī, he saw Iberian expansionism as a threat to the survival of Muslim society. He was also concerned about the large Andalusian refugee populations of Shafshāwan and Tetuan, who, while providing a welcome source of reinforcements for jihad, also introduced European customs that undermined traditional Islamic values. Al-Habṭī's efforts to purify Islam in the region of Shafshāwan were strongly resisted by the sharif Ibrāhīm ibn Rāshid, who repeatedly had the shaykh incarcerated. Al-Habṭī was to enjoy a free hand only after 948/1541, when the Banū Rāshid sharifs finally abandoned the Wattasids and pledged their allegiance to the Saʿdians. By this time, however, the injuries he had suffered from repeated beatings were so severe that he was barely able to walk.

In 956/1549 the Saʿdian sharif Muḥammad ash-Shaykh occupied Fez and began the political reunification of Morocco that would eventually be completed in 961/1554. Although al-Ghazwānī and his disciples had played an important part in this victory, its aftermath proved to be a bitter disappointment for the shaykhs of the Jazūliyya. Rather than seeing his Sufi mentors as the imams and guardians of Islam as they had hoped, Muḥammad ash-Shaykh prevented the Jazūliyya as an institution from entering the circle of power and asserted his own, exclusive claim to authority by divine right of birth. In doing so, he revived the early ideology of Hasanid Shiʿism that had prevailed under the Idrisids. As a descendant of the Prophet and *qāʾim* in the line of al-Ḥasan, he portrayed himself as the Just Ruler, Mahdī, and Imam of the Age, who would unify the Maghrib under his authority, expel the Christians from al-Andalus, and eventually free the Arabs of the Mashriq from the Turkish yoke. Instead of the Sufi Bell saint, Axis of the Age, or Jazūlite shaykh al-jamāʿa, Muḥammad ash-Shaykh now claimed the sole right to appropriate the Muḥammadan Inheritance.

By also demonstrating the power of his baraka on the battlefield, Muḥammad ash-Shaykh took the ideological high ground away from the Jazūliyya and promoted Saʿdian ideology in a way that was difficult to contest. The shaykhs of the Jazūliyya may have seen themselves as the axes of the spiritual realm, but in the material world—the *dunyā* that they as Sufis purported to reject—they were compelled to cede primacy of place. Although they could still be influential behind the scenes, the outward arena of political life was not traditionally seen as a proper environment for either scholars or saints. Here, it was the man of the sword (and increasingly the cannon or arquebuse) who had the advantage. This realpolitik of the *conditteri* was succinctly expressed by Muḥammad ash-Shaykh in a verse of his own composition:

> People are people, and the days they are as one;
> Time is time, and the world is his who has won![139]

No sooner had Muḥammad ash-Shaykh seized power in Fez than the Sufis of Morocco realized that they had been outdone by a monster of their own making. In 956/1549, the sharif ordered all of the shaykhs of northern

Morocco to formally pledge their allegiance to him in the conquered Wattasid capital of Fez. Those called to Fez included the Jazūliyya–Ghazwāniyya Sufis al-Yalṣūtī, al-Habṭī, and Ibn Khajjū, as well as the Zarrūqiyya shaykh Muḥammad ash-Shuṭaybī (d. after 960/1553). Only al-Habṭī and Ibn Khajjū saw fit to demonstrate their loyalty by complying with Muḥammad ash-Shaykh's command. As it turned out, al-Habṭī had to return to Shafshawān alone, for Ibn Khajjū died in Fez of natural causes.[140]

In 958/1551 sharifian suspicion fell on the followers of the Jazūlite shaykhs ʿAbd al-Karīm al-Fallāḥ and ʿAbd al-Munʿim al-Ḥāḥī, who were accused of withholding from the state the valuables entrusted to them by Wattasid officials.[141] The resulting persecution of the Tabbāʿiyya faction of the Jazūliyya was especially hard on the Ḥāḥiyya. Many of this taʾifa's most important figures were either executed by the Saʿdians or driven out of Morocco on the pretext of heresy. Although the initial excuse for this assault on the Jazūliyya was pecuniary, the real reasons for sharifian opposition appear to have been twofold. In the first place, the charismatic populism of Tabbāʿiyya doctrine posed a threat to the Saʿdian state, despite this faction's professed aversion to politics. This conclusion is supported by the fact that the most famous follower of ʿAbd al-Karīm al-Fallāḥ to be persecuted by the Saʿdians was ʿAbdallāh al-Kūsh (d. 961/1553), a shaykh of sub-Saharan African origin who enjoyed a broad following among the lower classes of Marrakesh. Second, both the Tabbāʿiyya and the Ḥāḥiyya were charged by the Saʿdian ulama with rejecting the authority of the four Sunni schools of law. Although this accusation did not represent the actual views of the Tabbāʿiyya, Ḥāḥiyya reformism did pose a threat to the hegemony of the Maliki school of jurisprudence, because it advocated abandoning the precedent of a single *madhhab* in favor of unanimity among the four Sunni schools in general.[142]

Muḥammad ash-Shaykh's persecution of the shaykhs of the Jazūliyya prompted a remarkable letter to the sharif from Mūsā ibn ʿAlī al-Wazzānī, a follower of the Jazūliyya–Ghazwāniyya faction and disciple of ʿAbdallāh al-Habṭī. This response of a fourth-generation Jazūlite shaykh to the actions of the Saʿdian autocrat provides a fitting symbolic epitaph to the Jazūliyya's involvement in Moroccan political life. It also illustrates the ambiguity that pertains when both Sufi saint and sharif lay claim to the same Prophetic Inheritance.

In his letter, al-Wazzānī uses the metaphor of the tree of life to describe the relationship between the Sufi saint and the state.[143] He begins by quoting Muḥammad ibn Yaggabsh at-Tāzī, who stated that "the obedience of a land and its people depends on a leader to whom they can turn in all affairs." According to al-Wazzānī, the leader referred to by at-Tāzī is the *quṭb,* the axial saint—the very person whom Muḥammad ash-Shaykh and his advisers most feared as a potential rival. Rather than fearing the *quṭb,* he responds, the just Islamic ruler should welcome this saint and cleave to him. Comparing the state to a tree, al-Wazzānī argues that the *quṭb* is the water that brings the state to life. Were it not for the water, the soil around the tree would not soften, thus preventing the tree from taking nourishment. Were it not for the life-giving soil, the tree's roots would not remain fixed and its branches would not grow. Were it not for the branches, the tree would produce no fruit. In this way, every part of the tree acts in concert with the other members to maintain the life of the tree as a whole. Thus, the place of the *quṭb* in the overall scheme of things is not to impart to the state its outward form, but rather to provide its life-giving essence. In like manner, the *quṭb* does not desire to assume outward political power, but rather is content to provide spiritual sustenance and moral guidance so that the state may live.

Every leader, says al-Wazzānī, is a *quṭb,* an axial figure for those who depend on him. For this reason, it is fully proper to consider the saints and Sufi shaykhs who sustain Morocco with their baraka as the *aqṭāb ad-dawla,* "axes of the state." The same is true of the major Sufi orders such as the Jazūliyya, which provide the means by which the saints and shaykhs disseminate their baraka to others. Rather than being enemies to the state, the Sufi orders help sustain and preserve it by keeping its political leaders on the right path, so that the state may benefit the land and its people for generations. The greatest source of this spiritual sustenance is the *quṭb az-zamān*—the Axis of the Age or paradigmatic saint—who derives his powers alchemically from the light of the Prophet Muḥammad. "Next to prophecy itself," concludes al-Wazzānī, "there is no other light that can illuminate the face of the earth."

CONCLUSION

Power and Authority in Moroccan Sainthood

The Introduction to this book posed a challenge for the study of Moroccan sainthood. There had to be a way of assessing a society's response to extraordinary individuals without falling back on inadequate and impressionistic concepts such as charisma or resorting to reductionistic theoretical models. Although finding an adequate way of dealing with the paranormal is difficult from a scientific point of view, it is necessary if one is to go beyond the current understanding of sainthood in Islamic Studies. Merely locating the saint in a particular social structure is not enough to conceptualize sainthood as a living phenomenon. Neither is it enough to conceptualize the holy person solely according to the tenets of mysticism. The study of sainthood must reconcile both social and doctrinal perspectives if it is to have any lasting value. This I have tried to do by making a diachronic and multidisciplinary study of sainthood in premodern Morocco.

To consider sainthood from the perspective of human experience, and not from some doctrinal ideal, one must first of all acknowledge that sainthood is a social phenomenon. In other words, the extraordinary is recognized in practice before it is defined in theory. To restate this point in the terms used by Moroccan Sufis: if the nature of a person's knowledge (*ʿilm*) is revealed through one's actions (*ʿamal*), then the nature of a person's sainthood (*walāya*) will also be revealed through the actions of the saint as experienced by others (*wilāya*). This interdependency of knowledge and praxis was fully understood by Moroccan Sufis, who remarked on it in their writings. An example of this understanding can be found in Aḥmad Zarrūq's statement, "The inner essence of the slave is known through his outward state,"[1] or in Aḥmad ibn ʿĀshir's "Knowledge without practice is like a tree without fruit."[2]

As a lived phenomenon, what most premodern Moroccans saw as sainthood was *wilāya,* not *walāya.* Within the symbolic universe of Moroccan Islam, each of these two terms symbolized a different province, or "enclave," of meaning.[3] These enclaves of meaning constituted the Moroccan version of the "two worlds of sainthood" observed by Weinstein and Bell in their studies of medieval Europe. Although the worlds of European and Moroccan sainthood were located in different cultural domains, they were similar in many respects. The main difference was that in Morocco the two worlds of sainthood were distinguished in doctrinal terms, whereas in Europe they were not. In Morocco, *walāya* connoted the internal visage (Ar. *bāṭin*) of sainthood. As such, it was the product of a particular mystical epistemology that relied on its own educational apparatus or regime of training. This epistemology contextualized the ideological, technical, and programmatic factors that entered into the Sufi definition of sainthood.[4] *Walāya* thus referred to the metaphysical essence of sainthood as seen from the perspective of Islamic mysticism—an ideological complex whose main function was to articulate and validate the premises of Sufism.[5]

Although *walāya* expressed the essence of sainthood for Moroccan Sufis, the concept of *wilāya,* the outward visage (Ar. *ẓāhir*) of sainthood, was phenomenologically "more real" to the general public. This was because the actions of the saint were experienced directly by the saint's audience, often before their interpretation could be passed through the filter of Sufi doctrine. This visible dimension of sainthood was primarily understood in terms of power. The sociological profile of Moroccan sainthood outlined in Chapter Four supports this conclusion by showing that the Moroccan saint was above all else an empowered person—empowered to perform miracles, empowered to communicate with God, empowered to help the weak or oppressed, empowered to act on behalf of others, empowered to mediate the course of destiny, and empowered to affect the behavior of other holders of power. Such a person was awe-inspiring to an audience because his or her powers, when viewed in the context of a systematic pattern of virtuous conduct, were believed to have come from God. The thirteenth-century jurist Aḥmad al-ʿAzafī summed up the "majestical power" of the Moroccan walī Allāh by saying that people learn to fear God through the power of His saints.[6]

The image of the Moroccan saint as an empowered person brings to mind Thomas E. Wartenberg's theory of situated social power.[7] For Wartenberg, power is a potentiality that is actualized through a network of social alignments that both restrict and empower the agent as he or she seeks to attain identified goals. The relationships that make up these alignments may be either dominant or subordinate, intentional or unintentional. Although these relations are oppositional by definition, in actual practice power can be exercised bidirectionally; even subordinates may affect the behavior of a dominant power holder because of their place in the network of power relations.

The value of Wartenberg's model for the study of sainthood is that it provides a perspective that is nonmetaphysical, yet is still congruent with the image of power relations that one finds in hagiographical texts. In Moroccan Sufism, the most powerful manifestation of the saint was what the shaykhs of aṭ-Ṭāʾifa al-Jazūliyya called *ash-shaykh al-wāṣil* and what al-Ghazwānī called *al-jaras,* the Bell. According to Jazūlite doctrine, such a person was a wielder of power over others (*ṣāḥib at-taṣrīf*) because the saint's "connections" to God allowed him to mediate between domains of reality much like a prophet. Whereas the Prophet Muḥammad received divine revelation, the *ṣāḥib at-taṣrīf* received divine inspiration; whereas Muḥammad used revelation to establish the laws of God, the *ṣāḥib at-taṣrīf* used inspiration to establish the way that led to God; whereas the Prophet acted as an exemplar by assimilating himself to the message of the Qur'an, the *ṣāḥib at-taṣrīf* acted as an exemplar by assimilating himself to the message of Muḥammad. Although Wartenburg would explain the "connections" of the *ṣāḥib at-taṣrīf* differently, he too would agree that such a person is an empowered individual. For Wartenburg, the connections of the *ṣāḥib at-taṣrīf* would position him in such a way as to understand the structure of power relations in society and thus manipulate the network of social alignments to his advantage. Although the ultimate source of power is different in these two explanations, the emphasis on power relations is the same.

Like Peter Brown's saints of late-antique Syria, the walī Allāh of Morocco was a "hinge man."[8] But the walī Allāh was more than just a social ombudsman or mediator. The saint was also a master of the knowable—a person who could mediate between different symbolic universes, whether they be urban–rural, esoteric–exoteric, literate–illiterate, Sufi–non-Sufi, or juridical–popular. This view of the Moroccan saint takes our understanding of Muslim sainthood well beyond Weber's concept of charisma. Rather than circumventing the issue of power and authority by reifying ineffabilities, we can now meet it head-on by examining the modalities of the saint's empowerment across time and in different literary genres. The hagiographical works utilized in this study demonstrate that in social terms, the Moroccan saint was primarily a broker. It is well known that brokers earn their profits from knowledge that others lack. For the Moroccan saint, as for any broker, to control knowledge was to possess the essence of power itself.

Most miracles of the Moroccan awliyāʾ Allāh involved the manifestation of extraordinary knowledge, such as reading thoughts, foretelling the future, or uncovering hidden secrets. These epistemological, *ʿilm*-based miracles were considered by hagiographers to be more fundamental than *ʿamal*-based action miracles, such as healing the sick, taming beasts, traversing long distances, or subduing spirits. Although I concluded at the end of Part I that being a person of knowledge was more important to the Moroccan saint than being a person of power, it would have been more correct to say that knowledge and power were interrelated. This was true even on the theoretical level, for the powers of the Moroccan saint were ultimately justified according to the views of right and truth that were expressed in Sufi models of *walāya*.[9] Ample illustration of this appears in the writings of the Jazūlite shaykhs ʿAlī Ṣāliḥ al-Andalusī and ʿAbdallāh al-Ghazwānī, for whom the main purpose of the theoretical discourse on sainthood was to confirm the worldly authority of the saint in a terrain of power that was the saint's property alone.

But the image of sainthood that is found in Moroccan hagiographies reflects more than just the Sufi perspective. For juridically minded ulama, who sometimes rejected the doctrines of Sufism, the saint's example had to conform to different, more widely accepted traditions. The most important of these were the traditions of uṣūl ad-dīn and uṣūl al-fiqh, which grounded the norms of Islamic thought and practice in the Sunna of the Prophet Muḥammad and his Companions. To be accepted by the ulama, a potential saint had to be recognized as a faithful adherent of the Sunna. This meant that the theoretical "meaning" of sainthood could never stray far from the perspective of normative Islam: even miracles had to conform to juridical ideals. Thus, Moroccan hagiographers typologized their subjects as quintessential Sunni Muslims and typified their actions according to the norms of Sunni conduct.

It was here that the juridical training and uṣūl-orientation of the earliest Moroccan hagiographers were most important. By reconciling Sufism with exoteric Islam in a common epistemological framework, orthodox-mystical hagiographers such as at-Tādilī, al-ʿAzafī, and Ibn Qunfudh could typify the traditions of Sufism and sainthood in such a way as to make them intersubjectively valid. This attempt to homogenize tradition is not limited to hagiography alone, but is part of the development of any institution. In this book I have used the term "typification" (derived from the sociology of knowledge) more often than the term "trope" (derived from literature), because typification deals with experience more than rhetoric and conveys a similar sense of the "sedimentation of meaning" without the negative connotation of fiction or falsehood.[10] To social theorists, the typification of habitualized actions by types of actors is integral to the process of institutionalization.[11] These typifications express the logic that defines an institution as a distinct social entity. In sociological terms, this is what is meant by "tradition."

The institution of Moroccan sainthood depended on transmitters of typified logic who defined the meaning of holiness for succeeding generations.[12] The most visible of these transmitters of typified logic were the authors of sacred biography. These legally trained scholars and Sufis legitimized Moroccan sainthood by integrating this phenomenon into the wider tradition of Sunni Islam. Another important group of transmitters, however, were the *rijāl* who were the subjects of the hagiographies themselves. By being made to uphold the tenets of Sunni tradition, the typified and typologized *rijāl* of hagiographical literature became the very embodiment of Islamic praxis. Once categorized as the bearers of normative tradition, they were no longer real individuals but ideal types that, in a process of circular logic, reconfirmed the values of their creators.[13] However, these typologized saints were more than just literary artifacts. The roles that they typified were real roles that were played by real people in Muslim society. Although the theoretical image of their sainthood may have been influenced by doctrinal concerns, their actions still reflected the collective recollection of social experience. In this case at least, the "fictions of factual representation" were based on recollected behaviors that were assumed to have been real. This is why the role typologies that emerge from the hagiographical record are useful in understanding the institution of Moroccan sainthood in general.

In the hagiographical works that are our main sources of information on Moroccan sainthood, eight role typologies stand out for their ability to summarize general trends. Besides reflecting modalities of power, these roles also typify modalities of authority. Like the roles themselves, these modalities are not mutually exclusive—a single saint may exemplify two or more of them at the same time. The conjunction of power and authority that is expressed in these ideal types supports the conclusion that sainthood as a lived experience reflects *wilāya* more than *walāya.* As a person's *ʿilm* is inductively derived from his or her *ʿamal* and the *bāṭin* is teased out of the *ẓāhir,* so *walāya* sainthood is inductively demonstrated by the *wilāya* sainthood that people actually perceive.

The most basic type of premodern Moroccan saint was the *ṣāliḥ,* a Qur'anic concept that goes back to the very origins of Sufism and reflects the Maliki tendency to favor praxis over doctrine. To the authors of Moroccan hagiography, the ṣāliḥ exemplified the *ethical authority* of sainthood. This authority was based on a moral commitment to carry out the commands of God and was actualized in behaviors that reaffirmed this commitment in numerous ways. In the Qur'an, the ṣāliḥ as an ideal type is linked to the prophets, who disseminate the word of God among humankind, the truthful, who submit themselves to the dictates of the word of God, and the martyrs, who put their lives on the line for the sake of God. As quintessential *rijāl,* the hagiographical tradition also links them in an "eternal present" to the precedent of *as-salaf aṣ-ṣāliḥ,* the "righteous forebears" of Islamic tradition who succeeded the Prophet Muḥammad as exemplars for the Muslim community.[14]

As an ideal type, the ṣāliḥ stood above all for social virtue (ṣalāḥ). Consequently, the ṣāliḥ was frequently associated with the Sufi traditions of futuwwa and the *ṭarīq al-malāma,* the path of blame. The relationship between the ṣāliḥ and the doctrines of futuwwa can be seen in the attention given by the Moroccan saint to the concept of ethical purity (*waraʿ*). It can also be seen in the saint's view of merit as based on altruism (*īthār*) and in the saint's mediation on behalf of the unempowered. The ṣāliḥ's relationship with the *malāmatiyya* tradition can be seen in the saint's tendency to act as a critic (*nāṣiḥ*) and in his or her advocacy of the Qur'anic injunction to "command the good and forbid evil." It was noted in Chapter One that an attitude of political dissent was more characteristic of the Moroccan *malāmatiyya* than was antinomianism, a rejection of the law.

As the prototypical walī Allāh, the ṣāliḥ exemplified Moroccan sainthood in its most basic form. Every Moroccan saint was a ṣāliḥ in some way. The Andalusian Sufis Aḥmad ibn al-ʿArīf and Aḥmad ibn ʿĀshir illustrate this point. Each of these saints was known for his ethical activism and played an important role in reconciling Sufism with exoteric Islam. Before achieving the status of sainthood, Ibn al-ʿArīf gained a widespread reputation as a reciter of the Qur'an, hadith transmitter, market inspector, and censor of public morals. His Sufism was grounded in an integrated approach to knowledge and practice and was firmly based on the principles of Sunni Islam. Because of this grounding, he could not readily be criticized by his exoteric opponents. In fact, his Sunni reputation was so impeccable that it is sometimes hard to imagine that the ṣāliḥ described by the Andalusian biographer Ibn Bashkuwāl in *Kitāb aṣ-ṣila* and the mystical author of *Maḥāsin al-majālis* are the same person. Yet the very normativeness of Ibn al-ʿArīf's persona also helped augment his saintly reputation to the extent where he became a danger to the Almoravid state. Even more, his interest in social justice led him to act as a spokesman for populist political aspirations and made him the ally of revolutionaries such as Ibn Tūmart and Ibn Qasī.

Ibn ʿĀshir, on the other hand, exemplified the ṣāliḥ in the role of critic. His sainthood was equally grounded in Sunni doctrine and practice, and he devoted himself to propagating the works of al-Ghazālī and al-Muḥāsibī, who were paradigmatic figures of orthodox mysticism. Although he went to great lengths to maintain his ethical purity by avoiding rulers and other authority figures, he did not hesitate to accuse the Marinid sultan Abū ʿInān of corruption and injustice. The letter in which he did so stands as a monument to the Moroccan Sufi tradition of political engagement.

The second ideal type of Moroccan saint was the *qudwa.* This person typified the *exemplary authority* of sainthood as conveyed by the prophets of Islam. Like the ṣāliḥ, the qudwa also symbolized the symbiosis of praxis and doctrine, since every saintly exemplar was, by definition, an exemplary Muslim. In fact, as a teacher of Sufis and hence of other potential saints, the qudwa was the exemplar par excellence. To put it another way, the qudwa was an exemplar for the exemplary.

Since the qudwa's role was built directly upon that of the ṣāliḥ, this saint was most of all an exemplar of God-conscious piety (*taqwā*). This spiritual attitude was also based on the example of the Prophet Muḥammad and as-Salaf aṣ-Ṣāliḥ. In the formative period of Moroccan Sufism, the qudwa often appeared as a defender of the faith, a martyr, or a scholar. As a scholar, the qudwa personified the universalistic aspirations of Islamic pietism and adhered to the doctrines of uṣūl ad-dīn and uṣūl al-fiqh. Although the uṣūl tradition owed its origins to Shafiʿism, the Moroccan saint tended to be non-sectarian with respect to *taqlīd,* loyalty to a single school of law. This attitude allowed the saint to place himself or herself at the cutting edge of doctrinal innovation. At times (such as in the Jazūlite doctrine of the imamate), the qudwa even espoused doctrines whose roots were located beyond the pale of Sunni normalcy.

Within the Sufi tradition, the qudwa was an exemplar of mystical practice. Here as well, this saint's example was based on the Muḥammadan paradigm, as illustrated by one of al-Jazūlī's most important maxims: "He who follows the example of the shaykh follows the example of his Lord. For the sacredness of the shaykh before his disciples is like the sacredness of the Prophet before the Companions."[15] The all-inclusive nature of the Muḥammadan paradigm was illustrated in the doctrine of aṭ-ṭarīqa al-Muḥammadiyya, which conceived of the spiritual master as a substitute for the prophets and as a mirror for the Muḥammadan Image.

The prophetic nature of the qudwa's exemplarity was known in earlier periods of Moroccan Sufism as well. This is amply illustrated by the case of the Berber saint Abū Yiʿzzā. Although he was dismissed by many exoteric scholars as an ignorant mountaineer, he was known to his fellow Sufis as the "shaykh of the shaykhs of the Maghrib." Abu Yiʿzzā's sainthood reflected two separate, yet complementary Sufi traditions. As a Sufi shaykh, he transmitted the Nūriyya tradition that came to dominate Moroccan mysticism after the end of the twelfth century C.E. As a worker of miracles, he was revered by Sufis for actualizing the prophetic archetype. Although he did not create an independent Sufi order, he was considered a paradigm for Moroccan Sufis because he was a symbol of God-consciousness and the universality of revelation.

Abū Yiʿzzā's sainthood was recognized by all types of people, from the intellectual to the illiterate, because it was based on the universally understood pedagogy of "look and learn." Rather than simply acting in accordance with the outward Sunna, his style was to model his inward state after the prophetic archetype. This was illustrated by his reputation for miracles of foreknowledge (*firāsa*), like the prophets of Israel, and his performance of healing miracles, like Jesus. His main link to the Prophet Muḥammad was in his belief that all miracles proceeded from the same divine source of knowledge (*ʿilm ladunnī*). Paraphrasing the Prophet, he proclaimed, "I have no knowledge other than what my Lord had made known to me."[16]

If Abū Yiʿzzā exemplifies the knowledge of the qudwa, Abū'l-ʿAbbās as-Sabtī exemplifies the qudwa's praxis. Although his miracles were just as unique and inimitable as those of Abū Yiʿzzā, the way of charity, good works, and social activism that these miracles expressed exemplified the social dimension of the Muḥammadan Sunna. This ethical view of saintly praxis was also shared by the authors of sacred biography. In recalling the virtues and exploits of Moroccan saints, these writers helped to maintain the institutional continuity of sainthood by inspiring their readers to follow the example of their subjects. Like other forms of exemplarity, the ethical path of sainthood was also made to lead back to the tradition of the prophets.

The role typologies of ṣāliḥ and qudwa converge in the third ideal type of Moroccan saint, the *watad.* As a holy faqīh and "anchor of the earth" who upheld the Sharīʿa in an urban locality, this figure exemplified the *juridical authority* of Moroccan sainthood. Like the qudwa, the key to the watad's authority was knowledge. But in this latter case, the saint's knowledge extended beyond the Sunna to the more professional knowledges of Sharīʿa and fiqh. Whether he was a non-Sufi, like Darrās ibn Ismāʿil, or a Sufi shaykh, like ʿAbd al-Jalīl ibn Wayḥlān, the watad was viewed as an "anchor of the earth" because he played two defining roles: that of *mujtahid,* interpreter of the law, and that of patron or protector of the community.

In ʿAlī ibn Ḥirzihim of Fez, the watad emerges as a key figure in the development of Moroccan Sufism. Like other *awtād* before him, Ibn Ḥirzihim was revered as the patron of his city. Also like his fellow awtād, he was juridically trained, having studied uṣūl-oriented Malikism under Abū Bakr ibn al-ʿArabī and the works of al-Ghazālī under his uncle, Ṣāliḥ ibn Ḥirzihim. By transmitting the orthodox mysticism of al-Ghazālī and legitimizing the dissident tradition of the *malāmatiyya,* he was more influential than all previous awtād except Darrās ibn Ismāʿīl. Just as Darrās earned a place in history by ensuring the primacy of the Maliki school of law and disseminating the *Mudawwana* of Saḥnūn, so Ibn Ḥirzihim became recognized as the father of Moroccan juridical Sufism by turning his rābiṭa into a major center for teaching al-Ghazālī's synthesis of Sufism and the Sharīʿa.

The fourth ideal type of Moroccan saint, the *murābiṭ,* was closely related to the watad in the functions he performed. However, two important differences separated these figures. First of all, the murābiṭ was an exclusively rural ideal type. Second, whereas the authority of the watad was based on the saint's knowledge of the Sharīʿa, that of the murābiṭ was largely dependent on the network of relations he maintained within a localized tribal context. The murābiṭ can thus be summarized as representing the *social authority* of Moroccan sainthood.

Many murābiṭūn, like the awtād of urban Morocco, were also specialists in the Sharīʿa. In the case of the murābiṭ, however, it was the ribāṭ as an institution, as much as the individual saint, that was believed to "anchor" the Sharīʿa to a particular locality. This point is illustrated by the case of Waggāg ibn Zallū al-Lamṭī, the most prominent teacher of Malikism in the Anti-Atlas region. In the generations after his death, he was remembered more for the ribāṭ he founded (Dār al-Murābiṭīn) than for his actual teachings.

The quintessential murābiṭūn of Morocco were the Banū Amghār of Tīṭ-n-Fiṭr. Unlike most of the ribāṭs of al-Andalus and Ifrīqīya, the main function of Tīṭ-n-Fiṭr was educational: to provide instruction in the Sharīʿa and Islamic theology. Also important to its role was the fact that it served as a hub in an important network of trade routes that passed through the region of Dukkāla. As the Berber name Banū Amghār (Sons of the Leader) implied, the masters of this ribāṭ exercised both religious and political authority over their clients, the pastoralist tribe of Ṣanhāja Azammūr. In doing so, they took on the roles of both religious leader (imām) and judge (*qāḍī*), and ensured the presence of Islamic law in a region that had only partially submitted to the authority of the state.

The murābiṭ's image as a saint was primarily based on his role as a broker. However, the murābiṭ was also an interpreter of culture who translated the urban-based logic of the Sharīʿa into the more restricted codes of tribal custom (Ar. *ʿurf, ʿāda*). To succeed as a broker, it was necessary to keep a foot in two environments at once: the normative and the normal. Both the urban-educated founders of ribāṭs and their descendants did their best to maintain the integrity of urban traditions in a rural setting. This is a major reason why ribāṭs often took on the appearance of administrative or educational centers rather than mere hermitages.

In at least three cases (Ribāṭ Tīṭ-n-Fiṭr, Ribāṭ Shākir, and Ribāṭ Āsafī), the doctrines of murābiṭūn became institutionalized to the point where they formed distinct Sufi traditions. This process is exemplified by the creation of the Ṣanhājiyya and Māgiriyya Sufi orders. In both groups, membership was predicated on the disciple's ethnic or tribal ties; whereas membership in the Ṣanhājiyya was limited to Ṣanhāja Berbers from the Dukkāla and Anti-Atlas regions, membership in the Māgiriyya was confined to the Maṣmūda Berbers of southern Dukkāla and Ragrāga.

The existence of these tribal Sufi orders illustrates an important difference between the doctrinal aspect of ribāṭ-based Sufism and institutional Sufism in general. Although the murābiṭ may at times have been a Sufi shaykh, his teachings had a limited appeal and were not widely popular outside of his home region. Abū ʿAbdallāh Amghār, the founder of aṭ-Ṭāʾifa aṣ-Ṣanhājiyya, was known by the limited appellation of *al-quṭb aṣ-Ṣanhājī,* the "Ṣanhāja Axis," instead of the more universal *quṭb az-zamān,* "Axis of the Age." The situation was somewhat different for Abū Muḥammad Ṣāliḥ, the founder of the Māgiriyya Sufi order, due to his subsequent development of the Ḥujjājiyya pilgrimage society and his training in Egypt in the way of Abū Madyan. Both of these factors linked his teachings to wider Islamic traditions that allowed his doctrine to transcend the restricted social universe in which he lived.

The fifth type of Moroccan saint was the *shaykh,* who personified the *doctrinal authority* of Moroccan sainthood. We have already seen how the shaykh as an ideal type could dovetail with other typifications of sainthood, such as when ʿAbd al-Jalīl ibn Wayḥlān combined the roles of shaykh and watad or when Abū ʿAbdallāh Amghār combined the roles of shaykh and murābiṭ. The shaykh is the most self-evident of all the categories of Moroccan sainthood, since the role of the saint is commonly assimilated to that of the spiritual master in Sufi treatises. It is important to remember, however, that the concept of sainthood is much broader than that of spiritual mastery, and that the shaykh is but one of several types of Moroccan saint.

The most prominent examples of the saint-as-shaykh in the premodern Maghrib were Abū Madyan and Muḥammad ibn Sulaymān al-Jazūlī. In both cases, the reputations of these saints were heavily dependent on their doctrinal legacy. Abū Madyan was the most important figure of the developmental period of Maghribi Sufism. His doctrinal influence extended from al-Andalus to Egypt and his spiritual method set the standard for North African mysticism for centuries to come. His Sufi training partook of all of the traditions that were available in his time: he learned juridical Sufism from Ibn Ḥirzihim, the Nūriyya tradition of the Moroccan ribāṭs via

Abu Yiʿzzā, and the doctrines of the Moroccan *malāmatiyya* through Abū ʿAbdallāh ad-Daqqāq of Sijilmāsa. In addition, his own writings had a great impact on future generations. These included the manual for novices, *Bidāyat al-murīd,* a collection of aphorisms, titled *Uns al-waḥīd wa nuzhat al-murīd,* and poems which are still recited in Sufi *zawāya* today.

One hardly needs to be reminded of the doctrinal significance of Muḥammad ibn Sulaymān al-Jazūlī. To this day, the rituals associated with his tomb in Marrakesh differ from other rituals of Moroccan saints because of his unique identification with the Muḥammadan paradigm. Unlike the tombs of other awliyāʾ (including those of his successors at-Tabbāʿ and al-Ghazwānī), al-Jazūlī's is never used for ecstatic performances. Public participation in Jazūlite rituals, such as the celebration of the Prophet's birthday and the recitation of *Dalāʾil al-khayrāt,* is in practice restricted to the "Mwālin Dalīl" (today's remnants of the Jazūliyya) and to people of known piety and virtue. No one is allowed to touch the embroidered cover of his catafalque, nor take a piece of it for blessings. When visitors (mainly women) attempt to do so, the *muqaddam* of the tomb drives them away with a wooden staff. It is ironic that a shaykh so long associated with "popular Sufism" is venerated in ways that are among the least "popular" of all.

Al-Jazūlī's unique position in the company of saints brings to mind the three most comprehensive types of Moroccan sainthood: the *ghawth,* the *imām,* and the *quṭb.* As the sixth ideal type, the *ghawth* represents the *generative authority* of the Moroccan saint. *Al-ghawth* was an early term for the axial saint in North Africa and is still used as a synonym for *quṭb.* It is also the most "feminine" type of sainthood, for the word carries the connotation of succor or nurturance. As an ideal type, the ghawth is best represented by Abū Madyan, who is still referred to in the Maghrib as "Abū Madyan al-Ghawth."

Abū Madyan was a generative saint on many levels. As a teacher, he was noted for "giving birth" to more than a thousand saints and shaykhs. He was also highly altruistic and made himself available to all classes of people. This same attitude also characterized his teacher Abū Yiʿzzā and Muḥammad ibn Sulaymān al-Jazūlī, who assimilated the way of Abū Madyan through the works of Abū Muḥammad Ṣāliḥ. The feminine side of Abū Madyan's spirituality can be seen in his frequent use of motherhood as a metaphor and in the fact that he had no sexual interest in women and never married. It is also visible in the following statement from *Bidāyat al-murīd:* "The similitude [of the saint] is like the Earth, which bears everything that is repugnant."[17] This comparison of the Muslim saint to the all-forgiving and generative Earth would reappear later in the teachings of Abū'l-Ḥasan ash-Shādhilī, who also saw himself as a generative saint who nourished his disciples through the "wealth in God" (*al-ghinā᾽ bi'llāh*) that came into his his hands.

Ash-Shādhilī's example brings to mind the seventh ideal type of Moroccan saint, the *imām*. This category typifies the *religiopolitical authority* of Moroccan sainthood. Examples of saintly imams include powerful murābiṭūn, such as Abū ʿAbdallāh Amghār and Abū Shuʿayb of Azemmour, who mediated both the religious affairs and the political relations of their clients. This type also characterizes ʿAbd as-Salām ibn Mashīsh, who combined the roles of Sufi shaykh and Idrisid imam, as well as his student ash-Shādhilī, who based his legitimacy on his sharifian lineage and referred to Sufi shaykhs as "kings in the guise of the poor."[18]

The clearest example of this type, however, can be found in the shaykhs of aṭ-Ṭā᾽ifa al-Jazūliyya. More explicitly than ever before in Moroccan Sufism, the leaders of this institution advocated an exalted role for the Sufi shaykh as the premier guardian of Islam, a role that evoked the image of the caliph as the imam of the Muslim community. Aṭ-Ṭā᾽ifa al-Jazūliyya was described by its founder as a "state" (*dawla*), in which the Sufis pledged their allegiance to the shaykh as their primary leader. The creation of this "state of salvation" out of the institutional structure of Moroccan Sufism, combined as it was with a mistrust of political authority that had long been part of the Sufi ethos, led to frequent conflicts between the leaders of the Jazūliyya and the government. These conflicts were only resolved when the Saʿdian ruler Muḥammadan ash-Shaykh brought his full power to bear on the *zawāya* of Morocco in the middle of the sixteenth century.

In al-Ghazwānī's doctrine of the Sovereignty of Saintly Authority (*siyādat al-imāma*), the authority of the saint-as-imam was conceived as a direct inheritance from the Prophet Muḥammad. Since a major source of this "prophetic inheritance" (*wirātha nabawiyya*) was genealogical, the Jazūlite ideology shared much in common with ʿAlid models of authority. Because al-Ghazwānī's Bell saint (*jaras*) assimilated many of the attributes of the imam of early Shiʿism, it was suggested that this might have been due to the influence of Idrisid ideology. Idrisid doctrine affirmed the divine right of the imam who arises against injustice or unbelief. This attitude is reflected in numerous statements by both al-Jazūlī and al-Ghazwānī, who claimed that their authority extended over the political rulers of their day.

Al-Jazūlī even went so far as to refer to himself as the Mahdī, a term which carries obvious political connotations.

By referring to himself as the Mahdī, al-Jazūlī staked his claim to the most comprehensive ideal type of saint, the *quṭb,* or axial saint. This paradigmatic figure exemplified the *inclusive authority* of Moroccan sainthood. By doing so, the quṭb became the prime exemplar of sainthood itself. Al-Jazūlī was perhaps the best example of a quṭb in the history of Moroccan Sufism, since both his historical presence and his doctrines mark a clear break between what preceded him and what came afterwards. Just as Abū Madyan personified the developmental period of Maghribi Sufism, so al-Jazūlī and his successors personified the apogee of Moroccan institutional Sufism.

In doctrinal terms, al-Jazūlī was an axial figure because he combined the competing traditions of Shādhilī and Qādirī Sufism into a single institution and thus set the doctrinal parameters for Moroccan Sufism for the next two hundred years. He was an axial figure in political terms because he and his successors were instrumental in the development of a new political ideology for Morocco at the dawn of the modern age. In addition, his successors facilitated the overthrow of the Marinid ancien régime and helped engineer the eventual victory of the Saʿdian sharifs. Because of their influence, Morocco took on a distinct political and religious identity that set it apart from other Muslim nations-to-be. Finally, the legacy of al-Jazūlī can be seen in many of the beliefs and practices that distinguish the popular aspect of Moroccan Islam today. He thus marks the boundary between premodern and modern Sufism in Morocco, and uniquely exemplifies the concept of sainthood in Moroccan society.

Notes

Introduction

1. See Philip E. Lewis, "The Measure of Translation Effects," in Joseph F. Graham, ed., *Difference in Translation* (Ithaca, New York and London, 1985), 37.

2. On the importance of context in translation, see Alasdair MacIntyre, *Whose Justice? Which Rationality?* (Notre Dame, Indiana, 1988), 370–388.

3. The term "double subjectivity" comes from Stanley Jeyaraja Tambiah, *Magic, Science, Religion, and the Scope of Rationality* (Cambridge, 1990), 111.

4. See, for example, the discussion of "saintship" in Toshihiko Izutsu, *Sufism and Taoism: A Comparative Study of Key Philosophical Concepts* (Berkeley and Los Angeles, 1983), 263–274, and "sainteté" in Michel Chodkiewicz, *Le Sceau des saints: Prophétie et sainteté dans la doctrine d'Ibn Arabî* (Paris, 1986), 29–39. Claude Addas (*Ibn ʿArabī ou La quête du Soufre Rouge* [Paris, 1989]) and William C. Chittick (*The Sufi Path of Knowledge: Ibn al-ʿArabī's Metaphysics of Imagination* [Albany, New York, 1989]) also make a point of using *walāya* as the "correct" term for Muslim sainthood.

5. The *maṣdar* (verbal noun) of the Arabic root *waliya* follows the grammatical form *faʿāla*. Thus, *walāya*, as a characteristic of the *walī Allāh*, means: "the state or condition of being a friend of God." The second term for Muslim sainthood, *wilāya*, follows another grammatical form (*fiʿāla*) and connotes the possession of authority or the consequence of friendship with God. See Hans Wehr, *A Dictionary of Modern Written Arabic*, J. Milton Cowan, ed. (Wiesbaden, 1971), 1099–1100. See also, Chodkiewicz, *Le Sceau des saints*, 34–35.

6. See, for example, Qur'ān, II [*al-Baqara*], 107; IX [*at-Tawba*], 74; and XXXII [*as-Sajda*], 4. See also, Edward William Lane, *An Arabic-English Lexicon* (Cambridge reprint, 1984), vol. 2, 3060.

7. Qur'ān VIII (*al-Anfāl*), 72; and XVIII (*al-Kahf*), 44.

8. Etymologically, the Qur'anic use of *walī Allāh* follows the Arabic root

walā, which means to "bestow," "entrust," or "commission." See Wehr, *Dictionary of Modern Written Arabic,* 1099–1100.

9. See, for example, Abū'l-Faḍl Jamāl ad-Dīn Muḥammad Ibn Manẓūr (d. 711/1311–12), *Lisān al-ʿarab* (Beirut, n.d.), vol. 15, 406–415. For a more extended discussion of the grammatical issues pertaining to *walāya* and *wilāya,* see Gerald Thomas Elmore, "The Fabulous Gryphon (*ʿAnqāʾ Mughrib*) on the Seal of the Saints and the Sun Rising in the West: An Early, Maghribine Work by Ibn al-ʿArabī" (Ph.D. dissertation, Yale University, 1995), 97–125.

10. Ibn Manẓūr, *Lisān al-ʿArab,* 407.

11. See Chodkiewicz, *Le Sceau des saints,* 35.

12. Bruce B. Lawrence, trans., *Nizam ad-Din Awliya: Morals for the Heart by Amir Hasan Sijzi* (Mahwah, New Jersey, 1992), 95.

13. Abū'l-ʿAbbās Aḥmad ibn Ibrāhīm b. Aḥmad b. Abī Muḥammad Ṣāliḥ al-Māgirī, *Al-Minhāj al-wāḍiḥ fī taḥqīq karāmāt Abī Muḥammad Ṣāliḥ* (Cairo, 1933), 80. My translation. Abū Muḥammad Ṣāliḥ will be discussed in Chapter Five.

14. F. V. Greifenhagen, "Traduttore Traditore: An Analysis of the History of English Translations of the Qurʾān," *Journal of Christian-Muslim Relations* 3 (2) (December 1992): 274–275.

15. Ibid., 275. See also, George Steiner, *After Babel: Aspects of Language and Translation* (New York and London, 1975), 72–74. Alasdair MacIntyre, who argues from the monadist premise, adds a further complicating factor, that of modernity, which distorts the terminology of premodern tradition as part of its hegemonic assertion of truth. See idem, *Whose Justice? Which Rationality?,* 370–388.

16. Lewis, "The Measure of Translation Effects," 38–39. See also John A. Coleman, "Conclusion: After Sainthood?" in John Stratton Hawley, ed., *Saints and Virtues* (Berkeley and Los Angeles, 1987), 213–217.

17. Lewis, "The Measure of Translation Effects," 39. This quotation comes from Derrida's essay, "Le retrait de la métaphore," translated as "The Retrait of Metaphors," *Enclitic* 2 (Fall, 1978): 5–33.

18. Tambiah, *Magic, Science, and Religion,* 3.

19. According to the Moroccan historian Mohamed Kably, the idea of the frontier in premodern North Africa was a psychological construct rather than a geopolitical reality. Since political entities and even geographical boundaries were ephemeral and thus subject to readjustment, all boundaries were open to dispute. Idem, *Société, pouvoir et religion au Maroc à la fin du Moyen-Age* (Paris, 1986), 93–94.

20. This is a major problem with Vincent Crapanzano's discussion of Sufism in *The Ḥamadsha.* Since Crapanzano was familiar with neither the history nor the doctrines of Moroccan Sufism, he was unaware of the concept of *walāya* and thus could not distinguish between the formal doctrines of a Sufi *ṭarīqa* and the less-systematic beliefs of a spirit cult. See idem, *The Ḥamadsha: A Study in Moroccan Ethnopsychiatry* (Berkeley and Los Angeles, 1973), 15–21, 30–56.

21. To give but one example: The section on *taṣawwuf* in the latest edition of

the Encyclopedia of Islam (in preparation) includes seven sections, which are organized as follows: (1) early period—up to Ibn ʿArabī; (2) Ibn ʿArabī and later; (3a) nineteenth- and twentieth-century Sufism: Africa; (3b) nineteenth- and twentieth-century Sufism: Persia; (3c) nineteenth- and twentieth-century Sufism: Egypt; (3d) nineteenth- and twentieth-century Sufism: Muslim India; (3e) nineteenth- and twentieth-century Sufism: Ottoman Empire and Turkey. Particularly noticeable in this list of topics are (a) the editors' use of the Andalusian mystic Ibn ʿArabī as a paradigm for premodern Sufism in general; (b) the complete exclusion of the Maghrib as a separate category; and (c) the inexplicable inclusion of nineteenth- and twentieth-century Persia, a region much less important to the development of contemporary Sufism than the Maghrib, which has produced at least three "international" Sufi orders in the last two hundred years: the Tijāniyya, the Aḥmadiyya-Idrīsiyya, and the Darqawiyya-ʿAlawiyya.

22. See, for example, R. S. O'Fahey, *Enigmatic Saint: Ahmad Ibn Idris and the Idrisi Tradition* (Evanston, Illinois, 1990), 1–26. O'Fahey now believes that neo-Sufism is little more than Moroccan Sufism internationalized (personal communication, May 1995).

23. See, for example, Chodkiewicz, *Le Sceau des saints*, 35.

24. A partial exception is Émile Dermenghem, *Le Culte des saints dans l'Islam maghrébin* (Paris, 1954 [reprint, 1982]), 26, who defines *wilāya* as "the sanctity of intimacy, which is considered susceptible to hereditary transmission" (my translation). Unfortunately, Dermenghem mistakes *wilāya* for *walāya* in this passage. Even worse, he proposes a paradigm for Muslim sainthood that depends for its meaning on the Christian categories of ascesis, grace, and virtue (27–33).

25. For the most thorough discussion of *baraka* and its manifestations, see Edward Westermarck, *Ritual and Belief in Morocco* (London, 1926), vol. 1, 35–261.

26. See, for example, Clifford Geertz, *Islam Observed: Religious Development in Morocco and Indonesia* (Chicago, 1971), 44, where the concept of *baraka* is used to symbolize the entire Moroccan *Lebensweld*. This interpretation is critiqued in Henry Munson, Jr., *Religion and Power in Morocco* (New Haven and London, 1993), 5–13. See also Ernest Gellner, *Saints of the Atlas* (Chicago, 1969), 75–77; Crapanzano, *The Ḥamadsha*, 19–20; and Michael Gilsenan, *Recognizing Islam: Religion and Society in the Modern Arab World* (New York, 1982), 75–94, 109–115. Although Dale Eickelman initially relied on a *baraka*-based model of sainthood in *The Middle East: An Anthropological Approach* (Englewood Cliffs, New Jersey, 1981), in the second edition of this work (1989) he chose not to characterize the Muslim saint as a possessor of *baraka*, but as a *ṣāliḥ*, or "pious one" (Ibid., 289–290, 297–304).

27. Westermarck, *Ritual and Belief*, vol. 1, 35–36. Since the feminine Arabic term, *shaykha*, refers to professional singers and dancers, and the Berber *tamghārt* means "mother-in-law," a female Moroccan saint is usually called a *ṣāliḥa*.

28. See, for example, Geertz, *Islam Observed*, 8, 43–54; and Eickelman, *Moroccan Islam: Tradition and Society in a Pilgrimage Center* (Austin, Texas, and

London, 1976), 6–7. Geertz (49–51) also uses *siyyid* as a synonym for *marabout,* while Eickelman (idem, *The Middle East* [1989], 297–304) pairs the term with *ṣāliḥ.*

29. See, for example, Ali Merad, *Le Réformisme musulman en Algérie de 1925 à 1940* (Paris and The Hague, 1967), 58; Abdallah Laroui, *The History of the Maghrib: An Interpretive Essay,* Ralph Manheim, trans. (Princeton, 1977), 245–246; and Mohammed Arkoun, *Rethinking Islam: Common Questions, Uncommon Answers,* Robert D. Lee, trans. and ed. (Boulder, Colorado, 1994), 82. For a critique of the Western treatment of subaltern terminologies, see Talal Asad, "The Concept of Cultural Translation in British Social Anthropology," in idem, *Genealogies of Religion: Discipline and Reasons of Power in Christianity and Islam* (Baltimore and London, 1993), 171–199.

30. Alfred Bel, *La Religion musulmane en Berbérie: Esquisse d'histoire et de sociologie religieuses* (Paris, 1938), 342. Bel's "substrate" model of Berber religion was influenced by the ethnographic studies of Auguste Mouliéras (*Le Maroc inconnu: Étude géographique et sociologique* [Paris, 1899]), Edmond Doutté (*Magie et religion en Afrique du Nord* [Algiers, 1908 (reprint 1984)], and Henri Laoust (*Mots et choses berbères* [Paris, 1920]). For a critical discussion of the ethnography of folk religion in colonial North Africa, see Abdellah Hammoudi, *The Victim and Its Masks: An Essay on Sacrifice and Masquerade in the Maghrib,* Paula Wissing, trans. (Chicago, 1993), 15–32.

31. Bel, *La Religion musulmane,* 330, 332.

32. Ibid., 361–362.

33. Ibid., 342.

34. Ibid., 379–381. See also Eickelman, *Moroccan Islam,* 25.

35. See Bel, *La Religion musulmane,* 17–30.

36. The French colonial view of Islamic law as an alien imposition on Berber customary practice can be seen in the following chapter title from Jacques Berque's first monograph: "Local Foundation and Oriental Importation" (*Fond local et Apport oriental*). See idem, *Structures sociales du Haut-Atlas* (Paris, 1955), 237–248. For the "state of nature" metaphor, see Gellner, *Saints of the Atlas,* 5. This same trope is also used in Francophone North African literature. See, for example, Driss Chraibi, *La Mère du Printemps (L'Oum-er Bia)* (Paris, 1982).

37. See, for example, Geertz, *Islam Observed,* 120, where Bel's study is praised as "the best book on the development of North African Islam, and indeed one of the finest books ever written on the area." See also John Waterbury, *The Commander of the Faithful: The Moroccan Political Elite—A Study in Segmented Politics* (New York, 1970); Kenneth Brown, *People of Salé: Tradition and Change in a Moroccan City, 1830–1930* (Cambridge, Massachusetts, 1976); and Shlomo Deshen, *The Mellah Society: Jewish Community Life in Sherifian Morocco* (Chicago, 1989). While Waterbury and Deshen rely directly on Bel's interpretations, Brown's more carefully nuanced work relies on studies of Moroccan Islam by colonial-era historians (e.g., Georges Drague, Roger Le Tourneau, and Evariste Lévi-Provençal)

who either studied under Bel or shared the same colonialist agenda. For an example of Bel's influence on contemporary Moroccan scholarship, see Kably, *Société, pouvoir et religion,* esp. 291–338. Eickelman (*Moroccan Islam,* 22–29) was the first to challenge Bel's model in detail, presenting it as a "'just so' story as interesting for the fact that it was still regarded as 'authoritative,' in spite of its obvious interpretive shortcomings" (personal communication, October 1996).

38. Gellner, *Saints of the Atlas,* 7–8. Gellner's "Protestant" approach to Islam is also apparent in his more recent *Muslim Society,* where he speaks of Muslim "Puritanism" and makes asides such as the following: "One wonders whether Knox's Scotland or Calvin's Geneva would surpass this fervour." Idem, *Muslim Society* (Cambridge, 1981), 131, 156. For a critique of Gellner's neo-Weberian methodology, see Munson, *Religion and Power,* 81–84.

39. Gellner, *Saints of the Atlas,* 8. Gellner's dichotomy of "doctor" versus "saint" was first used more than a decade earlier by Jacques Berque. See idem, *Structures sociales du Haut-Atlas,* 315–322.

40. Ernest Gellner, "Political and Religious Organization of the Berbers of the Central High Atlas," in idem and Charles Micaud, *Arabs and Berbers: From Tribe to Nation in North Africa* (London, 1973), 60.

41. Gellner, *Saints of the Atlas,* 11.

42. Dermenghem, *Le Culte des saints,* 24–27.

43. Eickelman, *Moroccan Islam,* 160. See also, idem, *The Middle East,* 298–302.

44. See, for example, Gellner, *Saints of the Atlas,* 179–278, where the Ḥansaliyya brotherhood is discussed on the basis of Weberian paradigms. For Weber's models in their original form, see idem, *Theories of Social and Economic Organization,* Talcott Parsons, ed., A. M. Henderson and Talcott Parsons, trans. (New York, 1964), 145–157. On charismatic authority and communal organization, see 358–363. For a neo-Weberian study of an urban Sufi order as a corporate institution, see Michael Gilsenan, *Saint and Sufi in Modern Egypt: An Essay in the Sociology of Religion* (Oxford, 1973).

45. Bryan S. Turner, *Weber and Islam* (London, 1978), 22–26. See also Geertz, *Islam Observed,* 45.

46. See, for example, Muḥammad Ḥajjī, *Az-Zāwiya ad-Dilāʾiyya wa dawruhā ad-dīnī wa'l-ʿilmī wa'ʾs-siyāsī* (Rabat, 1964). See also Jacques Berque, *Ulémas, fondateurs, insurgés du Maghreb, XVII*[e] *siècle* (Paris, 1982), 81–124.

47. See Gilsenan, *Recognizing Islam,* 116–141.

48. Turner, *Weber and Islam,* 56–67.

49. When the absence of exact European parallels leads one to assert, as in a recent study of the educated classes of medieval Syria, that "there was no 'system' of education, patronage, appointment, or of government" in premodern Damascus, this exceeds the bounds of both logic and common sense. See Michael Chamberlain, *Knowledge and Social Practice in Medieval Damascus, 1190–1350* (Cambridge, 1994), 177.

50. On the etymology of the word "religion," see Wilfred Cantwell Smith, *The*

Meaning and End of Religion: A New Approach to the Religious Traditions of Mankind (New York, 1963), 15–50. On "sainthood" (*sainteté*), see Hippolyte Delehaye, *Sanctus: Essai sur le culte des saints dans l'Antiquité* (Brussels, 1927), 2–58.

51. Turner, *Weber and Islam,* 62.

52. See, for example, Richard Kieckhefer, *Unquiet Souls: Fourteenth-Century Saints and Their Religious Milieu* (Chicago, 1987), esp. 21–49, 122–149, 150–179. See also André Vauchez, "Culture et sainteté d'après les procès de canonisation des XIIIe et XIVe siècles," in idem, *Religion et société dans l'Occident médiéval* (Turin, 1980), 271–290. One of the most provocative entries in this debate is Aviad M. Kleinberg, *Prophets in Their Own Country: Living Saints and the Making of Sainthood in the Later Middle Ages* (Chicago, 1992).

53. Even for Weber, charisma was a property of living beings. Thus, belief in the charisma of saints' tombs was seen by him as a posthumous extension of living charisma. See Weber, *Theories,* 359–360.

54. Dermenghem, *Le Culte des saints,* 11–21.

55. Geertz, *Islam Observed,* 8.

56. Delehaye, *Sanctus,* 109–161.

57. Ibid., 233–249.

58. Delooz's analytical method is based on the idea of "conjuncture," a concept that was pioneered by French economic historians. According to Pierre Chaunu, conjuncture involves "the desire to surpass the discontinuity between the various curves established by statisticians, to grasp the interdependence of the variables and factors isolated at a given moment, and to follow—hence predict—their evolution over time." See Paul Ricoeur, *Time and Narrative,* Kathleen McLaughlin and David Pellauer, trans. (Chicago, 1984), 106–107, 248 n. 23.

59. See Pitrim A. Sorokin, *Altruistic Love: A Study of American "Good Neighbors" and Christian Saints* (Boston, 1950). The most recent attempt to define sainthood as a form of radical altruism is Edith Wyschogrod, *Saints and Postmodernism: Revisioning Moral Philosophy* (Chicago, 1990).

60. The term "sacred biography" is borrowed from Thomas Heffernan, who sees it as a neutral way to conceptualize "a narrative text of the vita of the saint written by a member of a community of belief." See idem, *Sacred Biography: Saints and Their Biographers in the Middle Ages* (Oxford, 1988), 15–16.

61. Pierre Delooz, *Sociologie et canonisations* (Liège, 1969), 7. My translation.

62. Ibid., 7–14. Similarly "constructed" saints can also be found in Morocco. See, for example, Westermarck's discussion of "imaginary" saints such as "Lālla an-Nakhla" (Lady Palm Tree) and "Sīdī al-Makhfī" (the Hidden One) in idem, *Ritual and Belief,* 49–50. One of the most famous "constructed saints" in Morocco is Azemmour's "Lālla ʿĀʾisha al-Baḥriyya" (Lady ʿĀʾisha the Sailor). See Muḥammad ash-Shyaẓmī and al-Ḥājī as-Sibāʿī, *Madīnat Azammūr wa ḍawāḥīhā* (Salé, 1989), 147–148.

63. While Delooz is correct in claiming that saint cults in Europe arose as an expression of lower-class wishes, a prospective saint could not attain canonization

unless his or her cult received the backing of both the local clergy and the wider church hierarchy. See Kieckhefer, *Unquiet Souls,* 182–189.

64. Delooz, *Sociologie et canonisations,* 429. See also Kleinberg, *Prophets,* 21–39. This correlation of lower-class status and saint cults is still not sufficient to prove Michael Gilsenan's contention that sainthood is "part of the religious *bricolage* of the poor" (idem, *Recognizing Islam,* 115). On the contrary, it will be demonstrated in Chapter Four that Moroccan saint cults were supported by all classes of society.

65. Donald Weinstein and Rudolph M. Bell, *Saints and Society: The Two Worlds of Western Christendom, 1000–1700* (Chicago and London, 1982), 6.

66. A paradoxical example of this view can be found in Rudolph Bell's *Holy Anorexia* (Chicago, 1985). Could it be that this co-author of *Saints and Society* regards anorexia nervosa as an "active" form of piety?

67. Weinstein and Bell, *Saints and Society,* 5.

68. Ibid.

69. Ibid., 242–249.

70. See Kleinberg, *Prophets,* 13–17.

71. See also André Vauchez, *La Sainteté en occident aux dernier siècles du Moyen Age d'après les procès de canonisation et les documents hagiographiques* (Rome, 1981). This is the most thorough study of Roman Catholic sainthood in the *Annales* tradition.

72. See Richard W. Bulliet, *Islam: The View from the Edge* (New York, 1994), 8–12.

73. For an overview of problems in the social history of premodern Islam, see R. Stephen Humphreys, *Islamic History: A Framework for Inquiry* (Princeton, 1991), 187–308.

74. Aaron Gurevich, *Historical Anthropology of the Middle Ages,* Jana Howlett, ed. (Chicago, 1992), 19.

75. The term "tropics" comes from Hayden White, *Tropics of Discourse: Essays in Cultural Criticism* (Baltimore and London, 1978), 1–25.

76. See Bulliet, *Islam: The View from the Edge,* 8.

77. Richard Bulliet, *The Patricians of Nishapur: A Study in Medieval Islamic Social History* (Cambridge, Massachusetts, 1972), and L. Carl Brown, *The Tunisia of Ahmad Bey 1837–1855* (Princeton, 1974).

78. Carl F. Petry, *The Civilian Elite of Cairo in the Later Middle Ages* (Princeton, 1981).

79. A partial exception is ʿAbd al-Laṭīf ash-Shādhilī, *At-Taṣawwuf wa'l-mujtamaʿ, namādhij min al-qarn al-ʿāshir al-hijrī* (Salé, 1989).

80. Clifford Geertz, "Religion as a Cultural System," in idem, *The Interpretation of Cultures* (New York, 1973), 90. For a recent critique of this theory, see Asad, "The Construction of Religion as an Anthropological Category," in idem, *Genealogies of Religion,* 27–54.

81. On the relationship of conversion to identity development and reference-

group formation, see Robert W. Hefner, "World Building and the Rationality of Conversion," in idem, *Conversion to Christianity: Historical and Anthropological Perspectives on a Great Transformation* (Berkeley and Los Angeles, 1993), 25–28.

82. Alasdair MacIntyre sees the shortcomings of the "relativist" and "perspectivist" approaches to religion as lying in the fact that both doctrines are those of outsiders to tradition. Thus, "theirs is not so much a conclusion about truth as an exclusion from it, and thereby from rational debate." Idem, *Whose Justice? Which Rationality?,* 368.

83. See, for example, White, "Interpretation in History," in idem, *Tropics of Discourse,* 51–80.

84. This subject will be discussed in Chapters Two and Four.

85. This term is taken from Wyschogrod, *Saints and Postmodernism,* 235.

86. See Hans-Georg Gadamer, *Truth and Method,* Joel Weisenheimer and Donald G. Marshall, trans. (New York, 1994), 265–307, and MacIntyre, *Whose Justice? Which Rationality?,* 349–369.

87. White, "The Fictions of Factual Representation," in idem, *Tropics of Discourse,* 121–134. See also Ricoeur, *Time and Narrative,* vol. 1, 91–94.

88. This is a major problem in Thomas Heffernan's otherwise brilliant study of medieval hagiography: "Medieval authors, especially sacred biographers, saw little that need be contradictory between the worlds of fact and fantasy; both fact and fantasy were signs to the acute observer of the nature of things, different signs to be sure, but nonetheless signs revelatory of truth." Idem, *Sacred Biography,* 70–71.

89. See, for example, Weinstein and Bell, *Saints and Society,* 13.

90. See Kleinberg, *Prophets,* 59–62. A dogmatic skepticism which denies all possibility of transcendence is part of the antifoundationalism of postmodern analysis. Edith Wyschogrod characterizes postmodern thought as "henophobic" in its "antipathy toward the notion that there is a privileged source of truth and meaning, whether a transcendent divine Other or human consciousness." See idem, *Saints and Postmodernism,* 234.

91. See, for example, Frithjof Schuon, *Islam and the Perennial Philosophy,* J. Peter Hobson, trans. (London, 1976), 78–80.

92. Ibid., 78. See also, "Understanding and Believing" in idem, *Logic and Transcendence,* Peter N. Townsend, trans. (New York, 1975), 198–216.

93. See, for example, Seyyed Hossein Nasr, *Knowledge and the Sacred* (Albany, New York, 1989), 65–129, and idem, *Sufi Essays* (New York, 1977), 25–56.

94. Kleinberg, *Prophets,* 63–70.

95. See, for example, G. E. Van Der Leeuw, "Phenomenon and Phenomenology" in idem, *Religion in Essence and Manifestation,* J. E. Turner and Hans H. Penner trans. (Princeton, 1986), 671–678.

Chapter One

1. Bulliet, *Islam: The View from the Edge,* 9–10.
2. On the notion of the "symbolic universe," see Peter Berger and Thomas

Luckmann, *The Social Construction of Reality: A Treatise in the Sociology of Knowledge* (New York, 1967), 92–104.

3. Bulliet, *Islam: The View from the Edge,* 8.

4. According to Humphries, *Islamic History,* 187, the term "ulamology" was coined by Roy P. Mottahedeh. Dale Eickelman (personal communication, October 1996) recalls L. Carl Brown using the term well before Mottahedeh in 1974. Although one can argue that Brown's *The Tunisia of Ahmad Bey* (esp. 146–183) was the first "ulamological" work in American Islamic Studies scholarship, I have not been able to find the term itself in this text. See also, L. Carl Brown, "The Religious Establishment in Husainid Tunisia," in Nikki R. Keddie, ed., *Scholars, Saints, and Sufis: Muslim Religious Institutions since 1500* (Berkeley and Los Angeles, 1972), 47–92.

5. ʿAbdallāh ibn al-Mubārak, *Kitāb az-zuhd wa yalīʾuhu Kitāb ar-raqāʾiq,* Ḥabīb ar-Raḥmān al-ʿAẓmī, ed. (Beirut, 1949).

6. This attitude can be seen in the following statement by the Moroccan Sufi Aḥmad Zarrūq [*Qawāʿid at-taṣawwuf,* Muḥammad Zuhrī an-Najjār and ʿAlī Muʿbid Firghalī, eds. (Beirut, 1992), 111]: "The inner essence of the slave is known from his outer state" (*Yuʿrafu bāṭin al-ʿabd min ẓāhiri ḥālihi*) [Rule 144].

7. See Fritz Staal, *Exploring Mysticism* (Berkeley and Los Angeles, 1975), 60–70, who defines orthodox mysticism as the dialectical product of a confrontation between mysticism and scriptural dogmatism in the Western monotheisms. In the following pages, "orthodox" will be used to mean "correct doctrine" as defined by a majority of recognized authorities, whereas "orthoprax" will be used for "correct practice" as defined by the same authorities. Since these definitions are applicable to any religious context, there is little reason to confuse them with their more limited connotations in Greek Orthodoxy and Roman Catholicism.

8. For an overview of at-Tādilī's life and works, see Mohamed B. A. Benchekroun, *La Vie intellectuelle marocaine sous les Mérinides et les Waṭṭāsides* (Rabat, 1974), 95–98.

9. See as-Sulamī, *Ṭabaqāt aṣ-ṣūfiyya,* Nūr ad-Dīn Shurayba, ed. (Cairo, 1986).

10. See Abū Nuʿaym al-Iṣfahānī, *Ḥilyat al-awliyāʾ wa ṭabaqāt al-aṣfiyāʾ* (Cairo, 1932).

11. See Abū'l-Qāsim ʿAbd al-Karīm ibn Hāwāzin al-Qushayrī, *Risāla fī ʿilm at-taṣawwuf,* Maʿrūf Zurayq and ʿAlī ʿAbd al-Ḥamīd Beltarjī, eds. (Beirut, 1990).

12. The full name of this individual was Tāj ad-Dīn ʿAbdallāh ibn ʿUmar al-Fārisī, otherwise known as Ibn Ḥamawayh as-Sarakhsī (d. 642/1244–5). See Abū Yaʿqūb Yūsuf ibn az-Zayyāt at-Tādilī, *Kitāb at-Tashawwuf ilā rijāl at-taṣawwuf wa akhbār Abī'l-ʿAbbās as-Sabtī,* Ahmed Toufiq, ed. (Rabat, 1984), 35, n. 20. See also al-Qushayrī, *Risāla,* 389. On the Iranian scholarly diaspora after the eleventh century C.E., see Bulliet, *Islam: The View from the Edge,* 145–168.

13. On the importance of transmitters of tradition to the development of institutions, see Berger and Luckmann, *The Social Construction of Reality,* 70–71.

14. On the concept of "Sunni Sufism," see Muḥammad al-Manūnī, "At-

Tayyārāt al-fikriyya fī'l-Maghrib al-Marīnī," in idem, *Waraqāt ʿan al-ḥaḍāra al-Maghribiyya fī ʿaṣr Banī Marīn* (Rabat, 1979), 236–247. This term is not a neologism but was used by premodern North African jurists as an indicator of Sharīʿa-mindedness. See, for example, the *fatwā* by the jurist Aḥmad al-Qabbāb (d. 778/1376) in Aḥmad ibn Yaḥyā al-Wansharīsī (d. 914/1508), *Al-Miʿyār al-muʿrib wa'l-jāmiʿ al-mughrib ʿan fatāwī ahl Ifrīqīya wa'l-Andalus wa'l-Maghrib,* Muḥammad Ḥajjī et. al., eds. (Rabat, 1981), vol. 11, 121. The term "protégé of God" comes from Julian Johansen, *Sufism and Islamic Reform in Egypt: The Battle for Islamic Tradition* (Oxford, 1996), 3.

15. at-Tādilī, *at-Tashawwuf,* 31.

16. Qur'ān, IV (*an-Nisā'*), 69. My translation.

17. See, for example, at-Tādilī, *at-Tashawwuf,* 271 (119) and 303 (146). *Mar'a ṣāliḥa* ("virtuous woman") is the term most often used by at-Tādilī for the female saint.

18. See the discussion of these concepts in Toshihiko Izutsu, *God and Man in the Koran: Semantics of the Koranic Weltanschauung* (reprint, New York, 1980), 52–58.

19. ʿAbd al-Qādir al-ʿĀfiya, *Al-Ḥayāt as-siyāsiyya wa'l-ijtimāʿiyya wa'l-fikriyya bi-Shafshāwan wa aḥwāzihā khilāl al-qarn al-ʿāshir al-hijrī* (Rabat, 1982), 23–24.

20. Abū Muḥammad ibn Abī Zayd al-Qayrawānī, *Matn ar-Risāla* (Rabat, 1984), 12.

21. See Maribel Fierro, "The Polemic About the *Karāmāt al-Awliyā'* and the Development of Sufism in al-Andalus (Fourth / Tenth–Fifth / Eleventh Centuries)," *BSOAS* 55(1992): 238.

22. See Qur'ān, X (*Yūnus*), 62–65.

23. On the ethnic makeup of premodern Fez, see Roger le Tourneau, *Fès avant le protectorat: Étude économique et sociale d'une ville de l'Occident musulman* (reprint, Rabat, 1987), 190–208.

24. On early settlement patterns in Fez, see Abū'l-Ḥasan ʿAlī al-Jaznā'ī (fl. 766/1364–5), *Janā zahrat al-ās fī binā' madīnat Fās,* ʿAbd al-Wahhāb ibn Manṣūr, ed. (reprint, Rabat, 1991), 17–20, 24–26; and M. García-Arenal and E. Mantano Moreno, "Idrīssisme et villes Idrīssides," *Studia Islamica* (82), 1995, 15–20.

25. Abū ʿAbdallāh Muḥammad ash-Sharīf al-Idrīsī, *Description de l'Afrique et de l'Espagne* (*Kitāb nuzhat al-mushtāq fī ikhtirāq al-āfāq*), Reinhart Dozy and M. J. De Goeje, ed. and trans. (reprint, Leiden, 1984), 79.

26. E. Michaux-Bellaire, ed., "Les Confréries religieuses au Maroc," *AM* 27 : 19.

27. Abū'l-ʿAbbās Aḥmad ibn Khālid an-Nāṣirī as-Salawī, *Kitāb al-istiqṣā' li-akhbār duwwal al-Maghrib al-Aqṣā',* Jaʿfar an-Nāṣirī and Muḥammad an-Nāṣirī, eds. (Casablanca, 1954), vol. 1, 163.

28. See Muḥammad ibn ʿIshūn ash-Sharrāṭ, *Ar-Rawḍ al-ʿāṭir al-anfās fī akhbār aṣ-ṣāliḥīn min ahl Fās* (Rabat, BG ms. 525D), ff. 1r–4r. The juridical practice of the Idrisids appears to have been the same as that of the Zaydī Shiʿites.

29. See, for example, Muḥammad ibn Jaʿfar al-Kattānī, *Salwat al-anfās wa muḥadathāt al-akyās bi-man uqbira min al-ʿulamāʾ waʾṣ-ṣulaḥāʾ bi-Fās* (Fez lith. 1318/1900), vol. 2, 176. On the anti-Idrisid activities of Maliki jurists in tenth-century Morocco, see Halima Ferhat, *Sabta des origines au XIVe siècle* (Casablanca, 1993), 71–79.

30. al-Jaznāʾī, *Zahrat al-ās,* 21.

31. al-Kattānī, *Salwat al-anfās,* vol. 2, 176.

32. Ibid., 178. The claim that Darrās' *qibla* was more accurate than that of the Qarawiyyīn was a red herring in the Maliki ulama's attempt to portray the Idrisids as quasi-heretical innovators of Islamic doctrine (*mubtadiʿūn*). It has long been known that the *qibla*s of the earliest mosques in Fez were originally oriented toward the southeast (rather than due east) in imitation of Syrian precedent. Even after the triumph of Malikism, Moroccans continued to use the terms *al-qibla* for "the south" and *al-jawf* for "the north." For a critical examination of this issue in the Marinid period, see al-Jaznāʾī, *Zahrat al-ās,* 81–82.

33. See Georges Makdisi, *The Rise of Colleges: Institutions of Learning in Islam and the West* (Edinburgh, 1981), 21–23.

34. Moroccan Jews in the early modern period also shared a preference for private centers of worship. Although the earliest synagogues in Morocco appear to have been community-endowed institutions, by the eighteenth century most had been built by families of sages or were dominated by hereditary lineages. See Deshen, *The Mellah Society,* 90–96.

35. Makdisi, *The Rise of Colleges,* 37–38.

36. See David S. Powers, "The Maliki Family Endowment: Legal Norms and Social Practices," *IJMES* 25(3)(1993): 396.

37. The use of the masculine pronoun in the passage should not be taken to imply that mosques and hermitages were not, on occasion, endowed by women. However, most female-endowed institutions, such as the Masjid al-Qarawiyyīn, were not private but were instead nonfamilial public works created by the women of prominent or ruling families.

38. al-Kattānī, *Salwat al-anfās,* vol. 2, 178.

39. Ibid., 177–179.

40. Abūʾl-ʿAbbās Aḥmad ibn al-Qāḍī al-Miknāsī (d. 1025/1616), *Jadhwat al-iqtibās fī dhikr man ḥalla min aʿlām madīnat Fās* (Rabat, 1974), vol. 1, 107, and vol. 2, 506–507.

41. al-Jaznāʿī, *Zahrat al-ās,* 9.

42. A recently discovered fragment of Muḥammad ibn al-Qāsim at-Tamīmī's (d. 603–4/1206–7) *Kitāb al-mustafād fī dhikr aṣ-ṣāliḥīn waʾl-ʿubbād bi-madīnat Fās wa mā yalīhā min al-bilād,* the earliest Moroccan hagiographical work, mentions 13 arrivals from al-Andalus, 16 percent of the 80 surviving entries. *Al-Mustafād* will be discussed in greater detail in Chapter Four.

43. In its support of populism and Islamic universalism, the Almohad revolution in North Africa was analogous to the ʿAbbasid revolution of the eighth

century C.E., whose leaders also sought to overturn the privileges of the Arab ruling class. See M. A. Shaban, *The ʿAbbāsid Revolution* (Cambridge, 1979), esp. xiii–xvi, 138–168.

44. See Ted Robert Gurr, *Minorities at Risk: A Global View of Ethnopolitical Conflicts* (Washington, D.C., 1993). Communal contenders are found in states where "political power at the center is based on intergroup coalitions, usually dominated by a powerful minority that uses a mix of concessions, cooptation, and repression to maintain its leading role" (22).

45. See Ismāʿīl ibn al-Aḥmar, *Buyūtāt Fās al-kubrā* (Rabat, 1972). Begun in the late fourteenth century and completed before the year 880/1475, the anonymous *Mashāhīr Fās fī'l-qadīm* has been attributed both to the Granadan litterateur Ismāʿīl ibn al-Aḥmar (d. 807/1404) [see Benchekroun, *La Vie intellectuelle,* 329–337] and to the Fasi jurist and pro-sharifian demagogue ʿAbd al-ʿAzīz al-Waryāghlī (d. 880/1475–6). Despite the late date of its publication, it contains information from earlier sources that describe Andalusian society at the end of the ʿAmirid period. For more on this work, see Maya Shatzmiller, "Professions and Ethnic Origins of Urban Labourers in Muslim Spain: Evidence from a Moroccan Source," *Awrāq* 5–6 (1982–3), 154. Shatzmiller's views are reproduced in expanded form in idem, *Labour in the Medieval Islamic World* (Leiden, 1994), 327–346. For another perspective on this period, see Jacinto Bosch-Vilá, *La Sevilla Islámica, 712–1248* (Seville, 1984), 343–369. Much of the discussion that follows can also be found in Vincent J. Cornell, "Ḥayy in the Land of Absāl: Ibn Ṭufayl and Ṣūfism in the Western Maghrib during the Muwaḥḥid Era," in Lawrence I. Conrad, ed., *The World of Ibn Ṭufayl: Interdisciplinary Perspectives on Ḥayy ibn Yaqẓān* (Leiden, 1996), esp. 137–143.

46. Gurr, *Minorities at Risk,* 21. Ethnoclasses are culturally distinct populations that specialize in "distinctive economic activities, mostly of low status." See also, Ibn al-Aḥmar, *Buyūtāt Fās,* 23; and Mohammad Benaboud, *At-Tārīkh as-siyāsī wa'l-ijtimāʿī li-Ishbīlīya fī ʿahd ad-duwwal aṭ-ṭawāʾif* (Tetuan, 1983), 192–197. Benaboud's contention that Andalusian society was not rent by ethnic divisions seems to fly in the face of both the historical sources and the received wisdom of subaltern studies. See also M. Benaboud and A. Tahiri, "Berberising al-Andalus," *Al-Qanṭara* 11(1990): 475–487.

47. Ibn al-Aḥmar, *Buyūtāt Fās,* 24; Benaboud, *Tārīkh,* 176–177.

48. On the pre-Islamic use of the term *muwallad,* see Mahmood Ibrahim, *Merchant Capital and Islam* (Austin, Texas, 1990), 60.

49. Ibn al-Aḥmar, *Buyūtāt Fās,* 24.

50. Ibid., 25.

51. Although Peter C. Scales attributes the ethnic divisions surrounding the fall of the Umayyad caliphate to hatred for the Berbers who entered al-Andalus as soldiers of the ʿAmirids, his book *The Fall of the Caliphate of Córdoba: Berbers and Andalusis in Conflict* (Leiden, 1994) provides evidence of more long-lasting ethnic antipathies. See, for example, the Umayyad pretender Muḥammad al-Mahdī's (d. 400/1010) prohibition of Berbers riding horses or carrying arms, which implies

that they were relegated to the status of non-Muslims (68); the spread of the anti-Berber pogrom of Córdoba to Elvira and Málaga (70–71); and acts of ritualistic cannibalism on both sides during the wars of succession, such as when a *muwallad* woman of Elvira ate the corpse of Siwar, chief of the city's Arab elites (74 n. 139).

52. Thomas F. Glick, *Islamic and Christian Spain in the Early Middle Ages* (Princeton, 1979), 181.

53. The term *anṣārī* (helper), when used in a premodern Andalusian name as an unqualified attributive (i.e., *al-Anṣārī* as opposed to *al-Anṣārī al-ʿAwsī*) appears to have denoted prior convert status. The original *anṣār* were the inhabitants of Medina who helped the cause of Islam by taking the Prophet Muḥammad and his Meccan emigrants (*muhājirūn*) into their homes. In al-Andalus, the term *muhājir* referred to the descendants of Arab immigrants, while *anṣārī* referred to *mawālī* and *muwalladūn,* the descendants of native Iberians. Similar terms are still used in contemporary Pakistan to differentiate Indian Muslims who immigrated after 1947 from native Sindis and Punjabis.

54. Glick, *Islamic and Christian Spain,* 181–185. Post-Umayyad elitism is clearly visible in the *Kitāb as-siyāsa wa tadbīr al-imāra* of the Andalusian Abū Bakr al-Murādī (d. 489/1095–6). This "mirror for princes" counsels the Almoravid rulers of North Africa and Spain to seek the advice of the Andalusian ulama in all matters of state and social policy and to avoid at all costs "the ignorant, artisans, domestics, and slaves." See Ferhat, *Sabta,* 120–122.

55. On the concept of "Sunni internationalism" and the emergence of an integrated Islamic civilization, see Marshall G. S. Hodgson, *The Venture of Islam: Conscience and History in a World Civilization,* vol. 2, *The Expansion of Islam in the Middle Periods* (Chicago, 1974), 255–292.

56. For a thorough introduction to the methodology of *uṣūl al-fiqh,* see Mohammed Hashim Kamali, *Principles of Islamic Jurisprudence* (Cambridge, 1991).

57. See Dominique Urvoy, *El Mundo de los ulemas Andaluces del siglo V/XI al VII/XIII: estudio sociologico,* Francisco Panel, trans. (Madrid, 1983), 55–56. On the juridical practice of the early Maliki *madhhab,* see Yasin Dutton, "*Sunna, Ḥadīth,* and Madinan *ʿAmal,*" *Journal of Islamic Studies* 4(1)(January 1993): 1–31.

58. Abū'l-Qāsim Khalaf ibn ʿAbd al-Malik ibn Bashkuwāl, *Kitāb aṣ-ṣila fī tārīkh aʾimmat al-Andalus wa ʿulamāʾihim wa muḥaddithīhim wa fuqahāʾ ihim wa udabāʾ ihim* (Cairo, 1955), vol. 1, 271.

59. Ibid., 69–70.

60. Ibid., 48–49. See also Maria Isabel Fierro, "El proceso contra Abu Umar al-Talamanki a través de su vida y de su obra," *Sharq al-Andalus,* 9(1993): 93–127, and idem, "The Polemic about the *Karāmāt al-Awliyāʾ,*" 247–248.

61. Ibn Bashkuwāl, *aṣ-Ṣila,* 48. See also Urvoy, *El Mundo de los ulemas Andaluces,* 127, 153.

62. Urvoy, *El Mundo de los ulemas Andaluces,* 125, 127 n. 113. See also at-Tādilī, *at-Tashawwuf,* 61–62.

63. On the relationship of this development to the hadith-based Medinan

"school" of historiography (which was itself related to the Maliki school of *fiqh*), see A. A. Duri, *The Rise of Historical Writing Among the Arabs,* Lawrence I. Conrad, ed. and trans. (Princeton, 1983), 76–121.

64. For a politically contextualized discussion of al-Ghazālī's Sufism, see Mustapha Hogga, *Orthodoxie, subversion, et réforme en Islam: Gazālī et les Seljūqides* (Paris, 1993), 179–203.

65. Muḥammad ibn al-Munawwir, *Les Étapes mystiques du Shaykh Abu Sa'id (Asrār at-tawḥīd fī maqāmāt ash-shaykh Abī Saʿīd)*, Mohammad Achena, trans. (Paris, 1974), 36–40. Written by a great-grandson of Abū Saʿīd Abū'l-Khayr, this work presents a picture of Khurasani mysticism that is strikingly similar to Sufism in the Far Maghrib. For a summary of Abū Saʿīd's career and influence, see Terry Graham, "Abū Saʿīd ibn Abī'l-Khayr and the School of Khurāsān," in Leonard Lewisohn, ed., *Classical Persian Sufism: From Its Origins to Rumi* (London, 1993), 83–135. See also Margaret Malamud, "Sufi Organizations and Structures of Authority in Medieval Nishapur," *IJMES* 26 (3)(1994): 427–442. I do not agree with Malamud's contention that the institutionalization of Sufism was dependent on the spread of Shafiʿism per se. What attracted Sufis to Shafiʿism was rather its emphasis on uṣūl, which put a high premium on tradition and accentuated the rigor of Islamic practice.

66. See Miguel Asín Palacios, *The Mystical Philosophy of Ibn Masarra and His Followers,* Elmer H. Douglas and Howard W. Yoder, trans. (Leiden, 1978), 120–123.

67. In al-Andalus an *ʿarīf* was the commander of a *band* of forty men, a unit which roughly corresponded to the modern platoon. Each *band* was made up of five squads (sing. *ʿuqda*) of eight men each. See Weston F. Cook, Jr., *The Hundred Years War for Morocco: Gunpowder and the Military Revolution in the Early Modern Muslim World* (Boulder, Colorado, 1994), 34–35.

68. Ibn Bashkuwāl, *aṣ-Ṣila,* vol. 1, 52. On the juridical basis of Ibn al-ʿArīf's Sufism, see Cornell, "Ḥayy in the Land of Absāl," 145–155.

69. Aḥmad Bābā at-Timbuktī, *Nayl al-ibtihāj bi-taṭrīz ad-Dībāj* (Fez lith., 1317/1899), 30.

70. Abū ʿAbdallāh Muḥammad ibn al-Abbār al-Balansī, *Al-Muʿjam fī aṣḥāb al-qāḍī al-imām Abī ʿAlī as-Ṣadafī* (Cairo, 1967), 15–17. See also Ferhat, *Sabta,* 142–143.

71. al-ʿAbbās ibn Ibrāhīm (d. 1378/1959), *Al-Iʿlām bi-man ḥalla Marrākush wa Aghmāt min al-aʿlām* (Rabat, 1974–80), vol. 2, 6–7.

72. Aḥmad Bābā, *Nayl,* 30. This term refers to Ibn al-ʿArīf's reputation as a master of *adab,* the literary and intellectual arts in general.

73. In Sufi doctrine, *futuwwa* is a complex phenomenon that includes the practices of asceticism, scrupulousness, social awareness, preference for others, and institutionalized brotherhood. Since the commonly used terms "Sufi chivalry" or "spiritual chivalry" do not cover all of these practices, it is preferable to use the term *futuwwa* itself. On the Khurasanian background of *futuwwa/javanmardī,*

see Jaʿfar Mahjub, "Spiritual Chivalry and Early Persian Sufism," in Leonard Lewisohn, ed., *Classical Persian Sufism: From Its Origins to Rumi* (London, 1993), 549–582.

74. Although the Almoravids were Ṣanhāja Berbers, they claimed Arab descent by tracing their "noble" lineages to the South Arabian tribe of Ḥimyar. See H. T. Norris, *The Berbers in Arabic Literature* (London and Beirut, 1982), 32–40.

75. Paul Nwyia, "Notes sur quelques fragments inédits de la correspondance d'Ibn al-ʿArīf avec Ibn Barrajān," *Hespéris* 43(1)(1956): 219–220.

76. Ibid., 218. Asín Palacios, in the Appendix to his "El Místico Abū-l-ʿAbbās Ibn al-ʿArīf de Almería y su 'Majāsin al-Mayālis'" (*Obras Escogidas,* I [Madrid, 1946], 222), surmises that the name "Ibn Barrajān" is of North African origin. Although Asín cites no evidence for this assertion, he most likely took it from a biographical note in Ibn al-Abbār's *Takmila,* where Ibn Barrajān's ancestry is traced to a Lakhmid Arab who emigrated to Spain from Ifrīqīya (See Abū ʿAbdallāh Muḥammad Ibn al-Abbār al-Balansī, *Kitāb at-takmila li-Kitāb aṣ-Ṣila,* Francisco Codera, ed. [Madrid, 1887], vol. 2, 559). It must not be forgotten, however, that the name "Barragan" remains popular in Hispanic countries today and has been semantically linked to the same Celtic root as that of the name "Berrigan" of Ireland. Given the custom of Iberian *mawālī* to assume the tribal affiliations of their Arab patrons, it is possible that Ibn Barrajān's ancestor was Arab only by adoption or attribution and was actually *muwallad* by birth.

77. V. Lagardère, "La Tarīqa et la révolte des Murīdīn en 539H/1144 en Andalus," *ROMM* 35, (1983): 165–166. See also Addas, *Ibn ʿArabī,* 77–79. In her discussion of the intellectual ties between Ibn al-ʿArabī and Ibn Qasī, Addas points out that the former's opinion of the leader of the *murīdīn* changed from approval to disapproval over the course of his life. She does not, however, broach the subject of the influence that Ibn Qasī's book *Khalʿ an-naʿlayn* (Removing the two sandals) may have had on Ibn al-ʿArabī's mystical doctrines.

78. Lagardère, "La Ṭarīqa," 166. Many of Ibn Qasī's beliefs about the imamate are reminiscent of the Kaysāniyya–Hāshimiyya doctrines of the ʿAbbasids. See Farhad Daftary, *The Ismāʿīlīs: Their History and Doctrines* (Cambridge, 1990), 51–64. The Kaysāniyya movement, like that of Ibn Qasī, was popular among converts to Islam. The relationship (if any) between Ibn Qasī's *khātim al-wilāya* and the *khātim al-awliyāʾ* (Seal of the Saints), which was adopted by Ibn al-ʿArabī via al-Ḥakīm at-Tirmidhī (d. 298/910), is a subject that deserves further investigation.

79. Abū'l-ʿAbbās Aḥmad Ibn al-ʿArīf, *Miftāḥ as-saʿāda wa taḥqīq ṭarīq al-irāda* (Rabat, BH ms. 1562). This work has recently appeared in an edited version in Arabic under the erroneous title, *Miftāḥ as-saʿāda wa taḥqīq ṭarīq as-saʿāda,* ʿIṣmat ʿAbd al-Laṭīf Dandash, ed. (Beirut, 1993).

80. Ibid., 95. Dandash, ed., 210.

81. Ibid., 192. Dandash, ed., 208.

82. Ibid., 193–195. Dandash, ed., 208.

83. Ibn Ibrāhīm, *Al-Iʿlām,* vol. 2, 6. See also Asín Palacios, *Obras Escogidas,*

221. An overview of the political history of Almería in the Ṭā'ifa and Almoravid periods can be found in José Angel Tapia Garrido, *Almería Musulmana I (711–1172)* (Almería, 1986), 287–346.

84. On the social and political influence of jurists in Almoravid society, see Ferhat, *Sabta,* 128–144.

85. For al-Juwaynī's views on the role of the ulama in the post-caliphal sultanate, see Ann K. S. Lambton, *State and Government in Medieval Islam* (Oxford, 1981), 104–107.

86. For a discussion of Ibn Tūmart's critique of parochial Malikism, see Vincent J. Cornell, "Understanding Is the Mother of Ability: Responsibility and Action in the Doctrine of Ibn Tūmart," *Studia Islamica* 66(1988): 91–101.

87. My use of the archaic term *rābiṭa,* instead of the more commonly employed *zāwiya,* for an urban Sufi hermitage agrees with that of Muḥammad Miftāḥ (*At-Tayyār as-ṣūfī wa'l-mujtamaʿ fī'l-Andalus wa'l-Maghrib athnā'a al-qarn 8/14* [Ph.D. dissertation, Université Mohammed V, Rabat 1981]), who notes that the term *zāwiya* does not appear in Moroccan texts until the Marinid era. See ash-Shādhilī, *At-Taṣawwuf wa'l-mujtamaʿ*, 168.

88. at-Tādilī, *at-Tashawwuf,* 94. See also, ash-Sharrāṭ, *Ar-Rawḍ al-ʿāṭir,* 5r. Ibn Ḥirzihim's purported descent from the caliph ʿUthmān may have been a symbolic expression of loyalty to the Umayyad state rather than an actual genealogical link. The name *Ḥirzihim* is an Arabic expression meaning "their refuge" or "their charm" (*ḥirz*). *Aḥrāzem* is its Berberized plural.

89. at-Tādilī, *at-Tashawwuf,* 168–173.

90. Ibn al-Qāḍī, *Jadhwat al-iqtibās,* vol. 2, 466. See also Ibn Ibrāhīm, *Al-Iʿlām,* vol. 9, 52.

91. Ferhat, *Sabta,* 143–144.

92. Ibn al-Qāḍī, *Jadhwat al-iqtibās,* vol. 2, 464. Ibn Ibrāhīm, *Al-Iʿlām,* vol. 9, 49–52. Ash-Sharrāṭ, *Ar-Rawḍ al-ʿāṭir,* 6v.–11r.

93. This point is overlooked by ʿAbd al-Laṭīf ash-Shādhilī, who agrees that Ibn Ḥirzihim's biography in *at-Tashawwuf* is the first mention of the *malāmatiyya* in Morocco but links this method to the state of *jadhba,* "divine attraction." Later, however, ash-Shādhilī contradicts himself by asserting that *jadhba* was not a part of Moroccan *malāmatiyya* doctrine until the sixteenth century. In the end, he can find no other recourse but to fall back on psychological reductionism to explain the absence of antinomianism in the doctrines of early Moroccan *malāmatīs.* See idem, *At-Taṣawwuf wa'l-mujtamaʿ*, 91–94. Sara Sviri has recently challenged the association of the *ṭarīq al-malāma* with antinomianism, pointing out that it was not a characteristic of the early *malāmatiyya* of Khurasan. See idem, "Ḥakīm Tirmidhī and the *Malāmatī* Movement in Early Sufism," in Leonard Lewisohn, ed., *Classical Persian Sufism: From Its Origins to Rumi* (London, 1993), 583–613.

94. Ibn Ḥirzihim's description of himself as the "Axis of the Maghribis" appears in an ode (*qaṣīda*) that is edited and translated in Vincent J. Cornell, *The Way of Abū Madyan: Doctrinal and Poetic Works of Abū Madyan Shuʿayb ibn al-Ḥusayn al-Anṣārī (c. 500/1115–16—594/1198)* (Cambridge, 1996), 176–179.

95. Abū ʿAbd ar-Raḥmān as-Sulamī, *Uṣūl al-malāmatiyya wa ghalaṭāt aṣ-ṣūfiyya,* ʿAbd al-Fātiḥ Aḥmad al-Fāwī Maḥmūd, ed. (Cairo, 1984), 143. See also Ibn Ibrāhīm, *Al-Iʿlām,* vol. 9, 54. For more on Ḥamdūn al-Qaṣṣār, see as-Sulamī, *Ṭabaqāt aṣ-ṣūfiyya,* 123–129, and al-Qushayrī, *Ar-Risāla,* 426.

96. Ibn Barrajān was arrested and brought to Marrakesh during a period of social unrest in al-Andalus and was executed for either heresy or sedition (the actual charge is unclear) at the order of ʿAlī ibn Yūsuf ibn Tashfīn. His recently restored tomb can still be seen in Marrakesh.

97. at-Tādilī, *at-Tashawwuf,* 170. See also, Ibn al-Qāḍī, *Jadhwat al-iqtibās,* vol. 2, 465.

98. at-Tādilī, *at-Tashawwuf,* 95–101.

99. Qurʾān III (*Āl ʿImrān*), 104–105. For a discussion of Ibn Tūmart's interpretation of al-Ghazālī on the question of *al-amr bi'l-maʿrūf,* see Cornell, "Understanding Is the Mother of Ability," 89–91.

100. at-Tādilī, *at-Tashawwuf,* 96.

101. Ibid., 97. The "verse of Ḥassān [ibn Thābit]" mentioned in this poem is part of a hadith documenting the Prophet Muḥammad's destruction of a date orchard that belonged to the Banū Luʾayy, a Jewish family from the tribe of Banū Naḍīr. See Saḥnūn ibn Saʿīd at-Tanūkhī, *Al-Mudawwana al-kubrā* (Beirut, 1980), vol. 1, 372.

102. at-Tādilī, *at-Tashawwuf,* 97.

103. Ibid., 98–99.

104. Ibn al-Qāḍī, *Jadhwat al-iqtibās,* vol. 2, 458. Khayrūna al-Andalusiyya (d. 594/1198) also died in Fez and is buried near the tomb of Darrās ibn Ismāʿīl.

105. Ibid., vol. 1, 260.

106. at-Tādilī, *at-Tashawwuf,* 153–154.

107. Ibid., 155. See also Ibn al-Qāḍī, *Jadhwat al-iqtibās,* vol. 1, 260. At-Tādilī (*at-Tashawwuf,* 158) reports that during the same period another Sufi and political activist named Abū Muḥammad Ṣāliḥ u-Imlīl al-Munshīʾ (The Polemicist) was assassinated near the caravan center of Tazagūrāt (present-day Zagora) in the Darʿa valley. Al-Munshīʾ seems to have been a representative of the Ibn Ḥirzihim rābiṭa in the pre-Saharan oases.

108. Ibn al-Qāḍī, *Jadhwat al-iqtibās,* vol. 1, 259. Most of the information presently available about ad-Daqqāq is summarized in Alfred Bel, "Sîdî Bou Medyan et son maître Ed-Daqqâq à Fès," *Mélanges René Basset* (Paris, 1923), vol. 1, 31–68.

109. Ibid., 260. See also at-Tādilī, *at-Tashawwuf,* 156–157. Ad-Daqqāq's tombstone was found by French researchers in a small mosque dedicated to his disciple Abū Madyan. For a picture of this tombstone, see Bel, "Sidi Bou Medyan," 46. Abū Madyan will be discussed at length in Chapter Five.

Chapter Two

1. See, for example, Geertz, *Islam Observed,* 9, who claims that the countryside is Morocco's "cultural center of gravity."

2. In using the term "foundation metaphor," I follow Victor Turner, who saw the study of symbolic action as an investigation of "key words and expressions of major conceptual archetypes or foundation metaphors, both in the periods in which they first appeared in their full social and cultural settings and in their subsequent expansion and modification in changing fields of social relations." See Victor Turner, *Dramas, Fields, and Metaphors: Symbolic Action in Human Society* (reprint, Ithaca, New York and London, 1983), 28.

3. For example, despite Geertz's attempt, in *Islam Observed,* to portray *baraka* as a sort of "moral vividness," his failure to appreciate the link between the ethical dimension of Moroccan sainthood and its Qur'anic roots caused him to overlook the fact that *baraka* and *ṣalāḥ* typically go together. By not acknowledging scripturally based foundation metaphors, he was not in a position to appreciate the more universal aspects of Islamic sainthood. See idem, *Islam Observed,* 44, 54. Mark R. Woodward has identified similar problems with Geertz's analysis of Islam in Indonesia. See idem, *Islam in Java: Normative Piety and Mysticism in the Sultanate of Yogyakarta* (Tucson, Arizona, 1989), 53–79.

4. See, for example, P. M. Currie, *The Shrine and Cult of Mu'in al-din Chishti of Ajmer* (Delhi, 1989), esp. 66–96. The extralocality of maraboutism is also highlighted in ʿAbd al-Laṭīf ash-Shādhilī's critique of the Western study of Moroccan sainthood in idem, *At-Taṣawwuf wa'l-mujtamaʿ*, 8–25.

5. On the religious beliefs of the Barghwāṭa and their prophet Ṣāliḥ ibn Ṭarīf (d. 177/793), see Norris, *The Berbers,* 92–104. According to the Moroccan historian Ahmed Toufiq, the word *barghwāṭa* is an Arabization of the Berber *ilighwāṭen,* meaning "those who turn away." This is similar to the Arabic *khawārij* (secessionists), and it may indicate that *barghwāṭa* originally meant either Kharijism or apostasy in general. On the other hand, a group of people called *Baquates* were also known to have inhabited Morocco in Roman and late-antique times. See at-Tādilī, *at-Tashawwuf,* 52 n. 37. See also Oric Bates, *The Eastern Libyans* (reprint, London, 1970), 91–107, and Ferhat, *Sabta,* 79–84.

6. Ferhat, *Sabta,* 63–65.

7. D. Jacques-Meunié, *Le Maroc saharien des origines au XVIème siècle* (Paris, 1982), 203.

8. al-Idrīsī, *Description del' Afrique,* 66. See also Wilferd Madelung, "Some Notes on Non-Ismāʿīlī Shiism in the Maghrib," in idem, *Religious Schools and Sects in Medieval Islam* (reprint, London, 1985), 87–97.

9. From the late tenth century C.E., many "Andalusian" scholars were actually North African in origin, such as Abū Muḥammad al-Aṣīlī al-Andalusī (d. 392/1002), a native of the Moroccan town of Asila, who served as qāḍī al-jamāʿa of Saragossa. See Ferhat, *Sabta,* 72.

10. Ibn Bashkuwāl, *aṣ-Ṣila,* 349.

11. Ibid. See also Ibn al-Qāḍī, *Jadhwat al-iqtibās,* 344–345.

12. Norris, *The Berbers,* 110.

13. Ibn Bashkuwāl, *aṣ-Ṣila,* 349.

14. Halima Ferhat (*Sabta,* 112) asserts that a Veiled Ṣanhāja amir named Ibrā-

hīm al-Gudālī visited al-Qayrawān in 440 A.H., ten years after the death of Abū ʿImrān al-Fāsī. If this were true, he could not have been the person sent to Waggāg by al-Fāsī. Instead of al-Fāsī, Ferhat suggests that the Andalusian legist Abū'l-Walīd al-Bājī may have sent al-Gudālī to Waggāg. Al-Bājī was also an advocate of jihad and the political unification of the Maghrib, and he is known to have visited the Mashriq between the years 426/1035 and 440/1047.

15. Al-Fāsī's support for the ʿAbbasid caliphate was based on his alarm at the destruction caused by wars among Umayyad pretenders in al-Andalus between the years 399/1009 and 422/1031. His rejection of both the Umayyads and other pretenders to the caliphate, such as the Banū ʿAbbād of Seville and the Banū Ḥammūd sharifs of Málaga, may have been influenced by the political theories of his teacher al-Bāqillānī (another supporter of the ʿAbbasids), who refused to recognize more than one caliph at a time. See Lambton, *State and Government,* 75.

16. *Aggāg,* in the Tuareg dialect, signifies a minor teacher of the Qur'an or Islamic dogma. *U-aggāg,* therefore, would mean "Son of the Teacher." See Ahmed Toufiq's comments in at-Tādilī, *at-Tashawwuf,* 89n. 24.

17. Ibid., 89–90. On Ribāṭ Aglū and the tomb of "Sīdī Waggāg," see Muḥammad al-Mukhṭār as-Sūsī, *Khilāl Jazūla* (Tetuan, 1960), vol. 1, 74–78.

18. Norris, *The Berbers,* 130.

19. at-Tādilī, *at-Tashawwuf,* 89–90.

20. al-Idrīsī, *Description de l'Afrique,* 64.

21. at-Tādilī, *at-Tashawwuf,* 92.

22. Ibid., 93.

23. Ibid., 111.

24. Ibid., 110–111.

25. Ibid., 123. Among the modern Tuareg, who claim descent from the Lamtūna and Massūfa Berbers of the Almoravid era, chopping and carrying wood are occupations reserved for household slaves (*iklan*) or vassals (*imghad*) and would never be performed by veiled *imashaghen.* By performing such actions in front of his lineage mates, Ibn Yughān served notice that he wished to abrogate his clan prerogatives. See H. T. Norris, *The Tuaregs: Their Islamic Legacy and its Diffusion in the Sahel* (Warminster, United Kingdom, 1975), 5–15.

26. An example of the Andalusian use of the term *murābiṭ* can be found in the *laqab* of the twelfth-century Almerían scholar Abū ʿAbdallāh "Ibn al-Murābiṭ." See Urvoy, *El Mundo de los Ulemas Andaluces,* 116–119. For a discussion of the relationship between the terms *ribāṭ* and *jihād* in Islamic tradition, see Vincent J. Cornell, "Jihad: Islam's Struggle for Truth," *Gnosis* 21 (Fall 1991): 20–22.

27. Abū ʿUbayd ibn ʿAbd al-ʿAzīz al-Bakrī, *Description de l'Afrique Septentrionale* (*Kitāb al-mughrib fī dhikr bilād Ifrīqīya wa'l-Maghrib*), MacGuckin de Slane, ed. and trans. (reprint, Paris, 1965), 183.

28. Ibid., 182.

29. Ibid., 184–185.

30. Although the Moroccan historian ʿAbd al-Laṭīf al-Shādhilī sees the terms *ribāṭ* and *rābiṭa* as semantically equivalent, he distinguishes between them by size

and function. *Rābiṭa* (hermitage), the more basic term, referred to a privately built walled or fenced compound that was dedicated to worship or Sufi teaching. The term *ribāṭ* was used, however, after outsiders settled permanently in the vicinity of a *rābiṭa* for protection or blessing, thus expanding both the size and the social functions of the institution. See idem, *At-Taṣawwuf wa'l-mujtama'*, 171–172.

31. Muḥammad ibn ʿAbd al-ʿAẓīm az-Zammūrī (d. early ninth/fifteenth century), *Bahjat an-nāẓirīn wa uns al-ʿārifīn wa wasīlat Rabb al-ʿĀlamīn fī manāqib rijāl Amghār aṣ-ṣāliḥīn* (Rabat, BH ms. 1358).

32. It is necessary to point out that the transcription of "original" letters and documents in premodern Moroccan biographical and historical works is a rhetorical trope that goes back to the very beginnings of the Arabic historical tradition. In many cases, such documents were fabricated by later authors to justify the political or juridical status of certain individuals or institutions. There is thus no foolproof way of knowing whether the documents reproduced in *Bahjat an-nāẓirīn* are in fact genuine. For a detailed discussion of this issue, see Albrecht Noth and Lawrence I. Conrad, *The Early Arabic Historical Tradition: A Source-Critical Study* (Princeton, 1994), 76–87.

33. az-Zammūrī, *Bahjat an-nāẓirīn,* 14. Although the sharifian lineage of the Banū Amghār was officially confirmed in a decree issued by Sultan Abū ʿInān al-Marīnī in 755/1354, the eponym "Abū Zakariyya al-Ḥunayf" does not appear in any authenticated genealogy of the Prophet's descendants of which I am aware. In the opinion of Mohamed Kably, the Marinid sultans of Morocco granted sharifian status to the Banū Amghār in order to co-opt them into their spoils system and thus assure Marinid control over the grain-rich region of Dukkāla. See idem, *Société, pouvoir et religion,* 296.

34. az-Zammūrī, *Bahjat an-nāẓirīn,* 59. It is possible to conjecture, although impossible to prove, that the Banū Amghār had formerly been associated with the Fatimids, who dominated Egypt and the Hijaz during the late tenth and early eleventh centuries C.E. Hints of such a connection can be found in the names of the earliest Banū Amghār *murābiṭūn,* which recall those of Ismāʿīlī imams, as well as the foundation legend of Tīṭ-n-Fiṭr itself, which makes liberal use of the Ismāʿīlī motifs of light and revelation. For a review of Ismaʿīlī symbology, see Daftary, *The Ismāʿīlīs,* 91–144.

35. az-Zammūrī, *Bahjat an-nāẓirīn,* 59–62. ʿAbd al-ʿAzīz ibn Baṭṭān is considered by many to have been an actual leader of the Ṣanhāja Azammūr who flourished at the beginning of the eleventh century. His tomb can be found at Tīknī, a short distance from Ribāṭ Tīṭ. See Michaux-Bellaire, "Les Confréries religieuses," 37.

36. az-Zammūrī, *Bahjat an-nāẓirīn,* 55–56. ʿAbd al-Laṭīf ash-Shādhilī doubts the authenticity of this edict because it is not in the form of a tax exemption. See idem, *At-Taṣawwuf wa'l-mujtama'*, 209.

37. az-Zammūrī, *Bahjat an-nāẓirīn,* 20. Mohamed Kably's assertion that the Banū Amghār were allowed to dip into the *zakāt* funds of the Ṣanhāja Azammūr would have been impossible had they indeed been sharifs, since *zakāt* is forbidden

to descendants of the Prophet under Islamic law. See idem, *Societé, pouvoir et religion,* 296.

38. ash-Shādhilī, *At-Taṣawwuf wa'l-mujtamaʿ,* 210.

39. The use of the ʿ*aqīda* as a religiopolitical credo and polemic against Shiʿites, Muʿtazilites, and other so-called "heretics" was common among Hanbali reformers in the Mashriq during the fifth/eleventh century. See Georges Makdisi, *Ibn ʿAqīl et la résurgence de l'Islam traditionaliste au XIe siècle* (Damascus, 1963), 317–318.

40. See al-Qayrawānī, *Matn ar-Risāla,* 9–13.

41. The translated text of this ʿ*aqīda* can be found in Vincent J. Cornell, "Ribāṭ Tīṭ-n-Fiṭr and the Origins of Moroccan Maraboutism," *Islamic Studies* 27 (1) (1988): 29.

42. The Banū Amghār's conflict with the Barghwāṭa casts a certain amount of doubt upon their sharifian pretensions. Although the Barghwāṭa had formerly been close to the Umayyads of Spain, in the eleventh century C.E. they were allied with the Banū Ḥammūd of Málaga, a family of Idrisid sharifs who were deeply involved in caliphal politics. It is unlikely that a family of true sharifs would be attacked by the allies of other sharifs. See Ferhat, *Sabta,* 88–89. Tashelhit Berber definitions given in this book are taken from D. G. Hatt, *Tashelhit-English Dictionary: Based on the Work of Edmond D'Estaing* (Los Angeles, 1969). I am grateful to Professor Thomas Penchoen of UCLA for providing me with a copy of this work.

43. az-Zammūrī, *Bahjat an-nāẓirīn,* 64–67.

44. The Arabized Berbers of the Hashtūka and Shyāẓma regions, north of Dukkāla, believed that the well of Tīn Gīdūt was the southern outlet for the "Wādī aṣ-Ṣāliḥīn," an underground river that provided water for saints' shrines from Tīṭ-n-Fiṭr to Azemmour. See ash-Shyāẓmī and as-Sibāʿī, *Madīnat Azammūr,* 149.

45. az-Zammūrī, *Bahjat an-nāẓirīn,* 68–75. For a physical description of Tīṭ-n-Fiṭr and its ancient minaret, see Richard Parker, *A Practical Guide to Islamic Monuments in Morocco* (Charlottesville, Virginia, 1981), 69–73 plate 19. Parker incorrectly identifies Tīṭ-n-Fiṭr as a fortified ribāṭ for jihad, on the pattern of the ribāṭs of Monastir and Sousa in Tunisia. In fact, the wall that now surrounds the site has nothing to do with the original complex but was constructed at the beginning of the sixteenth century C.E. to defend against Portuguese raids.

46. The founding of aṭ-Ṭā'ifa aṣ-Ṣanhājiyya in the Almohad period disproves ʿAbd al-Laṭīf ash-Shādhilī's contention that Moroccan institutional Sufism was an exclusive product of the Marinid era. See idem, *At-Taṣawwuf wa'l-mujtamaʿ,* 131–135, 149.

47. Abū'l-ʿAbbās Aḥmad al-Khaṭīb ibn Qunfudh al-Qusanṭīnī (d. 810/1407–8), *Uns al-faqīr wa ʿizz al-ḥaqīr,* Muḥammad al-Fāsī and Adolphe Faure, eds. (Rabat, 1965), 64.

48. az-Zammūrī, *Bahjat an-nāẓirīn,* 30–31. This "letter" may be a trope rather than an actual document, since Abū'l-Walīd ibn Rushd the Elder died in 520/1126, two years before the letter was supposedly sent.

49. Ibid., 33. Abū ʿAbdallāh Amghār's otherworldliness is confirmed by his contemporary, the biographer at-Tamīmī, who describes the murābiṭ as having "the Hereafter between his eyes." See idem, *al-Mustafād,* 71–72 (biography 48).

50. az-Zammūrī, *Bahjat an-nāẓirīn,* 34. The minaret over the tomb of Mūlāy ʿAbdallāh Amghār, which resembles that of the Kutubiyya mosque in Marrakesh, dates from the Almohad period.

51. Ibid., 38. Only a generation later, the Banū Amghār were to abandon the Almohads and cast their lot with the Marinids.

52. at-Tādilī, *at-Tashawwuf,* 210.

53. az-Zammūrī, *Bahjat an-nāẓirīn,* 89, 91, 108.

54. Ibid., 79.

55. Ibid., 131.

56. See Von Franz Taeschner, "As-Sulamī's Kitāb al-Futuwwa," *Studia Orientalia Ioanni Pedersen* (Copenhagen, 1953), 348.

57. Ibid., 349.

58. Ibid.

59. Ibn al-Husayn al-Sulami, *The Way of Sufi Chivalry,* Tosun Bayrak al-Jerrahi, trans. (Rochester, Vermont, 1991), 108.

60. az-Zammūrī, *Bahjat an-nāẓirīn,* 24, 83. See also Annemarie Schimmel, *And Muḥammad is His Messenger: The Veneration of the Prophet in Islamic Piety* (Chapel Hill and London, 1985), 33; and Ferhat, *Sabta,* 146–156.

61. az-Zammūrī, *Bahjat an-nāẓirīn,* 92. It is possible that these contacts with Iraq and Yemen were part of the Banū Amghār's attempt to strengthen their claims to sharifian status. Contemporaries of Mūlāy ʿAbdallāh Amghār in Iraq included ʿAbd al-Qādir al-Jīlānī and Aḥmad ar-Rifāʿī. Both of these Sufi shaykhs made use of Prophetic genealogies to support their claims of religious authority. Yemen was known in this period as a center of both Zaydī and Ismāʿīlī Shiʿism and was the site of one of the earliest Qādirī ribāṭs outside of Iraq. See Yūsuf Muḥammad Ṭaha Zaydān, *Aṭ-Ṭarīq aṣ-ṣūfī wa furūʿ al-Qādiriyya bi-Miṣr* (Beirut, 1991), 178–179.

62. az-Zammūrī, *Bahjat an-nāẓirīn,* 9.

63. Despite certain problems on the level of theory, Ernest Gellner's *Saints of the Atlas* remains an important study of the sociopolitical functions of marabouts in segmentary societies (see esp. 78–139).

64. On the role of indispensability in brokerage, see A. P. Cohen and J. L. Comaroff, "The Management of Meaning: On the Phenomenology of Political Transactions," in Bruce Kapferer, ed., *Transaction and Meaning: Directions in the Anthropology of Exchange and Symbolic Behavior* (Philadelphia, 1976), esp. 88–95.

65. For a critical discussion of Weber's term, "qadi-justice," see Turner, *Weber and Islam,* 107–121.

66. The paradigm of the "opportunistic" North African marabout is based on the following models: (1) Alfred Bel's concept of the Muslim saint as an *homme fétiche,* detailed in the Introduction; (2) Clifford Geertz's trope of the "self-made warrior saint" (*Islam Observed,* 46–51); and (3) Ernest Gellner's polemical view of

"indulgent, socially acclimatised, illiterate, arbitration-oriented holy lineages" (*Saints of the Atlas,* 9, 140–154). Geertz's model is heavily influenced by the "utility maximization" perspective of transaction theory. For a critique of this perspective, see Bruce Kapferer, "Transactional Models Reconsidered," in idem, *Transaction and Meaning,* 1–24.

67. at-Tādilī, *at-Tashawwuf,* 209–211. See also at-Tamīmī, *al-Mustafad,* 71–72.

68. Cohen and Comaroff, "The Management of Meaning," 88.

69. Robert Paine, "Two Modes of Exchange and Mediation," in Kapferer, *Transaction and Meaning,* 74.

70. Ibid., 77.

71. See Jack Goody, *The Logic of Writing and the Organization of Society* (Cambridge, 1986), 144.

72. For the command to put contracts into writing, see Qur'ān, II (*al-Baqara*), 282. On the cultural effects of written contracts, see Goody, *The Logic of Writing,* 77–82, 144–147.

73. al-Bakrī, *al-Mughrib,* 306.

74. Ibid., 303. This mosque is also referred to as Ribāṭ ʿUqba. See Mohamed Kably, "Ḥawla baʿḍ muḍmarrāt 'at-Tashawwuf,'" in idem, ed., *Histoire et Hagiographie* (Rabat, 1989), 67.

75. at-Tādilī, *at-Tashawwuf,* 51–52, n. 36, 52. See also Ibn Ibrāhīm, *Al-Iʿlām,* vol. 9, 309–317.

76. See Ḥalima Ferḥat and Ḥamid Triki, "Kutub al-manāqib ka-mādda tāʾrīkhiyya," in Mohamed Kably, ed., *Histoire et Hagiographie* (Rabat, 1988), 57–60.

77. Muḥammad ibn Aḥmad al-ʿAbdī al-Kanūnī, *Āsafī wa mā ilayhā qadīman wa ḥadīthan* (Casablanca, n.d.), 22–24.

78. at-Tādilī, *at-Tashawwuf,* 86. *Tālaght,* in the Maṣmūda dialect of the High Atlas, signifies "red clay" or potter's clay (n. 11).

79. Ibid., 86.

80. Ibid., 86–87.

81. Ibid., 125, n. 126.

82. Ibid., 125–126.

83. Ibid., 125.

84. Extrapolating from times and itineraries supplied by the fourteenth-century Moroccan traveler Ibn Baṭṭūta, a trip from Fez to Alexandria would have taken about ninety days, barring storms at sea or bedouin raids. From Alexandria, one could travel up the Nile and take the Cairo Ḥajj caravan, which completed the journey to Mecca in forty to forty-five days. Allowing one month for visiting the holy places in Mecca and Medina, a pilgrim from the western Maghrib would have taken about nine months to complete the round trip. See Ross E. Dunn, *The Adventures of Ibn Battuta* (Berkeley and Los Angeles, 1989), 27–67.

85. Muḥammad ibn al-Muwaqqit, *As-Saʿāda al-abadiyya fīṭ-taʿrīf mashāhīr al-ḥaḍara al-Marrākushiyya* (Casablanca, 1936), vol. 2, 52.

86. at-Tādilī, *at-Tashawwuf,* 223.

87. This festival was held on Laylat al-Qadr, the "Night of Power," the night on which the Qur'an was believed to have been revealed.

88. at-Tādilī, *at-Tashawwuf,* 316. Munya's Arab ancestry can be deduced from the fact that her brother's son was nicknamed ʿAlī al-ʿArabī (317).

89. Ibn Ibrāhīm, *Al-Iʿlām,* vol. 7, 332.

90. at-Tādilī, *at-Tashawwuf,* 316. Halima Ferhat and Hamid Triki view at-Tādilī's use of the term *murīdīn* when speaking about Ribāṭ Shākir as evidence of a Moroccan movement analogous to Ibn Qasī's "Murīdiyya" political movement of al-Andalus. See idem, "Kutub al-manāqib," 57–58.

91. at-Tādilī, *at-Tashawwuf,* 316.

92. Ibid., 318.

93. Ibid., 350. Known today as "Sīdī Bū Brāhīm," the tomb of this saint can still be found in Addār (n. 89).

94. Ibid., 355. See also Ahmed Boucharb, *Dukkāla wa'l-istiʿmār al-Burtughālī ilā sanat ikhlāʾ Āsafī wa Azammūr (1481–1541)* (Casablanca, 1984), 90.

95. at-Tādilī, *at-Tashawwuf,* 350. Abū Ibrāhīm's states recall those of the Prophet Muḥammad as recounted in *sīra* (biographical) literature. See, for example, the discussion of prophetic revelation by Shams ad-Dīn Muḥammad ibn Yūsuf al-Kirmānī (d. 786/1384) in Izutsu, *God and Man in the Koran,* 166–168.

96. at-Tādilī, *at-Tashawwuf,* 350. The final sentence of Abū Ibrāhīm's statement is from Qurʾān, X (*Yūnus*), 62.

97. Ibid., 352–356.

98. Ibid., 355. The failure of the Berbers of Agawz to pay taxes to the Almohads reflected their opposition to the imposts used to finance Yaʿqūb al-Manṣūr's building programs and his prosecution of jihad in al-Andalus. See Ferhat, *Sabta,* 175–180.

99. Qurʾān, XL (*al-Muʾmin*), 28. This verse echoes a statement made by a member of Pharaoh's entourage when the latter sought to have the Prophet Moses executed. In modern times, Sayyid Quṭb (d. 1966) also used the Qur'anic account of the conflict between Moses and Pharaoh as a metaphor for the ethical imperatives of jihad and social reform. See Gilles Kepel, *Muslim Extremism in Egypt: The Prophet and Pharaoh* (Berkeley and Los Angeles, 1986), 43–67.

100. at-Tādilī, *at-Tashawwuf,* 355–356.

101. "Merging of horizons" is a translation of *Horizontverschmelzung,* a term adapted from phenomenology that Hans-Georg Gadamer uses to explain textual intersubjectivity. See David Couzens Hoy, "The Contingency of Universality: Critical Theory as Genealogical Hermeneutics," in idem and Thomas McCarthy, *Critical Theory* (Oxford and Cambridge, Massachusetts, 1994), 191–194.

102. Ibn Tūmart's companions included Maṣmūda, Ṣanhāja, and Zanāta Berbers, as well as some Berber-speaking "Arabs." This latter category included his successor as head of the Almohads, ʿAbd al-Mu'min ibn ʿAlī al-Gūmī, an Algerian Berberophone who claimed Qaysī descent. See Cornell, "Understanding is the Mother of Ability," 85–89. See also Abū Bakr ibn ʿAlī aṣ-Ṣanhājī al-Baydhaq,

Kitāb al-ansāb fī maʿrifat al-aṣḥāb, ʿAbd al-Wahhāb ibn Manṣūr, ed. (Rabat, 1971), 13–17, 28–32.

103. Ibn Ibrāhīm, *Al-Iʿlām,* vol. 8, 32. See also Michaux-Bellaire, "Les Confréries religieuses," 40. Abū'l-Faḍl al-Jawharī, the shaykh of ʿAbd al-Jalīl ibn Wayḥlān, was also the shaykh of the Andalusian Sufi and uṣūlī Aḥmad ibn Qarlumān aṭ-Ṭalamankī. For an introduction to the career and doctrines of an-Nūrī, see Annemarie Schimmel, "Abū'l-Ḥusayn al-Nūrī: 'Qibla of the Lights,'" in Leonard Lewisohn ed., *Classical Persian Sufism: From Its Origins to Rumi* (London, 1993), 59–64.

104. Ali Hassan Abdel-Kader, *The Life, Personality, and Writings of Al-Junayd* (London, 1976), 40–41. See also A. J. Arberry, trans., *Muslim Saints and Mystics: Episodes from the Tadhkirat al-Auliya' (Memorial of the Saints) by Farid al-Din Attar* (London, 1966), 222–230.

105. as-Sulamī, *Ṭabaqāt aṣ-ṣūfiyya,* 165. Hadith scholars consider this to be a weak tradition.

106. Ibid., 167–169.

107. Ibid., 169.

108. Ibn Ibrāhīm, *Al-Iʿlām,* vol. 8, 30.

109. Ibid.

110. Ibid., 31.

111. at-Tādilī, *at-Tashawwuf,* 149.

112. Ahmed Toufiq sees the Berber word *ilīskāwen* as referring to a pre-Islamic cult of the ram, which was revered in North Africa as a supernatural messenger or guide. See at-Tādilī, *at-Tashawwuf,* 131, n. 145.

113. *Mashanzāya,* the name of Abū Innūr's tribe, is an Arabization of the Berber *im.sh.n.zān,* which means "sellers" or "merchants." As late as the end of the fifteenth century, the town of al-Madīna al-Gharbiyya, in Mashanzāya territory, was an important center for the sale and export of the agricultural products of Dukkāla. See Ibid., 130, n. 141. See also Boucharb, *Dukkāla,* 81–82.

114. See Paine, "Two Modes of Exchange and Mediation," 79.

115. Ibn Qunfudh, *Uns al-faqīr,* 22.

116. at-Tādilī, *at-Tashawwuf,* 309.

117. Ibid., 187.

118. Ibn Ibrāhīm, *Al-Iʿlām,* vol. 1, 396.

119. at-Tādilī, *at-Tashawwuf,* 187.

120. Ibn Qunfudh, *Uns al-faqīr,* 22.

121. Ibn Ibrāhīm, *Al-Iʿlām,* vol. 1, 397.

122. Ibid., 396–397. See also at-Tādilī, *at-Tashawwuf,* 188.

123. Qur'ān, II (*al-Baqara*), 255 (*Āyat al-Kursī*).

124. Qur'ān, III (*Āl ʿImrān*), 18.

125. Qur'ān, CXII (*al-Ikhlāṣ*).

126. Ibn Ibrāhīm, *Al-Iʿlām,* vol. 1, 400.

127. See, for example, the sensationalized account of Ibn Yāsīn's educational methods in al-Bakrī, *al-Mughrib,* 319–323.

Chapter Three

1. Abū'l-ʿAbbās Aḥmad al-ʿAzafī, *Diʿāmat al-yaqīn fī ziʿ āmat al-muttaqīn,* Ahmed Toufiq, ed. (Rabat, 1989), 3.

2. See Kleinberg, *Prophets,* 21–39, 149–162.

3. Michel Foucault, *The Archaeology of Knowledge,* A. M. Sheridan Smith, trans. (New York, 1972), 38.

4. Ibid., 15 n. 2, 23–24.

5. The term "monographic biography" comes from Carl W. Ernst, *Eternal Garden: Mysticism, History, and Politics at a South Asian Sufi Center* (Albany, New York, 1992), 89.

6. Foucault, *The Archaeology of Knowledge,* 50–55. See also Paul Ricoeur, *Oneself As Another,* Kathleen Blamey, trans. (Chicago, 1992), 16–23.

7. An important exception is Ernst, *Eternal Garden,* 62–93.

8. See Heffernan, *Sacred Biography,* 3–37.

9. On the *imitatio Muhammadi,* see Schimmel, *And Muhammad,* 32. See also Frithjof Schuon, *Understanding Islam* (reprint, London, 1989), 91–94. This concept will be discussed further in Chapter Seven.

10. Heffernan, *Sacred Biography,* 34–37. On the influence of Aristotle's theories of rhetoric in Islamic philosophy, see Deborah L. Black, *Logic and Aristotle's* Rhetoric *and* Poetics *in Medieval Arabic Philosophy* (Leiden, 1990). The influence of Greco-Roman rhetorical models on Islamic biographical and historical literature is a subject that remains largely unexplored.

11. Jan Vansina, *Oral Tradition as History* (London and Nairobi, 1985), 27–32. My use of the word "tradition" in this book follows Vansina.

12. See, for example, Aviad Kleinberg's explication of Peter of Dacia's role in legitimizing the cult of Christina of Stommeln (d. 1312) in idem, *Prophets,* 71–98.

13. Kamali, *Principles of Islamic Jurisprudence,* 2.

14. In using the term "practitioners of *uṣūl al-fiqh,*" I am temporarily avoiding the word *faqīh.* This is because in Morocco, as in most of the Arabic-speaking world, a *faqīh* is often a mere imitator of juridical precedent (*muqallid*), and not necessarily a practitioner of the hermeneutical methodology that is stressed here.

15. See Th. Emile Homerin, "Ibn Taymiyya's *al-Ṣūfīyah wa-al-Fuqarāʾ,*" *Arabica* 32 (1985): 225–226, 233.

16. ʿAbd al-Ḥaqq ibn Ismāʿīl al-Bādisī, *Al-Maqṣad ash-sharīf wa'l-manzāʿ al-laṭīf fī't-taʿrīf bi-ṣulaḥāʾ ar-Rīf,* Saʿīd Aḥmad Aʿrāb, ed. (Rabat, 1982), 34, 69. On Ibn Sabʿīn's Hermetic mysticism, see Vincent J. Cornell, "The Way of the Axial Intellect: The Islamic Hermetism of Ibn Sabʿīn," *Journal of the Muhyiddīn Ibn ʿArabī Society* (forthcoming).

17. See, for example, Hodgson, *The Venture of Islam,* vol. 2, 218–219.

18. In using the term "courtroom," I do not mean to imply that trials and investigations of legal issues were carried out in a premodern version of the modern *maḥkama.* Rather, the rhetoric of dialectical disputation (*munāẓara*), long ac-

knowledged as an important aspect of pedagogy in the Islamic world, had more in common with modern legal disputation than with the present-day debate. For a description of this process in modern Qom, see Michael M. J. Fischer, *Iran: From Religious Dispute to Revolution* (Cambridge, 1980), 61–76.

19. For an overview of the life and works of al-ʿAzafī, see Benchekroun, *La Vie intellectuelle,* 99–108.

20. al-ʿAzafī's expertise in oral tradition is apparent in two of his less-famous works: *Minhāj ar-rusūkh ilā ʿilm an-nāsikh wa'l-mansūkh,* an examination of the concept of abrogation in Qur'an and hadith, and *Ithbāt mā lā minhu budd li-murīd al-wuqūf ʿalā ḥaqīqat ad-dīnār wa'd-dirham wa'ṣ-ṣāʿ wa'l-mudd,* a discussion of traditions on the weights of coins and solid measures. See Benchekroun, *La Vie intellectuelle,* 104–106.

21. Ibid., 103–104. *Ad-Durr al-munaẓẓam* has been edited by Fatima al-Yazidi as part of an unpublished doctoral dissertation at Université Mohammed V, Rabat (1987).

22. See, for example, al-Kattānī, *Salwat al-anfās,* vol. 1, 172; at-Tādilī, *at-Tashawwuf,* 213; ibid., Adolphe Faure, ed. (Rabat, 1958), 195; and at-Tamīmī, *al-Mustafād,* 7. Although in previous publications I have used the "Abū Yaʿzā" form suggested by Faure, I now prefer Ahmed Toufiq's "Abū Yiʿzzā," since it follows the most likely vocalization of the saint's name in Berber.

23. at-Tamīmī, *al-Mustafād,* 8.

24. See, for example, the biography of Abū Ḥafṣ ʿUmar al-Ḥuṣaynī in Muḥammad ibn ʿAskar al-Ḥasanī ash-Shafshāwanī (d. 986/1578), *Dawḥat an-nāshir li-maḥāsin man kāna bi'l-Maghrib min mashā'ikh al-qarn al-ʿāshir,* Muḥammad Ḥajjī, ed. (Rabat, 1977), 101.

25. A jurist and ascetic from Béja in al-Andalus, this Sufi lived in Seville and was an acquaintance of Ibn al-ʿArabī. See R. W. J. Austin, trans., *Sufis of Andalusia: The* Rūḥ al-quds *and* al-Durrat al-fākhirah *of Ibn ʿArabī* (Berkeley and Los Angeles, 1977), 136.

26. at-Tādilī, *at-Tashawwuf,* 215–216.

27. at-Tamīmī, *al-Mustafād,* 10.

28. Aḥmad ibn Abī'l-Qāsim aṣ-Ṣūmaʿī al-Harwī at-Tādilī, *Al-Muʿazzā fī manāqib Abī Yiʿzzā* (Rabat, BG ms. 299 K), 3.

29. at-Tādilī, *at-Tashawwuf,* 217.

30. aṣ-Ṣūmaʿī, *Al-Muʿazzā,* 3r.

31. Ibid. On the healing properties of Abū Yiʿzzā's bread, see at-Tamīmī, *al-Mustafād,* 11–12.

32. at-Tādilī, *at-Tashawwuf,* 218–219.

33. Arberry, *Muslim Saints and Mystics,* 222. A more plausible explanation for the derivation of an-Nūrī's nickname is that he was inspired by the "light" of divine knowledge. On the symbology of light in the Hermetic tradition, see Garth Fowden, *The Egyptian Hermes: A Historical Approach to the Late Pagan Mind* (Princeton, 1993), 104–115.

34. al-Kattānī, *Salwat al-anfās,* vol. 1, 172–174. The earliest confirmation of this miracle is by Ibn al-ʿArabī in *Al-Futūḥāt al-makkiyya* (The Meccan revelations). See Chodkiewicz, *Le Sceau des saints,* 95–96.

35. at-Tādilī, *at-Tashawwuf,* 213 n. 475.

36. See ʿAlī ibn ʿUthmān al-Jullābī al-Hujwīrī (d. 465/1072–3), *The Kashf al-Maḥjūb: The Oldest Persian Treatise on Sufism,* R. A. Nicholson, trans. (reprint, London, 1976), 189–190.

37. at-Tamīmī, *al-Mustafād,* 14–16. In *Le Sceau des saints* (106), Michel Chodkiewicz, relying uncritically on Ibn al-ʿArabī's interpretation of Abu Yiʿzzā's sainthood, portrays the Berber saint as a "veiled" *walī Allāh.* The testimony of *al-Mustafād,* however, makes it clear that Abū Yiʿzzā was "veiled" only from those who *chose* not to see him.

38. al-Kattānī, *Salwat al-anfās,* vol. 1, 174.

39. The political authority of Abū Shuʿayb was openly acknowledged by Abū Yiʿzzā, who exclaimed, upon hearing of his master's death: *Yimmūt umghār Abū Shuʿayb!* (Ber. "The leader Abū Shuʿayb is dead!"). See al-ʿAzafī, *Diʿāmat al-yaqīn,* 45.

40. Abū'l-ʿAlī ibn as-Sammāk (fl. 783/1381), *Al-Ḥulal al-mawshiyya fī dhikr al-akhbār al-Marrākushiyya,* Suhayl Zakkār and ʿAbd al-Qādir Zamāma, eds. (Casablanca, 1979), 146–147. The Almohads justified their contravention of the Islamic prohibition against making slaves of fellow Muslims by calling the Ṣanhāja Azammūr unbelievers for not accepting the divinely ordained mission of Ibn Tūmart. According to this interpretation, the women and children of their enemies could be sold as spoils of war (Ar. *ghanīma*).

41. aṣ-Ṣūmaʿī, *Al-Muʿazzā,* 3r. See also at-Tamīmī, *al-Mustafād,* 11.

42. Ibid., 4v–4r. Abū Yiʿzzā's political quietism is also noted by al-ʿAzafī. See idem, *Diʿāmat al-yaqīn,* 42.

43. This rābiṭa was supervised by Abū Yiʿzzā's Andalusian disciple Abū Madyan. See Cornell, *The Way of Abū Madyan,* 9–10.

44. al-Kattānī, *Salwat al-anfās,* vol. 1, 174.

45. Michaux-Bellaire, "Les Confréries religieuses," 44.

46. For a discussion of the symbolism of mountain and forest in the modern High Atlas, see Hammoudi, *The Victim and Its Masks,* 45–46.

47. See the introductory section to al-ʿAzafī, *Diʿāmat al-yaqīn,* 1–30. Al-ʿAzafī's negative image of the Banū Marīn, which differs greatly from that of official historiography, is supported by Mohamed Kably, who characterizes Marinid society as a semifeudal spoils system. See Kably, *Société, pouvoir et religion,* 3–15.

48. My translation of *muttaqīn* as "God-conscious" follows Muhammad Asad (*The Message of the Qurʾān* [Gibraltar, 1984], 3), who points out that the usual translation of the term as "God-fearing" does not convey the full sense of the concept of *taqwā* in Arabic.

49. al-ʿAzafī, *Diʿāmat al-yaqīn,* 3.

50. Ibid.

51. See Kamali, *Principles of Islamic Jurisprudence,* 48–61, for a discussion of

the truth-value of narratives in Islamic law. From the point of view of *fiqh,* the Qur'an is an unimpeachable source because the entirety of its text was transmitted via *tawātur.*

52. This term comes from Michael Morony of UCLA (personal communication), who uses it as a corrective for Hodgson's "Sharīʿa-mindedness." Morony's hypothesis, following Duri (*The Rise of Historical Writing,* 94, 111–120), is that the transmission of knowledge in Middle Period Islamdom, including the *rijāl* and *manāqib* genres of Moroccan sacred biography, was influenced by the hadith-oriented approach of the Medinan school of historiography.

53. For an anthropological study of Moroccan juridical practice in a modern context, see Lawrence Rosen, *The Anthropology of Justice: Law as Culture in Islamic Society* (Cambridge, 1989), esp. 20–57.

54. Al-ʿAzafī's concept of the discontinuity of tradition anticipates Michel Foucault's notion of the discontinuity of texts. See Foucault, *The Archaeology of Knowledge,* 6–11.

55. al-ʿAzafī, *Diʿāmat al-yaqīn,* 4.

56. Ibid., 5.

57. Ibid., 6–22. Al-ʿAzafī's inclusion of Ibn Abī Zayd al-Qayrawānī among the supporters of *karāmāt* is curious, since the latter did not believe in nonprophetic miracles. See Fierro, "The Polemic About the *Karāmāt al-Awliyāʾ*, 238.

58. al-ʿAzafī, *Diʿāmat al-yaqīn,* 23.

59. Ibid.

60. Ibid., 25–26.

61. On Abū Ṣabr Ayyūb al-Fihrī, see at-Tādilī, *at-Tashawwuf,* 415–416, and Ferhat, *Sabta,* 404–405.

62. al-ʿAzafī, *Diʿāmat al-yaqīn,* 38–39.

63. Ibid., 40–42.

64. For many generations, the custodianship of Abū Yiʿzzā's tomb was under the control of the Gnāwa, a hereditary confraternity of sub-Saharan healers and *jinn* devotees. On the importance of "Gnāwī" *jinn* in Moroccan healing rites, see Crapanzano, *The Hamadsha,* 140–149, and Dermenghem, *Le Culte des saints,* 285. In Tashelhit Berber, *gnawya* refers to the "African" red pepper known elsewhere in Morocco as *sūdāniyya,* while *ag.naw* signifies incomprehension: either a deaf-mute, or someone who speaks a dialect other than Tashelhit. Hatt, *Tashelhit-English Dictionary,* 8, 49.

65. On the Maṣmūda prohibition against marrying "Abyssinians," see at-Tādilī, *at-Tashawwuf,* 328, and Cornell, *The Way of Abū Madyan,* 14.

66. See, for example, at-Tādilī's notices in *at-Tashawwuf* on Abū Jabal Yaʿlā of Fez (101–105); Khamīs ibn Abī Zarg ar-Ragrāgī (113); Rayḥān al-Aswad as-Sabtī (158–159); and Mīmūn ibn Tīgrt (sic.) al-Ūrīkī (193).

67. Ibid., 214–215. For Abū Madyan's answer to these objections on behalf of Abū Yiʿzzā, see Cornell, *The Way of Abū Madyan,* 9–10.

68. al-ʿAzafī, *Diʿāmat al-yaqīn,* 53–54. Ibn Ṣanādīd was the commander of the Andalusian division of the Almohad army under ʿAbd al-Muʾmin (Ibid., n. 50).

69. See Abū Muḥammad ʿAbd al-Ḥaqq ibn ʿAṭiyya al-Gharnaṭī, *Al-Muḥarrar al-wajīz fī tafsīr al-kitāb al-ʿazīz,* al-Majlis al-ʿIlmī bi-Fās, ed. (Rabat, 1975–84).

70. al-ʿAzafī, *Diʿāmat al-yaqīn,* 66–67.

71. Ibid., 66.

72. Ibid., 42, 67. Ibn al-ʿArabī (a contemporary of al-ʿAzafī) discusses the "principial light" (*an-nūr al-aṣlī*) of the saints in his *Risālat al-anwār.* In this work, he also traces the origin of the "science of light" (*ʿilm an-nūr*) to al-Khiḍr. See below and Chodkiewicz, *Le Sceau des saints,* 71–72.

73. at-Tādilī, *at-Tashawwuf,* 215.

74. Ibn Ḥanbal, *Sunan* (5), 4, 5. See also Ibn Mājjah, *Sunan,* "Kitāb az-Zakāt," 1, 37. This hadith is also reproduced in *Diʿāmat al-yaqīn,* 91.

75. See, for example, al-Bukhārī, *Ṣaḥīḥ,* "Kitāb al-ʿilm," 15.

76. Perhaps because of Abū Yiʿzzā's close identification with the Muḥammadan paradigm, the folkloric tradition of the Maghrib has long associated him with ʿAbd al-Qādir al-Jīlānī (d. 563/1166), who claimed descent from the Prophet on both his mother's and his father's side. By the nineteenth century, the legend linking Abū Yiʿzzā to al-Jīlānī was so well-established that the normally careful biographer al-Kattānī was moved to report without comment an obviously spurious tradition in which the famous shaykh of Baghdad tells his followers: "There is an Abyssinian (*ḥabashī*) slave in the Maghrib, whose name is Āl an-Nūr and whose *kunya* is Abū Yaʿzā. He occupies a great station, which only a few of the First and the Last have attained" (*Salwat al-anfās,* vol. 1, 173). Similar traditions have also linked Abū Yiʿzzā's disciple Abū Madyan with ʿAbd al-Qādir al-Jīlānī. See Cornell, *The Way of Abū Madyan,* 10–11.

77. For a discussion of the concept of *ʿilm ladunnī* as applied to the Prophet Muḥammad, see Schimmel, *And Muḥammad,* 71–74.

78. On Ibn al-ʿArabī's concept of *ummiyya,* which Chodkiewicz defines as "spiritual illiteracy," see Michel Chodkiewicz, *An Ocean Without Shore: Ibn Arabi, the Book, and the Law* (Albany, New York, 1993), 31–33.

79. al-ʿAzafī, *Diʿāmat al-Yaqīn,* 78.

80. Ibid., 79.

81. Al-ʿAzafī's opinions are atypical for an uṣūlī scholar in that they contradict one of the most important tenets of *uṣūl al-fiqh*—namely, the nearly exclusive reliance on written traditions as precedents for legal reasoning.

82. See al-Bukhārī, *Ṣaḥīḥ,* "Kitāb al-ʿilm," (1) 27. The *isnād* of this hadith includes Ibn ʿAbbās and Ubayy ibn Kaʿb, both of whom were known to have transmitted traditions from Jewish sources. The youth who accompanies Moses to the "confluence of two seas" in the Qur'anic account is Joshua (Yushaʿa ibn Nūn). See also al-Tādilī, *at-Tashawwuf,* 46 n. 5.

83. al-ʿAzafī, *Diʿāmat al-yaqīn,* 82–83. One account even goes so far as to claim that al-Khiḍr's father was Persian and his mother Roman.

84. This point is clearly expressed in the hadith cited in n. 82 above, in which al-Khiḍr tells Moses: "Verily, I act on knowledge from the knowledge of God,

which He has made known to me but has not made known to you, while you act on knowledge that He has made known to you but has not taught to me."

85. al-ʿAzafī, *Diʿāmat al-yaqīn,* 93.

86. See Kleinberg, *Prophets,* 134–135.

87. at-Tādilī, *at-Tashawwuf,* 56–58.

88. Adolphe Faure, "Abū'l-ʿAbbās as-Sabtī (524–601/1130–1204), la justice et la charité," *Hespéris* 43(2)(1956): 450. My translation.

89. See Kleinberg, *Prophets,* 126–148.

90. This text can be found under its proper title in pp. 451–477 of the Ahmed Toufiq edition of *at-Tashawwuf.* In what follows, I will cite page references from the biography of as-Sabtī in al-ʿAbbās ibn Ibrāhīm's *Al-Iʿlām,* vol. 1, which provided the original text of *Akhbār Abī'l-ʿAbbās as-Sabtī* in the Toufiq edition.

91. This term comes from Serge Gagnon, *Man and His Past: The Nature and Role of Historiography* (Montreal, 1982), 36.

92. Ibn Ibrāhīm, *Al-Iʿlām,* vol. 1, 237.

93. Ibid., 286.

94. as-Sulamī, *Ṭabaqāt aṣ-ṣūfiyya,* 460.

95. Ibid.

96. See Taeschner, "As-Sulamī's Kitāb al-Futuwwa," 348.

97. Ibn al-Muwaqqit, *As-Saʿāda al-abadiyya,* vol. 2, 5.

98. Ibid., 7.

99. Ibid., 5.

100. Ibn Ibrāhīm, *Al-Iʿlām,* vol. 1, 242. See also a similar story related by Abū Madyan in Cornell, *The Way of Abū Madyan,* 2–3.

101. Ibn al-Muwaqqit, *As-Saʿāda al-abadiyya,* vol. 2, 4.

102. See also *Sunan* ad-Dārimī, "Kitāb as-siyar," 75, where the number of sects is given as 73.

103. Ibn Ibrāhīm, *Al-Iʿlām,* vol. 1, 242–243.

104. Ibid., 243–244.

105. Ibid., 238. See also Ferhat, *Sabta,* 172–173.

106. Ibn Ibrāhīm, *Al-Iʿlām,* 239. Whipping those who neglected to pray, a common practice in the early decades of Almohad rule, was the job of the Ḥizb Allah (Party of God), a futuwwa organization that assisted Almohad officials in applying Ibn Tūmart's rules of *ḥisba,* correction of deviant behavior. The region of Ajdīr, like other Berber areas in the Far Maghrib, fell under Almohad control before the cities of Morocco.

107. Ibid., 282–283.

108. Ibid., 36.

109. Ibid., 237.

110. Ibid., 282.

111. Ibid., 292.

112. Ibid., 294.

113. Ibid., 286–287.

114. Nearly three and a half centuries after as-Sabtī's death a similar method of "spiritual extortion" would be used by the ʿIsāwī Sufi Muḥammad Abū'r-Ruwayyin al-Miknāsī (d. after 950/1543). See Ibn ʿAskar, *Dawḥat an-nāshir,* 79–81.

115. Ibn Ibrāhīm, *Al-Iʿlām,* vol. 1, 262.

116. Ibid., 272.

117. Ibid., 265–266.

118. For a discussion of *qaḍāʾ* and *qadar* in Islamic theology, see W. Montgomery Watt, *The Formative Period of Islamic Thought* (Edinburgh, 1973), 82–118.

119. See Addas, *Ibn ʿArabī,* 213–214.

120. Izutsu, *Sufism and Taoism,* 176.

121. Ibid., 177–178.

122. Ibn Ibrāhīm, *Al-Iʿlām,* vol. 1, 252.

123. Thanks are due to Dr. Hassan ud-Din Hashimi of Gardena, California, for information on this aphorism.

124. Ibn Ibrāhīm, *Al-Iʿlām,* vol. 1, 238.

125. See Fowden, *The Egyptian Hermes,* 75–78, who notes that the concept of *sympathaeia* was central to Hermetic ritual.

126. Faure, "Abū'l-ʿAbbās as-Sabtī," 454.

127. Ambrosio Huici Miranda, *Historia política del imperio Almohade* (Tetuan, 1956), vol. 1, 338–340.

128. Ibn al-Muwaqqit, *As-Saʿāda al-abadiyya,* vol. 2, 7.

129. Ibid., 8.

130. Ibn Ibrāhīm, *Al-Iʿlām,* vol. 1, 284–285.

Chapter Four

1. See, for example, Qurʾān III (*Āl ʿImrān*), 184 and LI (*adh-Dhāriyāt*), 52.

2. See, for example, the notices on "unknown" (*majhūl,* fem. *majhūla*) saints in at-Tādilī, *at-Tashawwuf,* 94, 129–130, 139, 142–144, 159–160, 173–174, 176–177, 195–196, 203–205, 230, 265–266, 305, 330, 385–386, 423, 442–443, 445–446.

3. Quoted in Chodkiewicz, *Le Sceau des saints,* 53.

4. See, for example, Charles-André Julien's discussion of Almohad civilization in idem, *Histoire de l'Afrique du Nord* (reprint, Paris, 1978), 120–131.

5. Muḥammad al-Manūnī, *Al-ʿUlūm wa'l-ādāb wa'l-funūn ʿalā ʿahd al-Muwaḥḥidīn* (Rabat, 1977), 20–25.

6. The women of the caliphal household were particularly noted for their high level of literacy. See Ibid., 27–28, 33–34.

7. These works appear to have been lost. See Muḥammad ar-Rashīd Mūlīn, *ʿAṣr al-Manṣūr al-Muwaḥḥidī* (Rabat, n.d.), 168.

8. Ibid., 166.

9. al-Manūnī, *Al-ʿUlūm,* 58.

10. Ibid., 44.

11. In the Mashriq the hagiographical anthology was called *tadhkīrat al-awliyāʾ* (recollection of the saints) or *sīrat al-awliyāʾ* (biography of the saints). See Ernst, *Eternal Garden,* 84–93.

12. More than fifty entries in *at-Tashawwuf* illustrate at-Tādilī's critical approach to oral tradition. See Ahmed Toufiq's discussion of at-Tādilī's methodology in his Introduction to *at-Tashawwuf,* 13.

13. On this term, see Heffernan, *Sacred Biography,* 123–184.

14. Ibid., 123–132.

15. The desire to create a "city of God" on earth does not indicate, as Lamin Sanneh seems to believe, that Muslims have a "rather earthy understanding of virtue" or that the fulfillment of sainthood is in "the extreme of social eminence (*jāh*) and worldly acclaim." See idem, "Saints and Virtue in African Islam: An Historical Approach," in John Stratton Hawley, ed., *Saints and Virtues* (Berkeley and Los Angeles, 1987), 127–132.

16. At-Tamīmī's position as the founder of the *rijāl* tradition of hagiography in the western Maghrib has recently been challenged by Halima Ferhat, who notes the existence of an earlier Andalusian hagiography entitled *As-Sirr al-maṣūn fī mā ukrima bihi al-mukhliṣūn.* Although this work was composed a full generation before at-Tamīmī's *al-Mustafād,* the fact that it is more of a travel memoir (*riḥla*) than a true hagiographical anthology makes it difficult to assess its importance to the Moroccan *rijāl* tradition. See Halima Ferhat, "*As-Sirr al-Maṣūn* de Ṭāhir aṣ-Ṣadafī: un Itinéraire mystique au XIIe siècle," *Al-Qanṭara* 16 (2)(1995): 273–288.

17. For a general description of at-Tamīmī's work, see Mohammed Bencherifa, "Ḥawla Kitāb al-mustafād," *Daʿwat al-ḥaqq* 259: 26–31.

18. at-Tamīmī, *al-Mustafād,* 18.

19. For a discussion of this work and its author, see Benchekroun, *La Vie intellectuelle,* 195–200.

20. al-Bādisī, *Al-Maqṣad,* 16.

21. Ibid., 13–14.

22. Thanks are due to my student Scott Kugle for coining this term.

23. See Charles Tilly, "Computing History," in idem, *As Sociology Meets History* (New York, 1981), 53–83.

24. An "Arab" is defined in this survey as a person for whom recognizably Berber names in a given lineage disappear three or more generations prior to the subject, except in cases where tribal affiliation or residence indicates otherwise. Identifying ethnicity for this period of Moroccan history is easier than it is for later centuries because the bestowal of Arabo-Islamic names on Berber children had not yet become a universal practice. For example, Abū Ibrāhīm u-Gmāten ar-Ragrāgī (discussed in Chapter Two) is classified as a Berber, both because of his father's name (Gmāten) and because of his tribal affiliation (Ragrāgī). Similarly, Arabs can also be recognized by a well-known *nisba,* such as al-Khazrajī, al-Lakhmī, or al-Umawī. The scholar and legist Abū ʿImrān al-Fāsī, however, is considered "Arab," even though he traced his ancestry to the Berber Ghafjūma tribe, because his family's long residence in the city of Fez implied Arab enculturation.

25. The conversion of Berbers in the Far Maghrib did not necessarily include the adoption of Arabic or Islamic names, as Richard Bulliet has postulated for Middle Period Iran. Through the end of the Almohad period, it was common for

fully Islamized Berbers to retain names in their own language, such as Waggāg ibn Zallū al-Lamṭī (see Chapter Two). This problematizes Bulliet's proposed conversion curve for Muslim Spain, which fails to account for cultural differences in the ethnically heterogeneous population of al-Andalus. The findings presented here do agree, however, with Bulliet's conclusion that the Almohad era marked a watershed in the overall Islamization of the Maghrib—so long as "Islamization" is not equated with conversion. See Richard W. Bulliet, *Conversion to Islam in the Medieval Period: An Essay in Quantitative History* (Cambridge, 1979), 114–127.

26. It is significant that the leaders of nativist (*shuʿūbī*) movements in the Maghrib were fully aware of the Arab cultural content of hadith. In a treatise entitled *Aʿazz ma yuṭlab,* the Almohad leader Ibn Tūmart advocates relying only on *mutawātir* hadith when interpreting the Sharīʿa. If implemented, this restricted view of hadith would have given greater legitimacy to local, and hence non-Arab, custom. See Cornell, "Understanding Is the Mother of Ability," 91–92. See also Ignaz Goldziher, "Ibn Toumert et la théologie de l'Islam dans le Maghreb au XIe siècle," in idem, *Le Livre de Mohammed Ibn Toumert* (Algiers, 1903), 5–6.

27. This figure is almost identical to the 56.4% arrived at by ʿAbd al-Laṭīf ash-Shādhilī, who analyzed 525 hagiographical notices from fifteenth- through seventeenth-century Morocco. Although a clear majority in both samples have urban origins, ash-Shādhilī refuses to abandon the Bel thesis and continues to regard Moroccan sainthood as a rural phenomenon. He also implies that there is a correlation between the number of saints in a particular region and that region's percentage of the total Moroccan population. Such an assertion is impossible to corroborate statistically. See idem, *At-Taṣawwuf wa'l-mujtamaʿ*, 64–69.

28. See Makdisi, *The Rise of Colleges,* 9–34.

29. See Gellner, *Saints of the Atlas,* 5–12.

30. The category of "education abroad" was defined in this survey as including Andalusians studying in Morocco, residents of Morocco studying in al-Andalus, and residents of both regions studying in Ifrīqīya and beyond.

31. On the role of travel in the education of scholars in al-Andalus, see Sam I. Gellens, "The Search for Knowledge in Medieval Muslim Societies: A Comparative Approach," in Dale F. Eickelman and James Piscatori, eds., *Muslim Travelers: Pilgrimage, Migration, and the Religious Imagination* (Berkeley and Los Angeles, 1990), 59–64.

32. These findings refute Mohammed Arkoun's contention that "the ready-made clientele for mystics is clearly an impoverished urban milieu consisting of the members of marginal social categories and those who cannot rise into the privilege of the leisured classes of merchants, landowners, and 'intellectuals' associated with the exercise of power or protected by patrons." See idem, *Rethinking Islam,* 82. See also Gilsenan, *Recognizing Islam,* 115. They are more in line with the conclusions of Halima Ferhat, who links "popular" sainthood to the urban crafts and implies that Sufis functioned as unofficial ulama for the lower classes of urban society. See idem, *Sabta,* 317–320.

33. at-Tādilī, *at-Tashawwuf,* 227–230.

34. On the relationship between Sufi orders and occupational groups (*ḥirfa*, pl. *ḥiraf*) in precolonial Morocco, see Clifford Geertz, "Suq: The Bazaar Economy in Sefrou," in idem, Hildred Geertz, and Lawrence Rosen, *Meaning and Order in Moroccan Society* (Cambridge, 1979), 154–164.

35. For a modern discussion of the relationship between social pragmatism and Islamic thought, see 'Alija 'Ali Izetbegovic, *Islam Between East and West* (Indianapolis, 1993), 278–280.

36. ʿAbd al-Wāḥid al-Marrākushī (d. after 631/1233–4), *Al-Muʿjib fī talkhīṣ akhbār al-Maghrib,* Mamdūḥ Ḥaqqī, ed. (Casablanca, 1978), 400–401. Books that were ordered burned by Yaʿqūb al-Manṣūr included the *Mudawwana* of Saḥnūn, as well as the *Nawādir* and *Risāla* of Ibn Abī Zayd al-Qayrawānī.

37. See Turner, *Dramas, Fields, and Metaphors,* 292–294.

38. This argument owes an obvious debt to Pierre Bourdieu's concept of "symbolic capital." See idem, *Outline of a Theory of Practice,* Richard Nice, trans. (Cambridge, 1979), 179–183.

39. Miracles which impact the physical environment are the only *karāmāt* given serious attention by ʿAbd al-Laṭīf ash-Shādhilī, who finds it necessary to dismiss them with the argument that they reflect the universal human desire to solve intractable difficulties. This secularist bias prevents ash-Shādhilī from differentiating types of miracles and from even noticing epistemological miracles, which remained important throughout Moroccan history. See idem, *At-Taṣawwuf wa'l-mujtamaʿ*, 111–125.

40. For a transaction analysis of a modern Moroccan market, see Geertz, "Suq: The Bazaar Economy," 197–233.

41. Bourdieu asserts that symbolic capital, "which in the form of the prestige and renown attached to a family and a name is readily convertible back into economic capital, is perhaps *the most valuable form of accumulation*" in societies in which climatic and technological limitations compel collective activity. See idem, *Outline of a Theory of Practice,* 179.

42. Notices about women occur only six times in the three anthologies (four subjects being named and two unnamed), comprising a mere 1.9% of the notices. Among the five women whose place of origin is mentioned, four hailed from the Berber regions of Dukkāla and Haskūra, while the fifth was an immigrant from al-Andalus. None of the six came from the major urban centers where Arabo-Islamic culture predominated. These data, sparse as they may be, seem to confirm the contention made in Chapter Two that the high level of female participation at the Maṣmūda Berber Sufi center of Ribāṭ Shākir was unique for the region.

43. See S. D. Goitein, "The Mentality of the Middle Class in Medieval Islam," in idem, *Studies in Islamic History and Institutions* (Leiden, 1968), 249.

44. Qurʾān VI (*al-Anʿām*), 16.

Chapter Five

1. See, for example, Jamil M. Abun-Nasr, *A History of the Maghrib in the Islamic Period* (Cambridge, 1987), 102.

2. Kably, *Société, pouvoir et religion,* 222. A similar approach to premodern state building can be found in Charles Tilly, "War Making and State Making as Organized Crime," in Peter Evans, Dietrich Rueschemeyer, and Theda Skocpol, *Bringing the State Back In* (Cambridge, 1985), 169–191.

3. Kably, *Société, pouvoir et religion,* 179. Fees and services exacted by the Marinids from their subjects included the right of lodging (*inzāl*), the "welcoming" of Marinid elites on their travels (*ḍiyāfa*), the arbitrary "leasing" of livestock (Mor. Ar. *burnūs*), a ten-percent levy for each "horizon" crossed by itinerant Jewish merchants (Mor. Ar. *āfāq*), and the outright expropriation of goods (Mor. Ar. *khṭīya*). Ibid., 224–225.

4. Ibid., 223. See also Bel, *La Religion musulmane,* 361–362; Abun-Nasr, *A History of the Maghrib,* 102; and Laroui, *The History of the Maghrib,* 212–215, who adds an interesting wrinkle by blaming Marinid decadence on the influence of al-Andalus.

5. Kably, *Société, pouvoir et religion,* 219–220.

6. This term comes from Muḥammad al-Manūni, "Madkhal ilā taʾrīkh al-fikr al-Islāmī fī'l-ʿaṣr al-Marīnī al-awwal," in idem, *Waraqāt ʿan al-ḥaḍāra al-Maghribiyya fī ʿaṣr Banī Marīn* (Rabat, 1979), 192–211.

7. On the Mongol conquest of Baghdad, see ʿAlāʾ ad-Dīn ʿAṭāʾ Malik al-Juwaynī (d. 682/1283), *Taʾrīkh-i jahān-gushā,* in Bertold Spuler, *History of the Mongols* (New York, 1988), 115–120.

8. Kably, *Société, pouvoir et religion,* 55–57.

9. Abū ʿAbdallāh Muḥammad al-ʿAbdarī, *Riḥlat al-ʿAbdarī,* Muḥammad al-Fāsī, ed. (Rabat, 1968), 9, 11, 26–27, 64. On the literary importance of al-ʿAbdarī and his *riḥla,* see Benchekroun, *La Vie intellectuelle,* 117–125.

10. Kably, *Société, pouvoir et religion,* 10–12.

11. al-Manūnī, "Madkhal," 196–197.

12. Ibid., 196.

13. al-Manūnī, "At-Tayyārāt al-fikriyya," 246–247. Laxity in regard to sexual impurity (*najāsa*) is a common accusation in Muslim polemics against heterodoxy.

14. For an overview of Shiʿite revolts in Muslim Spain, see the relevant sections in Maria Isabel Fierro Bello, *La Heterodoxia en el-Andalus durante el periodo Umayya* (Madrid, 1987) and M. A. Makki, "At-Tashayyuʿ fī'l-Andalus," *Revista del Instituto Egipcio de Estudios Islámicos* (Madrid, 1954), 93–149.

15. Aḥmad ibn Ibrāhīm al-Qashtālī (d. early eighth/fourteenth century), *Tuḥfat al-mughtarib bi-bilād al-Maghrib li-man lahu min al-ikhwān fī karāmāt ash-shaykh Abī Marwān,* Fernando de la Granja, ed. (Madrid, 1974), 81–82.

16. al-Bādisī, *Al-Maqṣad,* 115.

17. Kably downplays the pro-Maliki stance of the Marinids, interpreting this as merely the latters' way of distinguishing themselves from their Hafsid rivals in Tunis. See idem, *Société, pouvoir et religion,* 279.

18. al-Manūnī, "ʿAlāqāt al-Maghrib bi'sh-sharq fī'l-ʿaṣr al-Marīnī al-awwal," in idem, *Waraqāt,* 130. According to Kably, these first Marinid contacts with the

Mamluks were meant to forestall an Egyptian takeover of the trans-Saharan trade routes. See idem, *Société, pouvoir et religion,* 99.

19. al-Manūnī, "ʿAlāqāt," 131–132.

20. Ibid., 132–133. On the pro-sharifian policy of the Marinids see Kably, *Société, pouvoir et religion,* 285–302.

21. al-Manūnī, "Madkhal," 199.

22. On Ibn al-Bannāʾ and his works, see Benchekroun, *La Vie intellectuelle,* 178–185.

23. al-Manūnī, "Madkhal," 200–201.

24. My view of the Moroccan madrasa as an institution in the service of orthodoxies-in-the-making is in general agreement with that of Fernando Mediano, who focuses on the monopolization of the Moroccan educational system by major families of ulama (see idem, *Familias de Fez (SS. XV–XVII)* [Madrid, 1995], 31–71). It differs markedly, however, from the opinions of Michael Chamberlain and Jonathan Berkey, who downplay (Berkey) or even negate (Chamberlain) the madrasa's educational functions. See Jonathan Berkey, *The Transmission of Knowledge in Medieval Cairo: A Social History of Islamic Education* (Princeton, 1992), 44–94; and Chamberlain, *Knowledge and Social Practice,* 69–90.

25. For an excellent architectural study of a Marinid madrasa, see Hamid Triki and Alain Dovifat, *Medersa de Marrakech* (Paris, 1990).

26. Benchekroun, *La Vie intellectuelle,* 67. See also Aziz al-Azmeh's discussion of Ibn Khaldūn's innovation of *uṣūl at-taʾrīkh* (science of the sources of history) in idem, *Ibn Khaldun* (London and New York, 1982), 153–155.

27. Benchekroun, *La Vie intellectuelle,* 65. See also Mediano, *Familias de Fez,* 43.

28. Muḥammad ibn Marzūq at-Tilimsānī, *Al-Musnad aṣ-ṣaḥīḥ al-ḥasan fī maʾāthir wa maḥāsin mawlānā Abīʾl-Ḥasan,* María-Jesus Viguera, ed. (Algiers, 1981), 307–309. On Ibn Marzūq and his works, see the bibliographical discussion in Benchekroun, *La Vie intellectuelle,* 283–293.

29. Ibn Marzūq mentions two students of Ibn Taymiyya, the brothers Abū Zayd ʿAbd ar-Raḥmān and Abū Mūsā ʿIsā al-Burashkī, who served as advisers to the Marinid sultan Abūʾl-Ḥasan. See idem, *Al-Musnad,* 265–266.

30. Benchekroun, *La Vie intellectuelle,* 488.

31. al-Wansharīsī, *Al-Miʿyār,* vol. 11, 30–31. See also Homerin, "Ibn Taymiyya's *al-Ṣūfīya,*" 225, 226, 233.

32. Abūʾl-Ḥasan ʿAlī ibn Abī Zarʿ al-Fāsī (fl. 726/1326), *Al-Anīs al-muṭrib bi-rawḍ al-qirṭās fī akhbār mulūk al-Maghrib wa tāʾrīkh madīnat Fās* (Rabat, 1973), 297.

33. al-Bādisī, *Al-Maqṣad,* 92.

34. On Ibn Rushayd and his works, see Benchekroun, *La Vie intellectuelle,* 186–194.

35. Ibn Marzūq, *Al-Musnad,* 262–265, 410–411.

36. Abū ʿAbdallāh Muḥammad ibn Ghāzī al-Miknāsī, *Fihris Ibn Ghāzī: at-*

Ta'allul bi-rusūm al-isnād ba'da intiqāl ahl al-manzil wa'n-nād, Muḥammad az-Zāhī, ed. (Casablanca, 1979), 91. On Ibn Ghāzī and his works, see Benchekroun, *La Vie intellectuelle,* 385–394. See also E. Lévi-Provençal, *Les Historiens des Chorfas* (reprint, Casablanca, 1991), 224–230. Khiḍrian Sufism was the Maghribi equivalent of the "Uwaysī" tradition in the Mashriq. Being "Khiḍrī" meant that one's chain of doctrinal transmission (*nasab* or *silsila*) went directly from the originator of one's spiritual method to al-Khiḍr, bypassing both the early masters of Sufism and the Prophet Muḥammad. Both Uwaysī and Khiḍrī forms of Sufism were often used as a means of validating a Sufi's *'ilm ladunnī,* the direct inspirational connection to God.

37. Ibn Marzūq, *Al-Musnad,* 162.

38. Ibid., 163.

39. al-Manūnī, "Madkhal," 206.

40. Ibid.

41. Ibid. See also az-Zammūrī, *Bahjat an-nāẓirīn,* 161.

42. al-Manūnī, "Madkhal," 207. Abū Zayd al-Hazmīrī is the source for the Khiḍrian *silsila* cited by Ibn Ghāzī. See n. 36 above.

43. For a detailed discussion of Sabta under Banū al-'Azafī rule, see Ferhat, *Sabta,* 203–269.

44. al-Bādisī, *Al-Maqṣad,* 69. See also Ferhat, *Sabta,* 405–407.

45. al-Bādisī, *Al-Maqṣad,* 63–64.

46. Ibn Qunfudh, *Uns al-faqīr,* 64–66. On Ibn Qunfudh and his works, see Benchekroun, *La Vie intellectuelle,* 358–363.

47. For a more complete account of Abū Madyan's life, see Cornell, *The Way of Abū Madyan,* 2–15.

48. Ibn Qunfudh, *Uns al-faqīr,* 14.

49. at-Tādilī, *at-Tashawwuf,* 322. See also Bel, "Sīdī Bou Medyan," 31–68.

50. Although I have previously written that Abū Madyan was Abū Yi'zzā's *muqaddam* in Fez (Cornell, *The Way of Abū Madyan,* 9), I now believe that his station was advanced enough at that time to train his own disciples. See, for example, at-Tādilī, *at-Tashawwuf* (323), where Abū Yi'zzā praises Abū Madyan's explanation of his idiosyncratic healing practices, saying, "It was as if he had improved upon my own answer."

51. See, for example, Abū 'Abdallāh Muḥammad ibn Maryam (fl. 1011/1602–3), *Al-Bustān fī dhikr al-awliyā' wa'l-'ulamā' bi-Tilimsān,* Mohammed Ben Cheneb, ed. (reprint, Algiers, 1986), 110; and Claude Addas, "Abu Madyan and Ibn 'Arabi," in S. Hirtenstein and M. Tiernan, *Muhyiddin Ibn 'Arabi: A Commemorative Volume* (Shaftesbury, United Kingdom, 1993), 169. Lending credibility to traditions about a meeting between Abū Madyan and al-Jīlānī is a report that Shaykh 'Abd al-Qādir initiated Sufis from different parts of the Muslim world during his second pilgrimage to Mecca. Although it is possible that North African Sufis were initiated into the Qādiriyya in Mecca, Qādirī historians themselves place their earliest non-Iraqi *zawāya* in Yemen, Syria, and Egypt—not in the Maghrib. See, for example, Zaydān, *Aṭ-Ṭarīq aṣ-ṣūfī,* 177–180, 185–190.

52. Ibn Qunfudh, *Uns al-faqīr,* 16.

53. Muḥammad al-Amīn al-Jīlānī (fl. 1272/1856), *Al-Mawāhib al-jalīla fī sharḥ Ḥizb al-wasīla,* in ʿAbd al-Qādir al-Jilani et al., *As-Safīna al-qādiriyya* (Tunis, n.d.), 94.

54. The Egyptian hagiographer Quṭb ad-Dīn al-Yunīnī (d. 726/1326) includes a notice on the second-generation Madyanite shaykh Abū Muḥammad Ṣāliḥ in his *Manāqib ʿAbd al-Qādir al-Jīlānī.* This work may also have contributed to the traditions linking Abū Madyan with al-Jīlānī. See the notes by Denis Gril in idem, *La Risāla de Ṣafī al-dīn ibn Abī l-Manṣūr ibn Ẓāfir: Biographies des maîtres spirituels connus par un cheikh égyptien du VIIe/XIIIe siècle* (Cairo, 1986), 220, 246.

55. Ibn Qunfudh, *Uns al-faqīr,* 37.

56. This work has been edited and translated in Cornell, *The Way of Abū Madyan,* 116–149.

57. See, for example, ibid., 150–175. On Abū Madyan's rules for the practice of *samāʿ,* see 80–95. Although in *The Way of Abū Madyan* I characterized *samāʿ* as an "ecstatic session" (80 n. 29), I now follow Bruce Lawrence's definition of the term: "Hearing chanted verse (with or without accompanying instruments) in the company of others also seeking to participate in the dynamic dialogue between a human lover and the Divine Beloved." See Bruce B. Lawrence, "The Early Chisti Approach to Samaʿ," in Joyce Irwin, ed., *Sacred Sound: Music in Religious Thought and Practice* (Chico, California, 1983), 93–109.

58. See Cornell, *The Way of Abū Madyan,* 156–159. As recently as 1984, *Al-Qaṣīda an-nūniyya* was being recited regularly in the Qādiriyya zāwiya of Marrakesh, Morocco. Abū Madyan's poems and aphorisms are also well-known among the ʿAlawiyya–Shādhiliyya of Mostaghanem in Algeria. See, for example, the commentary on *Uns al-waḥīd wa nuzhat al-murīd* in Aḥmad ibn Muṣṭafā al-ʿAlawī, *Kitāb al-mawād al-ghaythiyya an-nāshī ʿan al-ḥikam al-ghawthiyya* (Mostaghanem, 1942).

59. For pictures of the mosque and madrasa of Sīdī Bū Madyan, see Anthony Hutt, *Islamic Architecture: North Africa* (London, 1977), 43–45, 122–125.

60. Cornell, *The Way of Abū Madyan,* 60, 66.

61. See, for example, Ernst, *Eternal Garden,* 160.

62. Qurʾān II (*al-Baqara*), 143.

63. Fowden, *The Egyptian Hermes,* 158.

64. On the elitist ethos of the Athenian Academy and the Lyceum, see A. A. Long, *Hellenistic Philosophy: Stoics, Epicureans, Sceptics* (Berkeley and Los Angeles, 1986), 4–5.

65. A similarly egalitarian ideal was promoted by Saint Augustine, who conceived of humanity as united in a brotherhood of faith under Christ. See Peter Brown, *Augustine of Hippo* (New York, 1986), 224–225.

66. The juridical meaning of these terms even appears in the Islamic philosophical tradition itself. In his treatise on rhetoric (*khiṭāba*), Ibn Sīnā (d. 428/1037) discusses the "specialized disciplines" (*mawāḍiʿ khāṣṣa*) associated with this art and the "specialized classes of people" (*aṣnāf min an-nās khāṣṣa*) who are experts in them. See Black, *Logic and Aristotle's* Rhetoric, 120–121.

67. Cornell, *The Way of Abū Madyan,* 118.

68. To scholars of fiqh, the *ṣawm al-wiṣāl* is part of the nonjuridical portion of the Sunna. Thus, it is considered a praiseworthy act but is not enjoined on believers as an obligation. See Kamali, *Principles of Islamic Jurisprudence,* 52.

69. al-Māgirī, *Al-Minhāj al-wāḍiḥ,* 218–225.

70. Cornell, *The Way of Abū Madyan,* 118.

71. Ibid., 162.

72. Ibid., 90. This term comes from Qur'ān LVIII (*al-Mujādila*), 22.

73. See Cornell, "Understanding is the Mother of Ability," 95.

74. Cornell, *The Way of Abū Madyan,* 90.

75. Ibid., 96.

76. On the literary legacy of Abū Muḥammad Ṣāliḥ, see Benchekroun, *La Vie intellectuelle,* 109–112.

77. al-Māgirī, *Al-Minhāj al-wāḍiḥ,* 149. See also Gril, *La Risāla de Ṣafī al-dīn,* 208.

78. Long, *Hellenistic Philosophy,* 24–28.

79. For a description of ʿAbd ar-Razzāq al-Jazūlī's doctrine of the first impression, see al-Bādisī, *Al-Maqṣad,* 67–68. Benchekroun (*La Vie intellectuelle,* 111–112) believes that *Bidāyat al-murīd* was composed by Abū Muḥammad Ṣāliḥ rather than by Abū Madyan. This is unlikely, however, since the former was known to have written his own manual for novices entitled *Talqīn al-murīdīn.* See al-Bādisī, *Al-Maqṣad,* 102.

80. The local historian Muḥammad al-Kanūnī identifies modern Asafi as either Thimatria or Carcunticus, towns mentioned by Pliny the Elder as having been founded by the legendary Carthaginian admiral Hanno during his *periplus* along the African coast. He supports this assertion by the location of these ancient towns near Cape Solis (just north of present-day Asafi), and by the numismatic evidence of Roman coins found nearby. Al-Kanūnī, *Āsafī,* 77.

81. al-Māgirī, *Al-Minhāj al-wāḍiḥ,* 14. See also ash-Shādhilī, *At-Taṣawwuf wa'l-mujtamaʿ,* 154–160.

82. See, for example, al-Māgirī, *Al-Minhāj al-wāḍiḥ,* 149–151.

83. Ibid., 159–163.

84. On the Moroccan Hajj caravan, see Muḥammad al-Manūnī, *Rakb al-Ḥajj al-Maghribī* (Tetuan, 1953); Halima Ferhat, "Safi au XIIIe siècle: histoire sainte, histoire urbaine," in idem, *Le Maghreb aux XIIe et XIIIe siècles* (Casablanca, 1993), 79–90; and idem, "Le culte du Prophète au Maroc au XIIIe siècle: Organisation du Pélerinage et Célébration du Mawlid," in André Vauchez, ed., *La Religion civique à l'époque médiévale et moderne (Chrétienté et Islam)* (Rome, 1995), 90–91.

85. al-Kanūnī, *Āsafī,* 99–100.

86. On Aḥmad ibn Ibrāhīm al-Māgirī and *Al-Minhāj al-wāḍiḥ,* see Benchekroun, *La Vie intellectuelle,* 113–116. This work has recently been re-edited in a dissertation by Mohamed Rais. See idem, "Aspect du mysticisme marocain au VIIe–

VIIIe/XIIIe-XIVe siècle, à travers l'analyse critique de l'ouvrage *al-Minhāj al-wāḍiḥ fī taḥqīq karāmāt Abū Muḥammad Ṣāliḥ*" (Ph.D. dissertation, Université de Provence, Aix-Marseille I, 1995–96).

87. al-Māgirī, *Al-Minhāj al-wāḍiḥ,* 190–191.

88. Ibid., 144.

89. Ibid., 143. Another of Abū Muḥammad Ṣāliḥ's sons, ʿAbd al-ʿAzīz al-Māgirī (d. 646/1248–9), also settled permanently in Egypt. His tomb at al-Maḥalla al-Kubrā in the Nile Delta eventually became a pilgrimage center in its own right. See ibid., 145.

90. Ibid., 140–143. Aḥmad al-Māgirī at first contested his elder brother's claim to the leadership of Ribāṭ Āsafī. When he failed to win an election to the post held by the Māgiriyya fuqarāʾ, he cursed the representatives from Haskūra, whose lack of support had tilted the balance in his brother's favor. This malediction was assumed to have caused the drought and crop failures that afflicted Haskūra until shortly after Aḥmad's death. See Ibn Ibrāhīm, *Al-Iʿlām,* vol. 2, 187.

91. al-Māgirī, *Al-Minhāj al-wāḍiḥ,* 146–147. After the death of ʿĪsā in 698/1299, the Banū Abī Muḥammad Ṣāliḥ became a regional dynasty whose authority was more political than spiritual in nature. Subsequent murābiṭūn of Ribāṭ Āsafī, who were criticized by Sufis and dynastic historians alike for their cupidity and lust for power, had careers that were marred by treachery and fratricide. Even the Ḥujjājiyya pilgrimage organization fell victim to these influences. Aḥmad ibn Ibrāhīm al-Māgirī, the author of *Al-Minhāj al-wāḍiḥ,* reports that the Ḥujjājiyya in his time was no more than a heretical sect led by corrupt charlatans. See Ibn Ibrāhīm, *Al-Iʿlām,* vol. 1, 167–168, vol. 8, 215–216. Al-Bādisī (*Al-Maqṣad,* 115–116) opines that the Marinid sultan Abū Yaʿqūb Yūsuf an-Nāṣir suspected Ḥujjājiyya complicity in the Ghumāra revolt of al-Ḥājj al-ʿAbbās ibn Ṣāliḥ.

92. Ibn Qunfudh, *Uns al-faqīr,* 64–65. Although doctrinal exclusivism is a hallmark of North African Sufism today, it was the exception rather than the rule until the early modern period.

93. Ibid., 65.

94. See Benchekroun, *La Vie intellectuelle,* 258–264. For information about Ibn ʿĀshir, see also Paul Nwyia, *Ibn ʿAbbād de Ronda (1332–1390): Un Mystique prédicateur à la Qarawīyīn de Fès* (Beirut, 1961), 55–64.

95. Abūʾl-ʿAbbās Aḥmad ibn ʿĀshir b. ʿAbd ar-Raḥmān al-Ḥāfī as-Salawī (fl. 1141/1729), *Tuḥfat az-zāʾir bi-baʿḍ manāqib Sīdī al-Ḥājj Aḥmad ibn ʿĀshir* (Rabat, BG ms. 533D), 3v. This text is a recension of *As-Salsal al-ʿadhb,* by Muḥammad ibn Abī Bakr al-Ḥaḍramī (d. 787/1385). See Benchekroun, *La Vie intellectuelle,* 309–318.

96. as-Salawī, *Tuḥfat az-zāʾir,* 2r; Nwyia, *Ibn ʿAbbād,* 56.

97. Ibid., 2v–3v. See also Benchekroun, *La Vie intellectuelle,* 258–260. The tomb of "Sīdī al-Yābūrī," who was the patron saint of Rabat's sailors, remains extant today. It is located in the Bāb ʿAlū cemetery on the seaward side of the Casbah des Oudaïas. See Jacques Caillé, *La Ville de Rabat jusqu'au protectorat*

Français: Histoire et archéologie (Paris, 1949), vol. 1, 527. For a picture of the *qubba* of Sīdī al-Yābūrī, see Ibid., vol. 3, pl. lxxiii.

98. as-Salawī, *Tuḥfat az-zāʾir,* 3v–3r.

99. Ibn Qunfudh, *Uns al-faqīr,* 9. Benchekroun, *La Vie intellectuelle,* 259.

100. as-Salawī, *Tuḥfat az-zāʾir,* 4r.

101. Ibid. The tomb of Ibn ʿĀshir, now part of the old cemetery of Salé, is built on the site of the saint's retreat.

102. Ibid., 3r–4v.

103. Ibid.

104. Ibn Qunfudh, *Uns al-faqīr,* 9.

105. Ibid. See also as-Salawī, *Tuḥfat az-zāʾir,* 7r.

106. Ibid., 9v–9r.

107. Ibid., 9r–10r. See also Benchekroun, *La Vie intellectuelle,* 260–261. This is one of the few passages to be reproduced and translated in this bibliographical work. The caliphal title of "Commander of the Faithful" (*amīr al-muʾminīn*) was reinstated during the reign of Abū ʿInān's father, Abū'l-Ḥasan.

108. Benchekroun, *La Vie intellectuelle,* 262–263.

109. On the "totalitarian" reforms of Abū ʿInān and his father, Abū'l-Ḥasan, see Kably, *Société, pouvoir et religion,* 187–199.

110. See J. Spencer Trimingham, *The Sufi Orders in Islam* (Oxford, 1971), 31–104. For the Sufi use of the term *madhhab,* see ʿAlī al-Hujwīrī, *The Kashf al-Mahjūb,* 176–266.

111. See Annemarie Schimmel, *Mystical Dimensions of Islam* (Chapel Hill, 1975), 244–249, and Trimingham, *Sufi Orders,* 33–44.

112. See, for example, Schimmel's discussion of Abū Saʿīd Abū'l-Khayr's rules for Sufi novices in idem, *Mystical Dimensions,* 241–244.

113. Qādiriyya centers were established in Mecca and Syria in the generation after ʿAbd al-Qādir al-Jīlānī's death. See Zaydān, *Aṭ-Ṭarīq aṣ-ṣūfī,* 176–183. For a "Nāṣirian" approach to the creation of the institutionalized ṭarīqa, see Paul Nwyia, *Ibn ʿAṭāʾ Allāh (m. 709/1309) et la naissance de la confrérie šadilite* (Beirut, 1972), 17.

114. Some members of the modern Baṭawiyya–Shādhiliyya in Egypt maintain that the vocalization of ash-Shādhilī's name should be *ash-Shādhdhulī,* following an account in which God says to the shaykh, "Oh ʿAlī, you are the unique one for Me (*anta ash-shādhdhu lī*)." See ʿAbd Allāh Nūr ad-Din Durkee, *Al-Madrasa ash-Shādhdhuliyya (The School of the Shādhdhuliyya), Volume 1, Orisons* (Alexandria, 1991), 10. This opinion can be rejected for two reasons. First, it goes against the consensus of Shādhilī tradition, which sees this account from *Laṭāʾif al-minan* as making a rhetorical point alone. In other words, it is not to be taken as precedent-setting. Second, the grammatical form of the proposed vocalization, *ash-Shādhdhuliyya,* does not follow the rules of Classical Arabic grammar. In the title to Durkee's book, *Al-Madrasa ash-Shādhdhuliyya,* the second term of the construct is an adjective (*nisba*), which must be derived from a noun. But the phrase, *ash-shādhdhu lī,* as found in the original tradition, is a nominative sentence which acts

as a predicate. In Arabic, a nominative sentence cannot be made into a single word, as was apparently done to create *ash-shādhdhuliyya.* The only way to make an adjective out of this phrase would have been to create a new phrase: *al-madrasa ash-shādhdhiyya,* a construct which has never (to my knowledge) appeared in Shādhilī texts.

115. The tradition of Abū Madyan did have a number of adherents in Egypt. This was primarily due to the influence of three of Abū Madyan's disciples: ʿAbd ar-Razzāq al-Jazūlī (see above), Abū ʿAlī an-Nāsikh (d. 606/1209–10), and ʿUmar al-Ḥabbāk (d. 613/1216–17). See Gril, *La Risāla de Ṣafī al-dīn,* 134–135, 181–183, 208.

116. The full title of this work is *Kitāb laṭāʾif al-minan fī manāqib ʿilm al-muhtadīn wa qudwat as-sālikīn Sayyidī Abīʾl-ʿAbbās Aḥmad ibn ʿUmar al-Anṣārī al-Mursī wa shaykhihi quṭb al-aqṭāb wa dustūr ʿawārif al-maʿārif bilā irtiyāb, Sayyidī Abīʾl-Ḥasan ash-Shādhilī.* The fact that al-Mursī's name appears first is a clear indication of his centrality to the work as a whole. See Aḥmad ibn ʿAṭāʾillāh al-Iskandarī, *Laṭāʾif al-minan,* ʿAbd al-Ḥalīm Maḥmūd ed. (Cairo, 1974).

117. See Muḥammad ibn Abīʾl-Qāsim ibn aṣ-Ṣabbāgh al-Ḥimyarī, *Durrat al-asrār wa tuḥfat al-abrār fī manāqib dhī al-kaʿb al-ʿalī waʾl-fakhr ash-shāmikh al-jalī al-quṭb al-akbar waʾl-ghawth al-ashhar Sayyidī ʿAlī Abīʾl-Ḥasan ash-Shādhilī* (Tunis, 1304/1886–7). This work has recently been translated into English as Ibn al-Sabbagh, *The Mystical Teachings of al-Shadhili,* Elmer H. Douglas, trans., and Ibrahim M. Abu-Rabiʿ, ed. (Albany, New York, 1993).

118. Ḥasan ibn ʿAlī Wafāʾ, *Shajarat al-irshād* (Princeton, GC ms. 5916).

119. This conclusion is indirectly supported by the Egyptian hagiographer Safī ad-Dīn ibn Abīʾl-Manṣūr ibn Ẓāfir (d. 682/1283), who reports that ash-Shādhilī visited Egypt twice. His first visit—made early in life—was temporary, while the second was permanent and came on the heels of his expulsion from Tunis. It is likely that ash-Shādhilī's encounter with al-Wāsiṭī (if it happened at all) occurred during his first visit to Egypt. See Gril, *La Risāla de Ṣafī al-dīn,* 171–172, 177–178. Gril believes, however, that the al-Wasiṭī whom ash-Shādhilī met in Egypt could not have been the disciple of Aḥmad ar-Rifāʿī, because a notice in the work titled *Irshād as-sālikīn fī manāqib as-sayyid Aḥmad ar-Rifāʿī* contains a death date for al-Wāsiṭī of 589/1193 (Ibid., 204).

120. Trimingham, *The Sufi Orders,* 45–48.

121. Ibn Wafāʾ, *Shajarat al-irshād,* 4r. Aṭ-Ṭāhir al-Lihīwī, the modern historian of Jabal al-ʿAlam in Morocco, does not specifically link Ibn Mashīsh to the Rifāʿiyya, but he transmits accounts that refer enigmatically to an "Aḥmadī wisdom" (*al-ḥikma al-Aḥmadiyya*). He further claims that ash-Shādhilī was Ibn Mashīsh's only disciple, and that the young Abūʾl-Ḥasan was directed to his future shaykh by Aḥmad al-ʿAsalānī, Ibn Mashīsh's teacher of fiqh, who was from ash-Shādhilī's own moiety of Lower Akhmās in the Banū Ifrāḥ segment of the Ghumāra tribe of Banū Zarwīl. See al-Lihīwī, *Ḥiṣn as-salām bayna aydāy Mūlāy ʿAbd as-Salām* (Casablanca, 1978), 393–419, 436.

122. ʿAbd ar-Raḥmān al-Madanī has often been incorrectly identified as Abū

Madyan, who was actually separated from Ibn Mashīsh by two generations. See, for example, Trimingham, *The Sufi Orders,* 47–48.

123. Ibn ʿAlī Wafāʾ, *Shajarat al-irshād,* 7r.

124. Ibid. See also ʿAbd al-Ḥāfiẓ al-Fāsī, *At-Tarjumān al-muʿrib ʿan ashhur furuʿ ash-Shādhiliyya biʾl-Maghrib* (Rabat, BG ms. 4400D). Although al-Khuzāʿī has been mentioned as a disciple of Abū Madyan, Ibn ʿAlī Wafāʾ agrees with other Egyptian writers that Muḥammad ibn ʿAlī b. Ḥirzihim al-Fāsī (d. 633/1236) provided ash-Shādhilī's most direct link to this famous axial saint of the Maghrib.

125. Ibn aṣ-Ṣabbāgh, *Durrat al-asrār,* 16; Ibn al-Sabbagh, *The Mystical Teachings,* 28.

126. Ibn as-Sabbāgh, *Durrat al-asrār,* 5; Ibn al-Sabbāgh, *The Mystical Teachings,* 16. A different version of this account is given by al-Lihīwī, who places Ibn Mashīsh's son in the role of ash-Shādhilī's teacher: "Oh Abū'l-Ḥasan, the important thing is not to know the Name, but rather to be the essence (*ʿayn*) of the Name." See idem, *Ḥiṣn as-salām,* 410.

127. Ibn aṣ-Ṣabbāgh, *Durrat al-asrār,* 11–12, 14–15; Ibn al-Sabbāgh, *The Mystical Teachings,* 23–27.

128. See, for example, ʿAbd al-Ḥalīm Maḥmūd, *Al-Madrasa ash-Shādhiliyya al-ḥadītha wa imāmuhā Abū'l-Ḥasan ash-Shādhilī* (Cairo, 1967).

129. Ibn aṣ-Ṣabbāgh, *Durrat al-asrār,* 13–14; Ibn al-Sabbagh, *The Mystical Teachings,* 26–27. See also Trimingham, *The Sufi Orders,* 47.

130. Most of these mystics were members of aṭ-Ṭāʾifa al-Māgiriyya. Ṣafī ad-Dīn ibn Abī'l-Manṣūr ibn Ẓāfir mentions several disciples of Abū Muḥammad Ṣāliḥ in Egypt, including Abū'l-Ḥasan ibn ad-Daqqāq, Abū'r-Rabīʿ Sulaymān al-Marrākushī, and one Abū Lakūṭ. See Gril, *La Risāla de Ṣafī al-dīn,* 132–134, 171, 196–197.

131. Gril (ibid., 153–154, 215–216) agrees that Abū'l-Ḥajjāj al-Uqṣūrī was the main Egyptian transmitter of *al-Khirqa al-Madyaniyya* after ʿAbd ar-Razzāq al-Jazūlī.

132. Ibn aṣ-Ṣabbāgh, *Durrat al-asrār,* 15, 35; Ibn al-Sabbāgh, *The Mystical Teachings,* 27, 46–56.

133. Ibn as-Sabbāgh, *Durrat al-asrār,* 16; Ibn as-Sabbāgh, *The Mystical Teachings,* 28–29.

134. Ibn as-Sabbāgh, *Durrat al-asrār,* 25–26. In Ibn as-Sabbāgh, *The Mystical Teachings* (41–42), the term *ʿasākir awliyāʾ Allāh* is misinterpreted as "warrior-saints of God."

135. Ibn as-Sabbāgh, *Durrat al-asrār,* 11 and 24.

136. Ibn as-Sabbāgh, *Durrat al-asrār,* 6, 22, 160.

137. Ibn as-Sabbāgh, *Durrat al-asrār,* 21; Ibn as-Sabbāgh, *The Mystical Teachings,* 34–35.

138. Ibn ʿAṭāʾillāh al-Iskandarī, *Laṭāʾif al-minan,* 177.

139. Ibid., 164. See also Ibn aṣ-Ṣabbāgh, *Durrat al-asrār,* 25–26. On Abū Muḥammad al-Ḥabībī, see also Ibn as-Sabbāgh, *The Mystical Teachings,* 19–21.

140. Ibn as-Sabbāgh, *Durrat al-asrār,* 158. Ash-Shādhilī's "adoption" of Muḥammad ibn Sulṭān al-Masrūqī is not mentioned by Ibn ʿAṭāʾillāh, who reports instead that a similar filiation was established between ash-Shādhilī and Abū'l-ʿAbbās al-Mursī.

141. Ibn aṣ-Ṣabāgh, *Durrat al-asrār,* 158.

142. Ibid., 164. In 685/1286, Muḥammad ibn Sulṭān traveled to Alexandria in order to visit al-Mursī but found that the latter had died the previous year. This lack of communication between the *zawāya* of Tunis and Alexandria implies that the allegiance of the western branch of the Shādhiliyya to that of Egypt may have been more apparent than real.

143. On Abū Muḥammad al-Marjānī, see Nwyia, *Ibn ʿAbbād de Ronda,* xliv.

144. Muḥammad al-Manūnī, "aṣ-Ṣilāt ath-thaqāfiyya bayna'l-Maghrib wa Tunis al-Ḥafṣiyya," in idem, *Waraqāt,* 336.

145. Ibn aṣ-Ṣabbagh, *Durrat al-asrār,* 2; Ibn al-Sabbagh, *The Mystical Teachings,* 12.

146. A. L. de Prémare, *Maghreb et Andalousie au XIVe siècle* (Lyon, 1981), 121, 183–184 n. 215.

147. Ibn aṣ-Ṣabbāgh, *Durrat al-asrār,* 176.

148. For the *nasab* connecting Muḥammad ibn Marzūq at-Tilimsānī to Māḍī ibn Sulṭān, see al-Manūnī, "aṣ-Ṣilāt ath-thaqāfiyya," 336.

149. Much has been written about Ibn ʿAbbād of Ronda, both in Arabic and in European languages. The best modern work on his life is Paul Nwyia's *Ibn ʿAbbād de Ronda,* op. cit. A critical edition and translation of Ibn ʿAbbād's *ar-Rasāʾil aṣ-ṣughrā* was also published by Nwyia as *Lettres de direction spirituelle* (Beirut, 1971). An English version of Nwyia's translation has been published by John Renard under the title, *Ibn ʿAbbād of Ronda: Letters on the Ṣūfī Path* (New York, 1986). For Ibn ʿAbbād's commentary on Ibn ʿAṭāʾillāh's *Ḥikam* (full title of the commentary: *Ghayth al-mawāhib al-ʿaliyya bi-sharḥ al-Ḥikam al-ʿAṭāʾiyya*), see Abū ʿAbdallāh Muḥammad ibn ʿAbbād ar-Rundī, *Sharḥ al-ḥikam* (Cairo, 1939).

150. Nwyia, *Ibn ʿAbbād de Ronda,* lxix–lx.

151. Ibid., lix n. 2, 46, 54.

152. Ibid., 54. Sharaf ad-Dīn ash-Shādhilī lived in the city of Damanhūr during Ibn aṣ-Ṣabbāgh's lifetime and was known to the author of *Durrat al-asrār.* Also in Damanhūr was ash-Shādhilī's daughter ʿArīfat al-Khayr, who was the wife of the Egyptian shaykh ʿAlī ad-Damanhūrī. See above and Ibn aṣ-Ṣabbāgh, *Durrat al-asrār,* 15, 21.

153. Nwyia, *Ibn ʿAbbād de Ronda,* 54.

154. See Ali F. Khushaim, *Zarrūq the Ṣūfī* (Tripoli, 1976), 9–37. Khushaim is unclear as to whom Zarrūq's Shādhilī *nasab* should be traced.

155. Cf., Muḥammad ibn Qāsim ar-Raṣṣāʿ (The Ornamenter) of Tunis, whose craft consisted of working in gold inlay. See al-Manūnī, "Aṣ-Ṣilāt ath-thaqāfiyya," 335–336.

Chapter Six

1. See also, Wyschogrod, *Saints and Postmodernism,* 155–160.

2. See, for example, Victor Turner and Edith Turner, *Image and Pilgrimage in Christian Culture: Anthropological Perspectives* (New York, 1978), William A. Christian, *Local Religion in Sixteenth-Century Spain* (Princeton, 1981), idem, *Apparitions in Late Medieval and Renaissance Spain* (Princeton, 1981), and S. J. Tambiah, *The Buddhist Saints of the Forest and the Cult of Amulets* (Cambridge, 1984). One might also include in this list Jacques Berque, *Ulémas, fondateurs, insurgés.*

3. On the "root metaphor," see Stephen Coburn Pepper, *World Hypotheses: A Study in Evidence* (Berkeley and Los Angeles, 1948), 38–39. My own use of this term is taken from Turner, *Dramas, Fields, and Metaphors* (23–59), where it forms the basis of his theory of the social drama. Pepper's theory of world hypotheses is also central to Hayden White's "tropological" approach in *Tropics of Discourse.*

4. See Introduction for citations from Bel, *La Religion musulmane.* See also ʿAllāl al-Fāsī, "At-Taṣawwuf al-Islāmī fī'l-Maghrib," *Al-Muḥāḍarāt ath-thaqāfiyya* 10(1)(1969): 44. Despite their use of the same term, the concept of *la religion populaire* was understood very differently by these writers. For Bel, the term meant "popular religion" and denoted an illiterate, rural, and often antinomian type of religiosity. For al-Fāsī, it meant "the religion of the people" and was seen as a ideological expression of Moroccan nationalism.

5. White, *Tropics of Discourse,* 65–66, 73. White's concept of "emplotment" is Aristotelian in its ultimate origin. See Paul Ricoeur, *Time and Narrative,* vol. 1, 31–51.

6. *Pace* J. Spencer Trimingham, who claims that al-Jazūlī "formed neither *ṭarīqa . . .* nor *ṭāʾifa.*" Idem, *The Sufi Orders,* 85–86.

7. On the use of northern Moroccan ports as "free-trade zones" for weapons and other manufactured goods from Europe, see Cook, *The Hundred Years War for Morocco,* 178–182, 197.

8. On Muḥammad al-Mahdī al-Fāsī and aṭ-Ṭāʾifa al-Fāsiyya, see the Introduction to idem, *Mumtiʿ al-asmāʿ fī . . . al-Jazūlī wa at-Tabbāʿ wa mā lahumā min al-atbāʿ,* ʿAbd al-Ḥayy al-ʿAmrawī and ʿAbd al-Karīm Murād, eds. (Fez, 1989), i–vii. See also Lévi-Provençal, *Les Historiens des Chorfas,* 240–247, 264–269, 273–275, and A.-L. de Prémare, *Sîdi Abd-er-Raḥmân el-Mejdûb* (Paris and Rabat, 1985), 45–46. On Abū'l-Maḥāsin al-Fāsī, see Muḥammad al-ʿArabī al-Fāsī, *Mirʾāt al-maḥāsin fī akhbār ash-shaykh Abī Maḥāsin* (Fez lithograph, 1316/1898–9). See also Jacques Berque, *L'intérieur du Maghreb, XVe–XIXe siècle* (Paris, 1978), 146–150.

9. See, for example, Ḥajjī, *Az-Zāwiya ad-Dilāʾiyya,* 131–230. See also Berque, *Ulémas, fondateurs,* 81–123.

10. On ʿAlawite–ulama relations, see Berque, *Ulémas, fondateurs,* 161–229. See also Donna Lee Bowen, "The Paradoxical Linkage of the ʿUlamāʾ and Monarch in Morocco," *Maghreb Review* 10 (1)(1985): 3–9.

11. al-Fāsī, *Mir'āt al-maḥāsin,* 189.

12. See, for example, the criticism of the Jazūlite practice of head-shaving by the Libyan disciple of Zarrūq and part-time Ottoman ambassador Muḥammad al-Kharrūbī (d. ca. 963/1556) in al-Fāsī, *Mumti' al-asmā',* 16. See also Ibn Ibrāhīm, *Al-I'lām,* vol. 5, 129–131, who claims that the Ottomans exploited al-Kharrūbī's doctrinal links with Moroccan Sufism as a means of gaining access to the sharifian court.

13. Muṣṭafā Abū Ḍayf Aḥmad, *Athar al-qabā'il al-'Arabiyya fī'l-ḥayāt al-Maghribiyya khilāl 'aṣray al-Muwaḥḥidīn wa Banī Marīn [524–876/1130–1472]* (Casablanca, 1982), 79–80.

14. Ibid., 111.

15. The mother of sultan Abū Ya'qūb Yūsuf al-Marīnī (r. 685–706/1286–1307) was a Hasanid *sharīfa,* while the mother of Abū Sa'īd 'Uthmān I (r. 710–31/1310–31) was a woman of the Khuluṭ. See ibid., 162.

16. A preferential source of wives for the Wattasids was the 'Amārna faction of the Dhawī Manṣūr: "They are men who are noble and extremely brave. For this reason, the kings of Fez have the custom of taking nearly all of their wives from their girls so that they may establish familial connections." Jean-Léon l'Africain, *Description de l'Afrique,* A. Epaulard, trans. (Paris reprint, 1980), vol. 1, 32. This work has been translated into Arabic as al-Ḥasan ibn Muḥammad al-Wazzān al-Gharnāṭī, *Waṣf Ifrīqīya,* Muḥammad Ḥajjī and Muḥammad al-Akhḍar, eds. and trans. (Rabat, 1980), 2 volumes.

17. The Zayyanid sultan Abū Ḥammū Mūsā II (r. 753–88/1352–86) married the daughter of an imam from the nearby Idrisid village of al-'Alawiyyīn. See Aḥmad, *Athar al-qabā'il,* 147.

18. Ibid., 166, 224–227.

19. Kably, *Société, pouvoir et religion,* 229–257.

20. While living in Syria in the tenth century, many of the tribal segments of the Banū Hilāl supported Qarmaṭī Shi'ism. See Aḥmad, *Athar al-qabā'il,* 229, and Daftary, *The Ismā'īlīs,* 115–135.

21. Aḥmad, *Athar al-qabā'il,* 99.

22. Ibid., 100.

23. Ibid., 245.

24. Kably, *Société, pouvoir et religion,* 296–297.

25. The terms *musta'rab* (Arabized) and *musta'jam* ("foreignized" or Berberized) were used by the medieval North African historian Ibn Khaldūn. See idem, *Histoire des Berbères et des dynasties musulmanes de l'Afrique Septentrionale,* Le Baron de Slane, trans., and Paul Casanova, ed. (reprint, Paris, 1982), vol. 1, 6–7. On the abortive Portuguese attack on Tangier, see Cook, *The Hundred Years War for Morocco,* 86–87.

26. al-Manūnī, "At-Tayyārāt al-fikriyya," 245. Portuguese accounts claim that "40,000 to 50,000 Moors" came from the regions of ash-Shāwīya and Gazūla to relieve Tangier. See Vasco de Carvalho, *La Domination Portugaise au Maroc, 1415–1769* (Lisbon, 1936), 22–25.

27. Kably, *Société, pouvoir et religion,* 328–330.

28. Anonymous, *Ta'rīkh ad-dawla as-Saʿdiyya ad-Darʿiyya at-Tagmadertiyya,* Georges S. Colin, ed. (Rabat, 1934), 2. This seventeenth-century chronicle, although strongly biased against the Saʿdian dynasty, spares neither the Marinids nor their Wattasid successors in assigning blame for the political deterioration of Morocco in the fifteenth and sixteenth centuries C.E.

29. Aḥmad, *Athar al-qabā'il,* 190. See also Kably, *Société, pouvoir et religion,* 190–194.

30. Aḥmad, *Athar al-qabā'il,* 191, 211.

31. Gomes Eannes de Azurara, *Conquests and Discoveries of Henry the Navigator: Being the Chronicles of Azurara,* Virginia de Castro e Almeida, trans. (London, 1936), 95.

32. Ibid., 105–109.

33. Ibid., 126.

34. The best overall summary in English of the Portuguese domination of Morocco can be found in Cook, *The Hundred Years War for Morocco,* 83–163. The unfortunate number of mistakes in the transliterations of Arabic terms in this book should not cause the reader to underestimate its value as a source for early-modern Moroccan history.

35. Robert Ricard, *Études sur l'histoire des Portugais au Maroc* (Coimbra, 1955), 118–119.

36. Ibid., 124–127. See also Vincent J. Cornell, "Socioeconomic Dimensions of Reconquista and Jihad in Morocco: Portuguese Dukkala and the Saʿdid Sus, 1450–1557," *IJMES,* 22 (1990), 395.

37. Jean-Léon l'Africain, *Description de l'Afrique,* vol. 1, 191 and 203.

38. Ibid., 288, 285.

39. See Muḥammad ibn Sulaymān al-Jazūlī, *ʿAqīdat al-walī aṣ-ṣāliḥ Sīdī Muḥammad ibn Sulaymān al-Jazūlī* (Rabat, BH ms. 7245), 24. This work is reproduced in Ḥasan Jallāb, *Muḥammad ibn Sulaymān al-Jazūlī* (Marrakesh, 1993), 48–59.

40. See "Bāb mā waqaʿa min at-taghyīr fī muʿāsharat al-ajānib" (Section on the deviation that has occurred through association with foreigners), in Abū Muḥammad ʿAbdallāh al-Habṭī, *Al-Alfiyya as-saniyya fī tanbīḥ al-ʿāmma wa'l-khāṣṣa ʿalā mā awqaʿu min at-taghyīr fī'l-milla al-Islāmiyya* (Rabat, BH ms. 2808).

41. Al-Jazūlī's first name is sometimes vocalized in Moroccan sources as *Maḥammad.* This is an Arabized version of *Am'ḥammad,* a common rendering of Muḥammad in the Tashilḥīt Berber dialect.

42. See Bruce B. Lawrence, "The Chishtīya of Sultanate India: A Case Study of Biographical Complexities in South Asian Islam," *Journal of the American Academy of Religion—Thematic Studies* 68 (3–4)(1981): 53–54.

43. Ibid., 54.

44. Ibid., 54–55.

45. For the text of this prayer, see ʿAbd al-Qādir Zākī, *An-Nafḥa al-ʿaliyya fī awrād ash-Shādhiliyya* (Beirut, 1904), 15–16.

46. See Ricoeur's discussion of W. B. Gallie, *Philosophy and the Historical Understanding,* in *Time and Narrative,* vol. 1, 149–152.

47. Ibid., 38–45.

48. Traditions predicting the appearance of the Mahdī at Ribāṭ Māssa are found at least as far back as the thirteenth century C.E. See Mercedes García-Arenal, "*Mahdī, Murābiṭ, Sharīf:* l'Avènement de la dynastie sʿdienne," *Studia Islamica* 71 (1990): 82–83.

49. Muḥammad al-Mahdī al-Fāsī, *Kitāb mumtiʿ al-asmāʿ fī dhikr al-Jazūlī wa at-Tabbāʿ wa mā lahumā min al-atbāʿ* (Fez lithograph, 1314–15/1896), 15–16; al-Fasi, *Mumtiʿ al-asmāʿ*, 14.

50. al-Fāsī, *Kitāb mumtiʿ*, 2–3; al-Fāsī, *Mumtiʿ ʿal-asmāʿ*, 1.

51. al-Fāsī, *Kitāb mumtiʿ*, 1–2; al-Fāsī, *Mumtiʿ al-asmāʿ*, 1–2.

52. Jean-Léon l'Africain, *Description de l'Afrique,* vol. 1, 115–116.

53. al-Fāsī, *Kitāb mumtiʿ*, 6; al-Fāsī, *Mumtiʿ al-asmāʿ*, 5–6.

54. See Ibn Ibrāhīm, *Al-Iʿlām,* vol. 5, 49, who reproduces this account from Aḥmad Bābā's *Kifāyat al-muḥtāj.*

55. Ibid. See also al-Fāsī, *Kitāb mumtiʿ*, 6; al-Fāsī, *Mumtiʿ al-asmāʿ*, 6.

56. See, for example, Ibn al-Muwaqqit, *As-Saʿāda al-abadiyya,* vol. 2, 32. This source claims that al-Jazūlī was aided in writing *Dalāʾil al-khayrāt* by "Sīdī Shamharūsh," qāḍī of the Jinn and Companion of the Prophet Muḥammad.

57. See Ibn Ibrāhīm, *Al-Iʿlām,* vol. 5, 80. Aḥmad ibn Abīʾl-Qāsim aṣ-Ṣumāʿī was previously mentioned in Chapter Three, where he appears as a biographer of Abū Yiʿzzā.

58. Ibid. Although the phrase *marʾa ṣāliḥa* may connote nothing more in Arabic than a "righteous woman," in this context it is probable that the term refers to a female saint.

59. Abdellah Hammoudi suggests that women in rural Morocco have long played a sacerdotal role by officiating "between the human order and the dangerous and powerful supernatural order." See idem, *The Victim and Its Masks,* 131–133.

60. Al-Fāsī attributes the decision to include women as members of the Jazūliyya to the influence of al-Khiḍr. See idem, *Kitāb Mumtiʿ*, 16; al-Fāsī, *Mumtiʿ al-asmāʿ*, 17–18. Al-Jazūlī's open-mindedness in matters of gender may also have been due to the influence of the Sufi Ibn al-ʿArabī, who taught that female gnostics occupied stations of sainthood that were fully equivalent to those of men. See Chodkiewicz, *Le Sceau des saints,* 126–127.

61. al-Fāsī, *Kitāb mumtiʿ*, 7; al-Fāsī, *Mumtiʿ al-asmāʿ*, 6.

62. Ḥasanayn ibn Muṣṭafā Ghānim al-Manfalūṭī, *Tuḥfat al-kirām al-mabdhūla fī baʿḍ manāqib ghawth al-anām quṭb Jazūla or Manāqib Sīdī ash-Shaykh al-Jazūlī* (Rabat, BG ms. 925D), 5v.–5r. See also Cairo, DKM ms. Ṭalʿat 2052 film 18870. According to Denis Gril, al-Manfalūṭī was Maliki Muftī of Medina in the

nineteenth century C.E. (See idem, "Sources manuscrites de l'histoire du soufisme à Dār al-Kutub," *Annales Islamologiques* 28:132). Ibn al-Muwaqqit (*As-Saʿāda al-abadiyya,* vol. 2, 29–30) reproduces the same story but mentions a different prayer on the Prophet as the cause for the water miracle.

63. al-Fāsī, *Mirʾāt al-maḥāsin,* 137–138. For an English translation of *Dalāʾil al-khayrāt,* see John B. Pearson, trans., *A Guide to Happiness: A Manual of Prayer* (Oxford, 1907).

64. al-Kattānī, *Salwat al-anfās,* vol. 2, 218–219. Abū ʿAbdallāh Amghār aṣ-Ṣaghīr is buried not at Tīṭ-n-Fiṭr but in the Bāb Futūḥ cemetery in Fez.

65. See, for example, al-Fāsī, *Kitāb mumtiʿ,* 10; al-Fāsī, *Mumtiʿ al-asmāʿ,* 10.

66. Ibn al-Muwaqqit, *As-Saʿāda al-abadiyya,* vol. 2, 19. This account claims (rather implausibly) that al-Jazūlī would read *Dalāʾil al-khayrāt* twice each morning, after which he would make 100,000 *basmallāhs* and recite the Qur'an one and one-fourth times.

67. Abū Muḥammad Abdallāh ibn Muḥammad al-Ghazwānī, *An-Nuqṭa al-azaliyya fī sirr adh-dhāt al-Muḥammadiyya* (Rabat, BG ms. 2617K), 21. This tradition is also repeated by Muḥammad al-ʿArabī al-Fāsī in *Mirʾāt al-maḥāsin* (193–195).

68. Muḥammad al-Murtaḍā az-Zabīdī, *Itḥāf as-sādāt al-muttaqīn bi-sharḥ Iḥyāʾ ʿulūm ad-dīn* (reprint, Beirut, n.d.), vol. 3, 289. See also Ibn Ibrāhīm, *Al-Iʿlām,* vol. 5, 87. Az-Zabīdī is incorrectly identified by Ibn Ibrāhīm as the Shiʿite theologian ash-Sharīf al-Murtaḍā (d. 436/1044). According to Carl Ernst (personal communication), the only fifteenth-century Shirazi Sufi to attain fame beyond Iran was Shāh Dāʿī Shirāzī, who is not known to have composed a book of prayers on behalf of the Prophet.

69. See, for example, the introductory section to Muḥammad al-Mahdī al-Fāsī, *Maṭāliʿ al-masarrāt bi-jalāʾ Dalāʾil al-khayrāt* (Fez, private ms. dated 1310/1892–3), 1–2, and al-Fāsī, *Maṭāliʿ al-masarrāt bi-jalāʾ Dalāʾil al-khayrāt* (Cairo, 1970), 3–4.

70. See, for example, al-Magirī, *Al-Minhāj al-wāḍiḥ,* 4, where this author attributes his inspiration for writing *Al-Minhāj al-wāḍiḥ fī taḥqīq karāmāt Abī Muḥammad Ṣāliḥ* to Abū aṭ-Ṭāhir al-Baghdādī's *Al-Minhāj an-nāẓir fī karāmāt ash-Shaykh ʿAbd al-Qādir.*

71. al-Ghazwānī, *An-Nuqṭa al-azaliyya,* 21.

72. The Egyptian Sufi Ibrāhīm al-Matbūlī (d. 891/1486), a younger contemporary of al-Jazūlī and one of the masters of the Shādhilī shaykh ʿAbd al-Wahhāb ash-Shaʿrānī (d. 973/1565), used the same device to claim a direct connection with the Prophet Muḥammad. Ash-Shaʿrānī also professed a Shādhilī lineage *bilā wāsiṭa.* See Michael Winter, *Society and Religion in Early Ottoman Egypt: Studies in the Writings of ʿAbd al-Wahhāb ash-Shaʿrānī* (New Brunswick, New Jersey, 1982), 95–97.

73. See, for example, al-Jīlānī, *Al-Mawāhib al-jalīla,* in idem et. al., *As-Safīna al-qādiriyya,* 93.

74. al-Ghazwānī, *An-Nuqṭa al-azaliyya,* 140.

75. See Muḥammad ibn Sulaymān al-Jazūlī, *Dalāʾil al-khayrāt wa shawāriq al-anwār fī dhikr aṣ-ṣalāt ʿalā an-Nabī al-Mukhtār* (Cairo, n.d.), 82–83.

76. See, for example, Muḥammad al-Manlā (?), *Aṣ-Ṣalāt al-kubrā fī sharḥ aṣ-Ṣalāt aṣ-ṣughrā,* in al-Jīlānī et al., *As-Safīna al-qādiriyya,* 20–48.

77. Zaydān, *Aṭ-Ṭarīq aṣ-ṣūfī,* 186.

78. al-Jīlānī et. al., *As-Safīna al-qādiriyya,* 20.

79. Shams ad-Dīn Muḥammad ibn ʿAbd ar-Raḥmān as-Sakhāwī, *Aḍ-Ḍawʾ al-lāmiʿ li-ahl al-qarn at-tāsiʿ* (reprint, Beirut, n.d.), vol. 2, 237–239 (notice 613). Another possibility is ʿAbd al-ʿAzīz ibn Danyāl al-ʿAjamī al-Iṣbahānī (d. 811/1409) (Ibid., 218 [notice 554]). This second individual, however, lived in Mecca rather than Cairo and probably died too early for al-Jazūlī to have known him.

80. See al-Jazūlī, *Dalāʾil al-khayrāt* (Marrakesh, BY ms. 377). This manuscript is a reproduction of the Fāsiyya zāwiya's copy of *Dalāʾil al-khayrāt,* which was taken from as-Sahlī's original.

81. The title of this work is given in Ibn al-Muwaqqit, *As-Saʿāda al-abadiyya,* vol. 2, 35. Although sections of *An-Nuṣḥ at-tāmm* are extant in several manuscript collections, the complete work appears to be lost.

82. This mosque, originally called "Jāmiʿ al-Ḥurra," was endowed in 955/1587 by al-Ḥurra Masʿūda al-Wazgītiyya, the mother of the Saʿdian sultan Aḥmad al-Manṣūr. Manuscripts from this collection can presently be found in the Bibliothèque Ben Youssef in Marrakesh. See Muḥammad Ḥajjī, *Al-Ḥaraka al-fikriyya bi'l-Maghrib fī ʿahd as-Saʿdiyyīn* (Mohammedia, 1976), 185.

83. Muḥammad ibn Sulaymān al-Jazūlī, *Risāla fī'l-maḥabba* (Marrakesh, BY ms. 587/3), 49. See also Qur'ān, XII (*Yūsuf*), 21–34.

84. See, for example, Farīd al-Dīn ʿAṭṭār, *The Illāhi-nāma or Book of God,* John Andrew Boyle, trans. (Manchester, 1976), 112–113, 297–298, 327–328. In this work, Zulaykhā hints at the divine source of love and beauty when she says: "If I have the slightest information about my heart, I do not know why it fell in love, or if it fell in love whither it has gone. Though Joseph has no firm hold on my heart, yet Zulaykhā has not that heart either" (112).

85. See Reynold A. Nicholson, ed. and trans., *The Mathnawī of Jalālu'ddin Rūmī* (reprint, London, 1977), vol. 1, 25–41, 172–176; vol. 2, 34–42, 170–171, 305–329; vol. 3, 120–130, 198–200.

86. Abū'l-Faḍl Rashīd ad-Dīn al-Mībudī, *Kashf al-asrār wa ʿuddat al-abrār* (Tehran, 1982), vol. 5, 82–89.

87. ʿAbd ar-Razzāq al-Kāshānī [Ibn al-ʿArabī], *Tafsīr al-Qurʾān al-Karīm* (Beirut, 1968), vol. 1, 597–599.

88. See Carl Ernst, "The Stages of Love in Early Persian Sufism, from Rābiʿa to Rūzbihān," in Leonard Lewisohn, ed., *Classical Persian Sufism, From Its Origins to Rumi* (London, 1993), 444–455.

89. Ibid., 444–445. See also Masataka Takeshita, "Continuity and Change in the Tradition of Shirazi Love Mysticism—A Comparison between Daylamī's *ʿAtf al-Alif* and Rūzbihān Baqlī's *Abhar al-ʿĀshiqīn,*" *Orient* 23 (1987): 113–131.

90. al-Jazūlī, *Risāla fī'l-maḥabba,* 53–58.

91. Ibid., 57–58; Ernst, "The Stages of Love," 450–451.

92. al-Jazūlī, *Risāla fī'l-maḥabba,* 57–58.

93. al-Fāsī, *Kitāb mumtiʿ*, 10; al-Fāsī, *Mumtiʿ al-asmāʿ*, 10–11.

94. al-Manfalūṭī, *Tuḥfat al-kirām,* 7r–8v.

95. al-Fāsī, *Kitāb mumtiʿ*, 13; al-Fāsī, *Mumtiʿ al-asmāʿ*, 14. Mūlāy Muḥammad at-Tilmudī, the *muqaddam* of the shrine of Muḥammad ibn Sulaymān al-Jazūlī in Marrakesh, claims descent from the shaykh via al-Jazūlī's daughter.

96. Ibn Ibrāhīm, *Al-Iʿlām,* vol. 5, 80. See also Jallāb, *Muḥammad Ibn Sulayman al-Jazūlī,* 22; and al-Fāsī, *Kitāb mumtiʿ*, 13; al-Fāsī, *Mumtiʿ al-asmāʿ*, 14. The remains of Ribāṭ Asafi are known today as the "Retreat (*khalwa*) of Sīdī Slīmān al-Jazūlī."

97. Muḥammad ibn Sulaymān al-Jazūlī, *Risāla ilā ʿulamāʾ aẓ-ẓāhir* (Fez, BQ ms. 723/7), 131r–132v. Part of this work is also reproduced in al-Fāsī, *Kitāb mumtiʿ*, 15; al-Fāsī, *Mumtiʿ al-asmāʿ*, 16–17. *Maʿdin al-jawāhir* may be the work presently catalogued in the Bibliothèque Générale et Archives, Rabat (BG ms. 305Q) as Abū Muḥammad Ṣāliḥ, *Risāla fī'ṭ-taṣawwuf.* Its relationship to another work by Abū Muḥammad Ṣāliḥ, *Talqīn al-murīdīn,* is unclear. See al-Bādisī, *al-Maqṣad,* 102.

98. al-Fāsī, *Kitāb mumtiʿ*, 3–4; al-Fāsī, *Mumtiʿ al-asmāʿ*, 3.

99. ash-Shādhilī, *At-Taṣawwuf wa'l-mujtamaʿ*, 154–160.

100. Ibn Ibrāhīm, *Al-Iʿlām,* vol. 5, 61–62. See also al-Fāsī, *Kitāb mumtiʿ*, 17; al-Fāsī, *Mumtiʿ al-asmāʿ*, 16–17. To justify the practice of shaving the "hair of unbelief," al-Jazūlī cites the *Sunan* of Abū Dāwūd, Bāb aṭ-Ṭahāra, 127 and 129. A dissenting opinion is given by at-Tirmidhī, who quotes the Prophet as saying: "I did not say to shave the hair, but to beautify religion" (Bāb al-Qiyāma, 56).

101. See Chapter Five above and Ibn Ibrāhīm, *Al-Iʿlām,* vol. 5, 61. See also Cornell, *The Way of Abū Madyan,* 30–31.

102. Muḥammad ibn Sulaymān al-Jazūlī, *Risāla fī't-tawḥīd* (Fez, BQ ms. 723/7), 131v–131r. See also al-Fāsī, *Kitāb mumtiʿ*, 23; al-Fāsī, *Mumtiʿ al-asmāʿ*, 24. This text differs from the work under the same title (Marrakesh, BY ms. 587) that is reproduced by Jallāb in *Muḥammad ibn Sulayman al-Jazūlī,* 67–69.

103. al-Fāsī, *Kitāb mumtiʿ*, 28; al-Fāsī, *Mumtiʿ al-asmāʿ*, 29. See also Jallāb, *Muḥammad ibn Sulaymān al-Jazūlī,* 37.

104. For the complete Jazūlite invocation as practiced in Fez at the end of the sixteenth century, see at-Ṭālib, *Waẓīfat al-Jazūliyya al-Ghazwāniyya* (Paris, BNP ms. 1201, dated 1011/1600). The text of *Ḥizb al-falāḥ* can also be found in Jallāb, *Muḥammad ibn Sulaymān al-Jazūlī,* 95–97. Jallāb's version differs from that of the Paris manuscript in that it contains later additions made by the ʿĪsāwiyya brotherhood and also includes the text of *Al-Musabbaʿāt al-ʿashr.*

105. See Zakī, *An-Nafḥa al-ʿaliyya,* 2–9. *Ḥizb al-barr* is the counterpart for travel on land to ash-Shādhilī's equally well-known *Ḥizb al-baḥr,* which is to be recited at sea.

106. These invocations were to be recited seven times each. See Abū Ṭālib

Muḥammad al-Makkī, *Qūt al-qulūb fī muʿāmalat al-Maḥbūb wa waṣf ṭarīq al-murīd ilā maqām at-tawḥīd* (Cairo, 1884–5), vol. 1, 7. The version of *Al-Musabbaʿāt al-ʿashr* contained in this text differs slightly from that used by al-Jazūlī.

107. al-Fāsī, *Kitāb mumtiʿ*, 28; al-Fāsī, *Mumtiʿ al-asmāʿ*, 29–30. Also known as *Al-Ḥizb al-kabīr,* this litany is reproduced in Jallāb, *Muḥammad ibn Sulaymān al-Jazūlī,* 98–100.

108. See Ibn ʿIsā, *Ḥizb ash-shaykh al-jalīl ad-dāl ʿalā Allāh Abī ʿAbdallāh Sīdī Muḥammad ibn ʿĪsā raḍiya Allāhu ʿanhu* (Meknès lithograph, n.d.), 5–9. The remaining sections of the ʿĪsāwiyya invocation consist of additions by al-Jazūlī's disciples.

109. ash-Shādhilī, *At-Taṣawwuf wa'l-mujtamaʿ*, 159.

110. al-Fāsī, *Kitāb mumtiʿ*, 31; al-Fāsī, *Mumtiʿ al-asmāʿ*, 32.

111. al-Fāsī, *Kitāb mumtiʿ*, 6; al-Fāsī, *Mumtiʿ al-asmāʿ*, 4. See also Jallāb, *al-Jazūlī,* 31. Al-Jazūlī's mention of Baghdad in this passage may be taken as further evidence of Qādirī influence.

112. al-Fāsī, *Kitāb mumtiʿ*, 24; al-Fāsī, *Mumtiʿ al-asmāʿ*, 25.

113. al-Fāsī, *Kitāb mumtiʿ*, 25; al-Fāsī, *Mumtiʿ al-asmāʿ*, 26.

114. al-Fāsī, *Kitāb mumtiʿ*, 27; al-Fāsī, *Mumtiʿ al-asmāʿ*, 28.

115. al-Ghazwānī, the second shaykh al-jamāʿa of the Jazūliyya, taught that there are two separate types of prophecy (*waḥy*). The first, *waḥy al-kalām* (theological prophecy), ended with Muḥammad and was reserved for Prophets and Messengers alone. The second, *waḥy al-ilhām* (inspirational prophecy), is accessible to saints and Sufi shaykhs and lasts until the end of time. See Chapter Seven below and idem, *An-Nuqṭa al-azaliyya,* 142.

116. Abū Dāwūd, *Sunan,* 4/156, quoted in Ella Landau-Tasseron, "The 'Cyclical Reform': A Study of the *Mujaddid* Tradition," *Studia Islamica* 70 (1989): 79.

117. Ibid., 82–84.

118. al-Fāsī, *Kitāb mumtiʿ*, 26; al-Fāsī, *Mumtiʿ al-asmāʿ*, 27.

119. Similar states also inspired the writings and sayings of the Shirazi Sufi Rūzbihān, which may lend further credence to the hypothesis that al-Jazūlī was influenced by Persian Sufi traditions. In *Kashf al-asrār,* Rūzbihān describes being enveloped in an immense ray of light, from which God addresses him in the following *mukālama:* "Oh Rūzbihān, I have chosen you for *walāya* and I have singled you out for *maḥabba.* You are My friend (*walī*) and lover (*muḥibb*). You should not fear or grieve, for I have made you perfect and I will assist you in all that you desire." Chodkiewicz, *Le Sceau des saints,* 59.

120. al-Ghazwānī, *An-Nuqṭa al-azaliyya,* 31–32, 49–50.

121. The metaphor of *ʿIliyyīn* is also used by Abū Madyan in *Bidāyat al-murīd.* See Cornell, *The Way of Abū Madyan,* 58.

122. For a similar, divinely inspired polity, see Saint Augustine: "Two loves therefore have given origin to these two cities, self-love in contempt of God unto the earthly, love of God in contempt of one's self to the heavenly. The first seeks the

glory of men, and the latter desires God only as the testimony of the conscience, the greatest glory. That glories in itself, and this in God . . . That boasts of the ambitious conquerors led by the lust of sovereignty: in this all serve each other in charity, both the rulers in counselling and the subjects in obeying . . . in this other, this heavenly city, there is no wisdom of man, but only the piety that serves the true God and expects a reward in the society of the holy angels, and men, 'that God may be all in all." Idem, *The City of God (De Civitatae Dei),* John Healy, trans., R. V. G. Tasker, ed. (London and New York, 1950), vol. 2, 58–59.

123. al-Fāsī, *Kitāb mumtiʿ*, 3; al-Fāsī, *Mumtiʿ al-asmāʿ*, 4–5. See also Ibn Ibrāhīm, *Al-Iʿlām,* vol. 5, 48.

124. On previous mahdī–*mujaddid* correspondences in Morocco, see Cornell, "Understanding is the Mother of Ability," 101–102. See also Halima Ferhat and Hamid Triki, "Faux prophètes et mahdis dans le Maroc médiéval," *Hespéris-Tamuda,* 26–7 (1988–9): 5–23.

125. Ibn Ibrāhīm, *Al-Iʿlām,* vol. 5, 81; al-Fāsī, *Kitāb mumtiʿ*, 11; al-Fāsī, *Mumtiʿ, al-asmāʿ*, 12.

126. Ibn Ibrāhīm, *Al-Iʿlām,* vol. 5, 70.

127. al-Jazūlī, *ʿAqīda,* 26–27; Jallāb, *Muḥammad ibn Sulaymān al-Jazūlī,* 49 and 51.

128. al-Jazūlī, *ʿAqīda,* 27; Jallāb, *Muḥammad ibn Sulaymān al-Jazūlī,* 53–54.

129. Kably, *Société, pouvoir et religion,* 238.

130. an-Nāṣirī, *al-Istiqṣāʾ*, vol. 4, 96–97.

131. Ibid., 97. See also Kably, *Société, pouvoir et religion,* 330–332.

132. an-Nāṣirī, *al-Istiqṣāʾ*, vol. 4, 98.

133. Boucharb, *Dukkāla,* 90–94. Asafi became prosperous enough from its trade with the Portuguese to mint its own gold coins between the years 865/1460 and 914/1508.

134. Jean-Léon l'Africain, *Description de l'Afrique,* vol. 1, 117. Leo Africanus reports 4000 hearths in Asafi at the beginning of the sixteenth century. This would give the city an approximate population of between 20,000 and 25,000.

135. Ibn al-Muwaqqit, *As-Saʿāda al-abadiyya,* vol. 2, p. 28.

136. Ibid.

137. Jean-Léon l'Africain, *Description de l'Afrique,* vol. 1, 83–84.

138. The classic exposition of *liff* theory in Moroccan Studies can be found in Robert Montagne, *Les Berbères et le Makhzen dans le Sud du Maroc* (Paris, 1930). This work was updated and critiqued by Jacques Berque in idem, *Structures sociales du Haut-Atlas,* 424–439.

139. See Bernard Rosenberger, "Travaux sur l'histoire du Maroc au XVᵉ et XVIᵉ siècles publiés en Pologne," *Hespéris-Tamuda* 12(1971): 208. This article is a synopsis of Andrzej Dziubinski, "Les Chorfa Saadiens dans le Sous et Marrakech jusqu'en 1525," *Africana bulletin* 10(1969): 31–51.

140. Jean-Léon l'Africain, *Description de l'Afrique,* vol. 1, 80–81.

141. Ibid., 81–82.

142. Personal communication, February 1984.

143. See, for example, Gellner, *Saints of the Atlas,* 168–172. See also David M. Hart, *The Aith Waryaghar of the Moroccan Rif* (Tucson, Arizona, 1976), 187–188, 190–192; and Berque, *Structures sociales du Haut-Atlas,* 281–298, who describes the physical and ritual centrality of the female saint Lāllā ʿAzīza Tagurramt.

144. al-Fāsī, *Mirʾāt al-maḥāsin,* 207. This date, which agrees with the report in Zarrūq's *Al-Kunnāsh,* is considered definitive by most of al-Jazūlī's biographers.

145. See Jack Goody, *The Interface Between the Written and the Oral* (Cambridge, 1987), 107.

146. Aḥmad al-Burnusī al-Fāsī Zarrūq, *Al-Kunnāsh fī ʿilm āsh* (Rabat, BG ms. 1385 K), 66–67. For a summary of Zarrūq's account of Ibn as-Sayyāf's revolt, see García-Arenal, "*Mahdī, Murābiṭ, Sharīf,*" 86–87.

147. Zarrūq, *Al-Kunnāsh,* 67. This hadith may have come to Ibn as-Sayyāf's attention from the text of al-Jazūlī's *ʿAqīda.*

148. See Goody, *The Interface Between the Written and the Oral,* 157–161.

149. Zarrūq, *Al-Kunnāsh,* 67.

150. an-Nāṣirī, *al-Istiqṣāʾ,* vol. 4, 122.

151. Nehmiah Levtzion discovered in his studies of the Asante of Ghana that no less than ninety percent of the Arabic manuscripts in the tribe's possession were used for divination. See Goody, *The Interface Between the Written and the Oral,* 125–132.

152. García-Arenal ("*Mahdī, Murābiṭ, Sharīf,*" 85) is incorrect in claiming that Ibn as-Sayyāf may have been a nephew of al-Jazūlī. If his name were really "ʿAmr ibn Sulaymān" he could only have been the shaykh's great-uncle, since al-Jazūlī's full name was Muḥammad ibn ʿAbd ar-Raḥmān b. Abū Bakr b. Sulaymān. In addition, ʿAmr ibn as-Sayyāf was from Shyāẓma, not Gazūla.

153. an-Nāṣirī, *al-Istiqṣāʾ,* vol. 4, 123.

154. Ibn Ibrāhīm, *Al-Iʿlām,* vol. 5, 55.

155. Zarrūq, *Al-Kunnāsh,* 66.

156. Mūlāy aṭ-Ṭayyib at-Tilmudī, the eldest son of the *muqaddam* of the shrine of al-Jazūlī in Marrakesh, reports that King Hassan II of Morocco told his father that the name "Tilmudī" reflected the fact that the *muqaddam*'s ancestors had been Talmudic scholars before their conversion to Islam (personal communication, June 1994). See also al-Manūnī, "Madkhal," 196.

157. Zarrūq, *Al-Kunnāsh,* 123. Al-Jazūlī's is one of the few cases where a Moroccan saint can truly be characterized as an "homme fétiche." See Bel, *La Religion musulmane,* 342.

158. Ibn Ibrāhīm, *Al-Iʿlām,* vol. 5, 58. It is an open secret at al-Jazūlī's shrine in Marrakesh that the shaykh's body is not buried under the catafalque where most visitors pay their respects. Instead, it is located deep beneath the wall behind the catafalque. Jazūlite Sufis thus pay their respects to the left of the catafalque, facing the wall behind the *muqaddam*'s seat.

159. Jean-Léon l'Africain, *Description de l'Afrique,* vol. 1, 82.

160. Although Kably acknowledges that al-Jazūlī died after the revolt against ʿAbd al-Ḥaqq II, and not before this event, as most Western historians have as-

sumed, he is mistaken about the shaykh's death date, which he places in Rabīʿ al-Awwal 870/November 1465. See idem, *Société, pouvoir et religion,* 330–331. See also al-Fāsī, *Maṭāliʿ al-masarrāt* (Cairo edition), 4.

161. an-Nāṣirī, *al-Istiqṣāʾ*, vol. 4, 99–101. On ʿAbd al-ʿAzīz al-Waryāghlī, see al-Kattānī, *Salwat al-anfās,* vol. 2, 80–81. The most thorough study of this revolt is Mercedes García-Arenal, "The Revolution of Fās in 869/1465 and the Death of Sultan ʿAbd al-Ḥaqq al-Marīnī," *BSOAS* 41(1)(1978): 43–66.

162. Kably (*Société, pouvoir et religion,* 331–334), following García-Arenal, assumes that Zarrūq's opposition to this pogrom caused his sudden departure from Morocco. This may also explain why Zarrūq opposed the populism and political activism of Sufi orders such as the Jazūliyya.

Chapter Seven

1. Abū'l-Ḥasan ʿAlī Ṣāliḥ al-Andalusī, *Sharḥ Raḥbat al-amān* (Rabat, BH ms. 5697, dated 970/1562–3), 26.

2. On the concept of "maraboutic Sufism," see Bel, *La Religion musulmane,* 346.

3. See, for example, ash-Shādhilī, *At-Taṣawwuf wa'l-mujtamaʿ*, 74, where "popular Sufism" is translated into Arabic as *at-taṣawwuf ash-shaʿbī.*

4. de Prémare, *Sîdî ʿAbd-er-Raḥmân el-Mejdûb,* 74. My translation.

5. Zarrūq, *Qawāʿid at-taṣawwuf,* 15. On the life and works of Aḥmad Zarrūq, see Benchekroun, *La Vie intellectuelle,* 373–384, and Khushaim, *Zarrūq the Sufi,* 41–94.

6. Kably, *Société, pouvoir et religion,* 319.

7. Mercedes García-Arenal, "Sainteté et pouvoir dynastique au Maroc: la Résistance de Fès aux Sa'diens," *Annales ESC* 4 (July/August 1990): 1034.

8. Thomas S. Kuhn, *The Structure of Scientific Revolutions* (Chicago, 1970), 10, 16–17.

9. See Schimmel, *And Muhammad,* 32, 55, 61.

10. "Verily you have in the Messenger of God a good model (*uswatun ḥasanatun*) for one whose hope is in God and the Last Day and remembers (*dhakara*) God often" (Qur'ān, XXXIII [*al-Aḥzāb*], 21). My translation.

11. Schimmel, *And Muhammad,* 32. According to Richard Kieckhefer, the *imitatio Christi* is a paradigm that primarily models the attributes of patience, passion, and revelation. See idem, *Unquiet Souls,* 50–121, 150–179. On the relationship of martyrdom to the *imitatio Christi,* see Hippolyte Delehaye, *Les Origines du culte des martyrs* (Brussels, 1933), 1–24.

12. See Abū Naṣr ibn ʿAlī as-Sarrāj aṭ-Ṭūsī, *The Kitāb al-Lumaʿ fī'l-Taṣawwuf,* R. A. Nicholson, ed. (reprint, London, 1963), 93–95.

13. Ibid., 93.

14. Ibid., 94–95.

15. Although Hasanid Shiʿism has much in common with Zaydism, the two cannot be elided, as suggested by Richard T. Mortel ("Zaydi Shiʿism and the Ḥasanid Sharifs of Mecca," *IJMES* 19[4][1987]: 455–472). To give but one ex-

ample: the lack of interest shown by Idrisid historians in the revolt of Zayd ibn ʿAlī (d. 124/740) strongly suggests that the Idrisids did not consider themselves Zaydīs.

16. These uprisings took place in the year 169/785–6, and were precipitated by the anti-ʿAbbasid revolt of ʿAbdallāh al-Kāmil's nephew al-Ḥusayn in Medina. This revolt was followed by the abortive rising of Yaḥyā ibn ʿAbdallāh al-Kāmil in Daylam and that of his brother Muḥammad an-Nafs az-Zakiyya in Mecca. See al-Lihīwī, *Ḥiṣn as-salām,* 245–252.

17. ʿAbd al-Ḥamīd Ḥajjiyyāt, "Tārīkh ad-dawla al-Idrīsiyya min khilāl kitāb 'Naẓm ad-durr wa'l-ʿiqiyān' li-Abī ʿAbdallāh at-Tanasī (d. 899/1494)," *Majallat at-tārīkh* 9 (1980): 29. See also al-Lihīwī, *Ḥiṣn as-salām,* 256.

18. al-Lihīwī, *Ḥiṣn as-salām,* 272.

19. See, for example, Laroui, *The History of the Maghrib,* 109–112. See also Ibn Khaldūn, *Tārīkh Ibn Khaldūn: al-musammā Kitāb al-ʿibar wa dīwān al-mustadā wa'l-Khabar fī ayyām al-ʿArab wa'l-ʿAjam wa'l-Barbar wa man ʿāsarahum min dhawī as-Ṣulṭān al-Akbar* (Beirut, 1992), vol. 6, 256–260.

20. al-Lihīwī, *Ḥiṣn as-salām,* 278–285.

21. Ibid., 295–297.

22. Ibid., 300.

23. Ibid., 417–418.

24. Ibid., 392–439.

25. Ibid., 418.

26. Ibid., 419. ʿAbd ar-Raḥmān al-Madanī is buried in the region of Targha on the Rifian coast, where he is known as "the faqīh of Mūlāy ʿAbd as-Salām."

27. Ibid., 409.

28. See Benchekroun, *La Vie intellectuelle,* 103–104.

29. Muḥammad al-Manūnī, "Al-Mawlid an-nabawī ash-sharīf fī'l-Maghrib al-Marīnī," *Waraqāt,* 265–266. The Persian holiday *Mehrejān* was apparently celebrated as John the Baptist's birthday by the Mozarabs (Arabized Christians) of Muslim Spain.

30. Ibid.

31. On Abū'l-Qāsim al-ʿAzafī and the oligarchy of jurists and merchants (known locally as the *Shūra*) that ruled Sabta in the Marinid period, see Ferhat, *Sabta,* 232–242.

32. al-Manūnī, "Al-Mawlid an-nabawī," 267.

33. Ibid.

34. Ibid., 268.

35. al-Qashtālī, *Tuḥfat al-mughtarib,* 108–109.

36. Ibn Qunfudh, *Uns al-faqīr,* 71.

37. The most complete biography of Qāḍī ʿIyāḍ can be found in Ibn Ibrāhīm, *Al-Iʿlām,* vol. 9, 319–398. For a detailed account of his political activities as head of the ulama of Sabta, see Ferhat, *Sabta,* 146–161. Today, Qāḍī ʿIyāḍ is venerated as one of Marrakesh's "Seven Saints" (*sabʿatu rijāl*).

38. al-Qāḍī Abī'l-Faḍl ʿIyāḍ al-Yaḥṣubī, *Ash-Shifāʾ bi-taʿrīf ḥuqūq al-Muṣṭafā* (Beirut, 1979), vol. 2, 95–204.

39. Ibid., vol. 2, 95–97.

40. Ibid., 96–147.

41. Ibid., vol. 1, 335–360.

42. Ibid., 3–4.

43. Bernd Radtke and John O'Kane, *The Concept of Sainthood in Early Islamic Mysticism: Two Works by al-Ḥakīm al-Tirmidhī* (London, 1996), 105. I am grateful to Bernd Radtke for providing me with a prepublication copy of this work.

44. Ibid., 186.

45. Ibid., 186–187.

46. Izutsu, *Sufism and Taoism,* 218.

47. Muḥyī᾽ ad-Dīn Ibn al-ʿArabī, *Fuṣūṣ al-ḥikam,* Abū'l-ʿAlā ʿAfīfī, ed. (Beirut, 1980), 55. For a detailed study of the concept of *al-insān al-kāmil,* see Masataka Takeshita, *Ibn ʿArabī's Theory of the Perfect Man and its Place in the History of Islamic Thought* (Tokyo, 1987).

48. Ibn al-ʿArabī, *Fuṣūṣ al-ḥikam,* 50.

49. For further information on the concept of *al-ḥaqīqa al-Muḥammadiyya,* see Chodkiewicz, *Le Sceau des saints,* 79–94.

50. For a summary of Ibn al-ʿArabī's metaphysics, see William C. Chittick, *Imaginal Worlds: Ibn al-ʿArabī and the Problem of Religious Diversity* (Albany, New York, 1994), 15–29. Chittick prefers "Immutable Entities" to the more often used "Permanent Archetypes," because the former term better expresses Ibn al-ʿArabī's notion that all existent forms, and not just the forms *in principio,* are prefigured through *al-aʿyān ath-thābita.*

51. Izutsu, *Sufism and Taoism,* 236.

52. Ibn al-ʿArabī, *Fuṣūṣ al-ḥikam,* 162–163.

53. Al-Jīlī was a disciple of Sharaf ad-Dīn al-Jabartī (d. 806/1403–4), the founder of the Qādiriyya zāwiya of Zabīd in Yemen. The doctrines of this shaykh were heavily influenced by those of Ibn al-ʿArabī. See Zaydān, *Aṭ-Ṭarīq aṣ-ṣūfī,* 179.

54. ʿAbd al-Karīm ibn Ibrāhīm al-Jīlī, *Al-Insān al-kāmil fī maʿrifat al-awākhir wa'l-awā᾽il* (Cairo, 1981), vol. 1, 92–93.

55. Ibid., 94. Although this tradition is not found in the six "canonical" hadith collections, at least two versions of it appear in later works. According to Jalāl ad-Dīn as Suyūṭī (*Al-Itqān fī ʿulūm al-Qur᾽ān* [Cairo, 1985], vol. 1, 116–120), both versions of this hadith were transmitted on the authority of the Prophet's cousin Ibn ʿAbbās. Aṭ-Ṭabarī, however, rejects the tradition as *mawqūf* (i.e., it stops at a Companion without being linked directly to the Prophet), and implies that Ibn ʿAbbās may have forged it. Thanks are due to Alan Godlas of the University of Georgia for this information.

56. al-Jīlī, *Al-Insān al-kāmil,* vol. 2, 37. This interpretation is based on Ibn al-ʿArabī's concept of *al-ḥaqīqa al-Muḥammadiyya ar-raḥmāniyya.* See Chodkiewicz, *Le Sceau des saints,* 88.

57. al-Jīlī, *Al-Insān al-kāmil,* 46–47.

58. Ibid., 52.

59. Ibid., 59.

60. Ibid., 71.

61. Abū Bakr ash-Shiblī (d. 334/846) was governor of Damāvand in Khurasan before joining the circle of al-Junayd in Baghdad. As one of the earliest practitioners of *malāmatī* Sufism, he was notorious for his outrageous statements and may have ended his life in a mental asylum. See Arberry, *Muslim Saints and Mystics,* 277–286.

62. al-Jīlī, *Al-Insān al-kāmil,* vol. 2, 74–75.

63. al-Manūnī, "Al-Mawlid an-nabawī," 275–276.

64. al-Būṣīrī was a disciple of ash-Shādhilī's successor Abū'l-ʿAbbās al-Mursī (d. 684/1285). See Schimmel, *And Muhammad,* 181–187.

65. Abū'l-Qāsim Ibrāhīm ibn Ḥusayn al-Māgirī az-Zammūrī, *Uns al-waḥda fī sharḥ al-Burda* (Rabat, BH ms. 3210).

66. Abū Zayd ʿAbd ar-Raḥmān al-Maqūdī, *Maqṣūra nabawiyya ʿalā madḥ khayr al-bariyya* (Madrid, BN ms. 4956/3).

67. Muḥammad ibn ʿAbbād ar-Rundī, *Fatḥ at-tuḥfa wa idāʿat aṣ-ṣadafa li-taqaʿ al-muwāfaqa* (Madrid, BN ms. 4928). See especially the section, "Ghurbat ad-dīn wa anna amrahu fī naqṣin min ladun wafāt Rasūl Allāh" (The Disappearance and weakening of religion since the death of the Messenger of God).

68. al-Jazūlī, *Dalāʾil al-khayrāt,* 80.

69. Ibid., 98.

70. Ibn Ibrāhīm, *Al-Iʿlām* vol. 5, 47–48. See also al-Fāsī, *Mumtiʿ al-asmāʿ,* 4.

71. al-Fāsī, *Mumtiʿ al-asmāʿ,* 27.

72. al-Kattānī, *Salwat al-anfās,* vol. 2, 208.

73. al-Andalusī, *Sharḥ Raḥbat al-amān,* 2. Copyists' errors in the transcription of this passage were corrected according to the commentary on 56–67.

74. Ibid., 4–5.

75. Ibid., 9–14.

76. Ibid., 25–30.

77. Ibid., 20.

78. This phrase first appears in Ibn al-ʿArabī's *ʿAnqā mughrib.* See Chodkiewicz, *An Ocean Without Shore,* 35, 142 n. 1.

79. al-Andalusī, *Sharḥ Raḥbat al-amān,* 40–45.

80. Ibid., 54.

81. See, for example, Chodkiewicz, *Le Sceau des saints,* 95–110.

82. al-Andalusī, *Sharḥ Raḥbat al-amān,* 54.

83. Ibid., 58.

84. Ibid., 68.

85. For an overview of the "Light of Muḥammad" imagery in Sufism, see Schimmel, *And Muhammad,* 123–143.

86. al-Andalusī, *Sharḥ Raḥbat al-amān,* 71–74. See also Schimmel, *And Muhammad,* 125–126; and Gerhard Böwering, *The Mystical Vision of Existence in*

Classical Islam: the Qur'ānic Hermeneutics of the Sufi Sahl al-Tustarī (d. 283–896) (Berlin, 1979).

87. al-Andalusī, *Sharḥ Raḥbat al-amān,* 75.

88. al-Lihīwī, *Ḥiṣn as-salām,* 391–392. The pilgrimage to Mūlāy ʿAbd as-Salām ibn Mashīsh originated in the fourteenth century C.E., soon after the Shādhiliyya Sufi order was introduced into Morocco from al-Andalus. See al-ʿĀfiya, *Shafshāwan,* 284–285.

89. This work can be found under two separate titles in the Bibliothèque Générale et Archives, Rabat. The page numbers cited below refer to BG ms. 2617K. The second copy is cataloged under the title *Taḥbīr al-ajrās fī sirr al-anfās* (The Embellishment of the Bells in the Secret of the Souls) and corresponds to BG ms. 2002D.

90. See the discussion of *Raḥbat al-amān,* above, and al-Jazūlī, *Risāla fī't-tawḥīd,* 131v.

91. al-Ghazwānī, *An-Nuqṭa al-azaliyya,* 16, 19, 22.

92. Ibid., 12–13. Muḥammad al-Laqānī, a disciple of Aḥmad Zarrūq, was one of the most important Maliki legists of the sixteenth century. See Aḥmad ibn al-Qāḍī al-Miknāsī, *Durrat al-ḥijāl fī asmāʾ ar-rijāl* (Tunis and Cairo, 1971), vol. 2, 152–153, 152 n. 5.

93. See, for example, al-Bukhārī, *Saḥīḥ* (Kitāb al-waḥy), 2; Muslim, *Saḥīḥ* (Faḍāʾil), 87; at-Tirmidhī, *Sunan* (Manāqib), 7; and an-Nasāʾī, *Sunan* (Iftitāḥ), 27.

94. al-Jīlī, *Al-Insān al-kāmil,* vol. 1, 107.

95. Jean Canteins, *La Voie des lettres: Tradition cachée en Israël et en Islam* (Paris, 1981), 35–36.

96. al-Ghazwānī, *An-Nuqṭa al-azaliyya,* 30.

97. Ibid., 54–55.

98. Ibid., 15.

99. Ibid., 32, 245–250, 251, 315–320.

100. Ibid., 31.

101. Ibid., 54. This phrase is a paraphrasis of Qurʾān XXII (*al-Ḥajj*), 78: "It is [God] who has named you Muslims, both before and in this [Revelation], that the Messenger may be a witness for you (*li-yakūna ar-Rasūlu shahīdan ʿalaykum*) and that you be witness for humanity." My translation.

102. This aspect of al-Ghazwānī's theory of saintly authority appears to have been derived from al-Ḥakīm at-Tirmidhī's discussion of the relationship between the Prophet and the Seal of Sainthood. See Takeshita, *Ibn ʿArabī's Theory,* 135–148.

103. al-Ghazwānī, *An-Nuqṭa al-azaliyya,* 32.

104. Ibid., 32, 142.

105. Ibid., 56, 63.

106. Martin McDermott, *The Theology of al-Shaikh al-Mufīd (d. 413/1022)* (Beirut, 1978), 106–132.

107. Unlike the present author, Laroui considers Idrisid Shiʿism to have been a derivation of Zaydism (idem, *The History of the Maghrib,* 109–112). See also n. 15 above.

108. On the political activities and eventual martyrdom of ʿAbd as-Salām ibn Mashīsh, see al-Lihīwī, *Ḥiṣn as-salām,* 422–435.

109. al-Ghazwānī, *An-Nuqṭa al-azaliyya,* 141.

110. Ibid.

111. Ibid., 20.

112. Ibid., 142.

113. This verse alludes to Qurʾān XLVI (*Ḥāʾ Mīm*), 35: "So be patient, as were the Messengers of inflexible resolve, and be in no haste about them. For on the day that [the unbelievers] see what they were promised, it will be as if they had not tarried more than an hour of the day. [You are but] a proclaimer. Shall any but the immoral be destroyed?" My translation.

114. al-Ghazwānī, *An-Nuqṭa al-azaliyya,* 50.

115. On the relationship of the *aṭ-ṭarīqa al-Muḥammadiyya* to neo-Sufism, see, for example, Bradford G. Martin, *Muslim Brotherhoods in Nineteenth-Century Africa* (Cambridge, 1976), 71–72, 106.

116. See, for example, Trimingham, *The Sufi Orders,* 106–107; and Fazlur Rahman, *Islam* (Chicago, 1979), 206–239.

117. R. S. O'Fahey, *Enigmatic Saint,* 1–9.

118. The following discussion of al-Ghazwānī's model of *wilāya* sainthood is taken from idem, *An-Nuqṭa al-azaliyya,* 25–30.

Chapter Eight

1. Khushaim, *Zarrūq the Sufi,* 191. This passage has been corrected for orthographical and syntactical errors.

2. Ibid., 85. Manuscript copies of *ʿUddat al-murīd aṣ-ṣādiq* can be found in Rabat, BG mss. 1157D and 864G, and in BH mss. 5999, 5416, 992, 925.

3. Kably, *Société, pouvoir et religion,* 302–320.

4. On the fear of *fitna* among premodern Muslim ulama, see Chamberlain, *Knowledge and Social Practice,* 91–107, 167–174.

5. From the fifteenth century, the term *zāwiya* replaces both *ribāṭ* and *rābiṭa* in Moroccan Sufi texts. Accordingly, *zāwiya* will be used to designate Sufi institutions in what follows.

6. Muḥammad ibn Ibrāhīm al-Khayyāṭī ar-Rīfī, *Kitāb jawāhir as-simāṭ fī dhikr manāqib Sīdī ʿAbdallāh al-Khayyāṭ* (Rabat, BG ms. 1185D), 10r. See also Lévi-Provençal, *Les Historiens des Chorfas,* 331.

7. ar-Rīfī, *Jawāhir as-simāṭ,* 8v–10v.

8. Ibid., 4v–4r.

9. Ibid., 14v. Despite his quietism, al-Khayyāṭ may have been murdered by the Saʿdians because he did not support them strongly enough. See Ibn ʿAskar, *Dawḥat an-nāshir,* 83.

10. al-Jazūlī, *ʿAqīda,* 24. See also Jallāb, *al-Jazūlī,* 49.

11. Ibid.

12. Ibn al-Muwaqqit, *As-Saʿāda al-abadiyya,* vol. 2, 76.

13. Ibid.

14. Zarrūq, *Al-Kunnāsh,* 66.

15. ʿAbd ar-Raḥmān aṣ-Ṣumaʿī at-Tādilī, *At-Tashawwuf fī rijāl as-sādāt at-taṣawwuf* (Rabat, BG ms. 1103D), 76r.

16. al-Fāsī, *Mumtiʿ al-asmāʿ,* 37–38.

17. Ibid., 36–37.

18. For information on Muḥammad ibn ʿĪsā al-Fahdī and the origins of the ʿĪsāwiyya Sufi order, see Aḥmad ibn Mahdī al-Ghazzāl, *An-Nūr ash-shāmil fī manāqib fahl ar-rijāl al-kāmil Sayyidī Muḥammad ibn ʿĪsā* (Cairo, 1929), 2–15. See also Ibn ʿAskar, *Dawḥat an-nāshir,* 75–76.

19. See Kably, *Société, pouvoir et religion,* 335–336, where Aḥmad al-Ḥārithī is incorrectly linked to the Banū Maʿqil rather than to the Banū Hilāl.

20. al-Fāsī, *Kitāb mumtiʿ,* 32–33; al-Fāsī, *Mumtiʿ al-asmāʿ,* 35–36.

21. Ibn al-Muwaqqit, *As-Saʿāda al-abadiyya,* vol. 2, 59, 62.

22. al-Kattānī, *Salwat al-anfās,* vol. 2, 208.

23. See, for example, Ibn al-Muwaqqit, *As-Saʿāda al-abadiyya,* vol. 2, 62.

24. Ibid., 60–62.

25. At-Tabbāʿ is often considered by the people of Marrakesh to have been the shaykh of his actual master, Muḥammad ibn Sulaymān al-Jazūlī. His tomb is distinctive among those of the other "Seven Saints" of Marrakesh because its sanctuary is marked by four iron chains, which are believed to protect the tomb from the pollution of non-Muslims.

26. al-Fāsī, *Kitāb mumtiʿ,* 35; al-Fāsī, *Mumtiʿ al-asmāʿ,* 38.

27. Az-Zaytūnī, who was the first shaykh of Aḥmad Zarrūq, is often confused with the companion of al-Jazūlī, Muḥammad az-Zarhūnī, who may have been az-Zaytūnī's teacher. See, for example, the *silsila* of Aḥmad Zarrūq reproduced in Khushaim, *Zarrūq the Sufi,* 102–103.

28. Ibn ʿAskar, *Dawḥat an-nāshir,* 71–72.

29. Zāwiyat Bū Quṭūṭ had long been linked to the way of Abū Madyan. It was originally built by Abū'l-Ḥasan ibn Ghālib (d. 568/1172–3), an Andalusian hadith scholar and disciple of Ibn al-ʿArīf who taught Abū Madyan the *Sunan* of at-Tirmidhī. Its unusual name was due to its founder's fondness for cats. See Ibn al-Qāḍī, *Jadhwat al-iqtibās,* vol. 1, 241 n. 331.

30. See Muḥammad ibn aṭ-Ṭayyib al-Qādirī, *Nashr al-mathānī li-ahl al-qarn al-ḥādī-ʿashar wa'th-thānī,* Muḥammad Ḥajjī and Aḥmad at-Tawfīq, eds. (Rabat, 1977), vol. 1, 315.

31. Ibn ʿAskar, *Dawḥat an-nāshir,* 71.

32. Ibid., 66–71.

33. Abū Bakr al-Būkhuṣaybī, *Aḍwāʾ ʿalā Ibn Yaggabsh at-Tāzī* (Casablanca, 1976), 123. The complete text of at-Tāzī's *Kitāb al-jihād* is reproduced in this volume.

34. The conquest of Asila, the expulsion of its inhabitants, and the destruction of the city's mosque are all mentioned in the poem that closes *Kitāb al-jihād* (Ibid., 146). For an account of Portuguese adventurism in Morocco from the Christian

side, see Diego de Torres (ca. 1586), *Relación del origen y suceso de los xarifes y del estado de los reinos de Marruecos, Fez, y Tarudante,* Mercedes García-Arenal, ed. (Madrid, 1980).

35. al-Būkhuṣaybī, *Ibn Yaggabsh at-Tāzī,* 125–126.

36. Ibid., 126.

37. Ibid., 130.

38. Ibid., 132.

39. Ibid., 137. Note the semantic opposition between *imām ʿādil* and *sulṭān jāʾir* in this passage. Both terms have strong mahdist connotations and are employed in Sunni as well as Shiʿite political philosophy. For the most thorough discussion of these concepts in Imami Shiʿism, see Abdulaziz Sachedina, *The Just Ruler in Shiʿite Islam: The Comprehensive Authority of the Jurist in Imamite Jurisprudence* (New York and Oxford, 1988), esp. 4–8, 94–117.

40. al-Būkhuṣaybī, *Ibn Yaggabsh at-Tāzī,* 140.

41. Ibid., 140–141.

42. Ibid.

43. Kably bases his view on the opinion that sharifism did not emerge directly out of Moroccan culture but was the artificial creation of Marinid state policy. See idem, *Société, pouvoir et religion,* 296–302, 324–330.

44. Ibid., 320–324.

45. Much of the information in the following section can be found in Vincent J. Cornell, "Mystical Doctrine and Political Action in Moroccan Sufism: The Role of the Exemplar in the *Ṭarīqa al-Jazūliyya,*" *Al-Qanṭara* 13(1)(1992): 201–231.

46. Ibn ʿAskar, *Dawḥat an-nāshir,* 99–100.

47. al-Ghazwānī, *An-Nuqṭa al-azaliyya,* 201.

48. Ibn al-Muwaqqit, *as-Saʿāda al-abadiyya,* vol. 2, 73.

49. Ibid. The pronunciation of al-Andalusī's comment in its original Granadan dialect (*hūwa aʿrabī guwī*) is reproduced by Ibn Ibrāhīm (*Al-Iʿlām,* vol. 8, 249), who notes that the Granadan letter *qāf* was pronounced with a sound midway between a *kāf* and a *ghayn.*

50. Ibn Ibrāhīm, *Al-Iʿlām,* vol. 8, 239.

51. See, for example, Ibn al-Muwaqqit, *As-Saʿāda al-abadiyya,* vol. 2, 74.

52. On Muḥammad ibn Dāwūd ash-Shāwī, see Ibn ʿAskar, *Dawḥat an-nāshir,* 95. See also Muḥammad al-Jazūlī al-Laggūsī al-Ḥuḍaygī (d. mid-twelfth/eighteenth century), *Ṭabaqāt al-Ḥuḍaygī* (Rabat, BG ms. 2328K), 150.

53. al-Fāsī, *Mirʾāt al-maḥāsin,* 211.

54. Muḥammad ibn ʿAbd ar-Raḥmān al-Kurrāsī, *ʿArūsat al-masāʾil fī mā li-Banī Waṭṭās min al-faḍāʾil,* ʿAbd al-Wahhāb ibn Manṣūr, ed. (Rabat, 1963), 15. On the author of this work, see Benchekroun, *La Vie intellectuelle,* 416–419.

55. The passages from *Mirʾāt al-maḥāsin* that detail these events are also reproduced in Ibn Ibrāhīm, *Al-Iʿlām,* vol. 8, 249–251.

56. See al-Kurrāsī, *ʿArūsat al-masāʾil,* 17. In this passage, al-Kurrāsī describes a twenty-five-year truce between the sultan of Fez and the Portuguese. Since Ibe-

rian sources make no mention of such a truce, al-Kurrāsī must have been referring to the original twenty-year truce plus a five-year extension, which is permissible under Islamic law.

57. al-ʿĀfiya, *Shafshāwan,* 42–43.

58. Ibid., 73–74.

59. Ibid., 72.

60. Ibid., 87. On the repopulation of Tetuan, see an-Nāṣirī, *al-Istiqṣāʾ*, vol. 4, 124–125.

61. See al-Kurrāsī, *ʿArūsat al-masāʾil,* 17–18.

62. Ibid., 18. See also al-ʿĀfiya, *Shafshāwan,* 90–94.

63. Later, Ibrāhīm ibn Rāshid would help his brother-in-law Aḥmad al-Waṭṭāsī seize power from Abū Ḥassūn al-Waṭṭāsī by occupying Fez with 2,000 cavalry. See al-ʿĀfiya, *Shafshāwan,* 105–113.

64. On the Banū ʿArūs of Qasr Kutāma and their activities in the Gharb region of northern Morocco, see de Prémare, *Sîdi ʿAbd-er-Raḥmān el-Mejdūb,* 48–51.

65. an-Nāṣirī, *al-Istiqṣāʾ*, vol. 4, 140.

66. al-Kurrāsī, *ʿArūsat al-masāʾil,* 23–25. Cf. esp., 23, n. 21.

67. al-Fāsī, *Mirʾāt al-maḥāsin,* 211.

68. Ibid., 212. See also al-Lihīwī, *Ḥiṣn as-salām,* 391.

69. al-Lihīwī, *Ḥiṣn as-salām,* 391–392. Although al-Lihīwī claims that al-Ghazwānī spent thirty years in the region of Jabal ʿAlam, this does not seem probable, given the dates of other, better-known events in the shaykh's life.

70. Personal communication with al-Ḥājj al-M'thīwī, muqaddam of the tomb complex of Mūlāy ʿAbd as-Salām ibn Mashīsh, Fall 1983.

71. al-ʿĀfiya, *Shafshāwan,* 284–285.

72. al-Ghazwānī, *An-Nuqṭa al-azaliyya,* 128.

73. See al-Ḥasan ibn Muḥammad ibn Raysūn (d. mid-eleventh/seventeenth century), *Manāqib al-akhawayn* (Rabat, BG ms. 2286K). See also Ibn ʿAskar, *Dawḥat an-nāshir,* 18–19.

74. Ibn al-Muwaqqit, *As-Saʿāda al-abadiyya,* vol. 2, 76.

75. Ibid.

76. Ibid., 79.

77. Ibid.

78. For a description of these educational centers, see Ḥajjī, *Al-Ḥaraka al-fikriyya,* 452–643. For the names of Saʿdian officials of rural origin, see Muḥammad ibn ʿAbdallāh al-Ifrānī (d. before 1151/1738–9), *Nuzhat al-ḥādī bi-akhbār mulūk al-qarn al-ḥādī,* Olivier Houdas, ed. (reprint of 1888 Paris edition, Rabat, n.d.), 37–38.

79. Ibn ʿAskar, *Dawḥat an-nāshir,* 23–27.

80. See al-ʿĀfiya, *Shafshāwan,* 203–204, 223–227.

81. Ibn al-Muwaqqit, *As-Saʿāda al-abadiyya,* vol. 2, 81.

82. al-Ghazwānī, *An-Nuqṭa al-azaliyya,* 199–202. The appellation *Āyat an-Nūr* refers both to the "Light Verse" of the Qur'an (XXIV, 34) and the following

mukhāṭaba of God to al-Ghazwānī: "Oh my slave, be a sign (*āya*) in every thing so that one may be guided through you to everything in everything" (Ibid., 113v.).

83. Ibn al-Muwaqqit, *As-Saʿāda al-abadiyya,* vol. 2, 82. See also al-Ghazwānī, *An-Nuqṭa al-azaliyya,* 223.

84. al-Ghazwānī, *An-Nuqṭa al-azaliyya,* 223–229.

85. Ibn al-Muwaqqit, *As-Saʿāda al-abadiyya,* vol. 2, 78. Al-Januwī's recollections of al-Ghazwānī can be found in Muḥammad ibn Yūsuf as-Sijilmāsī (fl. ca. 1025/1616), *Tuḥfat al-ikhwān wa mawāhib al-imtinān fī manāqib Sīdī Riḍwān ibn ʿAbdallāh al-Januwī* (Rabat, BG ms. 114K).

86. al-Fāsī, *Mirʾāt al-maḥāsin,* 212.

87. Ibid.

88. This account is reproduced in full by Ibn Ibrāhīm, *Al-Iʿlām,* vol. 8, 250–251.

89. Ibn ʿAskar, *Dawḥat an-nāshir,* 45–46.

90. The nineteenth-century historian an-Nāṣirī adds to the confusion over this account by identifying the qāḍī al-jamāʿa of Fez as Aḥmad ibn ʿAbdallāh al-Ifrānī al-Miknāsī. See idem, *al-Istiqṣāʾ,* vol. 4, 146.

91. Ibn Ibrāhīm, *Al-Iʿlām,* vol. 8, 251.

92. Muḥammad al-Harwī aṭ-Ṭālib al-Fāsī, *Waẓīfat al-Jazūliyya al-Ghazwāniyya* (Paris, BNP ms. 1201), 1v–3r.

93. Aḥmad ibn al-Qāsim al-Ḥalfawī, *Shams al-maʿrifa fī sīrat ghawth al-mutaṣawwifa* (Rabat, BG ms. 764G), 37–38.

94. al-Kurrāsī, *ʿArūsat al-masāʾil,* 22–23.

95. Torres, *Relación del origen,* 58–61.

96. Weston F. Cook, Jr., "Warfare and State Building in Early-Modern Morocco (1497–1517)," *Jusūr* 4 (1988): 9–10.

97. an-Nāṣirī (*al-Istiqṣāʾ,* vol. 4, 147) has al-Ghazwānī leaving Fez for Marrakesh during the drought of 926–7/1519–20, which caused a famine so severe that Moroccan fathers sold their daughters to the Portuguese in exchange for bushels of wheat. Although this is possible, the preponderance of the evidence remains with the more contemporaneous account in *Shams al-maʿrifa.*

98. al-Fāsī, *Mumtiʿ al-asmāʿ,* 43. See also Ibn Ibrāhīm, *Al-Iʿlām,* vol. 8, 251. Note that the expression, *ayyā,* is Berber, which indicates that the Arabs of ash-Shāwīya were linguistically influenced by their neighbors, the Berbers of Tāmesnā.

99. See Kably, *Société, pouvoir et religion,* 250–255.

100. Ḥajjī, *Al-Ḥaraka al-fikriyya,* vol. 1, 41.

101. ʿAbdallāh al-Mʾḍaghrī was the teacher of Muḥammad ibn ʿAbd ar-Raḥmān's sons Aḥmad al-Aʿraj and Muḥammad ash-Shaykh. See al-Ifrānī, *Nuzhat al-ḥādī,* 25.

102. Ibid., 5–9.

103. Leo Africanus, *Description de l'Afrique,* vol. 1, 93.

104. al-Ifrānī, *Nuzhat al-ḥādī,* 11.

105. Torres, *Relación del origen,* 41 and n. 20.

106. Ibn ʿAskar, *Dawḥat an-nāshir,* 114.

107. Abū ʿAbdallāh Muḥammad al-Baʿqīlī, *Tarājim ʿulamāʾ wa ṣulaḥāʾ Banī Ultīta wa ghayrihā min al-bilād as-Sūsiyya* (Rabat, BH ms. 12,573), not paginated.

108. Torres, *Relación del origen,* 41–43.

109. al-Ifrānī, *Nuzhat al-ḥādī,* 16.

110. Ibid., 6.

111. See Mercedes García-Arenal, "Mahdisme et la Dynastie Saʿdienne," in *Mahdisme, crise et changement dans l'histoire du Maroc,* A. Kaddouri, ed. (Rabat, 1994), 95–117.

112. al-Fāsī, *Kitāb mumtiʿ*, 3; al-Fāsī, *Mumtiʿ al-asmāʿ*, 4–5.

113. García-Arenal, "Mahdisme et la Dynastie Saʿdienne," 101.

114. al-Ifrānī, *Nuzhat al-ḥādī,* 39. On the origins of the jihad state in Islam, see Khalid Yahya Blankinship, *The End of the Jihād State: The Reign of Hishām ibn ʿAbd al-Malik and the Collapse of the Umayyads* (Albany, New York, 1994), 11–35.

115. Anonymous, *Chronique de Santa-Cruz du Cap de Gué (Agadir),* Pierre Cenival, ed. and trans. (Paris, 1934), 77.

116. al-Ifrānī, *Nuzhat al-ḥādī,* 44. My translation.

117. al-Fāsī, *Mumtiʿ al-asmāʿ*, 48–49. Ibn ʿAskar, *Dawḥat an-nāshir,* 100.

118. al-Fāsī, *Mumtiʿ al-asmāʿ*, 50–51; Ibn ʿAskar, *Dawḥat an-nāshir,* 102–103. The *ʿAqīda* of al-Ḥāḥī can be found in the Biblioteca Nacional, Madrid (BNM ms. 5347).

119. al-Fāsī, *Mumtiʿ al-asmāʿ*, 49; Ibn ʿAskar, *Dawḥat an-nāshir,* 101. See also Muḥammad al-ʿArabī ibn Bahlūl ar-Raḥḥāl, *Manhaj al-irtiḥāl ilā maʿrifat ash-shaykh Sīdī Raḥḥāl* (Rabat, 1956).

120. See al-Fāsī, *Mumtiʿ al-asmāʿ*, 50.

121. al-Ghazwānī's symbolic demonstration of divine legitimation is strikingly similar to the Stoic philosopher Zeno's (ca. 310 B.C.E.) simile of cognition: the open hand stands for the percipient who is acted upon by external stimuli; the partially closed hand represents the assent of the mind to external stimuli; the closed fist represents cognition, or the "grasping" of a concept; and grasping the fist with the other hand represents the confirmation of knowledge by an external source. See Long, *Hellenistic Philosophy,* 126.

122. For the full text of the preceding story, see Ibn Ibrāhīm, *al-Iʿlām,* vol. 8, 253–254; al-Fāsī, *Mumtiʿ al-asmāʿ*, 44–45.

123. For the Wattasid version of Muḥammad al-Burtughālī's siege of Marrakesh, see al-Kurrāsī, *ʿArūsat al-masāʾil,* 28–29.

124. Ibn ʿAskar, *Dawḥat an-nāshir,* 97. According to the Portuguese captive Marmól de Caravajal, the siege of Marrakesh was only lifted when Aḥmad alʿ-Araj agreed to recognize the Wattasids as the rulers of Morocco and to pay them an annual indemnity. See also al-Kurrāsī, *ʿArūsat al-masāʾil,* 26 n. 23.

125. See al-Ḥudaygī, *Ṭabaqāt,* 251.

126. an-Nāṣirī, *al-Istiqṣāʾ*, vol. 4, 151. See also al-Ifrānī, *Nuzhat al-ḥādī,* 20. According to this latter source, some wags later remarked: "If the Banū Marīn had

understood anything, they would not have left Sīdī ʿUmar al-Khaṭṭāb buried, but would have placed his body in an ark" (20–21).

127. See de Prémare, *Sîdî ʿAbd er-Raḥmān el-Mejdūb*, 107–113.

128. ʿAbd al-Wārith al-Yalṣūtī, *Sullam al-murīd* (Rabat, BG ms. 3284K), not paginated.

129. Al-Habṭī's most important work on Sufi reform is the didactic poem *Shams aḍ-ḍuḥā* [cataloged as *Manẓūma fī'ṭ-ṭarīqa*] (Madrid, BNM ms. 4958–4).

130. al-ʿĀfiya, *Shafshāwan*, 368.

131. Ibid., 369–70. See also Ibn ʿAskar, *Dawḥat an-nāshir*, 7.

132. Ibn ʿAskar, *Dawḥat an-nāshir*, 7.

133. al-ʿĀfiya, *Shafshāwan*, 372.

134. ʿAbdallāh ibn Muḥammad al-Habṭī, *al-Alfiyya as-saniyya*. For a translation of this work, see Vincent J. Cornell, "The Sufi as Social Critic: The *Alfiyya* of ʿAbdallāh al-Habṭī," in Carl Ernst ed., *Sufism in Practice* (Princeton, forthcoming).

135. al-Habṭī, *Al-Alfiyya as-saniyya*, 34–35.

136. See Mūsā ibn ʿAlī al-Wazzānī, *Risāla fī taʿlīm al-ʿaqīda* (Madrid, BNM ms. 5168).

137. al-ʿĀfiya, *Shafshāwan*, 373–377. This information comes from the biographical monograph *Al-Muʿrib al-faṣīḥ ʿan sīrat ash-shaykh ar-raḍī an-naṣīḥ*, by al-Habṭī's son Muḥammad (d. 1001/1592–3). This manuscript is in a private collection and was unavailable for consultation by the present author.

138. Ibid.

139. al-Ifrānī, *Nuzhat al-ḥādī*, 24.

140. Ibn ʿAskar, *Dawḥat an-nāshir*, 5–6, 9, 14–16. Ibn Khajjū is buried in the Bāb Futūḥ cemetery of Fez, near the tomb of Ibn ʿAbbād ar-Rundī.

141. al-Ifrānī, *Nuzhat al-ḥādī*, 41.

142. Ibid. See also Ibn ʿAskar, *Dawḥat an-nāshir*, 102–104, 110–111.

143. The following section is a paraphrasis of Abū ʿImrān Mūsā ibn ʿAlī al-Wazzānī, *Al-Kurrāsa . . . li-mawlānā al-manṣūr as-sulṭān al-muẓaffar Muḥammad ibn Muḥammad ash-Sharīf al-Ḥasanī . . . fī masʾalat al-quṭb al-mushār ilayhi ʿinda ahl aṭ-ṭarīqa aṣ-ṣūfiyya* (Rabat, BH ms. 7585), folios not numbered.

Conclusion

1. Zarrūq, *Qawāʿid at-taṣawwuf*, 111.

2. as-Salawī, *Tuḥfat az-zāʾir*, 3r–4v.

3. The concept of "enclaves of meaning" comes from Alfred Schutz. See Berger and Luckmann, *The Social Construction of Reality*, 25–26.

4. See Richard Valantasis, "Constructions of Power in Asceticism," *JAAR* 63(4)(1995): 796–797.

5. The term "ideological complex" comes from social semiotics. See Robert Hodge and Gunter Kress, *Social Semiotics* (Ithaca, New York, 1988), 4–12, 266–267.

6. al-ʿAzafī, *Diʿāmat al-yaqīn,* 66–67. On the *majestas* ("overpoweringness") of the *mysterium tremendum,* see Rudolf Otto, *The Idea of the Holy,* John W. Harvey, trans. (Oxford, 1958), 19–23.

7. See Thomas E. Wartenberg, "Situated Social Power," in idem, ed., *Rethinking Power* (Albany, New York, 1992), 79–101.

8. Peter Brown, "The Rise and Function of the Holy Man in Late Antiquity," in idem, *Society and the Holy in Late Antiquity* (London, 1982), 119.

9. See, for example, Michel Foucault, *Power/Knowledge: Selected Interviews & Other Writings, 1972–1977,* Colin Gordon, ed. (New York, 1980), 94–95.

10. On the concept of "sedimentation of meaning," see Berger and Luckmann, *The Social Construction of Reality,* 69.

11. Ibid., 54–55.

12. Ibid., 67–70.

13. Ibid., 73–74.

14. On the concept of the "eternal present" in paradigmatic history, see Mircea Eliade, *The Sacred and the Profane: The Nature of Religion,* William R. Trask, trans. (San Diego and New York, 1959), 95–113.

15. al-Fāsī, *Kitāb mumtiʿ*, 27; al-Fāsī, *Mumtiʿ al-asmāʿ*, 28.

16. at-Tādilī, *at-Tashawwuf,* 215.

17. Cornell, *The Way of Abū Madyan,* 88.

18. Ibn aṣ-Ṣabbāgh, *Durrat al-asrār,* 25–26.

Glossary of Technical Terms

admiranda "things to be wondered at"; used in medieval Europe to describe the actions of a saint who is to be marveled at but not imitated. Cf. *imitanda.*

ʿālim (pl. *ʿulamāʾ*, anglicized: *ulama*) "person of knowledge" or "scholar," often designating an expert in the sciences of *ḥadīth, fiqh,* and/or *sharīʿa* (q. v.).

ʿamal "praxis," "practice" as opposed to "knowledge" or *ʿilm* (q. v.).

amghār Ber. "elder" or "leader." A term of primarily political connotation, roughly equivalent to the Arabic *shaykh* (q. v.).

ʿaqīda "creed," "doctrinal manifesto." A genre of religious literature usually devoted to doctrinal matters.

ʿārif "knower" or "gnostic," as in "knower of God" (*ʿārif bi'llāh*); a person who possesses spiritual knowledge or insight (*maʿrifa*).

awliyāʾ See *walī.*

baraka "spiritual potency" or "power" associated with holy individuals, places and/or objects. It is believed to have a tangible existence and can be transmitted to those who come into contact with the person or thing that possesses it.

bāṭin "inner," as in the inner aspect of religion or the knowledge of inner realities (*ʿilm al-bāṭin*); often opposed to *ẓāhir* (q. v.).

bayʿa "oath of allegiance" pledged to a political or spiritual leader.

dhikr lit. "remembrance" or "recollection," a Sufi ritual in which divine names or holy phrases are rhythmically chanted, bringing about a state of meditation or ecstasy.

faqīh (pl. *fuqahāʾ*) "legist" or "legal specialist," one who specializes in the science of *fiqh* (q. v.).

faqīr (pl. *fuqarāʾ*) "poor one," a person who is poor in spirit. In a Sufi context this term can be used to designate any Sufi, especially one who has transcended the world (regardless of his or her actual economic status). The term is sometimes used to distinguish rural Sufis (*al-fuqarāʾ*) from urban Sufis (*aṣ-ṣūfiyya*).

faqr "poverty" or "privation," the systematic practice of spiritual poverty.

fiqh the science of deriving legal rulings from the various sources of Islamic law.

firāsa in Sufism, "clairvoyance," an epistemological miracle involving mind reading or foreknowledge of coming events.

futuwwa a complex phenomenon, often translated as "Sufi chivalry" but also including the practices of asceticism (*zuhd*), scrupulousness (*waraʿ*), socially conscious virtue (*ṣalāḥ*), preference for others (*īthār*), and institutionalized brotherhood.

ghawth "succour" or "nurturer," often equated with the axial saint or *quṭb;* the *ghawth* practices *ighātha,* the nurturance of others through his knowledge.

ḥadīth (anglicized; *hadith*) the report of a saying or action attributed to the Prophet Muḥammad, passed down through a chain of transmission called an *isnād.* The term is also used for the collective body of Prophetic traditions.

ḥajj the annual pilgrimage to Mecca, enjoined upon each Muslim to undertake at least once in his or her lifetime (if physically and economically able).

ʿibāda "worship," "devoted servitude" to God.

iḥsān "virtue," "true goodness," the result of combining doctrine (*ʿilm*) with praxis (*ʿamal*).

ijtihād "independent judgment" or "independent reasoning," which one brings to bear on a legal or theological issue.

ʿilm "knowledge" or "science" (understood broadly). Often distinguished from praxis or *ʿamal* (q. v.).

imām "the foremost" or "prayer-leader"; also, the religious leader of a Muslim community.

imitanda "things to be imitated," used to designate the actions of saints who serve as behavioral exemplars. Cf. *admiranda.*

al-insān al-kāmil "the perfect human being," who in the doctrine of Ibn al-ʿArabī serves as the cosmic archetype, actualizing all the potentialities of existence. The concept was further developed by ʿAbd al-Karīm al-Jīlī and shaykhs of the Jazūliyya Sufi order.

iqṭāʿ a "quasi-feudal land grant"; in the Maghrib it is often used to designate a "grant of tribal usufruct."

īthār "altruism," "giving preference to others over oneself," one of the values of *futuwwa* (q. v.).

Islamdom a term coined by historian Marshall Hodgson to designate "the society in which the Muslims and their faith are recognized as prevalent and socially dominant in one sense or another—a society in which . . . non-Muslims have always formed an integral, if subordinate, element as have Jews in Christendom" (idem, *The Venture of Islam,* vol. 1, 58).

jaras lit. "bell." al-Ghazwānī employs this term to stand for the "Bell saint," or the unique and universal axial saint (cf. *quṭb*).

jihād "struggle" or "war" in defense of Islam. The "greater *jihād*" is waged against one's passional soul or *nafs* (q. v.), while the "lesser *jihād*" is waged against those who threaten the security of the Muslim community, or *umma* (q. v.).

juridical Sufism a praxis-oriented form of mysticism that submits to the authority of religious law.

karāma (pl. *karāmāt*) a "miracle" that a saint performs, often presented as proof of the saint's closeness to God. These saintly miracles are distinguished from the miracles performed by prophets, called *muʿjiza* (pl. *muʿjizāt*).

kharāj a tax levied on lands conquered by Muslims, and in principle paid to the Muslims who conquered them.

kharq al-ʿāda the "rending of custom" or "paranormal phenomenon," another term for a saintly *karāma* (q. v.).

khāṣṣ in the context of juridical discourse, which predominates in Moroccan Sufism, *khāṣṣ* means "something of specific application," as opposed to *ʿāmm* which means "something of general application." In other contexts the terms can mean "elite" and "common" respectively.

khirqa "mantle of initiation," passed on either literally or symbolically by a Sufi shaykh to a disciple. In Moroccan Sufism, the spiritual master who confers initiation in one's primary "way" (q. v. *ṭarīqa*) is called *shaykh al-khirqa.*

madhhab "methodology" or "school of thought," especially with regard to jurisprudence.

madrasa "study center" or "religious school," which in the Maghrib was usually state-sponsored. These schools promoted doctrinal orthodoxy through the teaching of a standardized curiculum based on abridged legal and religious texts (q. v. *mukhtaṣar*).

maghrib lit. "where the sun sets," "the west," here designating the entire region of western premodern Islamdom including North Africa and Spain. The "Far Maghrib," *al-Maghrib al-Aqṣāʾ*, roughly encompasses the boundaries of modern Morocco.

maḥabba "the path of love," which for al-Jazūlī expressed the highest station and quintessence of the Sufi way.

mahdī lit. "guided one," the expected messianic leader who will appear in the final days to command the forces of righteousness against the forces of evil, restoring justice to the world.

majdhūb "God-addicted lover," one "possessed" or "attracted [by God]."

manqaba (pl. *manāqib*) "hagiographical monograph" on the life of a single saint, containing biographical narratives and accounts of exemplary acts.

malāmatī one who follows the "path of blame," or *ṭarīq al-malāma.* This path is based on the appearance, but usually not the reality, of antinomian contravention of the *sharīʿa* (q. v.). In Morocco, *malāmatī* Sufism was often associated with social activism and political dissent.

marabout a Francophone corruption of the Arabic term *murābiṭ* (q. v.), first used in colonial Algeria to designate any rural holy man. Subsequently a number of scholars uncritically adopted the term and employed it for any type of North African "saint." Recently the term has become prevalent even among North Africans themselves.

mawlā (pl. *mawālī*) a non-Arab convert to Islam who becomes a "client" of an Arab family or tribe, associating with it for patronage and/or protection.

mawlāy (Mor. Ar. *mūlāy*) "master" or "lord," a title of address used for a descendant of the Prophet Muḥammad or *sharīf* (q. v.).

al-mawlid an-nabawī the birthday of the Prophet Muḥammad, the celebration of which was an innovation promoted by the Sunni legists of Sabta in the thirteenth century C.E. to mitigate the influence of Christianity on uneducated Muslims and new converts.

mawsim "season" or "yearly festival," for example an agricultural festival, or a festival to celebrate the anniversary of the death of a holy figure.

mujaddid "renewer," a person believed to fulfill for his period the *ḥadīth* (q. v.) which states: "God will send to this community at the turn of every century someone who will restore religion."

mujtahid an "interpreter of the law," who employs *ijtihād* (q. v.).

mukhtaṣar an "abridgement." Abridged texts were often used to facilitate instruction in the fields of grammar, theology, and law. The use of abridgments in the *madrasa* (q. v.) system of the thirteenth and fourteenth centuries C. E. contributed to an overall decline in religious and legal expertise but promoted the standardization of doctrine.

murābiṭ (pl. *murābiṭūn*) a technical term for a person associated with a *ribāṭ* (q. v.), a rural Sufi shaykh who maintained an "actionally formal" relationship with a tribe or group of tribes. Often the *murābiṭ* was an urban-educated intellectual who could translate the norms of "orthodox" Islam into terms that his pastoralist clients could understand and accept.

murīd (pl. *murīdūn*) lit. "desirer," a disciple or student of a Sufi shaykh or *murshid* (q. v.).

murshid lit. "guide," a Sufi teacher or spiritual master. Roughly equivalent to the term *shaykh* (q. v.) or *ustādh* (q. v.).

mushāṭara the ritualistic sharing of goods in proportionate measure, a characteristic of the Sufi practice of Abū'l-ʿAbbās as-Sabtī.

muwallad "half-breed," a term used in pre-Islamic Arabia for the offspring of slaves. Andalusian Arabs applied the label to new converts to Islam as an indication of their low social status.

nafs "ego" or "passional soul," which thrives on desire.

qāḍī "judge" in a Sharīʿa court, differentiated from *faqīh* (q. v.), or legist in general.

qudwa "exemplar," "model," a person who serves as a teacher of Sufis and hence of other potential saints. A *qudwa* is therefore an "exemplar for the exemplary."

quṭb lit. "tent-pole" or "axis." It is a term used for the saint who was deemed to be the greatest of his time and therefore held to be the metaphysical "Axis of the Age" (*quṭb az-zamān*, c.f. *ghawth*). Because the doctrine of *al-insān al-kāmil* (q. v.). allowed for multiple claimants to this title, in later years the station became applicable only regionally. This led the Jazūlite shaykh al-Ghazwānī to formulate a new title which could reclaim universal applicability, the "Bell saint" or *jaras* (q. v.).

rābiṭa "hermitage," a Maghribi term for an urban center of Sufi instruction, founded by a single shaykh, that was usually not associated with an "international" Sufi *ṭarīqa* (q. v.). It was replaced in the fifteenth century C. E. by the term *zāwiya* (q. v.).

ribāṭ lit. "place of attachment," an urban or rural center of instruction that provided religious education as well as Sufi training. As an institution, the rural *ribāṭ* was associated with a particular tribe or group of tribes and its leadership was usually inherited by the descendants of the founder. Also replaced by *zāwiya* after the fifteenth century C.E.

rijāl literature "hagiographical anthologies" devoted to the "men" (*rijāl*) who were deemed bearers of authoritative tradition. Originally the genre dealt primarily with the early "Righteous Forebears" of Islam (*as-salaf aṣ-ṣāliḥ,* q. v.), but Moroccan hagiographers such as at-Tādilī expanded the definition of *rijāl* to include Sufi saints. In this way the example of the saints was made as authoritative as that of *as-salaf aṣ-ṣāliḥ*.

aṣ-ṣaḥāba the Companions of the Prophet Muḥammad, who transmitted the Prophetic *ḥadīth* (q. v.). Many later Muslims, especially the followers of the *uṣūl* tradition (q. v.), regarded the sayings and acts of the Companions themselves to be instructive and authoritative.

as-salaf aṣ-ṣāliḥ "the Righteous Forebears," usually referring to the *ṣaḥāba* (q. v.), and the following two generations of Muslims. Along with the Prophet Muḥammad, *as-salaf aṣ-ṣāliḥ* were the chief exemplars of the *uṣūl* tradition (q. v.) and their time was thought to constitute a "golden age" of Islam.

ṣalāḥ "socially conscious virtue." Cf. *ṣāliḥ*.

ṣāliḥ (pl. *ṣulaḥā*ʾ, *ṣāliḥūn;* fem. *ṣāliḥa,* fem. pl. *ṣāliḥāt*) "virtuous one," a person who embodies *ṣālāḥ* (q.v.) by being a morally upstanding and socially constructive individual. The term *ṣāliḥ* epitomizes Moroccan sainthood in the early hagiographical texts.

sharīʿa "Islamic law" in the abstract, the entire body of rules governing a Muslim's life. The concrete applications of the Sharīʿa are worked out through the science of *fiqh* (q. v.).

sharīf (Mor. pl. *shurafā*ʾ) a "noble" person, in Morocco a descendant of the Prophet Muḥammad. The fifteenth century C. E. saw the popularization of "sharifism," an ideology in which religious and political authority were predicated on descent from the Prophet (i.e. being a *sharīf*).

shaykh lit. "elder" or "chief," used to mean political leader, scholar, or spiritual master. In Sufism, it is roughly equivalent to the term *murshid* (q.v.).

ṣūfī (anglicized: *Sufi*) a Muslim "mystic" and practitioner of *taṣawwuf.* Not every Muslim saint (*walī Allāh,* q. v.) was a Sufi, although most were. Likewise, many scholars (q. v. *ʿālim*) and legal specialists (q. v. *faqīh*) were also Sufis.

There was no rigid dichotomy or separation between a Sufi and a legist or any other type of Muslim intellectual.

ṭāʾifa lit. "faction" or "party." It can stand for any hierarchically organized corporate institution and was the most common term in premodern Morocco for an institutionalized Sufi order. In modern times this usage has largely been replaced by the term *ṭarīqa* (q. v.).

taqlīd loyalty to a single teacher, tradition, or *madhhab* (q. v.). Sometimes used disparagingly in the sense of "blind imitation."

taqwā "God consciousness," "God-conscious piety."

ṭarīqa a "hagiographically validated mystical tradition" or Sufi *madhhab* (q. v.). In modern times, this term is used to denote a Sufi order of international scope, made up of a number of individual groups or factions (q. v. *ṭāʾifa*).

aṭ-ṭarīqa al-muḥammadiyya the "Muhammadan Way," a term apparently originating with the tenth-century (A.H.) Jazūlite shaykh ʿAbdallāh al-Ghazwānī. It is a doctrine in which the social and religious dimensions of the Prophetic archetype were manifested in a single, multifaceted persona, the *jaras* (q.v.).

tawakkul "complete reliance on the will of God."

tawḥīd the doctrine of the unity and absolute oneness of God.

ulama See *ʿālim.*

umma the Muslim community as a whole, the paradigm of which is the *umma* established by the Prophet Muḥammad in Medina.

ustādh "teacher," used in the Maghrib as a synonym for *murshid* (q. v.) or Sufi shaykh.

uṣūl a methodology originally developed in the second century A.H. by Muḥammad ibn Idrīs ash-Shāfiʿī, who sought to unify Islamic practice by making legal reasoning dependent upon standardized sources of tradition. According to this method, the "roots" (*uṣūl,* sing. *aṣl*) of Islamic law were the Qur'an, Sunna (collections of Prophetic *ḥadīth*), analogical reasoning (*qiyās*), and the consensus of the community (*ijmāʿ*). This approach to legal reasoning was called *uṣūl al-fiqh.* The standardization promoted by the *uṣūl* approach was later applied to other forms of knowledge, including religious dogma (*uṣūl ad-dīn*), Qur'an interpretation (*uṣūl at-tafsīr*), and even Sufism itself. The *uṣūlī* (q. v.) approach to Sufism helped to draw mysticism into the fold of normative Islam.

uṣūlī an adjective applied to a person, doctrine, or approach that made use of the methodology of *uṣūl* (q. v.).

uswa ḥasana "beautiful example," referring to the example set by the Prophet Muḥammad, which all Muslims are enjoined to imitate.

vita (pl. *vitae*) lit. "life," a technical term for the sacred biography of a saint in Latin Christendom.

walī (pl. *awliyāʾ*) "manager," "guardian," "protector," or "intercessor" (terms in the semantic domain of *wilāya*); also "intimate" or "friend" (terms in the semantic domain of *walāya*). In this book, *walī* is used most often in the compound form *walī Allāh,* standing for a Muslim "saint" who is Allah's friend and thus able to protect or intercede for others as Allah's deputy or vicegerent.

waqf a "pious endowment" used to fund a mosque or another religious institution. In most schools of law, the *waqf* could provide sinecures for donors and their families and thus remain under their control for generations. Under the Maliki *madhhab,* however, the founder of a *waqf* was prohibited from serving as its initial beneficiary, and supervision of the *waqf* was transferred to the state upon its endowment.

waraʿ "scrupulousness" or "pious caution" in the quest for ethical purity, especially with regard to eating food grown or prepared by others.

watad (pl. *awtād*) lit. "tent-peg," "anchor of the earth." A member of the hierarchy of Muslim saints (cf. *quṭb*) who in Morocco was both a *mujtahid* (q. v.) and a patron or protector of the community.

ẓāhir "outer" or "apparent" in the sense of "exoteric knowledge" (*ʿilm aẓ-ẓāhir*). Often opposed to "inner" or *bāṭin* (q. v.).

zāwiya (pl. *zawāya*) lit. "corner," a term used to designate a Sufi institution. From the fifteenth century C. E., the term *zāwiya* replaces both *ribāṭ* (q. v.) and *rābiṭa* (q. v.) in Moroccan Sufi texts.

zuhd asceticism, the formal practice of self-denial.

Selected Bibliography

Manuscript Sources

al-Andalusī, Abū'l-Ḥasan ʿAlī Ṣāliḥ (d. before 914/1508–9), *Sharḥ Raḥbat al-amān* (Rabat, BH ms. 5697, dated 970/1562–3).

al-ʿArūsī, Baraka ibn Muḥammad (ca. 897/1491–2), *Wasīlat al-mutawassilīn bi-faḍl aṣ-ṣalāt ʿalā Sayyid al-Mursalīn* (Madrid, BNM ms. 4920).

al-Baʿqīlī, Abū ʿAbdallāh Muḥammad, *Tarājim ʿulamāʾ wa ṣulaḥāʾ Banī Ultīta wa ghayrihā min al-bilād as-Sūsiyya* (Rabat, BH ms. 12,573).

al-Fāsī, ʿAbd al-Ḥāfiẓ, *At-Tarjumān al-muʿrib ʿan ashhar furūʿ ash-Shādhiliyya bi'l-Maghrib* (Rabat, BG ms. 4400D).

al-Fāsī, Muḥammad al-Mahdī (d. 1109/1698), *Maṭāliʿ al-masarrāt bi-jalāʾ Dalāʾil al-khayrāt* (Fez, private ms. dated 1310/1892–3).

al-Ghazwānī, Abū Muḥammad ʿAbdallāh (d. 935/1528–9), *An-Nuqṭa al-azaliyya fī sirr adh-dhāt al-Muḥammadiyya* (Rabat, BG ms. 2617K).

al-Ghazwānī, Abu Muḥammad ʿAbdallah, *Taḥbīr al-ajrās fī sirr al-anfās* (Rabat, BG ms. 2002D).

al-Habṭī, Abū Muḥammad ʿAbdallāh (d. 963/1555), *Al-Alfiyya as-saniyya fī tanbīh al-ʿāmma wa'l-khāṣṣa ʿalā mā awqaʿa min at-taghyīr fī'l milla al-Islāmiyya* (Rabat, BH ms. 2808, dated 1273/1856–7).

al-Habṭī, Abū Muḥammad ʿAbdallāh, *Shams aḍ-ḍuḥā* (cataloged as *Manẓūma fī'ṭ-ṭarīqa*) (Madrid, BNM ms. 4958–4).

al-Ḥalfāwī, Aḥmad ibn al-Qāsim (d. after 1000/1590), *Shams al-maʿrifa fī sīrat ghawth al-mutaṣawwifa* (Rabat, BG ms. 764J).

al-Ḥuḍaygī, Abū ʿAbdallāh Muḥammad al-Jazūli al-Laggūsī (d. mid-twelfth/eighteenth century), *Ṭabaqāt al-Ḥuḍaygī* (Rabat, BG ms. 2328K).

Ibn ʿAbbād ar-Rundī, Muḥammad an-Nafzī (d. 792/1390), *Fatḥ at-tuḥfa wa idāʿat aṣ-ṣadafa li-taqaʿ al-muwāfaqa* (Madrid, BNM ms. 4928).

Ibn al-ʿArīf, Abū'l-ʿAbbās Aḥmad (d. 536/1141), *Miftāḥ as-saʿāda wa taḥqīq ṭarīq al-irāda* (Rabat, BH ms. 1562).

Ibn Raysūn, al-Ḥasan ibn Muḥammad b. ʿAlī (d. mid-eleventh/seventeenth century), *Manāqib al-akhawayn* (Rabat, BG ms. 2286K).

Ibn ʿAlī Wafā, Abū'l-Iqbāl Ḥasan (d. after 807/1404), *Shajarat al-irshād* (Princeton, GC ms. 5916).

al-Jazūlī, Muḥammad ibn Sulaymān (d. 869/1465), *ʿAqīdat al-walī aṣ-ṣāliḥ Sīdī Muḥammad ibn Sulaymān al-Jazūlī* (Rabat, BH ms. 7245, dated 1296/1879).

al-Jazūlī, Muḥammad ibn Sulaymān, *Dalā'il al-khayrāt wa shawāriq al-anwār fī dhikr aṣ-ṣalāt ʿalā an-Nabī al-Mukhtār* (Marrakesh, BY ms. 377, dated 11th/17th cent.).

al-Jazūlī, Muḥammad ibn Sulaymān, *Khiṣāl al-murīdīn* (Marrakesh, BY ms. 161).

al-Jazūlī, Muḥammad ibn Sulaymān, *Risāla fī'l-maḥabba* (Marrakesh, BY ms. 587/3).

al-Jazūlī, Muḥammad ibn Sulaymān, *Risāla fī'-tawḥīd* (Fez, BQ ms. 723/6).

al-Jazūlī, Muḥammad ibn Sulaymān, *Risāla ilā ʿulamāʾ aẓ-ẓāhir* (Fez, BQ ms. 723/7).

al-Manfalūṭī, Ḥasanayn ibn Muṣṭafā Ghānim, *Tuḥfat al-kirām al-mabdhūla fī baʿḍ manāqib ghawth al-anām quṭb Jazūla* (Rabat, BG ms. 925 D, dated 1302/1884–5).

al-Maqūdī, Abū Zayd ʿAbd ar-Raḥmān (d. 807/1404–5), *Maqṣūra nabawyya ʿalā madḥ Khayr al-Bariyya* (Madrid, BNM ms. 4956/3).

ar-Rīfī, Muḥammad ibn Ibrāhīm al-Khayyāṭī, *Kitāb jawāhir as-simāṭ fī dhikr manāqib Sīdī ʿAbdallāh al-Khayyāṭ* (Rabat, BG ms 1185D).

as-Salawī, Abū'l-ʿAbbās Aḥmad ibn ʿĀshir al-Ḥāfī (fl. 1141/1729), *Tuḥfat az-zāʾir bi-baʿḍ manāqib Sīdī al-Ḥājj Aḥmad ibn ʿĀshir* (Rabat, BG ms. 533 D).

ibn ʿIshūn ash-Sharrāṭ, Muḥammad (d. 1109/1697), *Ar-Rawḍ al-ʿātir al-anfās fī akhbār aṣ-ṣāliḥīn min ahl Fās* (Rabat, BG ms. 525 D).

as-Sijilmāsī, Muḥammad ibn Yūsuf (fl. ca. 1025/1616), *Tuḥfat al-ikhwān wa mawāhib al-imtinān fī manāqib Sīdī Riḍwān ibn ʿAbdallāh al-Januwī* (Rabat, BG ms. 114K).

aṣ-Ṣūmaʿī at-Tādilī, ʿAbd ar-Raḥmān ibn Abī Ismāʿīl (d. 1013/1604–5), *At-Tashawwuf fī rijāl as-sādāt at-taṣawwuf* (Rabat, BG ms. 1103D).

aṣ-Ṣūmaʿī at-Tādilī, Aḥmad ibn Abī'l-Qāsim, *Al-Muʿzzā fī manāqib Abī Yiʿzzā* (Rabat, BG ms. 299 K).

aṭ-Ṭālib al-Fāsī, Muḥammad al-Harwī (d. 964/1557), *Waẓīfat al-Jazūliyya al-Ghazwāniyya* (Paris, BNP ms. 1201, dated 1011/1600).

at-Tamīmī, Muḥammad ibn al-Qāsim (d. 604/1207–8) *Kitāb al-mustafād fī dhikr aṣ-ṣāliḥīn wa'l-ʿubbād bi-madīnat Fās wa mā yalīhā min al-bilād* (Rabat, BG ms. [copy provided by Ahmed Toufiq]).

al-Wazzānī, Abū ʿImrān Mūsā ibn ʿAlī (d. 970/1562–3), *Al-Kurrāsa . . . li-mawlāna al-manṣūr as-sulṭān al-muẓaffar Muḥammad ash-Sharīf al-Ḥasanī . . . fī masʾalat al-quṭb al-mushār ilayhi ʿinda ahl aṭ-ṭarīqa aṣ-ṣūfiyya* (Rabat, BH ms. 7585).

al-Wazzānī, Abū ʿImrān Mūsā ibn ʿAlī, *Risāla fī taʿlīm al-ʿaqīda* (Madrid, BNM ms. 5168).

al-Yalṣūtī, ʿAbd al-Wārith (d. after 960/1554), *Sullam al-murīd* (Rabat, BG ms. 3284K).
az-Zammūrī, Abū'l-Qāsim Ibrāhīm al-Māgirī, *Uns al-waḥda fī sharḥ al-Burda* (Rabat, BH ms. 3210).
az-Zammūrī, Muḥammad ibn ʿAbd al-ʿAẓīm (d. early ninth/fifteenth century), *Bahjat an-nāẓirīn wa uns al-ʿārifīn wa wasīlat Rabb al-ʿĀlamīn fī manāqib rijāl Amghār aṣ-ṣāliḥīn* (Rabat, BH ms. 1358).
Zarrūq, Abū'l-ʿAbbās Aḥmad al-Barnūsī al-Fāsī (d. 899/1493), *Al-Kunnāsh fī ʿilm āsh* (Rabat, BG ms. 1385 K).

Published Sources in Arabic

ʿAbd ar-Razzāq, Maḥmūd Ismāʿīl, *al-Khawārij fī bilād al-Maghrib ḥatta muntaṣif al-qarn ar-rābiʿ al-hijrī* (Casablanca, 1976).
al-ʿAbdarī al-Ḥayḥī, Abū ʿAbdallāh Muḥammad ibn Muḥammad (fl. 688/1289), *Riḥlat al-ʿAbdarī,* Muḥammad al-Fāsī, ed. (Rabat, 1968).
al-ʿĀfiya, ʿAbd al-Qādir, *Al-Ḥayāt as-siyāsiyya wa'l-ijtimāʿiyya wa'l-fikriyya bi-Shafshāwan wa aḥwāzihā khilāl al-qarn al-ʿāshir al-hijrī* (Rabat, 1982).
Aḥmad Bābā at-Timbuktī (d. 1036/1627), *Nayl al-ibtihāj bi-taṭrīz ad-Dībāj* (Fez, lith. 1317/1899).
Aḥmad, Muṣṭafā Abū Ḍayf, *Athar al-qabāʾil al-ʿArabiyya fī'l-ḥayāt al-Maghribiyya khilāl ʿaṣray al-Muwaḥḥidīn wa Banī Marīn [524–876/1130–1472]* (Casablanca, 1982).
al-ʿAlawī, Aḥmad ibn Muṣṭafā, *Kitāb al-mawād al-ghaythiyya an-nāshī ʿan al-ḥikam al-ghawthiyya* (Mostaghanem, 1942).
Anonymous, *Tāʾrīkh ad-dawla as-Saʿdiyya ad-Darʿiyya at-Tagmadertiyya,* Georges S. Colin, ed. (Rabat, 1934).
al-ʿAzafī, Abū'l-ʿAbbās Aḥmad (d. 633/1236), *Diʿāmat al-yaqīn fī ziʿāmat al-muttaqīn,* Ahmed Toufiq, ed. (Rabat, 1989).
al-Bādisī, ʿAbd al-Ḥaqq ibn Ismāʿīl (d. after 722/1322), *Al-Maqṣad ash-sharīf wa'l-manzaʿ al-laṭīf fī't-taʿrīf bi-ṣulaḥāʾ ar-Rīf,* Saʿīd Aḥmad Aʿrāb, ed. (Rabat, 1982).
al-Bakrī, Abū ʿUbayd ibn ʿAbd al-ʿAzīz (d. 487/1094), *Description de l'Afrique Septentrionale* (*Kitāb al-mughrib fī dhikr bilād Ifrīqiyya wa'l-Maghrib*), MacGuckin de Slane, ed. and trans. (reprint, Paris, 1965).
al-Baydhaq, Abū Bakr ibn ʿAlī aṣ-Ṣanhājī, *Kitāb al-ansāb fī maʿrifat al-aṣḥāb,* ʿAbd al-Wahhāb ibn Manṣūr, ed. (Rabat, 1971).
Benaboud, Mohammad, *At-Tārīkh as-siyāsī wa'l-ijtimāʿī li-Ishbīlīya fī ʿahd ad-duwwal aṭ-ṭawāʾif* (Tetuan, 1983).
Bencherifa, Mohammed, "Ḥawla Kitāb al-mustafād," *Daʿwat al-ḥaqq* 259: 26–31.
Boucharb, Ahmed, *Dukkāla wa'l-istiʿmār al-Burtughālī ilā sanat ikhlāʾ Āsafī wa Āzammūr (1481–1541)* (Casablanca, 1984).
al-Būkhuṣaybī, Abū Bakr, *Aḍwāʾ ʿalā Ibn Yaggabsh at-Tāzī* (Casablanca, 1976).
Farḥāt, Ḥalīma and at-Trīkī, Ḥāmid, "Kutub al-manāqib ka-mādda tāʾrīkhiyya," in Mohamed Kably ed., *Histoire et Hagiographie* (Rabat, 1988), 51–62.

al-Fāsī, ʿAllāl, "at-Taṣawwuf al-Islāmī fī'l-Maghrib," *Al-Muḥāḍarāt ath-thaqāfiyya* 10(1)(1969).

al-Fāsī, Muḥammad al-ʿArabī ibn ash-Shaykh Abī Maḥāsin Yūsuf (d. 1052/1642–3), *Mirʾāt al-maḥāsin fī akhbār ash-shaykh Abī Maḥāsin* (Fez, lithograph; 1316/1898–9).

al-Fāsī, Muḥammad al-Mahdī (d. 1109/1698), *Kitāb mumtiʿ al-asmāʿ fī dhikr al-Jazūlī wa't-Tabbāʿ wa mā lahumā min al-atbāʿ* (Fez, lithograph 1313/1896).

al-Fāsī, Muḥammad al-Mahdi, *Mumtiʿ al-asmāʿ fī . . . al-Jazūlī wa at-Tabbāʿ wa mā lahumā min al-atbāʿ*, ʿAbd al-Ḥayy al-ʿAmrawī and ʿAbd al-Karīm Murād, eds. (Fez, 1989).

al-Fāsī, Muḥammad al-Mahdī, *Maṭāliʿ al-masarrāt bi-jalāʾ Dalāʾil al-khayrāt* (Cairo, 1970).

al-Gharnāṭī, al-Ḥasan ibn Muḥammad al-Wazzān (Leo Africanus), *Waṣf Ifrīqīya,* Muḥammad Ḥajjī and Muḥammad al-Akhḍar, eds. and trans. (Rabat, 1980).

al-Ghazzāl, Aḥmad ibn Mahdī, *An-Nūr ash-shāmil fī manāqib faḥl ar-rijāl al-kāmil Sīdī Muḥammad ibn ʿĪsā* (Cairo, 1929).

Ḥājjiyyāt, ʿAbd al-Ḥamīd, "Tārīkh ad-dawla al-Idrīsīyya min khilāl kitāb 'Naẓm ad-durr wa'l-ʿiqiyān' li-Abī ʿAbdallāh at-Tanasī (d. 899/1494)," *Majallat at-tārīkh* (Algiers: Centre National D'Etudes Historiques) 9 (1989): 4–46.

Ḥajjī, Muḥammad, *Al-Ḥaraka al-fikriyya bi'l-Maghrib fī ʿahd as-Saʿdiyyīn* (Mohammedia, 1976).

Ḥajjī, Muḥammad, *Az-Zāwiya ad-Dilāʾiyya wa dawruhā ad-dīnī wa'l-ʿilmī wa's-siyāsī* (Rabat, 1964).

Ibn ʿAbbād ar-Rundī, Abū ʿAbdallāh Muḥammad, *Sharḥ al-ḥikam* (Cairo, 1939).

Ibn al-Abbār al-Balansī, Abū ʿAbdallāh Muḥammad ibn ʿAbdallāh al-Quḍāʿī, *Kitāb at-takmila li-Kitāb aṣ-ṣila,* Francisco Codera, ed. (Madrid, 1887).

Ibn al-Abbār al-Balansī, Abū ʿAbdallāh Muḥammad al-Quḍāʿī, *Al-Muʿjam fī aṣḥāb al-qāḍī al-imām Abī ʿAlī aṣ-Ṣadafī* (Cairo, 1967).

Ibn Abī Zarʿ al-Fāsī, Abū'l-Ḥasan ʿAlī (fl. 726/1326), *Al-Anīs al-muṭrib bi-rawḍ al-qirṭās fī akhbār mulūk al-Maghrib wa tārīkh madīnat Fās* (Rabat, 1973).

Ibn al-Aḥmar, Ismāʿīl (d. 807/1404), *Buyūtāt Fās al-kubrā* (Rabat, 1972).

Ibn al-ʿArabī, Muḥyī ad-Dīn (d. 638/1240), *Fuṣūṣ al-ḥikam,* Abū'l-ʿAlā ʿAfīfī, ed. (Beirut, 1980).

Ibn al-ʿArabī, Muḥyīʾ ad-Dīn [al-Kāshānī ʿAbd ar-Razzāq] (d. 730/1330), *Tafsīr al-Qurʾān al-Karīm* (Beirut, 1968).

Ibn al-ʿArīf, Abū'l-ʿAbbās Aḥmad (d. 536/1141), *Miftāḥ as-saʿāda wa taḥqīq ṭarīq as-saʿāda,* ʿIṣmat ʿAbd al-Laṭīf Dandash, ed. (Beirut, 1993).

Ibn ʿAskar al-Ḥasanī ash-Shafshāwanī, Muḥammad (d. 986/1578), *Dawḥat an-nāshir li-maḥāsin man kāna bi'l-Maghrib min mashāʾikh al-qarn al-ʿāshir,* Muḥammad Ḥajjī, ed. (Rabat, 1977).

Ibn ʿAṭāʾillāh al-Iskandarī, Abū'l-ʿAbbās Aḥmad (d. 709/1309), *Laṭāʾif al-minan,* ʿAbd al-Ḥalīm Maḥmūd, ed. (Cairo, 1974).

Ibn ʿAṭiyya, Abū Muḥammad ʿAbd al-Ḥaqq al-Gharnāṭī (d. 541/1146–7), *Al-*

Muḥarrar al-wajīz fī tafsīr al-Kitāb al-ʿAzīz, al-Majlis al-ʿIlmī bi-Fās, ed. (Rabat, 1975–84).

Ibn Bashkuwāl, Abū'l-Qāsim Khalaf ibn ʿAbd al-Mālik (d. 578/1183), *Kitāb aṣ-ṣila fī tārīkh āʾimmat al-Andalus wa ʿulamāʾihim wa muḥaddithīhim wa fuqahāʾihim wa udabāʾihim* (Cairo, 1955).

Ibn Ghāzī, Abū ʿAbdallāh Muḥammad al-Miknāsī (fl. 896/1491), *Fihris Ibn Ghāzī: at-Taʿallul bi-rusūm al-isnād baʿda intiqāl ahl al-manzil wa'n-nād,* Muḥammad az-Zāhī, ed. (Casablanca, 1979).

Ibn Ibrāhīm, al-ʿAbbās (d. 1378/1959), *Al-Iʿlām bi-man ḥalla Marrākush wa Aghmāt min al-aʿlām* (Rabat, 1974–80).

Ibn ʿĪsā, Muḥammad al-Fahdī (d. 933/1526–7), *Ḥizb ash-shaykh al-jalīl ad-dāl ʿalā Allāh Abī ʿAbdallāh Sīdī Muḥammad ibn ʿĪsā raḍiya Allāhu ʿanhu* (Meknès lithograph, n.d.).

ibn Khaldūn, ʿAbd ar-Rahmān, *Tārīkh Ibn Khaldūn: al-musammā Kitāb al-ʿIbar wa dīwān al-mustadā wa'l-khabar fī ayyām al-ʿArab wa'l-ʿAjam wa'l-Barbar wa man ʿāsarahum min dhawī as-Sulṭān al-Akbar* (Beirut, 1992).

Ibn Manẓūr, Abū'l-Faḍl Jamāl ad-Dīn Muḥammad (d. 711/1311–12), *Lisān al-ʿArab* (Beirut, n.d.).

Ibn Maryam, Abū ʿAbdallāh Muḥammad ibn Muḥammad b. Aḥmad (fl. 1011/1602–3), *Al-Bustān fī dhikr al-awliyāʾ wa'l-ʿulamāʾ bi-Tilimsān,* Mohammed Ben Cheneb, ed. (reprint, Algiers, 1986).

Ibn Marzūq, Muḥammad at-Tilimsānī (d. 781/1379), *Al-Musnad aṣ-ṣaḥīḥ al-ḥasan fī ma'āthir wa maḥāsin mawlānā Abī'l-Ḥasan,* María Jesus Viguera, ed. (Algiers, 1981).

Ibn al-Mubārak, ʿAbdallāh (d. 181/797), *Kitāb az-zuhd wa yalīʾuhu Kitāb ar-raqāʾiq,* Ḥabīb ar-Raḥmām al-ʿAẓmī, ed. (Beirut, 1949).

Ibn al-Muwaqqit, Muḥammad ibn Muḥammad b. ʿAbdallāh (d. 1368/1949), *As-Ṣaʿāda al-abadiyya fīṭ-taʿrīf mashāhīr al-ḥaḍara al-Marrākushiyya* (Casablanca, 1936).

Ibn al-Qāḍī al-Miknāsī, Abū'l-ʿAbbās Aḥmad (d. 1025/1616), *Durrat al-ḥijāl fī asmāʾ ar-rijāl* (Tunis and Cairo, 1971).

Ibn al-Qāḍī al-Miknāsī, Abū'l-ʿAbbās Aḥmad, *Jadhwat al-iqtibās fī dhikr man ḥalla min aʿlām madīnat Fās* (Rabat, 1974).

Ibn Qunfudh al-Qusanṭīnī, Abū'l-ʿAbbās Aḥmad al-Khaṭīb (d. 810/1407–8), *Uns al-faqīr wa ʿizz al-ḥaqīr,* Muḥammad al-Fāsī and Adolphe Faure, eds. (Rabat, 1965).

Ibn aṣ-Ṣabbāgh al-Ḥimyarī, Muḥammad ibn Abī'l-Qāsim (fl. 720/1320), *Durrat al-asrār wa tuḥfat al-abrār fī manāqib dhī al-kaʿb al-ʿalī wa'l-fakhr ash-shāmikh al-jalī al-quṭb al-akbar wa'l-ghawth al-ashhar Sayyidī ʿAlī Abī'l-Ḥasan ash-Shādhilī* (Tunis, 1304/1886–7).

Ibn as-Sammāk, Abū'l-ʿAlā (fl. 783/1381), *Al-Ḥulal al-mawshiyya fī dhikr al-akhbār al-Marrākushiyya,* Suhayl Zakkār and ʿAbd al-Qādir Zamāma, eds. (Casablanca, 1979).

al-Idrīsī, Abū ʿAbdallāh Muḥammad ibn Muḥammad ash-Sharīf (fl. 548/1154), *Description de l'Afrique et de l'Espagne* (*Kitāb nuzhat al-mushtāq fī ikhtirāq al-āfāq*), Reinhart Dozy and M. J. De Goeje, trans. and eds. (reprint, Leiden, 1984).

al-Ifrānī, Muḥammad aṣ-Ṣaghīr ibn ʿAbdallāh (d. before 1151/1738–9), *Nuzhat al-ḥādī bi-akhbār mulūk al-qarn al-ḥādī,* Olivier Houdas, ed. (reprint of 1888 Paris edition, Rabat, n. d.).

al-Iṣfahānī, Abū Nuʿaym Aḥmad ibn ʿAbdallāh (d. 430/1038–9), *Ḥilyat al-awliyāʾ wa ṭabaqāt al-aṣfiyāʾ* (Cairo, 1932).

Jallāb, Ḥasan, *Muḥammad ibn Sulaymān al-Jazūlī* (Marrakesh, 1993).

al-Jaznāʾī, Abū'l-Hasan ʿAlī (fl. 766/1364–5), *Janā zahrat al-ās fī bināʾ madīnat Fās,* ʿAbd al-Wahhāb ibn Manṣūr, ed. (reprint, Rabat, 1991).

al-Jazūlī, Muḥammad ibn Sulaymān (d. 869/1465), *Dalāʾil al-khayrāt wa shawāriq al-anwār fī dhikr aṣ-ṣalāt ʿalā an-Nabī al-Mukhtār* (Cairo, n.d.).

al-Jīlānī, Muḥammad al-Amīn (fl. 1272/1856), *Al-Mawāhib al-jalīla fī sharḥ Ḥizb al-wasīla,* in ʿAbd al-Qādir al-Jīlānī et. al., *As-Safīna al-qādiriyya* (Tunis, n.d.), 91–150.

al-Jīlī, ʿAbd al-Karīm ibn Ibrāhīm (d. 805/1402–3), *Al-Insān al-kāmil fī maʿrifat al-awākhir wa'l-awāʾil* (Cairo, 1981).

al-Kanūnī, Muḥammad ibn Aḥmad al-ʿAbdī, *Āsafī wa mā ilayhā qadīman wa ḥadīthan* (Casablanca, n.d.).

al-Kattānī, Muḥammad ibn Jaʿfar b. Idrīs (d. 1355/1926), *Salwat al-anfās wa muḥadathāt al-akyās bi-man uqbira min al-ʿulamāʾ wa'ṣ-ṣulaḥāʾ bi-Fās* (Fez, lith. 1318/1900).

al-Kurrāsī, Muḥammad ibn ʿAbd ar-Raḥmān (fl. 950/1534), *ʿArūsat al-masāʾil fī mā li-Banī Waṭṭās min al-faḍāʾil,* ʿAbd al-Wahhāb ibn Manṣūr, ed. (Rabat, 1963).

al-Lihīwī, Aṭ-Ṭāhir, *Ḥiṣn as-salām bayna aydāy Mūlāy ʿAbd as-Salām* (Casablanca, 1978).

al-Māgirī, Abū'l-ʿAbbās Aḥmad ibn Ibrāhīm b. Aḥmad (fl. 696/1297), *Al-Minhāj al-wāḍiḥ fī taḥqīq karāmāt Abī Muḥammad Ṣāliḥ* (Cairo, 1933).

Maḥmūd, ʿAbd al-Ḥalīm, *Al-Madrasa ash-Shādhiliyya al-ḥadītha wa imāmuhā Abū'l-Ḥasan ash-Shādhilī* (Cairo, 1967).

al-Makkī, Abū Ṭālib Muḥammad (d. 386/996), *Qūt al-qulūb fī muʿāmalat al-Maḥbūb wa waṣf ṭarīq al-murīd ilā maqām at-tawḥīd* (Cairo, 1884–5).

Makki, M. A., "At-Tashayyuʿ fī'l-Andalus," *Revista del Instituto Egipcio de Estudios Islámicos* (Madrid, 1954).

al-Manlā, Shaykh Muḥammad, *Aṣ-Ṣalāt al-kubrā fī sharḥ aṣ-Ṣalāt aṣ-ṣughrā,* in ʿAbd al-Qādir al-Jīlānī et. al., *As-Safīna al-qādiriyya* (Tunis, n.d.), 20–48.

al-Manūnī, Muḥammad, "Madkhal ilā tāʾrīkh al-fikr al-Islāmī fī'l-ʿasr al-Marīnī al-awwal," in al-Manuni, *Waraqāt ʿan al-ḥaḍāra al-Maghribiyya fī ʿaṣr Banī Marīn* (Rabat, 1979), 192–211.

al-Manūnī, Muḥammad, *Rakb al-Ḥājj al-Maghribī* (Tetuan, 1953).

al-Manūnī, Muḥammad, "At-Tayyārāt al-fikriyya fī'l-Maghrib al-Marīnī," in al-Manūnī, *Waraqāt ʿan al-ḥaḍāra al-Maghribiyya fī ʿaṣr Banī Marīn* (Rabat, 1979), 236–47.

al-Manūnī, Muḥammad, *Al-ʿUlūm wa'l-ādāb wa'l-funūn ʿalā ʿahd al-Muwaḥḥidīn* (Rabat, 1977).

al-Marrākushī, ʿAbd al-Wāḥid (d. after 631/1233–4), *Al-Muʿjib fī talkhīṣ akhbār al-Maghrib,* Mamdūḥ Ḥaqqī, ed. (Casablanca, 1978).

al-Mībūdī, Abū'l-Faḍl Rashīd ad-Dīn (fl. 520/1126), *Kashf al-asrār wa ʿuddat al-abrār* (Tehran, 1982).

Miftāḥ, Muḥammad, *At-Tayyār aṣ-ṣūfī wa'l-mujtamaʿ fī'l-Andalus wa'l-Maghrib athnāʾa al-qarn 8/14* (Ph.D. dissertation, Université Mohammed V, Rabat, 1981).

Mūlīn, Muḥammad ar-Rashīd, *ʿAṣr al-Manṣūr al-Muwaḥḥidī* (Rabat, n.d.).

an-Nāṣirī as-Salawī, Abū'l-ʿAbbās Aḥmad ibn Khālid (d. 1315/1897), *Kitāb al-istiqṣāʾ li-akhbār duwwal al-Maghrib al-Aqṣāʾ,* Jaʿfar an-Nāṣirī and Muḥammad an-Nāṣirī, eds. (Casablanca, 1954–5).

al-Qādirī, Muḥammad ibn aṭ-Ṭayyib (d. 1187/1773), *Nashr al-mathānī li-ahl al-qarn al-ḥādī ʿashar wa'th-thānī,* Muḥammad Ḥajjī and Aḥmad at-Tawfīq, eds. (Rabat, 1977).

al-Qashtālī al-Azdī, Aḥmad ibn Ibrāhīm b. Yaḥyā, *Tuḥfat al-mughtarib bi-bilād al-Maghrib li-man lahu min al-ikhwān fī karāmāt ash-shaykh Abī Marwān,* Fernando de la Granja, ed. (Madrid, 1974).

al-Qayrawānī, Abū Muḥammad ʿAbdallāh ibn Abī Zayd (d. 386/996), *Matn ar-Risāla* (Rabat, 1984).

al-Qushayrī, Abū'l-Qāsim ʿAbd al-Karīm ibn Hāwāzīn (d. 467/1074), *Ar-Risāla al-Qushayriyya fī ʿilm at-taṣawwuf,* Maʿrūf Zurayq and ʿAlī ʿAbd al-Ḥamīd Beltarjī, eds. (Beirut, 1990).

ar-Raḥḥāl, Muḥammad al-ʿArabī ibn Bahlūl, *Manhaj al-irtiḥāl ilā maʿrifat ash-shaykh Sīdī Raḥḥāl* (Rabat, 1956).

as-Sakhāwī, Shams ad-Dīn Muḥammad ibn ʿAbd ar-Raḥmān (d. 902/1497), *Aḍ-Ḍawʾ al-lāmiʿ li-ahl al-qarn at-tāsiʿ* (reprint, Beirut, n.d.).

as-Sarrāj aṭ-Ṭūsī, Abū Naṣr ʿAbdallāh ibn ʿAlī (d. 378/988), *The Kitāb al-Lumaʿ fī'l-Taṣawwuf,* R. A. Nicholson, ed. (reprint, London, 1963).

ash-Shādhilī, ʿAbd al-Laṭīf, *At-Taṣawwuf wa'l-mujtamaʿ, namādhij min al-qarn al-ʿāshir al-hijrī* (Salé, 1989).

ash-Shyāẓmī, Muḥammad, and al-Ḥājī as-Sibāʿī, *Madīnat Azammūr wa ḍawāḥīhā* (Salé, 1989).

as-Sulamī, Abū ʿAbd ar-Raḥmān (d. 412/1021–2), *Ṭabaqāt aṣ-ṣūfiyya,* Nūr ad-Dīn Shurayba, ed. (Cairo, 1986).

as-Sulamī, Abū ʿAbd ar-Raḥmān, *Uṣūl al-Malāmatiyya wa ghalaṭāt aṣ-ṣūfiyya,* ʿAbd al-Fātiḥ Aḥmad al-Fāwī Maḥmūd, ed. (Cairo, 1984).

as-Sūsī, Muḥammad al-Mukhṭār, *Khilāl Jazūla* (Tetuan, 1960).

as-Suyūṭī, Jalāl ad-Dīn, *Al-Itqān fī ʿulūm al-Qurʾān* (Cairo, 1985).

at-Tādilī, Abū Yaʿqūb Yūsuf ibn az-Zayyāt (d. 628/1230–1), *Kitāb at-Tashawwuf ilā rijāl at-taṣawwuf wa akhbār Abī'l-ʿAbbās as-Sabtī,* Ahmed Toufiq, ed. (Rabat, 1984).

at-Tādilī, Abū Yaʿqūb Yūsuf ibn Yaḥya, *Kitāb at-Tashawwuf ilā rijāl at-taṣawwuf,* Adolphe Faure, ed. (Rabat, 1958).

at-Tanūkhī, Saḥnūn ibn Saʿīd (d. 240/854), *Al-Mudawwana al-kubrā* (Beirut, 1980).

al-Wansharīsī, Abū'l-ʿAbbās Aḥmad ibn Yaḥyā b. Muḥammad (d. 914/1508), *Al-Miʿyār al-muʿrib wa'l-jāmiʿ al-mughrib ʿan fatāwī ahl Ifrīqīya wa'l-Andalus wa'l-Maghrib,* Muḥammad Ḥajjī et. al., eds. (Rabat, 1981).

al-Yaḥṣubī, al-Qāḍī Abī'l-Faḍl ʿIyāḍ (d. 544/1149), *Ash-Shifāʾ bi-taʿrīf ḥuqūq al-Muṣṭafā* (Beirut, 1979).

az-Zabīdī, Muḥammad al-Murtaḍā (d. 1207/1791), *Itḥāf as-sādāt al-muttaqīn bi-sharḥ Iḥyāʾ ʿulūm ad-dīn* (reprint, Beirut, n.d.).

Zākī, ʿAbd al-Qādir, *An-Nafḥa al-ʿaliyya fī awrād ash-Shādhilīyya* (Beirut, 1904).

Zarrūq, Abū'l-ʿAbbās Aḥmad ibn Aḥmad b. Muḥammad al-Barnūsī al-Fāsī (d. 899/1493), *Qawāʿid at-taṣawwuf,* Muḥammad Zuhrī an-Najjār and ʿAlī Muʿbid Firghalī, eds. (Beirut, 1992).

Zaydān, Yūsuf Muḥammad Ṭaha, *Aṭ-Ṭarīq aṣ-ṣūfī wa furūʿ al-Qādiriyya bi-Miṣr* (Beirut, 1991).

Published Sources in European Languages

Abdel-Kader, Ali Hassan, *The Life, Personality and Writings of Al-Junayd* (London, 1976).

Abun-Nasr, Jamil M., *A History of the Maghrib in the Islamic Period* (Cambridge, 1987).

Addas, Claude, "Abu Madyan and Ibn ʿArabi," in S. Hirtenstein and M. Tiernan, *Muhyiddin Ibn ʿArabi: A Commemorative Volume* (Shaftesbury, United Kingdom, 1993), 163–180.

Addas, Claude, *Ibn ʿArabī ou La quête du Soufre Rouge* (Paris, 1989), translated as *The Quest for Red Sulphur: The Life of Ibn ʿArabī,* Peter Kingsley, trans. (Cambridge, 1993).

Anonymous, *Chronique de Santa-Cruz du Cap de Gué (Agadir),* Pierre Cenival, ed. and trans. (Paris, 1934).

Arberry, A. J., trans., *Muslim Saints and Mystics: Episodes from the Tadhkirat al-Auliya' (Memorial of the Saints) by Farid al-Din Attar* (London, 1966).

Arkoun, Mohammed, *Rethinking Islam: Common Questions, Uncommon Answers,* Robert D. Lee, trans. and ed. (Boulder, Colorado, 1994).

Asad, Muhammad, *The Message of the Qurʾān* (Gibraltar, 1984).

Asad, Talal, *Genealogies of Religion: Discipline and Reasons of Power in Christianity and Islam* (Baltimore and London, 1993).

Asín Palacios, Miguel, ed., *Maḥāsin al-Majālis d'Ibn al-ʿArīf* (Paris, 1933).

Asín Palacios, Miguel, *The Mystical Philosophy of Ibn Masarra and His Followers,* Elmer H. Douglas and Howard W. Yoder, trans. (Leiden, 1978).

Asín Palacios, Miguel, *Obras Escogidas* (Madrid, 1946).

ʿAṭṭār, Farīd al-Dīn, *The Ilāhi-nāma or Book of God,* John Andrew Boyle, trans. (Manchester, 1976).

Augustine, Saint, *The City of God (De Civitatae Dei)*, John Healy, trans., R. V. G. Tasker, ed. (London and New York, 1950).

Austin, R. W. J., trans., *Sufis of Andalusia: The* Rūḥ al-quds *and* al-Durrat al-fākhirah *of Ibn ʿArabī* (Berkeley and Los Angeles, 1977).

al-Azmeh, Aziz, *Ibn Khaldūn* (London and New York, 1982).

Azurara, Gomes Eannes de (fl. 1448), *Conquests and Discoveries of Henry the Navigator: Being the Chronicles of Azurara,* Virginia de Castro e Almeida, trans. (London, 1936).

Barges, Abbé J. J. L., *Vie du célèbre marabout Cidi Abou-Médien* (Paris, 1884).

Bates, Oric, *The Eastern Libyans* (London, reprint 1970).

Bel, Alfred, *La Religion musulmane en Berbérie: Esquisse d'histoire et de sociologie religieuses* (Paris, 1938).

Bel, Alfred, "Sîdî Bou Medyan et son maître Ed Daqqâq à Fès," *Mélanges René Basset* (Paris, 1923), (1), 31–68.

Bell, Rudolph, *Holy Anorexia* (Chicago, 1985).

Benaboud, M., and A. Tahiri, "Berberising al-Andalus," *Al-Qanṭara* 11(1990): 475–487.

Benchekroun, Mohamed B. A., *La Vie intellectuelle marocaine sous les Mérinides et les Waṭṭāsides* (Rabat, 1974).

Berger, Peter, and Thomas Luckmann, *The Social Construction of Reality: A Treatise in the Sociology of Knowledge* (New York, 1967).

Berkey, Jonathan, *The Transmission of Knowledge in Medieval Cairo: A Social History of Islamic Education* (Princeton, 1992).

Berque, Jacques, *L'intérieur du Maghreb, XVᵉ–XIXᵉ siècle* (Paris, 1978).

Berque, Jacques, *Structures sociales du Haut-Atlas* (Paris, 1955).

Berque, Jacques, *Ulémas, fondateurs, insurgés du Maghrib, XVIIᵉ siècle* (Paris, 1982).

Black, Deborah L., *Logic and Aristotle's* Rhetoric *and* Poetics *in Medieval Arabic Philosophy* (Leiden, 1990).

Black, Max, *Models and Metaphors* (Ithaca, New York, 1962).

Blankinship, Khalid Yahya, *The End of the Jihād State: The Reign of Hishām ibn ʿAbd al-Malik and the Collapse of the Umayyads* (Albany, New York, 1994).

Bosch-Vilá, Jacinto, *La Sevilla Islámica, 712–1248* (Seville, 1984).

Bourdieu, Pierre, *Outline of a Theory of Practice,* Richard Nice, trans. (Cambridge, 1979).

Bowen, Donna Lee, "The Paradoxical Linkage of the ʿUlamāʾ and Monarch in Morocco," *Maghreb Review* 10(1)(1985): 3–9.

Böwering, Gerhard, *The Mystical Vision of Existence in Classical Islam: The Qurʾānic Hermeneutics of the Sufi Sahl al-Tustarī (d. 283/896)* (Berlin, 1979).

Bowersock, G. W., *Roman Arabia* (Cambridge, Massachusetts, 1983).

Brown, Kenneth, *People of Salé: Tradition and Change in a Moroccan City, 1830–1930* (Cambridge, Massachusetts, 1976).

Brown, L. Carl, "The Religious Establishment in Husainid Tunisia," in Nikki R. Keddie, ed., *Scholars, Saints, and Sufis: Muslim Religious Institutions since 1500* (Berkeley and Los Angeles, 1972), 47–92.
Brown, L. Carl, *The Tunisia of Ahmad Bey 1837–1855* (Princeton, 1974).
Brown, Peter, *Augustine of Hippo* (New York, 1986).
Brown, Peter, *Society and the Holy in Late Antiquity* (London, 1982).
Bulliet, Richard W., *Conversion to Islam in the Medieval Period: An Essay in Quantitative History* (Cambridge, 1979).
Bulliet, Richard W., *Islam: The View from the Edge* (New York, 1994).
Bulliet, Richard W., *The Patricians of Nishapur: A Study in Medieval Islamic Social History* (Cambridge, Massachusetts, 1972).
Caillé, Jacques, *La Ville de Rabat jusqu'au protectorat Français: Histoire et archéologie* (Paris, 1949).
Canteins, Jean, *La Voie des Lettres: Tradition cachée en Israël et en Islam* (Paris, 1981).
Carvalho, Vasco de, *La Domination Portugaise au Maroc, 1415–1769* (Lisbon, 1936).
Chamberlain, Michael, *Knowledge and Social Practice in Medieval Damascus, 1190–1350* (Cambridge, 1994).
Chejne, Anwar G., *Islam and the West: The Moriscos, A Cultural and Social History* (Albany, New York, 1983).
Chittick, William C., *Imaginal Worlds: Ibn al-ʿArabī and the Problem of Religious Diversity* (Albany, New York, 1994).
Chittick, William C., *The Sufi Path of Knowledge: Ibn al-ʿArabī's Metaphysics of Imagination* (Albany, New York, 1989).
Chodkiewicz, Michel, *An Ocean Without Shore: Ibn Arabi, the Book, and the Law* (Albany, New York, 1993).
Chodkiewicz, Michel, *Le Sceau des saints: Prophétie et sainteté dans la doctrine d'Ibn Arabî* (Paris, 1986), translated as *Seal of the Saints: Prophethood and Sainthood in the Doctrine of Ibn ʿArabī*, Liadain Sherrard, trans. (Cambridge, 1993).
Chraibi, Driss, *La Mère du Printemps (L'Oumer Bia)* (Paris, 1982).
Christian, William A., *Apparitions in Late Medieval and Renaissance Spain* (Princeton, 1981).
Christian, William A., *Local Religion in Sixteenth-Century Spain* (Princeton, 1981).
Cohen, A. P., and J. L. Comaroff, "The Management of Meaning: On the Phenomenology of Political Transactions," in Bruce Kapferer, ed., *Transaction and Meaning: Directions in the Anthropology of Exchange and Symbolic Behavior* (Philadelphia, 1976), 87–107.
Coleman, John A., "Conclusion: After Sainthood?" in John Stratton Hawley, ed., *Saints and Virtues* (Berkeley and Los Angeles, 1987), 205–225.
Cook, Weston F., Jr., *The Hundred Years War for Morocco: Gunpowder and the Military Revolution in the Early Modern Muslim World* (Boulder, Colorado, 1994).

Cook, Weston F., Jr., "Warfare and State Building in Early Modern Morocco" (1497–1517)," *Jusūr: The UCLA Journal of Middle Eastern Studies* 4 (1988): 1–30.

Corbin, Henri, *The Man of Light in Iranian Sufism* (London and Boulder, Colorado, 1978).

Cornell, Vincent J., "Ḥayy in the Land of Absāl: Ibn Ṭufayl and Ṣūfism in the Western Maghrib during the Muwaḥḥid Era," in Lawrence I. Conrad, ed., *The World of Ibn Ṭufayl: Interdisciplinary Perspectives on Ḥayy ibn Yaqẓān* (Leiden, 1996), 133–164.

Cornell, Vincent J., "Jihad: Islam's Struggle for Truth," *Gnosis* 21 (Fall 1991): 18–23.

Cornell, Vincent J., "Mystical Doctrine and Political Action in Moroccan Sufism: The Role of the Exemplar in the *Ṭarīqa al-Jazūliyya*," *Al-Qanṭara* 13 (1) (1992): 201–231.

Cornell, Vincent J., "Ribāṭ Tīṭ-n-Fiṭr and the Origins of Moroccan Maraboutism," *Islamic Studies* 27 (1) (1988): 23–36.

Cornell, Vincent J., "Socioeconomic Dimensions of Reconquista and Jihad in Morocco: Portuguese Dukkala and the Saʿdid Sus, 1450–1557," *International Journal of Middle East Studies,* 22 (1990): 379–418.

Cornell, Vincent J., "The Logic of Analogy and the Role of the Sufi Shaykh in Post-Marinid Morocco," *IJMES* (15), 1983, 67–93.

Cornell, Vincent J., "The Sufi as Social Critic: The *Alfiyya* of ʿAbdallāh al-Habṭī," in Carl W. Ernst, ed., *Sufism in Practice* (Princeton, forthcoming).

Cornell, Vincent J., *The Way of Abū Madyan: Doctrinal and Poetic Works of Abū Madyan Shuʿayb ibn al-Ḥusayn al-Anṣārī (c. 500/1115–16—594/1198)* (Cambridge, 1996).

Cornell, Vincent J., "The Way of the Axial Intellect: The Islamic Hermetism of Ibn Sabʿīn," *Journal of the Muhyiddīn Ibn ʿArabi Society* (forthcoming).

Cornell, Vincent J., "Understanding Is the Mother of Ability: Responsibility and Action in the Doctrine of Ibn Tūmart," *Studia Islamica* 66 (1988): 71–103.

Crapanzano, Vincent, *The Hamadsha: A Study in Moroccan Ethnopsychiatry* (Berkeley and Los Angeles, 1973).

Cruz-Hernández, Miguel, *Historia del pensamiento en el mundo Islámico* (Madrid, 1981).

Currie, P. M., *The Shrine and Cult of Mu'in al-din Chishti of Ajmer* (Delhi, 1989).

Daftary, Farhad, *The Ismāʿīlīs: Their History and Doctrines* (Cambridge, 1990).

Delehaye, Hippolyte, *Les Origines du culte des martyrs* (Brussels, 1933).

Delehaye, Hippolyte, *Sanctus: Essai sur le culte des saints dans l'Antiquité* (Brussels, 1927).

Delooz, Pierre, *Sociologie et Canonisations* (Liege, 1969).

Delooz, Pierre, "Towards A Sociological Study of Canonized Sainthood," in Stephen Wilson, ed., *Saints and Their Cults: Studies in Religious Sociology, Folklore, and History* (Cambridge, 1983), 189–216.

Dermenghem, Emile, *Le Culte des saints dans l'Islam maghrébin* (Paris, 1954 [reprint, 1982]).

Derrida, Jacques, "Le retrait de la métaphore," translated as "The Retrait of Metaphors," *Enclitic* 2 (Fall, 1978): 5–33.

Deshen, Shlomo, *The Mellah Society: Jewish Community Life in Sherifian Morocco* (Chicago, 1989).

Douglas, Elmer H., "Al-Shādhilī, A North African Sufi, According to Ibn al-Ṣabbāgh," *Muslim World* (38), 4, October, 1948, 257–279.

Doutté, Edmond, *Magie et religion dans l'Afrique du Nord* (Paris, reprint 1984).

Dunn, Ross E., *The Adventures of Ibn Battuta* (Berkeley and Los Angeles, 1989).

Duri, A. A., *The Rise of Historical Writing Among the Arabs,* Lawrence I. Conrad, ed. and trans. (Princeton, 1983).

Durkee, ʿAbd Allāh Nūr ad-Din, *al-Madrasa ash-Shādhdhuliyya (The School of the Shādhdhuliyya), Volume 1, Orisons* (Alexandria, 1991).

Dutton, Yasin, "*Sunna, Ḥadīth,* and Madinan *ʿAmal,*" *Journal of Islamic Studies* 4(1) (January 1993): 1–31.

Dziubinski, Andrzej, "Les Chorfa Saadiens dans le Sous et Marrakech jusqu'en 1525," *Africana Bulletin* (Warsaw) 10 (1969): 31–51.

Eickelman, Dale, *The Middle East: An Anthropological Approach* (Englewood Cliffs, New Jersey, 1981 [second edition, 1989]).

Eickelman, Dale F., *Moroccan Islam: Tradition and Society in a Pilgrimage Center* (Austin, Texas, and London, 1976).

Eickelman, Dale F., and James Piscatori, eds., *Muslim Travelers: Pilgrimage, Migration, and the Religious Imagination* (Berkeley and Los Angeles, 1990).

Eliade, Mircea, *The Sacred and the Profane: The Nature of Religion,* William R. Trask, trans. (San Diego and New York, 1959).

Elliot, William and Abdulla, Adnan K., *Maḥāsin al-Majālis, The Attraction of Mystical Sessions* (Amersham, Buckinghamshire, 1980).

Elmore, Gerald Thomas, "The Fabulous Gryphon (*ʿAnqāʾ Mughrib*) on the Seal of the Saints and the Sun Rising in the West: An Early, Maghribine Work by Ibn al-ʿArabī," (Ph.D. dissertation, Yale University, 1995).

Ernst, Carl W., *Eternal Garden: Mysticism, History, and Politics at a South Asian Sufi Center* (Albany, New York, 1992).

Ernst, Carl W., "The Stages of Love in Early Persian Sufism, from Rābiʿa to Rūzbihān," in Leonard Lewisohn, ed., *Classical Persian Sufism: From Its Origins to Rumi* (London, 1993), 444–455.

Faure, Adolphe, "Abū-l-ʿAbbās as-Sabtī (524–601/1130–1204), la justice et la charité," *Hespéris* 43 (2)(1956).

Ferhat, Halima, "Le culte du Prophète au Maroc au XIIIe siècle: Organisation du Pélerinage et Célebration du Mawlid," in André Vauchez, ed., *La Religion civique à l'époque médiévale et moderne (Chrétienté et Islam)* (Rome, 1995), 89–97.

Ferhat, Halima, *Sabta des origines au XIVe siècle* (Casablanca, 1993).

Ferhat, Halima, "Safi au XIIIe siècle: histoire sainte, histoire urbaine," in idem, *Le Maghreb aux XIIe et XIIIe siècles* (Casablanca, 1993), 79–90.

Ferhat, Halima, "*As-Sirr al-Maṣūn* de Ṭāhir aṣ-Ṣadafī: un Itinéraire mystique au XIIe siècle," *Al-Qanṭara* 16 (2)(1995): 273–288.

Ferhat, Halima and Hamid Triki, "Faux prophètes et mahdis dans le Maroc médiéval," *Hespéris-Tamuda,* 26–7 (1988–9): 5–23.

Fierro, Maria Isabel, "El proceso contra Abu Umar al-Talamanki a través de su vida y de su obra," *Sharq al-Andalus* (9), 1993, 93–127.

Fierro, Maribel, "The Polemic About the *Karāmāt al-Awliyā*ʾ and the Development of Sufism in al-Andalus (Fourth/Tenth–Fifth/Eleventh Centuries)," *BSOAS* 55 (1992): 236–249.

Fierro Bello, Maria Isabel, *La Heterodoxia en al-Andalus durante el periodo Umayya* (Madrid, 1987).

Fischer, Michael M. J., *Iran: From Religious Dispute to Revolution* (Cambridge, 1980).

Foucault, Michel, *The Archaeology of Knowledge,* A. M. Sheridan Smith, trans. (New York, 1972).

Foucault, Michel, *Power/Knowledge: Selected Interviews & Other Writings, 1972–1977,* Colin Gordon, ed. (New York, 1980).

Fowden, Garth, *The Egyptian Hermes: A Historical Approach to the Late Pagan Mind* (Princeton, 1993).

Gadamer, Hans-Georg, *Truth and Method,* Joel Weisenheimer and Donald G. Marshall, trans. (New York, 1994).

Gagnon, Serge, *Man and His Past: The Nature and Role of Historiography* (Montreal, 1982).

García-Arenal, Mercedes, "*Mahdī, Murābiṭ, Sharīf:* l'Avènement de la dynastie saʿdienne," *Studia Islamica* 71 (1990): 77–114.

García-Arenal, Mercedes, "Mahdisme et la Dynastie Saʿdienne," in *Mahdisme, crise et changement dans l'histoire du Maroc,* A. Kaddouri, ed. (Rabat, 1994), 95–117.

García-Arenal, Mercedes, "Sainteté et pouvoir dynastique au Maroc: la Résistance de Fès aux Sa'diens," *Annales ESC* 4 (July/August 1990): 1019–1042.

García-Arenal, Mercedes, "The Revolution of Fās in 869/1465 and the Death of Sultan ʿAbd al-Ḥaqq al-Marīnī," *Bulletin of the School of Oriental and African Studies* 41 (1)(1978): 43–66.

García-Arenal, M., and E. Mantano Moreno, "Idrīssisme et villes Idrīssides," *Studia Islamica* 82 (1995): 5–32.

Garrido, José Angel Tapia, *Almería Musulmana (711–1172)* (Almería, 1986).

Geertz, Clifford, *The Interpretation of Cultures* (New York, 1973).

Geertz, Clifford, *Islam Observed: Religious Development in Morocco and Indonesia* (Chicago and London, 1971).

Geertz, Clifford, "Suq: The Bazaar Economy in Sefrou," in idem, Hildred Geertz, and Lawrence Rosen, *Meaning and Order in Moroccan Society* (Cambridge, 1979), 123–264.

Gellens, Sam I., "The Search for Knowledge in Medieval Muslim Societies: A

Comparative Approach," in Dale F. Eickelman and James Piscatori, eds., *Muslim Travelers: Pilgrimage, Migration, and the Religious Imagination* (Berkeley and Los Angeles, 1990), 59–64.

Gellner, Ernest, *Muslim Society* (Cambridge, 1981).

Gellner, Ernest, "Political and Religious Organization of the Berbers of the Central High Atlas," in Ernest Gellner and Charles Micaud, *Arabs and Berbers: From Tribe to Nation in North Africa* (London, 1973), 59–66.

Gellner, Ernest, *Saints of the Atlas* (Chicago, 1969).

Gilsenan, Michael, *Recognizing Islam: Religion and Society in the Modern Arab World* (New York, 1982).

Gilsenan, Michael, *Saint and Sufi in Modern Egypt: An Essay in the Sociology of Religion* (Oxford, 1973).

Glick, Thomas F., *Muslim and Christian Spain in the Early Middle Ages* (Princeton, 1979).

Goitein, S. D., *Studies in Islamic History and Institutions* (Leiden, 1968).

Goldziher, Ignaz, *Le Livre de Mohammed Ibn Toumert* (Algiers, 1903).

Goody, Jack, *The Interface Between the Written and the Oral* (Cambridge, 1987).

Goody, Jack, *The Logic of Writing and the Organization of Society* (Cambridge, 1986).

Graham, Terry, "Abū Saʿīd ibn Abī'l-Khayr and the School of Khurāsān," in Leonard Lewisohn, ed., *Classical Persian Sufism: From Its Origins to Rumi* (London, 1993), 83–135.

Greifenhagen, F. V., "Traduttore Traditore: An Analysis of the History of English Translations of the Qurʾān," *Journal of Christian-Muslim Relations* 3 (2) (December 1992): 274–291.

Gril, Denis, *La Risāla de Ṣafī al-dīn ibn Abī l-Manṣūr ibn Ẓāfir: Biographies des maîtres spirituels connus par un cheikh égyptien du VIIe/XIIIe siècle* (Cairo, 1986).

Gril, Denis, "Sources manuscrites de l'histoire du soufisme à Dār al-Kutub," *Annales Islamologiques* 28 (1994): 97–185.

Guillaume, Arnold, *The Life of Muhammad: A Translation of Ibn Ishaq's Sirat Rasul Allah* (Oxford and Karachi, 1970).

Gurevich, Aaron, *Historical Anthropology of the Middle Ages,* Jana Howlett, ed. (Chicago, 1992).

Gurr, Ted Robert, *Minorities at Risk: A Global View of Ethnopolitical Conflicts* (Washington, D.C., 1993).

Hammoudi, Abdellah, *The Victim and Its Masks: An Essay on Sacrifice and Masquerade in the Maghrib,* Paula Wissing, trans. (Chicago, 1993).

Hart, David M., *The Aith Waryaghar of the Moroccan Rif* (Tucson, Arizona, 1976).

Hatt, D. G., *Tashelhit-English Dictionary: Based on the Work of Edmond D'Estaing* (Los Angeles, 1969).

Hawley, John Stratton, ed., *Saints and Virtues* (Berkeley and Los Angeles, 1987).

Heffernan, Thomas, *Sacred Biography: Saints and Their Biographers in the Middle Ages* (Oxford, 1988).

Hefner, Robert W., *Conversion to Christianity: Historical and Anthropological Perspectives on a Great Transformation* (Berkeley and Los Angeles, 1993).

Hodge, Robert, and Gunter Kress, *Social Semiotics* (Ithaca, New York, 1988).

Hodgson, Marshall G. S., *The Venture of Islam: Conscience and History in a World Civilization* (Chicago, 1974).

Hogga, Mustapha, *Orthodoxie, subversion, et réforme en Islam: Gazālī et les Seljūqides* (Paris, 1993).

Homerin, Th. Emile, "Ibn Taymiyya's *al-Ṣūfīyah wa-al-Fuqarāʾ*," *Arabica* 32 (1985): 219–244.

Hoy, David Couzens, and Thomas McCarthy, *Critical Theory* (Oxford and Cambridge, Massachusetts, 1994).

Huici Miranda, Ambrosio, *Historia política del imperio Almohade* (Tetuan, 1956).

al-Hujwīrī, ʿAlī ibn ʿUthmān al-Jullābī (d. 465/1072–3), *The Kashf al-Maḥjūb: The Oldest Persian Treatise on Sufism,* R. A. Nicholson, trans. (reprint, London, 1976).

Humphreys, R. Stephen, *Islamic History: A Framework for Inquiry* (Princeton, 1991).

Hutt, Anthony, *Islamic Architecture: North Africa* (London, 1977).

Ibn Khaldūn, *Histoire des Berbères et des dynasties musulmanes de l'Afrique Septentrionale,* Le Baron de Slane, trans., and Paul Casanova, ed. (reprint, Paris, 1982).

Ibn al-Munawwir, Muḥammad, *Les Étapes mystiques du Shaykh Abu Sa'id (Asrār at-tawḥīd fī maqāmāt ash-shaykh Abī Saʿīd),* Mohammad Achena, trans. (Paris, 1974).

Ibn al-Sabbagh, *The Mystical Teachings of al-Shadhili,* Elmer H. Douglas, trans., and Ibrahim M. Abu-Rabiʿ, ed. (Albany, New York, 1993).

Ibrahim, Mahmood, *Merchant Capital and Islam* (Austin, Texas, 1990).

Izetbegovic, 'Alija 'Ali, *Islam Between East and West* (Indianapolis, 1993).

Izutsu, Toshihiko, *God and Man in the Koran: Semantics of the Koranic Weltanschauung* (reprint, New York, 1980).

Izutsu, Toshihiko, *Sufism and Taoism: A Comparative Study of Key Philosophical Concepts* (Berkeley and Los Angeles, 1983).

Jacques-Meunié, D., *Le Maroc saharien des origines au XVIème siècle* (Paris, 1982).

Jean-Léon l'Africain, *Description de l'Afrique,* A Epaulard, trans. (Paris, 1956).

Johansen, Julian, *Sufism and Islamic Reform in Egypt: The Battle for Islamic Tradition* (Oxford, 1996).

Julien, Charles-André, *Histoire de l'Afrique du Nord* (reprint, Paris, 1978).

Kably, Mohamed, ed., *Histoire et Hagiographie* (Rabat, 1989).

Kably, Mohamed, *Société, pouvoir et religion au Maroc à la fin du Moyen-Age* (Paris, 1986).

Kamali, Mohammed Hashim, *Principles of Islamic Jurisprudence* (Cambridge, 1991).

Kapferer, Bruce, ed., *Transaction and Meaning: Directions in the Anthropology of Exchange and Symbolic Behavior* (Philadelphia, 1976).

Kepel, Gilles, *Muslim Extremism in Egypt: The Prophet and Pharaoh* (Berkeley and Los Angeles, 1986).
Khushaim, Ali Fahmi, *Zarrūq the Sufi* (Tripoli, 1976).
Kieckhefer, Richard, *Unquiet Souls: Fourteenth-Century Saints and Their Religious Milieu* (Chicago, 1987).
Kieckhefer, Richard, and George Bond, eds., *Sainthood: Its Manifestation in World Religions* (Berkeley and Los Angeles, 1988).
Kleinberg, Aviad M., *Prophets in Their Own Country: Living Saints and the Making of Sainthood in the Later Middle Ages* (Chicago, 1992).
Kuhn, Thomas S., *The Structure of Scientific Revolutions* (Chicago, 1970).
Lagardère, V., "La Tarīqa et la révolte des Murīdūn en 539H/1144 en Andalus," *Revue de l'Occident Musulman et de la Méditerranée* 35 (1983): 157–170.
Lambton, Ann K. S., *State and Government in Medieval Islam* (Oxford, 1981).
Landau-Tasseron, Ella, "The 'Cyclical Reform': A Study of the *Mujaddid* Tradition," *Studia Islamica* 70(1989): 79–117.
Lane, Edward William, *An Arabic-English Lexicon* (reprint, Cambridge, 1984).
Laoust, Henri, *Mots et choses berbères* (Paris, 1920).
Laroui, Abdallah, *The History of the Maghrib: An Interpretive Essay,* Ralph Manheim, trans. (Princeton, 1977).
Lawrence, Bruce B., "The Chishtīya of Sultanate India: A Case Study of Biographical Complexities in South Asian Islam," *Journal of the American Academy of Religion—Thematic Studies* 68(3–4)(1981): 47–67.
Lawrence, Bruce B., "The Early Chishti Approach to Samaʿ," in Joyce Irwin, ed., *Sacred Sound: Music in Religious Thought and Practice* (Chico, California, 1983), 93–109.
Lawrence, Bruce B., trans., *Nizam ad-Din Awliya: Morals for the Heart by Amir Hasan Sijzi* (Mahwah, New Jersey, 1992).
le Tourneau, Roger, *Fès avant le protectorat: Étude économique et sociale d'une ville de l'Occident musulman* (reprint, Rabat, 1987).
Lévi-Provençal, E., *Les Historiens des Chorfas* (reprint, Casablanca, 1991).
Lévi-Provençal, E., and Emilio García Gómez, eds. and trans., *El Siglo XI en 1ª persona: las "Memorias" de ʿAbd Allāh, último rey Zīri de Granada, destronado por los Almorávides (1090)* (Madrid, reprint 1982).
Lewis, Philip E., "The Measure of Translation Effects," in Joseph F. Graham, ed., *Difference in Translation* (Ithaca, New York and London, 1985), 31–62.
Long, A. A., *Hellenistic Philosophy: Stoics, Epicureans, Sceptics* (Berkeley and Los Angeles, 1986).
MacIntyre, Alasdair, *Whose Justice? Which Rationality?* (Notre Dame, Indiana, 1988).
Madelung, Wilferd, "Some Notes on Non-Ismāʿīlī Shiism in the Maghrib," in idem, *Religious Schools and Sects in Medieval Islam* (reprint, London, 1985), 87–97.
Mahjub, Jaʿfar, "Spiritual Chivalry and Early Persian Sufism," in Leonard Lewisohn

ed., *Classical Persian Sufism: From Its Origins to Rumi* (London, 1993), 549–582.

Makdisi, Georges, *Ibn ʿAqīl et la résurgence de l'Islam traditionaliste au XIe siècle* (Damascus, 1963).

Makdisi, Georges, *The Rise of Colleges: Institutions of Learning in Islam and the West* (Edinburgh, 1981).

Malamud, Margaret, "Sufi Organizations and Structures of Authority in Medieval Nishapur," *IJMES* 26 (3) (1994): 427–442.

Martin, Bradford G., *Muslim Brotherhoods in Nineteenth-Century Africa* (Cambridge, 1976).

McDermott, Martin, *The Theology of al-Shaikh al-Mufīd (d. 413/1022)* (Beirut, 1978).

Mediano, Fernando, *Familias de Fez (SS. XV–XVII)* (Madrid, 1995).

Merad, Ali, *Le Réformisme musulman en Algérie de 1925 à 1940* (Paris and The Hague, 1967).

Micaud, Charles, *Arabs and Berbers: From Tribe to Nation in North Africa* (London, 1973).

Michaux-Bellaire, E., ed., "Les Confréries religieuses au Maroc," *Archives Marocaines* 27.

Montagne, Robert, *Les Berbères et le Makhzen dans le Sud du Maroc* (Paris, 1930).

Mortel, Richard T., "Zaydi Shiʿism and the Ḥasanid Sharifs of Mecca," *International Journal of Middle East Studies* 19(4) (1987): 455–472.

Mouliéras, Auguste, *Le Maroc inconnu: Étude géographique et sociologique* (Paris, 1899).

Munson, Henry, Jr., *Religion and Power in Morocco* (New Haven and London, 1993).

Muslim, Abū'l-Ḥusayn ʿAsākir ad-Dīn ibn Ḥajjāj al-Qushayrī an-Nīṣābūrī (d. 261/875), *Ṣaḥīḥ Muslim (al-Jāmiʿ aṣ-ṣaḥīḥ)*, Abdul Hamid Siddiqi, trans. (New Delhi, 1978).

Nasr, Seyyid Hossein, *An Introduction to Islamic Cosmological Doctrines* (Boulder, Colorado, 1978).

Nasr, Seyyed Hossein, *Knowledge and the Sacred* (Albany, New York, 1989).

Nasr, Seyyed Hossein, *Sufi Essays* (New York, 1977).

Nicholson, Reynold A., ed. and trans., *The Mathnawī of Jalālu'ddin Rūmī* (London, reprint 1977).

Norris, H. T., *The Berbers in Arabic Literature* (London and Beirut, 1982).

Norris, H. T., *The Tuaregs: Their Islamic Legacy and its Diffusion in the Sahel* (Warminster, United Kingdom, 1975).

Noth, Albrecht, and Lawrence I. Conrad, *The Early Arabic Historical Tradition: A Source-Critical Study* (Princeton, 1994).

Nwyia, Paul, *Exégèse coranique et langage mystique* (Beirut, 1970).

Nwyia, Paul, *Ibn ʿAbbād de Ronda (1332–1390): Un Mystique prédicateur à la Qarawīyīn de Fès* (Beirut, 1961).

Nwyia, Paul, *Ibn ʿAṭā' Allāh (m. 709/1309) et la naissance de la confrérie šādilite* (Beirut, 1972).
Nwyia, Paul, *Lettres de direction spirituelle* (Beirut, 1971).
Nwyia, Paul, "Notes sur quelques fragments inédits de la correspondance d'Ibn al-ʿArīf avec Ibn Barrajan," *Hesperis* 43(1)(1956).
Nwyia, Paul, "Textes Mystiques inédits d'Abū-l-Ḥasan al-Nūrī (m. 295/907)," *Mélanges de l'Université Saint-Joseph* (Beirut, 1968), (14), fasc. 9, 117–154.
O'Fahey, R. S., *Enigmatic Saint: Ahmad Ibn Idris and the Idrisi Tradition* (Evanston, Illinois, 1990).
Otto, Rudolf, *The Idea of the Holy*, John W. Harvey, trans. (Oxford, 1958).
Paine, Robert, "Two Modes of Exchange and Mediation," in Bruce Kapferer, ed., *Transaction and Meaning: Directions in the Anthropology of Exchange and Symbolic Behavior* (Philadelphia, 1976): 63–86.
Parker, Richard, *A Practical Guide to Islamic Monuments in Morocco* (Charlottesville, Virginia, 1981).
Pearson, John B., trans., *A Guide to Happiness: A Manual of Prayer* (Oxford, 1907).
Pepper, Stephen Coburn, *World Hypotheses: A Study in Evidence* (Berkeley and Los Angeles, 1948).
Petry, Carl F., *The Civilian Elite of Cairo in the Later Middle Ages* (Princeton, 1981).
Powers, David S., "The Maliki Family Endowment: Legal Norms and Social Practices," *International Journal of Middle East Studies* 25(3)(1993): 379–306.
Prémare, A. L. de, *Maghreb et Andalousie au XIVᵉ siècle* (Lyon, 1981).
Prémare, A. L. de, *Sidi Abd-er-Raḥmān el-Mejdûb* (Paris and Rabat, 1985).
Radtke, Bernd, and John O'Kane, *The Concept of Sainthood in Early Islamic Mysticism: Two Works by al-Ḥakīm al-Tirmidhī* (London, 1996).
Rahman, Fazlur, *Islam* (Chicago, 1979).
Rais, Mohamed, "Aspect du mysticisme marocain au VIIᵉ–VIIIᵉ/XIIIᵉ–XIVᵉ siècle, à travers l'analyse critique de l'ouvrage *al-Minhāj al-wāḍiḥ fī taḥqīq karāmāt Abū Muḥammad Ṣāliḥ*" (Ph.D. dissertation, Université de Provence, Aix-Marseille I, 1995–96).
Raven, Susan, *Rome in Africa* (London and New York, 1984).
Renard, John S. J., *Ibn ʿAbbād of Ronda, Letters on the Sufi Path* (New York, 1986).
Renaud, H. P. J., "Ibn al-Bannâ de Marrakech, sûfî et mathématicien (XIIIᵉ–XIVᵉ s. J. C.)," *Hespéris* (25), 1938, 13–42.
Ricard, Robert, *Études sur l'histoire des Portugais au Maroc* (Coimbra, 1955).
Ricoeur, Paul, *Oneself As Another*, Kathleen Blamey, trans. (Chicago, 1992).
Ricoeur, Paul, *Time and Narrative*, Kathleen McLaughlin and David Pellauer, trans. (Chicago, 1984).
Rosen, Lawrence, *The Anthropology of Justice: Law as Culture in Islamic Society* (Cambridge, 1989).
Rosenberger, Bernard, "Travaux sur l'histoire du Maroc au XVᵉ et XVIᵉ siècles publiés en Pologne," *Hespéris-Tamuda* 12 (1971): 193–218.
Sachedina, Abdulaziz Abdulhussein, *The Just Ruler in Shīʿite Islam: The Com-*

prehensive Authority of the Jurist in Imamite Jurisprudence (New York and Oxford, 1988).

Sanneh, Lamin, "Saints and Virtue in African Islam: An Historical Approach," in John Stratton Hawley, ed., *Saints and Virtues* (Berkeley and Los Angeles, 1987), 127–132.

Scales, Peter C., *The Fall of the Caliphate of Córdoba: Berbers and Andalusis in Conflict* (Leiden, 1994).

Schimmel, Annemarie, "Abū'l-Ḥusayn al-Nūrī: 'Qibla of the Lights,'" in Leonard Lewisohn, ed., *Classical Persian Sufism: From Its Origins to Rumi* (London, 1993), 59–64.

Schimmel, Annemarie, *And Muhammad Is His Messenger: The Veneration of the Prophet in Islamic Piety* (Chapel Hill and London, 1985).

Schimmel, Annemarie, *Mystical Dimensions of Islam* (Chapel Hill, 1975).

Schuon, Frithjof, *Islam and the Perennial Philosophy,* J. Peter Hobson, trans. (London, 1976).

Schuon, Frithjof, *Logic and Transcendence,* Peter N. Townsend, trans. (New York, 1975).

Schuon, Frithjof, *Sufism, Veil and Quintessence* (Bloomington, Indiana, 1981).

Schuon, Frithjof, *Understanding Islam* (reprint, London, 1989).

Shaban, M.A., *The ʿAbbāsid Revolution* (Cambridge, 1979).

Shatzmiller, Maya, *Labour in the Medieval Islamic World* (Leiden, 1994).

Shatzmiller, Maya, "Professions and Ethnic Origins of Urban Labourers in Muslim Spain: Evidence from a Moroccan Source," *Awrāq* 5–6 (1982–3): 149–159.

Smith, Wilfred Cantwell, *The Meaning and End of Religion: A New Approach to the Religious Traditions of Mankind* (New York, 1963).

Sorokin, Pitrim A., *Altruistic Love: A Study of American "Good Neighbors" and Christian Saints* (Boston, 1950).

Spuler, Bertold, *History of the Mongols* (New York, 1988).

Staal, Fritz, *Exploring Mysticism* (Berkeley and Los Angeles, 1975).

Steiner, George, *After Babel: Aspects of Language and Translation* (New York and London, 1975).

al-Sulami, Ibn al-Husayn, *The Book of Sufi Chivalry: Lessons to a Son of the Moment,* Sheikh Tosun Bayrak al-Jerrahi al-Halvati, trans. (New York, 1983).

Sviri, Sara, "Ḥakīm Tirmidhī and the *Malāmatī* Movement in Early Sufism," in Leonard Lewisohn, ed., *Classical Persian Sufism: From Its Origins to Rumi* (London, 1993), 583–613.

Taeschner, Von Franz, "As-Sulamī's Kitāb al-Futuwwa," *Studia Orientalia Ioanni Pedersen septuagenario . . . dictata* (Copenhagen, 1953), 340–351.

Takeshita, Masataka, "Continuity and Change in the Tradition of Shirazi Love Mysticism—A Comparison Between Daylamī's *ʿAtf al-Alif* and Rūzbihān Baqlī's *ʿAbhar al-ʿĀshiqīn,*" *Orient* 23(1987): 113–131.

Takeshita, Masataka, *Ibn ʿArabī's Theory of the Perfect Man and its Place in the History of Islamic Thought* (Tokyo, 1987).

Tambiah, Stanley Jeyaraja, *The Buddhist Saints of the Forest and the Cult of Amulets* (Cambridge, 1984).

Tambiah, Stanley Jeyaraja, *Magic, Science, Religion, and the Scope of Rationality* (Cambridge, 1990).

Tilly, Charles, *As Sociology Meets History* (New York, 1981).

Tilly, Charles, "War Making and State Making as Organized Crime," in Peter Evans, Dietrich Rueschemeyer, and Theda Skocpol, *Bringing the State Back In* (Cambridge, 1985), 169–191.

Torres, Diego de, *Relación del origen y suceso de los xarifes y del estado de los reinos de Marruecos, Fez, y Tarudante,* Mercedes García-Arenal, ed. (Madrid, 1980).

Triki, Hamid, and Alain Dovifat, *Medersa de Marrakech* (Paris, 1990).

Trimingham, J. Spencer, *The Sufi Orders in Islam* (Oxford, 1971).

Turner, Bryan S., *Weber and Islam* (London, 1978).

Turner, Victor, *Dramas, Fields, and Metaphors: Symbolic Action in Human Society* (reprint, Ithaca, New York and London, 1983).

Turner, Victor, and Edith Turner, *Image and Pilgrimage in Christian Culture: Anthropological Perspectives* (New York, 1978).

Urvoy, Dominique, *El Mundo de los ulemas Andaluces del siglo V/XI al VII/XIII: estudio sociologico,* Francisco Panel, trans. (Madrid, 1983).

Valantasis, Richard, "Constructions of Power in Asceticism," *Journal of the American Academy of Religion* 63 (4)(1995) 775–822.

Van Der Leeuw, G. E., *Religion in Essence and Manifestation,* J. E. Turner and Hans H. Penner, trans. (Princeton, 1986).

Vansina, Jan, *Oral Tradition as History* (London and Nairobi, 1985).

Vauchez, André, *La Sainteté en occident aux dernier siècles du Moyen Age d'après les procès de canonisation et les documents hagiographiques* (Rome, 1981).

Vauchez, André, ed., *Religion et société dans l'Occident médiéval* (Turin, 1980).

Wartenberg, Thomas E., ed., *Rethinking Power* (Albany, New York, 1992).

Waterbury, John, *The Commander of the Faithful: The Moroccan Political Elite—A Study in Segmented Politics* (New York, 1970).

Watt, W. Montgomery, *The Formative Period of Islamic Thought* (Edinburgh, 1973).

Waugh, Earle H., "The Popular Muhammad," in Richard C. Martin, ed., *Approaches to Islam in Religious Studies* (Tucson, 1985), 41–58.

Weber, Max, *Theories of Social and Economic Organization,* Talcott Parsons, ed., A. M. Henderson and Talcott Parsons, trans. (New York, 1964).

Wehr, Hans, *A Dictionary of Modern Written Arabic,* J. Milton Cowan, ed. (Wiesbaden, 1971).

Weinstein, Donald, and Rudolph M. Bell, *Saints and Society: The Two Worlds of Western Christendom, 1000–1700* (Chicago and London, 1982).

Westermarck, Edward, *Ritual and Belief in Morocco* (London, 1926).

White, Hayden, *Tropics of Discourse: Essays in Cultural Criticism* (Baltimore and London, 1978).

Winter, Michael, *Society and Religion in Early Ottoman Egypt: Studies in the Writings of ʿAbd al-Wahhāb ash-Shaʿrānī* (New Brunswick, New Jersey, 1982).

Woodward, Mark R., *Islam in Java: Normative Piety and Mysticism in the Sultanate of Yogyakarta* (Tucson, Arizona, 1989).

Wyschogrod, Edith, *Saints and Postmodernism: Revisioning Moral Philosophy* (Chicago, 1990).

Yusuf Ali, Abdullah, *The Holy Qur'an: Translation and Commentary* (Plainfield, Indiana, reprint 1977).

Index

Maḥabba (love), 179
Malāmatiyya doctrines, 29–30, 196, 277–278, 280
al-Malīgī, Abū Zakariyya, 51–52
Maliki school of Islamic law, 4, 45, 99, 224
  in boarding schools, 128
  internationalism in, 15–19, 23–24
  introduction in Morocco of, 33–39
  under Marinids, 124
  in premodern Maghrib, 9–10
  sentiments against, 125–126
  state sponsorship of, 126–127
  versus Fatimid Shiʿism, 7
Mamluks of Egypt, 127
Manāqib (exploit narratives), 41–42, 98
  attributed to Abū Yiʿzzā, 74–75
al-Manṣūr, Sultan Yaʿqūb, 90, 91–92
Al-Maqṣad ash-sharīf (al-Bādisī), 100
al-Maqūdī, Abū Zayd, 212
Maraboutic crisis, xxxix, 231–232
"Maraboutic Sufism," 196
Maraboutism, xxvi–xxvii, xxix, 47–48, 117, 124
Marabouts, xxv, xxvi, xxx, 39. *See also* *Murābiṭ*
  as social brokers, 48–49
Marinid period, Moroccan Sufism during, 123–154
Marinid state, 42–43, 285
  educational system under, 128–129
  end of, 194–195
  establishment of, 123–124, 160–161
  al-Jazūlī versus, 187–188
  jurists in, 47
  Portugal and, 188–189
  propaganda against, 163
  sharifian policy of, 162–163
al-Marjānī, ʿAbdallāh, 152
Marrakesh
  Abū'l-ʿAbbās as-Sabtī at, 86–89
  following Almohad conquest, 96–97
  al-Ghazwānī in, 254–256, 263
  Kingdom of, 264
Maṣmūda Sufi tradition, 49–54, 57–58
Mawsim of Mūlāy ʿAbd as-Salām, 246
Mecca, pilgrimages to, 51–52, 127
al-Mībūdī, Abū'l-Faḍl, 178
"Middle path," 134–135
Midianite Mantle, 150
Miftāḥ as-saʿāda (Ibn al-ʿArīf), 21–22
al-Miknāsī, Aḥmad ibn al-Qāḍī, 99–100
al-Milyānī, Aḥmad ibn Yūsuf, 232
Miracles, 214, 275
  of Abū'l-ʿAbbās as-Sabtī, 86, 87–90
  of Abū Yiʿzzā, 72, 76
  as proofs of sainthood, 74, 112, 118, 119, 120
  types of, 115, 116
Monographic biography. *See also* Hagiographical anthology; Sacred biography
  knowledge, power, and authority in, 63–92
  in Latin Christianity, 64–65
  Sufi publicists and, 98
Moroccan Path of Blame, 25
Moroccan sainthood
  institutionalized, xxxviii, 123
  interpretations of, xxvii–xxviii
  middle class and, 109, 117–118
  power and authority in, 272–285
  social paradigm for, 3–6
Moroccan saints, 119–120
  affiliation of, 107–109
  occupations of, 109
  social status of, 119
  socioreligious activism of, 113
  spiritual practices of, 109–111
Moroccan Sufism, xxiv–xxv, xxxv, xxxviii, 4–6
  Arab flavor of, 102–104
  female participation in, 52–54
  formal education and, 105–107
  during Marinid period, 123–154
  rural traditions in, 32–62
  saints in, 7–9
  urban ethos of, 3–31, 93
Moroccan Sus, 97, 257–258